W9-BBE-593

THE ECONOMICS OF TASTE

Christie's : the great days of Mr. Woods. Woodcut from the *Graphic*, 10th September 1887. The original caption reads: 'The moment the picture comes upon the easel it is received with loud clapping of hands, repeated as often as the bidders outvie one another in their advances of perhaps a thousand guineas, and when the hammer falls at last to a lumping sum, there is a perfect uproar, just as the crowd roars its delight when the Derby is run, for the Christie audience revels in high prices simply for money's sake, though of course some of the applause is [illegible]'

THE ECONOMICS OF TASTE

The Rise and Fall of the Picture Market 1760–1960

BY

GERALD REITLINGER

HOLT, RINEHART AND WINSTON
NEW YORK CHICAGO
SAN FRANCISCO

First published in the United States October, 1964

Library of Congress Catalog Card Number: 64-21929

First Edition

87398-0114

Printed in the United States of America

IN MEMORIAM
HENRY REITLINGER
1885–1950

Acknowledgements

I have to thank Messrs. Christie, Manson and Woods for the use of their wonderful muniment room with its series of priced catalogues going back to 1766; the Courtauld Institute for the use of the Witt library; Mr. George Savage for the loan of numerous priced catalogues from several countries and much valuable advice. I must thank Mr. F. J. B. Watson for the resources of his encyclopaedic mind. Finally, I record my gratitude to Diana Imber, who typed my manuscript.

CONTENTS

LIST OF ILLUSTRATIONS

INTRODUCTION

How fascinating the price of pictures has become in this humdrum world. But in fact there has been a peculiar fascination in the price of pictures since the early sixteenth century. At a time when painters still charged a fixed rate for the job, as if they were making a pair of shoes, certain paintings began to acquire a prestige value. They were painted, not into the plaster of walls but on portable panels or canvases in order that their owners might trade them, if need be. These pictures began to change hands, as they do now, at higher and higher prices. Sometimes fantasy prices were paid by princes and cardinals, just to show that they were princes and cardinals, like Arab khalifs who filled the mouths of poets with gold. But quite often high prices were reached, because two or three magnates wanted the same picture. By the time that the collecting of pictures of the past as well as the present reached England, that is to say a hundred years later, in the reign of James I, there was already an international market. By 1650 the Raphaels of Charles I were sold for prices up to £2,000, his Correggios for £1,000 each, his commissioned works from living artists for anything from £40 to £200 according to the reputation of the artist and the magnitude of the work.

It is clear from memoir writers and letter writers that by the middle of the eighteenth century art-prices had the same interest for the informed public as they have to-day. Ambling through the Midlands in the 1780's Lord Torrington was shown a reputed Raphael in a squire's house. What could its value be? Stretching his imagination to the full, he suggested £7,000. It was widely known in those days that in 1754 the King of Saxony had given £8,500 for the *Sistine Madonna*, the highest sum that had ever been paid for any picture. When the name of Raphael was mentioned, people thought in those terms.

But what did this money value really mean? It was on the one hand a sum that only an absolute monarch could lay his hands on for such a purpose. It was also a yardstick of taste. At the time that the King of Saxony bought his Raphael, a gold-ground altarpiece of the Trecento or early Quattrocento could have been had for a few pounds. In this case the relationship of price is particularly interesting. It illustrates a whole system of aesthetic values, now extinct. The actual purchasing power of the money is immaterial for the purpose of the comparison. But one also wants to know how much works of art were really esteemed. One wants to know what sort of sacrifice the expenditure of £8,500 on a single picture entailed.

One wants to know, first of all, why so beggarly a sum should have been the wonder of the world. In the present century we are well used to pictures that fetch two or three hundred thousand pounds each, and yet these pictures are only the waifs and strays that have not yet been gobbled up by museums. Inside the museums there are pictures that could be worth a million each. Yet in the eighteenth century not very many pictures made as much as £1,000 each, and the man who could give such a sum for a picture was accounted a Nabob or a Croesus.

Does this mean that the eighteenth century failed to appreciate fine art, that the sums which were spent, even when the purchasing power of the money of the day is considered, were miserly and grudging? I think not. To measure the extent of eighteenth-century appreciation, it is not sufficient to work out a rate of exchange applicable to 1960. What has to be borne in mind is the shortage of fluid capital and the very low circulation of money. Two or three of the great landed estates of late-eighteenth-century England were worth actual millions in good gold guineas or sovereigns, yet their owners might find it difficult to negotiate bills of exchange for as much as £10,000. In inflationary times like the present there are financial operators who keep the greater part of their funds in liquidity, and who can write a cheque for a hundred thousand or two and remove the picture the same morning. Not only was such a thing unimaginable in the eighteenth century, it was something unknown even at the end of the nineteenth century. The art buyers then were no longer the nobility, whose fortune was frozen in entailed lands, but great merchants, industrialists and bankers, who could realise their capital. In actuality they could only do so in the most modest proportions, and in that year of great wealth, 1890, the payment of £30,000 or more for a picture was regarded as something stupendous.

If, therefore, we assume a certain rate of exchange between the values of the pound in 1760 and 1960, it still does not mean that a picture has retained its value, that a fashion has remained the same, simply because its price has advanced in this proportion. The enormous increase in the printing and circulation of money has to be considered as well. For a picture truly to have retained its standing over the past two hundred years, it will have multiplied its first price a hundred times over and more. A painting, which was unappreciated then, but is highly esteemed now, such as a Vermeer or a Frans Hals, may have advanced by 10,000 times or even 20,000 times.

Nevertheless, to make some sense out of the art prices which were paid by another age, one must have some idea what money could buy. There must be some kind of simple multiplication table.

A table of this sort is likely to be a more reliable indication for the present century, because, even in sixty years, ways of life among the higher income groups have not changed quite so enormously as in the past. For this reason it is more convenient to work backwards from 1960. If we take first the post-war period, it will be found that, since 1939, most wages and most food prices have multiplied by four, and in some cases by five. Manufactured articles have advanced rather less, while public utility services and inland transport have multiplied less than three times. I suggest that for the fairly static period, 1921–1939, prices can be multiplied by 3·7 to get present-day equivalents. The difficulty, of course, is that there has been no static period since 1939, and that the general index has advanced the whole time, though at varying speed. But, since the price of pictures did not begin an all-round advance till 1951 or later, I would be inclined to regard that year as a watershed between pre-war and post-war art prices.

To proceed beyond the 1921–1939 phase, we get the First World War, which raised the cost of living by more than 100 percent., but which was followed by partial deflation so that the increase fell to 60 or 70 percent. It is probable that, compared with 1900–1914, the cost of living to-day is six times as high. In fact, a gold sovereign in 1900–1914 did not buy a great deal more than its present value in paper money on the free gold market.

Travelling beyond 1900, one runs into difficulties. If we take as a starting point the Repeal of the Corn Laws in 1846, it appears that in the next half-century wages increased by more than 100 percent., whereas the cost of most articles of food and all manufactures actually fell. All sorts of things that had been too dear for the common man, such as sugar and tea and imported fruits, were now part of his life. For the lowest income groups the progression of the present century was reversed and money bought more. One cannot, however, estimate the relative value of picture-prices from the rise in a casual labourer's standard of living. With all deference to M. Maurice Rheims,[1] who uses the lowest wages of all as his truly remarkable yardstick for the value of money, casual labourers do not buy pictures, whether they

[1] *La Vie étrange des objets*, 1960.

make six shillings a week, as in 1760, or close on £9 a week as in 1960. The man whom we have to consider is rich or fairly rich, and for him the period 1850–1914 was a matter of swings and roundabouts: lower household bills, lower tailors' and dressmakers' bills, but a higher wages bill; cheaper travel, but dearer education; more charities but little taxation. On the whole I would call it an equilibrium.

The period 1815–1850 is very different, not a static period at all. At the beginning, there was the inflation of the Napoleonic wars, when shipyard workers could make £2 a day and the cost of food was at times trebled. Deflation followed much too fast with lowered wages, unemployment and food riots, to be followed by a costly form of protectionism, to be followed in turn by the dangerous and misapplied principles of Free Trade. Allowing for increases both in wages and in food after the deflationary years, the general rise between 1815 and 1850 may have been in the region of 50 percent.

The period 1760–1815 falls into two phases, first a static period between 1760 and 1795 or thereabouts, then successive waves of inflation during the wars. These wartime movements of price were so erratic that they must be left out of the account. It was however a fact that, after the post-war deflation had subsided, there was still some increase in the cost of living over the late eighteenth century, despite the cheaper manufactured goods. The carefully preserved travel bills of Viscount Torrington give a fair picture of the cost of living in the 1780's and 1790's. But in assessing the cost of living of a man in Torrington's position, the picture is rather too idyllic, since he always tried to avoid the expensive fashionable watering-places of the day. The country pubs, which provided him with large well-cooked dinners at a shilling or a shilling and sixpence a head with lodging thrown in, were just country pubs. At the 'hotel', in which Joseph Farington stayed at Lyme Regis in 1808, the dinner, which cost him six shillings, would have been considered an imposition in a place of this kind in 1939. And he paid half-a-crown a night for the use of a tent-bed in an attic with extra charges for fire and candles. And that was the year when Richard Arkwright's spinning jenny children at Cromford made 2*s*. 3*d*. to 3*s*. 6*d*. a week according to sex for seventy-two hours' work.

The trouble in finding a rate of exchange for the late eighteenth century lies in distinguishing on the one hand between 'passing rich on forty pounds a year' and 'dead drunk for tuppence' and on the other the cost of an influential man's establishment. What with armies of useless, though low paid, servants, expensive clothes, incredibly expensive travel and endless public obligations, one wonders whether a man's money really went much further than in the pre-inflationary early twentieth century. But, descending to the general, as opposed to the particular, cost of living, I suggest tentatively that the rate of exchange for 1760–1795 should be about twelve times to-day's purchasing power.

One is nevertheless up against many anomalies. Farington indicated the depths of Hoppner's poverty in the early 1780's, when he set himself up independently as a portraitist, by the fact that he 'did not get £400 a year'. But if this meant an untaxed income of £4,500 in to-day's money, one would have thought that Hoppner had nothing to complain of. In effect this money meant £4,500 only in the sense of the number of impoverished, barbarously living families which it could support in their usual condition. A portrait painter, in order to exist at all, had to receive his sitters in a presentable house, close enough to the fashionable part of London. He had to provide stand-in models, employ an assistant and spend as much or more on brushes, canvases and paints as he would have to spend to-day.

Whatever the period, the status of the living painter plays a very large part in determining the price of art, even when it is the work of old masters that is in question. It must not be forgotten that the starving artist in an attic was not a contemporary of the starving poet. He belonged to *la vie de Bohème*, he was a product and a victim of the rigorous exclusive Paris salon between the 1840's and the 1890's. He began with Meryon and ended with Van Gogh and in England he was a rarity. In late eighteenth-century England even a journeyman painter belonged to a prosperous class of tradesman. A fashionable portrait painter was a merchant prince, besieged by clients and dining with the great.

I would recapitulate the matter in this way. In the late eighteenth century, money for the richest class did not go nearly as far as is generally supposed. Therefore a general rate of exchange in present-day terms is least applicable to this class. A £1,000 picture could not have meant the equivalent of spending £100,000 to-day, because modern transactions of this kind involve realising a larger portion of a man's capital than would have been possible when capital was based on land. This difficulty created a very strict limit to what could be spent on a work of art, except in the case of Royalty. To the question whether collectors really spent as much as they could afford, the translation of a picture-price into food, clothes and necessities is not altogether relevant. Nevertheless for this purpose alone I offer these exceedingly tentative rates of exchange:

The pound in terms of 1960 values

1760–1795	Multiply by 12.
1795–1815	Fluid period; multiply by 12 to 10.
1815–1850	Fluid period: multiply by 10 to 8.
1850–1914	Multiply by 6.
1914–1921	Fluid period: multiply by 6 to 3.
1921–1939	Multiply by 3·7.
1939–1948	Fluid period: multiply by 3·7 to 2.
1948–1960	Fluid period: multiply by 2 to 1.

PART ONE

CHAPTER ONE

Art Collecting in the Late Eighteenth Century 1760–1792

1. The Italians — 2. The Northern Schools — 3. Paris taste; The Houghton Sale

---

1. *The Italians*

Though modern history is generally considered to have begun with the French Revolution, this story begins thirty years earlier. It is not simply because it marks a bicentenary that I have chosen the year 1760. In fact the 1760's were a turning point in the history of English taste, a decade which saw the first national academy, the first annual exhibitions and the first competition between the art-markets of London and Paris. In the period 1760–1790 this competition established a new scale of values, which continued to govern the London market when England was isolated from France by revolution and war. The London market then became paramount in Europe, the scene of an extraordinary episode in the history of taste. Yet, even in that age of war and adventure, only objects that had been in demand for generations were thought to be worth the trouble of removal from their ancient homes.

In an Italy overflowing with the works of the Quattrocento, thrifty, hard-bargaining Scots spent the first years of the nineteenth century combing the land for Van Dycks and Rubenses. That is not so surprising, seeing that in the more daring market of Paris between 1760 and 1792, a market much better documented than the London sales, it was always the same things that went round and round. Works which in Charles I's day were still treated with a certain *pietas* were now regarded as barbarous curios. The horizons of collecting had not expanded but shrunk. The first years of the sixteenth century, the manhood of Raphael, marked the extreme backward limits of serious collecting. Even the works of Mantegna, Giovanni Bellini and Perugino, revered in the days of Cardinal Richelieu, were now of no consequence.

It was an age of vigorous prejudices. While the late eighteenth-century market was restricted by a prejudice against early pictures, because they were 'hard and dry', there was a second prejudice against the brush that was too free and the colour that was too fresh and strong. When Titian's *Bacchus and Ariadne* was first shown in Buchanan's rooms in Oxendon Street in 1807, there were ladylike protests against the ultramarine sky. Though Thomas Lawrence recognised that this was the keynote of the picture, Benjamin West would not believe it. He decided that it was the work of Mr. Burch the picture-restorer.[1] This prejudice against *impasto* paint and strong colour was then nearly two generations old and its end was near at hand, but it had found exceedingly lucid expression in a powerful canonical pronouncement, Reynolds's Academy *Discourse* of December 1771, wherein the President laced into the entire Venetian sixteenth-century school, sparing neither Titian, Veronese nor Tintoretto, who were denounced relentlessly as mere decorators, obsessed with colour at the expense of form.

It was patently inconsistent to attack Titian for these qualities, while imitating Rubens and Van Dyck, yet Reynolds's teaching did actually debase the market for the Venetian school. It was possible to buy cheap Veroneses and Tintorettos and frequently cheap Titians well into the nineteenth century. On the other hand Reynolds's propaganda raised the price of the eclectic works of the seventeenth-century Italian masters, as it was intended to do. For these were the proud possessions of Reynolds's patrons, whose fathers had acquired them in the early years of the eighteenth century.

Considering the force of the example, one would expect these works to have influenced the disciples of Reynolds more than they did. In reality the menace of an Anglo-Bolognese school of painting was averted by the split personality of Reynolds himself. His own methods of painting were borrowed from Van Dyck and sometimes Rubens and later, as he succumbed to the lure of asphaltum, from Rembrandt. To the seventeenth-century Italians, whose worship he decreed, Reynolds

[1] The *Farington Diary*, IV.

certainly owed a great deal of monumental posturing and uplifted eyes, but not his technique. The real Italianist of the English school was not Reynolds but Benjamin West, who brought to England in the 1760's the pale flat mannerisms of Anton Raphael Mengs [1728–1779], a sinister force in international painting, Germano-Scandinavian though operating from Rome. And what that was may now be revealed, since the Fellows of All Souls have removed the *Noli me tangere* from the chapel roof, where Gilbert Scott[1] once pudically hid it, and have actually cleaned it. These gleaming slabs of apple-green, pink and violet should remind Reynolds's admirers how lucky they are that Reynolds only preached where Mengs practised.

In theory, but only in theory, the highest prized painters in 1760 were neither Guido Reni, Domenichino and the Carraccis, nor Titian, Rubens, Van Dyck and Rembrandt, but Raphael, Leonardo and Correggio. But it was impossible to put a price to these painters, since no authentic example of their work had been seen in a London saleroom. In particular, the name of Raphael was awesome and powerful. It was because Raphael had inspired them that the seventeenth-century Italians were so highly esteemed. As far back as the Commonwealth sales of 1651–1652 Don Antonio Cardenas had given £2,000 for Raphael's madonna, known as *La Perla*, perhaps £40,000 in modern currency. In 1754 King Augustus III of Poland and Saxony was reputed to have paid 17,000 gold ducats, or £8,500 English pounds, to the monks of Piacenza for the *Sistine Madonna*, and this may be considered as at least £120,000 to-day. Ten years later the *Ansidei Madonna* reached England through the clever fingers of Gavin Hamilton. This with the two *Panshanger madonnas*, which had been bought by Zoffany from Lord Cowper in Tuscany in 1773, were the only Raphaels in England till the end of the century and they were invisible to the general public since they were immured in remote country houses.

Painters and men of taste, unless they had travelled in Italy, only knew Raphael from engravings, and these generally derived from works in his most highly developed style. The price paid by Augustus III of Saxony for the *Sistine Madonna* was quite in keeping with the records, established by the *Ansidei Madonna* in 1885 and the *Alba Madonna* in 1931, and yet the eighteenth century found Raphael a grievous puzzle. Although the critics were obliged to accept Raphael at the valuation of Vasari and the Renaissance princes, most of what they saw had a hard, Gothic appearance that almost suggested the fourteenth- and fifteenth-century paintings with gold backgrounds, which could

[1] Sir George Gilbert Scott [1811–1878].

be had for a few guineas or a number of shillings, so unlike the gyrating God the Father of the *Loggie* of the Vatican, to which the engravings had accustomed them. Most of the Raphael pictures which came over with the Orleans collection in 1792 were therefore a disappointment, and early in the next century some of them left England for derisory sums.

With Correggio, however, eighteenth-century collectors were much happier. Since there was nothing Gothic about him, they were prepared to pay as much as for Raphael in his 'broad and grand manner'. In 1651 Jabach, the Antwerp banker, had paid £1,000 each for King Charles's three Correggios, which are now in the Louvre. When the pictures were in his possession, Cardinal Mazarin was said to have put a valuation of £5,000 on the *Jupiter and Antiope* alone, and it is even possible that Louis XIV paid this when he bought the picture from Mazarin's heirs. Most fantastic of all was the price of 27,000 Roman scudi or £6,500, which was paid to the Duke of Modena in 1746 by Augustus III, King of Poland and Saxony. The subject of this purchase was a little painting on copper, no more than 16 ins. × 12 ins., depicting a Magdalen, lying seductively on her stomach and reading a book. The thieves who once possessed themselves of the *Magdalen* could have spared themselves the trouble. The £6,500 picture is now generally regarded as a seventeenth-century copy of a lost Correggio. Morelli even declared it to be not Italian but Dutch.[1]

If that had been Correggio's prestige in 1746, how much more the glamour of the arrival of an important Correggio in London twenty years later. On 18th November 1771, Horace Walpole wrote to Sir Horace Mann: 'Mr. Hamilton's Correggio is arrived. I have seen it. It is divine—and so is the price; for nothing but a demi-god or a demi-devil, that is a Nabob, can purchase it. What do you think of three thousand pounds?'[2]

No one thought of three thousand pounds. The picture was sold to the painter-dealer Vandergucht for £1,500,[3] and poor Vandergucht lost on it. He kept it for a quarter of a century and, after his death in 1796, it was knocked down to Lord Radnor at Christie's for £630. Like the King of Poland's *Magdalen*, the *Venus, Cupid and Satyr*, which Horace Walpole found divine, was no Correggio. The commodity was rarer than was supposed. Of the ten pictures, which reached London in 1792 with the Orleans gallery, not one is nowadays accepted

[1] Georg Gronau: *Correggio (Klassiker der Kunst)*, p. 167.
[2] *Horace Walpole, Letters*, ed. Peter Cunningham, p. 350.
[3] Redford: *Art Sales*, II, p. 225. Source not disclosed.

in the Correggio canon. The real Correggios, the three pictures which depicted the irregular affections of Jupiter for Leda, Io and Danaë, had been disposed of by the Duke's father. He had ordered the painter Coypel to hack them to pieces in the presence of his confessor. Coypel had stuck the pieces together and restored them after his fashion. The *Leda* was sold to Frederick the Great, who gave it a new head. The *Danaë* was stolen from the Labbia palace in Venice. It was sold to John Udney, British Consul in Leghorn in 1780 and from 1793 it lived at Teddington. In 1802 this mutilated, overpainted picture, the only unquestionable Correggio in England, was sold for 200 guineas in the Robert Udney sale (see page 50). It was not till 1824 and 1833 that the National Gallery obtained three genuine and unmutilated Correggios.

Thwarted in their endeavours to find a Correggio, unmutilated and undoubted, which satisfied at all points, the English *cognoscenti* had to put up with the works of Girolamo Francesco Mazzuola or Parmigianino, a contemporary and disciple, who could at times be mistaken for the original. The big coffin-shaped *Vision of St. Jerome* in the National Gallery is an example. It was acquired in 1780 from a church in Città di Castelli by Jacob More, an Edinburgh house-painter who was permitted to paint the Pope. More sold the picture forthwith to the Earl of Abercorn for 1,500 guineas. In 1808 it was sold for £3,000. Later the picture was bought for the sugar-magnate, Watson Taylor, by William Seguier, the subsequent keeper of the National Gallery. At the Watson Taylor sale of 1823 it was bought for the British Institution by the Rev. Holwell Carr for £3,202 10*s*. On this occasion Holwell Carr told the poet, Thomas Moore, that the Parmigianino picture had cost Watson Taylor not less than £7,000.[1]

It cannot be denied that the *St. Jerome* is a good example of an attractive painter's work. But what was there about this picture that made it worth a whole gallery of Rembrandts in 1780 and as costly as any picture in England at the end of the Napoleonic wars? There seems to have been a special glamour, to-day somewhat unintelligible, surrounding huge soup-brown religious pictures that had been raided from the altar of a church or pledged by esurient monks or nuns. Till the end of the nineteenth century, English taste favoured very large pictures, and payment by size was all to the advantage of the seventeenth-century Italians, among whom life-sized figures had been an occupational disease. Moreover the huge well-smoked altarpieces went particularly well with even smokier ancestors. The taste was responsible for the Murillo cult as late as the 1840's and 1850's, and the market was only

[1] William T. Whitley: *Art in England*, II, p. 121.

killed by the demands of living art. In order to hang *Alpine Mastiffs*, 93 ins. × 75 ins., something else that was eight feet high had to go.

The collector of 1760, unable to discover Correggios, Leonardos and Raphaels, would find it natural to prolong the fashion for just those Bolognese and Roman painters who had been patronised by his grandfather during their own lifetimes. This alone would account for the high prices fetched by the 'eclectic' painters, quite apart from the praises of Joshua Reynolds and the exponents of 'ideal beauty'. In reality, however, this market in the 1760's was already becoming restless and choosy. Carlo Maratta, of whose work Robert Walpole had bought more than thirty examples, Luca Giordano, Pietro da Cortona and Andrea Sacchi, all showed symptoms of decline, whereas Guido Reni, Domenichino and Annibale Carracci, who were at least a generation older, were on the way up. In 1628, while Guido Reni was alive, Charles I had not had to pay more than a hundred guineas for *Venus attired by the Graces*. The King was prepared to spend double on a Van Dyck commission. Nevertheless, early in the eighteenth century, Guido Reni became the highest prize in the English market. In the 1730's the *Doctors of the Church* cost Robert Walpole £630, 'the first picture in England and equal to any in Italy, but Raphael's'. In 1758 Earl Spencer bought a Guido and an Andrea Sacchi at the Henry Furnese sale for 2,000 guineas.[1] While no other auction sale came up to this level, much higher prices were paid privately, as is always the case. Thus in August 1774 Mr. Duncombe of Duncombe Park, Yorkshire, paid reputedly £2,000 for a single Guido Reni, sent from Venice. Horace Walpole thought it much inferior to the *Doctors of the Church*, but this was nothing like the shock he suffered five years later, when his nephew sold the huge *Immaculate Conception* at Houghton to the Empress Catherine for £3,500. So far as I can tell, no Guido Reni fetched anything like this price again till the purchase of the Lichtenstein *Adoration* by the National Gallery in 1958.

The Empress's purchase bore no relation to the auction-room prices of Paris and London for the simple reason that auction rooms were incapable of handling such things. Invariably pictures that enjoyed so high an esteem had to be bought-in. Occasionally, indifferent works were sold for prices that seem quite breath-taking in terms of the purchasing power of the money of the day, but as a rule the case was opposite. A sale could continue for ten days without producing a single bid of 100 guineas. A bid of 1,000 guineas was considered gigantic, a bid of 1,500 guineas the talk of an entire generation. The typical London

[1] Horace Walpole to Horace Mann, 9th February 1758.

sale of the years 1760–1792 would be a collection of over-painted, dishonestly attributed daubs, among which a masterpiece passed unnoticed, unless it had been well puffed in advance. An illustrious collection did not necessarily attract buyers. In 1751 the Earl of Orford parted with four Van Dyck portraits for less than 100 guineas. The sale had not been announced well in advance, and it was the month of June, when persons of distinction were out of town. They were secondary works 'that had not found place at Houghton'.[1] Nevertheless a descendant of one of the buyers sold one of these portraits in 1922 for £3,990.

It is possible that such a fiasco could not have occurred forty years later, when men of wealth and fashion had become more conscious of artistic values, but the market in pictures was still temperamental in the highest degree even in the 1790's. It was long since the neo-classical movement had arrived from the Continent with an Etruscan urn or two for each bookcase, tall windows for the drawing room and a round temple for the plantation, but the neo-classic movement contributed nothing to picture-expertise. Even the Germans, who had pontificated on classical antiquities since the 1750's, could send no Dr. Waagen[2] to mislead the English nobility. The opinion of Benjamin West of the Royal Academy was much sought, but the president could no more see through those layers of sooty varnish than could the owners. If the thing had belonged to one of the Roman or Venetian princely families, it helped to sell the picture, but a new copy could be painted, dried, browned and baked to look much the same within a few weeks. The casualness of art collecting can be judged from the sale catalogue, dated March 1795, of Sir Joshua Reynolds's collection. The foremost art critic of his age and a good judge of an old drawing, Reynolds—or his executors—nevertheless believed that he possessed seventy Van Dycks, fifty-four Correggios, forty-four Michelangelos, twenty-four Raphaels and even twelve Leonardos. No less than four hundred and eleven pictures came under the hammer and the price that was realised represented less than £25 a canvas.[3]

This remoteness from reality disappeared at the turn of the century, after the sales in London of the Orleans collection and the loot from Rome, but it is incredible that it should have existed at all in a period

[1] *Op. cit.*, Walpole to Mann, 18th June 1751.

[2] See note, p. 110, *infra*.

[3] Redford; *op. cit.*, I, p. 33; William T. Whitley: *Artists and Their Friends in England*, II, pp. 194–6. There were nevertheless some good pictures, among them two famous Rembrandts, a Rubens self-portrait and probably versions of *The Agony in the Garden*, both by Giovanni Bellini and Mantegna.

when the Grand Tour, embracing Florence and Rome, was so popular with Englishmen. In the early 1790's there were no less than twenty-eight English and Scottish painters residing in Rome and trading in antiquities and old masters. To one of them, Gavin Hamilton, the Nation owes Raphael's *Ansidei Madonna* and Leonardo's *Virgin of the Rocks*. But it is significant that the one picture was bought in Perugia, the other in Milan. For in Rome the owners of the princely galleries were reluctant sellers and, besides, they were obliged to give the Pope a first option on their possessions. The objects were therefore smuggled through dishonest intermediaries. Rome, the artistic capital of the world, became such a spurious market that French collectors would have little to do with Italian painting—that is till 1797–1799, when they occupied Rome and helped themselves to what they could get.

But even if a More, a Jenkins, a Byres or a Gavin Hamilton succeeded in importing a masterpiece from Rome, there was still good reason for failing to understand Italian painting. Few people saw the masterpiece except its new owner, who could contemplate it among his staring 'Jacobethan' ancestors, his copies of the heads of the Kings of England and his occasional Van Dycks and Lelys, six deep on the walls and buried in cobwebs. These things were accessible only to young bucks, who were prepared to dispense a guinea or two among the staff.[1]

In London, where there were sometimes two or three exhibitions of the work of living painters in a year, old masters, such as they were, could only be studied in the auction rooms. There was not one permanent exhibition building in London. In 1787 this situation became ridiculous, when by disgraceful trickery the Vatican laws were evaded and a series of paintings, attributed to Nicolas Poussin and known as the *Seven Sacraments*, were sent from Rome by James Byres,[2] who had procured the Portland vase in 1770. The *Seven Sacraments* were possibly school pictures, since another series had been bought in Rome for the Duke of Orleans in 1715 for nearly three times the price. But, real or false, the newly arrived Poussins were news value. Sir Joshua Reynolds wanted King George III to see them, and he proposed to show them at the Royal Academy Summer exhibition. There was, in fact, nowhere else in London where the King could see the pictures properly

[1] In the 1830's, when the 2nd Duke of Buckingham cleared out some of the accumulations at Stowe, about 1,000 pictures were sent to Christie's, where they made £600, filling the junkshops of Wardour St. for months and years to come (*Introduction to the Stowe Catalogue*, 1848).

[2] Byres's paintings were sold to the Duke of Rutland for £1,500 which was £700 less than they had cost him. The *Seven Sacraments* in the Orleans collection were valued by Bryan for the Duke of Bridgewater in 1798 at £4,900.

displayed. But the Council of the Royal Academy, whose members disliked competition from the ghosts of the past, ruled that the proposal infringed their charter. The newspapers then took up the quarrel, and in the end Reynolds had to show the pictures to the King in the Council Chamber.[1]

2. *The Northern Schools*

The founding of the Royal Academy in 1769 took place at a time when there was a great deal of 'new money' in London, acquired both in the East and in the West Indies. For living English painters it heralded a golden dawn (see page 58). Not only the Nabobs and sugar kings but many of the noble houses who still owned the bulk of the country's wealth, showed themselves interested, more interested than in antiquarian collecting. And why not? The market could offer them nothing but dark and dubious, cooked and repainted pictures, no different from their own neglected possessions. Hence the usually poor level of prices in the rare priced eighteenth-century sale catalogues that have survived. They are the prices that a rich man might be expected to pay, provided he spent no more than at an evening's card-playing. Hogarth had no need to inveigh against 'the Black Masters', when his own works fetched no less than all these alleged Correggios. Buyers, who wanted something better than cheap and spurious Italian fare, had to look elsewhere.

Since the beginning of the eighteenth century there had been a steady rise in the value of Dutch *genre* paintings, because with these one at least knew where one stood. The best of the Dutch-Flemish painters belonged to the now classical age of Rubens and Van Dyck, of Guido Reni and Carlo Dolci, of Claude and the two Poussins. Little known in contemporary England and despised in France, some of these painters of middle-class and lower-class *genre* did, however, receive the patronage of the German princes and the Imperial court. In particular the Fleming, David Teniers the younger, enjoyed the Emperor's favours, covered, as he maintained, three leagues of canvas, and died in 1690 immensely rich. But Louis XIV regarded these levelling pictures with well-founded suspicion and is said to have uttered the words, 'Otez moi ces magots là'.

But the appeal of infinite dexterity was invincible. Opinions are divided in assigning the origins of the Dutch-picture cult to the prudery

[1] William T. Whitley: *Artists and their friends in England*, II, pp. 75-8.

of Madame de Maintenon, who disliked nudes about the place, or to the attractive loot that became available when Louis XIV's forces invaded the Netherlands. Whichever the explanation, the gulf between Dutch bourgeois taste and French Court taste had almost disappeared before the death of Louis XIV.

Of all the men of the Netherlands Teniers seems to have been the most honoured by the new taste, probably because Teniers, though the most uncourtly of painters, had been a court protégé. The record of the Paris auction sales is impressive. In 1737 the best Teniers in the Comtesse de Verrue's collection made £95, but in the Fontpertuis sale of 1748 a Teniers made £240, while no less than £1,248 was bid for Blondel de Gagny's *Prodigal Son* (now in the Louvre) in 1776. Not only was this the highest price ever paid at an open auction in London or Paris, but it was also not much less than Blondel de Gagny's picture would fetch to-day in pounds devalued to one twelfth or less. A *Fête de village*, hardly inferior to this picture, was in fact sold for £1,575 as recently as 1950.

The change in French taste also favoured Adriaen van der Werff, who continued to produce his slick silken draperies till his death in 1722. The Munich Pinakotek inherited thirty-nine of Van der Werff's works through his patron, the Elector Palatine. The Louvre obtained another nine through his English patron, Sir Gregory Page. They were bought for about £180 a picture, more than any Van Dyck or Rubens was worth in the 1720's. Fifty years later the Empress Catherine paid £700 for Lord Orford's *Bathsheba and Abishag*, but by the end of the century a Van der Werff was no longer worth more than any Rembrandt, because other painters, scarcely more capable of setting fire to Bond Street and King Street to-day, had caught him up. For instance, the name of Nicholas Berghem or Berchem had become as familiar to educated Englishmen as that of Raphael. Julius Caesar Ibbetson claimed that he was known the world over as the English Berchem, and since he had painted not a few of the works that passed as Berchem's, he had some title to the claim. Within a conveniently reduced canvas Berchem's Italianate ruins and neatly disposed shepherds provided all the elements of a big Claude or Gaspard Poussin. Between 1740 and the Revolution at least ten Berchems were sold in Paris at prices between £320 and £705, while a Berchem picture was bought by George III at the Trumbull sale of 1797 for £945.

With the taste for Berchem went the taste for Wouverman and the brothers Both, whose landscapes were something never seen in Holland, having kinship with Salvator Rosa's Calabria and Claude's Roman campagna. In fact they were bought because they were the least Dutch of Dutchmen, but there were other buyers who liked the traditions of the North for their own sake, though at this period they were not prepared to pay so much for them. The painters of conversation pieces were liked, inasmuch as they approached Teniers. That is to say drunken boors were considered more picturesque than clean honest burghers. There was little appreciation for de Hooch and not much more for Maes, Metsu and Jan Steen, but the real prizes were the infinitely niggling and highly polished works of Gerard Dou and the Mieris family. These with their minutely detailed shop interiors vied with the flowerpieces of Huysum, Rachel Ruysch and Van Os. The landscapes of Hobbema were still deemed insufficiently Italianate to command a market, but those of Cuyp and Potter appealed to a stock-breeding nobility, while the becalmed fleets of Willem van de Velde and the choppy seas of Backhuyzen had a strong appeal to fortunes founded on sea-borne trade.

With the exception of Rembrandt, whose peculiar case will be discussed, it was a prosaic list and interesting to-day chiefly for the names that were missing. If de Hooch and Hobbema were little appreciated, Frans Hals and Jan van Goyen were not appreciated at all. As to Vermeer, whose rare works have been more prized in the last two generations than those of any other painter that are likely to reach the saleroom, his very name had been forgotten. In 1763 the *Music Lesson* at Windsor was acquired by Consul Smith for George III as a Frans Mieris.

After 1795, when the French invasion of Holland brought several Dutch collections to London, the English cult for the Dutch school reached extravagant heights. Some of the prices, paid by the Prince Regent in 1811 and 1812 through the Marquess of Hertford and Sir Francis Baring, were not equalled till after 1900. At this time the Dutch paintings had become something more than substitutes for good examples of the Italian school that were unobtainable. They had become a form of political taste, a Whig taste. Painted by republicans, for the most part Protestants, at the time of the English Civil War and the Commonwealth, they acquired new virtues during the political struggles of Fox and Wilkes against court influence. It was a Hanoverian tradition that the heir to the throne supported the anti-court party. The Prince of Wales bought Dutch pictures because they were bought by his Whig friends. Nevertheless it was French taste, and court taste at that, which had originally made Dutch *genre* painting fashionable.

How odd that collectors who had been brought up on gods and goddesses, saints and angels, rolling on cotton-wool, should take to the two Flemings, David Teniers the younger and Adriaen Brouwer and to the Dutchman, Adriaen van Ostade. Their little stumpy figures smell of poverty and there is generally someone who vomits or relieves nature in a corner. These are not romantic pictures, nor are they sentimental like the peasant pictures of Greuze and Morland, nor moral like the later pastiches of Teniers, which were painted by David Wilkie. It is still more difficult to believe that anyone could have found them humorous. Yet the purveyors of *le chic* and *le bon ton* made Teniers an honorary Frenchman under the name of 'Tenière', and by a peculiar stroke of malice his little vomiting figures found their way to the Royal factory at Sèvres, where they were copied on *pâte tendre*, all frilled and petticoated with grounds of *rose pompadour* and *œil de perdrix*.

The answer to this riddle is, I think, that the growth of the French taste for Dutch and Flemish pictures of low company had become involved with politics, just as it had in England. In France the background was not fashionable Whiggery but fashionable rationalism. The Dutch and Flemish *genre* painters inflicted no dim religious light on their clients. The more their work recalled the daily scenes of life, the more their compatriots had liked it. To Gersaint, the agent of Watteau, the matter was once explained by Wassenaer of Opdam, an aged Dutch collector, who had known some of the great men in person: 'We may be wrong, but we love the kind of pictures which show us faithfully what we see every day. We perceive in these pictures the habits, pleasures and problems of our peasants, their simplicity, their jokes, their joy, their sorrows, their character, their passions, their clothes. All is expressed with the most exact truth. Nothing is affected. They are painted according to their nature. We feel that we are seeing them and hearing them. Everything speaks to us. That is what enchants us.'[1]

To a Frenchman of the generation of Diderot, realism meant something less wide-eyed, nordic and innocent than this. It was the partner of the cult of reason, of the desire to level and overthrow. It was welcomed because it stripped its subjects of the dignity of flowing draperies, clouds and ancillary cherubs. Realism was better still when it made the subject grotesque. It was a half-way house till the Revolution arrived, when the subjects were quite naked, though armed and helmeted as correctly as a Regiment of Guards.

But if that is where the little 'masters of the tight brush' were lead-

[1] Charles Blanc: *Le trésor de la curiosité*, Paris (1857), I, CXVIII.

ing, what are we to make of Rembrandt? Surely he has nothing to do with the terribly hard and neat painting that was encouraged by the Revolution. Yet before the Paris art market collapsed completely through emigration, confiscation and devalued *assignats*, the value of Rembrandt rose continuously: £240 in 1763, £555 in the famous Blondel de Gagny sale of 1776, £685 at the Choiseul-Praslin sale of 1793 on the very eve of the Terror. At that time no such market existed in England. Reynolds, for instance, appeared in his *Discourses* to have very little use for Rembrandt, criticising the blackness of his pictures in 1778 and his use of the palette knife in order to achieve 'accidental' effects in 1784. But with his habitual inconsistency it was Reynolds who made the English vogue for Rembrandt. While on a visit to Holland in 1781 or 1783, he bought the *Susanna and the Elders* and *The Vision of Daniel*, works of startlingly original composition, which clearly influenced Reynolds's later subject pictures. In the sale of Reynolds's collection in 1795 they made £163 15*s*. and £178 18*s*. These were low prices by Paris standards, but the English market was still restricted to practising painters, who could discern Rembrandt's experiments with pigment beneath the yellow gold layers of varnish and the dead cracked bitumen. Benjamin West and Lawrence were the chief addicts, and in 1797 Lawrence sold the *Jewish Merchant* of the National Gallery to Sir George Beaumont, himself an amateur painter. for £210.

The culmination of this vogue was reached some fourteen years later when the Prince Regent gave £5,250 for *The Shipbuilder and his Wife*, but the market was highly selective. A Rembrandt had either to be very large or full of small figures. For this reason in 1807 the Council of the Royal Academy hesitated and finally declined to buy the *Susanna* at £200. Together with *The Vision of Daniel*, it was bought by Lord Lechmere. In 1883 these two pictures, which had played a historic part in the formation of English taste, were picked up in Paris cheaply for the Kaiser Friedrich Museum.

The truth of the matter was that this taste of painters never truly established itself in England. Wilkie, who, like Reynolds, was tempted by Rembrandt into the use of bitumen, had to lighten his palette to suit the mood of the 1820's. And, with the advent of the rather gaudy pictures of the English Romantics, interest in Rembrandt flagged. After the Regent's purchase of *The Shipbuilder and his Wife* in 1811, no Rembrandt made 5,000 guineas in the London salerooms for another eighty years.

3. *Paris Taste; The Houghton Sale*

The success of the late eighteenth-century painters in creating a brief foothold for Rembrandt was all the stranger, because Rembrandt had sometimes tried the Grand Manner and this was by no means suited to his genius. On the Paris market, where the big baroque Italian pictures that appealed to English noblemen were scarcely to be found, the Grand Manner meant pre-eminently the religious subjects of Rubens and Van Dyck and the works of Claude and Nicolas Poussin. The market was created by a class that had no counterpart in England, the *Intendants Généraux* and *fermiers généraux*, who made fortunes collecting on commission the unstable revenues of the country. Clever men of low origin, their taste was vulgar and frilly, though it has remained the taste of financiers ever since. In England, where nobility and middle class alike were more puritanical in their nature, there was a different order of preferences, which had become very marked at the eve of the French Revolution. The French preferred Poussin to Claude, the English preferred Claude to Poussin. The English did not give much for Van Dyck either, even though he had passed a great part of his life in England, and had allowed the reticence of the English character to modify his style. But to a self-made *Intendant*, the great prize was Rubens. It had been perceived that Rubens's rosy expanses of flesh accommodated themselves in a singular manner to Gouthière mounts and slabs of green malachite—a function which is performed by Renoir to-day.

Not so in this country. The Englishman of sentiment and taste viewed Rubens with more inhibited feelings on the decidedly rare occasions when he had the chance of seeing his pictures at all. Since the paintings which Charles I had commissioned from Rubens had mostly left the country during the Commonwealth, the only English temple of Rubens at the end of the eighteenth century was Blenheim Palace, where picture-viewing was a costly experience. The love of the first Duke of Marlborough for Rubens had belonged to a rumbustious age, unperturbed by priggish notions of 'ideal beauty' and the 'sublime'. It had been so real a love that the Duke had actually paid for some of his possessions, a most unusual thing among the commanders of invading armies. Even so the Blenheim Rubenses were a mixed lot. Possibly only the *Garden of the Hesperides*, the *Drunken Silenus* and the *Andromeda Enchained* exhibited Rubens's hand as well as his direction. In 1781, John Byng, Viscount Torrington, could find nothing better to

Johann Zoffany: *The Tribunal of the Uffizzi Gallery, Florence*, 1774. Showmanship as the eighteenth century knew it, schools mixed indiscriminately, sculpture and paintings in one room; every inch of space is used. On the left the smaller Madonna of Raphael, once at Panshanger, which Zoffany had just bought for Lord Cowper. It was sold to P. A. B. Widener for £116,500 in 1913.

This picture is now in the Royal Collections at Windsor Castle and is reproduced by gracious permission of Her Majesty the Queen.

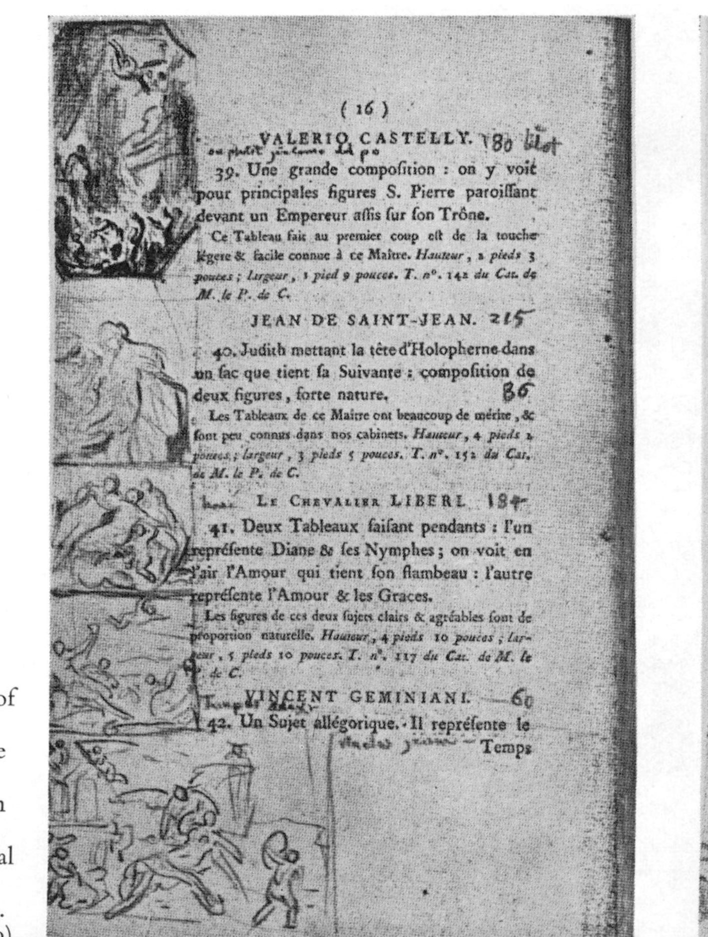

(16)

VALERIO CASTELLY.

39. Une grande compoſition : on y voit pour principales figures S. Pierre paroiſſant devant un Empereur aſſis ſur ſon Trône.

Ce Tableau fait au premier coup eſt de la touche légere & facile connue à ce Maître. *Hauteur*, 2 *pieds* 3 *pouces; largeur*, 1 *pied* 9 *pouces. T. n°.* 142 *du Cat. de M. le P. de C.*

JEAN DE SAINT-JEAN.

40. Judith mettant la tête d'Holopherne dans un ſac que tient ſa Suivante : compoſition de deux figures, forte nature.

Les Tableaux de ce Maître ont beaucoup de mérite, & ſont peu connus dans nos cabinets. *Hauteur*, 4 *pieds* 2 *pouces; largeur*, 3 *pieds* 5 *pouces. T. n°.* 152 *du Cat. de M. le P. de C.*

LE CHEVALIER LIBERI.

41. Deux Tableaux faiſant pendants : l'un repréſente Diane & ſes Nymphes ; on voit en l'air l'Amour qui tient ſon flambeau : l'autre repréſente l'Amour & les Graces.

Les figures de ces deux ſujets clairs & agréables ſont de proportion naturelle. *Hauteur*, 4 *pieds* 10 *pouces ; largeur*, 5 *pieds* 10 *pouces. T. n°.* 117 *du Cat. de M. le P. de C.*

VINCENT GEMINIANI.

42. Un Sujet allégorique. Il repréſente le Temps

(40)

116. Un grand Payſage répréſentant l'entrée d'un Village. Sur le premier plan, à droite, & près d'une maiſon, eſt un grouppe de quatre figures, dont trois cauſent enſemble : ſur le ſecond plan, on en voit quelques autres à table à la porte d'un Cabaret.

Ce morceau eſt agréable & du meilleur temps de ce Maître. *Hauteur*, 3 *pieds* 6 *pouces ; largeur*, 5 *pieds*. *T.*

BRAWER.

117. Un Tableau repréſentant une chambre où ſe voient ſix figures, les unes buvant & les autres fumant.

Il eſt bien touché & ſpirituellement fait. *Hauteur*, 1 *pied ; largeur*, 10 *pouces. B.*

F. VANDERMEULEN.

118. Deux petits Tableaux pendants. Tous deux repréſentent des combats de Cavalerie au paſſage d'un pont : dans l'un des deux on voit ſur la hauteur des bagages attaqués & ſurpris par l'Ennemi.

On voit dans l'un & dans l'autre une quantité prodigieuſe de figures, & par-tout l'ordre d'une compoſition heureuſe, quoiqu'en petit. Ils ſont d'ailleurs d'un tranſparent & d'une légéreté admirables. *Hauteur*, 8 *pouces & demi ; largeur*, 12 *pouces. B, n°.* 420 *du Cat. de M. le P. de C.*

Two pages from the catalogue of the sale of the Prince de Conti, Paris, 1779, one of the great sales of the eighteenth century. In the margins are drawings of the actual pictures by Gabriel de St. Aubin. (Sotheby's sale of 1959) say of them than this: 'Some of the apartments are newly furnished and abound with paintings of Reubens, not a favourite master of mine, as all his male figures are coarse and his women wet nurses.'[1]

In 1783 the Imperial Governor of the Netherlands confiscated the property of the Belgian monasteries and convents and a number of Rubens altarpieces came on the market. The great altarpiece of the Grosvenor family, which fetched £275,000 in 1959, was sold in Brussels for £700. Sir Joshua Reynolds, who had gone to Brussels on a bargain hunt, complained that he was asked £3,500 for *The Rape of the Sabines*, which was a private property belonging to Madame Bosschaert of Antwerp. The picture was bought by Angerstein and, since Angerstein's son accepted £2,500 from the British Government in 1824, it may be presumed that the lower rather than the higher sum was paid in 1785. Sir Joshua Reynolds spent no more than £1,000, but obtained a large number of pictures, among them several putative Rubenses, and the National Gallery's *Self-portrait*, which he believed to be a Van Dyck.

If the apostle of 'ideal beauty' himself could violate his principles sufficiently to join in the hunt, some re-appraisal of Rubens was inevitable, though hitherto English buyers had abstained altogether from the competition of the Paris salerooms. Very soon after 1800, several Rubens paintings, which reached London, fetched £4,000 each and more, but before 1792 it is doubtful whether any purported Rubens picture made more than 200 guineas at a London auction sale. Yet on the eighteenth-century Paris market the advance was continuous. *St. Cecilia* fetched £400 in the Carrignan sale of 1742 and more than £800 in the Tallard sale of 1756. *Helena Fourment and her Child*, now in the Louvre, made £832 in the sale of M. La Live de Jully in 1768, while a fellow financier, Randon de Boisset, gave close on £1,000 for it within a year or two, but was compelled to sell at a loss. This was not the dearest of Randon de Boisset's purchases. In 1766, while on a picture hunt in Flanders with the painter Boucher, he came across a battered altarpiece in the little church of Bourg St. Vinox. The elders of the village were prepared to sell the altarpiece in order to repair the church. It cost Randon de Boisset £880, but he had to spend another £370 on restoring it. £1,250 was an unthinkable sum, which his heirs never recovered.[2] On the other hand the success of the speculators in

[1] The *Torrington Diaries*, I, p. 53 (ed. 1934).

[2] It belonged later to Cardinal Fesch and Lucien Buonaparte. It made £1,260 in 1853 and £2,689 in New York in 1915. It is now regarded as a schoolpiece.

Belgium in 1783 can be judged from the fact that between 1798 and 1800 at least nine Rubens paintings which reached London from the Continent fetched over a thousand pounds, and one of them, the Duke of Orleans's *Judgement of Paris*, was valued for Lord Kinnaird at 2,000 guineas.

By contrast the English market in the works of Poussin lacked excitement. Eighteenth-century prices scarcely fulfilled the hopes that had been placed in Poussin by speculators in his own lifetime. Poussin had died in Rome in 1665, having seen his own work for years past frequently fetching more than the hundred guineas or thereabouts that was the sign of true success among the Italian painters of 'ideal beauty'. On one occasion during his life a picture by Poussin was auctioned in Rome for a thousand pistoles or £400. Fifty years after Poussin's death, the Regent, Duke of Orleans, gave 120,000 livres or £4,800 for the seven pictures illustrating the *Sacraments*. Nevertheless on the eve of the French Revolution, £800 would have been an exceptionally high price for a single picture. David and the neo-classicists paid due respect to Poussin's rhythmical lines of figures in the attitudes of Roman sculpture, but the market stayed curiously level.

Had it not been for English buyers, the market in Claude Lorrain might have stayed lower still. French neo-classicism was the enemy of atmospheric painting, and it must be added that Claude had used an impure palette, which had reduced his paintings to a dingy condition in a comparatively short time. There was less objection to this in England, where the climate and the coal fires has a levelling effect on all paintings. As early as the Verrue sale of 1737, when a Claude landscape with figures fetched the unprecedented sum of £320, the phenomenon could be accounted for by the all-embracing words 'pour l'Angleterre'. The knowing Mrs Jameson believed that the fashion had been started by Frederick, Prince of Wales, who died in 1751.[1] About the year 1770, the celebrated amateur French dealer, Noel Desenfans, brought a Claude painting from Paris which he sold to George III for £1,000.

It was the beginning of a wildly exaggerated English cult for Claude, whose origin was to be sought in the search for the 'picturesque', by which was meant the well-ordered landscape which men of sensibility liked to see round their houses. When the 'picturesque' had become an organised industry with its own landscape engineers and its ruin-and-temple architects, Claude was promoted to the rank of the

[1] Mrs Jameson's *Companion to the most Celebrated Private Galleries in London*, 1844.

highest-priced painter on the market. For while Poussin was no better than Titian, who painted landscapes to his figures, Claude actually painted figures to his landscapes. Moreover he had taken the trouble to record his larger pictures in a book of drawings, the *Liber Veritatis*, which was reproduced in a series of indifferent aquatint etchings by Earlom in 1771. Since the pictures tended to be all of the same dimensions, it was like buying a racehorse from a stud-book. You built your drawing room accordingly and waited till the space over the mantelpiece could be filled.

No one could buy a Rubens or a Titian this way. Consequently, long before the speculation in Claude paintings that followed the French occupation of Rome in 1797–1799, the price in London of a full-sized Claude had become fabulous. Let us take, for instance, the *Departure of St. Ursula*, which is perhaps the most popular to-day of the National Gallery's twelve Claude paintings. In 1760 it was bought in Rome by William Locke of Juniper Hall. During the 1770's Desenfans obtained it for £1,200 and sold it to the speculator Moore Slade of Rochester. Slade had to part with it at a loss to the Dutch dealer Hethyuzen and Desenfans then got it back only to sell it in 1786 to the financier, John Julius Angerstein, for £2,500. But this was a mere prelude to the story of the Altieri Claudes, which will be told in the next chapter, a pair of landscapes with figures, which Beckford bought for £6,825 in 1799 and for which Hart Davis paid £12,600 in 1808.

It is ironical that the great Turner, who constantly proclaimed himself the disciple, and who believed himself the rival of Claude, should have invented a style which killed the Claude market. In the 1830's a pair of country gentleman's Claudes was already less in demand. John Glover, who once copied a Claude and a Poussin at the same time, who could turn out an imitation Claude once a week, and who got more for them than Constable received for any of his landscapes, wisely emigrated to Tasmania in 1830.

From the 1840's onwards very few Claude paintings reached the £1,000 mark. In 1895 a full-sized Claude landscape, recorded in the *Liber Veritatis*, made only £472. Eventually a ridiculous situation was reached. In December 1935, *Hagar and Ishmael*, which had fetched £409 10*s*. in 1811, was sold for £220 10*s*., whereas in the following year a pen-and-ink study of two ships in the Oppenheimer Collection made £735. It looked like the funeral of the well-smoked chimney-piece Claude—but not quite. In April 1940 the 12,000-guinea Altieri Claudes reappeared in the saleroom and started the present recovery by making 2,500 guineas (see page 219).

With Nicolas Poussin the fall was still more catastrophic. In 1855, the Earl of Ashburnham's two 'Triumphs' could still fetch more than £1,200 each. But at the Miles sale of 1884, when the Altieri Claudes at least kept their value, the Poussin *Plague at Athens* had to be bought in at £420. In 1911 *Les funérailles de Phocion* was sold in London for £367 10*s*. In the Day and Robit sales of 1800–1801 it would have made at least 1,000 guineas. However, the purchase of this picture by the Louvre in 1921 heralded a Poussin revival which was stimulated by a peculiar piece of intellectual pretentiousness. This was the theory that Post-impressionism and Cubism were in the pure French classical tradition, as transmitted by David and Ingres. Even so, the National Gallery's *Adoration* was bought at Sotheby's in June 1956 for a great deal less than the price of a Braque abstract or a 'blue period' Picasso, namely £29,000.

Before passing from the saleroom favourites of the period 1760–1798 we have yet to consider the only Spanish painter whose name was one to conjure with.[1] Murillo, who was treated as an Italian painter, rated very high in the market for moist eyes and histrionic pathos. A 'Mr Mendez' had imported the first Murillos to London where they were bought in 1756 by Sir Samson Gideon.[2] In Paris Murillo was soon the rival of Rubens and Teniers, a picture in the Gaignat sale of 1768 fetching £730. At Desenfans's London exhibition of 1786 Calonne, the former French finance minister, gave £900 for the Dulwich Gallery *Flower Girl*, which Desenfans bought back in 1798 for £682 10*s*. But although Sir Simon Clark was said to have paid Bryan the astonishing price of 4,000 guineas for a pair of Murillo altarpieces in the Paris Robit sale of 1801 (see page 48), the real speculation in Murillo was early Victorian. Its height was reached in 1852–1853, when the Soult and Louis Philippe sales released a flood of altarpieces, which had been frozen off from the market since the Peninsular War.

Thus in the period 1760–1792 the northern schools reigned paramount in the Paris and London salerooms. Their advance was certain, whereas Italian works, imported according to the fashions of half a century ago and unrefreshed by new discoveries, wavered capriciously.

[1] But authentic Velasquez paintings had reached the country. Benjamin West valued the Houghton Hall portrait of *Innocent X* at only £60 in 1779. When it left Russia in 1931, eventually to join the Washington National Gallery, it cost Mr. Andrew Mellon nearly a thousand times as much. But in 1790 Vandergucht sold the National Gallery's *Admiral Pulido-Pareja* to Lord Radnor for 600 guineas, according to the newspaper reports of the day. (W. T. Whitley: *Artists and Their Friends in England*, I, p. 133.)

[2] One of them, a *Flight into Egypt*, made £3,360 at the Fremantle sale, 1945.

The period may be epitomised by one enormous transaction which took place in the very middle, for the collection, which Sir Robert Walpole had amassed at Houghton Hall in the 1720's and 1730's, was rich in both elements. In 1777, when he urged Parliament to buy the Houghton Gallery for the British Museum, John Wilkes declared that it was second only to the Orleans Gallery. It was not, however, the British Government that bought the pictures, but the Empress Catherine of Russia, who spent more than £40,000.

Horace Walpole, who disliked all this money going to his nephew, did not endorse Wilkes's description. In July 1779, when the pictures were still in England, he wrote to his friend, the Rev. W. Cole, that the best things had been sold off long ago, and that the Empress was being charged for the remains as much as his grandfather had spent on the whole collection. The prices for the individual works had, it is true, been fixed according to the exalted ideas of Benjamin West. In most cases they were two or three times as much as the auction-room maximum of the day. It is, however, the proportional values that are interesting, for none of the auction sales of the late eighteenth century gives so perfect a cross-section. The three Robert Strange sales in the 1770's are on too low a level, and the Calonne, Bryan and Dundas sales of the 1790's already show the results of wartime speculation.

The collection cost the Empress £40,555 on the valuation alone, without the transport costs, equivalent perhaps to half a million to-day and, though the largest of her block purchases, it was only one of six collections which she purchased between 1764 and 1779, spending altogether £150,000 or £1,800,000 by to-day's values. The Empress's position in the late eighteenth-century art market was consequently rather like that of the small group of American millionaires, who were managed by Duveen between 1901 and 1939, but the results were not at all comparable. There were competitors against Duveen, so that, although he wanted a high market, he did not always have to create it artificially. The Empress had no competitors. When her agents were absent, prices fell.

The purchase comprised 174 paintings, but only a small portion will be found recorded in the latest edition of the catalogue of the Hermitage Museum (1958). The survivors are clearly marked with the wonderfully phonetic designation ХОУТОН ХОЛЛ. Of the rest, many indifferent works were sold off or given away by the Imperial family, and a few of the very finest were sold to Mr. Andrew Mellon in 1931, at very high prices. Guido Reni's *Immaculate Conception*, which, as we have already seen, cost the Empress the unheard-of sum of £3,500, cuts but a poor figure among the marvels of the present-day Hermitage. But the next most expensive of the Houghton purchases, the Van Dyck *Holy Family*, and the Rubens *Magdalen Kissing the Feet of Christ*, which cost £1,600 each, are still among the museum's better-known treasures. West's valuations were on his usual high scale, but in the case of the *Holy Family*, nearly ten feet long, the figure may have been based on the £1,400 which Robert Walpole had paid the Princess of Friesland in the 1730's for a picture in such perfect eighteenth-century taste and swarming with cherubs like a Murillo. The price was far above the level of Van Dyck, whose most costly work at this time was the Duc de la Guiche's equestrian *Charles I*, now in the Louvre. It had been sold in 1771 for £708. That, however, was a portrait, and here we come across a peculiar kink in West's mind. He was determined that full-length portraits, painted by the illustrious dead, should not be esteemed higher than modern portrait commissions. So the dozen Van Dyck portraits were all priced at £200 or less. They were the very pick of Houghton Hall and had been spared the saleroom in 1751. Among them was the *Young Man carrying a Spear* (Philip, Lord Wharton), which left the Hermitage for the U.S.A. in 1931, costing Mr. Andrew Mellon £45,000. Yet West valued it at £200 with the rest.

After the two big Rubens and Van Dyck subject pictures, the next most costly picture in the list was most amazingly a Pietro da Cortona at £1,000. Pietro da Cortona [1599–1665] is remembered as a man who painted by the acre, crowding innumerable ceilings with his suspended baroque figures and knocking out of his way golden mosaics that might have been contemplated by St. Augustine. But the valuation was in the French fashion. *Jacob and Laban* was destined to be bought for Louis XVI in 1784 at £1,436, the auction record of the century. One has only to look at his easel pictures to see why 'Pierre de Cortone' became an honorary Frenchman. Nicolas Poussin, who had died in the same year, had borrowed a trick from him, that of rows of figures hurrying in opposite directions in the most demented fashion but *très correctes*, always in parallel lines. It was to become the most tiresome convention of the painters of the French Revolution, but uncommonly useful for battle-pictures and much in evidence in Singleton Copley's excellent *Death of Major Pierson* in the Tate Gallery (see page 68).

At £700 each, a Murillo and a Salvator Rosa were priced somewhat in advance of the times, while the French classicists were certainly based on the Paris market rather than on London: Nicolas Poussin at £900, £800 and £600; Lesueur and Sebastian Bourdon at £500 and £400. By contrast the Venetian painters were valued so low that Robert

Walpole himself could hardly have bought this school seriously. Evidently West believed the two Titians, which he valued at £100 each, to be copies, since the works of two school-painters, Palma Vecchio and Paris Bordone, were entered at £250 and £200. Of the three Veroneses at £100 each, one was thought by Horace Walpole to be a copy.

One may notice that a collection, which was typical of a time, thirty or forty years before Reynolds's famous lecture, contained so little of the Venetian school. By contrast obscure Roman painters, some of them alive in Robert Walpole's day, proliferated. That they should be forgotten to-day is only natural, but in fact the names of Carlo Cignani, Cantarini, Niccolo Berretone, Filippo Lauri, Giuseppe Chiari, Stella, Valerio and Matteo Ponzone could not have meant much in 1779 either. They were the heroes of Benjamin West's student days and he rated them high. Hardly any of these pictures cost the Empress less than £200 and the Cantarini *Holy Family* cost £300. On the other hand, a huge Francesco Albano and Pietro Mola's *Marcus Curtius*, works of men who were still esteemed giants, were valued at £700 and £400.

A fall in values since Robert Walpole's day may have been recorded in Benjamin West's valuation of the works of Carlo Maratta. At one time there had been thirty-five of them at Houghton in a special gallery, hung with green velvet. Half a century before the sale, Robert Walpole had obtained them from the Arnaldi Palace in Florence through a French painter. Now only eleven pictures were left, and the most expensive one (which Horace Walpole thought a copy) was sold for £300. The excellent portrait of *Clement the IXth* in the Hermitage Museum was valued at £250, and it may be recalled that another version, now in the Cassel Museum, was sold in London in 1894 for £84. Yet there has been a time when everyone knew who was meant by 'the divine Carlo'. And they did not confuse him with Carlino, who was *bien entendu* Carlo Dolci.

The Dutch-Flemish *genre* paintings were valued according to the disparaging taste of Benjamin West. The Teniers *Cookshop* cost £800 despite the £1,248 recently paid for Blondel de Gagny's *Prodigal Son*. It was hardly more than the £700 paid for the trivial *Bathsheba and Abishag* of Adriaen van der Werff, which had fitted so well into the Northern Italianising taste of Robert Walpole's day. The work of the mighty Frans Hals of Haarlem was in a less luxurious category. The so-called portrait of the painter's son was valued at £40. Like Velasquez's small head of *Innocent Xth*, it was destined to be sold to Mr. Andrew Mellon in 1931 for a little less than a thousand times what the Empress had paid for it. In 1779 Benjamin West must have found

Frans Hals a very vulgar painter, but the early Victorians found him still more so and were hardly prepared to give £5 for such a picture. Hals's soulless brilliance was essentially a late nineteenth-century cult. It was only towards 1900 that Lord Hertford's extravagant purchase of 1865, *The Laughing Cavalier* (so miscalled), began to brood over every schoolroom.

But the most astonishing of the valuations in the Houghton list is surely that of the two Van Huysum flowerpieces at £1,200 the pair, that is to say twice as much as the two Houghton Rembrandts, the *Portrait of Saskia* and the *Sacrifice of Isaac by Abraham*. One may be quite certain that, should there be another Hermitage sale in the 1960's, it would carry the latter picture beyond the £300,000 or even the £400,000 mark; but Huysum! One of the dearest is still William Beckford's *Splendid assemblage of flowers*, bought in 1793 for £368 and last sold in 1927 for £3,800. Possibly only one Van Huysum has fetched so much since.

The worship of Huysum, the most mechanical and the least inspired of the 'masters of the tight brush', showed eighteenth-century taste at its most deplorable. It may be slightly to the credit of Benjamin West that in this case he did not advise the Empress to buy much above the market, since 1,000 guineas had actually been paid for a pair of Van Huysums in London at the Liotard sale of 1773. All ages have failed to distinguish between skill and genius. But the eighteenth century cynically rated skill much higher than genius. Since Van Huysum died only in 1749, there was no element of antiquity or rarity in the valuation of 1779. A modern imitation, if sufficiently meticulous, could make as much. In 1801 the sum of £610 was bid for an imitation by the living Dutch painter Jan van Os, while in 1808 a near-Huysum, painted by the Bath coach-painter, James Hewlett, was bought for close on £800.[1] Wilkie and Haydon were much entertained that year by Hoppner's violence at Lord Mulgrave's table. Learning that Hewlett was now asking £945 for a single fruit-and-flowerpiece, Hoppner declared that 'Hewlett ought to be smothered'.[2]

Though this was the price of four or five fine Rembrandts or a large gallery of Italian primitives in the year 1808, one should not be too sanctimonious about the false gods of another age. Modern pundits of a standing equivalent to Beckford's no longer declare that Gerard Dou was 'the greatest of the Flemish masters' simply because his figures seem to lean out of the picture frame. This is not because the world has

[1] Whitley: *Art in England*, p. 117.

[2] Farington, *op. cit.*, V, p. 26.

grown more discriminating, but because in 150 or 200 years there have been enough masters of pure dexterity to debase the market.

It may occasion surprise that in a gallery of such typical eighteenth-century taste as Houghton Hall there should have been even one picture which by the standards of the time was almost 'Gothic'. It was a *Holy Family*, attributed to Giovanni Bellini, and it was valued at £60, which was Benjamin West's way of saying that it might be worth twenty. A far more sprightly valuation, £200, was put on the *Usurer and his Wife*, attributed to Quentin Matsys, which, though no older, was considerably more gothic. Northern primitives could fetch far more than Italian primitives in the eighteenth century for a number of reasons. The northern market was bolstered by an ancestor cult. If a Holbein or a Mabuse or even a Memling did not precisely portray an Englishman of the period, one could always paint a name on it. But no one could claim to be the descendant of a Botticelli, while the Italians themselves had become too infatuated with their post-Raphaelesque painters even to remember the names of the authors of many of their great frescoes and altarpieces.

But a northern picture was not unsaleable even if it dated from the fifteenth century. It could be called a Dürer or a Van Eyck. The market depended on that appeal of infinite dexterity in which the earlier Italians were lacking. The Castle Howard Mabuse, the *Adoration of the Kings*, made news enough in 1911 when it cost the nation £40,000. But who could have believed that it cost the 5th Earl more than the price of a fine Rubens in the 1790's? Sold by Prince Alexander of Lorraine in 1781 as a Dürer, it was brought to England in 1787 by a M. de Fulens and exhibited by John Greenwood, the American auctioneer, in Leicester Square at a shilling a head. After several attempts to auction it, the picture was bought by Bryan and sold to the Earl of Carlisle in 1795 for 500 guineas. The Earl prized it so much that it lived at Castle Howard in its own room, protected by a green silk blind.[1]

It was no ordinary Flemish primitive that could be worth a shilling to look at in 1787 or that could be reproduced in full-scale colour-photography to form a Christmas shopping display in 1958. More than half a century was to pass before a work of this kind could again command 500 guineas, but decidedly this purchase in the last years of the eighteenth century showed the shape of things to come.

[1] Whitley: *Artists and Their Friends in England*, I, pp. 191–3.

CHAPTER TWO

The Revolutionary and Napoleonic Period 1792–1815

1. *The Orleans Sales, 1792–1800* — 2. *The Rome and Genoa Dispersals* — 3. *From the Peace of Amiens to Waterloo*

---

1. *The Orleans Sales, 1792–1800*

The famous collection, whose arrival in London was to transform the market, was not an unblemished treasure. Out of 400 pictures, it is possible that not a twelfth part could find a place to-day on the walls of the six leading galleries of the world. Many can no longer be identified, and some that have been identified have fetched ludicrous sums in the present century, in one case 2 guineas.[1] And yet the Orleans gallery included several pictures which are to-day among the world's best-known.

Of twelve alleged Raphaels, no less than nine have stood up to 170 years of expertise, though three of them are only small predella panels. Of the twenty-seven Titians, nine are still admitted in the canon, and of these the four *Poesie*, which were picked by the Duke of Bridgewater, constitute a unique series. The four Veronese allegories in the National Gallery and the Tintoretto *Origin of the Milky Way*, which shares the room with them, are known to millions of people, though they were among the lowest-priced pictures in the collection. The Rubens pictures of the Orleans Gallery include the Windsor *St. George* landscape,

[1] Duke of Sutherland, Christie's, 1913: Ludovico Carracci, *Christ Crowned with Thorns* (£63 in 1798), £2 2*s*.

the National Gallery's *Judgement of Paris*, and the Boston Gallery's *Thomyris*. The Rembrandts include the Washington National Gallery's *Mill* from the Landsowne and Widener collections.

With not many exceptions the pictures had been bought between 1715 and 1723, when the nephew of Louis XIV, Philippe, Duke of Orleans, was Regent of France. The Duke was a bold bidder, but not, like Augustus III of Saxony, a wild bidder. In the 1730's Robert Walpole had paid £1,400 for his Van Dyck *Holy Family*, but the Regent never gave more than £1,000 for a picture. If he had better pictures than Walpole, it was because he had the advice of a truly-inspired man, Pierre Crozat, the banker and patron of Watteau. It was Crozat who in 1715 discovered for the Regent the forty-seven pictures of Don Livio Odescalchi and these were nothing less than the residue of the Gonzaga gallery after the purchases made by King Charles I in 1627. They had come to rest in Rome in the late seventeenth century after passing through the hands of two Imperial generals and Queen Christina of Sweden.

The Regent also acquired part of the lost British heritage of Charles I's collection since many of the King's pictures, which had been bought in London by the Antwerp banker, Jabach, had reached the Palais Royale gallery by purchase from the Mazarin, Richelieu and other families.

The motive of 'Philippe Egalité' for selling his grandfather's pictures was twofold. He was badly in debt and he was trying to finance a party in the National Assembly which would depose the King and make him Regent. The collection was offered in England as early as 1790, when a syndicate was formed to buy it for 100,000 guineas. When it was known that the Prince of Wales had put his name down for £7,000, and those of two of his brothers at £5,000 each, the prospect that the plums would go to the royal family discouraged further subscribers.[1] Furthermore Christie, who had despatched his agent, Philippe Tassaert, to Paris, learnt that the pictures, in spite of all that had been said about them, were not worth 100,000 guineas.

But the Duke's affairs became so pressing that, late in 1791, he pledged his French and Italian pictures alone to Walkuers, the Belgian banker, for 750,000 francs or £30,000. Walkuers sold them for 900,000 francs to a M. Laborde de Mereville, whose views were so liberal that, far from decamping with his treasures, he began to build a gallery in the Rue d'Artois as a tribute to the new constitutional state. But before the Terror was in full swing M. Mereville had got away to London with more than 300 pictures.

[1] Whitley: *Artists and Their Friends in England*, II, p. 180.

The Dutch and Flemish pictures were already in England. They had been on offer in May 1792, when an English syndicate sent Thomas Moore Slade to Paris to get them. This was the Slade who had owned Claude's *Departure of St. Ursula* and who was an experienced picture buyer. He reached Paris in the middle of June 1792, when the King was at Versailles, a prisoner of the National Assembly since his flight abroad. At this time the Duke of Orleans held a disreputable court in the Palais Royale, braving the heart of Revolutionary Paris, though he was to fall to the guillotine within eight months. The Duke believed himself to be virtually the Regent for the throne, and it had become less easy to do business with him. Finally he accepted Slade's bills of exchange for 350,000 francs, though the booty was nearly impounded by creditors.

At this point a new body of objectors appeared in the Palais Royale in the form of a band of art students from the Louvre, the pupils of Jacques Louis David, all national ardour in striped calico trousers and lank straight hair and probably as dirty as generations of their successors. The resourceful Chatham merchant dealt with these zealots by telling them that he had arranged for the pictures to go by Calais. In the meantime he packed them in a barge for Havre.

In London, Slade found sound backers in the persons of Lord Kinnaird and the amateur dealers, Morland and Hammersley, names that recur frequently in sales of the period. By March 1793 many of the pictures were on show at the old Royal Academy rooms in Pall Mall, where up to 2,000 people a week paid a shilling to see them. It was here that Mr. William Smith, M.P. for Norwich, bought the Rembrandt *Mill* for 500 guineas. In 1911 Lord Lansdowne sold it to Mr. P. A. B. Widener for £103,300.

But M. Mereville, who had spent by this time well over 1,000,000 francs, could not find a syndicate rich enough to buy him out. After two years had slipped by, there occurred the Calonne sale of March 1795 which showed only too clearly that the London market was not big enough to absorb a collection on the grand scale. The former French Minister of Finance, Charles de Calonne, had bought lavishly both in Paris and, since his emigration in 1787, in London. After the Revolution he mortgaged his pictures to Desenfans and the banker Herries in a desperate political bid for the leadership of the fugitive French *noblesse* at Coblenz. In 1794 the mortgagees foreclosed and the pictures were put on public exhibition. Desenfans, with his usual bad handling, refused good offers in the belief that the Empress Catherine would buy the collection. The Empress did not buy, and in 1795 Christie's held a dreary four-day sale. There were in fact few valuable pictures, and these were reserved for the last day. Scarcely a picture fetched as much as Calonne had given for it and the prices were not up to the Paris levels of the *ancien régime*. The Murillo *Flowergirl*, now at Dulwich, fell from £900 to £640, Reynolds's *Tragic Muse* from £735 to £320, the Poussin *Triumph of David* from £800 to £600, while another Poussin, which had cost Calonne £500, made only £125. Most of these pictures were bought in by the mortgagees.

Desenfans, who had a second unsold collection on his hands, which he had formed for the King of Poland, had the mortification of going to another dealer to dispose of his own wares. This dealer was Michael Bryan, the future author of the much re-issued *Dictionary of Modern Painters*. But the pictures, that had been bought in, fell still lower. The moment was the worst possible. In 1797 England had been at war for more than four years. The cost of living was rising, the Bank of England suspended payments, the Fleet mutinied, the French troops made a brief footing on the British mainland at Fishguard, and seemed to be on the point of swallowing Italy. The market for old masters was closely linked with the market for living painters, and this was wilting so badly that several Royal Academicians applied to their council for relief. Boydell, the successful print publisher, was driven into bankruptcy by the lack of foreign sales, and the studio effects of Gainsborough were auctioned off, some of them at a pound or two for each lot.

And even so, Bryan found the capital for Mereville's pictures. A single noble backer, the Duke of Bridgewater, put up the £43,000 and later he induced his nephew, Lord Gower, afterwards Marquess of Stafford, as well as the Earl of Carlisle, who had bought the Mabuse *Adoration of the Kings*, to come in with him. The man who could do all this in such a year as 1797 was certainly no ordinary person, but in fact not much is known of Michael Bryan. He was born in Newcastle in 1757, and in 1781 he settled in Bruges as an agent for his brother's cloth manufactory, having tried his hand as a schoolmaster and as an actor. Two years later, on a voyage to England, he was attentive to a sea-sick lady, who turned out to be a sister of the future Earl of Shrewsbury.[1] She married this man of obscure origin and bore him a large family. Bryan continued to live in Belgium. After the expropriation of the monasteries he started to deal in pictures. For some months he was interned by the French in Rotterdam, but was repatriated to England in 1794. He immediately opened a gallery in Savile Row, where he exhibited Dutch paintings, brought over by fellow fugitives. A French emigrant who had shared Bryan's captivity in Rotterdam introduced him to M. Mereville.

[1] Farington, *op. cit.*, III, p. 14.

The latter was not left a rich man after paying off his mortgages and the expenses of the lost years. He died in 1801, a lonely guest in an English country house. It had taken more than four years to raise £43,000, which was hardly more than the Empress Catherine had spent on the Houghton Gallery, but even in the prosperous year 1793 a collection, so predominantly Italian, was hard to handle, and it was over the Italian pictures in the collection that some of the later speculators burned their fingers.

The actual number of the pictures presented unheard-of difficulties. In 1798 when Bryan's backers decided to sell, two separate galleries in the Strand and Pall Mall had to be hired and, even after six months of continuous exhibition, large numbers of pictures remained unsold. Yet it is surprising how many people tried their hand at picture buying, both at the 1798 exhibition and at the auction of the unsold works, including those belonging to Moore Slade's syndicate, in 1800. The greater part were commoners, but the list of the chief buyers, printed by Buchanan, is so interesting sociologically that I have extracted most of the names in order to show the structure of the English market, which was quite unlike anything in Europe and grotesquely unlike pre-revolutionary France.

Nobility	*Art Dealers*	*Merchants*
Dukes of { Bedford, Bridgewater }	Cox	George Hibbert, M.P.
	Bryan	William Willett
Earl of Gower	Harris	Arnold Nesbitt, M.P.
Earl of Carlisle	Morland	William Smith, M.P.
Earl of Suffolk	Erard	Thomas Maitland, M.P.
Earl of Darnley	John Smith	Thomas Troward
Lord Berwick		Sir Abraham Hume
Lord Fitzwilliam		Hastings Elwyn
Lord Kinnaird		Sir George Hammersley
Lord Temple		Sir Philip Stephens
Lord Falmouth		
Lady Lucas		

Painters	*Bankers*	*Gentlemen Amateurs*
Walton	Thomas & Henry Hope	William Beckford
Udney	Julius Angerstein	Samuel Rogers
Cosway		John Davenport
Skipp		Justice Lawrence
		Charles Long, afterwards Lord Farnborough
		T. Fitzhugh

Under the heading of merchants are a number of men of social standing, all of whom seem to have been speculators rather than collectors and who disposed of their holdings at different times. Sir Abraham Hume seems to have become an amateur dealer who acted for Beckford. There was only one industrialist—and that, strange to say, was the great Duke who at one moment financed the entire speculation.

Francis Egerton, 3rd Duke of Bridgewater, was born in 1736 and became Duke at the age of twelve when his family considered him to be mentally defective—even more so, when in 1753 he returned from the Grand Tour under the care of the antiquarian Robert Wood of Palmyra fame. It seems that the young Duke was so bored with the tour that he did not bother to unpack his art-treasures, not even Palmyra Wood's portrait by Raphael Mengs. In 1758 he became engaged to one of the lovely Gunning sisters, Elizabeth, then the widowed Duchess of Hamilton. It appears that the Duke demanded a higher standard of moral conduct than the lady liked. The match was broken off and London Society blamed the Duke. In 1759, at the age of twenty-three, he quitted the London scene for his seat near Manchester, Worsley Old Hall.

For the rest of his life (he died in 1803) the Duke of Bridgewater had one passion—canals. A canal which carried coals from Worsley to Manchester was followed by a Manchester–Liverpool ship canal that nearly ruined him. In 1762 he had to cut his establishment to suit an expenditure of £400 a year. He spent £220,000 on his canal, but he lived to see it bring an income of £80,000 a year. In 1796, at the age of sixty, the child who had been judged mentally defective was experimenting with steam tugs. He had all the qualifications of millionaire eccentricity, wearing an untidy brown coat like Dr. Johnson's, smoking a navvy's clay pipe in public and talking of nothing but canals. And he remained a bachelor, not tolerating a single maidservant at Old Hall and hiring a friend's dining-room in order to entertain in London. But having been induced by the charm of Michael Bryan to speculate in old masters, the Duke of Bridgewater actually came to like them. In 1802 Joseph Farington found him reconciled to his town-house where a newly purchased Turner seascape, a daring patronage of youth, hung proudly with a Van de Velde fleet at anchor.

But the Duke was saving £20,000 a year of his income. Four years earlier, Farington had observed that he had insisted on defraying the cost of framing the Orleans pictures out of the exhibition receipts. The careful accumulation of an almost indestructible family fortune has had this result. Except for an occasional discarding of the less worthy purchases, the pictures, which the Duke left his nephews, have not quitted the Egerton family even to-day.

The pictures which the backers reserved for themselves cost them sums which were quite ludicrous even by the low standards of the late eighteenth century. A comparison between expenditure and receipts shows that the valuations which Bryan put on the reserved pictures had little meaning. Bryan valued the whole purchase at £72,000, of which the reserved portion (ninety-four pictures out of 305) accounted for £39,000. Of this portion, five-eighths were apportioned to the Duke of Bridgewater, a quarter was taken up by the Earl of Gower and an eighth by the Earl of Carlisle. The sale of the residue realised about £42,500 including exhibition receipts, and therefore practically covered the £43,000 paid to M. Mereville. The reserved pictures were not, however, an out-and-out free bonus, since there were Bryan's fees and expenses still to be accounted for, but these could not have involved many thousands. Thus the incredible valuation which Bryan put on Annibale Carracci's *Descent from the Cross*, though nominally £4,200, could not have meant more than a few hundreds to the Earl of Carlisle. But the point of the valuation still remains, namely that the Earl of Carlisle paid for this monstrous thing three and a half times as much as the Duke of Bridgewater gave for the most tender and poetical of Raphael's roundels, *Madonna with the Palm*.

Furthermore a price almost as high as the valuation of the Annibale Carracci was actually paid in ready money on the first morning of the exhibition, 26th December 1798, when John Julius Angerstein, that mysterious Germano-Russian foundling, walked into the Gallery and bought Sebastiano del Piombo's *Raising of Lazarus* for £3,750.[1] This picture, 12 ft. 6 ins. high, has been for 136 years the *Number One* of the National Gallery catalogue. As such, it was the picture to which the poet Tennyson would always take his children first. Its reputation dated from the day in 1519 when it was first displayed, for, according to Vasari, Sebastiano had been assisted by Michelangelo himself in order that he might surpass Cardinal Giulio di Medici's Raphael, *The Transfiguration*, a work the painter did not live to finish. The two pictures do indeed look so alike that Sebastiano was considered to have succeeded in his purpose. How the *Raising of Lazarus* reached the Chapter of Narbonne Cathedral is not quite clear, but in 1723 the Duke of Orleans bought it from the monks of the Chapter for 24,000 livres or £960.

[1] Why the backers let this picture go is a mystery. According to Farington, *op. cit.*, V, p. 183, the Duke of Bridgewater used to say. 'I ought to have bought that picture of Don Sebastian.'

One of the two 'Altieri' Claudes, *The Landing of Aeneas*. The second of the pair is *The Sacrifice of Apollo*. For the fabulous history of these two pictures, see pages 275-6. In 1808, when Philip Miles paid 12,000 guineas, they were the most expensive works of art in the world.

This picture is now in the collection of the Right Hon. the Lord Fairhaven, by whose courtesy it is published.

Frederick Mackenzie: *The Old National Gallery in Angerstein's House, No. 100 Pall Mall*, 1834. The big picture which is being copied is Sebastiano del Piombo's *Raising of Lazarus*, the Number One of the present National Gallery, which was then regarded as one of the three or four most valuable pictures in the world. For its story, see pages 409–10.

Mackenzie's picture is now in the Victoria and Albert Museum.

In 1814 the French government tried to recover *Lazarus*. Raphael's *Transfiguration* had been installed in 1803 in the *Salon Carré* of the Louvre after a triumphal procession through Paris. Louis XVIII believed that the powers would permit him to retain a picture that had merely been stolen from a Pope. In order that the two pictures might be shown together, Angerstein was offered £10,000. Angerstein declined not only this offer, but shortly afterwards an offer from Beckford of £16,000 if he would throw in the six Hogarth *Marriage à la Mode* pictures and Annibale Carracci's *St. John in the Wilderness*. Since these pictures were valued in Angerstein's estate at £2,700, he virtually refused £13,300 for the Sebastiano, the biggest offer that had ever been made for any picture in history.[1]

And yet, when Beckford made this offer, *Lazarus* had already been severely manhandled by Benjamin West, whom he detested. During the 1798 exhibition Sir Francis Bourgeois of the Royal Academy had observed that the picture lacked colour and character. So Lazarus was raised again from the dead by Benjamin West. The father of Sir Edwin Landseer used to declare that West had repainted the entire body of the resurrected man, as appears to be only too probable.

The incredible history of this work in the last manner of Raphael shows how lightly the genuine but immature Raphaels of the Orleans collection were esteemed. Even Bryan's valuations were in some cases very hesitant and, one might add, in inverse ratio to the merit of the works. First of all there was the Madonna, which the Duke of Orleans had bought from M. Seignelay and which had been known ever since as *La Belle Vierge*. It had been heavily repainted after its transfer from wood to canvas, and looked as fuzzy as a Correggio. Bryan, therefore, entered its value at 3,000 guineas. But the sad and moving little *Madonna del Passeggio*, which gleams like a jewel, was entered at only 300 guineas.[2] In between the two values the *Madonna with the Palm*, not quite a primitive and not quite a grand manner picture, was valued at 1,200 guineas. These pictures have never left the Egerton family, and to-day they must be worth well over a million pounds.

Yet the fate of the Orleans Raphael pictures, which were put on the open market, shows that Bryan's valuations had been too high. For instance, the Raphael of the present Duke of Westminster, a variant of

[1] W. T. Whitley: *Art in England*, II, p. 73.

[2] The figure of £315 for the *Madonna del Passeggio* is given by Buchanan and followed by George Redford. Writing in 1844 Mrs Jameson states that, like *La Belle Vierge*, it had been valued at 3,000 guineas but this seems most improbable in view of the fact that the *Madonna with the Palm* was valued at £1,260, and that this was clearly the more popular sort of picture.

the *La Vierge au Diadème* in the Louvre, was sold to William Willett for £735, whereas the much more individual *Virgin of the House of Orleans* was bought by George Hibbert at the 1800 sale for £525 but fell to £210 in 1829. It is now in the Condé Museum at Chantilly. Even this was not the lowest priced of the Raphaels. A badly damaged and overpainted picture, known as the *Madonna of the Tower*, was sold to Hibbert in 1800 for £157 10*s*. At the Henry Hope sale of 1816 the critic Samuel Rogers picked it up for £61 10*s*., and even at the Rogers sale in 1856 it made only £504. Presented to the National Gallery in 1906 it has long been recognised as the remains of a genuine early work.

Much less was thought of the three little predella paintings, which had originally belonged to the Colonna altarpiece, which Pierpont Morgan was to buy for £100,000 in 1901. They had been sold off to Queen Christina of Denmark by the nuns of San Antonio, Perugia, in 1663. The best preserved of these, the *Via Crucis* of the National Gallery, was sold to Hibbert in 1800 for £157 10*s*. The *Agony in the Garden*, much damaged, cost Hibbert only £44 2*s*., while the *Pietà* made £63 and was for a time in the possession of Lawrence, the painter. The last two are in the Fenway Court Museum, Boston.

The very high proportion of authentic pictures among the Duke of Orleans's Raphaels was due to the simple fact that an early Raphael was not considered worth copying. But Correggio's pictures were not only enormously in demand, but in their fuzzy, overpainted seventeenth- and eighteenth-century condition not difficult to manufacture. So the ten Orleans Correggios tell the same unhappy tale as Sir William Hamilton's picture and the Dresden *Magdalen*. *The Vierge au Pannier*, which Bryan valued for the Duke of Bridgewater at £1,260, was a copy of the National Gallery picture, which was then hidden in Spain (see page 53). In 1946 this copy was sold by Lord Ellesmere for £42. The *Danaë* was a school picture of a familiar Correggio subject. It remained unsold at Bryan's valuation of £1,100, but at the auction sale in 1800 Henry Hope bid as high as £682. At the Hope sale of 1816 it made only £183 15*s*. *The Education of Cupid* was believed to be none other than King Charles's picture, which Don Antonio Cardenas had bought in 1649, paying £1,000 on behalf of the Duke of Alba, but it was in a villainous condition when William Willett bought it at the exhibition for £367 10*s*. Fifteen years later *The Education of Cupid* dropped below £200, when it was realised that the original picture had been seized in Madrid by Marshal Murat.

To turn to the seventeenth-century Italian pictures which formed the bulk of the collection, Bryan hesitated to put a high value on the

Annibale Carraccis, probably because there were as many as twenty-five of them and because there was no other altarpiece comparable with the absurdly valued *Descent from the Cross*. Annibale Carracci appealed to eighteenth-century taste because he could paint in any manner he pleased with equal vigour. Reynolds explained to his Royal Academy audiences that this ability was not vulgar imitation, but the highest excellence in art. Although in 1798 this dry perfectionist cult encountered no opposition, the market may well have taken fright at a painter whose many styles were so hard to identify. As an example of this, one may take one of the more truly original Annibale Carraccis, a landscape, *Le Batelier*, valued for the Earl of Carlisle at 600 guineas. Its companion, now in the National Gallery, Washington, was in the Northwick sale of 1859, where it made £60 18*s*. as a Velasquez.

Most significant of this hesitance of the Annibale Carracci market was the valuation and sale of the *Vision of St. Roche* at £525, for it was the picture which the Duke of Orleans had bought from the Church of St. Eustache in Paris for £840, and that was eighty years previously. William Willett tried to sell it in 1814 but had to buy it in for £194. Yet in 1886 *St. Roche* was capable of making £231, for the real *nadir* of the Carracci family was not till the first quarter of the present century. In 1913, when the Duke of Sutherland vacated Bridgewater House, the Annibale Carracci *Riposo*, valued by Bryan at £735, was sold at Christie's for £36 15*s*., while the *Martyrdom of St. Bartholomew*, which Bryan valued at £105, made 5 guineas.

A disposition to fall after the Orleans sales was shown, not only by the works of the Carracci family, but also by those of Guido Reni, Albano, Domenichino and Guercino. This was caused, in part, by the arrival of more important and authentic examples from Italy. If the decline of the influence of Reynolds's teaching had also something to do with it, one must notice that Venetian painting fell too. Bryan's valuations were again much too high. Nominally the Duke of Bridgewater's Titians, the *Diana and Actaeon* and *Diana and Calisto*, were valued at £5,250, but in the saleroom they might not have fetched £1,000 each. Authentic Titians from the Orleans collection, which had to be auctioned, fetched a great deal less than that.

Thus, the smaller (brown but comely) *Diana and Actaeon*, which is now in the Harewood collection, was sold to Sir Abraham Hume for 200 guineas. The *Perseus and Andromeda* of the Wallace Collection was bought by Page Turner at the auction of 1800 for £325 10*s*. and acquired by the 3rd Marquis of Hertford in 1815 for £360. The *Noli me tangere* of the National Gallery was sold to Thomas Hope for £420, but bought by Samuel Rogers at the Champernowne sale in 1820 for £330. Almost the most magnificent of the Orleans Titians was the *Rape of Europa*, but Lord Berwick paid no more than £735 for it. Passed on shortly afterwards to Lord Darnley at £336, it was not on the market again till 1896, when Isabella Stewart Gardner bought it for £20,500. The present value of the *Rape of Europa* should exceed half a million.

Eighteen alleged Orleans Titian pictures have fallen out of the canonical list, but these were doubts which came slowly. In 1844, when Mrs. Jameson wrote her valuable commentary on the Orleans sales,[1] only four of the Titians had been rejected by the critics, but many of the doubtful pictures were protected from the cold wind of the saleroom for a century and a half. An outstanding example was *The Education of Cupid*, valued for Lord Gower at 800 guineas and hidden from the market till 1913 when the Duke of Sutherland sold it for £294. Similarly the portrait of *Pope Clement VII* was valued for the Duke of Bridgewater at 400 guineas and sold by Lord Ellesmere in 1946 for £84. One of the most famous of the Titians was the *Landscape with the Riposo*, which the First Duke of Orleans had bought from the Colbert family. It had got into a shocking mess. As a speculation the painter, Henry Walton, bought it at the 1798 exhibition for £262 10*s*. He succeeded in making the layers of varnish soluble and in removing them with breadcrumbs. The results were so attractive that Walton refused an offer of £840 and to the disgust of Sir Thomas Lawrence held out for £2,500. Finally he sold the *Riposo* to the eccentric Devonshire squire, Arthur Champernowne of Dartington Hall, for an unknown price.[2] Champernowne never kept his pictures long. In the 1840's the *Riposo* was acquired by Robert Stayner Holford, but at the great Holford sale of 1927 the picture made £3,570, hardly a Titian price in that memorable year.

Doubts darkened the prospect much earlier in the case of a small *Penitent Magdalen*, which Bryan sold to Thomas Maitland, M.P., for £367 10*s*. In 1831 Lord Northwick paid no more than £126, but was able to sell it in 1838 for £388 10*s*. When it appeared in the Yarborough sale of 1929, the picture had some backing as a Titian, but the price, £4,620, shows that once again it had fallen to the rank of a school-piece.

The pictures of Paolo Veronese, which had borne the full brunt of Reynolds's criticism, had a worse fate. There were allegedly sixteen of them, and the highest priced were the two huge works entitled *Wisdom*

[1] Jameson. *op. cit.*, p. xxix. [2] Farington, *op. cit.*, I, p. 282.

accompanying Hercules and *Mars and Venus united by Love*,[1] which were sold to Thomas Hope and Hastings Elwyn respectively for £525 and £315, but six other pictures, which Bryan had valued on this scale, were auctioned off in 1800 for derisory sums. Veronese's *Between Virtue and Vice*, valued at £367 10*s.*, sold for £63. The four big allegories of the National Gallery had been valued at £735. At the auction sale all four were bought by Lord Darnley for £178 10*s.* Even in 1890 they cost the National Gallery no more than £5,000. To-day they seem quite overwhelming in their poetic serenity, though *Scorn* and *Respect* are now thought partly to be schoolpieces. Relics of the Gonzaga Gallery and of Queen Christina of Sweden, the four canvases once formed the corners of a ceiling. It is possible that their disturbing perspective accounted for the peculiar price, both in 1800 and 1890.

Not all of the Veroneses were of this quality. The Duke of Bridgewater's *Venus and Adonis*, valued at £157 10*s.*, was sold in 1946 for the tell-tale price of £1,029, while *Christ and His Disciples*, valued for Lord Gower at £210, made £1,427 10*s.* In 1813 the *Rape of Europa* was bought by William Willett for £210, and in 1831 it was left to the National Gallery by the Reverend Holwell Carr, but this, too, is now regarded as a schoolpiece.

There were twelve alleged Tintorettos, mostly taken up by the three speculators at prices which Bryan made as low as possible, except for a very large work, *The Deposition*, which was valued for the Duke of Bridgewater at £630. Bryan bought for himself the picture which the Duke of Orleans had acquired from M. Seignelay, *The Nursing of Hercules*. Apparently he paid £52 10*s.*, selling it later to the Earl of Darnley. At the Darnley sale of 1890 the National Gallery paid £1,312 10*s.* This picture is none other than *The Origin of the Milky Way*. How a picture in such perfect eighteenth-century taste could have fetched only 50 guineas defies comprehension, but it is at least equally fantastic that in 1890 the National Gallery would have had to pay six times as much for Landseer's *Monarch of the Glen* as they paid for the noblest of Tintoretto's easel paintings.

In strong contrast to many of the Italian works, the pictures of the northern schools, which belonged to Moore Slade's syndicate, brought profit to the speculators. The Rubens *Judgement of Paris* of the National Gallery was valued for Lord Kinnaird at £2,100, sold in 1813 to the dealer Delahante for £2,625 and resold by him to Mr. Penrice of Yarmouth for £4,200, but it cost the gallery no more in 1844, when

[1] Washington National Gallery, Christie's, 1903, £6,300.

sentiment was moving away from Rubens. At the 1800 sale, Smith, the dealer of Marlborough Street, got the Windsor *St. George Landscape* for £1,050, Lord Berwick got the *Continence of Scipio* (destroyed in a fire in 1836) for £840, while Lord Darnley bid £1,260 for *Thomyris receiving the Head of Cyrus*, which was sold by Lord Harewood to the Boston Fine Arts Museum in 1940.

Rubens and Rembrandt were decidedly the painters most in demand among the new class of speculators, though the fame of the Orleans collection was based on the Italian pictures. All Bryan's experience had been acquired in dealing in the painters of the Netherlands. In 1798 he had sold Sir Francis Baring the Rembrandt *Centurion Cornelius* of the Wallace Collection[1] for £1,522 10*s*. At the 1800 sale Payne Knight paid £1,050 for *The Cradle*, double the price of *The Mill* at Moore Slade's exhibition of 1793.

It is curious that the Duke of Orleans collection included not a single Claude. Parisian taste of the early eighteenth century had preferred Nicolas Poussin, but it is doubtful whether the London market of 1798 would have supported the prices for Poussin paid by the 1st Duke of Orleans. Since he had given £5,000 for the seven pictures of *The Sacraments*, Bryan put the same valuation on them for the Duke of Bridgewater. By doing so Bryan created a Poussin vogue, pushing prices beyond the £1,500 mark, but this vogue, which was already out of date in Paris, failed to outlast the Napoleonic wars. Thus the *Birth of Bacchus*, for which William Willett paid £525 at the 1798 exhibition, made only £177 at Willett's sale in 1819. It was taken to Paris by Erard and it returned to England with the Montcalm collection in 1849. By that time Poussin was everywhere out of fashion, and the picture made only £144 10*s*.

'Philippe Egalité' had sold his pictures at a panic price. The English backers made a good profit, even though many of the Italian pictures were resold at prices lower than those given by the Duke's grandfather early in the century. The poor prices at the 1800 sale were partly the result of historic ill-luck. The French had occupied Rome before the 1798 exhibition and, by 1800, pictures that had been beyond the reach of the King of Poland or the Empress Catherine were already in London.

[1] Sold at Stowe in 1848 as *The Unmerciful Servant* and bought by Hertford for £2,300.

2. *The Rome and Genoa Dispersals*

The beginnings of this second diaspora of pictures must be traced to the year 1796 when General Bonaparte, the young conqueror of Northern Italy, had demanded an indemnity from the Pope in return for the inviolability of his territories. This indemnity included specified works of art. Just the same, Napoleon invaded the Papal States and by the Treaty of Tolentino in February 1797 he included 500 listed works of art in his demand for a second indemnity. But on the 27th August the murder of General Duphot provided an excuse for the occupation of the Holy City. In February 1798 General Berthier entered Rome, the Pope was arrested and sent into exile and a Roman republic was declared with all the operetta symbolism of the French Revolution. The policy of General Berthier and his army commissaries was to seize Papal properties but to respect private ownership. However, a large financial levy on the Roman princely houses for the benefit of the young Republic and the prospect of still further levies made the princes extremely amenable to sell their heirlooms in secret. The French army commissaries speculated on their own account and their competitors were the British artist colony who stayed on in Rome, spy-ridden but unmolested and free to exercise their former commerce.

Napoleon did not interfere, because his personal taste was for classical sculpture rather than old masters. It is true that by 1803 the Baron Vivant-Denon had seventeen looted Raphaels in the Salon Carré of the Louvre, including the *Madonna della Sedia* and the *Transfiguration*, but their bulk was small compared with the statues looted from the Vatican, which numbered over 400, on top of which Napoleon offered Prince Spadia 23,000 Roman ducats or £11,500 for the original statue of Pompey 'that all the time ran blood'. Fifteen years later, Napoleon had to restrain his classical passion rather than bid at an auction sale, held in Malta by the British Navy, and so the Munich Glyptothek obtained the Aegina marbles. It was one of the rare occasions when enemy trading was viewed with disfavour. Wars in those days were only total on the battlefield. In 1813 the casualties at Leipzig rivalled the first day of the Battle of the Somme, but the port, brandy and claret that filled Gilray's vast and patriotic stomachs came from France in neutral vessels operating under an excise licence.[1]

[1] 'Brandies and other articles are imported in English vessels under Prussian colours with the greatest security and are paid for through the medium of Hamburgh'. Farington, *op. cit.*, III, p. 11, 25th October 1804.

The French remained in Rome till September 1799. It was next to impossible during these nineteen months to remove the acquisitions to England. However, the retreat of the French did not end the buyers' opportunities. The new Pope, Pius VII, did not enter Rome till July 1800. In the meantime Rome was governed for Ferdinand IV of Naples by the Cavalliere Acton and during this period neither the papal option nor the strict papal laws on the alienation of heirlooms were enforced. Most of the treasures which reached England left Rome in 1800, but there was an interesting exception. In 1797, a few months before the entry of General Berthier, the architect Charles Heathcote Tatham had been implored by the blind Prince Altieri to buy the two landscapes that Claude had painted for his grandfather: *The Landing of Aeneas* and *The Sacrifice of Apollo*. Tatham would not undertake the risk, but two painters, Charles Grignon and Robert Fagan, not only paid 10,000 scudi or £2,250 for the Claudes, but smuggled them through the French lines and shipped them on a half-decked boat crammed with refugees to Palermo. Here Grignon received a commission to paint Nelson's portrait and so impressed his sitter with the importance of the pictures that a convoy was provided for them between Gibraltar and Falmouth. Notwithstanding the convoy, the *Tigre* narrowly escaped capture by a French frigate out of Brest and the two paintings took part in a sea-fight.

William Beckford, who had known the Altieri Claudes when he stayed in Rome in 1780, was determined to get them, even if he had to go to £10,000. In fact they cost him £6,825 in April 1799. Some years later Beckford declared that in 1803, during the Peace of Amiens, 'the museum in Paris' had offered him 500,000 or 600,000 livres (£20,000 to £24,000).[1] Outside this possible dream fantasy, Beckford discovered that his West Indian estates were not paying up. So in June 1808 he let the two Claudes go to Harris, the Bond Street dealer, for £10,500 and in that very month Harris sold them to R. Hart Davis, M.P., for £12,600. At some time between 1808 and 1816 Hart Davis sold them to his neighbour, Philip Miles of Leigh Court. Miles may very well have paid even more. Thus in the year 1808 two Claude paintings fetched a price that had only once been exceeded in the history of collecting, when Augustus III of Saxony paid £8,500 for Raphael's *Sistine Madonna*. Yet those who studied *The Landing of Aeneas* and *The Sacrifice to Apollo* at Burlington House in the winter of 1959 may well have wondered why Regency connoisseurship had been so captivated. The fact was that the pictures had reached

[1] Boyd Alexander: *Life at Fonthill, 1807–1822*, p. 47. Farington, *op. cit.*, V, p. 84.

England in a different state. Somewhere about the year 1816 the Miles family had sent them to be restored. Both Lawrence and West were said to have seen this sacrilege in progress and Lawrence is supposed to have remarked, 'I see, sir, that we have been where we were not wanted, and I am sorry, for this destruction will deprive me of my rest.'[1]

At the moment when the French quitted Rome, important pictures could still have been bought cheaply. Major Pryse-Gordon, agent for the Duke of Hamilton, entered Rome with the King of Naples's troops in 1799 and was offered the great Titian *Bacchus and Ariadne* for £700, but 'shortly after hordes of English arrived and the market rose five hundred percent'.[2] This is confirmed by the fact that the pictures from the Roman palaces, which reached England, were not very numerous, and that the asking prices were very high. The first to be auctioned publicly came under Christie's hammer in April 1800, barely two months after Coxe had auctioned the remainder of the Orleans collection. These had been obtained by John Udney, Consul in Leghorn and brother of the Royal Academician Robert Udney, but the most important spoils were brought back by Alexander Day, the miniaturist, a member of the Rome colony who stayed on throughout the French occupation. To sell these works Day had to keep them on exhibition at Henry Tresham's house in Lower Brook Street for close on a year, though Benjamin West thought them so splendid that he came from each visit 'feeling several inches taller'.[3] They had been bought mostly from the Colonna and Borghese palaces, except for the Annibale Carracci *St. Gregory*, which had been abandoned by the French on the quayside at Genoa on the approach of the Austrians.

Foremost was the alleged Leonardo of the Borghese Palace. *Christ disputing with the Doctors* was a small picture and almost quattrocento in appearance, yet Lord Northwick paid £3,150. It is in fact by Bernardo Luini and will be found under that name in the National Gallery, where it has been since 1831. But in 1800 there were only two Leonardos in England, Lord Lansdowne's *Virgin of the Rocks* and the uncoloured cartoon of the *Holy Family with St. Anne*, which the Royal Academy had acquired through Robert Udney before 1791. Leonardo was therefore the dearest of all the names that could be bought and generally it was no more than a name. Thus a beautiful fragment, which is also thought to-day to be by Luini, was bought by Beckford at Sir William Hamilton's sale in March 1801 for £1,365. The *Boy with a Puzzle*

[1] *Artists and Their Friends in England*, II, p. 359.
[2] Whitley: II, p. 227. [3] Whitley, *op. cit.*, II, p. 227.

remained a Leonardo till the end of the nineteenth century (see page 115).

As purchaser of the alleged Leonardo, Lord Northwick now emerges among the great picture-buyers of the early nineteenth century. He was already thirty-six years old, but he died in 1859 at the age of ninety-five, and the pictures, remaining in his two residences, Thirlestane House and Northwick Park, made over £100,000. Lord Northwick had lived in Rome from 1792 till the arrival of the French in 1797 and had known his pictures in their original homes. He must therefore have had good reason for paying more for this doubtful Leonardo than for either of his authentic Raphaels. For his middle-period Raphael, the *St. Catherine*, which he later passed on to Beckford, Northwick paid £2,625, but for the *Madonna, Child and St. John* of the Borghese Palace, an early work, he gave only £1,575. It was priced lower than the two Annibale Carraccis. These were the *St. Gregory* (which had been intended for Murat when it was captured at Genoa) at £2,625, and the *Domine quo vadis* of the National Gallery at £2,100.[1]

The great Angerstein, who had laid out £3,750 on the Sebastiano del Piombo within the past two years, now came forward with a block purchase of two Titians and a Gaspard Poussin from the Colonna Palace at £6,300. In 1824 the National Gallery paid for them as follows:

Titian: *Venus and Adonis* £3,500; *Rape of Ganymede* £2,000; Gaspard Poussin (Dughet): *Abraham and Isaac* £2,500.

The Gaspard Poussin was so like a Claude as to fetch a Claude price, but the *Ganymede* was an octagonal ceiling centre, painted by several hands and not by Titian. *Venus and Adonis*, the most reputable of the many replicas of this subject, must have cost Angerstein proportionally £2,750, a price which has a remarkable similarity to the valuation of Bridgewater's Titians as made by Michael Bryan. But Farington states in his diary that Day actually hoped to get £4,000 each for the Titians.[2, 3]

Another painter who stayed in Rome during the French occupation was William Young Ottley. At the age of twenty-eight, the future keeper of the British Museum print room was already generations ahead of his time. It was Ottley who found the Michelangelo and Raphael drawings for Sir Thomas Lawrence's collection and who made

[1] For the acquisition of the two Raphaels by the National Gallery, see p. 113.

[2] Farington, *op. cit.*, II, p. 306.

[3] Day's finances were quite a mystery. The sale of these pictures should have made him a fortune, but, when he died in 1807, he was working as picture restorer at the age of seventy-five, and his widow hoped to get a pension from the Royal Academy. Farington, *op. cit.*, V, p. 82.

a collection of medieval illuminations which Lord Northwick bought after his death. Ottley was also the first scholar to make any real sense out of the Italian Quattrocento, though this played but a small part in this first Roman speculation (see page 121).

In the Ottley sale which took place at Christie's in May 1801, the highest priced pictures were something totally different, namely two wild landscapes by the Neapolitan, Salvator Rosa, from the Colonna Palace. The *Finding of Moses* fetched £1,575, while the National Gallery's *Mercury and the Woodman* was bought by Sir Mark Sykes for £1,680, prices which were only twice excelled in the early nineteenth century and then not again till the 1950's. It is strange that Salvator Rosa's swarthy vigour should have remained something between a joke and a bore for a full century. Equally strange this first sudden appreciation. Between his death in 1683 and the 1790's any Salvator Rosa picture could have been bought for a hundred or two. Then at the Calonne sale in 1795 we get a seaport scene at £525 and in 1798 Sir George Younge's *Democritus* at £735. In this can be seen the beginning of the most notable trait of English collecting, literary influences. For the 1790's were the decade of popular fiction by Mrs. Radcliffe and her kin, concerning bandits, castles and Sicily. Salvator Rosa was so closely linked with banditry that he was said to have been a reformed bandit himself. That is why Sir W. Gilbert, the librettist, who was abducted by Sicilian bandits as an infant when Salvator Rosa was still in fashion, could only recall that the scenery was extremely picturesque.

There was a baroque and artificial character in these romantic landscapes just as there was in *The Mysteries of Udolpho*. In fact, Salvator Rosa did not survive the more thoroughgoing medievalist romanticism of Tennyson, the Pre-Raphaelites and Burne-Jones. Thus there were no more four-figure Salvator Rosas after the Ashburnham sale of 1850 and scarcely a vestige of a revival till 1953 (see page 226).

The most striking object of Ottley's discernment was one of the cheapest of the forty-nine lots in the sale. One has only to see the crowd round *The Vision of a Christian Knight* on any normal National Gallery day to perceive the veneration which that moment of enchantment in a young man's life 460 years ago can still inspire. But in 1801 it was a 'hard, dry' picture, even if it came from the Borghese Palace, and it measured barely 7 ins. square. Ottley had to buy the *Vision* in at £493 10*s*. At Ottley's second sale in 1811 the *Vision* did even worse. It fetched only £409 10*s*., and it would not have made even that if the buyer had not been Sir Thomas Lawrence, a collector of the rarest perception and a man of Ottley's own way of thinking. Finally the *Vision* *of a Christian Knight* was bought by the National Gallery in 1847 for 1,000 guineas. To-day there would certainly be buyers at £500,000.

In 1800, while Day's pictures were showing in London, a new speculative adventure was set afoot. An Edinburgh lawyer, William Buchanan, introduced one of his rich clients, Alexander Gordon, to the painter James Irvine, a member of the artist-dealer fraternity in Rome. Irvine was given a roaming commission, for everywhere in Italy the French retreat had left a trail of impoverishment. The capital was put up partly by Gordon and partly by Champernowne of Dartington Hall. Buchanan was to be the manager—so successfully that he abandoned his lawyer's practice to become a professional dealer and, after Bryan's bankruptcy, the foremost operator on the London market in the 1820's and 1830's. Some of these operations he described in a small two-volumed work, published by Ackerman in 1824. The *Anecdotes of Painting* dispense vital information in a dry, sententious, unsympathetic style, but they come to life in the parts which contain the letters of Irvine and Wallis, Buchanan's agents in Italy and Spain during the war years.

In October 1800, when Irvine reached Rome, a new Pope had been installed, the wave of panic selling had passed and the English dealer colony had to face the competition of art-struck members of Napoleon's family and staff. The new prices had little appeal to a commercial speculator. Thus Prince Justiniani demanded £3,000 each for a Domenichino and a Guido Reni. Two smaller Guidos were on offer at £3,000 the pair, and these Irvine eventually secured for £2,250; but not much was to be made on *Lot and His Daughters* and *Susanna and the Elders*. Nearly half a century later, when the National Gallery paid £2,940 for these two pictures, the wrath of the critics, including Ruskin, created a revolution in the management of the gallery (see page 125).

The greatest prize of all, Prince Justiniani's Domenichino, *The Vision of St. John*, reached England, but very obliquely. In June 1804 it was nearly bought by Joseph Bonaparte at the reduced price of £1,750. Then the Prince changed his mind and sent his whole collection to be sold in Paris. So in the year following Trafalgar the London French dealer Delahante obtained the 10-ft.-high *Vision of St. John*, and brought it somehow from Paris to England, where it was sold to Buchanan and by Buchanan to Harris of Bond Street and so to Hart Davis and, about the years 1808–1810, to Philip Miles's Leigh Court Gallery. According to family tradition, it cost Miles 12,000 guineas,[1] as much as his two Altieri Claudes put together. Yet in 1899 Sir Cecil Miles parted with *St. John* for 100 guineas, neither more nor less.

[1] *The Times*, 30th June 1884, in Redford, *op. cit.*, I, p. 388.

Having missed this opportunity, Irvine calculated rightly that Rubens and Van Dyck were a better speculation in London than the masters of 'ideal beauty'. He discovered that in 1800, when Massena's troops were besieged in Genoa, pictures in that city had been going cheap. A church, which Massena had used as a hospital, would have parted with a Guido Reni and two Rubenses for less than £1,000. In 1802 there were again French troops in Genoa, but the Treaty of Amiens was in force and pictures could be shipped openly to England. On his way to Genoa, Irvine stopped in Florence, where he was shown two Raphael *Madonnas*. They were 'painted on wood and admirable in their way'. Unfortunately they were only in the painter's first or second manner. 'I have some fears of acquiring Raphael's works of this time.' Met with the challenge that Lucien Bonaparte was after them, Irvine beat down the owners from 3,500 sequins to 1,450. Though the final cost of two supposed Raphaels was only £830 to Buchanan's syndicate, Irvine's premonitions proved to have been sound. Buchanan complained that he could not handle them, and sent the Raphaels, real or alleged, back to Italy. In June 1803 Irvine wrote an aggrieved letter to Buchanan, who had the commendable candour twenty years later to print it in his book.[1] 'As to an oil picture by Raphael in his great grand and broad manner, not above six perhaps exist in the world and are certainly not to be acquired for any money. . . . I am certain that if Raphael's works from the Vatican were to be carried to England without its being known that they were such, nobody would look at them. As to Sir Richard Worsley's observations, they give a just account of the present low state of taste in England and his preference of a *Magdalen* by Guido to the Raphaels does not surprise me, as that country has always been taken in by sleight of hand.'

In the meantime, Irvine had established himself in Genoa, and in September 1800 he secured a group of pictures that were closer to the hearts of the new English speculators. For the sum of £2,100 he was able to ship to London four splendid Rubens pictures from the Balbi Palace, for which the first price had been £3,000. They were the *Triumph of Julius Caesar* after Mantegna, the *Allegory of Peace and War* with Charles I's cipher still on the back of the canvas, and the two famous landscapes, known as the *Château de Steen* and the *Rainbow Landscape*. The last-named picture is in the Wallace Collection, the remainder in the National Gallery, the four pictures being worth to-day perhaps £750,000. Yet in the London of 1803 the treble profit, which the speculators demanded, was not easily to be had. William Pitt would

[1] For Buchanan's book, see Bibliography.

not buy pictures, which were not essential to the war effort. Even the stupendous Angerstein discovered that he had no picture room.[1] Finally Lord Gower came forward and added to his Orleans purchases the not very attractive *Allegory of War and Peace* at £3,000. As to the rest, the *Château de Steen* hung fire for a long time till Lady Beaumont bought it at £1,500 as a surprise present for her husband.[2] Champernowne paid Buchanan for *The Rainbow Landscape* with a Guido Reni and took over the *Triumph of Caesar* at a valuation of £800, but it was sold after his death in 1820 for £351 15*s*., and it cost the National Gallery no more than £1,102 10*s*. even in 1856. The *Château de Steen* was given to the infant National Gallery in 1826, but its companion, *The Rainbow Landscape* of the Wallace Collection, entered the higher domains of millionaire collecting when the Marquess of Hertford bid £4,777 10*s*. for it at the Orford sale of 1856. In 1802 Irvine had paid only £1,000 for the two landscapes with the *Triumph of Caesar* thrown in.

One of Irvine's purchases was too difficult for Buchanan to handle, and he had to put it in the saleroom in 1804. This was the treble portrait, *King Charles I in Three Positions*, which Van Dyck had made of the King to assist Bernini in modelling a bust. It was bought in at £514 10*s*., kept by Buchanan for some years and then returned to Champernowne, who had put up the money. It was bought by George IV after he had come to the throne and is now at Windsor.

In May 1803 England and France were once again at war. Though Irvine returned to Rome, another Scottish painter, Andrew Wilson, was able to stay on in Genoa by pretending to be an American citizen. Wilson worked for a rival syndicate, financed by Caleb Whitefoord, a wealthy Scottish laird residing in London. In the course of 1804 Wilson extracted a further sixteen pictures from the Balbi and Marana palaces at a cost of £5,000. In 1806, when these pictures arrived in London, Whitefoord expected to recover half the outlay on one picture alone, the *Brazen Serpent* of Rubens. A lottery, undertaken on the advice of Coxe, the auctioneer, failed to produce £2,500 or anything like it and the picture came under the hammer in May 1807 when it had to be bought in by Whitefoord at £1,260. There was a strong prejudice against this decidedly unbeautiful work, since Hart Davis had just paid £4,200 for the much inferior *Conversion of Saul*, now in the Kaiser

[1] Whitley: *Art in England*, I, p. 60.

[2] In 1803 it was borrowed by West, in whose house it was seen by James Ward [1767–1859]. Ward painted his *Fighting Bulls* in imitation of this picture, which had an important influence on the English romantic landscape.

Friedrich Museum. The *Brazen Serpent* was, however, sold to the National Gallery by Bulkeley Owen in 1837 for £3,675.

In the meantime Irvine had acquired his greatest treasure. In September 1803 he learned that both the Giovanni Bellini *Feast of the Gods*[1] and the Titian *Bacchus and Ariadne* were hidden in the Aldobrandini Palace, and were secretly on offer. The asking price for *Bacchus and Ariadne*, £700 in 1799, was now about £1,900. It is probable that Irvine got this reduced, since it was not until March 1806 that Buchanan had the picture in London, when Lord Kinnaird bought it for £3,150.[2] The price was quite unprecedented for a Titian, for the picture was by no means so universally acclaimed as it became in Victorian times. Yet Kinnaird could not have lost on his daring purchase, since in 1813 he received £6,825 from Delahante for *Bacchus and Ariadne*, together with the Poussin *Bacchanalia*,[3] which had cost him £1,575, and the Rubens *Judgement of Paris* which had been valued at £2,100 in 1793.

The cost of *Bacchus and Ariadne* to the nation in 1826, when it formed part of a block purchase from Thomas Hamlet the jeweller, seems to have been between £5,325 and £6,000. No such price was paid again for a Titian until seventy years later.

3. *From the Peace of Amiens to Waterloo—1801–1815*

Compared with the prices which they fetched in the 1820s and 1830's,' Buchanan seems to have sold his pictures very cheap. And yet he believed that he had come into the market at the end of a boom and that a slump followed, from which there was only a temporary recovery in 1810–1813. It is clear that apart from the three noble backers, Bridgewater, Gower and Carlisle, the Orleans speculators operated with insufficient capital to be tied up in pictures. Before the war was over three of the speculators, Bryan (in 1809), Moore Slade and Lord Kinnaird (in 1813), had been forced into bankruptcy, while Hastings Elwyn, Thomas Troward, George Hibbert and Sir Simon Clark had to sell

1 *The Feast of the Gods* was bought about the same year by the painter Vincenzo Cammucini, who sold it to the Duke of Northumberland in 1844.

2 Farington, *op. cit.*, IV, p. 115.

3 The *Bacchanalia* was in the Randon de Boisset Sale (1777), £600; Calonne Sale (London 1795), bought Walker £913 10*s*.; Walker Sale (1803), bought Troward £840; Troward Sale (1807), bought Kinnaird £1,575; Kinnaird Sale (1813), bought in £1,470; sold to Delahante as part of a block purchase, about £1,500; 1826 sold by Thomas Hamlet to the National Gallery as part of a block purchase, probably valued at £1,500; present-day value possibly £60,000–£70,000.

prematurely, as also had the older collectors, Ellis Agar and Walsh Porter.

There was no hint of this lack of money in the year that Buchanan sent Irvine to Italy. Within a few weeks of the Treaty of Amiens, which became effective in October 1801, a sale was rigged up in Paris to attract the now legendary number of English speculators. The Citoyen Robit had acquired a splendid collection through the forced sales and requisitions of the property of the *émigrés*. With the aid of two backers, Sir Simon Clark and George Hibbert, M.P., Bryan secured the greater part of the lots, a hundred and eighty-six in all. By the end of the year he had them on exhibition at the former Royal Academy rooms. Compared with the prices which Bryan obtained in London, most of the bids at the Robit sales seem very low, but it must be remembered that the biggest French speculators were Napoleon's family and Napoleon's generals, who did their buying outside the country. The Paris dealers were as depressed as twelve years of revolution and war could make them. Bryan was able to buy a Cuyp and a Murillo at 10,000 and 7,310 francs (25 to the pound) and sell them for £1,050 and £1,260. A Claude and three Poussins were sold at an almost threefold profit. Even adventures in war-worn Italy could bring no bigger rewards than these.[1]

It seems, however, that the French buyers, who failed to support such a traditional market as Nicolas Poussin, were more than ever inclined to favour Dutch painting, the taste of radicalism. Bryan allowed them to carry off the fairly expensive Teniers pictures as well as a Ter Borch, and a costly Paul Potter, which made £1,240. It would seem that, apart from Angerstein's Rembrandt, the Roman fever had momentarily devalued the Dutch school in London. In fact it did not recover till 1811, when the Prince Regent left his spectacular bids at the Lafontaine sale. Thus the record of the Walsh Porter and the Holderness sales in 1802–3 was depressing, particularly since many of the pictures had been much higher priced in 1794–1795, when they had been brought over by Dutch fugitives. At the Robert Heathcote sale in 1805 a pair of Wouvermans fell from £1,155 to £614 5*s*., and a Teniers from £1,050 to £225 15*s*. Bryan who had bought such pictures as these for his own stock, was bankrupted in 1809. The Robit speculation was his last fling.

In 1806 symptoms of stagnation were everywhere. But now there occurred the biggest sale of Italian and Italianate pictures since the Orleans exhibition of 1798. Luckily for Wellbore Ellis Agar, his sixty-five pictures were withdrawn from Christie's and sold *en bloc* to Lord Grosvenor for £31,500. Unfortunately for his chronicler, no detailed

[1] The French prices from Charles Blanc, *op. cit.*

valuer's list has survived, but Redford[1] had access to a sale catalogue, in which the dealer Smith of Marlborough Street wrote his own estimates on the basis that the collection was worth 50,000 guineas. It is curious to find that Rubens's *Ixion, deceived by Juno*, a very patchy work which was acquired by the Louvre before the First World War, was valued at £3,150, whereas only six weeks had elapsed since Lord Grosvenor had bought the Lansdowne *Adoration*, the £275,000 picture of 1959, for a mere £840.

Echoes of this remote forgotten transaction reverberated in 1959, when two of Ellis Agar's Claudes came on to the market, along with the Rubens *Adoration* and a number of earlier Grosvenor possessions. *The Worship of the Golden Calf* had been valued by Smith in 1806 at £3,100, *The Sermon on the Mount* at £525, in spite of a report that a titled lady had offered Ellis Agar an annuity for life, if only she might borrow it.[2] In 1959 the two pictures were almost level, making an all-time auction record for Claude at £36,000 and £35,000. But the two most valued Claudes of the Ellis Agar purchase, *Morning* and *Evening*, remain with the Grosvenor family to-day. They had been acquired by Ellis Agar soon after the Blondel de Gagny sale of 1776 where they had made £998. In 1803 Angerstein, who had just paid £8,400 for the *Bouillon* Claudes, *The Queen of Sheba* and *Isaac and Rebecca* of the National Gallery, was prepared to give as much for *Morning* and *Evening*. Some idea of the wild speculative nature of the Claude market may be got from the fact that, while Erard had tried in 1803 to hold out for £20,000 for the *Bouillon* Claudes, Smith in 1806 valued *Morning* and *Evening* at £6,300.[3]

Now that Ellis Agar's Claudes have established another landmark in their history, it would be intriguing to know what might be the fortune to-day of the picture which Smith clearly regarded as the chief treasure of the Grosvenor purchase of 1806, namely Berchem's seven-foot landscape, known as the *Château de Bentheim*. For Smith wrote in the margin of his catalogue '3,000 guineas' and that is about double the price any Berchem has fetched in the present century.

1807, a bleak year for the English speculators, was enlivened by Angerstein's Rembrandt. *The Woman taken in Adultery*, a possession of the famous Six family of Amsterdam, had arrived in London from Brussels, having mysteriously eluded the Continental blockade, and was in the hands of M. Lafontaine at a grubby Soho address. Like *Bacchus and Ariadne*, it had its friends and foes. Northcote preferred the

[1] Redford, *op. cit.*, p. 95. [2] Mrs. Jameson, *op. cit.*, p. 248.
[3] Farington, *op. cit.*, II, p. 90.

Susanna of the Reynolds collection, though he could not persuade the Academy to spend £200 on it. Other Academicians pronounced it a mere schoolpiece, perhaps because Benjamin West had declared it to be the greatest picture in the world. As to Lawrence, he took a chaise all the way to Blackheath in order to persuade the great Angerstein to buy it. He returned with a bidding commission of £4,000, but the Regency had traffic problems of its own, and he missed Christie's afternoon sale. Lawrence learnt from James Christie that Lafontaine had bought his picture in at £5,250 and was going to offer it to the Louvre at this price —another odd aspect of the intensified blockade of the Continent, that allegedly followed the victory of Trafalgar. Lawrence then accompanied Angerstein to Lafontaine's lodgings, where the deal was concluded for '4,000 pounds or guineas'.[1]

The renewed wartime boom, which Buchanan located in the years 1810–1813, can be seen in the second Walsh Porter[2] and second Lafontaine sales of April 1810, and June 1811. The first, a decease sale, comprised fifty-two pictures, and made more than £30,075. These, the average prices at an open auction sale, exceeded those paid by Lord Grosvenor in 1806, trebled those of the Orleans speculation and doubled even Benjamin West's inflated valuations of the Empress Catherine's purchases from Houghton Hall in 1779. As examples of the changed trend, Robert Udney's mutilated Correggio from Teddington (see page 7) rose from £210 in 1800 to £2,152 10*s*.,[3] a lesser-known Claude, *Sinon before Priam*, from the Chigi Palace, made £2,887 10*s*., and the Orleans Rubens landscape, the *St. George*, rose from £1,050 to £2,152. Furthermore, Buchanan must have had good reasons for paying £1,837 10*s*. in order to buy back one of his own pictures, the Domenichino *St. Cecilia*, which Irvine had found in Genoa.

The Dutch pictures, bought for the Prince Regent by Lord Yarmouth, later Marquess of Hertford, were at this stage still modestly priced things, such as Jacob Ruysdael's *Mill* at £304 10*s*. and a couple of Wouverman subjects at £400 each. The prices paid by the Prince in the following year are therefore mysterious. Both Buchanan and Mrs Jameson hint that these had been agreed beforehand and that the bidding against Yarmouth at the Lafontaine sale was therefore a piece of play-acting. On the other hand, Dutch prices had already been heading this way in the Calonne, Dundas and Orleans sales of the 1790's,

[1] Farington, *op. cit.*, IV, pp. 153–5.
[2] Walsh Porter had been the friend of the Prince of Wales and the arbiter of taste at Carlton House, but was considered a dealer rather than a collector (*The Farington Diary*, VI, pp. 25–6, 89).
[3] Resold in 1816 in Henry Hope's sale for £324.

though the past ten years had seen a set-back. The pictures in the June 1811 sale had just come through the Continental blockade from the famous Smet van Alpen Gallery in Amsterdam, and this fact alone would have stimulated prices, when the Baring and Hope brothers were in the market. In fact nothing like the prices paid by the Prince Regent was seen till the Patureau sale of 1857 and the San Donato sale of 1868, both of them in Paris.

In the first place, Angerstein's Rembrandt was outpaced by *The Shipbuilder and his Wife*, for which the Prince gave £5,250, a price not surpassed in the London saleroom till 1893, though Lafontaine had paid the Van Alpen family no more than £1,485 in 1810. Next came the Van Dyck, *Christ Healing the Lame Man*, according to Redford at £3,990. If this was indeed the price, it remained a record till the Duke of Marlborough's transactions of 1884 and a saleroom record till 1900.[1]

The Prince of Wales's remaining purchases at this extraordinary sale were as follows:

Wouverman: *The Hay Harvest*, £1,785, record price till 1854.
Adriaen van de Velde: *Landscape with Cattle*, £1,890, record price till 1875.
Adriaen van Ostade: *Flemish Interior*, £1,050, record price till 1844.
David Teniers the Younger: *A Village Festival*, £1,732 10*s*., record price till 1892.
Jan Both: *Philip Baptising the Eunuch*, £1,627 10*s*., record price till 1875.
Frans Mieris the Elder: *Lady Stringing Pearls*, £1,050, record price till 1875.

In the following year, 1812, the Prince bought the pictures, which Sir Francis Baring had acquired from the Geldemeester and Holderness collections in 1802, for £24,000 and the valuation seems to have been at the same high level, since a Paul Potter cattlepiece cost him £1,600, a record price till 1890. In 1817 Beckford had high hopes of selling Gérard Dou's *Poulterer's Shop* (National Gallery) to the Prince for 3,000 guineas,[2] but he failed and in 1823 he was able to buy it back from Farquhar's Fonthill sale for £1,365. The depression of the Dutch-Flemish *genre* market in the 1820's was probably due to modern competition. Wilkie's imitations, with their anecdotal and sentimental slant, were becoming more popular even among kings. And in the

[1] But did the Prince pay it? Mrs. Jameson (*op. cit.*) says that her catalogue was marked £346 (the figure copied by Roberts), but that she had heard from William Seguier that in reality the Prince had given over three thousand. Seeing that in 1821 the Prince paid M. de Burtin £2,625 for the Van Dyck *Marriage of St Catherine*, there is nothing improbable about Redford's figure.
[2] Boyd Alexander, *op. cit.*, pp. 205–7.

1840's a host of imitators of Wilkie, like Faed and Webster, killed the Dutch-Flemish *genre* market altogether.

Two years before the Bourbon restoration, in 1813, the very first of the Orleans speculators, Lord Kinnaird, became insolvent. Symbolically this marks the end of an era. The pictures in the Kinnaird sale maintained their value and the London market settled down to a period without violent movements, which lasted at any rate till the 1830's. But before finishing with the excitements of the Napoleonic age, something yet remains to be said of Buchanan's most difficult speculation.

Buchanan's decision to send a man to Spain was taken in October 1807, when there was no question yet of a forcible French occupation of the country, but only of a Franco-Spanish alliance against Portugal. But Jean-Baptiste Lebrun, the now emancipated husband of the formidable Madame Vigée Lebrun, was known to be on his way to Spain. As Napoleon's chief requisitioning expert, M. Lebrun was doubtless expected to bring the treasures of the Prado and the Escurial back to Paris. In reality M. Lebrun's acquisitions, which were neither costly nor important, found their way discreetly behind the smoke of battle and the shouting of the captains to Mr. Harris's shop in Bond Street. But, besides frustrating M. Lebrun, Buchanan had a second motive, and that was to recover some of Irvine's Genoese purchases, which had been taken as a prize of war into Algeciras.

In 1807 Buchanan made the acquaintance of an exceedingly *débrouillard* character, called George Augustus Wallis or the 'English Poussin'. Wallis had just reached London from Naples, having been in Rome almost continuously since 1788. During the French occupation of Rome he had been ostracised by his compatriots as a spy, which he may well have been, seeing how successful he was in the next seven years in living and in making money behind the French lines in Spain. But as told by his employer, Buchanan, the story has no particular moral.

Wallis reached Madrid early in 1808, but soon his researches were brought to a standstill by the popular fury which followed the French abduction of the Royal family to Bayonne. He saw some of the horrors of the *Dos de Mayo*, as painted by Goya. He saw the French momentarily expelled from the capital by Spanish patriots and the pictures of the pro-French Duke of Alcudia, 'the Prince of Peace', put up to auction. He also saw the French return to Madrid. The auction was then abandoned, to be resumed by the French themselves. But on the morning of the sale the best pictures were annexed for Napoleon's brother-in-law, Joachim Murat, now King of Naples. Murat obtained King

Charles I's Correggio, *The Education of Cupid*, a present to the 'Prince of Peace' from the Duke of Alba, but a second Correggio, *La Vierge au Pannier*, was bought by Wallis.

The fate of both these pictures, which are in the National Gallery, illustrates that 'Sibylline Books' principle on which nations acquire their treasures. In 1813, when Buchanan offered the *Vierge au Pannier* to the British government for £1,260, the price of an indifferent Teniers, he was refused. It was not till 1820 that he found a buyer in M. de Lapeyrière at £960. In 1825 Nieuwenhuys bought the Correggio at Lapeyrière's sale for £2,500, and at once sold it to the National Gallery for £3,800. As to *The Education of Cupid*, bought from the Marquess of Londonderry in 1834, it cost the National Gallery at least £9,000 (see page 115).

The owner of these pictures, the Duke of Alcudia, never got a penny for them, though he did not die till 1851. It was a fact that bothered few consciences, for the proper early Victorian view was that the Spaniards did not deserve to possess pictures. M. Lebrun had thought so as early as 1807 because there was no *libre entrée et sortie des monuments* in Spain, a matter which was soon put right. Mrs Jameson thought so in retrospect in 1844. She was *sure* that the spoliation had been right, because the pictures in Spain were so *neglected*. And she knew from the Countess Hahn-Hahn and her very pretty book, the *Reisebriefe*, that the occasional dishonesty of the guardians of these pictures should be welcomed. 'It is a matter of indifference that a Spanish *custode* more or less is *grillé* in the other world.'[1]

But the dishonesty of *custode* was not a matter of indifference to the doubtless primitive people, among whom the pictures were objects of veneration, and grilling not a matter for jesting. At the Convent of Loeches an infuriated mob tried to prevent the departure of six enormous cartoons, said to be by Rubens, which the monks had sold to Wallis. A French general provided Wallis with a heavily-armed infantry guard in return for two of the cartoons—this at a time when British troops were fighting the French on the Portuguese border. The bribe did not help, because Joseph Bonaparte seized the remaining four cartoons, but the 'English Poussin' found a way even out of that. Wallis had been partly financed by M. de Bourk, the Danish Minister in Madrid, because Buchanan had not been able to remit bills of exchange. De Bourk was therefore able to claim the cartoons as his property under diplomatic immunity. However, having done this to oblige Wallis, De Bourk kept the cartoons for himself, and in 1818 he sold them

[1] Mrs. Jameson, *op. cit.*, I, p. 192.

to Lord Grosvenor for £10,000. From 14 to 17 feet long, they became the chief glory of the original Grosvenor Gallery in Park Lane.

For this scabrous affair time exacted a comical revenge. In July 1924 the Duke of Westminster put three of the four cartoons, measuring more than 600 square feet, into Christie's, but had to buy them back, two at 650 and one at 1,000 guineas. And to-day Wallis's treasures form part of a gallery at Sarasota, Florida, the creation of the circus-king, Mr. Ringling. It seems that the cartoons had not been a gift of Rubens to the monks of Loeches and that his hand had hardly entered into them. They had formed part of a series of enlargements, made in Brussels from Rubens's sketches and intended to be copied as a tapestry for the Convent of the Clarissans in Madrid. When the tapestries were sent to Spain in 1648, the cartoons had been wrapped up with them and the Infanta had given them to the monks at Loeches because there was nowhere to put them.

The remaining negotiations, which Wallis conducted between 1809 and the flight of the French from Spain in 1813, were obscure and complicated. De Bourk was followed as Buchanan's agent by Coesvelt, the Belgian banker. Like de Bourk, Coesvelt broke away and treated the pictures which had been bought with his money as his own property. Moreover by 1813 the back of the English speculation had been broken. Not London, but the Tsar of Russia dominated the market, just as he dominated the combination against Napoleon. Coesvelt became pre-eminently a purveyor for the Russian court, with Buchanan only as his second string.

In 1801, long before Wallis's arrival in Spain, Coesvelt had been deep in the Spanish picture market, when residing in Madrid as Henry Hope's agent. He had bought through de Bourk from the Duke of Alba's physician the famous *Alba Madonna* of Raphael, paying £4,000 for this round picture in 'the grand and broad manner'. After keeping it thirty-five years, Coesvelt sold it to the Tsar for £14,000, and in 1931 this picture achieved a second world record when Mr. Andrew Mellon paid the Soviet government £240,000 for it.

To have obtained such a picture in Spain in 1801 was an uncommon stroke of fortune, but in 1812 when the French were forced to leave behind them the sequestered treasures of the Escurial, it was within the powers of Buchanan and Wallis to obtain a collection that rivalled the Vatican Gallery itself, though the Velasquez pictures meant little to them and the El Grecos nothing. There was, for instance, a series of Raphaels, of which the names alone were fabulous, *The Madonna della*

Rosa, del Pesce, del Legardo, del Cordero, della Tenda and *la Perla*, together with the vast *Visitation* and the *Spasimo da Palermo*.

Two only of these were in the consignments, which Wallis sent partly to Paris and partly to London. He seems to have moved back with the French in August 1812, when they evacuated Madrid. In order to find shipping for England, he had to take his pictures 1,600 miles overland as far as Stralsund on the Baltic, then the only neutral port on the European mainland. This consignment reached England in October 1813. Wallis himself, skipping with ease from one side to the other, crossed from Blucher's lines to the French on the Katzbach, stayed in Paris long enough to see his second consignment in the hands of the dealer Bonnemaison; then in some mysterious fashion this truly remarkable man made his way to London.

Coesvelt refused to sell the pictures, except as a collection. Buchanan then tried to raise £20,000 from seven backers, but only one share was taken up—by Lord Grosvenor. In 1798 Bryan had had to contend with a year of financial stringency, but Buchanan was now up against the weariness of spirit, caused by ten years of continuous war. Finally Coesvelt had to consent to separate sales, but the most costly works, which were only to have been brought from Paris when the full amount was raised, never came to England. Among them was the over ten-foot *Via Crucis* of the Escurial, known as the *Spasimo da Palermo*, Raphael's last finished picture, which Benjamin West valued at £10,000, but which Buchanan advertised at 7,000 guineas. It was so like Angerstein's *Raising of Lazarus* that it had been attributed to Sebastiano del Piombo. M. Bonnemaison, observing five huge vertical cracks, caused doubtless by bumping over the Sierras, transferred the picture on to canvas, but he found no customer. Finally in 1822 the Spanish royal family came to some arrangement with Coesvelt and recovered their property.

Nearly all the pictures which Wallis carted from Madrid to the Baltic in 1813 went back to the Continent. Most of the purchases which have enriched the British national collections had been despatched in 1810. They included the *Vierge au Pannier*, the Murillo *Holy Family*, the Titian *Apotheosis of Charles V*, and the Velasquez *Rokeby Venus*, all in the National Gallery. In the Wallace Collection there is the *Adoration* from the Duke of St. Iago's Chapel. As to the *Rokeby Venus* of Velasquez, its interesting history was somewhat overlooked during the controversy which circled round its merits, when in 1906 the nation acquired it for £45,000. In 1810 the picture had reached the Spanish royal family as a gift from the Duke of Alba, who used formerly to hang it in his study with the original picture that inspired it, Titian's *Venus with the Mirror*. In 1813 Buchanan was ready to sell both pictures for the inclusive price of 4,000 guineas. There were no offers, and the Titian remained with Bonnemaison in Paris till the Spanish royal family claimed it. Sold separately by Buchanan to a Mr. Moritt of Rokeby, it seems improbable that the Velasquez *Venus* could have made much more than 1,000 guineas. For the Velasquez *Self-portrait* and the *Duke of Olivarez* Lord Lansdowne paid Buchanan an inclusive 600 guineas.

Buchanan was more successful in finding a buyer in England for the Raphael *Madonna of the Curtain* (*Madonna della Tenda*) and a supposed Leonardo. The former is now considered to have been completed by Giulio Romano and to have been much repainted since, all of which was actually in its favour by the standards of 1813. Benjamin West decided that it was the finest Raphael to have reached England, and Buchanan advertised it at 5,000 guineas. Sir Thomas Baring, who bought it, actually obtained this price in 1818 from the King of Bavaria, and the picture is now in the Munich Pinakothek.

The Virgin with the Sleeping Child and St. John, which was attributed to Leonardo, was bought by Wallis from the French paymaster-general, M. de Crochart. Buchanan described it in his prospectus as equal to the *Virgin of the Rocks*, and valued it at 4,000 guineas.[1] It was sold, certainly for less, to Alexander Baring. It is known that the latter sold many of his pictures to Russia, and it should be possible to trace this work. It is tempting to identify it with the Benois *Madonna*, which was discovered in Astrakhan in 1824 and bought by the Tsar in 1914 for £310,400, but the description does not tally.

[1] According to Farington, the price paid by the Earl of Suffolk to Lord Lansdowne for the *Virgin of the Rocks* in 1810 was £2,000.

CHAPTER THREE

The Rewards of the Living Painter
The Georgians, 1760–1820

1. Portraits — 2. The Subject Picture — 3. Posthumous Fate of the Eighteenth-century Masters (up to 1862)

---

1. *Portraits*

These neatly rounded sixty years represent not only the reign-span of George III, but the working life of one man. No one to-day is disposed to call Benjamin West the best painter of his age or even to consider him a good painter. But he made more money than any other painter, his judgement on art was more valued than any other's and, though a foreigner, trained abroad, he somehow epitomised all that the English understood by art. The young Philadelphian had made his first paint brushes from the fur of his mother's cat, the camel not being indigenous to the North American continent, but in 1763 he was the spiritual heir of Guido Reni, newly come to town from Rome. And with him arrived an era that ended only with the Pre-Raphaelites.

The London that received the young Benjamin West possessed neither a National Gallery nor a Royal Academy, but it was by no means art-blind. Every year there was an exhibition or two, organised by the Free Society or the Incorporated Society. The English school had arrived and native artists, extremely scarce less than a generation before, now abounded. Hogarth died in 1764, but Reynolds and Gainsborough were in their prime and Romney had just started to practise. Not one of these three was a name to conjure with in 1763, nor was any other. There was a complete absence of any public personality cult. Everyone had a special preference of his own. The King would only be painted by Alan Ramsay because he was a Scot chosen by Lord Bute, but no one thought any the better of Ramsay for that. In 1763 Horace Walpole decided that Samuel Scott, the imitator of Canaletto, was the first painter of his age. Mason, Walpole's friend, thought that a Paul Sandby watercolour of *Snowdon* was the greatest picture of the century. Others extolled Richard Wilson as another Claude, and young West himself soon became the 'American Raphael'. It was all very simple-minded and it was still most attractively free of intellectual snobbery, for the latter was mostly practised by tiresome young men who had made the Grand Tour, and who had to justify all the money they had spent on the correct Roman taste.

All this was to change within the next quarter of a century. By the 1780's English painters were among the wealthiest men in the country, their names familiar to newspaper readers, their quarrels and cabals the talk of the town, their subjects known to everyone from the displays in the print-shop windows. The fortunate painters (but they were not *all* fortunate) believed that they owed it to the Royal Academy. Founded in December 1768, under the direct and exceedingly meticulous control of the Throne, the Academy undoubtedly gave painting a hierarchy, but it is doubtful whether it gave it much else. Royal patronage was certainly not responsible for the higher painters' fees. Veneration of the royal person was most unfashionable and royal appointments, as Reynolds was to find, could be a burden rather than an advancement to a painter. Nor were the Royal Academy exhibitions, hung six deep and up to the skylights, especially splendid. In 1768 the old independent association known as the Society of Incorporated Artists collected no less than 18,000 shilling entrance fees.[1] Those who think in terms of the Picasso exhibition of 1960, may reflect that the population of London was under a million, that there were no foreign tourists and that an entrance ticket cost quite 12*s.* in modern money, or the whole of a labourer's day-wage of that time. The success of this exhibition shows that in 1768 painters were on the eve of better days, even if that year had produced no royal chartered academy with its officers, teachers and lecturers.

The real source of the better rewards of painting was a fashion imported by Reynolds from Rome in 1753. This was the application of the picture-making recipes of seventeenth-century Italy, 'the Grand Manner' as it was called, to commissioned portraits. Reynolds had

[1] Whitley: *Artists and Their Friends in England*, I, p. 229.

undergone a long and searching period of study in Rome, but for this combination of methods he was chiefly indebted to Pompeio Battone, seventeen years his senior and himself an adept in glorifying the touring English gentry who sat for him. Under Reynolds's leadership English portraits were no longer set in puritanical interiors, from which the furniture seemed to have been removed to make room for the sitter. Henceforward the sitters, if they could afford the price of a whole-length, were flattered with subservient vegetation, with doves or cannon-smoke according to sex, with urns and pedestals, columns and curtains, cherubs and angels or disrobed and discountenanced naïads.

The 'grand manner' was not altogether new in England in 1753. In the reign of Charles I it had been partly acclimatised by Van Dyck, and after the Restoration it had been revived by Kneller and Lely, but in the reign of Queen Anne it began to lose ground. In the second quarter of the eighteenth century most English portraiture was bleak and utilitarian. There was no money in it and it tended to be practised by foreigners of journeyman status. But the extreme simplicity and honesty of the school had its own charm and it was a neglected challenge to genius. Neglected—yes, for it was only the most fleeting moment of time that saw the heart-rending integrity of *Mr. and Mrs. Andrews* and *Heneage Lloyd and his Sister*.

The English painters owed their enhanced status to the whole-length portrait in the Grand Manner, but these portraits, they hoped, would not be the sole purpose of their existence. Reynolds regarded the 200-guinea whole-lengths, for which commissions rained on him in the last ten years of his life, purely as pot-boilers. He believed that his greatest works were his religious, mythological and historical pieces. Mercifully their number was restrained by the demands of his portrait order-book, but for some of them he was able to charge far more even than for whole-length portrait groups. All the English eighteenth-century portraitists believed that they possessed the capacity to paint this sort of thing. Even Romney and Lawrence, tailors' and haberdashers' painters *par excellence*, occasionally attempted vast Miltonic *diableries*. In 1795 Lawrence produced the quite ludicrous fourteen-foot *Satan Summoning his Legions*, which is now in the Royal Academy, and even in 1838 his agent, Samuel Woodburn, was willing to pay £504 for it, when a Lawrence portrait could no longer be sold at all.

More will be said of the poor-relation status of portraits as compared with subject pictures, a relationship that had been completely forgotten in the 1920's, when portraits by Reynolds, Gainsborough, Romney, Lawrence, Raeburn and even Hoppner were shipped to the U.S.A. at the price of Raphaels. While whole-length portraits soared above the £100,000 mark, Reynolds's classical compositions actually fell. *Venus and the Piping Boy* made £6,720 in 1909, £1,575 in 1928 and £304 10*s*. in 1937. To-day the value of this mawkish thing might be no higher than the last figure. The millionaires of the 1920's probably never knew what little consequence the English eighteenth-century school attached to their normal portraiture routine. In terms of the 1920's, Reynolds's 200-guinea fee meant perhaps £800. Sargent, who died in 1925, had been known to receive 10,000 guineas for a portrait commission, and even in the 1870's Millais had sometimes obtained £2,000. Nor were 200 guineas (which was rarely exceeded before the inflationary phase of the Napoleonic wars) a remarkable sum in the late eighteenth century. More than one of Charles I's commissions had been as high. The point lay in the frequency with which 200 guineas could be earned under the new conditions and the ease with which orders could be accomplished. The 'broad free manner', which Reynolds so astutely commended, blinded the client to the fact that large areas had been filled in by studio-hands and apprentices. Often the fee was paid for no more than a few hours' original work. Alan Ramsay and Hoppner were the worst culprits of all, but none of the portraitists was immune. Even Gainsborough, who prided himself on painting his own draperies, farmed out many of his later pictures to his skilful nephew, Gainsborough Dupont.

In 1777 Reynolds wrote that, if necessary, a face could be begun and finished in a single day and the rest of the picture done without troubling the sitter.[1] It follows that most of the whole-length portraits required no more personal effort than a small head, which Reynolds would paint for from 25 to 40 guineas. The only extra expense would be the assistant's wages (seldom more than £100 a year) or the apprentice's keep and the cost of paint and canvas and a stand-in model. But if these were the rewards of practising the Grand Manner, even those who did not possess that facility could still make a prodigious amount of money. The Swiss Liotard was reputed to have made between £6,000 and £7,000 on crayon and pastel portraits in the course of a single year spent in London in the 1760's.[2] Francis Cotes, who painted moderate-sized and unpompous portraits, died in 1770, having for a few years rivalled Reynolds. He was only forty-five years old, but he died a rich man with a house and garden in Cavendish Square and a collection which it took several days to sell.[3] Reynolds, who, having lived in a very high style for over forty years, could still leave a fortune of well

[1] Whitley, I, p. 280. [2] Whitley, I, p. 268. [3] Whitley, I, p. 266.

over £100,000 in 1792, was in fact in modern terms a millionaire. Not far short of 4,000 pictures have been identified as at least partly by his hand. He must have produced fully a hundred pictures of various sorts every year, including at least half a dozen whole-length portraits or groups. In 1759, when Reynolds was not yet a wealthy man, he actually fulfilled over 150 orders.[1] For more than half of the thirty-eight years that he practised in London, Reynolds was able to charge fees higher than those of any other portraitist. According to the account-books, published by Graves and Cronin, Reynolds raised the price of his whole-length portraits from 60 guineas to 100 guineas as early as the year 1759 and from 100 guineas to 150 guineas in 1764, but already in 1762 George III paid 200 guineas for the double portrait of Lord Bute and the future Lord Liverpool. Reynolds raised his whole-length fee to 200 guineas in 1782, though there were still a few 150-guinea commissions. More than 200 guineas could only be earned when there was more than one personage in the picture. Thus in 1781 Warren Hastings paid 300 guineas for *Richard Barwell and his son* (£4,270 in New York, 1956), while *The Bedford Family*, an ill-balanced allegorical portrait group, in reality a fancy picture, which is now at Osterley Park, achieved Reynolds's record portrait-commission fee of 400 guineas in 1777. *The Lacemakers* (*The Ladies Waldegrave*), a big fancy portrait of his three Waldegrave great-nieces, cost Horace Walpole £315 in 1781. Fancy portraits of this kind could even increase their value in the saleroom. Thus *Garrick between Tragedy and Comedy*, for which Lord Rothschild was reputed to have paid £20,000 in 1886, was painted in 1762 for 200 guineas and auctioned twenty years later for 250 guineas. The robust and Rubenesque opera-singer, *Mrs. Billington as St. Cecilia with a Choir of Angels*, made £325 10*s*. in the saleroom in 1793.

Only one contemporary painter could command Reynolds's prices for large portrait groups, and that only for a restricted period. Between 1771 and 1779 Benjamin West painted a series of full-length groups of the Royal Family, ranging in price from 200 guineas to 300 guineas; of West's royal commissions more will be said, but it is possible that it was the machine-like productions, which were fobbed off by Ramsay and West on the Royal Family, which enabled Reynolds to earn more than royally-employed painters on his normal whole-length portraits. In the 1770's, for instance, Alan Ramsay had orders for ninety pairs of whole-lengths of the King and Queen at 200 guineas a pair. Ramsay diverted himself in Rome, while these things were churned out by his assistant,

[1] E. K. Waterhouse: *Reynolds*, 1941, p. 11.

Philip Reinagle, at 25 guineas a canvas and Ramsay pocketed the rest. Until the last five years of his life, Reynolds did not descend as low as this. At least he painted the faces and sometimes he had a hand in the draperies and background. But the office of King's Painter had become so prostituted by Ramsay that in 1784 Edmund Burke reduced the retaining fee from £200 to £50 a year. Reynolds, who succeeded Ramsay, was expected to paint the King, full-length, for £50 whenever required to do so. He became so worried that he applied for a sinecure office under the Crown to augment his income. He need not have worried. The King, who had liked Ramsay's portraits, made few calls on Reynolds's time.[1]

Reynolds's jealousy of Gainsborough was also ill-founded. Between 1772 and 1787 Gainsborough seldom received more than 100 guineas for a full-length and it was only in the last year of his life that he could raise the price to 160 guineas. Until the year 1800 Reynolds was unquestionably the only English painter who could charge 200 guineas as a standard fee. But the smallest sort of portrait head was painted by Reynolds right up to the year of his death for 40 or 50 guineas, and among these small heads are to be found the works that have the most aesthetic appeal to-day.

The progression, 1–2–4, for the prices of a head, half-length and whole-length, went back at least as far as the late seventeenth century. In 1714 Sir Godfrey Kneller charged 15, 30 and 60 guineas, a rate which would have been considered quite high sixty years later. In 1758, when he was over thirty, Gainsborough charged only 15 guineas for a half-length.[2] A hundred years after Kneller's day fees had not advanced much. For instance, in Edinburgh in 1801 Farington found the forty-seven-year-old Raeburn charging 25, 50 and 100 guineas; yet in 1911 Raeburn was ahead of Gainsborough and Reynolds as the first of the eighteenth-century British school to achieve £20,000 at auction. At the height of his powers, Raeburn charged no more than the homely 'Cornish Wonder' or 'English Rembrandt', John Opie, who received 100 guineas in 1805 for *Master Betty, the Young Roscius*.[3]

In 1779, when Benjamin West valued the best of the Houghton Hall Van Dyck portraits at £200 each, he surely intended that the highest fees of a Royal Academician should not be surpassed by the dead. It is peculiar that, with such a widespread urge to be painted and such an unquestioned supremacy, Reynolds was not able to increase his standard 200-guineas whole-length fee. The only exceptions were portraits that

[1] Whitley, II, p. 23. [2] E. K. Waterhouse: *Gainsborough*, 1958.
[3] Whitley: *Art in England*, I, p. 84.

were regarded as allegorical pictures and painted almost throughout by his own hand, like *The Tragic Muse*. It was not only strange but incongruous, for within a year of Reynolds's death Lawrence was already charging 160 guineas, and he was only twenty-four years old.

Lawrence was an incredible being. At twenty years of age he painted almost as well as at any period of his life. At sixty years of age he was able to take control of time and to prolong the eighteenth century thirty years into the nineteenth, painting men who grew ever more dramatic, proud and splendid and women whom he made more than ever dowdy, wooden and insipid. His fees, too, grew to heroic proportions and his inability to make a fortune out of them (or even to remain solvent) became one of the wonders of art-history.

The fees which Lawrence charged in middle life are recorded in the statements which he made to his bankers in 1806 and 1807.[1] They include 159 whole-length and three-quarter-length portrait commissions which were charged at 100 guineas and 200 guineas each. Two portrait groups were entered at £315 and £350. At that time most of Lawrence's commissions were probably charged no higher than those of his rival, the favourite of the Prince of Wales, John Hoppner. The death of Hoppner in 1810 left Lawrence the undisputed *doyen* of portraiture, and it enabled him immediately to raise his whole-length fee to 300 guineas, a fee which eventually Lawrence more than doubled. In the 1820's he asked 200 guineas for a head, 400 for a half-length and 600–700 guineas for a whole-length. This enormous increase began immediately after Lawrence's royal commissions for the Waterloo Chamber in 1818–1919. For these specially large whole-lengths, painted in Aix, Rome and Vienna, the Prince Regent paid £500 each, but he also paid out more than £1,000 for Lawrence's expenses, while the rings and gold snuffboxes, presented by the illustrious sitters, brought Lawrence's gains for that year up to £20,000, according to a tradition recorded by the Redgrave brothers.

In the 1820's Lawrence probably charged a special scale of fees for royal commissions, for in 1827 the Regent, now George IV, complained that he had paid Lawrence £24,000 in fees and had not yet received his pictures. 'All the world is ready to employ him at a thousand pounds and yet I am told he never has a farthing.'[2]

A thousand pounds was a price the King might be ready to pay Lawrence, but not all the world was able to pay it. *Master Lambton* or *The Red Boy* (originally a yellow boy), painted in 1825, was a normal

[1] Kenneth Garlick: *Sir Thomas Lawrence*, 1954, pp. 69–71.
[2] Whitley, p. 179.

600-guinea commission, though in 1932 the Earl of Durham bought it in at £95,000. Mr. Garlick, however, believes that in 1830, the year of Lawrence's death, his standard whole-length fee had been raised to 700 guineas, that is to say something near £6,000 in modern purchasing power. In 1830 Lawrence was easily the foremost portrait painter in the world. His successor in royal favour, David Wilkie, made less than half these fees.

The 1820's were an age of deflation rather than inflation; Lawrence's fees were a genuine tribute to an artist who was esteemed to have far excelled Reynolds. They were not rivalled either by Romney or Hoppner who survived Reynolds, the one by ten years, the other by eighteen. Romney, who refused to exhibit at the Royal Academy for the greater part of his life, seldom made over 100 guineas on a portrait. *Anne de la Pole*, for which Duveen bid £46,200 in 1926, was an ordinary 100 guineas commission in 1787. Probably the most popular picture Romney ever painted was his *Emma Hamilton as a Bacchante*, which made £131 5*s*. in 1805.

The fees which Reynolds, Gainsborough and Romney made in their prime of life, bore of course no relation to what they charged as beginners. In 1790 the twenty-one-year-old Lawrence sold his *Nelly Farren* for 100 guineas, but that was a year in which, as Wordsworth observed, to be young was very heaven. In 1743–1744 the twenty-year-old Reynolds had painted naval officers at Plymouth Dock for 3½ guineas each. In the 1780's, when he lost a royal allowance through marrying, Hoppner had to paint whole-length portraits at 8 guineas a time, and 'he did not get near £400 a year'.[1] Hoppner's later good fortune illustrates how particularly miserable was the fate of the young painter who remained an assistant. In 1808 Hoppner sold two replicas of full-length portraits of Pitt, which he had originally executed in 1804 for Lord Mulgrave at 200 guineas each. Philip Reinagle had painted replicas for Alan Ramsay; his son, gratefully christened Ramsay Richard Reinagle, painted replicas for Hoppner thirty years later at the advanced fee of 35 guineas. And for 20 guineas each Reinagle made thirteen replicas of Hoppner's half-length version of the Pitt portrait, which Hoppner sold for 120 guineas each. It meant that Hoppner made £1,300 on the copying rights of a single half-length portrait.[2]

One reason why Lawrence had so many unfinished portraits on his hands was that he frequently attempted to paint most of the picture himself. The strict limitation to 200 guineas on whole-length fees before Lawrence's day does therefore seem to have denoted a certain

[1] Farington, *op. cit.*, I, p. 84. [2] Whitley, p. 161.

realism on the part of the purchasers. In spite of the ease of the deception, they must have known that at best these things were only partly original. This view is borne out by the willingness of patrons to pay several times as much for subject pictures by the same painters. The critics of the day seem to have believed quite genuinely that these amateurish and frequently incompetent exercises were the equal of Raphael, Michelangelo or whom you will. But, once a painter had established a market for portraiture, he was not often tempted to take the risk of embarking on a task which required so much time and thought, however much he fancied his own ability. Certainly the rewards of historical painting were much higher, but they were not high enough, when good management might produce an income of from £5,000 to £6,000 a year (and you may call this £60,000 to £75,000 in modern values) by painting portraits alone.

There was perhaps another reason for pegging the price of portraits. In a famous passage in Sheridan's *School for Scandal* of 1777, Charles Surface sells his Great-aunt Deborah 'done by Kneller in his best manner', for £5 10*s*. A family investment would have been the last of considerations in choosing to have oneself painted. The day was far off when a self-made man would hope to acquire an aura of nobility by displaying the dearly-purchased ancestors of other people, who were not even of his own race. Furthermore, filial piety was not a conspicuous stage property in late eighteenth-century England, as witness the numerous commissioned and half-purchased portraits which after the death of Reynolds, Gainsborough and Romney were never redeemed by the sitters' families but allowed to depart for even less than Charles Surface's Aunt Deborah.

2. *The Subject Picture*

There was a big distinction in the year 1760 between conversation-pieces, which were deemed to be of only private interest, and history painting, by which mythological and religious subjects were chiefly meant. The latter were little attempted by English artists. Hogarth, who had been trained at the beginning of the century to paint ceilings in the manner of his master, Sir John Thornhill, occasionally produced historical paintings, but his talent was for satires on contemporary life which lent themselves to his craft as a popular engraver. Like the costume paintings of the nineteenth century, they were illustrations conceived in paint rather than pictures. They were the antithesis of the grand manner of the Italians and were made deliberately so. Consequently, when the engraving profits had been earned, the pictures themselves were of no interest to the galleries of the gentry and only unusual people like Garrick, Sir John Soane and Alderman Beckford cared to own them. In 1750 when Hogarth invited tenders for his six pictures, which formed the *Marriage à la mode* series, he was obliged to accept the only tender, 120 guineas. In the last years of his life Hogarth tried the experiment of a lottery (as Copley did later) to get rid of his four *Election* pictures. Less than a hundred 2-guinea tickets were subscribed, and Garrick was the only ticket-holder who took the trouble to draw a number.

Reproduction rights in the period 1730–1760 were not the gold-mine that they were to become a hundred years later, nor was the mass production of engravings possible. A thousand copies was generally the limit. Hogarth's attempt to paint for the common man was premature, and it did not make him rich. In the 1780's Hogarth's widow depended on a Royal Academy pension of £40 a year. It was an even more grievous error to be humorous in paint than it was to be common, though between the 1840's and the 1870's, Leslie and Frith imitated precisely this aspect of Hogarth's work. Like Hogarth, Frith lived to see how quickly his public wearied of light entertainment. For this reason Hogarth is even to-day an extremely under-priced painter. Frith, of course, is even more so.

The commodity that was required was neither meticulous detail nor a bitter sense of humour, but mythological, religious and historical painting as the Grand Tour snobs liked it. This accounts for the immediate success of Benjamin West, who arrived in London when Hogarth was still declaiming against the 'black masters' who had ruined his practice. West was to reform the English subject picture just as Reynolds ten years earlier had reformed the English portrait. In the 1760's the conversation-pieces of Highmore, Hudson and the elder Devis, though they possess such a disarming charm to-day, were most inadequate for the English culture addicts. On the other hand there was no precedent for selling gigantic historical subjects by a painter of an unmade reputation. So to enable the young American to paint such things in economic security, Archbishop Drummond of York attempted to raise a fund of 3,000 guineas. This subscription failed, but the King himself came to the rescue of historical painting. The result was that between 1768 and 1805 West drew £1,000 a year continuously from the royal purse.

In terms of the work carried out, the fee was fabulous, since West did much more work for other patrons, if one may trust John Galt's list.

West raised the value of historical painting to a plane that was peculiar to England and which was only exceeded by Napoleon's monumental commissions during the brief years of the Empire. It was also a heavy and enduring legacy to British taste. That peculiar British institution, *The Picture of the Year*, the huge narrative canvas that dominated the Royal Academy Exhibitions until the First World War, was West's invention.

In 1811 West sold *Christ Healing the Sick* for 3,000 guineas, with one exception the highest fee to be received by any painter in any country in his own lifetime before the year 1860. It is a very bad picture indeed, but West should not be judged by the ludicrous monsters which he produced between the ages of seventy-three and eighty. When free of his Italianising snobbery, West was an incredibly able and versatile painter, who invented the English battle-picture in modern dress, a man capable of that extremely original little picture, the *Kosciusko in London* of 1797, which looks for all the world like the work of a Pre-Raphaelite.[1]

Almost from the moment of his arrival in England West became known as the 'American Raffaele'. In 1820, after his death, he was compared in all seriousness by his biographer, John Galt, both with Raphael and Michelangelo. Forty years later Turner's biographer, Walter Thornbury, devoted an article to West under the heading 'West, the monarch of mediocrity?', a most ungrateful tribute to the man who had founded the school of historical painting that was most popular in 1860. In fact none of West's many styles had been conspicuously Raphaelesque, except that which he had practised in the last few years of his life. The kind of picture which West painted when he first came to England, such as the *Departure of Regulus*, for which George III paid £420 in 1769, was a Raphael Mengs version of the styles of Pietro da Cortona and Poussin. Two paintings in the same manner, *Elisha raising the Shunamite* and *Jacob blessing Ephraim*, departed from the Grosvenor family in 1959, after nearly two centuries' seclusion from the market, for £800 and £1,000. It would be rash, in that year of £50,000 abstract paintings, to describe this as a Benjamin West revival.

These three pictures, like the *Cleombrotus* of the Tate Gallery, all painted in the 1760's, are remarkable for attenuated statuesque figures which foreshadow the extreme classicist French style of Jacques Louis David. In fact they look like paintings of the French Revolution period. West's quarrel with the Royal Academy and the King, which led to the loss of his huge retaining fee and, for a time, to his retirement from the Presidency of the Royal Academy, began in 1803 over one of these

[1] Neeld sale, Christie's, 1945, £210. West sale, 1829, £42.

pictures. Having visited Paris during the Peace of Amiens, he refurbished his *Hagar and Ishmael* of 1776 in up-to-date French style and exhibited it at the Academy as a new picture. West's sympathy with France was well-known, and this was regarded in royal circles as a republican gesture.

Chiefly because of its flat dreary colouring, this early neo-classicist manner of Benjamin West had no influence on the English subject picture. But he soon drifted into a style, based on Guido Reni, which became the very foundation of the late-eighteenth-century subject picture. Moreover, throughout his life West produced battle-pictures in modern dress in a combination of modern portraiture and Poussinesque tricks. The prototype was the *Death of General Wolfe*, painted as early as 1771, a picture of which he made four versions. Lord Grosvenor, who bought the first of them for 400 guineas, also bought the *Destruction of the French Fleet off La Hogue* in 1780. It was the prototype of the many Trafalgar pictures of 1805, at which not only Turner tried his hand but also, strange to say, Constable; and in 1959 it made the quite interesting price of £2,000.

To have discarded togas, nudity and fireman's helmets for red coats and gaiters among the battle smoke was no small achievement for a disciple of Raphael Mengs and it may be noticed that the two most successful practitioners of this style in the eighteenth century, John Trumbull and John Singleton Copley, were Americans like West. Topicality was already a feature of American painting. It was found that such works could make more money as public exhibitions than as private commissions. In 1781 Copley's *Death of Chatham* was said to have made £5,000 in gate-money alone. In 1791 Copley's *Floating Batteries at Gibraltar* was shown in a tent in St. James's Park and made another £3,000. Reduced replicas for private patrons added to the painter's profits. For instance, in 1789 a quite small version of his *Sortie from Gibraltar* was sold by John Trumbull to Thomas Baring for £525. Then there were the profits from engravings. In 1806 Copley made £1,200 from engravings of his *Death of Nelson*, and in the same year he cleared £2,100 from a lottery for the original painting of *The Death of Chatham*, on which he had made £5,000 a full generation before.[1]

And yet Copley continued to complain of his inability to sell the original paintings on which he had made so much. There seems indeed to have been a slump in the battle-picture market between Trafalgar and Waterloo, but the giant religious picture, another of West's innovations, took the battle-picture's place and individual exhibitions

[1] Farington, *op. cit.*, III, p. 137.

continued to be very lucrative into the 1820's. That a fall in the popularity of this sort of entertainment took place between the 1820's and the 1860's was due less to lack of public interest in painting than to the growing number of competitors.

West himself had no need to compete with such raree-shows until after 1805 when the state of insanity of George III permitted his enemies to put an end to his embellishments of Windsor Castle and the Chapel Royal. The scale of West's emoluments may be gauged from the fact that less than a dozen old master pictures made as much as 1,000 guineas each in the London and Paris salerooms of the eighteenth century. West himself sent a carefully audited account to the King in 1801 in order to remind him how he had earned his allowance of £1,000 a year.[1] It appeared that in 1779–1780 West had painted eight pictures for the Royal apartments, commemorating the victories of the founder of Windsor Castle, Edward III. Three of these were accepted at £1,365 each, the remainder at 500 or 600 guineas. For the Chapel Royal eight pictures, celebrating the *Triumph of Revealed Religion*, were accepted between 1780 and 1801 at 1,000 guineas each, besides one at £1,260. In addition to the paintings, West made three full-size cartoons on paper to be copied by Jervase in stained glass for the chapel windows, and for these, too, he received 1,000 guineas each, though he complained to Farington in 1804 that he had been underpaid. In fact these were by no means West's highest fees, for in 1794 he received £1,300 for a large painting in the Royal Naval Hospital chapel at Greenwich, in addition to 125 guineas for preparing the necessary oil-sketches.[2]

According to John Galt, the pious biographer, West refused the offer of a knighthood, made to him through the Duke of Gloucester in 1791, because he considered that his position in art was such that it could only be commemorated by a title that was hereditary. Although the Royal Duke approved the nobility of this sentiment, the President of the Royal Academy remained Benjamin West Esquire for the rest of his days.

In 1811 West was able to test his popularity with the art-world, even when the royal patronage had been withdrawn. He had been asked to contribute to a hospital for his native city, Philadelphia. With his usual prudence West, offered a picture in place of money. *Christ Healing the Sick* was a relatively modest-sized picture for West, 16 ft. × 12 ft., and not very much bigger than Sebastiano del Piombo's *Raising of Lazarus*, which it imitated. Instead of sending it to Philadelphia, West showed it

[1] John Galt: *Life and Works of Benjamin West*, 1820, Vol. 2.
[2] Farington, *op. cit.*, I, p. 83.

at the British Institution's exhibition. This body was West's brain-child after he had observed, during the Peace of Amiens, that the French government not only exhibited works of living artists but also bought them. The British Institution acquired *Christ Healing the Sick* for £3,150 through the medium of sixty private subscribers. Only one painter had ever received a fee comparable to this, but the example must have been dear to West's heart, for it was the Emperor Napoleon who had paid 100,000 francs or £4,000 for David's *Sâcre de L'Empereur*, painted between 1805 and 1807. *Le Sâcre* was, however, a far more elaborate and accomplished work than *Christ Healing the Sick*, and it measured 31 ft. × 20 ft. 4 ins. Politics have been hard on it. Twice in history *Le Sâcre* has had to be cut up, rolled and hidden, in 1814 and 1870.

The more remarkable feature of the purchase of *Christ Healing the Sick* was that the British Institution recouped most of this money as well as a 1,500-guinea engraver's fee by selling 840 extremely indifferent prints of the picture at the astonishing price of 5 guineas each. William Hazlitt alone dissented from the chorus of praise by declaring that West was 'great only by the acre'. As to the picture, it went in 1825 to the National Gallery, who nowadays keep it discreetly hidden. The Philadelphia hospital received a replica, instead of the promised original.

The reader may be reminded at this point that, two years after the British Institution's 3,000-guinea purchase, Titian's *Bacchus and Ariadne* was bought-in at the Kinnaird sale for £2,625. But West continued to receive every encouragement to remain a megalomaniac. In 1814 he organised a one-man show in order to exhibit *Christ Rejected by Caiaphas*, 34 ft. × 16 ft., with 120 figures in it and in a frame modelled after the gate of Theseus at Athens, but, if anything, larger. The 'American Raffaele' was reputed to have refused 10,000 guineas (but from whom?). The picture remained with the painter, who followed it up with another just as big, which he exhibited in the old Royal Academy rooms in November 1817, when he was seventy-nine years old. *Death on the Pale Horse*, an interpretation of the Apocalypse, was based on Raphael's *Victory of Constantine* in the Vatican, but even more muddled and a bit crazy at that.

In 1820 Benjamin West died worth more than £100,000. There was no need for an executors' sale, and his works remained with his sons in Newman Street. The fact that one of the executors, Henry Fauntleroy, a pioneer collector of Dresden porcelain, was hanged for forgery some years later after the failure of the bank which he owned may explain why West's sons were forced to hold a sale in 1829. On paper the sale made £20,000, but since the auctioneer was the famous George Robins, much bidding may have been done by the chandelier. *Christ Rejected* and *Death on the Pale Horse* were bought-in. It is most unlikely that the figures of 3,000 and 2,000 guineas were reached by genuine bidding in a year when fashion had already changed radically. The fact remains that six years later both pictures were discovered in small shops, rolled up for lack of space. They made their way to West's home town of Philadelphia where the Pennsylvania Institute of Art still owns them.

Most of the pictures and designs which West had made for George III had been returned by George IV to the painter's family. Some of them, *The Times* complained, were 'literally given to the public'.[1] *Moses and the Brazen Serpent*, one of the 1,000-guinea commissions, must, I think, be the painting which covered the end-wall of the lounge of a hotel in the Isle of Wight when I was a small boy. It was said to have been put there to save the cost of papering.

The logical progeny of these enormous exhibition-pieces was not a picture at all but a panorama, an institution that reached its highest popularity before the end of the wars. The panorama of London, known as the *Eidemetropolis* of 1802, measured 108 ft. × 18 ft. and was the work of Girtin, the water-colourist, of all people.[2] The *neoramas* of Jean Pierre Alaux, which came to London in the 1820's, were even bigger. For instance, the *Westminster Abbey*, which is rolled up in the cellars of the Louvre, was designed to form a rotunda 57 ft. high. The *Padorama* of 1831 was a continuous landscape strip, representing the view from the first railway carriages travelling between Liverpool and Manchester. These contraptions had ceased to be high art, even as the age understood it, and therefore it became unwise to drag *historical* painting down to the same level in competing exhibitions. Yet works of quite obscure men, Dubost's *Damocles* of 1807 and Count Strohling's *Daniel in the Lions' Den* of 1810, had made 1,600 guineas apiece, even when sold after the exhibitions, while this vogue lasted.[3] Benjamin Haydon, despite his endless lamentations, cleared £2,000 on the *Entry of Christ into Jerusalem* as late as 1820.

When the panorama craze died down, the giant religious picture returned. Haydon would certainly have envied the rewards of Holman Hunt and Gustave Doré in the 1860's and 1870's, but in the period of this chapter engraving rights were, on the whole, a more secure source of profit for the painter than a raree-show exhibition. Those who were

[1] Whitley: *Art in England*, II, p. 170. [2] *Ibid.*, I, pp. 40–1.
[3] Whitley, I, pp. 214, 216.

not in the special position of Benjamin West, relied on the print-publishers to buy their subject-pictures as book illustrations in subscribed editions. A handsome, expensive mezzotint by Valentine Green, taken from a Reynolds full-length portrait, brought less to the painter or to the owner of the original than a commission for a poorly-engraved illustration to Macklin's *Poets' Gallery* or Boydell's *Shakespeare Gallery*.

Macklin, who died in 1800, spent the last fourteen years of his life producing an *Illustrated Bible*, on which he spent £30,000 in painters' commissions alone. The price stands comparison with the £40,000 paid by the Empress Catherine for the Houghton Gallery in 1779, or the £44,000 paid for the Orleans Gallery in 1798. Even the most indifferent painters benefited from this munificence. Some of the following commissions were for Macklin's Bible and some for his *Poets' Gallery*. All relate to the period 1784–1800.

Reynolds:	*Holy Family*, £500 (engraving fee £700)
	The Cottagers, 1788, £500 (engraving fee £252 10s.)
	The Fortune Teller, £150
Gainsborough:	*Hobinol and Gambaretta*, £350 (engraving fee £250)
	Lavinia, £300 (engraving fee £250)
Opie:	*The Freeing of Amoret*, £200
William Hamilton:	*Palamon and Arcite*, £100
	The Ancient English, £200
William Peters:	*The Death-bed of the Just*, £400 (engraving fee £350)
Thomas Stothard:	*Death of Lord Robert Manners*, £200 (engraving fee £700)
Benjamin West:	*The Witch of Endor*, £400
George Morland:	*The Farmer's Stable*, £200
Thomas Barker of Bath:	*The Woodman and His Dog*, £300
H. W. Bunbury:	*The Mouse's Petition* and *Marian*, £300 each

The obscure Bunbury, the pedestrian Barker and the cheaply sensational Peters ranked with Gainsborough. The elaboration of the subject alone seems to have dictated the fee, and in two cases the engraver made more than any of the painters. Macklin's prices were certainly no guide to the normal fees of the lesser painters, but all were capable of surprises. George Stubbs, for instance, was regarded as no more than a gentleman's horse painter, and it was not until 1929 that his true position in art was recognised. Yet there were times when he made as much as Reynolds received for his big portrait groups. From the lawsuit which he won against Sir Vane Temple in 1801, it appears that Stubbs could get 300 guineas for a horse portrait when he was seventy-seven years old.

At £500, Reynolds's *Holy Family*, a dull imitation of Correggio and Murillo, which is now in the Tate Gallery, was no more than a normal subject-picture commission, and Macklin was able to sell it later to Sir Peter Burrell for £735. But Reynolds had no fixed rate for such things. The price depended on the folly and the enthusiasm of the customers, and in this respect Reynolds sometimes shared the good fortune of Benjamin West. In 1779 Reynolds painted his largest work of this kind, the Guido Reni-like *Nativity*, for which the Duke of Rutland reputedly paid £1,200, but the sum was probably more. The numerous Reynolds portraits which were destroyed in the fire at Belvoir Castle in 1813 were insured at no more than Reynolds's normal commission fees. Since the huge *Nativity* was insured for £1,400, it is a fair inference that this was the cost in 1779.[1]

A picture which did not try to look like a raided altarpiece, stood less chance of making such a price. The famous *Mrs. Siddons as the Tragic Muse*, for which Reynolds asked 1,000 guineas in 1784, was really no more than a large seated whole-length with some Italian accessories. It remained in the painter's hands till 1790, when it was sold through Desenfans to M. de Calonne[2] for £735. At open auction in 1795 it made only £336 10*s*., but twice in its history the *Tragic Muse* has become the highest priced of Reynolds's works in 1823 when Lord Grosvenor bought it for £1,837 10*s*. and in 1921 when his descendant sold it to Duveen, who charged Henry Huntington £73,500.

Reynolds was destined to receive one other four-figure fee before his death. In 1786 he was commissioned by the Empress Catherine to paint any subject he liked for her and to name any fee he liked. The subject which Reynolds chose was the *Infant Hercules strangling the Serpents*, an allegory of the Empress's struggles to make Russia a great power. The picture was exhibited with loud acclaim at the Royal Academy in 1788 before its despatch to Russia. In March 1790 Reynolds received through the hands of Count Voronzov a golden box studded with diamonds and a letter of gratitude from the Empress. Voronzov was instructed to pay Reynolds's bill, which was 1,500 guineas. For one of the most unsatisfactory examples of Reynolds's most unsatisfactory style the price was exorbitant enough, but in the last years of the Napoleonic wars it was far outstripped by the giant historical pictures which have been mentioned.

If size and pomposity determined the value of a subject-picture in the

[1] An eye which fell right out of the *Nativity* in 1809 was replaced by the Reverend Peters. (Farington, *op. cit.*, V, p. 186).
[2] Whitley, II, p. 10.

late eighteenth century, minute finish and crowded detail commanded a price that was almost as high. For Zoffany's ludicrously crowded '*Tribuna' of the Uffizi Gallery at Florence* George III paid £800, but he had previously allowed Zoffany £1,500 for his expenses for the year which he spent in Italy in 1772–1773, so that this single picture, which the King did not like, cost the royal family £2,300. We have already seen how this love of the meticulous raised the price of a niggling imitation of Van Huysum by Hewlett or Van Os to something more than Reynolds's biggest portrait group (see page 24).

On the other hand, pure landscape was the Cinderella of the art world. It was the domain of topographical draughtsmen and water-colourists with a strong element of the lady and gentleman amateur, seeking the picturesque in a medium that did not spoil their fine clothes.[1] A large landscape had therefore to contain figures, if it was expected to sell better than such light affairs. It was a convention which derived from the seventeenth-century Italians, who could only express themselves in landscape if some scriptural or mythological incident was thrown in. Gainsborough, who derived his landscape style from Wynants, Hobbema and Ruysdael and sometimes Rubens, would have preferred to leave out the figures. Not caring at all for scriptural and mythological subjects, he tended to reproduce the same incidents, hence a profusion of market carts, river fords and cottage doors. On the other hand, Richard Wilson, who headed the Italianists, derived his style from Claude and had to introduce mythology into his bigger landscapes to make them sell. For full-length landscapes without historical figures, he only got 40 guineas. With figures, the price was more than doubled.[2]

The wretched convention continued into the nineteenth century. Turner had the cunning to sub-title a straightforward harbour scene, *Van Goyen looking out for a Subject*. A few daubs in the foreground of a view of the Forum were alleged to represent Raphael in the company of La Fornarina carrying his canvas to the Vatican. Whether the practice helped Turner's market is a matter of dispute, but it is certain that Constable, who despised such artifices, hardly ever made more than 200 guineas even in the 1830's.

Reynolds, whose lectures quite often reveal a streak of honest good sense, was not happy about the situation. In 1788, in his 14th Royal Academy *Discourse*, he remarked that Richard Wilson 'our late ingenious academician' had introduced gods and goddesses into scenes

[1] In 1809 Lady Lonsdale was of the opinion that painting in oils would ruin her daughter's health. (Farington, *op. cit.*, V, p. 179.)
[2] Farington, *op. cit.*, V, p. 183.

that were by no means prepared to receive them and he hinted that even the great Claude might have been better without them. But, a few years after Reynolds's death, Claude had become enthroned as the greatest painter in the world, and anything that imitated Claude must be good. It was now that John Glover began to ask 500 guineas for his emasculated Claude imitations. The effect on the Wilson market was interesting. In 1755 the Duke of Gloucester had paid the painter the altogether exceptional price of 150 guineas for *Landscape with the Death of the Children of Niobe*, the very landscape which Reynolds attacked in 1788. On the Duke of Gloucester's death in 1806 there was a movement among the Royal Academicians to buy *Niobe* for 1,000 guineas, though poor Wilson had not been able to earn as much money for three years' work. The picture was sold in the end to Sir Francis Baring for £840.[1]

In 1808, at the absolute height of the Claude cult, Payne Knight complained that landscapes, for which Wilson 'had but thirty or forty guineas', were now only to be got for 'three or four hundred'.[2] As late as 1827 a *View on the Arno* made £493 10*s*. at the de Tabley sale. After that, Wilson's pictures went out of fashion with Claude's, though the Prince Consort bought a landscape when he came to England in 1840.

Gainsborough had not committed the crime in Reynolds's eyes of introducing mythological personages into landscapes that were not designed for their reception. In 1785 Reynolds generously bought his rival's *Landscape with a girl tending pigs*—but only for 100 guineas. It is strange to have to record that this fee was exceptionally high for a man whose landscapes were head and shoulders above those of any of his contemporaries. In the following year the Prince of Wales paid 80 guineas for *The Market Cart*, for which Duveen gave £74,400 in 1928. Professor Waterhouse mentions three landscapes which Gainsborough sold in 1785 for 200 guineas between them. In 1753 he had asked 15 guineas and in 1766 40 guineas for mantelpiece-sized works. The prices fixed by Gainsborough's widow at the Schomburg House exhibition in 1789 were too high, since most of the 200-guinea landscapes were bought-in. An unaccountable price, £525, appears to have been paid for a picture, called *The Woodman*, whose attractions can no longer be judged since it was destroyed in a fire in 1810. The fact was that as late as 1787 or 1788 Gainsborough had accepted £78 15*s*. from Alderman Boydell for the Hobbema-like *Cornard Wood* which is now in the National Gallery.

[1] Bonham's Rooms, 1961, £2,000.
[2] Farington, *op. cit.*, V, p. 14.

3. *Posthumous Fate of the Eighteenth-century Masters (up to 1862)*

The sale of the remains of Gainsborough's studio in 1797 shows that the landscapes alone survived the total eclipse which was then habitual after a painter's death. The families of the sitters, as we have seen, could not be induced even to redeem the works, on which half the commission had been paid. Thus the full-length *Henry Duke of Gloucester* (£22,000 in 1958) made £6. The *Duchess of Gloucester* (£12,705 in 1904) made £2 10*s*. The almost monochrome full-length in the National Gallery, known as *Mrs. Graham as a housemaid*, had been left unfinished two years before Gainsborough's death. It was bought by Bryan for £4 15*s*. 6*d*. and passed on to his backer, the Earl of Carlisle. Other unfinished full-lengths were sold for a pound or less and three unfinished portrait heads made thirteen shillings between them. In the previous year Arnold Nesbitt, M.P., the speculator of the Orleans sale, had bought *Master Jonathan Buttall*, to-day better known as *The Blue Boy*, for £36 15*s*. The Gainsborough collapse was therefore not a surprise. Out of 103 lots in the 1797 sale there were only five that exceeded £16 and only one, a landscape, made a normal commission price, £101 17*s*. *The Mall in St. James's Park*, an over-ambitious theatrical monstrosity, which Gainsborough should never have attempted, made a specially high price, namely 30 guineas. In 1916 it cost Duveen £62,000.

A few months before this sale, Reynolds's studio effects went through the same experience. The finished portraits, which the executors had been trying to negotiate with the sitters' families for the past five years, were sold for 'little more than half a crown a foot'. Exceptionally the Marquis of Hertford paid a sentimental price of 50 guineas for *Perdita Robinson*, who was no Great-aunt Deborah. The same thing happened in 1807 at Romney's executors' sale. Three *Lady Hamiltons* went for £36 between them, and a *Mrs. Siddons* for £4 6*s*. Only seven pictures fetched over £20 each, and the dearest was again a fancy picture in Romney's least happy vein, *Titania*, at £68 5*s*.

In those days death was no advantage to the value of a painter's work as it was in 1925, when the assortment of odds and ends in Sargent's studio made £146,000 (gold standard pounds). Thirty years after the death of Reynolds, the high-piled head dresses, the powdered wigs and long embroidered waistcoats had become as comically outdated as flounces, wasp waists, pyramid collars and walrus moustaches in the knowing 1920's. To William Hazlitt in 1824 Reynolds's pictures had something old-womanish about them. They had an obsolete affected air, reminding him of antiquated ladies of quality. They were somewhere between the living and the dead, by which presumably Hazlitt meant that Reynolds was not yet dead enough to be judged as an old master.[1]

The Reynolds and Gainsborough executor sales demonstrated at least that in future these painters would be judged by their subject-pictures and landscapes with figures. But the cult of pure landscape was still a long way off. It began with the French republicanism of 1848–1852, the revival of interest in the Dutch school and the recognition of its Barbizon imitators. In the intervening period, therefore, the scales were heavily weighted for Reynolds against Gainsborough. The balance was not in fact redressed till the 1870's, when it became fashionable to buy other people's ancestors and Gainsborough was judged by his portraits.

At a period when the saleroom reception of Reynolds's whole-lengths was mediocre, his subject-pictures actually advanced. In 1805 they stood up to the severe test of Alderman Boydell's bankruptcy. All the pictures, which had been painted since 1787 for the famous Shakespeare Gallery, were brought under the hammer after James Tassie, the Scottish gem-engraver, had won the complete collection in a lottery. Not even Reynolds had ever painted pictures less suited to his style than these. Nevertheless, *Macbeth and the Witches* made £578 and the *Death of Cardinal Beaufort* £525, that is to say as much as Boydell had paid in 1789, though the pictures had long ago earned all that was possible in engraving rights. Samuel Rogers bought *Puck* for £215. The Shakespeare Gallery had made this obese imp so famous that people called to each other 'There it is', as a Rowlandsonian porter bore it in front of the yellow-faced sage from Pall Mall to St. James's Square.[2]

In contrast with these 'fancy picture' prices, the *Nelly O'Brien* of the Wallace Collection, one of the most famous of all Reynolds's portraits to-day, was bought by the Marquess of Hertford at Caleb Whiteford's sale in 1820 for £62 1*s*. However, in 1813 the British Institution held a memorial banquet and an exhibition of no less than 150 Reynolds pictures. The owners of Reynolds portraits certainly profited by the publicity, for in 1816 a portrait from this exhibition made £378. It must be added that it was of exceptional literary interest, being the head of Dr. Johnson painted for Mrs. Thrale.

But the real Reynolds year was 1821, when a big sale followed the

[1] Whitley: *Art in England*, II, p. 205.

[2] J. T. Smith: *Nollekens and His Times*, ed. 1920 with notes by Wilfred Witten, II, p. 227.

death of the painter's niece, Mary Palmer, who became Countess of Thomond. The sale took place at Christie's in a singularly modern aura of fashionable hero-worship. The porters had to shout the bids for the gentry who were unable to squeeze past the ante-room. Gilt chairs and a television screen were yet to come. If, however, the sale is compared with the Carnarvon and Michelham sales in the 1920's, it becomes clear that the buyers were looking for something very different. Straightforward full-length portraits, forty years old and more, made no more than their original commission prices, though two portraits of 'fancy-picture' status fetched over £300 each. Mythological pictures did a great deal better with an eight-foot *Dido on her Funeral Pyre* at £735 and the smaller *Snake in the Grass*, a version of a several times repeated subject, at £536 10*s*. The prizes that brought fashionable London to the sale were, however, eleven broadly painted colour cartoons in oils, from 7 ft. to 13 ft. high, which Reynolds had designed for a gothic stained-glass window in New College chapel. They had been Reynolds's one thorough attempt to put the theories of his lecture of 1771 into practice by going all out to imitate Guido Reni. In fact he completed the cartoons eight years later. At the 1821 sale the single figures in gothic niches, known as the *Seven Virtues*, were bought by Lord Normanton for £5,565, the figure of *Charity* alone fetching £1,155, while the central cartoon, the *Adoration of the Shepherds*, cost Lord Fitzwilliam £1,575. Nor was this all. In 1827 George IV offered 10,500 guineas for the *Seven Virtues*, hanging very handsomely in Normanton's long gallery at Somerley, while in 1831 the trustees of the National Gallery offered 16,000 guineas—and even this was refused.[1]

It is remarkable that the first of Reynolds's works to make four-figure prices in the saleroom should have been quite untypical, in a foreign mannerism and of eccentric shape. But in 1821 Benjamin West had just died, revered as the greatest painter of all time, and these works had been the rivals of West's window at Windsor. The New College windows, when they were first installed, had enjoyed no such popularity. Horace Walpole complained in 1782 of the badness of Jervase's technique and the poor light. It had been easier to see the window design when the glass had been shown in a darkened room in Pall Mall. As to the style, John Byng, later Viscount Torrington, who was always wonderfully English in his tastes, had compared Reynolds's figures in 1781 to half-dressed languishing harlots. He supposed 'that men had been consulted who determined them to be in the Gothic taste, else they never would have been introduced into this beautiful chapel'.[2]

[1] J. T. Smith, *op. cit.*, II, p. 231. [2] *The Torrington Diaries*, I, p. 55.

The resale of the *Tragic Muse* in 1823 for £1,837 10*s*. was surpassed at the Gwydyr sale of 1829, when the British Institution paid £1,995 for *The Holy Family* or *Riposo* of the Macklin *Bible*. But the eight Reynolds paintings in the Thomas Lawrence sale of the following year were all portraits and only one made the original commission price of a normal whole-length. The period 1830–1860 was a very flat one for most picture prices. Yet the Reynolds 'fancy pictures' retained their high valuation, though in 1824 *Lord Heathfield* cost the government no more than £400, the price Angerstein had paid Lawrence who bought the picture in 1809 for £300.[1]

The Reynolds 'fancy pictures', like Murillo's, fitted so perfectly into the early Victorian taste that the wonder was that more did not reach the salerooms. The National Gallery *Age of Innocence* fetched £1,596 at Jeremiah Harman's sale in 1844. In 1850 the Marquess of Hertford paid £1,070 for *Miss Bowles and her puppy*,[2] while at Samuel Rogers's sale in 1856 he gave £2,205 for the *Strawberry Girl*, an extraordinary price for a picture only 25 ins. × 30 ins., seeing that the Reynolds market had always been governed by size. Lord Hertford bought this rabbit-faced child (Reynolds's niece, Offy Palmer) without having seen it on the strength of a letter from Thomas Lawrence to Rogers, which was printed in the sale catalogue. According to this letter, Reynolds had regarded the *Strawberry Girl* as one of the half-dozen great things he had ever painted. Nevertheless it had made only £81 18*s*. at the 1796 sale and it was more browned and flaked and faded than was habitual, even with Reynolds.

Samuel Rogers [1763–1855] not only left ten Reynolds pictures, which were sold at auction, but he had actually known Reynolds personally, a fact which gave the sale tremendous romantic significance. The revival of interest in the English eighteenth-century school and its build-up into a millionaire market dates properly from 1856, though Gainsborough's work did not appreciate till rather later. Gainsborough had indeed failed to keep up with Reynolds's prices even for his fancy landscape pictures, which rarely made more than a hundred or two till 1827. In that year William Seguier bid £1,182 18*s*. for *The Market Cart* at the de Tabley sale. Two years later, when the National Gallery took over the purchase, there were loud accusations of jobbery. Seeing that Seguier was both a dealer and Keeper of the National Gallery, the accusations may have been well founded.

The purchase of *The Market Cart* bore not the least relation to the

[1] Farington, *op. cit.*, V, p. 181.
[2] Engraved under the title, 'Love me, Love my dog.'

real market. In 1841 another *Market Cart* made £651 while portraits by Gainsborough, which seldom found their way to Christie's, continued to fetch very little in early Victorian times. In 1843 a whole-length of William Pitt fetched 23 guineas and in 1845 a head of Lord Clive made £3 10*s*. In 1834 *The Morning Walk* could not find a bidder. It was sold in the Northwick sale of 1859 for £735 to a member of the sitter's family. The high price may have been due to romantic associations for, like Samuel Rogers, Lord Northwick had lived in Gainsborough's time. The sale certainly triggered-off a new market for Gainsborough. In 1862 the National Gallery recognised the old master status of family portraits by paying £1,000 for Gainsborough's whole-length of *Dr. Ralph Schomburg* which had failed to make 50 guineas in 1836. From another source the Gallery acquired at the same price the famous half-length portrait of Mrs. Siddons.

It was the beginning of close on seventy years' enthronement of the English eighteenth-century portrait, but it was not till the late 1870's that the revaluation extended to Lawrence, Hoppner, Raeburn and Romney. Generally speaking, it was not considered worth the trouble to put their pictures in the saleroom. As late as 1872, Mr. Woods of Christie's bought a big imposing Romney family group, which had been withdrawn from the saleroom, for 28 guineas. After his death in 1906 it made £4,830. The whole subject of the revival of the English eighteenth-century school in the latter part of the last century is, however, bound up with the opening of the American market and will be studied in Chapter Seven.

CHAPTER FOUR

The Rewards of the Living Painter
The Proto-Victorians (1800–1860)

1. *Painter's Fees* — 2. *Posthumous Adventures*

---

1. *Painters' Fees*

It was a dynamic half-century that began with Romney, Hoppner and Lawrence in full practice and ended with the Pre-Raphaelites. And for more than half the time two utterly different civilisations overlapped. For while Turner and Constable exhibited before 1800 and Wilkie in 1806, Romney worked until 1802, Hoppner until 1810, Benjamin West until 1820, Raeburn until 1823 and Lawrence until 1830.

Lesser survivals bordered on the humorous. Sir William Beechey exhibited at the Royal Academy almost continuously from 1776 to his death in 1839, while Philip Reinagle, who had painted Alan Ramsay's whole-lengths of the Royal Family, when Beechey was a mere beginner, died in 1833. As to Ramsay Richard Reinagle, who fulfilled the same office for Hoppner in 1808, he did not die until 1862. And three years after Reinagle there died 'the English Wouverman', James Leakey, who had been accepted by Sir Joshua Reynolds as an assistant in 1791. Both Reinagle and Leakey lived right into the era of Leighton, Burne-Jones and Alma Tadema. Then there was John Linnell senior, the friend of Blake, who attracted the notice of Wilkie and Haydon as an infant prodigy of fourteen years in 1806. Yet he lived till 1883—lived to reprove Millais for forsaking Pre-Raphaelitism.

And perhaps one should add to this fascinating company of Rip van Winkles the name of Joshua Shaw of Bath, who startled Benjamin West in 1807 by the speed and facility with which he turned out pseudo-Berchems and pseudo-Ibbetsons, and who was engaged in drawing Mississippi paddle-steamers at the time of his death in 1860 at Burlington, New Jersey.

Lesser men could accommodate themselves to the times, but Lawrence's way of painting remained completely eighteenth-century to the last, though black coats and poke-bonnets lent themselves ill to the Grand Manner. Since Lawrence was the only man in Europe who could perform this tight-rope walking feat, portraiture declined at his death to a second- or third-rate branch of art for want of competent practitioners. It had become impossible for painters to cope with the puritanism of dress, particularly since the new garish style of interior decoration was the enemy of dark pictures. On every possible ground the public wanted its pictures brightly coloured. Not only did the brightly coloured picture stand up better to the coal-soot, but it lent itself to the technique of steel engraving and in Tractarian times it had the sanction of the age of faith.

The portrait painter had to get round the dress difficulty as best he could, but portraits stayed steeped in gloom. To the subject-painter frock-coats and chimney-pot hats were banned altogether. The past was considered not only more colourful than the present, but also more improving to the mind. This belief became so deep-seated that in the late 'forties, when he began to paint contemporary Cockney life, William Frith considered himself a Columbus of the paint-brush. For a generation the dullest of Royal Academicians had banded together to denounce contemporary subjects as vulgar, the reason being that they found them too difficult to paint, unless in peasant dress and foreign at that. To paint contemporary clothes needed the genius of Manet and Whistler, but the clue to the modern portrait was only discovered through a revival of interest in Velasquez in the Paris of the 1860's and in Frans Hals in the Munich of the 1870's. Once again portraiture was to become dashing, fashionable and more than ever expensive.

At the time of Lawrence's death the mania for fancy-dress pictures had unquestionably dethroned the contemporary portrait. Wilkie, who painted a few royal and noble portraits in the eleven years that followed Lawrence's death, received much lower fees. George IV was painted in Highland dress in 1830 for 500 guineas, but only three other of Wilkie's whole-lengths brought him 400 guineas. Wilkie's standard whole-length fee seems to have been 300 guineas, but for his extra whole-length royal portraits of 1834 and 1838, 500 guineas the pair. Sir Francis Grant, who succeeded Wilkie as the most fashionable English portraitist, charged less than Wilkie and at his death in 1879 his famous portrait of Palmerston made 300 guineas. The drabness of English portraits in the 'forties and 'fifties (best studied in the Reform Club) impelled Queen Victoria and the Prince Consort to patronise the glossy Winterhalter with his shining cheeks and bouquets of flowers. Even Millais at the height of his success in the 'seventies and 'eighties complained of the boredom of painting black-coated statesmen and bishops and only relished the task when he painted women sitters or children.

The romantic movement stifled portraiture, because it could find no formula to replace the Grand Manner. In other directions the Grand Manner was in no need of replacement. The romantic movement simply gave it a new twist. In the hands of Barry, Fuseli, Romney and even Lawrence the big religious or mythological picture had become horrific before the end of the eighteenth century. West himself, the first importer of the Grand Manner, succumbed to this impulse in his gigantic *Death on the Pale Horse* of 1817. In the previous year the young undiscovered John Martin had exhibited *Joshua commanding the sun to stand still* at the British Institution, selling this unassuming theme for 200 guineas, but in the twenty years that his fashion lasted, Martin did better than Turner. Still wilder than Martin was the Irishman, Francis Danby, whose small *Deluge* picture was bought by the Tate Gallery in 1953, an unforgettable salad of clammy nude bodies which seem to be struggling in the lurid blue light of London's first gas-lamps. Danby, too, till he became involved in a scandal and fled abroad, had the patronage of the gentry. Beckford bought the *Opening of the Sixth Seal* in 1827, as mad a picture as ever was painted, while in 1821 the Marquess of Stafford paid 500 guineas for *Pharaoh's Host Overwhelmed*.

The end of this extraordinary vogue can be seen in the famous Stowe sale of 1848, where Martin's *Destruction of Herculaneum* fell to an eighth of the 800 guineas paid in 1823. It may seem strange that these doom-sodden works, which express so well one aspect of early Victorian England, should have passed out of fashion so soon. But in fact they were killed by another by-product of Benjamin West's supreme versatility, the 8- or 10-ft. coloured illustration of lower-form history. *Cromwell dissolving the Long Parliament* is still to be found in elementary lesson books to-day, but in spite of its air of Victorian instruction, West painted it in 1810. In this picture the attitudes are not Guidoesque or Raphaelesque, but quietly subordinated to a display of knowledge of costume, furniture and architecture. Here the heirs of Benjamin West were not Martin and Danby, but Leslie and Maclise.

In religious painting the last and most baroque of the many styles of Benjamin West survived into the 1840's, oblivious of the fact that *Christ Rejected* and *Death on the Pale Horse* had found no buyer. The faithful practitioners were William Hilton and Benjamin Robert Haydon. Both these men continued to paint pictures on so vast a scale that only State patronage could have kept them alive. Haydon was driven to suicide in 1846 at the age of fifty-three. For a time Haydon had thrived on his peep-show exhibitions and Hilton had benefited from the generosity of the British Institution, who gave £525 for *Mary anointing the feet of Christ* in 1821 and £1,050 for *Christ Crowned with Thorns* in 1825.[1] For a few years after West's death such prices were not altogether unrealistic, for in 1823 Graves, the print-seller, paid £2,100 for a work in the style of West's 'medieval' pictures, *Stephen Langton and the Barons*, by Arthur Devis the younger [1763–1822]. The change can be detected in 1834 when Hilton's *Finding of Harold's Body* made only £200. Yet this work and its companion, *The Citizens of Calais delivering their keys to Edward III*, were used to misinstruct children for at least another century.

Despite the failures of Haydon and Hilton, the giant religious picture made its return to London in 1868, when Gustave Doré exhibited the first of the pictures which later constituted the Doré Gallery. For many years a series of 30-ft., somewhat West-like works were exhibited in the rooms that are at present the scene of the *Son et lumière* triumphs of Messrs. Sotheby. It was doubtless their edifying influence which made Lord Leighton buy poor Hilton's *Christ, Crowned with Thorns* as the Nation's first purchase under the Chantrey Bequest in 1878.

But so far as the private patron was concerned, the deaths of Hilton and Haydon ended the English Grand Manner in painting in the form that the eighteenth century had known and loved it. In the 1840's even the Italian originals went out of favour. Those who had formerly bought great smoky altarpieces, now bought the fancy-dress historical pictures, sometimes with a preference for the French and Belgian schools. Those who had once favoured the English Whig taste for the seventeenth-century Dutch school bought Wilkie and his followers. At one end of the scale Turner imposed the maximum of intellectual strain when he painted *The Burning of the Ships*; at the other end of the scale Thomas Webster, in *Roast Pig*, imposed no intellectual strain at all.

[1] In 1821 they gave £1,000 for James Ward's monstrous *Allegory of Waterloo*, which was presented to the Greenwich Hospital.

But even in the 1840's there was not yet a high church and a low in painting. The same patron might purchase both. There was no sign of the day when English art patronage would be split in two and the aesthete would flee from the vulgarian to seek refuge in the fairyland of *Laus Veneris* and *Beata Beatrix*.

It was hardly more than an accident that the peasant subjects of Wilkie and Mulready became a royal taste. The Prince of Wales bought Dutch paintings in the early 1800's because they were the taste of his Whig friends (see page 13). The Prince seems to have been incapable of distinguishing between the original and the pastiche. Wilkie to him was a second Teniers and even a better Teniers—as if nostalgic memories of apple-stealing and playing truant from school had anything in common with the dry remorseless observation of human life of a seventeenth-century Fleming. In the 1820's three kings competed for the possession of Wilkie's works, a fairly creditable taste, but neither St. Louis paperweights nor Fabergé toys were yet available for the indulgence of Royal appetites. It was a little more remarkable that Turner's works should have been bought by the conservative patrons of the Grand Manner Italians. For, even though Turner in his early paintings rang the changes between Claude and Backhuyzen, his handling was already broad and free and his colour sometimes violent and disconcerting. Mostly, however, Turner's paintings disconcerted Royal Academicians like Joseph Farington, whose mind was almost on as small a scale as the style which he practised, or the tiresome amateur artist, Sir George Beaumont, a sort of permanent public school prefect.

From the beginning of their painting careers Turner and Wilkie benefited from the relatively high value which late-eighteenth-century taste set on subject pictures. Their talent was so quickly recognised that age and inexperience did not count against them. In 1800, when Turner was twenty-five years old, Beckford paid £157 10*s*. for the *Fifth Plague of Egypt*, a work in the spirit of his own *Vathek*. In the following year the Duke of Bridgewater admitted Turner's works into his Orleans Gallery, paying £262 10*s*. for *Dutch Boats in a Gale*, which he hung next to a Willem van der Velde. In 1803 Turner held out in vain for 300 guineas for his *Calais Pier*, which remained with him all his life. But next year, Turner certainly got this price and perhaps more from Lord Yarborough for the *Festival at Macon*, for which he had already demanded 400 guineas from Lord de Tabley.[1]

In 1806 Turner sold the impressive 8-ft. *Falls of the Rhine at Schaffhausen* of the Boston Fine Arts Museum (by means of a part-exchange)

[1] A. J. Finberg: *The Life of J. M. W. Turner*, p. 106.

for 350 guineas. This was the beginning of a period of standard charges, 350 guineas for a specially large picture, 200 guineas for pictures 3 ft. × 4 ft., a size for which Gainsborough had been glad to accept 75–80 guineas twenty years earlier. It is difficult to establish how far this enormous advance in the value of landscape was due to the belief in the genius of a painter barely thirty years old, how far it was mere homage to Claude and how far it was wartime inflation. Occasionally even higher fees could be earned. In 1813 Sir John Swinburne paid Turner £577 10*s.* for *Mercury and Hersé*, while in 1818 Walter Fawkes gave £525 for *View of Dort*, 'the challenge to Cuyp'. In 1824 George IV reluctantly disbursed £630 for a commissioned work, *The Battle of Trafalgar*, while Turner refused to part with *Dido building Carthage* at £787 10*s*. It is possible that there were even higher bidders for this picture, which was in Turner's most popular post-Claude style. Turner had long been addicted to the practice of hoarding works like this, with which he was in love, and on which no one would give him his own price.

In 1811, however, Turner had checked his output of these big oil-paintings, which he painted largely for his own delectation. He had found that watercolour views, painted in sets, made all the money he wanted. The prices were low, at first 25 guineas and by 1823 60 guineas for large examples, not more than 80 guineas even in 1842. But they did not take long to make, while engraving rights could be as high as on an oil painting. By contrast there was no real rise in the basic price of Turner's oil paintings between 1813 and his death in 1851. A fee of 500 guineas was rarely earned, whereas mere imitators like Callcott and Stanfield could make it with ease. Yet Turner never became embittered like Constable. He was insensitive to criticism and indifferent to rewards. On the other hand, he hated to see his work underpriced, and of this noble trait he gave the world a memorable example. In 1827 there was a panic among English painters. The executors of Sir John Leicester, who became Lord de Tabley, suddenly ordered the sale of his collection. A financial depression, following the several bank failures of 1825, had already subdued the art market, but, as it turned out, de Tabley's modern pictures were well supported. The famous Joseph Gillott, the pen-maker, appeared among the new speculators; but the best supporter was Turner, who bought-in *Dutch Fishing Boats, Sun rising through Vapour* for £514 10*s*., which was half as much again as he had been paid for it. A clumsy and derivative composition, though magically lit, Turner kept it all his life and it was believed that he meant to be buried in it. Towards the year 1850 Elhanan Bicknell, the speculator, was so challenged by the old man's obstinacy that he was said to have offered him £1,600.[1]

The gesture was quite in keeping with Bicknell's habits. In March 1844, for instance, he paid Turner £1,050 for the 8-ft. *Palestrina* (National Gallery, Dyson Perrins Bequest, 1959), which had been rotting in the neglected Turner Gallery in Queen Anne Street since 1830. It is probably quite untrue that the propaganda contained in the volumes of Ruskin's *Modern Painters*, between 1843 and 1851, was the chief cause of the speculation in Turner's works during the last years of his life. The speculators, Bicknell, Gillott, Windus, Meigh and Newington Hughes, bought only Turner's more easily intelligible early works, whereas Ruskin praised only Turner's last style. The success of the speculators was seen in the years 1872–1878, when some of their Turner oil paintings made from £6,000 to £8,000 apiece. But it must be appreciated what these works were. They had none of the dazzling, astonishingly modern qualities, which were noticed in 1910 when the unsold late works, which Turner had left to the Nation, were shown for the first time in the new Tate Gallery rooms, properly cleaned and properly lighted—and it was just then that some of the swarthy, badly decayed favourites of the mid-Victorian saleroom began to decline.

The speculation was the triumph of astuteness rather than taste. In 1844 when he paid Turner 1,000 guineas for *Palestrina*, Bicknell had already paid as much for works by Callcott and Stanfield. And from this point we get a symptom which has a decidedly modern flavour. While Turner was selling the products of his daring new style for 300 or 400 guineas, if at all, his apprentice-pictures were making more in the saleroom. In 1845 *Walton Bridges*, sold in 1806 for £210, made £703 10*s*. Two more of Turner's earliest pictures were auctioned for £593 and £577 10*s*. in 1848, three years before his death.

The speculation of the 1840's in Turner's works continued unabated after the painter's death in 1851. Yet the very reverse happened in the case of David Wilkie, who had been able to make two or three times as much as Turner in his own lifetime. Wilkie's rise had been meteoric. In 1806 as a Scottish youth of twenty-one, newly arrived in London, Wilkie had sold *The Blind Fiddler* to Sir George Beaumont for £50. In the following year he sold two pictures at 150 guineas each. In 1813, when he was twenty-eight years old, Wilkie received fees, which for mere 'cabinet' pictures, had not been attained even by Reynolds. The Prince Regent paid him £525 for *Blind Man's Buff*, while in 1811

[1] *Art Journal*, 1862.

Angerstein gave no less than £840 for the *Village Festival*. In recent times the picture has been banished from the National Gallery to the Tate Gallery. Separated by a thin sanitary cordon from the Picasso exhibition of 1960, it looked as brown and homely as a cottage loaf.

In 1824, when the *Village Festival* was taken over by the Nation at a price much higher than Van Dyck's portrait of *Van der Geest*, Wilkie had just achieved his greatest triumph, the placing of a rail at the Royal Academy exhibition round his diffuse, crowded and unsatisfactory picture, *Chelsea Pensioners reading the Gazette of Waterloo*. It had taken Wilkie six years to complete and the fee of £1,260, which the Duke of Wellington had proposed in 1816, was no longer a commensurate reward. But when he began it, Wilkie was only thirty years old. It was not till after 1860 that painters, so young, could hope to make a thousand pounds on a single work—and then only two or three painters. During the Regency, patronage was in the hands of far fewer people than was the case fifty years later, but it was unquestionably more adventurous. It was also, as Turner had just learned, very capricious. While he was at work on the *Chelsea Pensioners* Wilkie's fees began to fall. The brown Teniers-like pictures of milling peasants went out of fashion after a vogue of barely ten years.

The trouble began with Charles Leslie who, only a few years younger than Wilkie, had come to London from Philadelphia in 1811 to sit at the feet of his great fellow-townsman, Benjamin West. Leslie's point of departure was that remarkable newly painted costume-piece of West's, *Cromwell dissolving the Long Parliament*. Leslie now made the fancy-dress picture his special study, and in 1821, two years before Wilkie's *Chelsea Pensioners*, he sent his *May Day in the Time of Elizabeth* to the Royal Academy, selling it for £315. Pseudo-Elizabethan pageantry had been a cult among English painters since the days of Boydell's *Shakespeare Gallery*, but Leslie's conception was a novel one. He discarded the Shakespearean fantasy costumes of the eighteenth-century stage and attempted to introduce authentic period dress and authentic architecture. Leslie's compositions were as laboured and old-masterish as Wilkie's, but there was a conscious avoidance of murkiness and *chiaroscuro*. His faces were full and high-lighted and they shone as if the mantle of prophecy had descended on them. Much care was taken over accessories. Leslie himself rarely succeeded in mixing fewer than three periods of costume together, unless his subject was located in the eighteenth century in which he happened to have been born, but Leslie's followers had to fulfil more exacting standards. For instance, in

1827, when he painted *Les Enfants d'Edouard*, Paul Delaroche produced something very different from Leslie's *Princes in the Tower*. The costumes and the furniture were, it is true, no more in period than Leslie's, but they were so conscientiously painted from life that they appear now as if photographed. In fact the work could be mistaken for a Salon picture of the 1880's.

If he expected to sell to the nobility and the more sophisticated merchants, who favoured the historical as opposed to the peasant-anecdotal setting, the English painter of the 1830's had to reckon with competition from the French school and the Dutch-Belgian school, the competition of schools with much higher academic standards of training and much too much knowledge of national history. He had to be conversant with *Don Quixote* and *Gil Blas* and Molière's plays. He had to know the fashions of the period and to invest in Wardour Street studio properties. He had also to master a laborious technique. Bright and sparkling pictures to suit gold and plush rooms meant painting on a pure white ground in successive glazes, whose transparency could be observed. These were the methods which enabled the Pre-Raphaelite pictures to survive so much better than those of Wilkie.

There are few subject-pictures of the period 1820–1860 which are not vulgar and silly, as painted according to the standard prescription. But it must not be forgotten how abominably bad most subject-pictures had been in the late eighteenth century. Vulgarity and sloppiness were a great deal older than industrialism. Noble patronage was still strong in 1820–1850. Some of the collectors who invested in Leslie, Maclise or Clarkson Stanfield had bought in the days of Reynolds and Gainsborough. The Great Reform Bill of 1832 stopped a great deal short of destroying the influence of the entire nobility in English politics. It changed art patronage still less. Joseph Gillott of Edgbaston, whose speculations began with the de Tabley sale of 1827, was a small manufacturer rather than an industrialist. Sheepshanks, Vernon, Bicknell and Windus were wholesale merchants. The fabulous William Wells of Redleaf was a shipbuilder and a member of an old naval family. Living painters were equally well patronised by the Duke of Bedford and the Marquess of Stafford, and also by Lords Northwick, Lansdowne, Egremont, Yarborough and Monson and, it may be added, by Sir Robert Peel. Only in the early 'forties do we find the first cutlery and cotton kings in the market; the ironmasters came even later.

The most pernicious influence on the painters of this period was that of a single man, not a painter or even interested in painting, but a writer of romances. Costume painting or romantic landscape painting, as inspired by the numerous works of Sir Walter Scott, dominated everything from the 1820's onwards. William Etty's nudes, the scriptural calamities of Martin and Danby were a mere blind alley. In 1833 Wilkie had to give up his work in order to design 'tableaux vivants' from Scott's novels for the Marchioness of Salisbury. Scott dominated the painting of his age as much as its literature, the continent of Europe as much as England. Scott wrote whole chapters on end to read like costume-pictures; painters filled 14-ft. canvases to look like Scott's descriptions.

Wilkie could no longer paint his happy villagers. In 1827–1828, still loyal to Rembrandt and *chiaroscuro*, he hunted Spain for romantic material. He chose subjects from the still freshly remembered Peninsular War, using a new technique which, though his patrons found it too streaky, showed Wilkie for the first time as a true painters' painter, a man of the age of Delacroix. To this period belongs the Tate Gallery's *First Earring*, which Wilkie sold at the oil-sketch price of 100 guineas. But for his larger works Wilkie could now charge on a scale approaching that of the late Benjamin West. In 1832 he received £1,260 from Sir Robert Peel for *John Knox preaching before the Lords of the Congregation*. In 1839 Lady Baird-Preston paid £1,525 for the *Finding of Tippoo Sultan's Body* (11½ ft. × 9 ft.), while Wilkie's royal commission of 1830, *George IV receiving the Scottish Nobility at Holyrood*, brought him £1,680, though quite modest in size.

These remained the highest rewards of any painter till the late 1850's, but the rewards of the true inventors of this style were on a very different plane. In 1828 when the young Bonington died, his father had to buy-in the most important picture of the sale, *Henry IV and the Spanish Ambassadors*, for £84. In the same year Delacroix, exhibiting in England, failed to find a purchaser for *The Execution of the Doge Marino Faliero* at the British Institution. The picture, for which the Marquess of Hertford was to pay £4,000 in 1869, was taken back to France by Delacroix and sold for £72. Wilkie also surpassed the English rivals who had threatened to supplant him. Landseer received only £420 in 1834 for *Scene of the Old Time at Bolton Abbey*,[1] while Leslie in 1840 got £630 for his painting of the *Coronation of Queen Victoria*. Mulready, who had seemed to be cutting Wilkie out in 1820, when he sold George IV that surprisingly Victorian-looking picture, *The Wolf and the Lamb*, got no more than £714 from Lord Northwick for *The Convalescent from Waterloo* of 1838, a far more touching and sincere work than Wilkie's fussy *Chelsea Pensioners*. Mulready did, however, live to

[1] Sold in December 1960 for 60 guineas.

see this picture make £1,239 in 1859 after Lord Northwick's death.[1]

Towards the end of the period 1820–1850 there may have been four, at the most five, painters who could on occasion make £1,000 on a single picture. The rewards were still small, compared with those of the late 'fifties and 'sixties when the popular reproduction market fell into more competent hands—foreign hands. Most of the painters of the 1820–1850 generation were affected by this increased market only posthumously, while the highest prices for their work were paid after the deaths of their chief patrons, when whole collections came into the saleroom, particularly in 1863 and 1872.

For such a formidable series of dispersals to sustain the market, it was necessary that the pictures should be those which were in fashion at the time of the first sale. In 1863, the year of the Bicknell sale, Wilkie, Mulready and Leslie were not only dead but heavily eclipsed by their followers. Hence their very moderate rating in the mid-Victorian art boom. For Mulready the highest price was £1,585 10*s*. paid in 1886 for his *Idle Boys*. Leslie's *Falstaff impersonating the King* made £1,522 in 1877, while the best price for Wilkie was (and still is) £2,152 10*s*., paid in 1893 for the charming and witty *Letter of Introduction*.[2] It was a long way from the £8,000 *Monarch of the Glen*, which Landseer had painted in 1851. On the other hand, the highest price for a school painting in Wilkie's anecdotal manner was the sum of £3,727 10*s*., which was paid in 1872 for Thomas Webster's *Roast Pig*, a rustic revel for which Gillott had given £735 in 1862. But Thomas Webster [1800–1886] was still at work when the picture was sold.

The strictly historical paintings of Leslie and Maclise were eclipsed by the enormous prices which were paid in the 1870's for fancy-dress affairs by contemporary artists. But if George Redford is to be trusted, one work by Maclise foreshadowed these prices as early as 1854. This was the *Marriage of Strongbow*, 10 ft. × 16 ft., for which the Earl of Northwick was reported to have paid £4,000, though it was bought by Flatou, the print publisher, at the 1859 sale for £1,785 and sold in 1879 when there were no more reproduction rights, for £840.[3] In 1862 Maclise received £2,500 from the government for the mural painting of *Wellington greeting Blücher*, which may still be noticed by an occasional tourist visiting the House of Lords. And it may be added that in

[1] Now in the Victoria and Albert Museum.

[2] Sold in 1814 to Samuel Dobree for £262 10*s*. For the curious history of this subject see Alan Cunningham: *Life and Letters of Wilkie*, 1848.

[3] Now in the National Gallery, Dublin.

1937 one of Maclise's fancy-dress pictures, *Ordeal by Touch*, 10 ft. × 7 ft., made £2 12*s.* 6*d.*

Sometimes a landscape painter felt constrained to imitate these performances—for, instance Sir Augustus Wall Callcott [1777–1844], whose *Raphael and the Fornarina*, and the *Blind Milton dictating to his Daughters*, painted in 1837 and 1840, remained among the torments of the nursery till the early 1900's. Callcott made his real reputation with his staid imitations of Turner, which he had been producing as early as 1806, when he emerged from the studio of Hoppner. 'They never gave me a knighthood,' Turner remarked, but he bore no grudge against a man who lived by copying him and made more money. In 1845, a few months after buying *Palestrina*, Bicknell paid £997 10*s.*, almost the same price, for a Callcott landscape in the saleroom. At Bicknell's sale in 1863 a Callcott landscape of the late 1830's, to which Landseer had added cattle, made as much as £3,097 10*s.* In 1947, however, a large and typical Callcott landscape in oils was sold at Christie's for 6 guineas.

It is curious that the fancy-dress painters of this generation should have begun to decline in the 1860's, just when their French and Belgian counterparts, Delaroche, Delacroix, Ary Scheffer and Baron Leys, were making fabulous prices. Partly this was because of the greater and more deserved popularity of the Pre-Raphaelites and partly because of the immensely enhanced prestige of the figured landscapes, which followed the Turner cult. In the 1860's even landscape painters with the least anecdotal interest, like Linnell, Nasmyth, David Cox and Copley Fielding, came to rate only a little below Callcott, Clarkson Stanfield and William Collins and only a little below the romantic illustrators of Spain and the Near East, John Philip, David Roberts, William Muller and John Frederick Lewis. Yet, with the exception of Callcott and Stanfield, none of them had been able to compete with the fancy-dress painters before 1850.

The pioneer of this most characteristic style of the period fared the least well. William Collins [1788–1847] had been brought up by his picture-dealing father in the company of George Morland. Collins's developed style was therefore a combination of Morland's sentimentalised eighteenth-century scenes of humble life with Bonington or Constable backgrounds. He was the very essence of small beer, hardly above the level of the *Keepsake Annual*, and only to be studied in that unspoilt period-piece, the Sheepshanks Bequest of the Victoria and Albert Museum. Yet in 1872 Collins's *Cromer Sands* made saleroom history by fetching £3,780. In the late 1830's Joseph Gillott had paid £315 for it. Only once had Collins been able to make 500 guineas on his own and that was in 1827 when he sold his *Frost Scene* to Sir Robert Peel. In the 'thirties and 'forties £200 was a high fee for William Collins, but the price climbed within a year or two of his death and in 1856 the once-famous *Skittle Players* made £1,210.

At least a dozen pictures by William Collins made four-figure prices in mid-Victorian times, but the fashion was wholly posthumous, Collins having died just when the revaluation of the whole school was beginning. By living a great deal longer, John Linnell senior secured some of the new values for himself. In 1859 the *Art Journal* observed that, while Linnell had not been honoured by the Royal Academy, with him 800 to 1,000 guineas was no uncommon fee. David Cox, on the other hand, who died in that year and whose pictures often looked like Linnell's, if not quite so dull, was reputed never to have achieved his ambition of earning a hundred guineas. But then Cox's oil paintings always appeared to be painted in water-colours and so commanded a water-colour price.

The rival of Callcott, who could make more money out of landscape than Turner and many times more than Constable, was Clarkson Stanfield [1794–1867], who had been born in Sunderland, the son of an Irish hack-writer. A seaman in the Navy at the end of the Napoleonic Wars, then a scene-painter at Drury Lane and a designer (with David Roberts) of panoramas, Stanfield became a professional painter in the middle 1820's. The death of Bonington in 1828 made Stanfield's career, for if Bonington could no longer turn out Boningtons, Stanfield certainly could. In 1832 *Wreckers off Fort Rouge, Calais* made the lively price of £435 6*s*. among the old masters of the now bankrupt George Watson Taylor. Stanfield was then an Associate of the Royal Academy and the only painter protégé of William IV, the sailor king who liked seapieces. He was paid 500 guineas apiece by Lord Lansdowne for a series of ten seascapes at Bowood, and in 1838 he charged Bicknell £735 for his landsman picture, the *Pic du Midi*. Before the year 1850, Stanfield had charged 1,000-guinea fees. In 1863 he saw his *Pic du Midi* fetch £2,677 10*s*. The *Beilstein*, a mountainous Turnerish landscape, sold in 1837 for £267 10*s*., made £1,575. Nothing like that had ever happened to Lawrence, Turner or Wilkie. The dullest of the dull of the early nineteenth-century school, Stanfield died in 1867, appropriately in Belsize Park. After his death several of his pictures made over £3,000 each.

Although he straddled both halves of the nineteenth century, Sir Edwin Landseer [1802–1873] belongs spiritually to the first half. In the last fifteen years of his life he painted little and hardly changed his style. The prices paid for Landseer's work have been much multiplied by legend, but in any case the highest saleroom prices, from 5,000 to 7,000 guineas, were all paid in 1875–1895, the twenty years immediately following his death. The Landseer of the period 1830–1850 was a fashionable but not particularly high-priced painter. When Landseer broke away from Shakespearian and medieval subjects in Leslie's manner, it was not at first in his favour that his new inspiration was Dutch-Flemish. But even if his skies came from Dujardin, his beasts from Cuyp and his horsemen from Wouverman, he made them Victorian enough. Contrary to popular belief, Landseer's most highly valued works were neither dogs wearing wigs and spectacles, nor monkeys torturing cats, but scenes from the life of Highland crofters and pictures which celebrated the killing of game. The former belong to Landseer's middle period, the latter to his last and gloomiest phase, although Landseer had discovered Scotland as early as 1824 through an excursion in the company of Leslie, when the mania for Scott and Wilkie was at its height.

Landseer's market was built up by print-publishers and by a few speculative business-men like Jacob Bell, the wholesale pharmacist. But by the nature of the subjects his pictures came to rest finally in noble and even royal houses among the trophies of weapons, the stags' heads and the varnished pitch-pine. Till well into middle age, Landseer's prices advanced cautiously. In the 1820's his pictures rarely made more than £100 each. But the highly successful *Bolton Abbey Revels* of 1834 made 400 guineas, and in the following year Sheepshanks paid 500 guineas for the first of the Highland crofter pictures, the large and muddled *Departure of the Drovers*, which had been commissioned first by the Duke of Bedford. The most famous of the anthropomorphic dog pictures, the *Dignity and Impudence* of 1839, made, by contrast, only £50 when sold to Jacob Bell without the copyright.

In 1847 *Van Ambergh the Lion-tamer* was commissioned by the Duke of Wellington for 600 guineas, but Landseer maintained that the Duke had sent a cheque for double the amount. Apart from this extravaganza, Landseer's normal fee for a large painting of figures or animals in 1852, when he was fifty years old, was probably under 400 guineas. *The Lost Sheep* was bought by Bicknell in 1850 for £262 10*s*., while the *Monarch of the Glen*, which had been refused by the British government as a mural decoration for the House of Lords at £500, was bought by Lord Londesborough at the 1851 Royal Academy exhibition for £362 10*s*. By 1854, however, there were two £800 or 800-guinea commissions,

Lord Aberdeen's *Otter Hunt* (sold twenty years later for £10,000) and Bicknell's *Harvest in the Highlands*. In 1856 Landseer sold his Academy picture, *Saved*, for 1,000 guineas.

Landseer's rivals were now only Millais and William Frith. In 1860 *Titania and the Fairies*, sold to Brunel the engineer in 1851 for 400 guineas, made £2,940 at auction, while in 1858 Jacob Bell made £2,100 on a picture for which he had paid £100 in the 1830's. In 1868 Landseer saw the picture of stags, known as *Braemar*, which he had exhibited in 1857, sold for £4,200. It is uncertain whether Landseer in the rare painting moments of his last years was capable, like Millais, of earning a 4,000-guinea commission on his own, but it is not impossible. In 1867 Millais had actually been paid 4,500 guineas for his heavy unpleasing *Jephthah* (see page 152), and it is at least known that in 1856 Landseer refused £2,000 for the ridiculous quite small picture, *Noble Connoisseurs*, which he presented to the Prince of Wales.[1]

Landseer also received £6,000 for modelling the originals of the Trafalgar Square lions, but this was not a formidable sum, seeing that the lions occupied most of the periods between 1859 and 1865 when Landseer was not melancholy-mad. Half Landseer's income, according to the life by James Manson, was derived from the sale of copyrights and to such good purpose that in 1876 his executors had to re-swear his estate at £200,000.

To draw a contrast between Landseer's prices and Constable's is not altogether valid, since Constable died in 1837 when Landseer was still finding his way. It is nevertheless true that Constable could not have lived even in his own modest style on the money he made from painting. And yet he was not entirely a *peintre maudit*. Although most of the time abusive, the Press was on occasions quite kind to him. Not only had Constable several very loyal patrons, but his landscape details were borrowed by every painter of the day who needed a background of a native English kind. Mulready and William Collins were particularly in his debt.

Constable's prices were consequently those that a Royal Academician could expect for landscapes which lacked the all-essential figure groups of anecdotal interest. It must not be forgotten that, low as these prices appear, the big Constable landscapes of the 1820's and early 1830's fetched two or three times as much as any landscape which Gainsborough had sold in his own lifetime. Landscapes without figures were not a fashionable taste in England till the 1870's, when the Barbizon

[1] Richard and Samuel Redgrave: *A Century of British Painters*, Phaidon ed., p. 419.

cult had been absorbed from France and when Millais was at work on his dour Scottish autumnal scenes.

Though not, therefore, victimised financially, the lack of support for Constable among colleagues, who borrowed his imagination, was sinister. Turner, Lawrence and Wilkie became full Academicians before they were thirty, but Constable was not made an A.R.A. until he was forty-three and an R.A. not until he was fifty-three. It seems that the apparent ease of Constable's methods created jealousy. In the 1820's a painter's training had ceased to be as slipshod as it was at the end of the eighteenth century when Constable studied. Fancy-dress pictures required years of training, besides months of preparation for the individual painting. The career of painting offered no attraction to a well-bred man. Much more than in the past, the young painters came from artisan or small tradesman families and had been inured to arduous hours of labour since early childhood. Constable, however, was a rich miller's son who had been intended for the Church and who had generally some means of his own. Hence accusations of amateurishness and of sketching, almost a form of cheating. With Turner, slapdash methods mattered less because his work was always dramatic. But when Constable tried to be dramatic, he painted at his worst. Constable just did not belong to the Romantic Movement.

Constable was a late starter. In 1810 at the age of thirty-four it was a novelty for him to sell a landscape to Lord Dysart for 30 guineas.[1] In 1813 he relied on painting portrait-heads at 15 guineas each for a living, and in the following year he got no more than 20 guineas for one of his first large-scale pictures, the *Lock on the Stour*. In 1817, when he moved to London, Constable did not reckon to contribute more than £100 a year to his family budget from painting.

In 1819 and 1820 the exhibition of rather larger works at the Royal Academy brought him better clients, since *The White Horse* and *Stratford Mill* were sold for £100 each. Yet the great *Haywain* of the National Gallery received no better offer in 1822 than £70, which Constable refused. In 1824 he sold his Academy picture, *Boat passing a Lock*, to a Mr. Morrison for 150 guineas and next year he was at last able to dispose of the *Haywain*. It was bought by the dealer Arrowsmith, together with the *View on the Stour* and a small seascape, for £250. Arrowsmith exhibited the pictures at the Salon in Paris and got £400 for the *Haywain* alone, more money than Constable made on a picture in his life. In the 1830's the highest fee for Constable's overworked 6-ft. Academy landscapes remained £250; at a time when Wilkie could

[1] Farington, *op. cit.*, VI.

make £1,650 on a single picture, it was rare for Constable to earn even £200.

On Constable's death in 1837 his friends banded together to spend 300 guineas on the *Cornfield* as a memorial picture for the Royal Academy. But the collecting world put a lower valuation on his work. At the executors' sale of 1838 only the *River Stour, Horse on a Barge* made 150 guineas. *The Lock* made £120 15*s*., and the stupendous *Weymouth Bay* of the Tate Gallery, ranking only as an oil sketch, made 4 guineas. A few years later there was a modest rise in Constable's saleroom prices, but it was not till 1866 that the resale of the *Haywain* at £1,365 registered a belief that Constable might have been as good as some of his contemporaries.

As the first half of the century neared its end, the dynamic spirit that had slain the gods of the eighteenth century died with it. Between 1825 and 1849 there was scarcely a new name among the annual Royal Academy exhibitors that means anything to-day, except for Landseer and Frith. Outside the Academy, Samuel Palmer and George Richmond pursued their Blake-like style in almost total obscurity. By demanding a pedantic literary standard of the works to be exhibited, the Academy condemned painting to stagnation and the market reflected this. With one uncertain exception in 1854, there was nothing before the year 1860 to compare with Benjamin West's 3,000-guinea sale of *Christ Healing the Sick* in 1811. Even a fee such as the Empress Catherine paid Reynolds in 1790, may only have been earned two or three times between 1811 and 1860. A thousand guineas remained the symbol of the maximum success a painter could hope to attain. Anything beyond it was a freak price or perhaps a saleroom tribute to a style of which he was no longer capable.[1]

At the end of the half-century, art in England was ripe for a rebellion, but what a rebellion! The Pre-Raphaelites abandoned the artificial old masterish grouping of the standard fancy-dress pictures; they introduced minute detail, stereoscopic lighting and some tiresome fifteenth-century attitudes, yet they left the literary convention, by which a painting was nothing more than a large illustration for a book, more enthroned than ever. It was a revolution to suit the demands of the time and not to dictate them, for Pre-Raphaelitism arrived just at the moment when the framed engraving was at its height. The so-called rebel style of the Pre-Raphaelite Brotherhood was everything that the publishers of steel engravings welcomed.

[1] One may contrast this with the auction price of Ingres's *Stratonice* in 1852 in Paris—namely, £2,500. Ingres had still another sixteen years' work before him.

The possibility of selling a highly finished engraving in tens of thousands of impressions existed already in the 1840's, but publishers were slow to take advantage of it, while artists were slow to see how increased distribution had affected the value of their works since the days of Macklin and Boydell. For instance, in 1813 William Collins sold *The Pet Lamb* to a print-publisher for a fee well above the 20 or 25 guineas that were then usual with him, namely £147 10*s.*, but, seeing that the print, originally a magazine illustration, was reissued in 15,000 impressions, the price was ludicrously low.

It was Turner who conceived the idea that the painter should be his own engraver, but his experiments proved generally a loss to his publishers, who preferred to farm the work out to less exacting professionals. In 1821 John Martin had the same experience as Collins. A small engraving of his *Marcus Curtius* picture, originally an illustration to the *Forget-Me-Not* annual, was re-cut several times and sold in 10,000 extra impressions. Martin was determined to seize this market for himself. In 1826 he began issuing his own prints, huge affairs in a combination of mezzotint, etching and steel engraving at 3½ guineas each and, in the case of the *Fall of Nineveh*, at 5 guineas for the ordinary lettered proofs. Between 1826 and 1840 Martin claimed to have made £21,000 either in royalties or in direct sales of prints from his pictures. Considering their immense popularity, an average yearly income of £1,500 does not appear a very high reward. In fact, for the purchasing power of the day the price of a print was much too high and Martin had to reduce it. In 1843 he complained that copies of the *Eve of the Deluge* were not selling, though the price had been reduced to 2 guineas, lettered, and in 1849 he wrote that he had been driven from the market through the sale of inferior pirated engravings of his pictures, made in infringement of a weak law of copyright.[1]

In reality Martin's works had quite simply gone out of fashion. The time was at hand when men like Gambart and Flatou would pay 5,000 guineas simply for the right to employ their own engraver to copy a popular picture, which event occurred in 1860 in the case of Holman Hunt's *Infant Saviour in the Temple*.

In 1845 the process of electrotyping made immensely bigger editions of steel engravings possible without any loss of the refinements of detail. The same year saw an even more important innovation. The duty on glass, which made framing a print eight times as dear as it was on the Continent, was abolished.[2] A 5-guinea proof in a 2-guinea frame

[1] Mary L. Pendered: *John Martin, Painter*, 1923, pp. 148-62.

[2] Paul Oppé in *Early Victorian England*, II, p. 122n.

was not within the reach of modest lower middle-class households in the 1840's, though in the early 1920's you could have bought almost any of Martin's monster prints in their original bird's-eye maple frames for one shilling. But the two-guinea proof in a five-shilling frame, published by Gambart or Flatou in the 1860's, that was true popular art. We are too accustomed to think of that decade as one of sweated labour and mass destitution, forgetting that, compared with the Continent, England had a much higher national standard of living. The popular framed print certainly became a distinctly English feature of life and its impact on taste something peculiar to these islands. In the period which we have been examining, this impact was not very noticeable. For better or for worse, *Well-bred Sitters* and *Uncle Toby and the Widow Wadman* were a wealthy and even a noble taste. That in England there was to be no emancipation from this sort of thing, not even the equivalent of a Barbizon school, was a tribute to the power of the now much-praised common man.

2. *The Proto-Victorians (1800–1860) — Posthumous Adventures*

It may be thought that enough space has already been given to a period which produced little that is of consequence to-day outside the works of Turner, Blake, Cotman, Bonington, Samuel Palmer and Constable. But the adventures of the more popular pictures in the saleroom have a certain bearing upon the mysteries of the modern art market. In the 1870's prices equivalent to £50,000, even £70,000 according to our present money, were paid for works by Turner and Landseer, which were not as old then as the best work of Braque and Picasso is now. But, in reality, the £10,000, which Baron Grant was said to have paid for the *Otter Hunt* in 1874, or the £20,000 which Vanderbilt paid for the *Grand Canal* in 1885, meant much more than the most dazzling prices of to-day's favourite modern painters. For in the 1870's and 1880's these things were not bought simply because the great masters of the past were unprocurable. On the contrary they were bought because they were much preferred to the great masters. In 1876, for instance, Titian's *Man in the Red Cap* of the Frick Foundation made £94 10*s*. In the most open and public competition in 1874 the Botticelli *Mars and Venus* cost the Nation no more than 1,000 guineas, while in 1884, when a Rembrandt portrait actually made more than £1,000, *The Times* observed that it was enough in all conscience.

Furthermore, when comparing past booms in modern art with the present boom, it should be borne in mind that this was the first time in the history of the English school that paintings went up in value instead of down, as soon as their makers had ceased to produce them. In the late eighteenth century, just as in previous ages, there had been no virtue in the mere fact of a painter being dead. On the contrary, Van Dyck portraits had been despised as soon as Kneller and Lely portraits came in. These in turn were despised when Gainsborough and Reynolds practised, while in the 1820's and 1830's these portraits in their turn became frumpish and outmoded.

What happened in the 1850's was something quite new. The conviction that Turner had been underrated in his own lifetime became so strong that even his followers achieved old-master status. The case is therefore precisely comparable with that of the French Impressionists in the 1950's, except that the rise in the market was in genuine gold sovereigns. Between 1850 and 1863 the prices of Turner's paintings were multiplied fifteen times, by 1900 after a long pause about twenty times. For water-colours the rate of increase was doubled. Water-colours, bought by Gillott in the 1830's, had increased their value by thirty to forty times at the 1872 sale. In the 1890's some of these water-colours had gone up eighty times.

Still more astonishing increases occurred in the values of the lesser landscape painters, who had first excited the local patriotism of the industrial Midlands. For instance, David Cox in his later years was almost unknown outside Birmingham and in 1870 his prices astonished the London market when the collection of his patron, Edward Bullock of Handsworth, was sold at Christie's. It was then that a water-colour landscape, which had been bought towards 1840 for 6 guineas, made £433. And there were others at about the same price, dearer than the Botticelli cassone panels of the Barker sale of 1874 and more sensational in their promotion than David Cox's most famous work, *The Vale of Clwyd*, which rose from £278 5*s*. in 1860 to £4,725 in 1892, or the water-colour *The Hayfield* which was bought in 1850 for £50 and sold at the Quilter sale of 1875 for £2,950.

Between the middle 'eighties and the early 'nineties the whole of this market began to fall, with the exception of Turner, whose highest market was reached about 1913, and Constable, whose market is still rising to-day. The rest of the pictures which we have been studying went out of fashion when realist painters, like Alma Tadema and the later Millais, or belated Pre-Raphaelites like Burne-Jones, ruled the London market. These, in turn, were demoted about 1910 when the Barbizon school became fashionable, though the decline was not absolute till the 1920's when Impressionism and Post-Impressionism at last penetrated to England.

In France the process of posthumous worship, followed by demotion, was more rapid and much more like the eighteenth century. The romantics of the Turner-Constable generation, Delaroche, Delacroix, Decamps, Ary Scheffer, achieved their highest prices in the 1860's and 1870's, but in the 1880's and 1890's they fell as Millet, Courbet, Bastien Lepage, Breton and the Realists advanced. These in turn fell in the early 1900's with the rather more belated advance of Corot, Daubigny and Théodore Rousseau, who began to fall with the rapid revaluation of the Impressionists soon after the First World War.

Though 1863, which saw the Bicknell sale, was the Turner year, the advance in Turner's prices had been continuous since the 1840's. Five pictures, which Turner's patron, B. G. Windus, had bought at Royal Academy exhibitions between 1841 and 1846, were auctioned in 1853 at prices ranging from £546 to £850, Windus having probably paid from 350 to 400 guineas each. *The Ducal Palace, Dogana, with part of San Giorgio, Venice*, had been commissioned from Turner by Sir Francis Chantrey in 1841 and may have cost considerably more. In 1853 it was bought by the painter Augustus Egg for £1,155, but next year at the Wadmore sale three Turners fetched four-figure prices, Mr. Grundy of Liverpool paying 2,000 guineas for *Cologne—Tower of St. Martin's Church above City Walls*. In 1856 Lord Delaware sold another early Backhuyzen-like Turner of 1804, *Carrying out an Anchor to a Dutch Man-of-war*, Mr. Benoni Whyte paying £3,000. This was a truly extraordinary price, actually higher than anything in either of the subsequent Bicknell sales—so high that at Whyte's sale in 1879 it fell to £1,575. Finally, in 1860 one of the smaller pictures which lay neglected in the uninhabited town house of Turner's Scottish Laird friend, Monro of Novar, came under the hammer. Gambart paid £2,520 for *The Grand Canal*, but Sam Mendel, the Manchester cotton king, to whom he sold it, got £7,350 for the picture in 1875.

By 1863 the rise in prices had been so continuous that the sale of Elhanan Bicknell's Turners turned out to be a disappointment. Bicknell was a schoolmaster's son who, having married the sister of Hablot K. Brown ('Phiz', the Dickens illustrator), made a fortune, selling whale-oil for the patent-lamps of the period. He was not rich enough to start buying till 1838, when he was fifty, but in the 1840's he gave a thousand pounds for a single picture on more than one occasion. The 145 pictures which this homely Maecenas had kept in his suburban villa at Newington Butts made £58,639, that is to say half as much again as the Empress Catherine had paid for the Walpole collection in 1779 and a lot more than the Duke of Bridgewater and his partners had paid for the Duke of Orleans collection in 1797. Yet the Turners, which were expected to realise £25,000, made only £17,000, and *Palestrina*, which failed to double its purchase price, was bought-in, together with a number of others, to be re-sold in 1865.

The highest prices were paid for Turner's imitators rather than for Turner: £3,097 5*s*. for Callcott's *Landscape* (with cattle by the living Landseer) and £2,677 10*s*. for the *Pic du Midi* of the living Stanfield. The dearest of the Turners was *Van Goyen looking out for a Subject*, at £2,635, a picture which Turner had let Bicknell have, according to his habit in the 1840's, for £420.

Turner's water-colours had cost Bicknell at the most 80 guineas each and generally less. The dearest, *Lucerne*, one of the famous 80-guinea Swiss views of 1842, made £735, not a surprising price seeing that *Bamborough Castle* and *Grenoble Bridge* had made 500 guineas each in 1860 and 1861. The dearest of Bicknell's water-colours were again not by Turner but by an imitator. The Marquess of Hertford gave £2,436 for five water-colours by Copley Fielding and one of them, the 2-ft. *Crowborough Hill* of the Wallace Collection, which is hardly one of the gallery's treasures, cost him £798. It had been commissioned by Bicknell in his early buying days in 1838 at 25 guineas.

Most of the minor artists of the 1800–1850 period reached their apogee in the saleroom in 1872 when Joseph Gillott's collection came under the hammer. Gillott, the Sheffield man who invented the steel pen, had been born in the eighteenth century and had begun his collecting before the De Tabley sale of 1827. In a decade which was dominated by Landseer and Rosa Bonheur, Gillott's executor sale included little that was later than the period, 1800–1850, of which it was a true epitome. The sale produced £164,530, the equivalent of at least a million pounds of to-day's money. On 29th April 1872 the *Daily News* reported that King Street was completely blocked by ladies and gentlemen who had come on foot to hear what the Turners had fetched and had been unable to get inside Christie's rooms.[1]

Turner's water-colours had now all but caught up with his oil-paintings. *Bamborough Castle* rose from £525 in 1860 to £3,307 10*s*., one of the most reckless bids of the Earl of Dudley, now made still more reckless by the death of his rival, the Marquess of Hertford. The 80 guinea *Rhine Tour* views of 1841–1842, *Ehrenbreitstein* and *Heidelberg* made £2,782 10*s*. each, having risen much more rapidly than the

[1] Redford, *op. cit.*, I, p. 184.

£5,250 *Walton Bridges* and the £4,567 10*s*. *Junction of the Thames and Medway*, though these early Turner oil paintings were certainly the dearest works of the nineteenth century to have come under the hammer in 1872.

Gillott had once offered Turner £35,000 for the entire contents of the neglected Turner Gallery in Queen Anne Street, but in actuality only twenty-three of the 525 pictures in the sale were by Turner. Many of the works, which achieved high prices, were by men who are now virtually forgotten. Some of these were bought by Isaac Holden and, since they were put on the market in 1913 by the first Lord Holden, they afford a unique view of the decline of this taste:

Gillott Sale, 1872	£	*Holden Sale, 1913* £
Thomas Faed: *Walter Scott and His Friends*	955 10*s*.	99 15*s*.
William Frith: *Merry Wives of Windsor* (oil sketch)	126	15 15*s*.
John Linnell Senior: *Eve of the Deluge*	1,092	189
Daniel Maclise: *Gipsies*	934 10*s*.	199 10*s*.
Erskine Nicol: *Country Booking Office*	1,155	388 10*s*.
Clarkson Stanfield: *Wooden Walls of England*	2,835	168 (Sampson)
Thomas Webster: *Travelling Jeweller*	556 10*s*.	44 2*s*.
Ditto: *Roast Pig*	3,727 10*s*.	262 10*s*.

Two other revaluations of Gillott's pictures tell the same story. William Muller's *Chess Players*, painted in the early 'forties and bought by Gillott for £300, made £3,950. Two years later it was resold for £4,052 10*s*., and in 1931 it was bought by the Bristol City Gallery for £78 15*s*. David Cox's *Lancaster, War and Peace*, painted in 1846, made £3,601 and was resold in 1908 for £945. Of Gillott's Constables, bought by him from the painter before 1837, the dearest was *Weymouth Bay* at £735. This is the picture now in the Louvre, for which that in the Tate Gallery is believed to be a study.

Till the end of the nineteenth century, Turner, Constable and Landseer rose fitfully, but their contemporaries declined. For instance, at the Mendel sale of 1875 Turner's *Grand Canal*, which had made £2,520 in 1860, was bought by Agnew for £7,350, sold to Lord Dudley for £8,055 and resold after Lord Dudley's death in 1885 to Cornelius Vanderbilt for £20,000. It took the American market another twenty-eight years to catch up with this purchase. Yet Turner had become an American taste in his own lifetime. In 1845 James

Lennox had bought *Staffa, Fingal's Cave* from the painter Leslie for £500, while in 1850 he bought *Fort Vimieux* at the Meigh sale for £693. In 1956 the two pictures were sold in New York by Parke-Bernet for £17,000 and £20,000. The Metropolitan acquired a Turner at its first foundation, bidding £2,835 for *Kilgarren Castle* at the Gillott sale of 1872. On the strength of this purchase Gillott's executors sent some further Turners to be auctioned in New York.

The top prices for Turner's works at the 1875 sale were hardly exceeded before the American buying of the late 'nineties in spite of the huge collection of Monro of Novar, which came on the market in 1878. It was Mr. James Christie's belief[1] that the Scottish Laird had not spent more than £4,000 on his sixteen oil paintings and seventy-nine water-colours, which made £88,185 10*s*., but the dearest hardly exceeded £5,000 each and in 1884 a year, of financial panic, the Orme and Skipper sales showed the first declines.

The year 1890 restored the balance, when the collections of two of Turner's patrons, Walter Fawkes and William Wells, were sold by descendants, but if *Sheerness* and *Walton Bridges* made £7,450 each, these prices paled before the £48,000 which M. Chauchard was reputed to have paid that year for Millet's *La Bergère* and the £32,000 which he certainly paid for the *Angelus*.

In 1897 four large oil paintings by Turner in Sir John Pender's sale fetched £30,450 between them. The prices were not higher than Lord Dudley's purchases in 1875, but one of the four pictures, the £7,140 *Giudecca*, had made only £2,100 at Bicknell's sale in 1863. The *Dogana*, which Sir James Ross bought in 1899 for £8,620, had risen in the same proportion from £2,698 in 1870. But A. C. R. Carter reported in *The Year's Art* that much higher prices than this had been paid in private negotiation. Turner, like Gainsborough, was moving into the millionaire market which culminated in the sale of *Mortlake Terrace* to Frick in 1913 for £30,000.

In terms of our inflation pounds Turner has slumped. In the 1950's no oil painting fetched more than £20,000 and no water-colour much more than £11,000. The brilliant late and impressionist Turners are probably all frozen from the market. It would therefore be impossible to say how much such an astonishing work as the unfinished *Landscape with Aqueduct* of the 1856 bequest would fetch to-day—perhaps no more than a minor Renoir, a thing which Renoir himself would have been the first to deplore.

[1] In 1885, quoted by Redford, *op. cit.*, I, p. 399, from the *Daily News*.

Landseer's works, as we have seen, passed the £4,000 mark in his own lifetime. In 1877, four years after Landseer's death, there came the sale of the famous *Otter Hunt* of 1844, which Ruskin had attacked in *Modern Painters* for its beastly savagery. In 1860 Agnew had bought it from Lord Aberdeen's executors for £2,500. After passing through other hands it had been bought by the mysterious Albert Gottheimer, known as Baron Grant, probably in the year of Landseer's death, and he was reported to have paid £10,000. At the Baron's sale in 1877 *The Otter Hunt* made £5,932, was bought from Agnew by Isaac Holden for £6,815 and sold by Lord Holden in 1913 for £1,260.

In 1879 the National Gallery paid £9,000 for Leonardo's *Virgin of the Rocks*. As usual, the expenditure of public money was thought extravagant. Nowadays one is tempted to wonder how many fearless bidders there were in London in 1879, who could have made a million for their grandchildren by such a purchase. But the search for life-sized beasts, either slaying or slain, continued unchecked. In May 1881 the executors of the mustard-king E. J. Colman sold three Landseers at over 5,000 guineas each, the latter price being paid for the *Fatal Duel*, the 8-ft. outline for a picture which Landseer had drawn in Colman's house in 1866 in three hours and sent to the Royal Academy just as it was. Another of Coleman's pictures was *Man proposes, God disposes*, in which two life-sized polar bears are shown positively eating the Franklin expedition of 1845 down to the last wishbone. It was bought by Thomas Holloway, the pill-king, for £6,615 to grace the advanced women's college which he was shortly to found. The pictures were chosen for instruction and edification, though the only lesson the advanced women could have learned from this work was to keep away from the North-west Passage.

The Monarch of the Glen, the 350-guinea picture of 1851, had its turn in 1884, when the heirs of Lord Londesborough put this leaden, menacing beast into Christie's. Sir Cuthbert Quilter had just paid Agnews 7,000 guineas for *Titania*, for which Brunel had given £420 in 1850. It was predicted that a work with so celebrated a history as the *Monarch of the Glen* would fetch very much more than *Titania*; 8,000 and even 10,000 guineas were named. But it has been the fate of this picture always to disappoint its vendors—except in 1916 when the worst was anticipated but not fulfilled. In 1884 *The Monarch of the Glen* was knocked down to Sir Charles Eaton (Lord Cheylesmore) for £6,510. At the Cheylesmore sale of 1892 it was bought by Agnew for £7,245 and sold to Mr. Barratt of Pear's Soap for £8,000.

This was the pinnacle of the Landseer boom. In 1895 the sum of

£5,985 could still be paid for *Chevy Chase*, surprisingly a fancy-dress picture in the Leslie manner of 1826. But it was the last of the five thousand pound Landseers, except for *The Monarch of the Glen*, which Barratt was able to sell to Sir Thomas Dewar for 5,000 guineas as late as 1916. The fall began about the year 1900, though at first it was not violent:

		£		£
1873	Lady Godiva's Prayer	3,360	1916	943
1875	Children of the Mist	1,239	1937	21 4*s.*
1877	Otter Hunt	6,215	1913	1,270
1885	The Fatal Duel	5,250	1933	39 8*s.*
1886	The Deer Family	3,255	1937	252
1887	Taking a Buck	2,047 10*s.*	1930	27 6*s.*
1892	Monarch of the Glen	7,245	1916	5,250
1895	Chevy Chase	5,985	1923	1,050
1890	None but the Brave	4,620	1935	152 10*s.*
1897	The Lost Sheep	3,150	1943	315
1890	The Roebucks	4,042	1945	440

This short table tells the full story. Till 1923 the old Landseer favourites fetched serious prices, though the popularity of the Barbizon school had relegated them to a less informed taste. By the 1930's the cataclysm was complete. A drawing or a small oil sketch of Landseer's first years might have made as much as these great machines. At this point the Second World War introduces the element of general scarcity. There is a small rise in prices, but the big pictures are kept away from the sales. Yet owners of Landseer's pictures may take heart. In November 1959 Christie's sold a large and singularly harmless Landseer picture of an old grey mare in a stable for £1,260.

Should not Rosa Bonheur be considered with Landseer? To treat a painter who died in 1899 as part of the school of the first half of the nineteenth century seems illogical. But where else are we to put her? She was exhibiting in 1841 and by 1850 she imitated Landseer as much as Constantin Troyon. In 1853 Gambart the print-seller conducted Rosa Bonheur to the Highlands in order that she might paint the subjects which Landseer now only produced at rare intervals. Although Landseer met her but once, it was said that he was going to marry her. When Frith challenged Landseer with this story, it is noteworthy that Landseer, though as fanatically celibate as Lawrence, Reynolds and Turner, declared that it was a good idea. It would certainly have been a good business partnership, for in 1865 two of Rosa Bonheur's cattle-pieces made 2,000 guineas each in the London saleroom. In 1887

Denizens of the Highlands made £5,827. The triumph which was anticipated for the *Monarch of the Glen* in 1884 was reserved for Rosa Bonheur's 16-ft. *Horsefair.* It was auctioned in New York in 1886 for £10,500 and then sold to Pierpont Morgan for £12,000, while a small replica was sold in London for £3,150. Disaster came swifter than for Landseer. Not many pictures have fallen as violently as *Pâturages Nivernaises,* £4,410 in 1880 and £48 3*s.* in 1929.

This chapter must conclude with the fate of Constable, the lowest-priced of the painters who achieved fame between 1800 and 1850, the slowest to attain old-master status and to-day the only English painter of his time to approach the £50,000 region.

This first picture to obtain a price that was outside Constable's range in his own lifetime was *The Lock.* It was sold after his death in 1838 for £131 and it made £860 in 1855. The great *Haywain* of the National Gallery made £1,365 in 1866, but no other comparable price appeared until the *Dell in Helmingham Park,* sold in 1886 for £1,627 10*s.* (£9,160 in 1954). In 1893 Lord Revelstoke's *Hampstead Heath* made £2,625 (£63 in 1838), while in 1894 and 1895 we have *On the Stour with White Horse,* £6,510 and the *Young Waltonians,* £8,925, a price which was not surpassed for a Constable picture until 1944. This stagnation is not easily explicable. In the 1890's the high price may have reflected a return to pure landscape by the exceedingly popular Millais, who in his own turn may have been struck by the Barbizon school. But in the early 1900's, when the Barbizon school of painters of pure landscape became a rich international taste, Constable's prices failed to keep up with them.

The big rise in the Constable market began with the purchase of the *Vale of Dedham* by the Scottish National Gallery in 1944 for £20,000, and its culmination was Sir Walter Gilbey's purchase of the *Young Waltonians* in 1951 for £44,100. It might be rash to draw conclusions from prices which were paid during a period of enforced insularity and economic isolation, for Constable has never been an international taste. The homage of the French Impressionists in the 1870's was perfunctory, and in the 1920's the American millionaires found Constable's merits insufficiently spectacular.

CHAPTER FIVE

The Old Masters 1815–1884

1. *Rubens and the Italians* — 2. *The Return of the Primitives* — 3. *Spain* — 4. *Holland*

---

1. *Rubens and the Italians*

In 1815 a very high price for any picture was still indicated by the almost mythical and unattained figure, £10,000. But in 1884 the British government paid £70,000 for Raphael's *Ansidei Madonna* and Alfonse de Rothschild paid £35,000 for a doubtful Rubens. From these figures one could infer that these were seventy years of rising prices. Yet the very reverse was true. Till the Marlborough sales of 1884–1886 the best of Rubens and Van Dyck failed to exceed the prices of the Napoleonic wars. Rembrandt and Titian fell miserably, the favourite seventeenth-century Italian painters were seldom in demand, Claude and Poussin hardly ever. By contrast Italian primitives rose steeply in the 1840's, Dutch seventeenth-century *genre* and landscape paintings went up in the 'fifties and 'sixties and Murillo had a frenzied vogue which extended from the 'thirties to the 'seventies. But none of these movements of fashion gave any real indication that the great masters of the past had become rarer, that the opportunities of the Napoleonic wars could never be repeated.

A flat market was to be expected after the Napoleonic wars, if only for the fact that the laws of property became effective again. But for the prevailing flatness of the London old-master market almost throughout the next seventy years there were deeper causes. It would seem that pictures continued to come to London, but that London did not really want them. At first it was the instability of France that kept London in the position which it had reached during the wars, particularly in 1830 and 1848. But, with the advent of the Second Empire in 1852, Paris became more truly cosmopolitan than ever and her position as the art centre of Europe so assured that even defeat, foreign occupation, revolution and another republic created nothing more than a brief interregnum. Paris recovered in the 1870's, though this was probably the most depressed decade the London old-master market had ever known.

At the beginning of the period there was undoubtedly a sense of insecurity. There were food riots in the decade following Waterloo, a rumble of revolution in 1832, corn law and Chartist agitations in 1846 and 1849, but their effect on the art market was either momentary or non-existent. In reality the causes of flatness and decline were within the market itself. Throughout this period the London market was continuously dominated by living art at the expense of the old and for this there were three separate causes.

The inflation of living painters' prices through the engraving copyright market has been studied in the previous chapter. Its effect on old-master sales was obvious. The copyright market appealed to short-term speculators, the very people who had created the 'post-Orleans' picture boom of 1798–1813. It was almost inconceivable that an old-master painting, which if it had any popular appeal, must have been engraved time and time again, could compete with new works that had never been seen.

The next point that told against the old masters was the loss of the mood of over-confident optimism, in which so many works had been bid-up beyond their merits. The first speculators had failed to distinguish between original and schoolpiece; for the experts at the turn of the century, though painters themselves, seem to have been ignorant of the fact that Rubens and Titian had indulged in the same bad practices as Alan Ramsay and Hoppner. The vogue for *mellow* pictures, that is to say thoroughly browned and obscured with successive layers of varnish, made it impossible to examine the individual handling of the paint. For this reason the speculators, who paid £4,000 and more for alleged Rubens paintings that are no longer included in the canon, might have paid some attention to what Rubens's contemporaries had to say. There was, for instance, the letter of Lord Danvers, concerning Charles I's first Rubens purchase, the *Judith and Holofernes* of 1621:

'But now for Reubens; in every painter's opinion he hath sent hether, a peece scarse touched by his own hand, and the postures so forced, as the Prince will not admit the picture into his galerye.'

Benjamin West should have read this. He remained the expert-in-chief till his death in 1820, yet West's great Titian discovery, the *Death of Actaeon*, for which he refused an offer of £4,000, was sold by his descendants in 1898 for 250 guineas.[1] Other impostor works revealed themselves even in the lifetime of the buyer. An alleged Rubens, *Cupid, Mars and Vulcan*, for which the Marquess of Lansdowne had given £1,575 in the early 1800's, was allowed to go for 50 guineas in 1834. At this time, purchasers, armed with John Smith's *Catalogue Raisonné*, were certainly growing more wary of the snares of the 'black masters'.

The third reason for the stagnation of the market was in fact the very crude one that the 'black masters' were going out of favour just because they were black. The gold and plush school of decoration, which forced Wilkie to abandon the murkiness of his palette, was inimical to old-master collecting, except for the primitives. These three impediments could have depressed the old-master market indefinitely, if foreigners had not sought opportunity in the English salerooms, for with a very few exceptions British patronage became incredibly insular. Neither the amateurish and erratic expertise of Dr. Waagen,[2] nor the literary rhapsodies of John Ruskin, stimulated the new race of industrialists to try their hand at old-master collecting. In the late 'seventies it was possible that one or two old masters might be sold at Christie's in a given year for more than a thousand pounds each, but the number of four-figure purchases of works by living or recently dead English painters could run to twenty or thirty. In 1879 only one old master made a thousand guineas and that was a picture barely a hundred years old, Reynolds's *Robinetta*. Of this entire period between 1815 and 1884 it can be said that the very finest things were generally bought cheaply. They were bought by exceedingly wise curators, like Eastlake or Burton, and they were bought by a few discriminating collectors who were by no means of the wealthiest class.

Already in 1813 and 1814 the experience of Buchanan and his backers had been extremely disappointing. It was the best hope now of any importer of a masterpiece from Italy or Spain to sell it to the Tsar of Russia, the Prussian Royal Gallery, or the King of Holland. Each had

[1] Whitley, II, pp. 31-4.

[2] Gustav Friedrich Waagen [1794–1868], director of the Royal Gallery, Berlin. His *Treasures of Art in Great Britain* (1854) still provides pedigrees for old-master pictures that reach the saleroom.

his supplier: Coesvelt for the Tsar, Edward Solly for the King of Prussia and the young Nieuwenhuys[1] for the King of Holland. It was only when there were possibilities of an exhibition success that it was worth the trouble to bring an expensive picture to London. An instance was the portrait of *Susanna Fourment* by Rubens in the National Gallery, misnamed *Le Chapeau de Paille*. In 1817 Buchanan made a fruitless journey to Antwerp, hoping to get this picture for £2,000. In 1822 it cost Nieuwenhuys £3,190; the picture was then taken over by the famous John Smith of the *Catalogue Raisonné* at £4,000 as an exhibition piece at half-a-crown a head. Smith next tried to sell it to George IV for £7,000 and finally parted with it to Sir Robert Peel for £3,600. Although losing money on it, Smith had certainly sold the most expensive straightforward portrait that had ever been on the London market.

Why were people prepared to pay what was then the price of a lavish dinner to look at an agreeably painted but decidedly plain woman? Why was the King expected to find £7,000 for it? The fame of this work is fraught with mystery. In 1827 the Rubens *Triumph of Silenus* cost Sir Robert Peel no more than £1,100, while Angerstein's *Rape of the Sabines* was bought by the Nation in 1824 for £2,500, which was no more than Angerstein had given in 1785. The only explanation that seems to work is that the *Chapeau de Paille* was that rarest of things, a perfectly decorous Rubens, and that this was what the age required. A landscape or a fully-clothed portrait was the only sort of Rubens which lacked that fleshly appeal which was beginning again to be viewed with disfavour.

Hence, too, the superior fortunes of the Rubens *Rainbow Landscape* which Irvine had acquired in Genoa. In 1808 it made £1,500, in 1823 £2,730 and in 1856 it cost the Marquess of Hertford £4,777 10*s*. It was thus a much dearer picture than either the *Brazen Serpent* (£3,675 in 1837) or the *Judgement of Paris* (£4,200 in 1844), the chief Rubens purchases of the National Gallery. It also remained the costliest example of Rubens till 1882, though more than one Rubens picture had been sold for £5,000 during the Regency.

The downward movement in Rubens prices was an example of a prejudice that began to affect all schools, almost a full generation before Queen Victoria came to the throne. Ruskin's diatribe against the National Gallery's purchase of two Guido Renis in 1845 gave it wings,

[1] Nieuwenhuys was born in 1799. In 1821 he sold the wings of the Van Eyck *Adoration of the Lamb* from Ghent to Edward Solly. He died in 1883 in Wimbledon, a link between the world of the Prince Regent, Angerstein and the Barings and the world of Mr. Pooter.

but its more consistent exponent was Mrs. Jameson, an amateur artist and self-constituted expert, the bane of living painters, whose opinions were much in demand among the fashionable. Writing in 1844, Mrs. Jameson informed the world that she had not made up her mind to blame the son of the Regent Duke of Orleans for mutilating the three pictures which depicted the irregular loves of Jupiter, because 'the memory of Correggio would surely have been fairer had he never painted them'.[1]

Passe pour Correggio! There were so few of his works available that the market could survive this form of moral censorship, but among the later Italian painters it made the buying extremely selective. It seemed that, like Correggio, they had all painted two sorts of picture. Guido Reni had painted at least ten different sorts of picture, but the age could not be asked to approve the long white elegant bodies of *Atalanta and Hippomenes*. On the other hand, there were no cries from the guardians of chastity in 1840, when the National Gallery bought Sir Simon Clark's moist-eyed *Magdalen* for £430 10*s*.; and less still in 1856 when the Gallery accepted the schoolroom picture of all time, Samuel Rogers's *Ecce Homo*.

It is an error to suppose that the eighteenth-century passion for the Bolognese school was killed by the Romantic movement. Religious sentiment could, on occasions, bring this market to life even at the end of the nineteenth century. For instance, in 1886 the Duke of Marlborough's Carlo Dolci, the *Madonna con Stelle*, was bought-in at £6,930. For this octagonal *Madonna* with a bright blue mantle and starred halo Redford believed that the Earl of Dudley had offered 20,000 guineas, though it had been relined and overcleaned.

The treasure of Blenheim Palace was not the *Madonna con Stelle* but Raphael's *Ansidei Madonna*, whose purchase by the Nation in 1884–1885 for £70,000 marks the end of an epoch or rather the end of a fool's paradise. In that year Parliament and the Press had to realise that the most celebrated works of the past could no longer be kept in the country at a fraction of the cost of a Landseer or an Edwin Long. Covetous eyes had observed the Englishman's indifference. The Cumaean Sibyl had only three books left, but Tarquin must pay the price of nine.

It could only have been a Raphael that fetched such a price, for Raphael was the one painter who had proved immune to changes of fashion, immune to depressed markets, the one painter, whose prices —for his fully developed work at any rate—had always gone up. No one had ever questioned the right of Raphael to command several times

[1] Jameson, *op. cit.*, p. xxix.

as much as any other painter. In 1813 when the dearest of all the Raphaels, the *Alba Madonna* and the *Via Crucis* or *Spasimo da Palermo*, were on offer, the British government decided not that they were not worth the money but simply that they could not afford them (see page 55). And the view that the Nation could not afford Raphael persisted for another twenty-five years. In 1818 Sir Thomas Baring's *Madonna della Tenda* went to the Crown Prince of Bavaria for £5,000, while in 1836 the *Alba Madonna* finally left London for Russia at £14,000. The National Gallery was founded in 1824, but only got its first Raphael in 1839, not through the exertions of the Trustees, but through a sudden impulse of the Chancellor of the Exchequer. *St. Catherine of Alexandria* was part of a block purchase from the ageing Beckford and cost about £6,000.

In 1841 the nation acquired the *Buonvisi Altarpiece* from Lucca, the work of Francesco Francia, paying £3,500 presumably because it looked like a fairly mature Raphael. Having been so extravagant, the Trustees decided in 1845 not to buy the Prince of Canino's *Crucifixion*, a real and important Raphael, for which they were asked only £2,400, but this of course was a *primitive* picture, for which conservative taste was not fully prepared. The *Crucifixion* (which the Nation did finally get in 1924) went to the future Earl of Dudley.

In 1847 the *Vision of the Christian Knight* (see page 43) cost the Nation a thousand guineas. This price, paid for a picture only six inches square, was a sign that the early Raphaels were beginning to be appreciated at last. Consequently, the *Garvagh Madonna* of 1865 cost £9,000, about six times its price to Lord Northwick at the Day exhibition of 1801. The *Costabile Madonna*, another early work from Perugia, but in bad condition, went to the Tsar of Russia four years later for £12,400. These prices for small works gave some indication of what the impact on the market of a historic Raphael altarpiece might be. It was not, therefore, altogether surprising that in 1869 the exiled Neapolitan Duke of Ripalda wanted £40,000, when he deposited his *Colonna altarpiece* with the Louvre. It was the first full-scale Raphael altarpiece to come on the market since 1754, when the King of Saxony had paid £8,500 for the *Sistine Madonna*.

The Colonna altarpiece is, it must be confessed, a dull picture. At the outbreak of war in 1870 the Louvre had not found the money. The picture had to be hidden in a gun casemate at Cherbourg. And after the war public money was scarce, so the Duke now lent his picture to the National Gallery. When the ownership of the picture came into dispute, it descended to the Gallery cellars. In 1884 it was adjudicated to the ex-King of Naples and till his death in 1894 it was on loan at the Victoria and Albert Museum. Sedelmeyer, the Paris dealer, acquired the Colonna altarpiece in 1896, though whether for the original £40,000 or for more is not certain. In 1901 James Pierpont Morgan bought the altarpiece for £100,000, but it stayed in the National Gallery till Morgan's death in 1913.

A slow progress for a work, whose authenticity had never been in doubt, but the story ended happily ever after in the Metropolitan Museum, whereas an equally famous work fell a prey to the new and powerful race of specialists. Its history is worth telling.

The pretty roundel Madonna, known as the *Madonna of the Candlesticks*, had been sold from the Borghese Palace during the French occupation of Rome in 1797–1799. Through Lucien Buonaparte it gravitated to the Duke of Lucca and in 1841 to William Buchanan, who sold it for £1,500, not as a Raphael but as Giulio Romano. The purchaser, who was Turner's Scottish Laird patron, Monro of Novar, promoted it to a Raphael and it was sold as such in 1878. Before the sale, it had been seen by Adolf Rosenberg, J. P. Richter and other experts, who thought it a schoolpiece, only partially painted by Raphael. Nevertheless the bidding at Christie's began at 15,000 guineas and at £20,475 (19,500 guineas), the highest figure ever pronounced in an English saleroom up to that date, the picture was proclaimed to have been bought-in. It was afterwards believed that the reserve had been £35,000, and that a bank had actually advanced this sum on the picture, but that dealers had been deterred by the rumoured discovery of another version, bought cheaply by J. C. Robinson, the critic. In point of fact the Robinson version, which was for some time on loan to the National Gallery, was much inferior.

The semi-Raphael proved an unlucky picture for Monro's heir, H. A. Monro Butler-Johnstone. He took it to New York in 1882, hoping, as the Duke of Ripalda had hoped, for £40,000. In 1884 he had to mortgage the *Madonna of the Candlesticks* to a London bank, who advanced not more than £10,000. Eventually the bank foreclosed, and in 1901 the picture was sold to Henry Walters of Baltimore for an unknown price.

It will be noticed that throughout the period 1815–1884 Raphael paintings were always in supply, whereas the hope of obtaining a Leonardo or a Correggio dwindled very early. The last appearance of unquestionable Correggio works was in 1834, when the National Gallery bought *The Education of Cupid*—though the *Ecce Homo*, that went with it, was far from unquestionable. The price of £12,075 for the two was recommended to the Keeper and Trustees by David Wilkie and four other Academicians.[1] When it is considered that *The Education of Cupid* had been one of the most costly of Charles I's treasures, the price does not seem to have been exorbitant, even though the *Ecce Homo*, which was known to be one of several replicas, could not have accounted for more than a quarter of the purchase-money. The two pictures had been confiscated in Madrid on behalf of Marshal Murat when King of Naples (see page 53). After Murat's execution in 1815 they had been acquired from his widow, the younger sister of Napoleon, by the Marquess of Londonderry. The cost of the *Education of Cupid* alone can perhaps be reckoned at £9,000, that is to say more than the National Gallery's Sebastiano del Piombo but a lot less than the *Alba Madonna*.

Since these sums represented the highest picture values in the world in the 1830's, it is surprising to find that, as late as 1879, the National Gallery could still obtain its only Leonardo da Vinci, *The Virgin of the Rocks*, from the Earl of Suffolk for £9,000. Undoubtedly the market value of the *Virgin of the Rocks* was depressed by whispers that it was a mere replica of the Louvre picture, though that is no longer the prevailing view to-day. The market was even more depressed by doubts concerning all Leonardo attributions. Forty-eight works had been listed by William James Browne in 1828, but by the end of the century the canon had been reduced to ten. Even in 1882 Beckford's treasure, the famous *Laughing Boy*, which Sir William Hamilton had brought back from Naples in 1801, was sold for the un-Leonardesque price of £2,205 (see page 42). Together with *Christ Disputing with the Doctors*, for which Lord Northwick had paid 3,000 guineas even in 1801, it has now become a Bernardo Luini.

Another of these ill-fated Leonardo attributions was the *Vierge au Bas-relief*, a picture which the dealer Woodburn sold to Lord Monson of Gatton Park in the early 'forties for £4,000. Shortly after the National Gallery's acquisition of the *Virgin of the Rocks*, it was offered to the Berlin Museum for 12,000 guineas and refused. At the Viscount Oxenbridge sale of May 1888, the picture made only £2,520. Still worse was the fate of the version of the lost picture which Leonardo made for Francis I of France, *Leda and the Swan*. Apparently it was something like the large version of *Leda and the Swan*, which is still in the Borghese Gallery. The picture came to Christie's from Italy in 1825 and an attempt was made to obtain £7,000 for it by private sale. Some thirty or forty years later *Leda and the Swan* came into the hands of

[1] W. T. Whitley: *Art in England*, II, p. 271.

Alexander Barker, the great mid-Victorian collector of Italian primitives. At the Barker sale of 1874 it was bought-in at £178 10*s*. At the second sale of 1879 it was let go at £84.[1]

The only authentic works of Leonardo which reached the Victorian salerooms were drawings. The finest of them were dispersed with the collection formed by Sir Thomas Lawrence, but not all that most fabulous horde of drawings of all time was a treasure-house. For instance, in 1838 Samuel Woodburn tried to sell a parcel of not less than seventy-five alleged Leonardo drawings for £1,500. Excluded from this parcel were the once famous life-sized heads of the Apostles for *The Last Supper*. These Woodburn had bought at Lawrence's executor sale in 1830 for about £550, an enormous sum in those days for eight drawings which were not finished works in themselves. Woodburn sold them to the King of Holland, at whose sale in Amsterdam in 1850 they were bought by the Duke of Weimar for 10,000 gulden. They can be found illustrated in old-fashioned text-books, sadly over-restored objects and probably not even of the period.

The whole of Lawrence's collection of close on two thousand drawings, which by his own estimation had cost him £40,000, could have been bought by the Nation in 1834 for £18,000. It was in fact bought for £15,000 by Samuel Woodburn, who had found many of the drawings for Lawrence and to whom Lawrence's estate still owed money. It took Woodburn many years to sell the drawings, and the Nation obtained only a small portion of them. In 1838 Woodburn exhibited a hundred and twenty alleged Michelangelo drawings and two hundred which were attributed to Raphael. Among them were many genuine works, some of which were obtained by private subscription for the Ashmolean Museum in 1842, but the government's failure to stop the dispersal fully justified Talleyrand's warning, 'Si vous n'achêtez pas ces choses-là, vous êtes des barbares'.[2]

The 1840's also saw the two only probable Michelangelo paintings that have ever been available for sale. The *Entombment* had disappeared from the huge collection of Cardinal Fesch, who died in 1839. In 1846 it was found in Rome by the painter-dealer Robert Macpherson, when it was in use as the backboard of a market stall. It took Macpherson more than twenty years to establish his title and to get the picture out of the country. The price paid by the National Gallery in 1868 was £2,000, a ridiculous sum for a truly magnificent work, which was not

[1] W. L. Roberts: *Memorials of Christie's*, 1896, I, p. 113.

[2] Recollection of Sir Charles Eastlake, April 1834. See Whitley, *Art in England*, II, p. 278.

then considered to be a Pontormo or Sebastiano del Piombo, as was later suggested. The same absurd price was paid in 1870 for the unfinished *Holy Family* from Lord Taunton's collection, and in this case it was a picture which had been on offer to the Nation as early as 1844, when the beggarly sum of £250 was proposed to a previous owner. It must be added that Sir Charles Eastlake believed this picture at that time to be a Ghirlandajo, for which £250 was a quite exceptionally high price.

The real authorship of the two pictures is still a matter of controversy, but their beauty remains unaffected by the problem. Both the doubts and the absurd low price were the results of a bigoted belief that Michelangelo had disdained painting easel-pictures altogether, and had only provided cartoons for others to work from, a belief due to a too literal acceptance of contemporary sources.

After all, the highest-priced English purchase in the entire period which ended with the £70,000 *Ansidei Madonna* of 1884 was neither a Raphael, a Leonardo nor a Correggio, but a Veronese, *The Family of Darius*, purchased by Eastlake in Venice in 1857 from Count Vittorio Pisani. The size was close on 8 ft. × 16 ft., the price £13,650. In permitting so much money to be spent on the work of a painter, who was still under the cloud of the disapproval of Reynolds, the Trustees of the National Gallery must have been influenced by rivalry with the Louvre. For in 1799 Napoleon had seized as reparations that incredible work, *The Marriage Feast of Cana* from the convent of San Giorgio Maggiore in the Venetian lagoons. The picture was 33 ft. × 13½ ft. and, sooner than have the trouble of moving it, the reparations-commissioners of 1815 accepted a less gigantic religious work by Charles Le Brun.

The Trustees were fortunate in getting the only big decorative work of Veronese that was still available. As to raising the price level of the Venetian school generally, neither this purchase nor the propaganda of Ruskin's *Stones of Venice* of 1851–1853 were at all effective. For instance, Ruskin's new-found enthusiasm for Tintoretto was not shared by the National Gallery Trustees, who in 1853 declined to spend £12,000 on the two great altarpieces from San Cassiano and the Salute. Not only Tintoretto and Veronese remained cheap painters till the end of the nineteenth century, but even Titian. *Bacchus and Ariadne* cost the National Gallery in 1826 less than £6,000, but no Titian in England fetched a comparable price for another seventy years. Probably the most expensive Titian purchase was the Gallery's *Tribute Money*, bought at the Soult sale in Paris in 1852 for £2,604 and immediately pronounced to be by Paris Bordone.

The real Titians—and there were several very great ones sold between 1826 and 1896—were inconceivably cheap. After doubts had assailed some two-thirds of the twenty-seven Orleans Titians in England, no one attempted any longer to master the subject. To distinguish between master and pupils was bad enough; to risk the revelations of thorough cleaning was worse. Some of the prices sound barely credible. The *Perseus and Andromeda* of the Wallace Collection, a picture hidden for generations in a bathroom, was bought by Lord Yarmouth[1] in 1815 for £302. The *Noli Me Tangere* of the National Gallery, a picture that has the perfection of a sonnet, cost Samuel Rogers £330 15*s*. in 1820. *Daniello Barbaro*, which made £7,560 in 1928, was bought in the Paris Tarral sale of 1847 for £39 18*s*. In 1852 the Earl of Darnley paid £288 10*s*. for the Orleans *Rape of Europa*, which was sold by the family to Isabella Stewart Gardner in 1896 for £20,500. The sketch for *The Apotheosis of Charles V*, known as *La Gloria*, made £283 at the Rogers sale of 1856 and was bought by the National Gallery in 1927 for £11,000. In 1870 Lord Grosvenor bought the *Duke of Urbino and His Son* in Paris for about £700. At the Westminster sale of 1959 it made £24,000. The *Man in a Red Cap*, which Hugh Lane sold to Frick in 1915 for £50,000, was bought in 1876 for no more than £94 10*s*. Only at the Dudley sale of 1892, where Ludwig Mond bought the National Gallery's *Holy Family* for £2,520, did the bidders at Christie's seem to show a bit of sense.

The poor bidding merely repeated the same lack of true appreciation which had been apparent among the Orleans speculators. Till the end of the nineteenth century neither Titian's smaller canvases nor his earlier works were understood. Just as a hundred years before, Titian remained 'caviare to the general'. It had been observed in 1805 that the pundit Payne Knight 'did not notice pictures by Titian to which Rubens would have bowed'.[2] Yet these particular Titians were the pick of the Orleans collection. In the nineteenth century Titian rated in practice very much below Rubens. The Titians of the 1930's at £100,000 and more had only reached this position after the disentangling labours of Bernard Berenson.

[1] The future 3rd Marquess of Hertford and father of the co-founders of the Wallace Collection.

[2] Farington, *op. cit.*, III, p. 99.

2. *The Return of the Primitives*

From the adventures of the earlier works of Raphael in the saleroom it is easy to reconstruct the very slow demise of the prejudice against 'hard, dry pictures'. The attitude of the late eighteenth century was not complicated. Seeing that painters in Raphael's day had already learned how to paint closer to nature than ever before, why bother about those who did not possess this advantage? Scholars could assemble materials for the study of the development of the art of painting. That was their affair. Collectors required perfection or something as near perfection as they could get.

In the year 1844, when the Quattrocento was almost fashionable in England, the magisterial Mrs. Jameson observed that it was just as well that this had not happened during the Napoleonic wars, for 'if we had not then been in the shadow of ignorance, the frescoes of Angelico and Ghirlandajo would have been torn down and sold by the square foot in Pall Mall'.[1]

It was, however, only the English collectors who had been, with two or three honourable exceptions, 'in the shadow of ignorance'.[2] In the course of Napoleon's depredations there had been a considerable movement of Italian primitives to the Louvre, partly as war indemnity payments. In 1815 the restitution commissioners of the easy-going but victorious allies did not think it worth the trouble to demand the return of such inferior objects; but it is quite evident that the requisition experts of the Revolution, Consulate and Empire had thought differently of them. The official neo-classicist art teaching of Louis David, the republican enemy of *impasto* in painting, had already found an affinity with the hard sculptural quality of the primitives. Some of David's disciples practised a kind of earlier Pre-Raphaelitism. And even Ingres, the classicist of all classicists, sent pictures to the Salon during his residence in Florence in 1820–1824, which owed much to Fra Angelico and which, like his *Francesca da Rimini*, were denounced as gothic.

It is not altogether surprising that the Baron Vivant-Denon, who advised Napoleon so wisely on his cultural annexations, should have had a discriminating eye for quattrocento painting. During the French occupation of Genoa, he bought the retable of the Fregoso family, the

[1] Jameson, *op. cit.*, p. xxxi.

[2] One of the exceptions was the 4th Earl of Bristol, Bishop of Derry, whose Trecento paintings were seized by the French in Rome in 1798 and never returned to him.

beautiful Ligurian *Annunciation with St. Benedict and Augustine*, for £8 10*s*. Among the spoils of war which arrived in Paris in 1799 were the early Mantegna *Crucifixion* of 1459 from the Correr altarpiece in Verona and also Mantegna's *Madonna of the Victory* from Mantua. From Parma came the Cima da Conegliano *Holy Family*, and from a convent of French monks in Rome the great *Madonna* in the Louvre by Piero di Cosimo.

In 1801 the requisition commission brought to Paris among the ancient possessions of the Richelieu family the two famous Mantegnas, the *Parnassus* and *Wisdom triumphing over the Vices*, as well as Perugino's *Combat of Love and Chastity*. In 1803 the loot from Florence and Pisa included fourteenth- and even thirteenth-century paintings, Fra Angelico's *Coronation of the Virgin*, Giotto's *St. Francis* and the supposed Cimabue *Madonna*. In 1812 a horde of cheap purchases in Florence included such treasures as Filippo Lippi's *Santo Spirito* altarpiece, Benozzo Gozzoli's *Triumph of St. Thomas Aquinas* and Ghirlandajo's *Visitation*.

It is easy to contrast Vivant-Denon's astuteness in building up a historic collection with the action of Buchanan and other English speculators, who re-shipped reputed early Raphaels back to Italy because they could not sell them (see page 45). But, since there was no National Gallery before 1824, English speculators, who assumed the cost and the risk of importing pictures from Italy, could not dispose of them to the State. Even in France, state acquisition was only enlightened when Vivant-Denon was in charge. Few Italian primitives were acquired under the restored Bourbons, and there was no comparable movement of Italian primitives to France until Napoleon III's block purchase of the Campana collection in 1863. So little had the French acquisitions of the Consulate and Empire affected the market for Italian primitives that in 1834 the Louvre could still acquire the entrancing Simone Martini *Calvary*, a jewel-like painting, 8 ins. × 10 ins., for 200 francs (£8).

Even English late-eighteenth-century taste had not absolutely ignored the Italian primitives.[1] The subject was quite sensibly discussed in 1795 in William Roscoe's *Life of Lorenzo di Medici* and in 1784 Reynolds himself praised Masaccio's frescoes of the Brancacci Chapel in his 12th *Discourse*—but purely as an illustration intended to justify his own practice of borrowing from the masters of the past. He justified Raphael for

[1] It would seem that Hogarth had heard of the Quattrocento. In his famous attack on 'picture jobbers from abroad', which he published in 1737 under the pseudonym 'Britophil', he makes his picture-jobber say, 'O Lord, Sir, I find that you are no connoisseur—that picture, I assure you, is in Alesso Baldovinetto's second and best manner, boldly painted and truly sublime'. Did picture-dealers really talk about Alessio Baldovinetti in 1737?

introducing some of Masaccio's figures, dating from 1426, into the great tapestry cartoons for the Vatican which were then at Hampton Court. Reynolds described the superiority of Masaccio's figures to those of the Trecento, 'when the best of painters could not foreshorten a foot, but every figure appeared to stand on his toes'.

Reynolds, who had not been to Florence for more than thirty years, could not have remembered the almost invisible figures of the Brancacci Chapel. Either, trusting Vasari, he imagined that Masaccio's figures and Raphael's looked exactly alike or he relied on the grotesque etchings of Thomas Patch. Reynolds mentioned no other quattrocento painter, nor did Benjamin West, who parroted the praise of Masaccio in his discourse of 1811. But this was enough to make Masaccio a frequent saleroom attribution, the coveted prize of the few amateurs of the quattrocento.

One of the first English collectors of Italian primitives was the Hon. Charles Greville, second son of the Earl of Warwick and nephew of Sir William Hamilton, who had himself imported a gold-ground Giottesque picture from Naples in 1801. In Greville's decease sale of 1810 there were twenty-six Italian primitives, which he had arranged as a comparative historical museum in his house at Paddington Green. One would like to know more about a roundel *Holy Family*, attributed to Ghirlandajo, at 16 guineas, the big Cimabue *Madonna* at 12 guineas, the Giotto fresco fragment at £1 11*s*. 6*d*. But we do know something of the two alleged Masaccio apostle heads which were said to have come from the Brancacci Chapel (10 guineas). For in the following year two whole figures from this series which Greville had sold to Young Ottley made £42. They were in fact by Masaccio's disciple, Masolino, and formed part of the *Santa Maria Maggiore* altarpiece. In 1950 they cost the Nation £15,750.

It was also in the 1811 Young Ottley sale that the first authentic Botticelli appeared on the English market. It was the National Gallery's small *Nativity* and Ottley had obtained it from the Villa Aldobrandini, an extremely rich picture full of figures, for which he evidently expected to get a good price. But at £42 the picture was bought-in and in 1837 after Ottley's death, it was sold to a dealer for £25 4*s*. In 1878 the *Nativity* cost the Nation £1,500, and to-day it might be worth £100,000, or even £150,000. It was not the only Botticelli to leave Italy during the Napoleonic wars, for in 1808 the Hermitage *Adoration* was bought in Florence for the Tsar Alexander I for about £50. In 1931 it cost Mr. Andrew Mellon £173,600. There was also the Munich *Pietà*, bought by the Crown Prince of Bavaria in Florence before 1816.

The Greville and Young Ottley sales of 1810 and 1811 covered almost the whole of the English speculation in Italian primitives, such as it was, during the Napoleonic wars. From now on to the early 'forties such works appeared rarely in the saleroom, and they continued to fetch the prices of mere curios. The arrival of the first early Raphael Madonnas in England with the Orleans collection in the 1790's had done nothing to raise the value of the Italian primitives, but on the contrary had devalued Raphael himself. Only very late fifteenth-century works with a strong sixteenth-century flavour, such as Mantegna, Perugino and Giovanni Bellini, were capable of real appreciation. Since the early eighteenth century Charles I's Mantegna cartoons, the *Nine Triumphs of Julius Caesar*, had been restored to Hampton Court. In 1627 they had cost the King 10,500 ducats or about £5,000. Cromwell's commissioners had valued them at £1,000, but during and after the Napoleonic wars it is doubtful whether they would have been worth £400. For instance, Giovanni Bellini's incredibly beautiful *Agony in the Garden*, which was understandably sold as a Mantegna at the Fonthill sale of 1823, was bought back by Beckford for £52 10*s*.[1] Bellini's *Doge Loredano* of the National Gallery, which Beckford had bought in 1807, cost him only 13 guineas. But the rise in Perugino, Mantegna and Bellini in the early 1840's was truly impressive. In 1844 the *Doge Loredano* cost the National Gallery £630. The Perugino *Holy Family*, bought back by Beckford in 1823 for £33 12*s*., cost the Gallery £800 in 1841, though six years later Ruskin wrote that 'the attribution to Perugino of the wretched panel, which now bears his name, was a mere insult'.

As the earlier Raphael pictures returned to favour, provincial north Italian works of a Raphaelesque flavour rose with them. As early as the first Young Ottley sale of 1810, the *Ecce Homo* of the decidedly second-rate Mazzolino of Ferrara made £450. The most startling purchase of this kind, quite out of line with the saleroom values of the day, was the £3,500 paid by the Nation in 1841 for the Francia *Buonvisi* altarpiece, already mentioned, while a much smaller Raphaelesque altarpiece, the *Nativity* of Giovanni lo Spagna, was bought by King Louis Philippe in 1843 for £1,000.

Works of a more truly quattrocento, or worse still trecento, character continued to go for nothing. Beckford's alleged Orcagna *Crucifixion* was sold in 1823 for £19 9*s*. 6*d*. There was no question of the National

[1] In one of his fits of financial panic, Beckford had sold Fonthill Abbey and part of its contents to John Farquhar, the East India millionaire, who immediately auctioned off the art collection. Many of the objects were bought back either by Beckford or his son-in-law, the Duke of Hamilton. A considerable number reappeared at the Hamilton Palace sale in 1882. The *Agony in the Garden* had been sold at the Joshua Reynolds sale of 1795 for £5.

Gallery, which was founded next year, absorbing such things cheaply as a historic collection, though this is precisely what the Berlin gallery did in 1821, when it bought *en bloc* the stupendous collection of the English merchant, Edward Solly. Sir Robert Peel, the chief arbiter of the nation's purchases, regarded anything older than the first years of the sixteenth century as *curiosities*.[1] With the exception of two wings of a Lorenzo Monaco altarpiece, which came as a gift in 1849, the National Gallery acquired nothing older than the year 1500 until 1853.

The turning point in taste, which led to the revolution in the National Gallery's affairs, began with the dispersal of the Cardinal Fesch collection in 1843–1845. Exiled in 1815 from power but not from wealth, Napoleon's uncle had died in Rome in 1839, the possessor of 3,330 pictures. To make his collection complete, the Cardinal had acquired 'works even of the Greek painters of the twelfth and thirteenth centuries'. At one of the Fesch sales in Rome in 1845 the first high price was paid for an early quattrocento painting, £708 for Fra Angelico's sadly mutilated altarpiece the *Last Judgement*. It was resold in England to Lord Ward, the future Earl of Dudley [1817–1885], for £1,500. The 'mighty and perfect work', which Ruskin thought the National Gallery should have bought instead of spending £4,200 on the *Judgement of Paris*, 'a coarse and unnecessary Rubens', had been bought by the Cardinal from a Roman baker for a few pounds. But if it now cost Lord Ward £1,500, it was because of the competition of German galleries. In Germany, under the influence of the Nazarener painters Fra Angelico had already created a mania. The earliest monograph, *Johann von Fiesole*, was published by Schlegel in 1846, and it was to the Kaiser Friedrich Museum that the *Last Judgement* went on Dudley's death in 1885.

The German interest in Italian primitive paintings dated from the 1790's when the Dane, Asmus Carstens [1754–1798] startled the Roman colony by abandoning tiresome outline drawings, that derived from late Greek vases, for imitations of the young Raphael. His example was followed in Vienna in 1806 by a group of students, who regarded the neo-classic teaching of the day as French, atheistic and alien to the Germanic *ethos*. They concocted a wonderfully Savonarola Brown synthesis of Holbein, Perugino, Dürer, Memling and Raphael. In 1810, under the leadership of Johann Friedrich Overbeck [1789–1869], the circle removed themselves to Rome, where Overbeck completed the picture he had begun in Vienna, *Christ's Entry into Jerusalem*, an overcrowded pseudo-primitive picture, crammed with borrowings from Perugino and the young Raphael and with portraits of Overbeck's

[1] Holmes and Baker: *The Making of the National Gallery, 1824–1924*.

friends—and, it must be admitted, a truly remarkable work.

Rome was an international meeting-place for artists. The Nazarener painters in the 1820's influenced Ingres and, in the early 1840's, G. F. Watts. Yet, if it had not been for the wave of German patriotic feeling at the end of the Napoleonic wars, this quaint and rather charming earlier Pre-Raphaelite movement would have had no more ultimate significance than that of a school of painting in some small Himalayan state. But because of the general strengthening of the institution of monarchy in 1815, the German princes were moved to become patrons of native art, of art untainted by any unshaven French republican evocations of Brutus and Demosthenes. In this way Edward von Steinle [1818–1886], who became the master of Lord Leighton, was invited to Frankfurt. Peter Cornelius [1783–1867] was invited to Munich, Julius Schnorr von Carolsfeld [1794–1872] to Dresden, and Wilhelm von Schadow [1789–1866] to Berlin. These former Nazarener painters now executed huge mural painting projects for benevolent despots, who were beyond the reach of waspish newspaper letter-writers. But these paintings became less and less quattrocento in feeling. Only Overbeck remained in Rome, distilling the pure essence of 'primitive Christian art', just as Holman Hunt was to remain at the end of the century.

Between her recurrent bouts of xenophobia, the England of the 1840's professed an exaggerated admiration for the very modest success of the Germans in evolving various labour-saving media in imitation of true fresco painting. It became a weapon, levelled at the parsimony of successive governments, who, not being out of the reach of newspaper critics, were disinclined to finance the 'historical' performances of Hilton and Haydon (see page 84). In 1843 mural painting was the subject of a royal commission under the chairmanship of the Prince Consort, but practical and disillusioning results did not appear until the mural embellishments of the Houses of Parliament in 1858–1864.

While the Nazarener painters had mostly lost their quattrocento mannerisms, their influence on the German courts caused a prodigious number of primitive paintings, both Italian and North European, to be bought. But this German background to the quattrocento taste did not tell in its favour in England. 'Historical' painting in England in the 1840's was still bound up with the eighteenth-century cult of Shakespeare and not with the Middle Ages. Painters had not yet begun to hanker after the Holy Graal. You could paint any number of Titanias and Rosalinds in the costume of a children's pantomime, but when the Pre-Raphaelites introduced a little Fra Angelico and Botticelli, it was considered a bad intellectual pose. The Pre-Raphaelites were led to protest that they had no connection with 'the encaustic painters of Germany', an echo of 1843 when the Prince Consort had been attacked for plotting to introduce German artists to paint the Parliament murals.

In 1848 there was a graver accusation that the Prince was forcing the nation to buy the possessions of his German relatives. The storm arose from an exhibition which he had arranged at Kensington Palace. The not altogether first-rate collection of Northern primitives, formed by Prince Oettingen-Wallerstein, was in very truth for sale, and exceedingly cheap.[1] Yet even the consequent typhoon of xenophobia could not arrest the flood of romantic medieval taste, particularly since the Arundel Society began in that year to bring out the first of their popular prints, which reproduced the jewel-like colours of the primitive masters in the tints of old faded office blotting paper.

The sale of the Edward Solly collection to the Royal Gallery in Berlin had passed unnoticed in 1821. What could this eccentric English merchant have signified at the end of the Napoleonic wars? On the other hand, the young Lord Ward's princely purchases at the Fesch sale were of national interest, particularly in 1851, the year of the Great Exhibition when 50,000 people paid to see his Raphael *Crucifixion* and Fra Angelico's *Last Judgement*, which were shown at the Egyptian Hall.

This, coupled with the success of the British Institution's exhibition of primitives in 1848, increased the pressure on the Trustees of the National Gallery, who had been reproved by a Parliamentary commission, already in 1836, for their failure to establish a true historical collection, representing the early schools. To little purpose. In 1846–1847 more Guido Renis, picked by fox-hunting squires over the heads of a helpless Keeper, had excited the ire of J. Morris Moore and John Ruskin. Eastlake resigned the Keepership, but more attacks during the Keepership of Thomas Uwins elicited a second Government Inquiry in 1853, this time with practical results. One of them was that Eastlake returned with the firm, deciding powers of a Director. There was also for the first time an annual grant of purchase. And the Select Committee strongly recommended the acquisition of the earlier Italian masters.

Between 1855 and 1865 when he died at Pisa, Eastlake made an annual shopping expedition to Italy and there was little among his purchases that the nation need regret to-day, though it is a question whether the deciding voice was not Lady Eastlake's, rather than the Director's. Some of these purchases were for sums so modest that it is difficult to credit them to-day. At the same time, it became apparent

[1] A few pictures, bought by the Prince Consort, were given by Queen Victoria to the National Gallery in 1862.

from the beginning that the competitive buying of the German princes had raised the price of large and suitably royal possessions. Whereas Dudley had bought the Fra Angelico *Last Judgement* in 1845 for £1,500, in 1860 the nation had to pay, together with the papal government's export fees, no less than £4,200 for the five surviving panels from Fra Angelico's altarpiece of San Domenico in Fiesole. In an age when piecework was the usual yardstick, a picture which contained 266 figures was irresistible. In 1860 such a price was lavish for any old master, but prices on the same scale had already been paid for Italian primitives. In Milan in 1856 Eastlake paid £3,571 for the three surviving panels of Perugino's Pavia altarpiece. In 1857 the Pucci family in Florence received £3,155 for the 9½-ft. *St. Sebastian* of Pollaiuolo. Count Mocenigo's alleged Carpaccio, the *Holy Family*, was bought in Venice in 1865 for £3,400. The Crivelli Demidoff altarpiece was bought in Paris at the San Donato sale of 1868 for £3,360. The far more exciting Crivelli *Annunciation* from Ascoli had been given to the gallery by Lord Taunton in 1864 and it should be noticed that in 1847 Taunton had given only £325 10*s*. for it at the Edward Solly sale. After Eastlake's death the policy of securing the costly space-wasting altarpieces continued under Sir Frederick Burton, In 1879 Burton bought the larger Perugino *Holy Family* for £3,200, and in 1882 an Ercole di Grandi altarpiece was bought in Ferrara for £2,970.

All these prices were paid for altarpieces from churches, some of them of vast size. The full height of the Demidoff altarpiece is 16 ft. In other words the eighteenth-century predilection for huge religious works with the guilty glamour of violated sanctity had simply transferred itself to the Primitives (see page 7). But when it was a matter of buying roundels or detached panels or cassones or works which were not religious at all but pagan, it is astonishing how little the Nation had to pay for the venerated objects that now bring visitors from the ends of the earth, and which appear annually on hundreds of thousands of Christmas cards.

Here are a few examples of Eastlake's purchases in Italy. In 1855 the most famous of the Botticelli roundel Madonnas was bought in Bologna for £331, but the Mantegna *Madonna Enthroned*, being a late work and more Renaissance-looking, cost £1,152 12*s*. Quite incredibly, Eastlake obtained the Piero della Francesa *Baptism of Christ* in 1861 by bidding £241 10*s*. at a Florence auction. When it is considered that Duveen bid £77,500 in 1938 for the Piero della Francesca small *Crucifixion*, which is now at Washington, a half-million might be a low estimate of the present value of Eastlake's purchase of a hundred years ago. And in the following year, when Eastlake returned to Florence, the most touching of all the early Renaissance works in the National Gallery, the *Cephalus and Procris* of Piero di Cosimo, fell into his hands for £171 6*s*. Then there is that Florentine lady with the world-famous high forehead and sharp profile, now ascribed to Alessio Baldovinetti. It was bought from a Florence dealer in 1866 for £160.

Low as these prices were, they were paid in Italy where buyers from several European governments were on the prowl. When a collection of primitives came under Christie's hammer, prices could be lower still. The excitement of the late 'forties and early 'fifties over Italian primitives was shortlived[1] and again it only affected objects of important appearance. For instance, the poetic little Pollaiuolo panel, *Apollo and Daphne*, which was left to the National Gallery in 1876, had been bought by Wynn Ellis at the William Coningham sale of 1849 for 13 guineas. Broadly speaking such purchases were possible right up till the end of the century. Small trecento and quattrocento works were an inexpensive scholar's taste. The primitives at the William Graham sale of 1886 cost only a fraction of the prices that were fetched by Burne-Jones's imitations (see page 165).

Important works were nevertheless bought from time to time by the National Gallery in the London salerooms. In 1874 Benjamin Disraeli, as Chancellor of the Exchequer, accompanied Sir Frederick Burton to Christie's and insisted on spending £10,000 at the Alexander Barker sale. The most enlightened buyer of his age, Barker was the son of a fashionable bootmaker of Ludgate Hill. The *Daily News* displayed the most odious side of Victorianism in its snobbish and facetious jokes about the dead collector, but for the money that Baron Grant had spent on Landseer's *Otter Hunt* the nation obtained the following pictures, five of which rank among the best-loved works in the National Gallery:

	£
Piero della Francesca: *Nativity*	2,415
Pinturicchio: *The Return of Ulysses* (fresco)	2,152
Botticelli: *Mars and Venus*	1,050
Jacopo del Sellaio: *Venus reclining with amorini*	1,627
Luca Signorelli: *The Triumph of Chastity*	840
Umbrian School: *The Story of Griselda* (3 panels)	724 10*s*.
Benvenuto di Giovanni: *Madonna Enthroned*	525
Carlo Crivelli: *Immaculate Conception* (altarpiece with wings)	577 10*s*.
Two smaller panels from ditto	210
Cosimo da Tura: *small Madonna*	84

[1] The enthusiasm was certainly fostered by the Oxford Movement, and died when Puseyite practices were no longer popular with young intellectuals.

Ridiculous as these prices seem, they were inflated by the presence of the Nation as a buyer. Witness the fate of the four long cassone panels by Botticelli which illustrated Boccaccio's *Story of Nastagio*. Made for a lady of the Pucci family in 1487 as a pair of marriage casquets, Barker had bought them in 1868 from the house which they had never quitted. Yet for a total sum of £2,730, all four were bought in. At the second executors' sale in 1879 there was no Chancellor of the Exchequer present and the panels were allowed to go for £1,086. The four panels went abroad, three of them to end in the Prado Museum in Madrid. But the *Wedding Feast of Nastagio degli Onesti* returned to England and rose from £294 to £1,365 at the Frank Leyland sale of 1892. Exhibited at Burlington House in January 1960, the picture appeared quite ravishing, despite the accusations of repainting that had been levelled against the *Nastagio* panels in 1874. And who could believe that, almost within living memory, it had been allowed to escape abroad for less than £300?

On one other occasion the opportunities of the first Alexander Barker sale were repeated. At the Hamilton Palace sale of 1882 the National Gallery bought fourteen pictures, including the £6,300 Velasquez whole-length of Philip IV of Spain. Much of this collection, the most magnificent that has ever been sold in London, was formed by Beckford, in the early part of the century. Beckford's Louis XVI furniture and Sèvres urns, some of the pieces not even a hundred years old, fetched prices that seem high even in the 1960s. Many thousands were paid for the crystal vases and mounted celadons which Beckford had amassed like a ninth-century Khalif. But for the Italian primitives, bought by Beckford and his son-in-law, the sale was not even a landmark.

The highest priced picture was the National Gallery's *Assumption of the Virgin*, bought as a Botticelli but nowadays ascribed to Botticini. A dull work, over 12 ft. long and containing several hundred angels, the *Assumption* had all the characteristics of an overrated national treasure, and it was expected to fetch at least £10,000. On 25th June 1882 Christie's had the appearance of a formally aligned battlefield. Sir Frederick Burton and two seconds from the Board of Trustees faced M. Gauchez of the Louvre and his myrmidons, flowing locks and Dundreary weepers against Mephistophelian pointed beards. *Que Messieurs les Anglais tireront les premiers.* Yet the National Gallery won at not more than £4,777 10*s.*

As to the other national purchases, the Luca Signorelli *Circumcision* fetched a price that had been standard for a 9-ft. late quattrocento altarpiece for the past forty years, namely £3,150. The two exquisite gold and *grisaille* Mantegna panels, *Tuccia* and *Sophonisba*, made £1,785 as a pair. Then there was the Botticelli *Adoration*, which had been acquired by the foreseeing Beckford, perhaps before the eighteenth century was out. With its crowded figures and fantastic rocks it looked very like Young Ottley's *Nativity*. It was now called Filipino Lippi and, as such, it made £1,227 10*s*. After a brief career under the name of *Amico di Sandro*, a discovery of Berenson's, the picture is now dubbed by the National Gallery as a schoolpiece.

When Antonello da Messina's *Portrait of a Young Man* was knocked down to Sedelmeyer of Paris for £514 5*s*., the name of the purchaser 'was received in ominous silence'.[1] Mr. Woods from his rostrum had remarked according to his habit, that the Nation ought to have it, since Sir Charles Eastlake had been outbid by the Louvre for the last Antonello in the saleroom. By this was meant the so-called *Condottiere*, one of the most haunting portraits of all time, which had cost the Louvre at the Pourtalès sale of 1865 no less than £4,540. But why could not the British Government find a few hundred pounds for this second signed and dated Antonello, which seven years later was snapped up by the Kaiser Friedrich Museum? It must be answered that in 1882 the primitives were in decline. English indifference was due, on the one hand, to the disillusionment that followed faulty attributions and on the other hand to jingoism at the expense of other times and nations. In the next few years the collections of William Russell, Fuller Russell[2] and William Graham went for trifling sums. The absolute nadir was reached at the Henry Doetsch sale of 1895 when hardly a single quattrocento picture made £50. The situation was only redeemed when the young Berenson captured the confidence of the American millionaires —but that is a matter for the next chapter.

If the history of the North European primitive masters in the saleroom followed the same pattern, the extremes were less dramatic. The National Gallery did not have to wait for a public scandal and a Parliamentary commission before it bought a Van Eyck. As we have already seen, there was an element of regional patriotism and ancestor-worship in North Europe, which had created a demand for gothic pictures even in the eighteenth century. The names of Holbein, Dürer and Mabuse

[1] The habit of cheering a popular purchase was general in the 1880s, when the Nation had not yet discovered that it was strong and silent. Popular too were short speeches from the rostrum and even from successful bidders.

[2] In 1885, the two beautiful Ugolino da Siena panels were bought by the National Gallery for 25 guineas the pair. The probable value of these panels today would be £15,000 to £20,000.

had always commanded a price, and even those of Van Eyck, Quentin Matsys and Hans Memling. The long years of struggle against French-imposed rationalism in 1792–1815 fomented these gothic yearnings. Thus in 1821 Edward Solly paid Nieuwenhuys £4,000 for the six wings of Van Eyck's altarpiece, the *Adoration of the Lamb*, which had been pawned by the Vicar of the Diocese of Ghent in 1815 for £240. For some months Solly's panels were in London, but the government was not interested. Solly therefore sold them to the King of Prussia for £16,000. In 1919 they were returned to Ghent under the terms of the Versailles Treaty, but in the meantime they had been the palladium of the Nazarener school and, at £2,600 a panel, quite. the dearest Flemish primitive paintings until the end of the century. In 1934 the small *grisaille* panel, which was stolen from one wing, had been insured for £70,000, and it was declared that the entire altarpiece was insured for £1,400,000.

The market value of a Van Eyck between 1815 and 1884 was something very different from the King of Prussia's purchase. In 1828 Sir William a' Court bought *St. Francis receiving the Stigmata* in Portugal for £8. In 1894 it was sold to John J. Johnson of Philadelphia for £700. In 1842 the National Gallery paid £630 for *Jan Arnolfini and his Wife*, to-day worth possibly a million, and even then known to have been continuously in the possession of kings till its removal from the Royal Palace of Madrid during the Peninsular War. In 1872 Francis Cook bought the *Three Maries at the Tomb* at the Middleton sale for £336. In 1940 the Baron von Beuningen refused an offer of £300,000 from Goering for the same work.

The virtual failure of these pictures to advance at all during the second and third quarters of the nineteenth century was part of the general stagnation of the art market, from which at first not even living painters were exempted. But it might be thought that works, which meant so much to the Continental romantic movement in painting, would have done better than other old masters. It appears that the sentiment for northern gothic, which had been so strong during the North European coalition against Napoleon, weakened considerably when the Italian primitives were found to be not only attractive but abundant. The English market remained weak, when the German Princes were not in competition, as the following examples will show. In 1802 Beckford bought a splendid picture at the Bessborough sale, *The Exhumation of St. Hubert*, which was long thought to be by Van de Weyden, for £96 12*s*. The companion panel, *The Dream of Pope Sergius*, was sold in 1850 for no more than £112 7*s*. Though in 1868 the National Gallery were willing to give £1,500 for Beckford's picture, they were not willing to bid beyond £14,700 for the companion in 1938. Beckford's Dürer, the *Adam and Eve*, which he bought from Delahante in 1814, cost him £147. The National Gallery's first Dürer portrait (actually by Hans Baldung) was bought at the Marquis Joly de Bammeville's sale in 1854 for £145 7*s*. Beckford's Memling, the *Madonna with the Apple*, was sold as a Van Eyck in 1823 for £74 12*s*., while Samuel Rogers's Memling, the alleged self-portrait, made £90 6*s*. in 1856.

In 1850 there came the sale of the Dutch Royal collection, patriotically stocked with Northern primitives in the 1820's and 1830's, when Belgium and Holland were under one crown. The market was flat even under these unusual conditions. Out of twelve alleged Memlings the two panels of the *Life of St. Bertin* made £1,916, the others from £167 to £538.[1] The Tsar bought the Hermitage *Annunciation* of Van Eyck for £448, while a Dirk Bouts made £750.

In 1886 it was still possible for a brilliant picture which everyone considered a Van Eyck, actually the small *Madonna* of Petrus Christus in the Metropolitan, to go to America for £315. At the Reverend Fuller Russell's sale in 1885 one of the greatest works of the German renaissance, Altdorfer's picture of *Christ taking Leave of His Mother*, which is now at Luton Hoo, was sold for 23 guineas. For once it can be recorded that the Berlin Museum had been caught napping and at a moment when patriotic purchases of the national school were at a very high level. For instance, in 1883 Berlin had paid £3,200 for Dürer's portrait of *Jakob Muffel* from the Narishkin collection, while in 1884 *Hieronymus Holzschuher* was said to have cost them £10,000. Occasionally this frenzied activity ruffled the surface of the London market, where Fairfax Murray held a watching brief. In 1888 he bought the Earl of Exeter's Petrus Christus, the *Virgin St. Barbara and Carthusian Monk*, for the Kaiser Friedrich Museum, paying £2,625. To some extent the National Gallery made up for the loss of a picture, which was no doubt considered costly, by paying only £2,000 in 1894 for Lord Northbrook's unattributed early Flemish masterpiece, the *Legend of St. Giles*. In 1934 the companion panel, the *Mass of St. Giles*, cost the gallery £10,000, but long before this time the Trustees had realised that this sort of thing could no longer be bought for the price of a David Cox water-colour. That sad thought must have occurred in 1911, when it cost £40,000 to save the early Mabuse *Adoration of the Kings*.

[1] The St. Bertin panels, which were bought-in by the king, are now attributed to Simon Marmion.

3. *Spain*

The prejudice against the fleshly school of painting, which preceded the accession of Queen Victoria, fell heavily on the seventeenth-century schools, but it left out one notable exception, namely Murillo. In the late eighteenth century, Murillo had been prized as highly as any of his Italian contemporaries, and his reputation suffered no decline from the overloading of London and Paris with his works in 1810–1813 (see page 55). If some indifference followed, it was chiefly because of the belief that the best of the loot of Lucien Bonaparte and Marshal Soult was being withheld. But the market for Murillo recovered in the 1840's, long before the dispersal of the Soult and the Louis Philippe collections. More even than in the late eighteenth century, it was Murillo's sentimental quality that now appealed to the taste of the day.

The quality can be studied in the National Gallery's *Holy Family* with its sentimentalised central figure of the child Christ. The picture had been bought from the Pedroso family of Cadiz by the painter Wallis in 1810. Buchanan sold it to the Earl of Berwick in 1813 for £2,500. Even at that date this was not the highest priced Murillo, for Lord Grosvenor paid Buchanan £3,000 for a much less striking work, *Laban seeking his Household Gods*. The *Holy Family* reappeared at Bulkely Owen's sale in 1837 and, appropriately in this year, the early Victorian mania for Murillo began with its purchase by the National Gallery for £3,675. It was also said in 1837 that a small *Assumption of the Virgin* on copper, which was bought in at a Paris auction for £290, was sold in England *à l'aimable* for £2,400.[1]

In 1840 the costly Simon Clark purchases of 1801 (see page 48) reappeared, James de Rothschild paying £3,045 for the *Good Shepherd*, a much restored work with a decidedly Anglo-Saxon physiognomy. This was a market made by nature for the Marquess of Hertford. In 1846 he gave £3,018 for Edmund Higginson's swarthy 7-ft. *Adoration*, while in 1848 he paid £2,992 10*s*. for the *Charity of St. Thomas of Villanueva*, an Irvine Genoa purchase of the early 1800's which had passed to William Wells of Redleaf. In 1850 the dealer Roos paid about £3,000 for another Murillo altarpiece, the *Assumption of the Virgin*, at the King of Holland's Amsterdam sale.

It will be noticed that £3,000 had become a standard price for a Murillo altarpiece in the 1840's, which in other respects were one of the dullest of decades in the salerooms. These were, in fact, among the

[1] Charles Blanc, *op. cit.*, II, p. 480.

dearest pictures of their day, but everyone expected higher prices, when the collection of Marshal Soult, Duke of Dalmatia, came on the market. So in 1852 the National Gallery Trustees authorised Mr. Samuel Woodburn to go as high as £7,000 for the *Immaculate Conception*.

Murillo and his assistants had painted several dozen *Immaculate Conceptions* for the churches of Seville alone, but there was no question that the altarpiece of the church of the *Venerabiles* was the finest and the one that owed most to Murillo's own hand. It was 9 ft. high and was painted in the fuzzy gold to coffee-coloured pigment which was characteristic of Murillo's work in 1678, when he was over sixty. Bilious in complexion, though Théophile Gautier called her 'rose-coloured like a vapour of the dawn', the Virgin is surrounded with a tumbling torrent of corpulent cherubs. Who could have failed to ecstasize over a picture which the far-seeing Murillo appeared to have designed for the year of the Great Exhibition and the subsequent emulation of William Adolphe Bouguereau?

Unfortunately for the hopes of the Trustees of the National Gallery, a Bonaparte prince was President of the French Republic. Within a few months a national plebiscite was to make him Emperor. He was almost an emperor already and unlikely to let such a treasure go to other emperors. The Tsar bid, but not high enough, and the *Immaculate Conception* entered the Louvre at a cost of 615,300 francs or £24,600.

There had been nothing like it before; there was to be nothing like it again till the sale of the Blenheim pictures in 1884–1885. It was in every respect, except the precedent which it set, a freak. The horde of Murillo pictures in the Louis Philippe sale of 1853 provided in fact an anti-climax. But it was a long time before the Soult Murillo was forgotten. In 1860 a less gigantic *Immaculate Conception* was sent to Christie's by Sir Culling Eardley. In the belief that the triumph of the Soult sale would be repeated, the bidding started at 5,000 guineas,[1] but at £9,450 the picture had to be withdrawn. It was nevertheless the highest figure for a picture that had ever been named in an English saleroom, and it remained so until 1876.

Victorian taste died hard. As late as 1909 one of these *Immaculate Conception* pictures from Seville made £5,040 at the Cuthbert Quilter sale, but the same picture was sold in June 1944 amid the flying bombs for £525. Even the Baroque revival among modern speculators has not made Murillo's religious works very popular. One of Soult's better Murillos, *Christ healing the Paralytic*, cost the National Gallery not more than £8,000 in 1950. This price suggests that the Louvre *Immaculate*

[1] As related in the *Art Journal*, 1860.

Conception could still make £24,600 and perhaps a bit more—but what pounds!

While this seems very small beer for a painter who was the rival of Raphael a hundred years ago, there is another sort of Murillo which would be very highly prized to-day if it could be found, namely the painter's realistic portrayals of beggars, gypsies, urchins and peasant girls. In Reynolds's day they were well appreciated. Calonne gave £900 in 1795 for the Dulwich *Flower Girl*, but in early Victorian times they were absurdly cheap. The finest of these Murillos fetched from £200 to £400, in spite of the fact that they were imitated by Alexandre Decamps and even reproduced as wallpapers for middle-class homes. They were in the taste of the day, but a lower plane of taste.

One of these cheap Murillo purchases of the 1840's was Robert Stayner Holford's oil sketch of a gypsy girl seductively baring a shoulder. It made £5,880 at the great Lindsay Holford sale of 1928, but £25,000 at the Goldschmidt sale of November 1956. Not a great deal perhaps for a brilliant little masterpiece in an inflationary decade which saw a very dull Rubens make more than ten times as much; but how perverse the price would have seemed in the year when three nations competed for the *Immaculate Conception*.

That Velasquez in the 'fifties and 'sixties should have rated well below Murillo was due partly to the large number of false attributions and partly to the fact that he had not painted sentimental angels. In the 'forties Velasquez still ranked very high. Inasmuch as the *Rokeby Venus* had been sold in 1813 or 1814 for at least £1,000 and possibly £2,000, in 1846 the executors of Lord Cowley felt entitled to ask £3,000 for the famous *Boar Hunt*, which had been presented to the late Ambassador by King Ferdinand of Spain. Although the picture had been seriously damaged and repainted since its arrival in England, the National Gallery paid in the end £2,200. This was more than the £1,610 which the Tsar gave in 1850 for each of the King of Holland's portraits, the *Philip IV* and the *Duke of Olivarez*.

The Louis Philippe sale in 1853 at Christie's included thirty pictures, attributed to Murillo and sixteen attributed to Velasquez. Some of these had been bought in Spain by the eccentric Lincolnshire Squire, Frank Hall Standish, who would have left them to the National Gallery if Lord Melbourne had supported his claim to a baronetcy. But in 1841 Standish left his pictures to the French King, because the French were more polite. The pride of the collection was an alleged Velasquez *Adoration* from the Aguilar family of Seville, for which the King was believed to have paid £4,800 in 1835. It now cost the National Gallery only £2,060, but it is no longer considered to be a Velasquez. The equestrian *Don Baltasar Carlos*, another doubtful picture, went to Lord Hertford for £1,680. The only two paintings which have received a modicum of critical backing in modern times were among the cheapest in the sale. They were whole lengths of *Philip IV* and the *Infanta Isabella* at £257 10*s*. and £315; both pictures were on the London market again in 1951.

Velasquez again appeared in the saleroom in 1865 when the National Gallery bought the bust portrait of *Philip IV* for £1,200 and the splendid, though now rejected, *Orlando Muerto* for £1,549. The pictures were part of the loot from the Royal Palace in 1810–1813 and were acquired at the Pourtalès sale, one of the great artistic events of the Paris of the Second Empire. The *Orlando* inspired Manet's *Dead Bullfighter* and played a part in the evolution of Impressionism, but its performance in the saleroom was hardly exciting. There was no furious competition for these controversial works till the Hamilton Palace sale of 1882, when the National Gallery had to give £6,300 to get possession of the full-length portrait that had once belonged to Beckford, the '*Silver Philip*'.

In early and mid-Victorian times El Greco was always called by his true name of Theotocopuli on the few occasions when his work was not sold as that of Titian or Tintoretto. The name first appeared in the London saleroom in 1849 when William Coningham's *Vincentio Anastagi* made £115 10*s*. In the Louis Philippe sale of 1853 there were at least seven El Grecos. *Don Alvaro de Basan* made £155 and the so-called *Portrait of the Artist's Daughter* £133. Both pictures have since remained with the Stirling-Maxwell family, and the second subject is exceedingly famous to-day as the *Lady in the Silver Fox Fur*, surely one of the most beautiful sitters to any old master. The fact that these two pictures were almost Titianesque in feeling brought them the dignity of at least a three-figure price. But five paintings of El Greco's disturbing later style left the country after the 1853 sale, having fetched £64 10*s*. between them.[1] One of them was almost the most exciting of all El Grecos, the *Adoration of the Shepherds*, $11\frac{1}{2}$ ft. high × $4\frac{1}{2}$ ft. wide. It fetched 10 guineas. In 1868 it was bought in Sicily by King Carol I of Rumania, who became eventually the owner of eight El Grecos. Another El Greco fetched only £18 7*s*. 6*d*. as late as 1888. *Christ healing the Blind* was then sold as a Tintoretto. It was sold again at Christie's in 1958 for £37,800 as a Veronese, before it was recognised as a close replica of the early El Greco picture at Parma.

[1] According to A. C. R. Carter in *The Year's Art*, 1939.

When the loot of the Peninsular War was dispersed, El Greco was so little known outside Spain that only a specialised scholar could have traced his style in the early works which alone attracted a market. Thus the National Gallery's *Ludovico Cornaro* made as much as £619 10*s*. in the Hamilton sale of 1882 because it was believed to be a Titian. The hunt for really typical late and wild El Grecos only began about 1900, when the market was rapidly built up by Mr. and Mrs. O. Havemeyer, who ransacked Spain with the aid of the Impressionist painter, Mary Cassatt.

The 'discoverers' of El Greco assumed that he had been a neglected, abused genius whose works had slumbered for more than three centuries before the kindred spirit of Cézanne made it possible to appreciate him. The cash account sometimes deals harshly with such convenient legends. The fact was that the number of commissions, which El Greco executed in his late style after he came to Spain, was very large, that he was paid for them all and that he refused to accept the low remuneration which was typical of the day. In fact he was better paid than Titian. While the mid-nineteenth century, which rated Murillo the greatest painter on earth, had little use for El Greco, it also had very little use for El Greco's master, Tintoretto. Evidently this prejudice was regarded as much older than it really was. Those who swallowed the El Greco legend might have reflected that El Greco's works had been piously preserved by the doubtless ignorant religious fraternities, for whom they had been painted, and that the esteem in which these works were held had even persuaded the liberators of the country's art treasures during the Napoleonic Wars to carry quite a number of them off.

4. *Holland*

Genius was not an easily marketable commodity in early and mid-Victorian times. No painter fared worse in the salerooms, compared with the previous age, than Rembrandt. But this was largely due to the artificial character of the Rembrandt boom during the Regency. The Barings, the Hopes and Angerstein, together with the Prince Regent himself, who were inspired by the enthusiasm of Lawrence and Benjamin West, had no successors. The Prince's acquisitions were safe and so were Angerstein's, but as the patrons died the saleroom told a dismal story. In 1816 Henry Hope's *Burgermaster Pancras and His Wife* made only £290. In 1831 Lawrence's *Joseph and Potiphar's Wife*, now in the Kaiser Friedrich Museum, made £498 10*s*., though at one time it had almost been sold to the Prince Regent for £1,500. Lawrence's *David and Bathsheba*, now in the Metropolitan Museum, made £157 10*s*. In 1841 it was sold in Paris for £350 and in 1913 it cost Benjamin Altmann £50,000.

Until the 1860's the very best of Rembrandt's paintings could be had for less than £700, unless they were of exceptional size. This was the period in which the Holford family Rembrandts were acquired, and their record is illuminating. The *Lady with the Handkerchief*, sold in 1928 for £31,000, was bought by Robert Stayner Holford at the Fesch sale in Rome in 1843 for £630. The *Portrait of Martin Looten*, sold in 1928 for £27,300, was bought in 1849 for £735. At the King of Holland's sale in 1850, where the Marquess of Hertford competed against several kings, several Rothschilds and a Tsar, the prices were even lower. Hertford paid £1,500 for the two groups of the *Pelicorne Family*, but they had cost the King twice as much at the Valckenier sale in 1841. The *Portrait of a Rabbi*, for which Beckford had paid £882 in 1807, was bought by Théodore Pâtureau for £283. The Munich Pinakothek's *Head of an Oriental* was bought by the King of Bavaria for £375. The same price was paid by Adrian Hope for *Nicolas Ruts*, the portrait in the Metropolitan Museum, which cost Pierpont Morgan £30,000 in 1904.

Exceptionally a large or a crowded Rembrandt could still command a fantasy price. At the 1843 Fesch sale the future Earl of Dudley paid £3,080 for *St. John Preaching in the Wilderness*, a picture in which 110 personages were counted. This was actually more than the price (£2,625) for which the family sold the picture to the Berlin Museum in 1892. In 1848 the 7-ft. picture of the Wallace Collection, *The Unmerciful Servant*, was bought for the Marquess of Hertford at the Stowe sale for £2,300. This was probably none other than the *Centurion*, which Bryan had sold to Sir Francis Baring in 1798 for £1,522 10*s*. If so, it was a unique instance of a Rembrandt of the first English speculation actually increasing its value.[1]

The change began for Rembrandt, as it did for the entire Dutch school, in 1865, when the Duc de Morny sold the unusually fresh and clean portrait of *Herman Doomer the Gilder* for £6,200. Emboldened by this saleroom wonder, William Boxall began his Directorship of the National Gallery in 1867 by recommending the payment of £7,000 for *Christ Blessing Little Children* from the famous Suermondt Collection at Aachen, most of which was acquired by the Berlin Museum seven years later. The Trustees agreed to the purchase, probably because the picture was as sentimental as Murillo, for which reason it could not

[1] The problem is discussed in the Wallace Collection catalogue, p. 235.

possibly be by Rembrandt. The name of Fabritius has been suggested perhaps unfairly.

Discouraged by a costly false step, English buyers fought shy of Rembrandt altogether. For seventeen years no Rembrandt reached £1,000 in London. In 1884, when Albert Levy's *Man in a Black Cap* made £1,890, Redford observed in *The Times* that this was very expensive and a proof that the doubts concerning the picture were ill-founded.[1] Yet this was precisely the period when strong German and American markets were developing. A portrait had fetched £6,800 at the Lissingen sale in Paris in 1876. The *Lucretia*, now at Minneapolis, made £5,840 at the third San Donato sale in 1881. The *Herman Doomer* portrait doubled its price in 1882, when Henry G. Marquand paid American Excise Duty on £12,400.

The indifference of Paris and London now created a positive exodus of Rembrandts. Between 1880 and 1910 Berlin acquired sixteen, while in 1909 *Klassiker der Kunst* recognised the existence of fifty in the U.S.A. By 1892 the prices had at last risen at Christie's, for the *Hendrickje Stoffels* of the Edinburgh National Gallery made £5,250 at the sale of the dealer, Samson Wertheimer. Eighty years had passed since such a price had been bid for a Rembrandt. In 1893 Lord Clifden's *Vrouw Six* made £7,035, but in 1894 the Earl of Ashburnham's *Rainer Ansloo* went straight to Berlin at £9,000.

The strong rise of the market for Dutch paintings in the 1860's, though stimulated by German buying, originated in the Paris of the Second Empire. The previous flatness of the Dutch market during the Bourbon restoration had little that was political about it and was in fact universal. A strong factor in producing the much higher prices in the Pâtureau (1857) and Pourtalès and Morny (1865) sales was the growing recognition of the Barbizon school of landscape-painters, particularly the Ruysdael-inspired Thèodore Rousseau and the Cuyp-inspired Troyon and Brascassat. The Dutch cult among these French painters was only political in the sense that it expressed a revolt against the French official school of 'classico-romantic' historical pictures, huge and pretentious. As such, the Barbizon painters were somewhat in favour under the brief republic of 1848–1852, and under a cloud during the subsequent imperial system. Nevertheless they expressed recognisably the taste of the peasant proprietor class that still predominated in France. And at the turn of the twentieth century when that class ceased to predominate, these paintings acquired a tremendous nostalgic value

[1] G. Redford, *op. cit.*, I, p. 372, quoting *The Times* of 12th May 1885. Yet in 1887 a mere etching, the first state of the *Hundred Guelder piece*, made £1,365.

on that account. Thus the Barbizon painters brought back the traditional French fashion for Dutch pictures, but not quite in the form that the *ancien régime* and the Revolutionary Napoleonic age had known it.

The Italianising Dutchmen, who had affected the airs of Claude, Salvator Rosa and Gaspard Poussin, now rated well below the true realists. In mid-Victorian times Berchem, Wouverman and the brothers Both were no longer considered the greatest painters of Northern Europe. Furthermore, David Teniers the Younger and his imitators were not as highly rated as formerly, perhaps because they painted the poor without any social conscience as demanded by the age. Cuyp and Paul Potter were of course the Barbizon favourites and Hobbema now achieved a vogue that bordered on the fantastic. In all this, London followed Paris.

Hobbema had risen very strongly during the Regency. In the late eighteenth century £60 was still a high price in London, but in 1807 Peter Coxe sold a landscape for £588. In 1820 Watson Taylor's *Watermill* from the Smet van Alpen collection made nearly £1,000. Between 1824 and 1829 the market was sustained by Sir Robert Peel's several purchases, which reached the National Gallery in 1871. That outstanding picture, the *Avenue at Mittleharnis*, was bought in 1829 for £840. It had been sold in Holland in 1815 for only £90. Yet it was cheaper than most of the six National Gallery variants of the *Cottage in the Woods* theme, which look as if they had been painted by the yard. Such examples had a most depressing effect on the work both of Constable and the Barbizon school.

Between 1829 and 1860 the advance of the Hobbema landscapes was continuous, a rare phenomenon in that age. The *Watermill* of the Wallace Collection was bought at the King of Holland's sale in 1850 for £2,250, half as much again as the dearest of the King's Rembrandts and five times as much as the Hermitage Van Eyck *Annunication*. The peak was reached at the last of the San Donato sales in 1881, when M. Secrétan paid £8,400 for *The Cornfield*, which had made £294 at the Holderness sale of 1802. In 1880 barely a dozen pictures had achieved such a price since the sale of the *Sistine Madonna* in 1754. There was no fall in the Hobbema market until after 1928, when the Six family *House in the Woods* was sold in Amsterdam for £33,000. Thus Hobbema's vogue outlasted the vogue for the heavy nineteenth-century French landscapes which he had inspired.

In the 1820's there was already a tendency for middle-class *genre* pictures, soft in tone and fresh in colour, to gain ground from the grubby paintings of low company, which had been so popular in the eighteenth century among the classes who were not obliged to meet the original models. Drunken boors had then been considered picturesque, whereas the clean house-proud burghers lacked *le bon ton*. Pieter de Hooch was so little appreciated that in 1779 an interior, which made £8,925 in New York in 1958, fetched only the equivalent of £7 17*s*. 6*d*. at the Paillet sale. In London during the Napoleonic wars a de Hooch picture could barely make £200 at best, but in 1820 Smith of Marlborough Street sold the King one of those miraculous backyard pictures for £400. In 1829 the second of the National Gallery's two brilliant variants on this theme was bought by Sir Robert Peel for £945. The first version was bought for the Gallery at the Paris Delessert sale of 1869 for £1,722, a price that reflected the popularity of contemporary realist painting. By 1937 a much less interesting member of the 'backyard' series could make £17,500 at the Rothschild sale at Sotheby's. The two versions in the Washington National Gallery may have cost Mellon and Widener more than twice as much. Nowadays Hooch's later paintings of interiors with somewhat grander company but murkier in colour, fetch a great deal less, yet one of these at the Secrétan sale of 1889 achieved the record for any Dutch picture in the last century at £11,040.

To-day the most universally loved of all the Dutch painters is no longer de Hooch, but Jan Vermeer of Delft, but in the period of this chapter Vermeer was absurdly underrated. Till the middle of the nineteenth century his style was seldom recognised, and some of the most famous Vermeers were sold as the work of Maes or Metsu or, like the Windsor *Music Lesson*, which was sold to George III in 1763 by Consul Smith, as Frans van Mieris. The first attempt to sort out Vermeer's works was made by the collector-critic Théophile Thoré, who wrote under the name of 'W. Buerger'. Thoré had been bowled over in the early 'fifties by the sight of the great *View of Delft* in the Rijksmuseum. He bought both the *Girl with the Pearl Necklace* of the Kaiser Friedrich Museum and *The Lady at the Virginals* of the National Gallery. In 1866 Thoré published an article in the *Gazette de Beaux Arts*, listing seventy-seven of Vermeer's works, which Charles Blanc in a terse rejoinder cut down to twelve. The situation to date is not as bad as that. Discounting at least three ladies in large and fanciful hats, whose high cost suggests that Meegeren had a successful predecessor, there may be thirty-five survivors to-day.

The market created by Thoré-Buerger was not very impressive, but before 1872 only the great *View of Delft* (£242 in 1822) and the *Woman with a Pitcher* (£175 in 1813) had made three-figure prices. In 1870 the *Lacemaker* of the Louvre, the highest perfection of Vermeer's art, fetched only £51 in Rotterdam, whereas in 1872 the *Geographer* of the Staedel Institute made £652 at the Isaac Péreire sale. In 1876 Lord Powerscourt bought the *Woman with the Pewter Ewer* of the Metropolitan Museum as a Metsu for £404 5*s*. The picture was sold to Henry Marquand in 1888 for about £2,000, and in the following year a new scale of saleroom prices was inaugurated with the *Love Letter* of the Beit Collection, bought at the Paris Secrétan sale for £2,580.

Of the new valuations of the mid-Victorian period the most interesting is certainly Frans Hals. In the late eighteenth century Hals was very little esteemed. His hard realism was displeasing and his slashing use of paint did not accord with the 'tight brush' which was so admired in the Dutch school. In 1774 the famous *Laughing Cavalier* was sold in Holland for £15, while in 1779 even the Empress Catherine's *Officer at a Window* from Houghton Hall was valued by Benjamin West at no more than £40, though it cost Mr. Andrew Mellon £35,000 in 1931. To the early Victorians, all out for sentiment and romance, Hals was more displeasing still. In 1855 Ralph Bernal's *Lady in a Black Dress* made £2 15*s*., while at the Stowe sale of 1848 two portraits made £7 7*s*. and £11 0*s*. 6*d*. They were recognised, when they appeared again in 1899, by Mr. Woods of Christie's, who had been brought up at Stowe as the son of a gamekeeper. Correctly catalogued, their price was now £2,100 and £3,150. For a picture to multiply its value 300 times in half a century is something to which we are beginning to get accustomed; yet quite a number of instances can be cited from an age which never knew the shadow of inflation.

Lord Hertford's purchase of *The Laughing Cavalier* at the Pourtalès sale of 1865 for £2,040 was an isolated millionaire escapade, since the price was a full fifteen years ahead of its time. The real interest in Frans Hals did not begin till after 1874, when the Berlin Museum acquired six first-rate examples with the Suermondt Collection. In 1876 the National Gallery was able to get its first fat old woman for £105, but Frans Hals could still pass unnoticed in the London salerooms. It was one of Mr. A. C. R. Carter's recollections that the painter's name used to get confused with Frank Holl, A.R.A. [1845–1888]. The *Man in Black*, which made £9,450 at the Glanusk sale of 1913, was actually bought at the William Russell sale of 1884, with a still-life thrown in, for 5 guineas. Even Picassos do not multiply their value by 1,800 times in thirty years.

The sale of the quite astounding *Pieter van der Broeke*, now at Kenwood, for £4,420 at the Secrétan sale of 1889 was an acknowledgement that Frans Hals fitted perfectly into the realist and early impressionist mood. For many years past homage had been paid to Hals by Manet and Sargent and even by Millais, but the great days for Frans Hals in the saleroom were in the reign of Edward VII, an age for which nature seems almost to have intended him.

CHAPTER SIX

The Golden Age of the Living Painter 1860–1914

1. *Millais, Holman Hunt and Frith* — 2. *Realism and Classicism, 1860–1887* — 3. *Secession. Insularity's Rearguard Action, 1884–1914* — 4. *Impressionism and Post-Impressionism, 1872–1914*

---

1. *Millais, Holman Hunt and Frith*

It may be that some of the Royal Academicians of the 1850's believed themselves to be living in revolutionary times, but revolution was far from the salerooms, which were dominated by the living painters, Landseer, Maclise, Leslie, Mulready, Stanfield and Linnell, and the dead painters, Turner, Wilkie and Callcott. As to the rebellious Pre-Raphaelites, their market was neither that of rejected outcasts nor of pampered geniuses. The truth was that from the very beginning they were paid reasonably, that few of the works of the Brotherhood lacked customers and that speculators were quick on the scene. The sum of £150 was certainly not a very large recompense for a picture as elaborate as *Christ in the House of His Parents*, contemptuously named *The Carpenter's Shop* by the opponents of the Pre-Raphaelite movement, but Millais, in 1849, was only twenty years old. Turner and Wilkie would have counted themselves lucky to have made a third as much at that age.

Less than ten years separated the first purchase of *Christ in the House of His Parents* from the sale of Holman Hunt's *Finding of Christ in the Temple* to Gambart for £5,750, a proof that it was a print-seller's revolution that had conquered the public rather than a critic's revolution;

a proof that the new style was not the creation of rare minds living among abstractions, but a popular style. The original purpose of the Brotherhood had been to get back to the fifteenth century, as the German Nazarener had tried to do during the Napoleonic wars. But within three or four years it became clear that pedantic medievalism had given way to a fifteenth-century insistence, Flemish and not at all Italian, on the close observation of nature. Writing in the 1890's in pious praise of his father, John Guille Millais, a sort of Gilbert and Sullivan guardsman, would not admit that Rossetti, that Bohemian fellow, who went on painting fifteenth-century attitudes till his death in 1882, had ever been a Pre-Raphaelite at all.

Holman Hunt, who had invented the term and who liked to think of himself as a Pre-Raphaelite to the last (he died in 1910), never cared to admit that he had borrowed the idea from the German Nazarener. It is true that there was no very startling similarity between the works of the Brotherhood and those somewhat schoolmasterish German medievalists. Yet undoubtedly the German painters had been responsible for the veneration of the Quattrocento among English artistic circles in the 1840's. The veneration had already attracted inartistic circles too, because of the appeal of bright colours. But the Brotherhood could not seriously have believed that they were going back in time beyond Raphael. They were repudiating not Raphael, who was no longer imitated, but Leslie and Maclise, whose archness and theatricality had travelled a long way from Raphael and even from Benjamin West.

As an episode in the history of taste, the saleroom fortunes of Millais's pictures are particularly interesting. Little as Millais may be appreciated to-day, he straddled the second half of the nineteenth century in English painting like a Colossus of Rhodes. There was nothing like this Englishman of partly French Channel Islands stock even in France, where dextrous virtuosity abounded in that flatulent age. In the end, dextrous virtuosity found its level, for nowadays only Millais's first Pre-Raphaelite pictures and his truly poetic book illustrations continue to attract interest. To most people the name Millais means Pre-Raphaelitism, though Millais painted in this formula for barely five years. *The Order of Release* of 1853 was no longer a Pre-Raphaelite picture except for the meticulous painting of a lock and key; and five years later in his *Vale of Rest* all pretence at meticulousness was abandoned. In that year, 1858, Millais wrote that he had had to give up his ideals, because of the hostility of critics and Academicians. In order to be able to live, he had decided to give the public what it wanted.

Millais was surely the champion self-dramatiser of his age. Almost in the same breath he wrote that his pictures were making more than those of anyone except Landseer. The truth was that the Pre-Raphaelite ideals were not his own but Holman Hunt's and, though they provided the most brilliant episode of his career, they were only one of many borrowings. Millais understood the currents of taste of his own time so perfectly that he could even anticipate them. The *Mrs. Bischoffsheim* of 1873 is in some respects more like a full-blooded Renoir than the work of Renoir himself at this early date. The *Thomas Carlyle* of 1877 with its slashing Frans Hals-like brush strokes is almost a Sargent. Millais, like Picasso, used his talent to do anything he pleased, a facility which posterity inevitably judges ill, and for this reason the later Millais is now only associated with his most blatant vulgarities, the *Cherry Ripe* of 1879 and the *Bubbles* and *Lilacs* of 1886. Yet it was precisely in 1886 that he achieved a work of such singular freedom as his *Head of Portia.*

At some time before his death in 1883, the veteran John Linnell reproached the painter in his thin quavering voice. 'Mr. Millais, you have lost your first love, you have lost your first love'. This is precisely what Millais believed himself. The sight of his early works at the commemorative exhibition of 1886 moved him to tears of genuine humility and contrition. But there never was a first love, unless it was those Maclise-like pictures which Millais had painted in his 'teens. The trouble was that Millais loved every kind of painting that others could do well. In the 1870's, when Gainsborough and Reynolds returned to fashion, he painted Gainsboroughs and Reynoldses, and when the Germans rediscovered Frans Hals, Millais painted like Frans Hals. In 1887, nine years before his death, Millais painted one of the last of his little-girl pictures, *Penseroso.* In this white dress against a white background with faint Japanese sprays of foliage in one corner there is an unquestionable debt to the anathematised Whistler.

Had Millais been a less versatile painter, he might have gone on painting according to Holman Hunt's formula, but that would not have made him rich. For the *Hireling Shepherd* of 1853 Hunt got £315, for the *Light of the World* of 1856, £420, and for the hideous *Scapegoat* £472 10*s.*, but this represented two years' work. You could not rent a deer shoot in Scotland at the age of twenty-six on that sort of thing. Millais's fees in the 1850's show a more interesting progression. In 1851 *Mariana in the Moated Grange* made only £150, the same fee that Millais had got for *Christ in the House of His Parents* in 1849. In 1852 Benoni White paid him £300 for the *Huguenot* and, next year, Joseph Arden of Rickmansworth paid £420 for the *Order of Release,* for which the founder of the Tate Gallery gave £5,250 in 1898. It was in this year, 1853, that Millais became an A.R.A. in spite of Gambart's tempting offer to pay double for his pictures, if he would boycott the Royal Academy and give him the first exhibition rights.

In 1855 Arden bought that singularly unrealistic work, *The Rescue*, for £580, but in 1860 Millais wrote that he had actually seen the owner refuse an offer of £2,000 from Gambart for this picture. In 1856 Miller of Preston bought *Peace Concluded*. Millais seems to imply in the letter he wrote to his wife that Miller had paid £945. Between his sobs of self-pity Millais mentioned that only Landseer's picture had done better in that year's Academy. Evidently this was the famous St. Bernard dog and the drowning child, known as 'Saved'. The following year saw the young painter writhing at the general disapprobation (including Ruskin's) which greeted his least happy picture, *Sir Isumbras at the Ford*. Even so, it was bought by Charles Reade, the novelist, for £800, the price at which Gambart had repudiated it. It was Millais's last thing of its kind. In 1859 the *Vale of Rest*, bereft of medieval attitudes and microscopic detail, went to Windus, the early speculator in Turner, for a comfortable £735, while the *Love of James I of Scotland* brought at last the long-coveted £1,000 fee from Lord de Grey. In 1860 the *Black Brunswicker* was sold to Gambart for £816, but passed on at £1,150 to T. E. Plint, an enterprising stockbroker from Leeds, who had been hoarding Pre-Raphaelite pictures since 1851.

The year 1862 was a testing time for all Pre-Raphaelite painters, for, at the end of 1861, Plint died suddenly, heavily in debt to clients and leaving his eleven children with no assets except his pictures, on which he was said to have spent £25,000.[1] In fact the collection fetched no more than £18,000 in the saleroom, but the worst falls were not among Plint's Pre-Raphaelite works. He had invested heavily in the latest Continental wonder, the Baron Jean Auguste Henri Leys [1815–1869]. It was said that the *Preaching of Capestro, the Carpenter of Antwerp* had cost Plint £5,000, and it made £892 10*s*. Millais's *Proscribed Royalist*, for which Plint had given £1,000 in 1860, was also down to £551, while the *Black Brunswicker* fell from £1,150 to £819. But *Christ in the House of His Parents* was up to £525 and the *Escape of a Heretic*, another early work, was bought by Gambart for £673.

Tom Taylor of *The Times* wrote tolerantly about the sale and had even some rather sniffy praise for Plint, distinguishing his adventurous buying from the uncultivated patron who wanted something as safe as

[1] Has there been another age when a speculating stockbroker would have had eleven children?

Consols or cotton-bales.[1] Taylor was particularly struck by the market for other Pre-Raphaelites, including the water-colours of Mr. Rossetti and Mr. Jones, which he found poetic though wilfully cramped by medievalism and quite dear at £30 to £40 for the biggest of them. With these works he contrasted the 'moderates' of Pre-Raphaelitism, by which he meant Ford Madox Brown, whose *Last of England* was bought by Gambart for £430 10*s.*, and Henry Wallis, whose *Elaine* made nearly £500.

Holman Hunt was represented at the Plint sale by some meticulous small landscapes which he had painted in the Holy Land in 1854–1856. The spectacular sale of Hunt's *Finding of Christ in the Temple* in 1860 throws into relief the fact that the famous *Nazareth* made only £150. But there was nothing incompatible about this. Hunt had spent six years painting the first of his crowded religious canvases. Part of the time he had roamed the Near East in search of biblical atmosphere. Part of the time he had supported himself on minor works, while completing his masterpiece. He calculated that he had spent £2,000 on it. Gambart was shrewd enough to see the publicity value of all this, and the mere fact that it was Dickens who proposed the terms made them acceptable. After paying Hunt £5,775, Gambart collected £4,000 in shilling exhibition fees, £5,000 in profits on the engraving, and was still able to sell the picture itself for £1,500.

It was, after all, a modest reward for six years' labour. And, having achieved public success this way, there was no retreat, so that Hunt spent most of the rest of his working life producing no more than three finished pictures. They had become part of the economics of his disregard for time, and in spite of their record-breaking nature, Hunt was the only well-known painter of his age who did not die immensely rich.

The product of Hunt's second residence in the Holy Land was not sold till 1874, when Agnew paid £11,000 for *The Shadow of the Cross*, which is now in the Manchester City Gallery. The sum included, besides the entire rights, an elaborate primary study in oils. Inasmuch as five years' work was involved, the remuneration was not remarkable. Millais would not have been content with £2,000 a year, paid to him five years in arrears. It was in the years 1868–1874 that Millais certainly raised his income to £20,000 a year, if not £25,000. He had written in 1867 that he could make £100 a day, if he liked, by executing water-colour copies of his more popular works. In the 1880's he could exceed

[1] The lugubrious history of the safe investment, with particular reference to Consols and cotton-bales, has yet to be written, but not by a thesis author.

that without any such drudgery, declaring on one occasion that his past year's income had been £40,000.[1]

Though Holman Hunt seems to have been ill-paid by comparison, it was probably not till the inflationary 1950's that a painter—but certainly no English painter—could again make £11,000 on a single sale. In the late 1880's and early 1890's there were £20,000 Meissoniers and perhaps a £48,000 Millet, but neither Meisonier nor Millet received the money, whereas in 1874 *The Shadow of the Cross* was possibly the fourth most expensive picture that had ever been sold in the history of collecting, ranking next to the £13,650 Veronese, *The Family of Darius*, bought by the National Gallery in 1856. And yet Hunt's picture was uncompromisingly Pre-Raphaelite. The composition was deliberately unattractive, the colour harsh, and in order to ensure an accurate cross-shaped shadow, the principal figure was improbably posed. But Agnew had no cause to regret his purchase. The steel engravings were now as cheap as 2 guineas each, and working-men's clubs offered to subscribe to them on the instalment plan.

A year later, Holman Hunt was again in Jerusalem at work on a picture which was to take him not six years to complete but nine, a picture which was to exhaust his powers prematurely and eventually to induce a state of blindness, though he did not die till 1910. Naturally *The Triumph of the Innocents* shows many signs of mental aberration. Composition and atmosphere both suggest Blake, who was hardly a popular artist in 1884, but Blake would have said it all with a few hours' effort. Here the dead, overworked pigments and the endless altered passages tell the desperate story of that native-made linen canvas which warped. Probably the picture made even more money than *The Shadow of the Cross*, for after several profitable exhibitions and a large edition of 3-guinea steel engravings, Hunt was still able to sell the original to the Walker Art Gallery of Liverpool for £3,750.

With *The Triumph of the Innocents* was reached the very peak of the market for the 2- and 3-guinea steel engraving. In 1884 it was already giving way to the chromo-lithograph, which could be reproduced by the hundred thousand and sold for a shilling, requiring neither high finish in the original painting nor fine work in the reproduction. Beginning in 1880 with *Cherry Ripe*, Millais had been selling his popular paintings of children to the proprietors of the *Graphic*. *Cherry Ripe* sold in 600,000 impressions as a Christmas supplement and the owners could have sold a million.

[1] William Gaunt: *The Pre-Raphaelite Tragedy*, p. 155, quoting a recollection of Kegan Paul, the publisher.

William Holman Hunt: *The Shadow of Death* or *The Shadow of the Cross*. For the full rights and ownership of this picture, which it took Hunt more than six years to paint, the firm of Agnew paid £11,000 in 1874. It is probably the highest fee, even now, that has ever been paid to an English painter, but it took Hunt a long time to earn it.

This picture is now in the City Art Gallery, Manchester, and is reproduced by courtesy of the Director.

Sir Edward Burne-Jones: *Love and the Pilgrim*. It was bought by the Duchess of Sutherland at the sale of Burne-Jones's executors in 1898 for £5,775. In 1942 the picture, 16 ft. long, was bought in at £21.

This picture is now in the Tate Gallery, London, and is reproduced by courtesy of the Trustees.

Edwin Long, R.A. : *The Babylonian Marriage Market*
Bought by Edward Hermon, M.P., at the Royal Academy in 1875 for 7,000 guineas. In 1882 it established an auction record for a living English artist by fetching £6,615. And yet today the name of Edwin Long is completely forgotten.

[illegible] by courtesy of the Council

The practice had unforeseen consequences. In 1886 *Bubbles* was sold to Sir William Ingram, proprietor of the *Illustrated London News*, but, to Millais's surprise, picture and copyright were resold to Mr. Barratt of Pear's Soap. 'Some natural tears they shed but wiped them soon'—tears not from Millais, but from Marie Corelli, authoress of *The Sorrows of Satan*. Millais was almost able to convince the lady that a poster, 8 ft. high, was as good a way of bringing this deep message to the heart of the people as any other.[1]

But it was the beginning of the end of the swollen value of copyright, which had made mid-Victorian artists' fees what they were. A bad hastily-produced picture looked no worse as a coloured Christmas supplement than a Raphael which had been subjected to the attentions of the Arundel Society. And the next step was the basically photographic heliogravure. Reproduction was no longer an additional source of profit, but an eagerly-sought free advertisement for the original picture. If you wanted to publish the 'Moderns' in the 1920's, the art galleries gladly presented you with a fine glossy photograph.

Before we leave the steel-engraved picture, we must consider the case of William Frith, for he was the first to profit in this enormous way from the ventures of Gambart and Flatou. Frith was not, as some people have concluded from the shiny faces of *Derby Day*, a Pre-Raphaelite. Though Frith was only three years older than Holman Hunt, he retained a deep-seated hatred of the Brotherhood all his days. Frith was in fact a pre-Victorian survival, spiritually a contemporary of Leslie and Mulready. In the late 'forties Frith had abandoned his Leslie-like themes from popular classics in order to paint life in contemporary dress. But when the first excitement caused by *Ramsgate Sands*, *Derby Day* and *The Railway Station* had passed, he had to go back to fancy-dress pictures. The reason for this was that pictures in modern dress had now to teach a sociological lesson and of that Frith was incapable. But while the prints sold, his market was astonishing. First of all, *Ramsgate Sands* was sold in 1853 in all innocence to the dealer Lloyd for 700 guineas. Lloyd surrendered his picture to the Queen at cost price, but retained the rights, on which he was said to have made over £3,000. Next year, when he began *Derby Day*, Frith had learned his lesson. The picture was commissioned by Landseer's patron, Jacob Bell, for eventual delivery at £1,500, but the picture was not ready for exhibition till four years later. In the meantime Frith sold the engraving rights to Gambart for another £1,500 and the exhibition rights (after the picture had been

[1] J. G. Millais: *Life and Letters of Sir John Millais*, p. 307 in the one-vol. edition of 1905.

shown at the Royal Academy) for £750. Total: £3,750 on a single picture and a triumph for Yorkshire good sense.

For *The Railway Station* Frith made an agreement with Flatou in 1860 for £4,500, plus £750 for exhibition rights. This is Frith's own version, though in 1862 the *Art Journal* was convinced that the first sum was £8,000. It would seem in fact to have been rather less than the sum which Holman Hunt received for the *Finding of Christ in the Temple*.

Rather unwisely, Frith turned down Flatou's offer of 1863 for a series of four pictures at £16,000. He preferred the glamour of a court appointment, painting the *Marriage of the Prince of Wales* for £3,150. But no knighthood followed, and Flatou's next commission was less lavish. In 1868 Gustave Doré had exhibited a painting at the German Gallery, the *Gambling Rooms at Homburg*. In 1870 Flatou paid Frith £4,000, inclusive of rights, for a picture of the same subject, the *Salon d'Or*. Four years later Flatou was able to get £1,995 for the picture alone but, alas, in 1932 the *Salon d'Or*, 8 ft. 6 ins. long, was sold for £48 6*s*. It is now in the Rhode Island School of Design.

In 1868 Frith had painted a picture for the cotton king, Sam Mendel, *Before Dinner in Boswell's Lodgings*. This was a reversion, and not the first, to Frith's early fancy-dress subjects. In 1875 *Boswell* actually achieved the English saleroom record for the work of a living painter by making £4,567 10*s*. and beating Millais's *Jephthah* of 1867. In the pride of this achievement, Frith forgot to mention in his autobiography that it fell to £3,150 two years later.

Frith made two more attempts to revive the contemporary setting and the contemporary story. The four pictures of the *Road to Ruin* series were commissioned by Flatou at £2,000 each and sold in 1878 after the publication of the prints for £6,300 to a Mr. Joel, who was known as Colonel Ellis. By 1919 this set of pictures had fallen to £460. In the meantime Flatou had commissioned the five pictures of the *Race for Wealth* in 1880. Hastily painted and indifferently engraved, this pictorial record of a swindling Victorian financier was to be had 'ex rights' in 1887 for £787 10*s*. In 1925 the complete *Race for Wealth* made £168.

Frith died in 1909 at the age of eighty-five, having ceased to paint since the late 'nineties. In 1909 the aimless period charm of *Derby Day* was almost beginning to be appreciated again, but the Frith market had all but disappeared. There are occasional petulances in Frith's autobiography, directed against the Pre-Raphaelites, Whistler and what Frith believed to be the French Impressionists, but not a word against the revivalists of classic drama and the high moral purpose, who had killed his market stone dead. But then Frith never admitted that this had happened to him.

2. *Realism and Classicism, 1860–1887*

We have come a long way from the *Eve of St. Agnes*, which Holman Hunt sold in 1848 for £70. Within twenty years of that first Pre-Raphaelite sale, the entire basic valuation of living art had been changed. In 1848 there was hardly a painter capable of making more than 1,000 guineas on a single work. But in 1868 both Millais and Landseer had achieved 4,000 guineas; by 1874 three pictures, Landseer's *Otter Hunt*, Holman Hunt's *Shadow of the Cross* and Alma Tadema's *Roman Picture Gallery* may have made £10,000 apiece and more. This was the price of valuable reproduction rights; it was often, when the rights had been sold, the price of glory alone. The nobility, who liked their pictures to be French or Belgian, paid almost as much as the cotton kings. The Marquess of Hertford paid £4,000 for Delacroix's *Marino Faliero* at the Pérere sale of 1868 and at the San Donato sale in 1870 he paid the same price for Ary Scheffer's heavy and Teutonic *Francesca da Rimini*, while at the same time Lord Cheylesmore gave £4,400 for Delaroche's *Death of Lady Jane Grey*.

One is almost surprised to find a good picture, the *Marino Faliero*, in this millionaire company, for the noble buyers showed no more refinement of taste than the cotton kings. If it is asked why many of the prizes of the mid-Victorian art-speculation were such bad pictures, it can be answered that works of art which have been bought in this way have been bad in all ages, the present not least. The men who paid these prices, Hermon, Mendel, Levy, Bolckow, Barratt, Holloway, Baron Grant and the rest, made no pretence to being men of taste. Unlike their predecessors in the businessman art-speculator's world, Plint, Bicknell, Gillott and Bullock, they did not follow their own fancy. They bought under the best-esteemed London advice and they expected the best value for their money. It was for the dealer and the painter to provide it. If they paid 7,000 guineas for pictures like Long's *Babylonian Marriage Market*, rather than for the *Little White Girl*, it was because that was what the whole apparatus of informed taste told them to do. They were not buying intimate homely objects for their cosy dens, but the equivalent of the Grand Manner, something very large and showy that was expected to enhance their status.

It would have been possible to sell them Titians. For the money that Holloway, the pill-king, spent in a mere two years, he could have made his women's college a rival to the National Gallery, instead of a very large and dimly intelligible joke. But to have persuaded the new rich to do just that would have meant puncturing their illusion that modern English painting was the culmination of all the painting that ever was. It would have upset the immensely valuable copyright market. If even the staid and stodgy established dealers, who were not at all in the class of Gambart and Flatou, had persuaded clients such as these to bid each other up for old masters, instead of for the Royal Academy 'Picture of the Year', they would have lost the most perfect working arrangement between painter and dealer that has ever existed. They did not lose it. Incredible treasures went abroad for derisory sums to end up anywhere, a stupendous El Greco in Rumania, three Botticelli panels in Spain, but faith in the nineteenth-century English realist school remained invincible. Even after the First World War it was battered, but unbowed.

Realism, extreme realism was the keynote of the new prices, but it was realism in a great variety of forms. No particular style dominated the market, and Millais, the most popular of all contemporary painters, practised almost every style that was going, though he became more and more occupied with portraits. In the 1860's these had still something Pre-Raphaelite about them. Not till the 1870's did he produce his endless little girls, wearing Reynolds's mob cap most of the time, the grand ladies in Gainsborough's luscious hats, the black-coated statesmen and professors, ringing the changes between Frans Hals and, alas, Hubert von Herkomer.

The Gainsborough style began with *Hearts are Trumps*, the three pretty Armstrong girls whom he painted in 1872, but the composition was Reynolds's, being derived from the *Lacemakers* at Strawberry Hill. It was the first of the really costly modern portraits, the forerunner of Sargent. 'Some say 2,000, some say 5,000', wrote *The Times* in 1876. 'We believe the true price to the painter was 2,000 guineas.' But Sir William Armstrong failed to sell his daughters. He bought them in at £1,365 and in 1944 the Chantrey Bequest acquired the picture for the Tate Gallery at £1,000.

Subject-pictures still brought Millais more money than his portraits. Here the great change began in 1867, when Sam Mendel paid him £4,200 for *Jephthah's Daughter*, the first truly elaborate work since Millais's Pre-Raphaelite days with more than a trace of Frederick Leighton's newly imported German classicism. Two years later the picture had gone up to £4,500, while in 1874 Bolckow, the ironmaster, paid Millais £4,930 for the tremendously popular *North-West Passage*, now in the Tate Gallery. At Bolckow's death in 1888 the picture made £4,200 and there were cheers in King Street from the fashionable mob who had failed to squeeze into Christie's. And yet the picture had dropped 700 guineas.

The highest price, recorded in the saleroom, for any of Millais's works during his own lifetime was paid, not for a painting made nation-famous by cheap reproductions, but for a somewhat austere landscape, *Over the Hills and Far Away*, for which £5,250 were bid in 1887.[1] Like the more famous *Chill October*, this was one of a series of Scottish landscapes, painted in the 1870's for £1,000 each near Millais's shooting lodge at Murthly in Perthshire. They recall no particular artist and are almost devoid of style, looking for all the world like very large daguerrotypes of not outstandingly attractive places. The weather is generally very bad:

> Tired we are of summer
> Tired of gaudy glare
> Showers soft and steaming
> Hot and breathless air.

Kingsley's verses to the North East Wind were prophetic, though written at a time when all that was Italian was glamorous and when Turner's southern sunsets were still copied. *The Times* observed that the price paid for *Over the Hills and Far Away* had been exceeded only by the landscapes of Turner. The works of David Cox, Stanfield, Linnell, Collins, Constable and Copley Fielding had come nowhere near it. The fact was that Millais's chilly landscapes adapted themselves far better than his subject-pictures to the new mood of social realism, moreover the painters of the Turner–Bonington formula were already on the way out in 1887. Since the 1860's their style had only been kept alive by painters of 'keepsake-pictures', like Birket Foster and Callcott Horsley.

There was no mistaking the mood to which Millais's landscapes had adapted themselves. In 1886, the year of Millais's memorial exhibition, *Christ in the House of His Parents* made no more than £892 10*s*. The commodity which was required was realism, but not the realism of the Pre-Raphaelites. If you sat for Herkomer or Frank Holl, it was improbable that a Venetian Doge or a crusading knight would emerge, while the rich spoilt women, who sat for Sargent, looked unlike Titania or Rosalind in a children's matinée and uncommonly like rich spoilt

[1] The heavy landscape-realism of Théodore Rousseau had cost the Louvre a similar sum in 1881.

women. In 1889 the *Saturday Review* voted Sargent's *Ellen Terry as Lady Macbeth* the most hated picture of the year. It was remarkable, all the same, how easily the hideous vulgarity of this picture was accepted among all the honey. Crude realism now permeated every subject, contemporary, historical, mythological or religious. It was essential that not an inch of the canvas surface should be left to conjecture. Thus when Orchardson depicted the social world of Voltaire and Alma Tadema the social world of Tacitus, it was all there, including the model's varicose veins, dandruff and bad teeth. And often it was the same model.

It was not that every painter tried to paint like a daguerreotype, as William Dyce had done in his *Pegwell Bay* of 1858. The rôle of photography took a different direction. It enabled the old masters to be studied in a more intelligible form than in the awful text-book engravings of the previous generation. It revealed new sources of inspiration to be tapped—by portraitists in particular. There was the terrible problem of the rich industrialist sitter with an uninspiring face and a long black morning coat. If you painted him like a photograph, he might in the end prefer to be photographed. Fortunately there was Frans Hals, who had painted entire town councils that were positively porcine, and yet he made a lively enough affair of them. Frans Hals was now in.

With the subject-picture there was no need to be so old-masterish. Having painted each object and figure accurately beneath the same top light, only a little fuzzing of the outline was needed to give them patina. The newspaper critics of the 1870's and 1880's hardly concerned themselves with artists' values, such as tone, colour, composition, drawing and quality of paint. The test with the critics, as with the public, was whether the picture conveyed its message. The subject was expected to be original but not the treatment, and a great fuss was made if some detail did not explain itself readily to the least receptive mind. Such an obsession with the literary content of the picture meant a broadening of the accepted iconography. An exhibition-success could always be achieved with some straightforward anecdote, in which the models acted their part with the aid of the skilful stage management of the painter. But with the dwindling of reproduction rights the popular subject was no longer necessarily the best seller. If the rich patron rather than the print publisher was to be wooed, a little, a very little, had to be done to flatter the client's intelligence.

For this it was necessary to find a formula. William Quiller Orchardson's first exhibit in London in 1868 was a straightforward Shakespearian subject. But as walnut succeeded oak and pitch-pine, the

Georgian scene succeeded the Shakespearian scene. *The Queen of Swords* of 1877 therefore paid homage to the Gainsborough revival, but it is not a bit like an eighteenth-century picture. In this collection of mincing overdressed models, lit as in the finale of a musical comedy, the influence was the theatre and to the theatre Orchardson adhered. In 1884 he began his contemporary dramas of high life, the *Mariage de Convenance*, and the *First Cloud*, always in mid-stage, always in evening dress. The rewards were solid for these thinly scumbled, colourless productions. *Napoleon on Board the 'Bellerophon'* was bought by the Chantrey Bequest in 1880 for £2,000. *Hard Hit*, painted in 1879, reached £3,460 in 1908, when Orchardson was still alive. Three years after his death, in 1913, *Master Baby* and the *Young Duke* made £4,620 each.

The formula of the 'strenuous-life' school of mid-Victorian painters was the precise reverse of the pernickety dressing-up of Orchardson, Pettie and Marcus Stone. It was all nature in the raw; the storm-bound rocks and sea birds of Peter Graham, the deep sea fishermen of James Clark Hook and Napier Hemy, the wild beasts of Briton Rivière and James Swann, the Highland cattle in mist and snow by which everyone knew David Farquharson. Invariably the weather was at least as bad as in *Chill October*, but in those days of St. John's Wood studios it was seldom depicted out of doors. All these painters had begun by imitating Landseer, but by the later 'sixties they had parted for good from the stilted attitudes and elaborately constructed compositions which distinguished the early Victorians from the late. Hook and his disciple sea-painters certainly leaned heavily on the Dutch realist painter, Josef Israels [1824–1911], whose *Drowned Fisherman* was sold in London as early as 1865 (National Gallery).

With the exception of David Farquharson, whose very titles, such as *Cauld blaus the Wind frae East to West*,[1] were enough to put the drawing-room fire out, all these painters were oddly popular with the richest class of patron, who erroneously supposed that their children would live as happily as they, along with storm-racked cliffs that loomed out of the billiard room and life-sized man eating tigers that sprang from the mantelpiece. All these painters had their loyal devotees. At the Matthews sale of 1891, three pictures by James Clark Hook fetched over £1,700 each, and next year the death of James Pryce of Paignton revealed that the good man had bought ten of them. In 1884 the executors of Edmund Crompton Potter, the Manchester calico-printer, put eleven Briton Rivières in the saleroom in the same afternoon,

[1] McCulloch sale, 1913, £283 10*s*.

all big animal subjects. Although the season had been hit by the beginnings of a famous three-year trade depression, the pictures averaged £1,000 each, even when sold *en gros*, while *Daniel* with a great many lions was bought by Agnew's for the fourth time since 1872 for £2,625.

Briton Rivière, who had begun to exhibit in 1860, died in 1921 when some of the Christmas magazine favourites were already down to £100 or less, but that was not the end of the decline of the English realists. A picture ironically entitled *Come Back!* was sold in 1934 to the highest bidder at £2 10*s*., but among the Briton Rivière pictures in the Crompton Potter sale of 1884 it had made £745 10*s*.

Different again was the social realist formula, a product of the political liberal reforms and uneasy consciences of the early 1870's and also a sort of backwash of French Republican art. Misery-painting had been launched by Millet as early as 1848, in England the Pre-Raphaelite year. Jean François Millet [1814–1875] was a true painter, who never lost sight of a painter's business among the moralising, but it was the moral purpose and not the aesthetic quality that made *L'Angélus* and *La Bergère* in 1890 the most costly modern works that had ever been sold (see page 161). The two figures in *L'Angélus* are impoverished, hard-working and religious, the background is muddy, the evening air chilly. The moral lesson is therefore complete. To rub the lesson in even harder with funerals, sick-beds, meagre fare, ragged children and with even worse weather, was the work of Bastien Lepage, Leon L'Hermitte and Jules Breton. The last-named [1827–1906] had a small market in England, beginning with a peasant picture sold to Lord Grosvenor by Gambart in 1861.

The first of the English Breton-inspired misery pictures seems to have been *The Lord Giveth and Taketh Away* by Frank Holl [1845–1888], exhibited at the Royal Academy in 1868. It was followed in 1873 by the *Pawnbroker's Shop* and in 1878 by the famous *Newgate, Committed for Trial*. In spite of the stir created by this dramatic, though shapeless and colourless work, it was bought by Edward Hermon for not more than 1,000 guineas, and it came to rest at Holloway College in 1882 at £808 10*s*. By this time it was complained that Holl painted nothing that was not inspired by the coffin or the gallows and that his Academy pictures gave everyone the creeps. Wisely he took to portraiture, somewhat in the manner of Millais. Holl died prematurely in 1888, having made his peace with capital by painting Mr. James Pierpont Morgan. But Holl's executor sale was overshadowed by *Newgate*, of which a perfect replica made £231, while the portraits in his studio made only £20 to £50, a matter which was regarded by sophisticated buyers of the French Barbizon school as a portent of the fall of the story-telling painters.[1]

A more successful practitioner of the social realist style was Sir Luke Fildes [1844–1927], partly because he made his name with a picture that exposed a real scandal and partly because he modified his style subsequently. Luke Fildes should not be judged by the famous *The Doctor* in the Tate Gallery, which was painted as late as 1891 in a watered-down Jules Breton style, sentimental and not indignant. The picture that brought him into the limelight in 1874 bore the uninviting title *Applicants for Admission to the Casual Ward at St. Martin in the Fields.* It was, nevertheless, so popular that it followed Wilkie's *Chelsea Pensioners* and Frith's *Derby Day* and *Salon d'Or* as the fourth picture in the history of the Royal Academy to require a rail round it. *The Casuals* was bought by Thomas Taylor, the Wigan cotton-spinner, for 2,500 guineas. Holloway, who bid the picture up to £2,100 at Taylor's sale in 1883, declared that he would have given £4,000 for it.

Poor in pigment, alternately brown and chalky in colour, the big dramatic picture looks like an enlargement of some murky Victorian woodblock—which it is, for the composition first appeared as an illustration in the *Graphic* in 1869. It is one of the exceedingly few works of the 'establishment' since the 1850's which show traces of genius. Fildes's work in the *Graphic* illustrates the simple fact that illustrations look better on a 4 in. block than on a 9 ft. canvas, and that painting can follow a false scent. Nevertheless, one of Fildes's admirers was Vincent Van Gogh—of all people.

Fildes painted few pictures that even attempted this manner. Most of his later work was based on journeys to Italy—what Charles Kingsley had called 'beggars, fleas and vines', but somehow Fildes's Italian peasant beauties seemed more flea-bitten than any others; the shadow of *The Casuals* hung over them.

As the 1880's opened, the Royal Academy subject-picture dominated the salerooms, rivalling the Turner cult and almost extinguishing the old masters, which by-passed the saleroom on the way to Germany and America. Since 1878 the annual purchases of the Chantrey Bequest had demonstrated that there could be no higher flight of genius than these works. Yet to the more sensitive sort of patron the pictures were distressing. But unless he moved in a very sophisticated circle, escape was not easy for him. To travel in the company of Burne-Jones and Rossetti into the world of Dante and the *Mabinogion* was to invite the reproach

[1] A. C. R. Carter: *The Year's Art*, 1888.

of being artistic, the greatest insult which could be hurled at a middle-class family in the classic age of the British matron, when to admire Botticelli was to be thought a cissy. The alternatives were the fuzzy, supposedly Titianesque, allegorical pictures of George Frederick Watts and the reconstructions of the ancient world of Leighton, Poynter, Alma-Tadema and Edwin Long, nudes, togas or chitons, white marble, basins and cypresses.

London had no Ingres to perpetuate the prim, statuesque pre-French Revolution manner of Jacques Louis David, no official art schools which tried to stifle the free handling of paint. The classical revival of the 'sixties was a sort of accident. Although Frederick Leighton [1830–1896], its leading exponent, had spent some years in Rome before 1855, the outcome of his German and Roman studies was the picture *Cimabue*, Pre-Raphaelite in theme, but in style somewhere between Ford Madox Brown and Delacroix's *Marino Faliero*. It was probably Leighton's hearty dislike of the Burne-Jones Rossetti association that made him give up medieval subjects. *The Sargonsian Bride leading Wild Beasts in Procession to the Temple of Diana* (12 ft. × 5 ft.) was the first expression of this new trend and easily the winning picture of the year in 1866. It seems hardly a subject to have evoked cheers from manly British hearts, but it was bought by Agnew for £1,200 and in 1874, when Frank Leyland got rid of it, the dealer Vokins gave £2,677 10*s*.[1] Then there was *The Daphnephoria*, illustrating one of those classical passages lost to most people through the mercies of amnesia after the age of nineteen. But it was bought by Lord Revelstoke in 1876 for £1,500 and by McCulloch, the king of Broken Hill, in 1893 for £3,937 10*s*., just as if it had been some rousing patriotic Millais subject.

Three years later, at Leighton's executor sale, Mr. A. C. R. Carter drew attention in *The Year's Art* to the cool reception that had been given to the completed works from Leighton House—for instance, only £651 for *Perseus and Andromeda*. But chitons and chlamyses had mysteriously won the affection of the islanders. Even in 1925 the *Music Lesson* of the Denny sale cost Lord Bearsted £3,255.

A different sort of being was Sir Lawrence Alma-Tadema [1836–1913], a native of Friesland, trained by the famous Baron Leys of Antwerp to paint the dark annals of Frankish history; the creator of pictures with obscure titles, such as *Gonthramu Bosé and His Daughters, A.D. 572*. In 1861 the young Friesian was persuaded by Ernest Gambart to exhibit *The Children of Clothild* at the Royal Academy. It was a success. The picture was bought by the Catalan banker, José Murrieta

[1] But in January 1961 it was sold by Knight, Frank and Rutley for £200.

(later Marquis de Santurce) and sold in 1873 for £1,102 10*s*. But the customs of the Merovingians were more remote from St. John's Wood than those of the Syracusans and much less appetising. Aided by a steady contract with Gambart, Alma-Tadema changed towards the year 1866 to the ancient Romans, beginning with *Horace's Lesbia* and the *Proclamation of Claudius*, but drifting steadily towards the Late Empire. The reign of Elagabalus was reached in 1888. There was much sense in this. Not only did it avoid doubling Leighton's subjects, but for an indifferent anatomist the late Romans had the advantage of being less addicted to undressing on official occasions. And since they were much richer than the Greeks of the Periclean age, many more delectable bronze and marble objects could be painted into the background. And this was well, since usually Alma-Tadema's archaeology was sound, but his figures were so closely painted from life that neither breastplate nor toga ever hid an air of waiting for the Swiss Cottage omnibus.

But there was no doubt of the success of the Dutchman's formula. Long before the end of the century he had rivalled the highest fees of Sir John Millais and in 1874 he may even have come close to rivalling Holman Hunt's *Shadow of the Cross*, for Gambart was said to have given £10,000 for the exclusive rights of the *Roman Picture Gallery*. Alma-Tadema was generally higher priced than Leighton and, by living sixteen years longer, he postponed the fall of the market. For instance, in London in 1903 his *Dedication to Bacchus* made £5,880, while his *Reading from Homer* made £6,060 in New York. In 1904 the Nile engineer, Sir John Aird, paid all Alma-Tadema's expenses for a long stay in Egypt, and in addition paid a 5,000 guinea commission fee for *The Finding of Moses*, a reversion to a biblical theme in Alma-Tadema's last painting years. Alma-Tadema died in 1912 and in the following year there was a tremendous memorial exhibition of all his works at the Royal Academy, followed by the purchase of the *Sculpture Gallery* in the McCulloch sale at £2,730.

From this point it is the familiar story of the subject-picture in decline. *Love in Idleness* could still make £1,050 in 1925. The 5,000 guinea *Finding of Moses* made £861 in 1935, but in 1942 it fell to £273 10*s*. And in the winter of 1960 it still hung around at £252. *An Audience with Agrippa*, which had made £2,675 at the Santurce sale of 1891, fetched £94 10*s*. in 1947.

The highest price for a picture of the ancient world was achieved neither by Alma-Tadema nor by Leighton, but by a mere imitator. Edwin Long [1829–1891] had begun with imitations of Mulready, followed in the 1860's by imitations of John Philip's Spanish subjects and in the 1870's by imitations of Alma-Tadema, painting anything from dynastic Egypt to the Christian martyrs. A dingy Philip or an anaemic Alma-Tadema will often be found to bear Long's signature in exceptionally large letters. Long's *Babylonian Marriage Market* was a newspaper success at the Royal Academy in 1875. Mr. Edward Hermon, M.P., who had bought a big house at Henley, paid the painter £7,350. In 1882 Hermon put the picture up at Christie's, where it made £6,615, a saleroom record for a living English painter until the First World War, when two Sargent portraits were auctioned for the Red Cross at 10,000 guineas each.

Holloway bought *The Marriage Market* for his women's college with ambiguous intent. The subject derived from a passage in Herodotus and showed a polygamous Babylonian paterfamilias auctioning his prettier daughters in order to provide dowries for the plainer ones, an arrangement more practical than anything the Holloway students could expect. Holloway also bought *The Suppliants* of 1879, a picture almost as big, which Long had sold for £1,575 and which now made £4,305, though the copyright had long been disposed of. There could be no higher tribute than that.

Holloway was that recurrent phenomenon, the millionaire who turns the market upside down for a couple of years and then departs. Even so, the hopelessly second-rate Long saw two more of his pictures auctioned for 2,500 guineas. And in 1890, just before his death in the grand house he had built in Fitzjohn's Avenue, he was said to have refused £5,250 for the *Parable of the Sower*, 17 ft. × 9 ft. It remained with Long's widow, at whose death in 1908 it was sold for £131 5*s*.[1]

3. *Secession—Insularity's Rearguard Action, 1884–1914*

The trade recession of 1884–1887 was notable for the number of treasures from the great houses that came on the market and for the much accelerated drift of old masters to America. By contrast there was little disturbance of the typical English businessman's market for modern or almost modern works, except for the decline of Frith and the earlier storytelling painters. On the whole the absence of private commissions was made up for by the continued competition of dealers, who dared not go short of stock. Moreover, during the three slump years the copyright market for popular reproductions was stronger than ever. The most ominous side of the recession was that the Americans, who were

[1] A. C. R. Carter: *Let Me tell You*, p. 39.

not affected by it, were buying furiously at prices which were much inflated by their ridiculous tariff laws; and they were buying French paintings. The demand was for Corot above all and also for the Barbizon landscape painters, for Jules Breton and his followers, for Rosa Bonheur, Millet and Meissonier. The newest rich bought the works of William Adolphe Bouguereau [1825–1905], one of whose deplorable rubber *baigneuse* subjects was auctioned in New York in 1886 for £4,400. But even the Bouguereau-fanciers were not patrons of Edwin Long.

In London, prices for the still-enthroned British favourites became strong again in 1887. The fantastic picture deals of 1874 were recalled in 1892, when Mr. Barratt of Pear's Soap bought Landseer's *Monarch of the Glen* for £8,000. By this time, however, the competition between American millionaires and patriotic French buyers had sent the modern French school sailing high above the level of English prices. In the year 1887 alone, Cornelius Vanderbilt paid £13,500 for Meissonier's *Friedland*, £12,000 for Rosa Bonheur's *Horse Fair* and over £10,000 for Jules Breton's *Communiantes*. Already in 1885 the dealer Durand Ruel had paid £9,520 for this picture. In 1889, when Cornelius Vanderbilt wanted M. Secrétan's Millet, *The Angélus*, Knoedler was prepared to travel to Paris for this one picture, braving a whole series of Phileas Fogg adventures, which included a slow passage to Queenstown, a special train from Shrewsbury to Dover in order to catch the Channel boat and an arrival at Sedelmeyer's auction room with only twenty minutes to spare.

In 1859 poor Millet, forty-five years old, had sold his most famous picture for £72. A subsequent owner parted with it, having been driven to the verge of insanity by his guests, all of whom made the same remark: 'You can hear the Bells.' In 1881 the picture was bought by M. Secrétan, the cartridge king, for £6,400. The cartridge king tried to become a copper king. His monopoly reduced the armament-makers of the world to melting copper saucepans and then M. Secrétan's credit broke. A collection of unbelievable costliness came swiftly under the hammer.

Knoedler was prepared to bid *The Angélus* up to 100,000 dollars. In fact he lost it to M. Gauchez of the Louvre at 550,000 francs or £22,120. But the Chamber of Deputies would not ratify the purchase of a picture which they considered too clerical. A M. Chauchard, owner of *Les Grands Magasins du Louvre*, got it in the following year over Knoedler's head and presented it to the Louvre, after paying Secrétan's receivers 800,000 francs or £32,000. It was also believed that in the same year Chauchard paid a much larger sum, according to Maurice Rheims,[1] not less than 1,200,000 francs or £48,000 for a much inferior Millet picture, *La Bergère*.

Next to Millet, Meissonier [1815–1891] was certainly the most popular painter on the international market of the 1880's and 1890's. In England his first reception had been cool. In 1860 the *Art Journal* waxed indignant at the price of £630 for a picture, exhibited at Manchester, which was 'no bigger than a man's hand'. But Meissonier soon became the favoured painter of those, who, like Ruskin, deplored the lack of fine detail and close observation among most of the English realist school. He was given the rare new title of H.F.R.A., or Honorary French Royal Academician. That Meissonier was a painter of tailor's dummies, obsessed with costume and accessories and devoid of lyrical powers, was no obstacle to Ruskin's later artistic philosophy. In 1869 Ruskin impetuously spent a thousand guineas at the French Gallery on a Meissonier picture, *Napoleon in 1814*, only 12 ins. × 9 ins. and as intricate as the inside of a watch. In 1882 Ruskin put it into Christie's, where the Pre-Raphaelite painter, Henry Wallis, paid £6,090. About this time Bolckow, the iron-master, gave £8,400 for the *Signpainter*, while Alma-Tadema's patron, Murrieta, may have given even more for a second version of Vanderbilt's huge water-colour, *Friedland*, 1813. Murrieta sold this in 1892 to M. Jean Balli, reputedly for £20,700. It was the high watermark for Meissonier, but as late as 1920 *Le Guide* could still make 5,000 guineas at Christie's, while to-day an occasional minor work of Meissonier may cost £500 as a piece of manual dexterity. The larger works keep away from the saleroom.

By contrast with the popularity of Meissonier in England, neither Jean-Baptiste Corot [1796–1875] nor Charles Francis Daubigny [1817–1878] found much of a market in the London of the 1880's. As early as 1890 Corot's *Danse des Amours* made £7,200 at the Crabbe sale in New York, but there were no comparable sales in London till the 1900's. On his death in 1896 Leighton's four big allegorical landscapes by Corot, which hung at Leighton House, made only £6,300 between them. In the 'eighties and 'nineties English taste favoured Corot and Daubigny a great deal less than the decidedly turgid works of Constantin Troyon [1810–1860], some of which had been brought to England by Ernest Gambart before 1860. Troyon's cattle pictures had been copied by Rosa Bonheur and possibly by Landseer, but the fact that a landscape painter as stodgy as the 'French Cuyp' could compete with Millais himself was disturbing to the subject-picture buyers. Even an iron-

[1] *Op. cit.*, p. 284.

master like Bolckow could be persuaded to buy Troyons, and his *Going to Market* lived up to its name in 1890 by fetching £4,920 at Christie's.

The landscape painters, French and Dutch, of the Barbizon group had mostly begun to paint in the 1840's. Creators of a freely painted but realistic kind of landscape, originally closely based on Ruysdael, Hobbema and Cuyp, they had at first been execrated, particularly when the romantic historical painters were paramount, but the Second Republic [1848–1852] gave these painters, none of whom made much money, a little encouragement. The Third Republic of 1871 offered them meagre official commissions in their old age. Only in the early 1880's did their work begin to get expensive and only in the 1900's did it become truly a millionaire taste, with the exception, of course, of Troyon, who had always been popular in England, and of Corot, who had become popular in America in the late 'seventies.

Although this somewhat unexciting taste developed so late, all the Barbizons were certainly known in England in the 1870's, and their stolid worthiness helped to spread the suspicion that there was something intrinsically wrong with the Royal Academy selections. One of the most assiduous buyers of Academy pictures had been the notorious Baron Grant, 'Mr. Albert Grant' to *The Times*. In April 1877 a collection, which was said to have cost the ruined financier £150,000, was dispersed for £106,000. George Redford tried to account for the worst falls by the great size of the pictures, 'because those who already had fine possessions could not find room for such things'. Repeating this charge in his criticism of the Royal Academy in May 1884, Tom Taylor attacked the standard of execution as well. A financial depression, he remarked, was not a bad thing because prices had been too high. Fashionable painters were tempted to work fast and carelessly.[1] It occurred to neither writer that the fault lay in taste and style more even than in technical execution.

In France still larger pictures were regularly shown at the Salon in the hope or with the promise of public commissions. In England there were few such commissions, but private enterprise was encouraged to buy works of monumental size through the example of the annual Chantrey Bequest purchases. The sum that became available under Chantrey's will in 1877 was not large and it yielded an income of little more than £2,000 a year. The selection was made by Royal Academicians, who lived in the world of their studenthood, when monumental size offered the highest prizes within a painter's reach. It was better,

[1] Redford, *op. cit.*, p. 382.

Sir Frederick Leighton thought, to encourage such works by spending the whole annual income on four pictures at most and occasionally on one picture. But in this there were the makings of a racket, because the purchases were chosen exclusively from the exhibits at the Royal Academy, where the Academicians had prior right to space. Leighton's own example could not have been worse. He allowed three years' income of the fund to be pledged in advance in order that the first purchase should include his own bronze figure of an athlete at £2,000.

In 1897, when the new Tate Gallery was opened, the results of twenty years' buying policy could be seen for the first time as a whole. There were sixty-five works, nearly all of them subject-pictures. They ranged from Yeames's ghastly life-sized corpse of *Amy Robsart* to the arch, embarrassed puritan of Frances D. Millet, *Between Two Fires*. Rossetti, Burne-Jones, Whistler, Fred Walker, even Holman Hunt were conspicuously absent. But it was not till 1905 that the first Parliamentary Commission sat, and not until 1920 that a system was devised by which the Bequest was used for the purpose that Chantrey had intended.

Despite its air of devastating unassailable State art, the Chantrey Bequest display of 1897 was already an experiment that had failed. For the past twenty years secessionist painters had been edging their way to the rich man's table. In the first place the Royal Academy had never enjoyed such a monopoly as the Paris Salon. Even in 1806 the British Institution had offered a formidable challenge. But till the later 1860's there had been no need for a rebel art centre. In spite of the whining and unworthy letters of Sir John Millais, the Academy had treated the Pre-Raphaelites well. But with the advent of extreme realism, and the Academy's blatant encouragement of Christmas magazine standards, Rossetti, Burne-Jones, Whistler and Albert Moore became an opposition. Good or bad, their works asserted the painters' right to select what they needed to express. Popular gibes at 'art for art's sake' and aestheticism could not hide this fact.

In 1875 Sir Coutts Lindsay founded the Grosvenor Gallery. His aim was not to form a *Salon des Indépendents*, but to run a gallery in which every work that was hung stood an equal chance with the others, neither skied nor on the floor nor wedged between objects that submerged it. Because Academicians were allowed to exhibit, Rossetti and Holman Hunt foolishly boycotted the gallery, but it was dominated by Burne-Jones and Whistler. Despite obtuse critics, it became a smart thing to be seen there. The 'greenery yallery Grosvenor Gallery young man' of W. S. Gilbert was a fashionable person (1881).

The first to benefit by the new current of fashion was Rossetti, despite his refusal to exhibit. In 1882, a few months before his death, the Walker Gallery of Liverpool paid £1,575, a price Rossetti had never dreamed of, for his only big picture, *Dante's Dream at the Death of Beatrice*. But the executor sale of the following year was not brilliant. It raised £5,000 and the dearest item was a replica of *Beata Beatrix*, sold for £661 10*s*. The real reappraisal dated from 1886, when the pictures of William Graham of Stobhall came on the market. Graham, a passionate, if profuse, lover of painting, had been a Trustee of the National Gallery and, since 1860, a patron both of Rossetti and Burne-Jones. His modern pictures, including several costly works of Millais and Fred Walker, made over £45,000, of which £27,000 were attributable to Burne-Jones and Rossetti alone, a lively contrast to some three hundred and twenty-three old-master paintings, largely quattrocento works of high quality which made only £23,000 (see pages 127 and 199).

The Graham sale put Burne-Jones in the class of Leighton, if not of Millais, when *Laus Veneris* and *Le Chant d'Amour* made £2,677 10*s*. and £3,307 10*s*. The prices reflected the extraordinary standing of a man who had just been made a full Academician without ever having exhibited a picture at the Academy. The conscientious resignation of Burne-Jones in 1893 portended still further triumphs. In 1898, following the painter's death, *The Mirror of Venus* made £5,727 and *Love and the Pilgrim* £5,775. Twentieth-century prices lowered this princely status, but not much. In 1913 *Love among the Ruins* made £5,040 and in 1918 the *Beguiling of Merlin* made £2,730.

When a more serious revolt against literary pictures ruled the London market, the fall became serious. The £5,775 *Love and the Pilgrim* was bought in at the Colman sale of September 1942 for £21. Who wanted a 16-ft. pane of glass when the blitzes were expected to recur? The picture was negotiated privately by the Tate Gallery. The last word had, however, not been said, for in December 1957 *Laus Veneris* was bought by Agnew for £3,400—more than it had made at the triumphant Graham sale of 1886, but of course not the same pounds.

Lacking the finish and the glamour of Burne-Jones, William Graham's Rossetti pictures fetched less, though they had probably increased in value in the same proportion. Joseph Ruston, the manufacturer of agricultural machinery, bought the *Beata Beatrix* of 1872 for £1,207 10*s*. and *La Ghirlandata* of 1877 for £1,050. In 1898, after Ruston's death both pictures made 3,000 guineas. At the Graham sale of 1886, Mr. Agnew had removed his top-hat to announce the news that *Ecce Ancilla Domini* (*The Annunciation*), the most Pre-Raphaelite of all Rossetti's pictures, had gone to the National Gallery at £840. There were rounds of applause, but the unthinkable scene would have been better appreciated four years earlier in the epic disorder of Rossetti's complicated life.

The fall of Rossetti's pictures began early. With the strong insistence on painterlike qualities in the 1900's, it was remarked more even than in Rossetti's own lifetime that his drawing was often feeble and that he had never mastered his pigments to the extent of distinguishing between an oil painting and a water-colour. It was the fashion to consider Rossetti a poet-painter rather than a painter-poet. Already in 1907 *Veronica Veronese* had fallen from £3,954 to £2,883 10*s*. in four years. *Beata Beatrix*, which had fetched £1,207 10*s*. at the Graham sale, made £293 at the Fairfax Murray sale of 1920. In 1927 an important work, *Bocca Bacciata*, made only £168, while in 1935 a small oval girl's head, a picture and not a study, though said to have been completed by Madox Brown, was sold for £1 11*s*. 6*d*. However, in July 1939 *Paolo and Francesca*, a distinguished early work of 1862, was bought at the Edmund Davis sale for £420.

In the 1950's Rossetti's works shared the mild revival of market interest in Burne-Jones and the later Pre-Raphaelites, but the prices denoted little more than a recognition that these objects have their place in art-history. Of the London painters of the late nineteenth century only the American Whistler can compete to-day with even quite lesser French impressionist painters. There was only one Whistler work among Graham's Burne-Jones and Rossetti pictures. In 1886 Whistler had long lost the Pre-Raphaelite atmosphere of his early Thames-side etchings and his opinion of Dante or indeed any other literary source as the inspiration of a painting was very low. The companionship of the Grosvenor Gallery did, however, link the two tastes together. But there was no doffing of top hats when Graham's Whistler *Nocturne* came under the hammer.

'When this lot came up, there was a slight attempt at an ironical cheer, which, being mistaken for serious applause, was instantly suppressed by an angry hiss[1] all round, such as had never been heard before in these solemn precincts. The incident was enlivening and did not damage the sale of the drawing, for it brought the respectable price of 60 guineas and was bought by Mr. R. C. H. Harrison.'[2]

Redford believed that the *drawing*, by which name he deliberately

[1] The hissing may have created a precedent. In February 1892 they hissed Degas (see p. 173).

[2] Redford, *op. cit.*, p. 432.

misdescribed an oil-painting, called *Nocturne in Silver and Blue*, was the 'pot of paint flung in the face of the public', over which Whistler had failed to recover damages from Ruskin in 1878. In fact, the libelled picture had been in the same Grosvenor Gallery exhibition and had been described as *Nocturne in Black and Gold, the Falling Rocket*, price 200 guineas. Graham's picture, for which he paid £157 10*s*., had however figured at the trial as an exhibit. Whistler had explained that the blobs on the bridge were 'what you like'. *Nocturne in Blue and Silver* is better recognised to-day as *Old Battersea Bridge*. It was bought for the Tate Gallery in 1905 against heavy American competition for £2,000. To-day it might be worth from £10,000 to £20,000.

Before leaving the Graham sale, the four Fred Walker landscapes should be mentioned. Fred Walker, who died at the age of thirty-six, is said to have been the 'little Billee' of du Maurier's *Trilby*. Chiefly remembered to-day for his very poetic book illustrations, his figured landscapes seem heavy and mannerised, owing quite a bit to Millais. Fred Walker fitted neither into the Royal Academy story-telling taste nor into the Grosvenor Gallery. Yet the prices were very high. *The Bathers*, those ill-nourished street Arabs, made £2,625. In 1909 Mr. Barratt failed to get the ablutionary subject as a soap advertisement, even at £3,000. The year 1909 was the beginning of an even stronger cult for Fred Walker. French painting of the Barbizon school dominated the London salerooms. Generally it was felt that no Englishman of the 'sixties and 'seventies had painted nature like that, unless it could be Fred Walker and perhaps the equally short-lived Cecil Lawson.

There was the *Harbour of Refuge*, a huge water-colour which looked like an oil painting, bought by Sir William Agnew in 1908 for £2,709. In 1912, when he presented it to the Tate Gallery, it was reported (and no one denied it) that Agnew had refused an offer of £10,000 from the Duke of Westminster. Then there was *The Plough*, bought by Lady Wernher at a Christie Red Cross sale in 1917 for £5,670, and *Marlow Ferry*, sold several times at £2,000 and £3,000, and still able to command £798 in September 1945.

It was an oddly conservative taste that made the bright wonder of the 1886 Graham sale also the bright wonder of 1917. It was, of course, a year of forced isolation and forced chauvinism, but the sale was none the less a true symptom. To study it better we most go back a little way to the eve of Armageddon, to May 1913 and the George McCulloch sale.

George McCulloch was a king among collectors who was reputed to have spent more than £200,000 on modern art. He had once owned

Whistler's portrait of himself, but he had not kept it. A man of the open spaces, who had won the Broken Hill gold-mine in Australia in a game of penny nap, McCulloch had been attracted to the views of William Morris, who also fancied the open spaces in his way. No. 184, Queen's Gate, was a treasure house of Merton Abbey tapestries, cassones and high-backed settles, which had expanded over the back garden. There were two hundred easel pictures which made £129,220, and the whole three hundred and twenty-six lots made £136,859. In the year 1913 the collection would have bought a new destroyer for the Navy or a small passenger liner. If it were sold to-day, it might buy a smart motor-launch.

The following prices will show what the great dealers were recommending to their richest clients in a year when a Cézanne had already made £3,600 and when Matisse and Picasso could be studied at Mr. Frank Rutter's exhibition in Bond Street. It was a year when Sherlock Holmes observed a suspicious breeze coming up from the East, but to Mr. A. C. R. Carter it was the return of the good old times. The sale was a proof that the best of the living British artists had not shared the downfall of the Frith generation:

		£
Millais	*Sir Isumbras at the Ford* (1858)	8,190
Edwin Abbey	*Richard of Gloucester and the Lady Anne*	5,670
	Scene from King Lear	5,040
Burne-Jones	*Love among the Ruins*	5,040
Orchardson	*The Young Duke*	4,620
	Master Baby	4,620
Cecil Lawson	*Marshlands*	2,940
Alma-Tadema	*The Sculpture Gallery*	2,730
	Love's Jewelled Fetter	1,992
Lord Leighton	*The Daphnephoria*	2,625
	Garden of Hesperides	2,625
James Waterhouse	*St. Cecilia*	2,415
	Flora and the Zephyrs	1,785
G. F. Watts	*Fata Morgana* (1865)	1,785
John Macmillan Swann	*Orpheus*	1,832 10*s.*
Peter Graham	*Caledonia stern and wild*	1,522 10*s.*
Millais	*Lingering Autumn* (1890)	1,522 10*s.*
Luke Fildes	*Alfresco toilet*	1,575

McCulloch also bought French or near-French paintings. Those who think that they are well up in the French school of the 1870's and 1880's, should look at this very abridged list:

		£
Jacob Maris	*Dutch Landscape with Windmills* (1873)	6,930
Bastien Lepage	*Potato Gatherers* (1878)	3,255
	Pauvre Fauvette	1,470
	Pas mèche	2,005 10*s.*
Rosa Bonheur	*The Lion at Home*	966
M. Munkaczy	*After the Dessert*	966
Leon L'Hermitte	*The Harvesters*	1,783
	Noonday Rest	1,312
Dagnan-Bouveret	*Dans la Forêt* (1892)	1,050
August Rodin	*The Kiss* (sculpture)	3,045

In 1913, that year of new values in French painting, there was only one artist in this list whose prices were positively going down, and that was Rosa Bonheur. Of the Bastien Lepage pictures *Pas mèche* had cost McCulloch only £441 in 1885. The Jacob Maris [1838–1899], which made nearly £7,000, had been bought from Sir Henry Thompson at the turn of the century for £880. As to the English school, some new names will be noticed, but new blood would be too strong an expression. Who was Sir Edwin Abbey [1840–1911], whose *Richard of Gloucester* could make the equivalent of £35,000 in to-day's money? He was a quiet American, who lived at Broadway (not New York, but the Cotswolds), and who did not upset the natives like his own friend Sargent or like Whistler. Having covered the walls of the Boston Public Library with the history of the Holy Graal, he painted the Coronation of King Edward VII and was knighted by that un-Arthurian monarch.

As to John William Waterhouse [1840–1917], he also affected a belated Pre-Raphaelite manner, somewhat recalling the flat mural style of Ford Madox Brown's later public commissions. John Macmillan Swann [1847–1910] was a milder Briton Rivière and a great one for tigers. In 1912 his *Polar Bears* had made £1,627. Cecil Lawson [1849–1882] painted very large brown-looking landscapes, inspired partly by Constable, partly by Millais. Having lived only thirty-three years, he was accounted a boy wonder, another 'Little Billee' of whom great things had been prophesied; a Grosvenor Gallery young man at that, who had begun in 1870 on absolutely the right lines, when he did a back view of Thomas Carlyle returning to Cheyne Walk.

The McCulloch sale was not the finale of the fifth act for any of these painters, for there can never be a finale. The act is still in progress and some of the characters of this opening scene make their appearance from time to time. In 1913 the Melbourne Gallery at once honoured an Australian Maecenas by buying the Cecil Lawson and the Bastien

Lepage *Potato Gatherers*, while the Metropolitan bought Abbey's *King Lear* scene. Lord Leverhulme bought the two Leightons and *Sir Isumbras*, which cost him £9,000, whereas the *Daphnephoria* cost only £3,000 as against £3,937 10*s.* in 1893. The Scottish National Gallery acquired *Master Baby*, but the *Young Duke* descended to £1,900 at the Blakeslee sale in New York within two years. Watts's *Fata Morgana* was sold in 1934 for £240 and Burne-Jones's *Love Among the Ruins* in 1958 for £480. As to *Lingering Autumn*, it lingers—but where? For of all Millais's pictures those chilly landscapes have proved the most unsaleable. In 1946, for instance, *Flowing to the River*, 1871, better painted and less sombre, made only 14 guineas.

No collection comparable with McCulloch's has ever been sold in its entirety. The wonder to-day is not perhaps that he bought it, but that he lived with it in that Norman Shaw house that I still vividly recall. Did McCulloch sit down to dinner every night with Lot No. 53, the Hon. John Collier's *A Glass of wine with Caesar Borgia*, £367 10*s.*?

4. *Impressionism and Post-Impressionism, 1872–1914*

In 1917, when *The Plough* made £5,670, no British schoolboy was allowed to doubt that the nineteenth-century realist painters embodied all the wisdom, skill and genius of the ages. There were those blue-and-gold books which were still given as Christmas presents, *A Hundred Great Masterpieces of the World*; *The Laughing Cavalier* and *Victory, O Lord*, *The Last Supper* and *Two strings to Her Bow*, *Prima Vera* and *When did you last see your father?* It seemed as natural a state of marriage, not to say divinely ordained, as three pages of abstract paintings and a Fabergé jewelled Easter egg in Messrs. Sotheby's *Forthcoming Sales*.

The illusion was fed on the absence of true fanaticism. There was nothing in England like the French Impressionists and their enemies, who were truly savage in their antipathy, so that when Impressionism conquered, the triumph was all the more overwhelming. In the early 1920's compromise over the Chantrey Bequest, compromise over the Royal Academy exclusions, compromise everywhere, induced the feeling that a French Revolution had been avoided, complete with tumbrils. It also hid the fact that secession had not gone anything like far enough. It hid the fact that the whole of British art since the death of Turner in 1851 had been a backwater, dotted here and there with beautiful water-lilies, but a backwater all the same.

In 1884 the contents of Manet's studio were sold by the painter's executors. I select the following:

	£
Olympia (1866)	400
Argenteuil	500
Le bar aux Folies Bergères	234
Chez le père Lathuile	200
La servante de bocs	100
Le Balcon	100

Here are six of the most famous paintings in the world, to-day worth perhaps a million and a quarter and then worth £1,534. This, however, is not the reason for printing the list. The reason is that as long ago as 1924, *La servante de bocs* cost the Tate Gallery Courtauld Fund £10,000 when there was no inflation and no buying on taxation account. The Impressionist market was not created by Greek shipowners in the 1950's. Degas, Manet and Renoir were respected by all serious French critics towards 1890, Cézanne, Van Gogh, Gauguin and Seurat not long after 1900. Before the First World War Impressionism and Post-Impressionism had become an international market and after 1920 it was useless to expect undiscovered masterpieces.

What was the position of England in this competition? The reader will not find many French Impressionist and Post-Impressionist items in the London salerooms before the 1930's. But those who are too young to recall the 1920's should not infer that there were no such paintings in England. Magnificent things were seen in the showrooms of London dealers year after year. If few of them found their way to Christie's or Sotheby's, it was because the market was too uncertain. In fact most of these works returned to the Continent. And this was something that had been happening since the very birth of Impressionism in the early 1870's.

In 1954 this subject was meticulously analysed by Mr. Douglas Cooper in his brilliant introduction to the catalogue of the Courtauld Collection. Mr. Cooper concluded that, though Durand-Ruel showed Impressionist works in London as long ago as 1872, very few works were bought before 1905 or, if they had been bought in London, they had gone abroad. In the late 'nineties the author George Moore, together with Lord Grimthorpe and Sir William Eden, acquired a few works each, mainly of Degas and Manet, but there was no important collector before Sir Hugh Lane. The Lane Bequest of 1915, which is now shared between the National Gallery and Dublin, was acquired between 1905 and 1912. The rival collection, the pictures of the London

University Courtauld Gallery, were bought by Samuel Courtauld between 1922 and 1929. The pictures, which the Tate Gallery acquired through the Courtauld and other funds, date back no further than 1923.

This record may be compared with the fact that even in Russia, the Tschoukine collection was begun as far back as the 'nineties, that Impressionist works were first bought by the Berlin Nationalgalerie in 1896; that, in spite of the U.S. tariff, Durand-Ruel built up a profitable clientele in New York from 1886 and that the Metropolitan Museum accepted two Manets in 1889.

If in the endless vista of the future, the work of this one group of painters is to retain the same status as to-day (a thing which has never happened to *any* school of painting), then the excessive British provincialism or conservatism, for you can call it either, will always remain a tragedy. It is certainly considered a tragedy in most quarters to-day, though the eccentric few may believe that the country owns enough Impressionist pictures already and that no tears need fall into the ritual champagne, when another well-publicised canvas goes off to its unpublished destination. The thought that the same canvas was in London in the 1870's, waiting a buyer at 100 guineas, may be galling; but it is equally galling that some of the finest Italian primitives of the German and American galleries were in England too in the 1870's and that they were sold for even less.

The greater tragedy is surely the absolute lack of English works which can challenge the French Impressionists on their own ground. The Impressionist experiment was first seen in London at a time when native subject-pictures, realistic and full of moral purpose, were rated so high as to make everything else wellnigh invisible. In the late 1880's this was no longer true. The creed of art for art's sake had spread very widely, but it was too late to expect that the imitation of a French point of view could produce masterpieces. All such attempts were now dogged by the sense of *hubris* of a dominant nation, which saw itself becoming provincial, haunted by the fear of being merely Parisian.

In the late 1880's the New English Art Club hesitantly took up the French challenge, while trying to remain English, producing works which Mr. Cooper so rightly calls *genteel*. But it is useless to suppose that these works could have been anything else. If only something had arisen, ferocious enough to be persecuted, some foundation for the future might have been laid. Instead, in the 1890's, when Millais and Burne-Jones and Leighton died, there was no rebel generation to occupy their thrones. A slice had been cut out of time. Sargent, alone of the next generation, was a man of equal calibre and after 1925, when

Sargent died, leaving £146,000 worth of odds and ends in his studio, there were no more painter-princes in England. To-day one may see the results of this slice cut out of time. At no period has the value of native modern art been so depressed. While the works of Picasso, Braque, Matisse, Rouault and Modigliani can make from £30,000 to £60,000, our leading Impressionist, Walter Sickert, and our leading Post-Impressionist, Sir Matthew Smith, barely reach the £2,000 mark.

In the 1870's the precious, 'arty', drift of English secessionism already spelt doom. Neither intolerance nor defiance were strong enough on English soil. After all, the storm in 1878 was not because Whistler's *Rocket* was so daring, but because he put so little into it. In 1862, when Whistler not only painted like the outrageous Courbet, but also invented strange stalagmite rocks that seemed to anticipate Cézanne, the Royal Academy accepted *Alone with the Tide* without demur. The indifference of selection committees to technical methods permitted all sorts of Impressionist devices, provided that the story was there. There was another instance in 1887 when Sargent's *Carnation, Lily, Lily, Rose* was accepted. The picture had not only a Whistlerish title but owed something to Manet and Renoir as well. Yet Sir Frederick Leighton recommended its purchase by the Chantrey Bequest at £700.

Better still, this English indifference to technical innovation can be illustrated by Degas's famous painting, *L'Absinthe*, now in the Louvre. Somewhere in the 1870's it was bought at a Durand-Ruel exhibition in Bond Street by Mr. Henry Hill of Brighton for £200. In 1889 it appeared at Christie's where, like Whistler's *Old Battersea Bridge* three years earlier, it was hissed. It was, nevertheless, bought by Alexander Reid, the Glasgow dealer, for 180 guineas. Why then should this picture, which Degas had not called 'a harmony in grey and black' or anything like that, have been hissed at all? By calling his picture *L'Absinthe*, Degas drew a moral lesson which should have been acceptable in London. It was as good as calling it *The Effects of Intemperance*. But he had omitted to include a neglected, ailing child, a crushed rose and a pawn-ticket sticking out of the man's pocket. So the bare statement, concerning these two bedraggled human beings, was found profoundly shocking.

So much for Degas. The market for the more truly Impressionist painters in 1872–1914 found no echo at all in the London salerooms, but for those who study this exciting market to-day, the following comparative scale for the end of the nineteenth century should be interesting. All but Manet and Van Gogh were still at work, and the saleroom prices (with these exceptions and one other) may be taken as typical of the fees the painters could earn:

			£
1899	Cézanne	*Neige fondante*	270
1900	Degas	*Le Ballet*	564
1895	Gauguin	*Manao Tapapau*	36
1900	Van Gogh	*Hollyhocks*	44
1898	Manet	*The Alabama off Boulogne*	800
1898	Monet	*Au jardin*	880
1900	Pissarro	*River Bank*	320
1899	Renoir	*Déjeuner des canotiers*	884
1900	Sisley	*Inondation*	614

The most remarkable feature of this list is Renoir's *Canotiers*, one of his most famous works and to-day worth quite a quarter of a million, but ranking no higher than Monet and only a little above Sisley. The Cézanne price is deceptive, because Monet bought the picture and, to help Cézanne, he employed someone to bid against himself.

Between 1900 and 1912 the advance in these values was only moderate, though in 1907 the Metropolitan Museum paid £3,500 for Renoir's *Les enfants de Mme. Charpentier*. Serious acceleration began after 1910, when a spate of Fauvist, Cubist and Futurist exhibitions threatened to do for traditional European civilisation all that Prinzip's hand-bomb did at Sarajevo in 1914. It was no doubt an advantage to the market of the Impressionists that the young men had begun to abuse them. Of Corot's works (they generally lumped him with Impressionism on the English and American markets) no less than six made from £12,000 to £17,000 in 1910–1912. In 1913 it was said that Senator Clarke had given £33,000 for *The Fisherman*, the work of the pioneering, but oh so dull, Théodore Rousseau.

1912 saw the legendary Rouart sale. It cost Mrs. Montgomery Sears £21,000 to win the *Danseuse à la barre* of Degas and to present it to the Louvre. Manet's *Buste de Femme* was bought in at £3,880 and Cézanne's *Baigneuses* went to the Barnes Foundation at £720 'amidst applause and admiration'. But that was a mere foretaste of the sale in Paris in 1913 of the collection of Count Mariczell de Nemés of Budapest. There were five expensive Cézannes, and the famous *Boy in the Red Waistcoat*, which made £220,000 in 1958, fetched £3,600. A Van Gogh still-life made £1,450 and Manet's *Rue de Berne*, which had been bought for £540 in 1899, now made £3,180.

That was in June 1913, three weeks after the great McCulloch sale.

CHAPTER SEVEN

The Treasures Depart
1884–1929

1. The Marlborough Sale: Rubens and Van Dyck — 2. The Return of the Eighteenth Century — 3. The Early Continental Schools

---

1. *The Marlborough Sale: Rubens and Van Dyck*

We have seen something of the indifference with which the emigration of the rarest works was regarded in mid-Victorian England. Those who might have been shocked to know the truth comforted themselves with a thought, which one sometimes finds expressed in newspaper articles of the period. It was that the real treasures of the country were so heavily protected by entail or by the mere strength of family sentiment as to be inviolable. Before the year 1882 it was very rare in London for even part of a noble inheritance to come under the hammer. The collections that were dispersed belonged chiefly to out-and-out speculators or they belonged to scholars, whose heirs could not afford to retain their possessions. In spite of a very considerable movement of works of art, families that had amassed immense collections over the ages, such as the Churchills, Grosvenors, Cavendishes, Russells and many others, were far from having to part with anything. Thus the doctrine of inviolable security was still expressed even in the early 'eighties, when the Americans began to show their hand as a nation prepared to buy at any price.

But it was precisely at this moment that events conspired to demolish the last bulwark of complacency. Since the opening up of the prairie lands in the early 'seventies, the Americans had been exporting wheat at a cut-throat price. No British government of the day would have dared to stop the entry of this wheat by restoring the hated tariff that had been repealed in 1846. Fatalistically, Liberal and Conservative governments alike watched the decline of English agriculture and the population-drift to industry. Wheat fell from 56*s*. 9*d*. a quarter in 1877 to 31*s*. 6*d*. in 1886. By the year 1880, 28½ percent of British wheat-bearing land had gone out of cultivation and 65 percent of the nation's wheat came from across the Atlantic,[1] a higher proportion than to-day. The consequent fall in rents was far more damaging to the position of the great hereditary estates than the Reform Bill of 1832. Unable to sell off settled land or heirlooms, many families found it impossible to maintain their homes.

To meet the emergency, the Settled Lands Act of 1882 made it possible for the trustees of settlements, on application to Chancery, to sell off both land and chattels, provided that the proceeds remained under trusteeship.[2] Some of the results were perceived in March 1884, when *The Times* published an important article mentioning in covert fashion Henry G. Marquand's purchases of the previous year from the Marquess of Lansdowne at Bowood, objects 'whose owner most persons would have supposed to have been as likely to part with the bones of his ancestors as to part with the family collection to a foreigner'. The article declared that 'the tide had set in a contrary direction, but not as yet in overwhelming force'. The nation must make up its mind to buy these treasures or to 'see them lost for ever'.

In June 1884 Sir James Robinson of the Victoria and Albert Museum pointed out in *The Times* that it was now easy to alienate an heirloom. The Leigh Court and the Blenheim collections were about to come under the hammer, and there was a danger that the finest works would 'go to the Rothschilds or to Vanderbilt'. Some action followed this letter. At the Fountaine sale, a few days later, a syndicate of collectors and curators attempted to buy the finest lots of maiolica, sixteenth-century French faïence and Limoges enamels, with the intention of offering them to the nation at cost price. The 'syndicate' found guarantors for £24,000, but were only able to spend £10,000, so fantastic had prices become. Some of them have not been equalled even in the 1950's. Ferdinand de Rothschild paid £7,350 for an oval Limoges

[1] R. C. K. Ensor, *England, 1870–1914*, p. 116.

[2] Legally an heirloom could already be disposed of where there was no trusteeship. See the highly diverting counsel's opinion on this subject in Anthony Trollope's *Eustace Diamonds* of 1873.

enamel dish of the Henri II period. The Vienna Rothschilds gave £4,452 for a sixteenth-century ivory hunting horn. A St. Porchaire pottery *flambeau* of fearsome intricacy went to Paris at £3,675. Never have the stage properties of Alexandre Dumas been so highly esteemed.

A year later, on the eve of the Beckett Denison sale, *The Times* observed that, in spite of the trade depression (see page 160), the Act of 1882 was still securing the prosperity and popularity of the saleroom. But the writer had mistaken the symptoms. Both the old-master and the *objets d'art* market needed the competition of the Rothschilds to stop the downward drift. The Earl of Dudley and the Marquess of Hertford were both dead, and there was no other English collector like them. At the Hamilton Palace sale of 1882 the mysterious and ill-fated Beckett-Denison had spent more than £100,000. Yet in one of the most disappointing of Christie's recorded sales all these purchases declined in value. The trade depression had been underestimated.

In the following year, 1886, a General Election took place in June on account of Gladstone's defeat over the Irish Home Rule Bill. The most spectacular product of the Settled Lands Act, the sale of treasures from Blenheim Palace, was due. Wisely the Duke of Marlborough postponed the sale till the end of July. But the more important pictures had already been sold by private negotiation. It was indeed the beginning of a period in which the salerooms played a minor part in the movement of works of art from England. In the salerooms a Landseer or a Millais could be left to take its chance among several competing dealers, who knew their clients, but all through the 'nineties the works of the past were difficult to handle. It was not till after 1900, when Duveen Brothers had established a strong American market, that London again became the centre for old-master sales, which it had been before the Second Empire. It is remarkable that as late as 1901 Mr. A. C. R. Carter could not record more than one sale that brought in £20,000 in the course of the year.

In the 'eighties and 'nineties the drift was not yet mainly towards the U.S.A. Apart from Rembrandt, the emphasis among American collectors was towards the modern French school and only in a very small degree towards the English eighteenth century. The obvious clients for freed British heirlooms were the branches of the House of Rothschild and the 'Berlin Museum'. Most of the *objets d'art*, as opposed to paintings, went to Paris, where the market was very much stronger. Hence the depressing reiteration of the names of French dealers at the Hamilton Palace, Andrew Fountaine and Hollingworth Magniac (1892) sales.

But there was nothing till the end of the century to equal the incredible sales which were negotiated by the Duke of Marlborough in 1884–1885. It was known early in 1884 that proceedings were on foot to free the picture gallery at Blenheim Palace. At once Sir Frederick Leighton petitioned Gladstone to rescue for the nation a group of pictures which included Raphael's *Ansidei Madonna* and Van Dyck's equestrian *Charles I.* But, in May 1884, the Trustees of the National Gallery were informed abruptly by the Treasury that the purchase was out of the question. It was then a matter of twenty-three pictures costing £400,000, or six specially selected pictures costing £165,000 and averaging £27,500 each. The reader may be reminded that at this moment only one picture in the whole of history had fetched more than £20,000 and that was Soult's Murillo, the *Immaculate Conception,* in 1852.

The Treasury now relented to the extent of allowing Sir Frederick Burton to put his own valuation on the pictures. This came to £264,875 for the eleven best pictures, including £115,500 for the *Ansidei Madonna* alone. But even for this reduced number the Duke still wanted £367,500. Gladstone was prepared to recommend to Parliament the purchase of the *Ansidei Madonna* at £70,000 or alternatively the expenditure of £100,000 on this picture, together with the Van Dyck *King Charles* and the Rubens *Garden of the Hesperides.* The Duke replied, declaring that better offers had been received already, and that the trustees of the Blenheim Estate would not be content with less than double this sum for the three pictures alone. The Treasury's next move was to knock out the second most costly picture, the Rubens *Garden of the Hesperides* and to offer £85,000 for the Raphael and the Van Dyck. Somewhat unexpectedly, the Duke telegraphed from Switzerland his acceptance of £70,000 for the *Ansidei Madonna.* Later he accepted £17,500 for the Van Dyck.

Seeing that the dull *Colonna Altarpiece* was on offer in 1884 for £40,000 and that the Metropolitan Museum had just been asked the same price for the *Monro Madonna,* the acceptance of £70,000 for the *Ansidei Madonna* was more than fair. The actual Treasury Grant, required for the two purchases, was £83,250, but Parliament did not pass the supplementary estimate till 6th March 1885, when the Opposition complained that even the notorious *Immaculate Conception* had not cost the Louvre more than £24,600. Mr. William Agnew then rose to point out that 'there was a great gulf in point of educative value between a Raphael and a Murillo'. Remarking that there were now national galleries even in Boston and St. Louis, Mr. Agnew gave his view that 'within the past twenty-five years the value of high class art had quintupled'.

The estimate was passed, though the Hon. Member for West Surrey said that King Charles's horse was not fit for a knacker's yard. And on the whole the economists had little of which to complain, for they stopped the National Gallery Grant in Aid for the next two years. The Duke of Marlborough, who had hoped to get £367,500 for eleven pictures outside the saleroom, sold them for £223,000, but even that much-reduced sum was something beyond all precedent in 1884–1885. For the picture of the *Family of Rubens* together with *Helena Fourment and a Page*, Alfonse de Rothschild of Paris paid £57,750. For the *Garden of the Hesperides*, which is now at Waddesdon Manor, Christie's negotiated a price for Ferdinand de Rothschild of £26,250. The Kaiser Friedrich Museum paid over £15,000 for the *Andromeda*, Rubens's most attractive single nude, £10,000 for the too exuberant *Drunken Silenus*, £5,000 for a small Holbein of a young man, and £11,000 for the reputed Raphael portrait of *La Fornarina*, now ascribed to Sebastiano del Piombo, an ample lady looking rather like Ingres's portrait of Mme. Moitessier. The Van Dyck double portrait of *Lady Morton and Mrs. Killigrew* and the Reynolds fancy portrait, *The Little Fortune Teller*, were said to have been negotiated at 5,000 guineas each. For yet another Rubens, *The Venus and Adonis*, a copy of the picture at Düsseldorf, the Duke failed to get £15,000 from M. Sedelmeyer, as the Press believed, and at the 1886 sale it had to be bought-in at £7,560 (now Metropolitan Museum).

The five privately sold pictures by Rubens from Blenheim Palace were not only several times as costly as any previously sold Rubens paintings, but they were also without rival till 1935 when the Metropolitan Museum paid over £50,000 for Pierpont Morgan's portrait of *Anne of Austria*, despite the fact that *Klassiker der Kunst* listed it as a good school-replica of the Prado picture. At the 1886 Blenheim sale it had been bought-in for £3,885. Nowadays, when a very humdrum Rubens altarpiece can make £275,000 in open competition, it is hard to realise that between 1885 and 1935 it was very rare for a Rubens picture to make £10,000 even by State purchase. Throughout this period Rubens prices were flat, because the puritanical taste of American millionaires was against masses of flesh. Instead of being dominated by the traditional association between Rubens and the taste of courts, the world market was dominated by the Anglo-Saxon prejudice against Rubens, which had prevailed in the mid-eighteenth century and in early Victorian times.

The unique prices of 1884–1885 had been entirely due to the Rothschilds. The family passion for objects with royal and noble pedigrees had always been extravagant, and never more than now. Redford believed that Alfonse de Rothschild had paid £35,000 for the *Family of Rubens* alone. Yet in 1931 *Klassiker der Kunst* placed it firmly in the category of doubtful pictures, 'probably by Bockhorst'. The companion picture, which cost apparently £22,750 in 1884, has none of the splendour of other Helena Fourment portraits and is not universally accepted in the Rubens canon; nor is the *Garden of Hesperides*, which Gustav Gluck in 1920 described as a concoction, based on the Prado Museum picture. £84,000 for three dubious pictures and only forty years had passed since Ruskin had attacked the National Gallery for spending £4,200 on one of Rubens's absolute masterpieces, *The Judgement of Paris*.

Eighteen Rubens paintings were left to face the saleroom, most of them works painted only under Rubens's direction and some of them copies. The best was *Lot and his daughters leaving Sodom*, for which Sedelmeyer had been wrongly reported to have given £10,000. Bought by Charles Butler for only £1,942, it made £6,825 in 1911. In December 1912, when it was exhibited in Toronto as the property of Sir James Ross, it was believed by *American Art News* that *Lot and his daughters* had cost 500,000 dollars. It was, none the less, sold at Christie's in 1927 for £2,205.

Next to Wilton, Blenheim Palace had more alleged Van Dyck portraits than any house in the country, and twelve remained to be disposed of. Only one made over a thousand pounds, the whole-length portrait of the *Duchess of Lennox and Richmond with Mrs. Gibson the dwarf*, now at Wilton (£1,207 10*s*.). Although to-day considered a second replica of a picture in America, it was just the sort of work that might have changed hands in the early 1900's at £70,000. Millais paid only £241 10*s*. for *Time clipping Cupid's Wings* (Musée Jacquemart-André), a picture not in Van Dyck's happiest vein but considered perfectly authentic. *The Times* nevertheless thought that the Van Dycks had done much better than the Rubens pictures. It was not thought worthy of comment that a *Visit to the Harem*, by Henrietta Brown [Sophie Desaux, 1829–1901], had just made more than the *Duchess of Richmond*, but 1886 was such a depressed year that no one could think beyond Clark Hook and Briton Riviére (see page 155).

The Americans were not yet interested in Van Dyck, nor was there any improvement in prices till 1900 when two of Van Dyck's very finest portraits, *The Genoese Senator and His Wife*, came to Christie's.

Imported by Buchanan through Irvine in the early 1800's, they had been bought by Sir Robert Peel in the 1830's on Wilkie's strenuous recommendation for £800. They now cost the Kaiser Friedrich Museum £24,250. In 1905 Lord Ashburton's portraits of *Charles I* and *Henrietta Maria* were expected to fetch at least as much, but they were school-pieces which would not have made £17,850 if the young Duveen had not stepped unwarily into this dangerous territory.

But it was now possible to play off four multi-millionaires against one another: Pierpont Morgan, P. A. B. Widener, Benjamin Altman and Henry Clay Frick. To-day, when it must be twenty years since a Van Dyck last fetched £10,000, it is hard to realise that in 1906 Van Dyck became the highest priced painter in the world when P. A. B. Widener paid Knoedler £103,300 for the *Marchesa Grimaldi-Cattaneo*. Only one other picture had made £100,000 and that was Raphael's *Colonna Altarpiece*, bought by Pierpont Morgan in 1900 (see page 114). The craze for Van Dyck in 1906 resembled the craze for Rubens in 1884 and for Murillo in 1852, but in this case there was also the spice of adventure. It seems that Widener's five Van Dycks and several others, all from the Cattaneo, Durazzo and Adorno families, had been sold to a French dealer by the Marchese Cesare Imperiale. According to legend, the strict Italian export laws had been evaded by taking the pictures from Genoa to Nice, one by one, concealed in an additional exhaust pipe attached to a vast touring car of interesting vintage.

What may be called the exhaust-pipe plot had an astonishing effect on Van Dyck prices for a whole generation. The two small, but very fine, Cattaneo portraits, which the National Gallery was able to obtain from the leavings in 1907, cost the nation £27,000. A full-length portrait from the Genoese series, which had been in England since the early nineteenth century, the Earl of Abercorn's *Paolina Adorno*, cost Henry Clay Frick £82,400 in January 1914. As much, or more, was paid by Widener in 1909 for a very much finer portrait of this lady from the Earl of Warwick's collection. As late as 1928 the *Abbé Scaglia* could make £31,500 at open auction in London, while in private Duveen sold the Earl of Northbrook's *Henrietta Maria with Geoffrey Hudson the dwarf* to Randolph Hearst for £77,500.

The startling innovation of paying high prices for portraits of the ancestors of perfect strangers had begun at the King of Holland's sale of 1850, when Lord Hertford gave £5,300 for Van Dyck's by no means aristocratic likenesses of *M. and Mme. Leroy*. In the 1870's and 1880's the Van Dyck portrait cult wilted and lagged behind the English eighteenth-century cult, then overtook it and finally shared its apogee and its decline. Nevertheless, the inspiration of the two cults was not quite the same. At some time after 1909 Mr. Widener might have learned that his *Lady Brook* from the Warwick Collection was another *Paolina Adorno*, that the great Dr. Waagen had mistaken the physiognomy of his hosts. More than ever since the affair of the extra exhaust pipe, it must have been realised that the finest of the Van Dyck portraits had been painted, not in England, but in Genoa, where Van Dyck had spent five years as a young man [1622–1627]. You could not create for yourself the right sort of English ancestor out of Durazzo's, Imperiales and Cattaneos. Probably, therefore, it was wish-fulfilment rather than ancestry building which made a truly extravagant cult of Van Dyck. A millionaire of the second generation would have liked to have posed for Van Dyck with a wolfhound or a dwarf beside him. A millionaire of the first generation would not have had the nerve. He would have preferred to be painted by Frans Hals.

2. *The Return of the Eighteenth Century*

It is still a little inexplicable that the art market should have been so dominated by portraits between the 1870's and the 1920's. It is equally mystifying that among the new prices in the region of £70,000 to £100,000, which began soon after 1900, there should have been several Van Dycks, a number of Gainsboroughs, two Romneys, a Lawrence, a Reynolds and even a Hoppner.

While the movement became a craze after 1870, it was already apparent in the 1850's, though the real causes had not yet manifested themselves. The first impulse was a form of sentimentality. The executor sales of Samuel Rogers in 1856 and of Lord Northwick in 1859 created romantic values for Reynolds and Gainsborough, because these almost centenarian collectors had been their last living contemporaries. But it needed something more than that to release the positive mania for the eighteenth century, that beset the late 'sixties and early 'seventies, a mania that embraced Thackeray's later novels, the creation of the so-called Queen Anne house, the replacement of Jacobean oak and pseudo-gothic pitch pine with cream panelling and walnut furniture; a mania that embraced the Gainsborough pastiches of Millais, the eighteenth-century subjects of Orchardson and Marcus Stone and the jolliest and most expensive revival in women's fashions that ever was.

Writing in 1926 in his history of Christie's, Mr. H. C. Marillier pointed out rather ingeniously that,[1] while a man does not normally sell his mother's portrait or his grandmother's, he has no qualms about his great-grandmother. For this reason the cult of Reynolds and Gainsborough started earlier than the cult of Hoppner, Raeburn, Beechey and Lawrence. Now this makes a good enough explanation for a sudden spate of Reynolds or Gainsborough great-grandmothers on the market in the 1860's, but it does not explain why strangers were prepared to buy them and at tremendous prices. When Marillier wrote, the cult was over sixty years old and was no doubt expected to last for ever. In fact, anticipating a never-ending demand for British ancestor paintings, Marillier provided old masters for the future—the things we are expected to buy in 1962—from among the portraitists of the early Victorian age. His choice was Watson-Gordon, Daniel Macnee, Thomas Philips, John Linnell Jnr., James South and G. F. Watts.

The same assumption had been made by A. C. R. Carter, writing in *The Year's Art* in 1911. Noting that even a Raeburn picture had now reached the five-figure class, he commented that 'the market which depletes must fill'. In order to satisfy the apparently permanent and insatiable American demand for the English school, Carter proposed, not early Victorian portraitists, but minor late eighteenth-century ones whom the saleroom had not yet conspicuously honoured; Lemuel Abbott, Daniel Gardner, William Hobday, John Downman, the Rev. Peters, John Highmore, William Owen, James Rising, Francis Cotes.

At this distance of time we can see that out of Marillier's list, only Watts excites a mild and strictly insular interest, while out of Carter's list there is in fact a modest home market for Gardner, Downman, Highmore and Cotes. Both assumptions were faulty. No rule exists by which portraits become suitable for millionaires at a given age, nor does such a rule exist for anything else—otherwise Queen Victoria's Balmoral gothic furniture of the 1860's would be making as much in modern money as the commode and secretaire of Marie Antoinette made at the Hamilton Palace sale in 1882, that is to say about £60,000 apiece. It may well be that, when a historical taste such as this is traced to its ultimate source, it will be found that the source is nothing but an accident.

That the taste for these portraits should have appealed to the Rothschild dynasty sprang from the fact that the Rothschilds were representatives of a social group, among whom the love of an eighteenth-century *décor*, not English, but French, had never died. Although the

[1] H. C. Marillier, *op. cit.*, p. 244.

taste for French painting of the *ancien régime* was completely extinguished by the Revolution and the Empire and did not recover till the 1840's, the taste for the ormolu-mounted furniture and Sèvres porcelain, that went with it, survived in exile. In England under the Regency these objects, which had been so costly to make, could be had fairly cheaply. In the 1820's the price rose through the competition of Beckford, Watson Taylor, the Duke of Buckingham and the father of the collecting Marquess of Hertford. The vast forced clearance sale of the Duke of Buckingham at Stowe in 1848 was remarkable both for the profusion of objects of this kind and for the competition of several branches of the Rothschild family. But the Paris market remained astonishingly low even under the restored Bourbons. It was only in the late 1850's, when the Rothschilds began to plan whole palaces designed to go with their furniture, that the Paris market came into line with London. The neglected French painters of the eighteenth century had now returned to fashion—as decorator's accessories.

While the buying of English portraits had a snobbish motive, the French works were bought for their decorative qualities. These qualities were not apparent under the Empire, when the *décor* was Pompeian, nor under the restored monarchy, when it was Renaissance or early Louis XIV. Even in 1826, Watteau's *Carnival*, sold at the death of his solitary admirer, the Baron Vivant-Denon, made only £26. The rich relations of *Le cousin Pons* (published, 1847) had not even heard of Watteau's name. The revival of Watteau really began with the Fesch sale of 1845 when the *Fête in a Park* and *Halt during a Hunt* made £1,175 the pair.

Even now the market for Watteau and his school was English or cosmopolitan rather than French. In 1848, when the Marquess of Hertford paid £945 at Phillips's rooms for the *Champs Elysées* of the Wallace Collection, the *Art Union Magazine* described the price as outrageous and the climax of imbecile judgement. However, in 1852 Hertford paid the same price when the Fesch *Fête in a Park* reappeared. In 1857 Théodore Pâtureau's *Les deux Cousines* fetched £2,200, a price equivalent to those of the costliest Reynolds pictures at the Rogers and Northwick sales. Rather grudgingly M. Charles Blanc, former Directeur des Beaux Arts, wrote 'passe pour Watteau', but he exploded at the thought that Hertford had spent £1,160 on two pairs of decorative panels by Boucher. 'Only thirty years ago you could have got a pair of *dessus de porte* like these for £20.' And when four paintings by Pater made £1,800 between them, he declared that it was an insult to the masters of art.[1]

[1] Blanc, *op. cit.*, II, p. 533.

At this same sale in 1857 Hertford paid £1,100 for Gréuze's moist-eyed, soulful *Psyche*, almost a replica of another Greuze for which he had paid the same price in 1846. That did not upset M. Blanc. Greuze was the Murillo of the French eighteenth-century school, fitting the early Victorian age so well as to be proof against devaluation. By shuttlecocking between Hertford and Dudley, Greuze's young women, generally tearful and always *enceinte*, stayed in the higher regions of the art market for the next thirty years. Hertford bought at least twenty-nine Greuze heads, not all of them in the Wallace Collection. He spent on Greuze more than £20,000. In 1845 the *Votive Offering to Cupid* cost £1,540, in 1852 *La Pelottoneuse* cost £3,360, in 1870 *Les Œufs Cassés* cost £5,040. And all this was capped in 1876 when Dudley paid £6,720 for *A Girl carrying a puppy*, now in the Bearsted Collection at Upton.

The subject of Blanc's rage in 1857 had been the bidding up of mere decorator's pictures, pagan and frivolous in content, when so much uplifting sentiment was to be had. Millionaire taste was already changing, though for some time to come it accepted both worlds. Of this market Watteau was not the key-painter, for his subjects were seldom painted on the decorator's scale and his faulty pigments had browned rapidly. It was François Boucher [1704–1770] who showed the change to perfection. At the Gore House sale of 1849 two oval portraits of the Princesse de Croy made only 12 and 18 guineas. At the Montlouis sale in Paris in 1851 the oval panels, *Diana and Calisto* and *Angelica and Medora* made £130 the four. In New York in 1957 they made £25,000. The first important price for Boucher was paid in 1860, £1,260 for Sir Culling Eardley's large painting of nymphs. In 1874 Alexander Barker's eight big upright panels from the Château de Crècy (and later at Wilton) made £6,352. In 1903 five of these panels were bought for Sir Joseph Robinson at £23,415. In the meantime Wertheimer had bought one of the big Pompadour portraits for Maurice de Rothschild at the Lonsdale sale of 1887 for £10,395. The climax of this decorator's market was reached in Europe at the Michelham sale of 1926, when Captain Jefferson Cohen paid £47,250 for the two panels *La Pipée aux Oiseaux* and *La Fontaine d'Amour* in order that they might remain on the staircase of Arlington House.

The works of Jean Honoré Fragonard [1732–1806] show very much the same pattern. In 1841, when the Paris market was dominated by Murillo and Greuze and the modern romantic painters, the small *School-mistress* cost Hertford no more than £15 10*s*. But at the Morny sale of 1865, two quite small panels, *Le Souvenir* and *Les Plaisirs de l'Escarpolette*, cost him £1,400 and £1,208. As to Fragonard's big decorative panels, which were much rarer than Boucher's, the history of the ten panels called *Roman d'Amour de la Jeunesse* will suffice. They were obtained by Agnew from M. Malvitain in 1898 and sold to James Pierpont Morgan for £64,000. In 1915 they were bought by Joseph Duveen and sold to Frick for £205,500—more than £20,000 a panel.

It seems now almost inconceivable that Boucher could ever have rated higher than Watteau. *The Luteplayer*, bought by the Stockholm National Museum in America some years ago, was said to have cost close on a quarter of a million pounds. Yet the great *Enseigne de Gersaint*, one of the masterpieces of all time, was sold in Paris in 1886 for about £350 and went quietly to Charlottenberg. The highest English auction price for a Watteau painting is still the £6,510 which was made by a *Fête Champêtre* in 1913. The two paintings in the National Gallery, *L'Accord parfait* and *La Gamme d'Amour*, were sold, the one in 1891 for £3,675, the other in 1895 for £3,517 10*s*. More than this would be paid to-day for one of Watteau's drawings.

Mid-Victorian and late-Victorian prices for the best works of the French eighteenth-century school were certainly not high even by the standards of the day and, despite their greater rarity, they seldom competed with the most expensive of the English portraits. The excessive valuation of the English school must have owed a great deal to the residence of the Vienna-born Baron Ferdinand de Rothschild in England, particularly after 1874, when he began the construction of Waddesdon Manor, a fantasy palace, externally a French Renaissance château, but decorated internally in the strictest, most perfect mid eighteenth-century French taste.

The original plan may have been to fill this setting with French paintings. Several examples of Watteau and Boucher, as well as tapestries after the same school, were bought. In giving pride of place to English whole-length portraits, Ferdinand de Rothschild followed the example of the head of the English branch of the family, Lionel Nathan de Rothschild [1808–1879], who had paid £3,150 for Reynolds's *Miss Stanhope* in 1872. In 1873 Ferdinand de Rothschild bought Gainsborough's flamboyant and rather shallow portrait of *Mrs. Sheridan* for the same price. It was the beginning of the Gainsborough portrait cult, for Gainsborough portraits then rated well below those of Reynolds, as they had done in Gainsborough's own lifetime. Hertford had paid £2,771 10*s*. for Reynolds's *Mrs. Richard Hoare and her child* as far back as 1859, whereas the most that had been paid for a Gainsborough portrait before 1872 was the sum of £1,000 each which the National

Gallery had given in 1862 for *Dr. Ralph Schomburg* and *Mrs. Siddons seated.*

In fact in the early 'seventies Gainsborough's landscapes fetched more than his portraits, in keeping with a general English preference for landscapes. In 1867 Lord Tweedmouth gave £3,147 for one of the several versions of the *Harvest Wagon* theme, while in 1875 the Earl of Dudley, now past his thirtieth year of picture-buying, gave £3,640 for *Returning from Market.* High as these landscape prices were in comparison with any of the orthodox old masters, the Rothschild family's interest now drove Gainsborough's portraits much higher. In 1873 the Baron Ferdinand failed to get the *Misses Ramus*, which made more than any of Gillott's Turners, £6,615. He retrieved the picture in the saleroom in 1887 at £9,997 and three years later lost it in a fire at Waddesdon.

Till his death in 1885, the Earl of Dudley fought the Baron for these newly-esteemed treasures. The most famous of these duels, in which neither won, was in 1876, the year of the disappearing *Duchess.*

The sale of Wynn Ellis's *Duchess of Devonshire* was one of the most completely irrational things that have happened in the history of collecting. It was well known that the Gainsborough attribution was flimsy, that the only recorded version of the subject was at Althorp, that the picture was much cut down and heavily restored. A few could even have noticed that the parts which were not restored looked hardly worthy of Gainsborough's brush at its best. Yet the picture made more than the work of any British painter of the past, more than any picture that had been sold at a British auction, more than any Rubens, Titian, Van Dyck or Rembrandt. But Dudley was after it, Rothschild was after it, Agnew was after it and an unknown got it.

Wynn Ellis, the silk-manufacturer and radical M.P., who died in 1875, had bought hundreds of old-master paintings, some of which he left to the National Gallery, besides several expensive Turners and the *Duchess.* Such was the glamour of the eighteenth century in 1876 that for the sake of a likeness of the famous Georgina the whole of King Street was blocked with carriages, which overflowed into St. James's Square. Wynn Ellis's picture had been bought in the 1850's from a picture-restorer, named Bentley, for £63. Bentley had reduced it to a half-length, because the Duchess had already been deprived of her foot in order to accommodate her to the modest mantelpiece of a Mrs. Magennis, a schoolmistress, who, strange to say, had bought the huge thing at an auction in 1839 for £50. In the late 1880's the knowing Mr. A. C. R. Carter was acquainted with a certain Partington, who claimed that he had been employed as a youth by Bentley to 'paint the *Duchess*'.

What was the real truth about this picture, which looks like a copy of the Althorp picture with a large hat clapped on it? Henry Labouchére maintained that it was not the famous Georgina, wife of the 4th Duke, but the portrait of Lady Elizabeth Forster, who was destined to marry the 5th Duke, though not till 1809. It was a fact that in 1778, five years before painting the Althorp picture, Gainsborough had done a whole-length of Lady Elizabeth Forster. It has been suggested that Wynn Ellis's picture was an unfinished replica of this work, which someone, either Gainsborough's nephew, Gainsborough Dupont, or another, had converted into an imitation of the Althorp *Georgina*. Nothing so ingenious had been thought out in 1876, and the lack of record was not in itself a disproof of authenticity. But the painting spoke for itself. Millais, who had been studying Gainsborough's methods pretty hard in the 1870's, strode down Christie's great staircase, shouting to George Redford,[1] 'I don't believe Gainsborough ever saw it.' Some of those who noted the niggled, fussy appearance of the picture, when it faced the public at the Metropolitan Museum in January 1913, were inclined to agree.[2]

In a spellbound saleroom, where the bidding shot from 1,000 guineas to 3,000 at a single call, the *Duchess* was knocked down to Mr. Morland Agnew for 10,100 guineas (£10,605). It was then disclosed that the Earl of Dudley had been the underbidder at 10,000 guineas.

Agnews had bought the picture for stock, and they kept in on exhibition in Bond Street for three weeks. On the 29th May the American banker, Junius Spencer Morgan, accepted Agnew's price. He had decided suddenly to give the picture to his son, James Pierpont Morgan. With dealer's commission and U.S. excise duty, the picture would have cost him £14,000 or £15,000 at the very least. Thus the schoolmistress's mutilated picture had multiplied its value 300 times in thirty-seven years to become the second most expensive picture in the world, or rather it would have done had it not been stolen from the gallery that very night. It was not seen again until 1901.

During these twenty-five years it was known that the thieves had attempted to obtain ransom from Agnews, but that Scotland Yard had intervened and that the picture had then been smuggled out of the country. The most probable reconstruction of the events[3] is that Adam Worth and his international gang hid the *Duchess* in the lining of a mattress in lodgings in St. John's Wood. They hoped to get enough from Agnews to bail out an accomplice, who was in Newgate waiting

[1] Redford, *op. cit.*, p. 220 (1888). [2] *American Art News*, XI, 15.
[3] A. C. R. Carter: *Let me tell you*, 1942.

extradition to the U.S.A. The failure of the blackmail and the unexpected release of the accomplice deprived the theft of all meaning. The *Duchess* became a dead weight to the thieves, hidden uselessly in a Chicago warehouse. Only when the gang were all dead was it thought safe to resume negotiations. Agnews received their picture in a Chicago hotel, the *Duchess's* homecoming was greeted with a music-hall song and Pierpont Morgan was so determined to have the picture, which his father had intended for him, that he paid a price for this disreputable object which has been estimated at £32,000 and even £35,000.

The 10,000-guinea bid of 1876 had now established a precedent. In 1886 Redford believed that the 1st Lord Rothschild (Nathaniel Meyer Rothschild) [1840–1915] had paid £20,000 for Reynolds's picture of *Garrick between Tragedy and Comedy*, a price that was perhaps inspired by the recent family purchases from Blenheim Palace. Even more impressive was the price, paid in 1895, for the oval Gainsborough portrait of *Lady Mulgrave*. Measuring 29 ins. × 24½ ins., Gainsborough had probably received no more than 25 guineas for it. But it was bought by M. Camille Groult, a rival and contemporary of Prince Florizel of Bohemia, who produced £10,500 in banknotes and took the picture to Paris in a private steam-launch which he had moored by the Embankment.[1]

In 1894 Samson Wertheimer bid £11,150 for Reynolds's large and simpering *Mrs. Delmé and her children*. The real client was James Pierpont Morgan, who had inherited a fortune in 1890, estimated at £2,600,000, an event which he celebrated by offering £15,000 for Gainsborough's *Beggar Boy and Girl* at Knole. It was a portent that the Rothschild market had given way to the Americans. In 1896 Isabella Stewart Gardner offered £40,000 for the Duke of Westminster's *Blue Boy*,[2] more even than Morgan paid five years later for the erring *Duchess*.

In the 1890's American buyers were interested for the first time in Romney, Hoppner, Raeburn and Lawrence, whose market had hitherto been far below that of Reynolds and Gainsborough. Since their work had been almost entirely restricted to portraiture, it had been practically worthless before the 1870's. The portraits of Lawrence, commissioned in many cases at 700 guineas, only once made £300 between 1831 and 1872. Hoppner's portraits fetched so little that Graves found only three worth recording at all between 1804 and 1887. In 1852, in the last few months of his life, the Duke of Wellington bought Lord Liverpool's

[1] A. C. R. Carter: *Let me tell you*, 1942.
[2] Aline B. Saarinnen: *The Proud Possessors*, 1959, p. 34.

portrait of Pitt for £157 10*s*. As to Raeburn, there was an awakening of interest in 1877, when the Raeburn family executors put a collection of forty-nine works into Christie's, clearing about £6,000. Previous to that year Redford could record only William Russell's portrait of Walter Scott as a young man, bought-in at £3 5*s*. in 1863. Romney did a little better. Though even his big portrait groups usually fetched under £100 till 1875,[1] *Lady Hamilton as St. Cecilia* made £472 10*s*. in 1860 and *John Wesley* made £556 10*s*. in 1872.

The entry of Lawrence, Raeburn, Romney and Hoppner into the millionaire market is generally credited to one man, namely Joseph Duveen, Jnr., later Lord Millbank. But it will be clear by this time that the basis for a revaluation of the entire English late eighteenth-century portrait school existed in the 1870's, if not the 1860's. The firm of Duveen had grown from small beginnings in 1869, but hardly handled pictures at all before 1901 and certainly not English eighteenth-century pictures. In 1901 when the future Lord Millbank paid £14,752 for Hoppner's *Lady Louisa Manners*, the auction record then for any English picture, the firm paid for entering the territory of others. Pierpont Morgan failed to purchase this indifferent performance, and *Lady Louisa Manners* was sold at a loss.[2] It was in reality Samson Wertheimer who created a millionaire's market in Gainsborough's contemporaries. In 1896, for instance, Samson Wertheimer paid £11,025 for Romney's big group, the *Spencer Sisters, Allegory of Music*. He had given £2,850 for *Lady Hamilton in a Welsh hat* as early as 1889. In 1902 he gave £6,825 for the Raeburn group, now at Washington, *The Sons of D. N. Binning*. Raeburn had died in 1823, Lawrence in 1830. Both these painters were therefore hardly of old-master status in the 'nineties. Nevertheless in 1897 the famous *Nelly Farren* of 1790, the picture that had made Lawrence's reputation, fetched as much as £2,415. But within a few years it was bought by Pierpont Morgan, reputedly for £20,000.

Doubtless Lawrence had attractions as a link between a past that had now become very romantic indeed and a generation that was still living. About the year 1900 Morgan bought the portrait of *Miss Croker*. Lawrence had painted it as a gift in 1827, but had subsequently asked 150 guineas, because he was being dunned by creditors. But the lady was alive. She was ninety-three years old and she sent the millionaire her photograph, which he hung with the picture at Prince's Gate.

[1] *The Stanhope Children* (£4,835 in 1906) was bought privately by Mr. Woods of Christie's in 1872 for 28 guineas.

[2] It was bought back by the firm in 1926 for £18,900.

This innocent romanticism played a large part in an episode in the history of taste that has become unintelligible to younger generations. In 1960, when some 6,000 people daily swallowed each other's carbon dioxide at the Tate Gallery Picasso exhibition, you could have proposed marriage or composed a sonnet in perfect peace among the adjoining Gainsboroughs, blissfully ignored by columns of organised youth who had come a long way to look at pictures. But if it was an aberration of taste, there have been worse aberrations. The article was perhaps a 90 percent commercialised product, but the gods that were worshipped varied in their falsity and the falsest were worshipped most.

Even so, between the 1870's and the 1920's, it was the best painter of the school, Gainsborough, who was generally at the top of the list, but the relative prices show a dismal lack of true discrimination. While the meretricious *Blue Boy* was sold in America in 1921 for £148,000, the National Gallery paid only £3,349 two years later for the smaller, unfinished and even more moving version of *The Painter's Daughters*. It is probable that in the 1920's *Mr. and Mrs. Andrews*, sold in 1960 for £130,000 and then acquired by the Nation, would not have fetched more than four or five thousands. Probably the Gainsboroughs that found their way to Frick and Huntington will have depreciated less than some of their other purchases, but it would have been a feat of the highest ingenuity, if not a technical impossibility, to have persuaded even the richest men on earth to choose from Gainsborough's works more injudiciously.

The competition of two men above all, Henry Clay Frick and Henry A. Huntington, both of them collectors for the sake of prestige and not for love of art, lifted the price of Gainsborough portraits into what may be called the Raphael class. This began in 1913, when Huntington, aged sixty-three, but as yet uninterested in the English eighteenth-century school, married the widow of his uncle Collis P. Huntington, the railway king. The first honours were with Frick, who paid Duveen that year, if the *American Art News* is to be credited, not less than £82,700 for Gainsborough's portrait of the *Hon. Frances Duncombe*. The picture had been through several hands, including that of Lionel de Rothschild, but was only a second replica of a portrait at Longford Castle. If it was a matter of paying a fortune for second replicas, Huntington was able to win the next round in 1915 by paying £50,000 for Lord Bessborough's replica of the Reynolds portrait of *Lavinia, Countess Spencer*. In 1916 it was Frick's turn, when he paid £62,000 for *The Mall in St. James's Park*, the most theatrical and superficial work of Gainsborough's worst period for which Duveen had had to give the same price.

If such things could be done during the full fury of Armageddon, it was not long afterwards that Huntington showed the world that he could sell out a hundred or two hundred thousand pounds' worth of shares as if he were paying for a dinner party. After having sounded Huntington while travelling to England on the *Aquitania* in 1921, Duveen persuaded the Duke of Westminster to part with Gainsborough's *Blue Boy* and *Cottage Door* together with Reynolds's *Mrs. Siddons, the Tragic Muse* for 620,000 dollars, or about £148,000 at the rate of exchange of the day. Duveen then sold Huntington *The Blue Boy* for the cost of the whole collection. The picture, which had been bought by the Duke's ancestor in 1802 for £68 5*s*., was now the second most expensive work of art in the world; dearer than the Colonna and Panshanger Raphaels, and surpassed only by the late Tsar's Leonardo, the *Benois Madonna*.

This legendary sale violated most of the rules of the game, for the subject was not a noble ancestor, but the son of Gainsborough's grocer. Moreover the code of the English portrait market has always been chivalrous; women and children first. In 1959, for instance, the ratio between the Earl of Chesterfield and his Countess was 2 : 7. In 1910, when the Gainsborough market had already soared into the higher regions, *Raphael Franco*, interesting in race as well as sex, was reputed a record for a male Gainsborough portrait at no more than £6,510.

Subsequently Huntington took *The Cottage Door* and *The Tragic Muse* at about £73,500 each, but the price of the latter was not a surprise. In July 1919, in the middle of the crazy wave of art speculation which followed the Armistice, the Duke had withdrawn *The Tragic Muse* from the saleroom at £54,600, Messrs. Gooden and Fox having bid up to £52,500. It is possible that at that moment Huntington might have had to go even higher for *The Tragic Muse*, for the time was much more propitious than 1921, a year of labour convulsions, inflated currencies and short credit everywhere.

Most of Huntington's Reynolds purchases were made in January 1925, that is to say, two years before his death. They came from the Spencer family at Althorp and they included a second *Lavinia, Countess Spencer*, the *Little fortune teller* (see page 179), *Lady Bingham* and the *Duchess of Devonshire*. It is probable that these were £50,000 to £60,000 pictures, but there was also a second *Duchess of Devonshire* by Gainsborough, none other than the original work, with which Wynn Ellis's notorious picture had become confused in 1876. This may have cost Huntington over £70,000, and when it was sold to Andrew Mellon after Huntington's death, probably £100,000.

The lower level of Reynolds will be noticed, but in the open saleroom the level was lower still. In the none too subtle millionaire décor Reynolds's famous *flying colours*, his deadened shadows, cracked asphaltum glazes and flaked high-lights told against him, whereas the French frilliness of Gainsborough's portraits, which had condemned them both in the artist's lifetime and for the next eighty years, was now his main attraction. As to Reynolds's sentimental fancy portraits of children, which had kept his reputation alive in early Victorian times, they hardly partook of the millionaire's feast. In May 1922 Christie's sold the Reynolds pictures that had belonged to the Baroness Burdett-Coutts. Nothing more romantic could be conceived than the background of this sale. The owner, who had just died at the age of ninety, had bid in person at the Samuel Rogers sale of 1856; she had known Rogers intimately as a girl and Rogers had known Reynolds. As Miss Angela Burdett-Coutts, she had virtually started the entire eighteenth-century revival on that memorable day, sixty-six years past. Yet the *Mob Cap*, so famous, so often imitated, rose from £819 to no more than £2,100, while *Cupid and Psyche* rose from £420 to £2,520. Only the *Girl Sketching*, in which Reynolds had refrained from sentiment, showed a substantial increase from £383 10*s*. to £5,460.

Even to-day the saleroom record for a Reynolds picture, as opposed to Huntington's purchases, is still the £19,425 which was paid in 1927 for *Lady Anne Fitzpatrick*—not by an American but by Lord Leverhulme. Since 1929 no Reynolds has fetched more than the £4,270 paid in New York in 1956 for the big double portrait of *Richard Barwell and his son*. The price, paid by the Edinburgh National Gallery in 1952 for *The Lacemakers, the Sisters Waldegrave*, was probably much less than the £20,000 which Lord Rothschild was said to have paid for the rival picture, *Garrick between Tragedy and Comedy*, in 1886.

Apart from *The Blue Boy*, which got all the publicity, several other Gainsborough paintings may have reached the £100,000 mark, since, after his deal with the Russian government in 1931, Andrew Mellon thought little of spending that sum on a single picture. Mr. Behrman asserts that in 1936 Duveen sold Mellon forty-two pictures for twenty-one million dollars and this purchase included the Gainsborough *Landscape with a bridge* at Washington. Of Mellon's other Gainsboroughs it may be that the Althorp *Duchess of Devonshire*, the *Mrs. Sheridan* (bought by Duveen from Lord Rothschild in 1936 for £50,000), the *Mrs. John Taylor* and the *Miss Catherine Tatton* (bought by Duveen at the Michelham sale of 1926 for £46,000 each), were all £100,000 purchases.

The *Landscape with a bridge* was not the only Gainsborough landscape to reach these higher regions. There was also another *Market Cart*, practically a replica of the picture in the National Gallery. It had been commissioned by the Prince of Wales in 1786 and given to Mrs. Fitzherbert. In 1841 this picture had been bought-in at a price that was lively for the period, £651. It was bought by Sir Lionel Philips in 1894 for £4,725 and by Duveen in 1913 for £20,160. Duveen sold it to Elbert H. Gary for £34,200. At the Gary sale in New York in 1927 Duveen paid £74,400 to get the picture back, later selling it to Charles T. Fisher of Detroit. Finally the *Market Cart* reached the Canadian National Gallery via Mr. Frank P. Wood of Toronto. In the late 1920's this version of the *Market Cart* must have been an £80,000 or £90,000 picture at the very least, yet it is no better than the version sold to the Barber Institute in 1946 (£20,475) and the version sold to Mr. Paul Getty in 1953 for £27,300.

At certain moments Lawrence, Romney and even Raeburn became the rivals of Gainsborough, the factors governing the incidence of this phenomenon being almost too complicated to trace. Even in the case of Raeburn, who as an exclusively Scottish painter had his own special niche, it is not at all clear whence the millionaire market first sprang. It was not originally American. The portrait of *Lady Raeburn*, which just missed breaking the sound barrier of £10,000 in 1905, stayed in England and now belongs to the Mountbatten family. In 1909, when *Sir John Sinclair* made £6,510, it was said that the owner had been asking £15,000, which was more or less what Duveen paid in 1911 for *Lady Janet Traill*. By 1912 when Duveen gave £22,260 for *Mrs. Hay*, the client for Scottish ancestors was E. T. Stotesbury of Philadelphia. Another Raeburn, which had reached America in 1913, was *Mrs. Hart*, which was said to have been sold by the Blakeslee Galleries in Chicago for £31,000. The same work had been sold in London in 1907 for £6,930. Even now the new buyers were not all American. The famous portrait of *The McNab in the Uniform of the Breadalbane Fencibles* was sold in July 1917, at the high tide of war when its owner, Hugh Lane, had gone down in the *Lusitania*, to Dewar, the whisky king, for £25,140. So, too, the *Macdonald Children* was sold to Lord Bearsted in 1920 for £21,000. Probably no Rubens and certainly no Impressionist painting would then have fetched as much as these pink and pasty portraits.

It was nevertheless American competition which kept Scottish lairdry on such an exalted plane. Consequently the American slump showed itself very plainly in the case of Raeburn. For instance, *Miss Lilias Campbell*, which made £8,800 in 1929, the last year in which that was possible, was bought-in for £945 in 1934. Six portraits of the Mackenzie family were sold in 1932 at Sotheby's for £2,290, one of them fetching only £90. To-day the kilted whole-lengths are shy of making an appearance. The market is probably more than ever American, but it has become modest. *Mrs. Robertson Williamson*, bought by Knoedler at the Michelham sale of 1926 for £24,675, made £5,000 in New York in 1957, the price of a pretty doodle by Paul Klee.

For Romney the great revaluation began in 1913, when Duveen bought the small half-length *Anne de la Pole* at the Oppenheim sale for £41,370. In September 1914, during the German advance on Paris, *Miss Penelope Lee-Acton* was bought for Frick at £45,000, while at the second Hamilton Palace sale of November 1919, the *Misses Beckford* was bought by Duveen for £54,600. For this work Huntington paid over £70,000, the price Stotesbury may have paid for Hoppner's *Girl with a Tambourine* in 1914. But even at £70,000 these were not such appalling purchases as the so-called *Kemble Sisters*, which Huntington had bought in London in 1913 at the beginning of his collecting adventure—for £20,000. A famous English lawsuit in 1917–1918 decided that the picture was not a Romney, but an Ozias Humphrey, and in July 1944 it made £63.

At the Methuen sale of June 1920, it was regarded as a sign of financial depression that Romney's *Sir Christopher and Lady Sykes* made only £28,350. All was put right in July 1926, when Duveen bid £60,900 at Christie's for *Mrs. Davenport*, very smart, very wooden-faced and not ostentatiously human. Nevertheless, Mr. A. C. R. Carter wrote, 'it won all hearts and a rousing cheer went up.'

Suddenly some of Duveen's dearest purchases were back under the hammer, but the time was November 1926. The scene at Arlington House, the home of the late Lord Michelham where Messrs. Hampton auctioned these dangerous treasures, was something straight out of *Vile Bodies*. The party just couldn't go wrong. Even *Lady Louisa Manners*, the Hoppner picture on which he had come a cropper in 1901, was bought back by Duveen and this time at £18,900, while Romney's *Anne de la Pole* rose from £41,370 in 1913 to £46,200. Three other portraits made 40,000 guineas each, two Gainsboroughs and Romney's *Lady Hamilton as an Ambassadress*.

In the case of the Lawrence portrait of a small girl, *Miss Mary Moulton-Barrett*, known as 'Pinkie', Duveen had no need to force the pace artificially. He had sold the picture to Lord Michelham in Paris in 1920 for £60,900, and Knoedler had a brief from Andrew Mellon to go well beyond this price. Mellon and not Huntington was the ruler of the Lawrence market, as Duveen knew, for in 1924 he had bought *Lady Templeton and Her Son* from Lady Carnarvon on Mellon's behalf, paying over £40,000. Nevertheless, Mellon was unwilling to take over a picture which had cost Duveen no less than £77,700 in the heady atmosphere of the Michelham sale. In the end it was Huntington who adopted *Pinkie* at a little over cost price, to be enthroned where she now is at San Marino, California.

Huntington paid the equivalent of £300,000 in modern money, a sum which seems out-and-out madness for this pretty superficial thing. But, though Huntington died in 1927 and the American slump began in 1929, there remained this extraordinary market for Lawrence whenever Andrew Mellon was interested. For instance, in 1935 it cost the Metropolitan Museum £41,200 to retrieve Pierpont Morgan's £20,000 *Nelly Farren*. It was also said that as late as 1931 Duveen was prepared to pay £80,000 for *Master Lambton* or the *Red Boy*, belonging to the Earl of Durham, but the asking price was £200,000. It was known as 'the million-dollar picture', though in 1825 Lawrence had been glad to paint it at £630. In April 1932 it was actually under the hammer in an auction at Lambton Castle, which was carried out by a Newcastle firm. Presumably it was Duveen's bidding with Mellon in view which made the buying-in price for the owners as high as £95,000.

The number of pictures of the English eighteenth-century school which finally changed hands at prices from £70,000 to £100,000 will probably never be known. Certainly it exceeded twenty, while more than half of them must have been bought between 1919 and 1927. A £70,000 picture of the 1920's means at least a £250,000 picture today; the £148,000 *Blue Boy* was equivalent to about £525,000. No other single school of painting has ever achieved such values, and certainly not the French Impressionists. Nor have we seen anything like it in the post-war era. Since the 1940's only two pictures in the salerooms of the world have made over £200,000 each. Possibly a dozen have made such prices outside the saleroom, but they are pictures of *all schools and all periods*.

It is impossible to judge the present-day value of these particular eighteenth-century works, except by analogy, because towards the end of his life (he died in May 1939) Joseph Duveen succeeded in persuading almost all his greater clients to offer their collections to posterity. Thus Duveen made certain that he would never again have to perform such feats as were demanded of him at the Michelham sale of 1926. In 1929–1933, when a slump came, the rap was taken by lesser works of which the price had become inflated through Duveen's operations. These falls were inevitable and to some extent they were foreseen, but it is much less likely to-day that this can happen again, simply because so much more is frozen off the market for ever than was the case in 1929–1933.

3. *The Early Continental Schools, 1884–1929*

The dullness of the Continental old-master market in the 1890's has already been noticed, and it was not confined to the Northern schools. Just as the market for Rubens and Van Dyck failed to respond to the extraordinary private sales from Blenheim Palace, so did the great Italian masters fail to respond to the £70,000 sale of the *Ansidei Madonna*.

The record of the National Gallery's purchases of the Italian school until the Titian *Ariosto* of 1904 is a record of prices that might have been paid at any time since the 1850's and in some cases since the 1840's. If pictures of the early Italian school fetched more, they eluded the British Nation altogether and went to Berlin or the Metropolitan or to Mrs. Isabella Stewart Gardner in Boston. It is true that in 1890 part of the Earl of Darnley's inheritance from the Orleans sale came to the National Gallery, but fantastically cheap—the Tintoretto *Origin of the Milky Way* at £1,312 10*s.* and the four big Veronese allegories at £5,000. But from the possessions of the fabulous 2nd Earl of Dudley [1817–1885] the nation got nothing. Having just swallowed the *Ansidei Madonna*, there was some excuse for not competing for the late Earl's more costly treasures, which rivalled the Duke of Marlborough's that were sold the same year. Among the Dudley pictures, sold in 1885, were Turner's *Dogana and Salute*, sold to Vanderbilt for £20,000, Reynolds's *Garrick between Tragedy and Comedy*, sold to Lord Rothschild for £20,000, and Raphael's *Three Graces*, sold to the Duc d'Aumale for £25,000. For Dudley's famous Fra Angelico *Last Judgement* the Berlin Museum paid £10,000.

There was much less excuse for the failure to bid at the Dudley sale at Christie's in 1892, when the Carlo Crivelli *Holy Family* and the Rembrandt *Preaching of St. John the Baptist* were bought for Berlin by Sir James Fairfax Murray for £7,350 and £2,625. Though an infinitely more interesting Raphael than the *Colonna Altarpiece*, for which Pierpont Morgan was soon to give £100,000, the Dudley *Crucifixion* was allowed to escape for a second time to Dr. Ludwig Mond at £11,130. It was no promissory note but good fortune alone that enabled the National Gallery to get the picture in the Mond bequest of 1924, together with the Titian *Holy Family* (£2,520 in 1892).

The Blenheim Palace negotiations of 1884–1885 were no prelude to any sort of Government policy, directed against the indiscriminate export of art treasures. But from time to time the Press would get wind of some imminent transaction and subscribers would come forward to assist the Treasury in outbidding the foreigners. Naturally, the cost of rescuing pictures, which had already achieved high publicity value, was enormous and therefore productive of hostile criticism. Mostly the critics missed a point, which now seems obvious, namely that sums so large could have shown a vastly better return, had they been applied to stopping the annual outflow of objects of less popular interest.

Despite the dire warnings of impending national spoliation, which had followed the Act of 1882, the British attitude in the 1890's and the early 1900's seems to have been that the building up of the Metropolitan Museum and the Kaiser Friedrich Museum was a commendable form of export trade. The Kaiser Friedrich Museum directors, in particular, were such good customers that from time to time British dealers and collectors sent them substantial gifts of pictures in order to encourage them. In the catalogue of 1911 there are twenty such acknowledged gifts, all made in the previous thirty years. And then in 1909, amid these showers of gifts, the British press was convulsed with yawps of Yahoo laughter. It had been discovered that the great Dr. Wilhelm Bode, the archimandrite of German expertise, had spent £9,000 of the German Government's money on an alleged Leonardo wax bust of *Flora*. It appeared that *Flora* had been acquired by the first vendor in Southampton for 35*s*. and that, being hollow, she contained part of the quilted early Victorian waistcoat of her maker, Richard Cockle Lucas.

Dear me, those were the days. But in retrospect one may think that the Kaiser Friedrich Museum directors in 1909 could well afford to drop a clanger even of these dimensions, considering the amount of Italian Renaissance art they had received from England either through Mr. Edward Solly in the distant past, or recently through Sir James Fairfax Murray. If Dr. Bode had claimed that *Flora* had been something less than a Leonardo, no one in England would have noticed if she had gone to Patagonia.

In the 1890's far fewer early Italian pictures reached the National Gallery than in the days of Eastlake and only moderately-priced purchases were sanctioned. From the Northbrook collection came the Mantegna *Agony in the Garden*—at £1,500, a price more worthy of 1850 than 1895. As to the Sebastiano del Piombo *Holy Family*, which looked very like a mature Raphael, it cost the nation hardly any more than the Earl of Northbrook had paid in 1849, namely £2,000. On the other hand, the naïve simplicity, now so much more fashionable, of Pisanello's *Vision of St. Eustace* was considered to be worth £3,000. Finally we have the Lorenzo Monaco *Coronation of the Virgin*, an altar-piece over 7 ft. high and one of the most conspicuous of the gold-back-ground pictures in the Gallery. It was bought in Florence in 1902 for £2,739.

These were the prices at which nations competed. In the London saleroom a Quattrocento painting could at times make no more than the cost of a new frame. In April 1886 the executors of William Graham, Trustee of the National Gallery and patron of Burne-Jones and Rossetti, put three hundred and twenty-two mainly Italian pictures into Christie's, all of them of the fourteenth, fifteenth and sixteenth centuries. Attributions have changed much since Christie's printed their catalogue seventy-five years ago, but it is clear that these were works chosen by a scholar, with scarcely a truly false picture among them. A few were relatively expensive, a Ghirlandajo double portrait making £777 and a Filippino Lippi, which Graham had bought in Paris in 1885 for £90, going to Germany for £661 10*s*. Nevertheless the sale made only £23,409, hardly more than £70 a picture. In 1927 the hundred and fourteen early Italian paintings of the Robert Benson collection were bought by Duveen for £620,000 and sold over the years for well over a million. Some of these pictures, like Piero di Cosimo's *Triumph of Chastity*, had been bought at the Graham sale of 1886. Forty years later their value had multiplied fully forty times, if not fifty.

Conceivably there are one or two men still living who recall the art sales of the first years of the century, as A. C. R. Carter used to recall the sales of the 1880's. In 1906, for instance, the sum of £23 2*s*. could buy a Sienese Trecento triptych, which was thought cheap fifty years later when it was sold for £3,570. Those were years of opportunities rare, favoured by ignorance superlatively blissful. There was still no Late Night Final edition of the *Burlington Magazine* to bring the glad news of a hitherto unrecorded *bozzetto* of the Master of the Bambino Vispo. And the first essay in expertise of the young Bernard Berenson was regarded with what seems to have been malevolent suspicion—to judge from the story of the Doetsch sale of June 1895.

Henry Doetsch had formed his collection within the previous twenty years and had opened it to the public in his house in New Burlington Street. It was even bigger than William Graham's. There were four hundred and forty-eight pictures, chiefly primitives, Northern and Italian, but also a few Dutch pictures. Doetsch was believed to have spent more than £100,000. Apparently these pictures had been notorious for over-restoration and foolish attributions. Christie's therefore took the then quite revolutionary course of having them all reattributed by Professor J. P. Richter, who also contributed an introduction to the catalogue. The preface was particularly resented. It was stated most unfairly that all this was being done to bolster up something inferior. Even W. L. Roberts, who published his highly adulatory *Memorials of Christie's* the following year, spoke of 'a superfluous preface and pedigrees more or less imaginary'. In later years A. C. R. Carter described the experienced Mr. Woods, snorting like an old war-horse at the glaring frames on the walls. In the middle of the sale he stood down in disgust and left the rostrum to a newly joined partner. In three arduous days the four hundred and forty-eight lots made only £12,970, less than £30 a picture.

Yet the profuse and quite adequate original photographs, which were pasted into the special edition of the catalogue, suggest that there were many works which, if not masterpieces, would be welcomed in the better provincial galleries to-day and at four-figure prices. Some were far better than that. The portrait of an ill-tempered man with a scruffy beard had been very cautiously attributed by Berenson to Jacopo dei Barbari. As such it made £23 2*s*., but it is now in the National Gallery, Washington, as a Giorgione.[1] Several other pictures had been mentioned in Berenson's *Venetian Painters*. For instance, a 6-ft. *Adoration* had been attributed by him to Cariani. It made £105. A full-sized altarpiece of the Holy Family and saints, which Berenson had attributed to Lorenzo Lotto himself, made £53 11*s*. Of the paintings of other schools, for which names had been supplied by Richter, I cannot help thinking that the man who bought a roundel *Holy Family* for 13 guineas, whether or not it was by Raffaelino del Garbo, was exceedingly lucky.

It is hard to resist the impression that a dead set was made against this sale, because the pictures belonged to a foreigner and had been assembled according to erudite German principles. It is true that the best of Doetsch's two Frans Hals portraits made £672 at a time when such things were fetching £2,000 or £3,000—but if only there had been a few David Coxes!

It would be a mistake to suppose that Berenson's work on the Italian schools was unknown in London in 1895. He had already contributed an introduction to the exhibition of Venetian paintings at the New Gallery and he had advised Mrs. Gardner of Boston to pay £3,500 for

[1] Langton Douglas in the *Connoisseur*, 1949.

the Earl of Ashburnham's small *Lucretia* panel by Botticelli. In fact, not long after the Doetsch sale, Berenson's influence created a new scale of values. For instance, in 1899 Mrs. Gardner paid the Chigi family £14,500 for Botticelli's *Madonna of the Eucharist.* In 1908 she gave £10,000 for the Piero della Francesca fresco fragment, the *Young Hercules,* and in 1909 about £12,000 for the Pollaiuolo *Lady in Profile.*

By this time there were other American buyers for Italian primitives besides Mrs. Gardner and Pierpont Morgan. Duveen, who had bought the collections of Oskar Hanauer, Rodolf Kann and Maurice Kann *en bloc* between the years 1907 and 1909, now retained Berenson as a permanent expert, an indication that the taste of scholars had become effectively introduced to the millionaires. Furthermore, it was almost time for the works of Titian, ludicrously underestimated since the National Gallery purchase of *Bacchus and Ariadne* in 1826, to make their return.

Mrs. Gardner had shown the way in 1896, when she was reputed to have spent £20,600 on the Earl of Darnley's Titian from the Orleans Collection, *The Rape of Europa.* Titian's portrait, known as *Ariosto,* was bought at the same time by Sir George Donaldson certainly for less than £5,000. In 1904 the National Gallery Trustees, helped by some private subscriptions, raised £30,000 in order to secure a picture which had probably cost the Earl of Darnley in the early nineteenth century a hundred or two. But a precedent had been set as far back as 1890, when the State had contributed £25,000 towards a £55,000 purchase from the Earl of Radnor at Longford Castle. The purchase comprised Holbein's *Ambassadors,* Velasquez's *Admiral Pareja* and Moroni's *Italian Nobleman.* The Holbein alone may have accounted for £35,000 of the total.

The Titian purchase of 1904 turned out to be the beginning of another desperate effort to close the stable door, similar to the purchase of the *Ansidei Madonna* in 1884–1885. It was followed by the purchase of Holbein's *Duchess of Milan* in 1909 for £72,000 and of the Mabuse *Adoration of the Kings* for £40,000 in 1911.

The year 1913, the most lavish in all the recorded annals of art history, saw the positions of the great Italian painters largely re-established, even though no Titian could fetch as much as Frick's latest Gainsborough. Hugh Lane sold Mrs. Emery of Cincinnati the Augsburg *Portrait of Philip II* for £60,000. He also bought back the *Man in a Red Cap* for £13,650. In 1915 it was on its way to Frick at £50,000 when Lane went down with the *Lusitania.* For *Caterina Cornaro* Sir Herbert Cook paid £36,000 in 1913, believing that the picture was not a Titian, but a Giorgione.

The Venetians had even now not lost their secondary status, for in 1913, the year of his death, Benjamin Altmann was prepared to give Duveen three times as much (£103,300) for a large Mantegna *Holy Family*, which had only just been auctioned at the Weber sale in Berlin for £29,500. For the smaller Raphael *Madonna* from Panshanger £116,500 was paid to Duveen by P. A. B. Widener. Altmann, had he lived, would have given £150,000, half as much again as Pierpont Morgan had paid for his big altarpiece in 1900. Even this was far from the limit for the greatest of names. At the end of that incredible year, 1913, the Tsar of Russia suddenly exercised his right to an option on the recently rediscovered Leonardo *Madonna* of the Benois family—at a million and a half dollars or £310,400. Duveen had already paid a deposit and the picture was in Paris, waiting to go to Henry Clay Frick. At a price equivalent to £1,862,400 in to-day's money, it is still the most expensive picture that has ever been sold.[1]

Compared with 1913, an *annus mirabilis*, the 1920's were fairly static years for the Italian masters. Only in 1929, when the National Gallery paid £122,000 for the Duke of Northumberland's *Cornaro Family*, and in 1931, when Andrew Mellon paid £112,250 for the Leningrad *Venus with the Mirror*, did Titian become a serious rival to the English eighteenth-century school. The Althorp *Venus and Adonis*, bought by Joseph E. Widener in 1925, probably cost no more than the Reynolds portraits which left Althorp for Huntington's gallery at San Marino, California. Moreover, the day of underpriced Italian primitives was not yet past. In 1914 the Ashmolean Museum's Uccello, the *Battle of Anghiari*, was bought by Hugh Lane at the Grenfell sale for £1,522 10*s*. In 1916 the National Gallery acquired the Masaccio *Holy Family with Angels* from Canon Sutton for £9,000. Part of the much-scattered Carmine altarpiece from Pisa, it had been sold as a Gentile Fabriano in 1860 for £70. For the much less attractive *Madonna of Humility*, a recent discovery of Berenson's, Andrew Mellon paid at least £100,000 in 1936.

In the 1930's the incredible spending power of Andrew Mellon dictated the prices for the last important early Italian works before world famine set in. This will be studied in the next chapter. The scale of the famous Leningrad purchases of 1931 was already established in 1929, when Mellon paid £172,800 for the larger Raphael *Madonna* from Panshanger.

The advance in the value of the primitives of Northern Europe followed the same pattern as the Italian school during the period 1884–

[1] S. W. Behrman: *Duveen*, p. 155. See also *supra*, p. 56.

1929, but the realisation of the rarity of these works was more tardy and the reaction more severe. It is still incredible that Mr. John G. Johnson of Philadelphia could have acquired the Van Eyck *St. Francis* in 1894 for £700 (see page 130), or that Marquand could have bought the Petrus Christus *Madonna* of the Metropolitan Museum in London in 1886 for £315. The high cost of rescuing the Mabuse *Adoration of the Kings* in 1911 seems to have altered the balance, for in 1912 the Memling *Man with a Love Letter* of the Taylor sale made £3,990 and in 1913 a French school *Madonna*, attributed to Jean Malouel, cost Carlos de Besteguei £5,700. In 1921 the Melbourne National Gallery paid £31,395 for the little Van Eyck *Madonna* of Ince Hall, a price that seems as absurd to-day as the failure of the British Government to keep such a picture in the country. It was a poor substitute for the National Gallery to spend £19,000 in Berlin in 1925 on two panels by the Master of Moulins and Geertgen Tot Sint Jans respectively.

The Petrus Christus *Man in a Doublet* of the 1927 Holford sale was another picture for which some effort might have been made. But since it graduated through Duveen and Andrew Mellon to the Washington National Gallery it would have required far more than the £14,700 that were bid. In the following year it needed no less than £90,000 to keep the Wilton diptych at home, a sum which was paid for the earliest English royal portrait which was at the same time an outstanding work of the earliest French school. However, much more was paid within a few months for a pair of portrait-panels of infinitely less importance. These, the discovery of the Curator of the Dijon museum, were attributed to the Master of St. Jean de Luz and bought by Duveen for J. D. Rockefeller, Jnr., for £155,000.

Though bought on the eve of the great recession, the Wilton diptych purchase set the pace for a revaluation of the Northern primitives. The rarest and greatest primitive master of them all was by a singular freak still on the market. In 1931 Andrew Mellon paid £103,500 for the Leningrad Van Eyck *Annunciation*, for which the Tsar had paid £448 at the King of Holland's sale in 1850, while in 1940 Von Beuningen was to give £225,000 for the Doughty House *Three Maries at the Sepulchre*, which had cost £336 in 1872.

The market for the Dutch seventeenth-century masters has always tended to be unexciting, with the exception of Rembrandt. In the middle 1920's most of the *genre* painters reached their highest valuation and some have declined badly since. It seems a characteristic of this school never to be able to hold the gains that have been registered at the best sales, perhaps because it is only then that the market is truly international. To-day the Dutch school, except for Rembrandt and Vermeer, has fallen from grace. When translated into modern terms, the prices of the Six and Holford sales of 1928 seem very high indeed, though in some cases they were not higher than those of the Neumann sale of 1919, the Steengracht sale of 1913 and even the Secrétan sale of 1889.

The importance of the Dutch portion of the Holford collection at Dorchester House in 1928 arose from the fact that it had remained intact since the purchases of Robert Stayner Holford in the first few years of Queen Victoria's reign, when he had been the saleroom rival of Sir Robert Peel. The comparison of the changed values of this group of pictures is of such special interest as to merit even to-day some detailed study. Here are a few examples:

AELBERT CUYP: *Panoramic View of Dortdrecht from the Maas*, 6 ft. long. £21,000. The picture had been bought in 1841 for £1,522 10*s*. In the Brownlow sale of 1923 Duveen had paid £18,735 for a rather similar picture, which is now in the Mellon Bequest in Washington. Although a much smaller view of Dortdrecht fetched £24,000 at the Duke of Westminster's sale, 1959, the price was only equivalent to £7,000 in 1928 purchasing power. Before 1923 very few Cuyp paintings made more than £5,000.

ADRIAEN VAN OSTADE: *Interior with Peasants*, £4,200. Still a record price to-day for one of the great late eighteenth-century favourites, but what a poor record! A tavern scene by Ostade had made £4,120 as early as the 'Schneider of Creuzot' sale of 1876. The second Ostade in the 1928 sale had been Robert Holford's dearest acquisition in 1844 at £1,386, but it made no more than £3,675 in 1928 and in 1934 it was down to £1,400 again.

JAKOB RUYSDAEL: *Le Coup de Soleil*, £6,300. There has been only one price like this for Jakob Ruysdael since the Holford sale, because Jakob (waterfall and ruins) Ruysdael has been overtaken by his uncle Salomon (ferry boats) Ruysdael. The decline had already begun in 1928, for at the Neumann sale of 1919, a picture of *Ruins* had made £12,600.

PAUL POTTER: *The Rabbit Warren*, £8,400. This again seems to be an absolute record price for Paul Potter, whose pictures fetched over £1,000 each even in the late eighteenth century and over £6,000 in 1890. For Paul Potter the picture is quite exceptionally pretty, whereas since the war only very average and very cheap works have reached the salerooms. In 1838 *The Rabbit Warren* had cost £409 10*s*.

DAVID TENIERS, the younger: *Le Bonnet Rouge*, £3,360. Probably also a record price. Although the *Prodigal Son* of the Louvre cost £1,248 in 1776, when it was one of the most expensive pictures in the world, very few of David Teniers's pictures have exceeded £2,000 in the present century, and in the 1960's a good Teniers costs no more than a cheap mass-produced car of the more pretentious kind. *Le Bonnet Rouge* had cost Robert Holford £693 in 1844, when Teniers was out of fashion.

PHILIPS WOUVERMAN: *La Course au Hareng*, £4,200. Sold by the famous Randon de Boisset in 1777 for £480 and bought by Robert Holford in 1841 for £409 10*s*. This too may be the highest priced Wouverman to-day. The Wallace Collection *Horse Fair* cost £3,200 even in 1854.

		£
REMBRANDT:	*Young Man with a Cleft Chin*	46,200
	Portrait of Martin Looten	27,300 (£700 in 1849)
	Lady with a Handkerchief	31,500 (£630 in 1845)
	Self-portrait with a Sword Scabbard	50,400
	Portrait of Maurits Huyghens, drawing in heightened chalk	10,500

Bearing in mind that none of these is an outstandingly brilliant Rembrandt portrait, or exceptional in scale, they must be considered the most expensive that have ever been sold at auction and comparable with the prices which Duveen obtained in the early 1920's in America. In terms of to-day's money, the self-portrait made about £180,000. It would be absurd to compare this somewhat ugly work, about 28 ins. × 41 ins., with the Panshanger *Horseman* of the National Gallery, which probably did not cost much more in real values in 1960, or even with the Van Aalst *Juno*, which failed to find a buyer that year at £52,500. At present, however, this is a starved market and it would be impossible to predict what might happen if four such portraits came into the saleroom together in the 1960's. *Maurits Huyghens* was, of course, astonishingly priced, but as a record for a single drawing it was capped in June 1936, when Duveen paid £10,710 for a fifteenth-century pencil portrait, attributed to Jean Fouquet.

In this early-Victorian collection of Dutch masters there was naturally neither Frans Hals nor Vermeer of Delft. The rise of Frans Hals was closely bound up with the career of Sargent, that is to say Hals became expensive in the 'eighties and 'nineties, when Sargent was painting smart people, and much more expensive from 1907 onwards, when Sargent was painting multi-millionaires. In 1907 Duveen paid over £30,000 for the *Artist's Family*, while Benjamin Altmann, a decidedly Frans Hals subject himself, paid a lot more. In 1910 an unattractive old woman from the Yerkes sale cost Frick £31,000, while altogether at least half a dozen portraits made such prices before the 1929 depression, which Frans Hals survived very well. The appeal of this prodigious but rather soulless artist has kept pace with the speed of inflation. In 1958 the brilliant little portrait of *Frans Post* was sold at Sotheby's for £48,000, and in 1960 a by no means laughing cavalier made £182,000.

With Vermeer the situation has been very different. The fact that the existence of several works of the most modern-minded of Dutchmen was discovered, just when this seemed no longer possible, created in the first place several daring buyers and in the second place the most daring forgeries in history. In 1888–1892, in spite of a more serious attitude to the subject, Vermeer prices were still dull and five of the very finest changed hands at £2,000 to £2,600. The soft tonal fashion in painting of the *fin du siècle* then gave Vermeer pictures a tremendous boost. In 1907 the *Woman with a Pitcher* of the Six Collection cost the Dutch nation more than £30,000. What P. A. B. Widener paid for the *Goldweigher* in 1910 and what Joseph Widener paid for the *Girl with a Flute* in 1925 are matters of conjecture, but some clue is offered by the fact that it cost Sir Henri Deterding £75,000 to present the Six family's little *Street in Delft* to the Rijksmuseum in 1930. *The Girl in the Red Hat* certainly cost Mr. Andrew Mellon £100,000 in 1931. In fact in 1937 the Boymans Museum and its benefactor, the Baron von Beuningen, must have found their forged *Christ in the House of Emmaus* an inexpensive picture at 550,000 gulden or £55,000.

CHAPTER EIGHT

Slump, War and Inflation 1929–1960

1. *Recession and Recovery, 1929–1939* — 2. *War and Aftermath, 1939–1952* — 3. *Taste on the Expense Account, 1952–1960*

---

1. *Recession and Recovery, 1929–1939*

Since the effects of the Wall Street collapse were not felt before November, the year 1929 was still typical of the pre-recession era. As such, it is worthy of individual study as the last of its kind, for, when the recovery began, the emphasis was quite different and is still more different now. The prices, which I shall give, must be multiplied by about 3·7 to arrive at their equivalent in to-day's money. This should dispel the illusion that the taxation-account Maecenases of the new age have been exceptionally reckless.

As was more often the case before the 1950's, the most expensive objects in the saleroom in 1929 were not pictures but *objets d'art*. The *Bedford Book of Hours* and the *Luttrell Psalter* were bought by James Pierpont Morgan, Jnr., at the sale of the Weld family of Lulworth Castle for £33,000 and £35,000. In reality this was a generous holding brief for the British Museum, who found the money later for these national treasures. The next most expensive object was the Portland vase, which, despite the fact that it had been smashed by a maniac in 1845, was run up to £30,450 before it was bought-in for the second time in its history by the Duke of Portland. It only became national property in 1945.

These were the dearest things in the saleroom in 1929. Outside the saleroom, the Nation paid £122,000 for the Alnwick Titian, *The Cornaro Family*, and £90,000 for the *Wilton Diptych*, while an anonymous donor spent £27,000 in order to present the Victoria and Albert Museum with the sixteenth-century German stained-glass windows from Ashridge Chapel.

The dearest picture, which was sold at auction in London, was Lord Brownlow's *M. le Roy, Sieur de Ravels*, a variant of the Van Dyck portrait in the Wallace Collection, which went to America at £17,850. English eighteenth-century paintings were headed by Gainsborough's *Colonel Craggs-Nugent*, which was sold at Puttick and Simpson's to Baron Thyssen for £15,225, rather less than the £16,380 given for the Rembrandt portrait of the year, the *Man in Armour*. But the Gainsborough was the last to reach a five-figure price till 1946. In the U.S.A. Messrs. Ellis and Smith were reported to have found a customer for Stubbs's *Eclipse and Jockey* at £15,500. At the Gilbey sale of 1915 it had made barely a twentieth of this sum. Hoppner's *Cust Brothers* made £10,500, Morland's *Dancing Dogs* £9,040, while Richard Wilson's *Thames at Twickenham*, a humble guest at the eighteenth-century banquet, made a price that is still a record, £6,720. As to Reynolds, the once-famous *Mob Cap* rose from £2,100 in 1922 to £6,300, but it is even now the last Reynolds to have made over £5,000 under the hammer.

The beautiful little Holbein portrait of *Edward VI as a Child* made only £9,975 at the Yarborough sale, because another version existed at Hanover, but it cost Mr. Andrew Mellon several times as much as this in 1931. The Yarborough Turner, the big *Vintage Festival at Macon*, made £9,030, a pale reflection of the £30,450 paid in 1927 for Sir James Ross's *Dogana and Salute*, but there is little reason to think that this sort of Turner would fetch any more to-day than in 1929.

Impressionist and Post-Impressionist pictures were not abundant in the London saleroom in 1929, but among the excellent drawings of the Vicomte Bernard d'Hendecourt was Cézanne's large water-colour of the *Mont St. Victoire*, which made £400 at Sotheby's and which might make £20,000 to-day. Hardly a single work by a living painter made over £500, and it may be added that in 1927, an 'annus mirabilis' second only to 1913, only six had done so, and not one of them was by a painter of the modern French school. Yet in 1927 *The Year's Art* recorded the sale of a hundred and thirty old-master paintings at upwards of 1,400 guineas each. *Nous avons changé tout ça.*

The world recession of 1929–1933 still awaits a historian. No one will disbelieve to-day that such a thing can happen again; and no one will believe that it can happen in the same way. It is hard to imagine the conditions in which a Budget deficit of a mere 100 millions made Socialists and Conservatives rally to a National Government. It is harder still to realise that the first naval mutiny since 1797 was caused by a Socialist Chancellor of the Exchequer who knocked a shilling a day off the sailors' pay as a small part of a plan for saving 70 millions a year. In a world so utterly different it is hardly surprising that prolonged financial depression sent art-prices down, whereas to-day buyers are convinced that the next depression will send their treasures up.

Not that *everything* went down. The highest class of transaction was actually a product of the stringency of the times. Andrew Mellon could not have bought twenty-one pictures from the Hermitage Museum in 1930–1931, spending about £1,400,000, if the Soviet Union had not suffered from the prevailing malady of shortage of foreign currencies. The sudden liquefaction of such an enormous sum by a single owner took place moreover when capital throughout the world was as firmly ice-bound as the St. Lawrence in winter. This incident too belongs to a different age, for, if the Russian government were to sell such a collection to-day, no single buyer could bid high enough for it.

The transaction was isolated from the market. In 1929–1933 millionaires no longer bid each other up for pictures at £100,000 each. At first the result of this was to keep pictures out of the market, rather than to bring down prices. In the season ending in July 1930 the London stock market was still not entirely overturned by the first series of Wall Street crashes, but the number of pictures auctioned in London at 1,400 guineas and over, a hundred and thirty in 1927, was now down to sixty-three. In the season ending July 1931 it dropped to thirteen. In August there occurred the credit crisis, the suspension of bank-payments and the creation of the National Government. On 21st September, before the next season opened, the pound was devalued from 4·86 dollars to 3·23. Most Continental currencies remained linked to the dollar, and the pound did not recover its position till the devaluation of the dollar itself as part of Roosevelt's emergency measures of 1933. For the next two seasons, therefore, London was theoretically a cheap market which must attract foreign buyers till prices forced themselves up. Nothing of the kind happened. In the 1931–1932 sales season only eight pictures exceeded 1,400 guineas, the lowest number since the early 1870's, except for the first season of the First World War. The highest priced picture, Frans Hals's *Smuggler*, made only £3,600. At the exchange rates of the day level prices meant a 40 percent. fall.

In 1932–1933 international buyers remained reluctant to exploit the low London market and only ten pictures exceeded 1,400 guineas. The

Lambton Castle sale and the failure to get rid of Lawrence's *Red Boy* has been mentioned in the previous chapter. An underbid of £90,000, if there really was one, would have meant not more than 305,000 dollars, whereas in 1926 the final price of *Pinkie* had been well over 400,000 dollars for a picture which the *Red Boy* was expected to surpass. An attempt to make use of the rate of exchange, then running at 3·48 dollars to the pound, by sending treasures to New York proved equally fruitless when the Earl of Lothian's illuminated manuscripts crossed the Atlantic the same month. Even at the reduced value of the pound, the *Tickhill Psalter*, which was expected to fetch as much as the £33,000 *Bedford Book of Hours* of 1929, was bought for the New York Public Library at £17,579.

By 1931 most European countries had imposed restrictions on the export of currency, a further reason why the exchange rates failed to make London a substitute for the lost Paris market. While the French eighteenth-century furniture market had shown itself to be in a state of collapse at the Founés sale of 1929, in London it was no longer worth the trouble to send such things to the saleroom. During the Armistice celebration of the 1918–1919 season no less than fifty-two lots of French furniture had made from 1,000 to 9,000 guineas each. In the season ending July 1933 only four lots made over £200 each. There could be no better barometer of the state of high finance in those days than the sales of tapestries. In 1920 some thirty-two lots of various periods made from £1,000 to £7,000 each. In 1931, 1932 and 1933 not more than three or four a year were capable of exceeding £1,000.

When recovery began, it was gradually discovered that some of the casualties of the depression bore a permanent look, not only English eighteenth-century portraits, but also Italian majolica, tapestries and Renaissance works of art in general. To other items, which had already been on the way out, the French paintings of the Barbizon school and the English subject pictures of the late nineteenth century, the depression gave the *coup de grâce*.

To take first the English eighteenth-century school, in 1930 the market almost retained its old look, when Duveen paid a support price of £14,700 at the Breitmeyer sale for a Hoppner he had once sold, *Miss Papendieck as a Child*. There was also Raeburn's *Miss Inglis* at £7,140 and Zoffany's *Bradshaw Family* at £5,880. The year 1931 saw only one high-priced portrait, Romney's *Richard Mayler* at £6,825, while in 1932 there were the first spectacular falls, Romney's *Mrs. Jordan* descending from £5,040 in 1909 to £1,680. In 1933 the *Gunning* portraits were sent to New York, but even at 3·50 dollars to the pound, five Romney and Hoppner portraits produced only £20,000, while Hoppner's *Louisa Countess of Mansfield* made just over £10,000.

The worst falls in the English eighteenth-century school began in 1934, which was technically a year of recovery. Being a dealer's stock, which had been acquired with the American market in view, the sale of the late A. J. Sulley was particularly disastrous. Raeburn's *Lilias Campbell*, sold as late as 1929 for £8,400, was bought-in at £945, while Romney's *Miss Anne Warren*, sold in 1928 for £6,090, was bought-in at £819.

Duveen, of course, attempted to support his own prices. In May 1935 he paid £12,075 for Hoppner's *Portrait of his Wife* and £9,975 for Lawrence's child-portrait, called *The Woodland Maid*, but it was the last occasion that either Lawrence or Hoppner fetched anything like these prices, though in the same year the Metropolitan Museum, with the lesser flexibility of a public body, could still find £41,200 for Lawrence's *Nelly Farren*.[1] In reality the year 1935, so buoyant in other respects, was one of the worst for the English school. Romney's *Lady Hamilton as Cassandra* fell from £8,925 in 1929 to £1,260, while *Mrs. Charlton and her Children*, which had been bought at the same time by Solly Joel for about £15,000, made only £588. In 1937 Reynolds's *Venus and the Piping Boy*, which had made £6,720 in 1909, fell to £309 10*s.*—the even more disastrous fall of the Reynolds fancy pictures, that had meant so much to the early Victorians. Worst of all was Lawrence's *Lord Castlereagh*, sold in 1928 for £4,410, even as a replica of the Londonderry House picture, and in 1938 down to £567.

The lowest levels for the English eighteenth-century school were reached during the Second World War, when Reynolds fared worst of all. For instance, at the Carnarvon sale of 1925 the twin whole-lengths of the *Earl and Countess of Carnarvon* made £16,695, but in December 1941 they were bought-in at £400 the pair. Andrew Mellon, before his death in 1938, was still capable of sustaining the old Gainsborough prices, for instance, £50,000 in 1936 for Lord Rothschild's *Mrs. Sheridan*,[2] but in the same year the National Gallery took advantage of the times to acquire *Viscount Kilmorey*, less attractive in person but much more honest in craftsmanship, for £5,000.

Inevitably the fall of the English portraits dragged down the rival millionaire market in Van Dyck. The *First Earl of Denbigh* dropped from £6,615 at the Fielding sale of 1919 to £1,995 in 1938. Since 1929 there have been no five-figure Van Dyck portraits in the saleroom, though in 1938 the Melbourne National Gallery gave £12,500 for the

[1] See Chapter 7, p. 190. [2] See p. 186.

least attractive of the Wilton portraits. But the lack of high prices to-day denotes only the absence of good examples. The reappearance of some of the Genoa portraits might prove exciting. Not so, however, those later schools which had been honoured at the time of the Van Dyck boom of the early 1900's; neither the Sargent portraits and the Barbizon landscapes, nor the romantic English landscapes that had still been the prizes among Midland businessmen. For instance, David Cox's *Flying the Kite*, the Mona Lisa of the Birmingham market, fell from £4,620 in 1926 to £290 in 1933.

Most of the falls in the English nineteenth-century school had been long overdue when the depression set in. Already in 1927 the situation was not happy. Sir James Murray's sale may well be compared with the great McCulloch sale of 1913, except that it was smaller and that, since Murray lived later, there were some French Impressionists—about £20,000 worth—among all the 'pictures of the year'. Van Gogh's *Vase of Flowers* at £1,260 rubbed noses with Swann's polar bears, *Adrift* (and more than they thought) at the same price. Of Orchardson, still respected north of the Tweed, there was *The Borgia* and *The Lyric* in mitigated prosperity at £924 and £840. Waterhouse's *The Danaïdes* made £1,050, Edward Stott's *The Kiss* £1,102 10*s*., and Peter Graham's *Moorland Lovers* £1,155. A selection of Bastien Lepage, Charles Jacques, Jakob Maris and Anton Mauve rang the changes between £1,622 10*s*. and £2,100. It was less than two years since Sargent's prodigious executor-sale and a small oil sketch could still make £3,780, but it is sad to record the prices of the living English painters, who in 1927 were at the height of their fashion. Five of the lively early works of Augustus John aggregated only £2,350, and made no more when they were put up again in 1933. Orpen's *Roscommon Dragoon* at £1,122 10*s*. was the highest priced work of a living English painter to appear in the sale-room before the 1950's.

In 1927 the painters who had been represented in the McCulloch Collection appeared to have fallen to a third of their value, but three years later, that is in April 1930, when there was no real general slump, the scene of devastation was far worse:

		£	£
Millais	*Murthly Water* (landscape)	41 8*s*.	(1,512 10*s*. in 1892)
	The Proscribed Royalist	168	(2,100 in 1897)
Briton Rivière	*Union is Strength*	12 12*s*.	(315 in 1903)
David Farquharson	*Full moon and spring-tide*	3 3*s*.	(178 10*s*. in 1913)
Alma-Tadema	*Thou Rose of all the Roses*	110 5*s*.	(1,155 in 1909)
Meissonier	*Advanceguard of an Army*	67 4*s*.	(535 10*s*. in 1903)

Later in the season, a well-known Landseer picture, *Taking a Buck*, made £27 6*s*., the price of its big gold frame, though in 1888 it had cost £2,047 10*s*. Burne-Jones, a later comer, made a sturdier resistance, since the famous *Chant d'Amour* (£3,360 in 1898) was still good for £620, but that was only 1930. The depression was to prove a great leveller. *Love and the Pilgrim* (£5,775 in 1898) made £210 in 1933 and £21 in 1941.[1] The belief that there was more than meets the eye in the paintings of G. F. Watts was still to come, for in June 1934 *The Rain Cloud*, a work which had fetched £420 in 1906, was bought for £10.

Even Turner was of this company. The full tide had been reached in 1927 with the *Dogana and Salute* at £30,450 and the *Red Righi* water-colour at £8,925. The falls, which began in 1929, were steeper for the water-colours, many of which had faded since they were last in the saleroom. In 1930 one of the famous Swiss views of 1842, *Lausanne from le Signale*, fell from £1,732 10*s*. in 1912 to £577 10*s*., while the *Lake of Thun* fell from £1,417 10*s*. to £294. In June 1939 the *Double Rainbow* at Nottingham was bought by the Nottingham Gallery for £110, though it had made £1,155 as far back as 1877. Devaluation to a fifth or a tenth was now quite common, and in 1942 the *Red Righi* itself made only £1,155.

The fall in Sargent was the most significant, showing that it was not only an economic system but the gods of an age that were changing. At Sargent's death in 1925, his works had been no violet-scented Victorian memories, but so much an expression of the time that a hundred and sixty-two scrapings from his studio made £146,000, equivalent to £540,000 in to-day's money, and they were all water-colours, small oil-sketches or studies. The only portrait, the unfinished *Mme. Gautreau*, was withdrawn from the sale and presented by Duveen to the Tate Gallery. He was said to have paid £20,000. The splashy oil landscapes sold for anything up to £7,000, the water-colours made as much as £7,350 in the case of *San Vigilio*, and even a student copy of Velasquez's *Don Baltazar Carlos*, which I well recall, made £6,300.

For five years Sargent's position remained unchallenged except by Renoir. The enormous Reynoldsian *Wyndham Sisters* was said to have fetched £18,000 in New York in 1928. One of the first warnings that all was not right must have come in 1931, when a standard 21-in. water-colour of Majorca made not 2,000 guineas, but £115 10*s*. In the immediate pre-war years they were to be had sometimes for 50 guineas, while the efficient charcoal portrait of *Marie Lohr* was sold in 1944 for £5 10*s*.

[1] Subsequently acquired by the Tate Gallery, see page 165.

The financial recovery of 1933–1936 tempted a few of the 5,000–10,000-guinea whole-lengths into the open, with dire consequences. In 1933 *Cora, Countess of Stafford* made £609, in 1935 *Mme. Errazuriz* made £885, and in 1936 *Mme. Helleu* made £975. Thereafter the great whole-lengths stayed under cover. Even the last few years, which have seen the return of four-figure prices for some of Sargent's smaller works, have not brought them out again.

In the 1930's, Impressionist and Post-Impressionist pictures, rare in the London salerooms of the 1920's, became a little more common, though by no means proof against the depression. At the end of the summer season of 1939, both Van Gogh's *Olive Trees at St. Remi* and Cézanne's *Mont St. Victoire* had to be bought-in at £4,000 and £4,200 at Sotheby's. Nevertheless, the National Gallery, Melbourne, paid £9,735 that year for Cézanne's *Route montante*, while in June 1940 Parke-Bernet of New York sold a portrait of *Mme. Cézanne* for £5,700. On the whole this market remained in a starved condition not only during the moratorium of the war but for seven years afterwards. There was no real leap forward till the Cognacq sale of 1952. On the other hand, post-Cézanne paintings now began to appear at infrequent intervals in the London salerooms. In 1934 the Tate Gallery bought its first Picasso, a conservative flowerpiece of 1901, for £700. In 1935 Sotheby's sold the entire collection of the late Roger Fry, the begetter of the celebrated modernist exhibitions of 1910 and 1911, for £248. A Rouault head, an object that would be much publicised to-day, made £20. In 1937 the first Picasso to reach Christie's, a female head, made £157 10*s*., but generally the saleroom was the graveyard of such works. Thus, in April 1937 Christie's sold six fairly consequential works of Braque and Juan Gris for approximately a thousand pounds all told. The two Braque paintings, which made £220 10*s*. each, might possibly fetch from £35,000 to £50,000 to-day.

While the auction market of the late 'thirties was not ready for abstract or semi-abstract pictures, the Post-Impressionists were nevertheless gaining over the Impressionists. Compared with Van Gogh and Cézanne, the true Impressionists remained static. The market for Degas never caught up with the £21,000 paid for *Danseuses à la barre* in 1912. In 1927 a big dancer subject could make £7,560 at the Murray sale, but in 1938 the very popular *Woman combing her Hair* cost the Tate Gallery's funds no more than £4,083 14*s*. 4*d*. According to M. Maurice Rheims, the larger ballet subjects were still on Durand-Ruel's books in 1940 at about £6,000 each.

Renoir is not to be judged from the occasional freak prices which were paid for his larger and more splendid works, for instance £50,000 which was said to have been paid by Duncan Phillips of Washington for *Les Canotiers* in 1923[1] or £38,250, which Albert Barnes gave for *Mussel Fishers at Berneval* in the U.S.A. in 1942. *La première sortie* was bought for the Tate Gallery for £7,500 in 1924 and it would have had to be a very exceptional Renoir to make £10,000 in the 1930's. Moreover, till 1930 the lush millionaire taste still favoured Sargent.

At least the Impressionist cult was now strong enough to make the fall of the Pre-Impressionist French painters dramatic. As late as 1911 Frick had paid £31,000 for Millet's *Femme à la Lampe*, and in 1914 Sir James Ross paid £12,000 for the quite small and slight *Oedipus taken from the Tree*. But in 1934 a much more important work, one of Millet's finest, the Chardin-like *Knitting Lesson*, was sold in New York for only £3,200. A Corot, which made £3,320 in New York in 1938, was reputed to have been the dearest in five years. Three years earlier the famous *Ronde des Nymphes* was sold for £525, a 'gout americain' Corot which had made £6,830 in 1913. Corots of this kind have still not recovered. *Les baigneuses des îles borromées* was one of the last really expensive nymph-ridden Corots at £8,440 in January 1930, but in 1952 it made £2,500—and in New York at that.

The worst hit were the lesser Barbizon painters, the companions of the Edwardian leather sofa and the Edwardian big cigar. In 1919 Sir George Drummond's Daubigny, *Le Retour du Troupeau*, made £8,190. Such a picture would barely achieve £2,000 to-day, and in the middle 'thirties a few hundreds. In fact, in 1935 an exceedingly large Daubigny of the inevitable flock of sheep, but in this case a *Nocturne*, which is always asking for trouble, made 3 guineas.

In the later 1930's the recovery was selective even for the old masters of the Continental schools, strong for Rubens, strong for the early Italians, weak for Rembrandt and the Dutch school in general. The day was past when big mythological subjects by Rubens could still reach the saleroom, but the last of the great landscapes to become available, the *Watering-place* of the Duke of Buccleuch, cost the nation an extremely reasonable £20,000 in 1936. In 1935 the Metropolitan Museum were prepared to go to £51,500 for Pierpont Morgan's dull school-replica of the Prado portrait of *Anne of Austria*, which had been bought in by the Duke of Marlborough in 1886 at £3,885.

Rembrandt appeared with fair frequency, neither at the high prices of the 1928 Holford sale nor at prices that appeared to be affected by the depression. In 1930 Lord Scarsdale's *Portrait of an Old Man* made

[1] Rheims, *op. cit.*, p. 322.

£19,950, while Mellon was reported to have paid at least £40,000 apiece for the *Polish Nobleman* and *Joseph and Potiphar's Wife* from the Hermitage Museum. In 1933 the Melbourne National Gallery bought the *Self-portrait* from Welbeck and in 1936 the *Two Philosophers*, both at £21,500. In 1938 the National Gallery bought the Duke of Buccleuch's *Saskia as Flora* for £28,000 and in 1940 Lord Crawford's *Margarete Tripp* at £20,000.

The inference from these prices is that Rembrandt did no more than preserve a steady market after the slump, whereas Frans Hals remained on the upgrade until the war, mainly through the purchases of Andrew Mellon. *The Painter's Son* and *The Officer at the Window* from the Hermitage cost £35,000 each, while the *Baltazar Coymans* of the Rodolfe Kann Collection cost Mellon via Duveen £87,500 according to the Washington National Gallery valuation. Prices outside the Andrew Mellon market were on a lesser plane, but stiff. In 1935 the Metropolitan paid £62,000 for Pierpont Morgan's two *Bodolfe* portraits.

Italian primitives now reached their highest level, for nothing since the war has been important enough for comparison. The English habit of regarding quattrocento pictures as inexpensive curios was, however, by no means dead in 1934 and 1937, when the National Gallery acquired seven Sassetta panels at £43,000 and four small cassone panels, attributed to Giorgione, for £14,000. Criticism was hottest concerning the latter, *The Loves of Damon and Thyrsis*, because the attribution was under fire as well as the price. It was alleged that they were by Andrea Previtali, from whose hand the National Gallery already possessed half a dozen not too exciting works. As to the Sassetta panels, it seems peculiar to-day that £6,000 each should have been thought too much for anything so miraculously beautiful. But they had been sold by Duveen to Clarence H. McKay, who had sold them back to Duveen—and Duveen was himself a Trustee of the National Gallery. So exit Lord Duveen of Millbank as Trustee of the National Gallery, despite his numerous benefactions. In 1958 a single small panel of no more importance than any of the Sassetta panels, the *St. George*, attributed to Uccello, was bought for the Gallery at £35,000 without a murmur, but the deaths of the vituperative generation of art-experts have been a sad loss to the British Press.

In the middle 1930's much higher prices for the Italian primitives were inevitable, since few important works still remained free and the American museums and their benefactors were determined to get them. The Mellon Hermitage purchases set the standard: the £240,000

Raphael *Alba Madonna* (see page 54) and the £154,600 Raphael *St. George*, the £173,000 Botticelli *Adoration* and the £60,000 Perugino *Crucifixion*. The Metropolitan's purchases from the Pierpont Morgan estates in 1935 included a Lippo Lippi triptych at £50,000, while the Ghirlandajo portrait of *Giovanna Tornabuoni* cost Andrew Mellon £103,300. The dearest quattrocento portrait in the world has certainly cost more since and is now at Lugano. In 1876 the lovely *Giovanna* was bought in Paris by William Willett of Brighton for £600. It was actually on the National Gallery's walls till 1896 and they could have bought it for £1,200.

In 1938 Duveen-Mellon prices appeared in the open saleroom, when Duveen bought the Piero della Francesca *Crucifixion* for his client at the New York Carl Hamilton sale. The picture measured 14 ins. × 16 ins., and it cost £77,400, but Duveen paid a lot more in damages, settled out of court, because his expressions of opinion were alleged to have harmed the price.[1]

Opportunity was fading just as fast for the primitive paintings of Northern Europe. In 1933 the National Gallery were fortunate indeed in getting the Weydenesque *Mass of St. Giles* for £10,000, having spurned it when it made £3,570 at the Dudley sale of 1892.[2] But how irritating that the *Dream of Pope Sergius* should have been allowed to go abroad in 1938 at £14,700. The companion panel had been bought for the National Gallery in 1868 for £1,500 and surely this famous work, *The Exhumation of St. Hubert*, known in England since Beckford had bought it in 1802, might have been mated. It must have been apparent in 1938 that things of this kind would not float round the world at less than £20,000 much longer. Only a momentary depression, caused by an exodus of collections from Germany, made it possible for the Hans Memling *Descent from the Cross* to go for £17,130 in New York early in 1939. *The Three Maries at the Sepulchre* of Jan van Eyck, bought by Sir Francis Cook in 1872 for £336, was already under negotiation with the Baron von Beuningen at £225,000, and in 1940 the latter refused an offer of £300,000 from none other than Hermann Goering.

The most interesting revaluation that followed the 1929–33 recession was in the market for old-master drawings. It had been realised already at the beginning of the nineteenth century, in the days of Lawrence, Samuel Woodburn and Young Ottley, that the old masters had left behind them brilliant untarnished drawings in which their handwriting could be far better perceived than in the present condition of their paintings. But apart from a few Leonardos, Michelangelos, Dürers and

[1] Behrman, *op. cit.*, p. 199. [2] See p. 131, *supra*.

Raphaels, old-master drawings throughout the nineteenth century were ludicrously cheap. In the sale of the late Sir Edward Poynter in 1918, a drawing by Dürer actually made over £2,000, but in 1936 the number of drawings which had achieved such a price could almost have been numbered on one's fingers. In 1929 the magnificent Ingres drawing of *Mme. Reiset and her Daughter* could still be got for £940, but in 1959 a drawing by Ingres that can hardly be compared with it, *Mme. le Gallois*, was sold in Paris for £6,650.

The pre-war market was still very like that of the late eighteenth century. The best prices were made by drawings which could be shown on a wall like a picture. Thus the French eighteenth-century school rated especially high. At the Faucher-Magnan sale at Sotheby's, in December 1935, three Watteau drawings made £1,300 each and a Fragonard drawing £1,100. After the recession years, the ascent was very apparent in this school. At Sotheby's, in July 1937, a sheet of Watteau studies made £5,800 and a big bistre drawing by Fragonard £2,900. At the Mortimer Schiff sale of 1938 two drawings by even such a secondary artist as Lavreince made nearly £2,000 apiece, a step towards the sums of £6,000 and £7,000 which were paid for the highly finished Moreau le Jeune drawings at the Chanter sale of 1959.

Quite distinct from this traditionally rich man's market were working drawings and studies, of which it was quite unbelievable what a few pounds could buy in the 1920's and sometimes even in the 1930's. The point of change was the Oppenheimer sale of July 1936. Oppenheimer had spent £48,000 on drawings, including £32,000 for the single block purchase of the drawings of John Postle Heseltine. In spite of this uneconomic method of collecting, practically everything showed gains. Leonardo's *Rider on a Rearing Horse* from the Wilton sale of 1917 rose from £735 to £4,305, and to-day would doubtless be assessed between £35,000 and £50,000. A sheet of grotesque heads by Michelangelo had been bought in 1913 for £960 and now made £3,570, while a silverpoint portrait, attributed to Dirk Bouts, rose from £715 to £4,200. The Wolf Huber drawing of Luther had been bought for £700 from Heseltine and now made £3,255, while a study for *Tantalus* by Holbein rose from £152 in 1920 to £1,522 10*s*. Oppenheimer had paid most—£2,800—for a portrait-drawing on vellum of a papal legate, ascribed to Jean Fouquet. For this Duveen bid £10,710 against the competition of the erudite Mr. Lugt of Amsterdam, the highest price paid for any drawing before 1959.

2. *War and Aftermath, 1939–1952*

To compare the movement of art prices during the two world wars is not to compare like with like. At no time in 1914–1918 was Britain an island fortress. Communication with neutral countries was comparatively simple, and till 1917 the U.S.A. remained a buyer's market, some very highly priced English eighteenth-century works crossing the Atlantic even in 1915 and 1916. Still more different was the moral climate. Except for a brief period between March and May 1918, it never occurred to anyone that the war could be lost. And it was never imagined that victory would be followed by a less secure world with changes in the distribution of wealth. Except for some of the nineteenth-century English painters, price-levels did not fall, nor did they rocket up as a hedge against inflation. The market was normal, but reduced in volume. Big gains were registered among Sir Joseph Beecham's Constables in May 1917, and among the Linnell family Blake water-colours and tempera paintings in May 1918. But the nostalgic Midland market for Birket Foster was really a post-war creation, an Armistice spending spree, which created the first four-figure prices.

In other fields of collecting, the Greek and Roman marbles of the Hope family fetched prices in the summer of 1917, which seem quite astonishing, when compared with the sale of the Lansdowne marbles in 1930 and even when compared with the odds and ends that come on to the market to-day.

To come to the Second World War, the phase that was called 'the phoney war' faithfully reflected the conditions of 1914–1915. Few sales, few important works, steady prices. In April 1940, the paintings of Claude recovered from a century of almost continuous neglect when the Duke of Kent bought the famous Altieri landscapes for £2,625.[1] But by the end of May a different feeling was in the air. Capitulation to the enemy was hardly expected, but most people imagined vast destruction, mass evacuation of the towns and buying and selling restricted to the bare necessities of life. This fear was dispelled a year later and yet the market showed no elasticity. Logically there should have been plenty of buying as a hedge against inflation, particularly since so many dealers had come to England who had experienced real inflation in the Germany of the early 1920's. But capital was short, credit was shorter and there was a feeling of guilt in buying fine things among the destruction and the sacrifices. Prices stayed dull until the landings in Italy in September 1943, but during the particularly trying weeks of

[1] See pp. 19 and 40.

the flying-bombs in the summer season of 1944 it will be recalled that the salerooms were well stocked. Even then works of art barely achieved the levels of 1934–1939, though the cost of the ordinary wants of life had more than doubled.

The first years after the capitulation merely prolonged these conditions, because there was no sense of confidence in the future, nothing in the least like the mood of November 1918. The buyers, though they were more than ever international, had no notion of the demands of a reconstituted European society, while entire economic systems lay in ruins. On the one hand, the Midland industrialists were not forcing up the price of David Cox and Birket Foster; the Americans were not scrambling for English eighteenth-century portraits. On the other hand, the Continental old-master market remained completely enigmatic. Without some free movement of currency, paintings and drawings of the Continental schools could not find their true level by becoming once again an international market.

Virtually the market remained rationed until at least 1951. In the previous years heavy price rises could only be sustained by purely native or resident buyers in such protected areas as the U.S.A. In the early 'fifties it was still said that the cheapest thing you could buy was a work of art. In 1953–1954, however, the speed of revaluation was so rapid that people mistook the symptoms. It was not inflation that was running away any faster, but a demand that had been artificially held in check. Nor were the prices of the later 'fifties, particularly the prices of nineteenth- and twentieth-century French art, altogether the 'coup de foudre' which the popular Press made them to be. In the dull 1939–1952 phase of collecting there was certainly some intelligent anticipation, an intuition that the extremer forms of modern painting were the only ones that belonged truly to their own time, and that the Impressionists and Post-Impressionists on that account would acquire the status of the last great 'visual' painters.

Outwardly, however, in this dull period the only things in the salerooms which seemed to keep pace with devaluation were those that could not be dispensed with: the furniture, china, glass and carpets that had been destroyed in large quantities and that could not be replaced by anything new. For art that was bought for its own sake, the period was one that the small collector, a class now threatened with extinction, will look back to with singular wistfulness.

The pitiful sacrifice of the Eumorphopoulos collection of Asiatic art at the time of the fall of France and the evacuation of the British forces will be recalled, though it is outside the scope of this book. Other things were thrown away during the months of preoccupation and anxiety. In July 1940 Eumorphopoulos's Modigliani portrait made £530 and Monet's famous view of *Hyde Park* was sold at Sotheby's for £640. In 1941 an excellent Hubert Robert, *La Pèche à la Ligne*, made £270. Ipswich Museum bought Constable's *Willy Lott's House* for £1,400 and Gainsborough's *Coast Scene* for £797. Lincoln Museum bought De Wint's reputed masterpiece, a big view of *Lincoln*, which had made £1,753 5*s.* in 1889, for £378. While provincial museums snapped up bargains, the National Gallery wisely secured Rembrandt's *Margarete Tripp* at £20,000. But for the ordinary stuff of the saleroom there was the perfect English barometer. Only one Birket Foster was sold—for £75. In a boom year like 1920 as many as forty could be sold, and all at three-figure prices.

In New York, the season which ended in July 1941, was said to have been the best since 1929, a sad proof of how little Europe meant now in the top market. Goya's portrait of the child, *Victor Guye*, made £8,500, a Matisse £2,600 and a Blake water-colour £2,520. A single sale, that of Mrs. Henry Walters of Baltimore, cleared 646,684 dollars, or something like £180,000. By contrast the blitz-free London sales season, 1941–1942, though it brought out a few more objects, was still very depressed. The *Self-portrait in the Robes of an LL.D.*, presented by Reynolds to the Corporation of Plymouth when he was made Mayor, fell from £5,985 in 1919 to £2,520. Nattier's *Marquise de Tournelle* fell from £3,255 in 1913 to £525, while Turner's *Red Righi* water-colour, £8,295 in the 1912 Taylor sale, now made £1,155. At the Edmund Davis sale the National Gallery acquired Hogarth's *Staymaker*, which is the last important work of that rare painter to have appeared on the market, for £3,255. Surprisingly a Paul Potter could still make £3,500, but a very large dark Italian painting, considered to be by Luca Giordano, made one guinea.

In 1942–1943 there was rather more animation. The first £5,000 picture to be sold since 1939 appeared on 14th September 1942, before Alamein or Stalingrad, an Adriaen Isenbrandt *Triptych* at £5,880. An unattributed quattrocento portrait made £3,300, Ben Marshall's *Gentleman on a Grey Hunter* made £2,940, the Rothschild early fifteenth-century *Book of Hours* £5,800, and a big elaborate Guardi £4,200. The next season opened on 17th September 1943, a week after the landings at Salerno, the first on the continent of Europe. And most symbolically there were forty-five Birket Fosters, all from West Hartlepool and sold in a single morning. The dearest made £945: it was as good as ringing the church-bells.

In March and June 1944 there were two big sales in Christie's war-time rooms, and now at last prices began to catch up with the late 'thirties. The sale of James Pierpont Morgan Jnr., who died in 1943, consisted of objects from Wall Hall, Aldenham, many of which had been bought thirty to fifty years ago by the elder Morgan. The National Gallery obtained four Giovanni di Paolo panels for £12,000, the Barber Institute a Matteo da Sienna panel for £5,460, and Duveen Brothers a Duccio-school *Triptych* for £5,670. Among the modern English paintings, which Morgan had bought in his earliest collecting days, was Landseer's *Lost Sheep*, for which £3,255 had been paid in 1897. It now made £315.

The second sale was of the Neeld pictures from Grittleton Manor and included, besides Dutch paintings of the early nineteenth-century choice, Romney's *Lady Hamilton as Ariadne*, quite the sweetest of all the Lady Hamiltons and at the very healthy price of £4,725. The best of the Neeld Constables, *The Vale of Dedham, 1828*, had been negotiated for the National Gallery of Scotland at £20,000, but there was the English saleroom record for a Rubens portrait, £16,800 for *Peter Pecquius, Chancellor of Brabant*. The first of the new valuations appeared for Van Goyen, when one of his thin, subtle, almost monochrome landscapes made £4,410. On the other hand, one of the best Teniers pictures to appear for many years, *The Temptation of St. Anthony*, made £1,323, no more than an early nineteenth-century price. But before concluding with 1944 one must mention Mr. Leopold Sutro's Van Gogh, *View in a Park at Arles*, which made £1,550. In October 1958 another Van Gogh view of this park made £132,000.

The season, which saw the end of the war in Europe, was not rich in pictures and singularly unlike the Armistice season, 1918–1919. It seems incredible that the National Gallery should have been able to acquire the Doughty House Dürer, *The Madonna of the Irises*, for £12,000. But the *objets d'art* of the R. M. Walker sale yielded £156,000 and English Tudor silver show-pieces fetched little less than they would have done fifteen years later. But the season 1945–1946 opened on a less confident note. During the recess a Socialist Government had come to power. The Hiroshima bomb had blown the lid off Pandora's box and the rift between the war-time allies was widening. There was nothing spectacular about this season. In the summer of 1946 the good-quality Dutch pictures, acquired by the Swaythling family in late-Victorian times, showed how little these works had advanced to meet the reduced value of money. The de Hooch *Woman nursing a Child* had advanced from £2,940 in 1893 to £7,875, the Jan Steen

Greeting had risen from £724 10*s.* in 1893 to £7,140, while the Hobbema *Wooded Landscape* had advanced very much less, from £4,725 in 1893 to £11,025.

A good deal of Turner was seen in the 1945–1946 season, so that the present pattern became clear for perhaps the first time. While the big oil paintings, particularly the early seascapes, continued to decline, smaller water-colours, like *Quillebœuf* at £3,465, were worth several times as much as in late-Victorian times. Thus *Mercury and Hersé*, sold in 1897 for £7,875 and now grown somewhat swarthy, made £2,623. *Van Tromp's Shallop*, sold in the Novar sale of 1878 for £5,460, made £2,730. *The Nore*, sold in 1893 for £5,040, was sent over from America in 1945 in search of the best market, and made only £1,785. [In 1961 *Mercury and Hersé* was sold for £8,190.]

There now began the real recovery of Gainsborough. The Barber Institute bought the Swaythling *Harvest Wagon* (the picture that had started the boom in 1867 by making £3,147 10*s.*) for £20,745. It was the first five-figure Gainsborough since 1929 and a better landscape than the version which Duveen had sold that year for £80,000 or £90,000. A little sense had been introduced into the former Californian playground. *Viscountess Tracey*, sold in 1906 for £6,300, now made £1,050.

The highest price of the summer in 1946—indeed, the highest price in the London saleroom for anything since 1928—was paid for Constable's big, over-laboured landscape, *The Young Waltonians*, at £43,050. In the late 1950's not much would have been thought of that, for pictures were fetching £40,000 on occasions six times in a morning. But *The Young Waltonians* had been bought in 1895 by the 1st Lord Swaythling for £8,925 and it was not expected to fetch a great deal more than the £20,000 *Vale of Dedham* of 1944. It was announced in the saleroom that the buyer, Mr. Walter Hutchinson, had bought the picture for the Nation, and gratitude was recorded in *The Times* by the President of the Royal Academy. For a few years *The Young Waltonians* was on view in an institution, calling itself rather oddly the 'National' Gallery of British Sports and Pastimes. This did not alter the fact that the picture was back in the saleroom at the owner's death. The price fetched in 1951 was somewhat higher, £44,100, but it is impossible to forecast what such a Constable would fetch in the 1960's, since by every indication there are no more works on this scale to come. On the other hand, small oil studies, painted out of doors, continue to advance and may well reach these higher regions too.

In 1946–1947 Impressionist and Post-Impressionist paintings

reappeared, but without the least hint of the market that was building up; a good Cézanne water-colour of 'V-shaped' trees at £304 10s., a Rouault head at £880, a Renoir landscape at £819 and a Braque at £280. In those days it was still dearer to buy an old master, and yet the prices of 1947 look very old-fashioned now. For instance, a reasonably attributed Botticelli roundel of the *Holy Family* made £5,880 in October 1946; a Rembrandt self-portrait was bought for the Glasgow City Gallery for £13,125 and a Velasquez portrait of *Count Olivarez*, with fair claims to authenticity, cost £11,000. The lively little Frans Hals portrait of the fishwife *Hille Bobbe* seems to have been an absurdly cheap picture at £3,360, but the Poussin *Moses sweetening the Waters of Mariba* at £6,930 and the reappearance of the Altieri Claudes showed interesting revaluations. The Claudes made their third bow to the public at Christie's in 1947. At £3,045 *The Sacrifice to Apollo* cost less than Beckford had paid in 1799,[1] and only half the auction price of 1884. It was none the less the first £3,000 Claude in sixty-three years. In 1960 tribute was paid to the rarity, if not the popularity, of these former household gods by the purchase of *Apollo and the Muses* for the National Gallery, Edinburgh, at £47,000.

The year 1948 saw the beginnings of the most depressing symptom of the present era, the upgrading of journeyman painters. It was due to the plain impossibility for a private individual to obtain works by more inspired masters. In 1941–1942 seven flowerpieces by Fantin-Latour made £4,500 between them. In 1948 almost as much was paid for Sir Bernard Eckstein's *Hollyhocks* alone, a picture which had been dear for a Fantin-Latour in 1933 when it made £819. After 1954 almost any of these tasteful but far from inspiring exercises could make from £3,000 to £5,000, while in April 1961 an unusually profuse example made £21,000.

There was this about Fantin-Latour. His pictures could be spotted by the dullest visitor to any smart flat. So too could Boudin's. In the 1920's it was rare for a Boudin to attain £100. In 1936 a collection of these very pretty but extremely standardised beaches and harbours aggregated £7,500 for twenty-three pictures, while in March 1942 eighteen Boudins could be had for £6,700, and in the spring of 1945 fourteen for £4,735. Being halfway to an Impressionist, the boom in Boudin began later, at the Cognacq sale of 1952, where a *Regatta Scene* made £4,800. By 1957 *Trouville*, a beach scene in the usual formula, could make £13,800.

Not many painters have repeated themselves quite so conveniently as

[1] See p. 40.

Zuccarelli, an Italian working in London in Reynolds's day, when he was considered to be no more than a decorator. His lacy, small-minded pastiches of Claude and the two Poussins were usually sold, like partridges, by the brace. Before 1914 the normal price was £100 a pair, and in the 1920's from £150 to £300. A pair of Zuccarellis was sold for £168 as late as 1944, but in 1953 a pair fetched £4,200 and in 1958 another pair was sold at Sotheby's for £6,500.

Francesco Guardi is hardly to be written down to the same level as Zuccarelli, but the inflated esteem which his work acquired after the Second World War sprang from the same appeal of a smart, easily recognised style and an obvious decorative quality. In Paris his *Capriccios* were a discovery of the 1860's, but they were hardly known on the London market before the Lord Frederick Cavendish Bentinck sale of 1891, when, among eleven Guardis a large Venetian view made £756 10*s*. It was this picture which started the new boom by making £10,290 in 1948. Between 1948 and 1959 eleven Guardis have been auctioned in London at prices between £4,500 and £14,500, and these include three showy drawings in bistre wash. While £14,500 was an auction record in 1959, the unusual large panels which were rediscovered in 1956 at Bantry House in Ireland and shown at Burlington House in 1959 were sold for a great deal more. Dramatic as it was, the discovery in no way altered Guardi's status as a decorator-painter. In spite of their magnificence of colour, the Bantry House panels showed up the painter's poor slapdash drawing through their very size, in one case 15 ft. long. Clearly, however, Guardi's works must continue to enjoy their exaggerated esteem, so long as each year produces one or two showy examples to feed a very smart market.

In 1873, when good examples of Guardi could have been had for £150 and the very finest on the Paris market had not exceeded £1,000, the Earl of Dudley paid £3,360 for a Canaletto. Thereafter Canalettos went out of fashion till 1928, when the four Tatton Canalettos made £25,750 between them. There ought not to be any question of comparing Guardi with Canaletto's best period, but the fact is that the record price for a Canaletto, £32,500 paid in March 1960 for a latish Venetian subject, is still not much more than double the highest priced Guardi *Capriccio*. Moreover, the same barbarous preference for quite obvious picturesque effects has elevated the stagey *Pulcinello* drawings of Domenico Tiepolo far above the real draughtsmanship of Giovanni Battista Tiepolo.

A phase more creditable to the age than this upward grading of journeyman work has been the reappraisal of painters whose work has been unjustly neglected for the past century or more. In addition to Claude and Poussin, Salvator Rosa made his come-back in the 1950's. The paintings that fetched almost as much as any Rubens at the end of the eighteenth century had indeed fallen on evil days. The Lansdowne *Diogenes*, sold in 1810 for £997 10*s*., made £51 9*s*. in 1885. Beckford's 8½-ft. *Job and His Companions* was sold in 1912 for £33 12*s*., while in 1930 a landscape, which was to make £735 in 1958, was sold for £7 17*s*. 6*d*.

Symbolically the Salvator Rosa revival began in 1953, when the two Ashburnham landscapes, that had been bought in for £1,050 in 1850, were sold on the death of Lady Catherine Ashburnham for £6,300. In 1957 the *Death of Regulus* made £4,800 and in 1958 *l'Umana fragilta* was bought by the Fitzwilliam Museum for £3,360. These prices have still not tempted more than a few of the numerous privately-owned Salvator Rosa pictures into the market. Fewer still of Salvator Rosa's more famous Italian contemporaries have ventured their way into the saleroom, despite a spate of baroque exhibitions and much scholarly propaganda. The purchase of the National Gallery's huge and none too pleasing Guido Reni, the *Adoration of the Shepherds*, from the Lichtenstein collection in 1959, was certainly a landmark, but the saleroom prices of Guido Reni, the Carracci family, Guercino, Domenichino, Albano, Pietro da Cortona and Carlo Dolci are as yet scarcely up to late-eighteenth-century levels.

The march of inflation has demonstrated very plainly that it is useless to expect the fashionable masters of the past to appreciate merely because their works are more than a hundred years old. Even the best of the romantic English water-colourists, including Turner himself, have not kept abreast of inflation. The French social realist painters, not excluding Millet, are as flat as ever and so are the Barbizon landscapes. The one exception here is Corot. Although the incredible prices paid in America in 1910–1913 were depressed by the later success of the Impressionist market, it was on the Impressionist wave that Corot returned. The *Paysage à Morvans*, which was sold for £4,500 at the Cognacq sale of 1952, was the first Corot to make such a price since 1930. Yet, a month later, *Baigneuses de l'Ile Borromée* was sold in New York for a third of the price it had fetched at the Rouart sale of 1912. The market is highly selective; silvery nymph-haunted Corots are not in demand. The highest post-war price is still that of *Venus au bain*, bought for the Maharanee of Baroda at Sotheby's in 1956 for £27,000. Completed in the last year of his life, when Corot was close on eighty, it is one of the most memorable nudes ever painted, despite its sombre colour. But, before 1914, several of Corot's pot-boiling nymphs and glades had fetched as much in the U.S.A.

Apart from Blake and Samuel Palmer, there has only been one truly substantial revaluation among the English school since the war, namely that of George Stubbs [1724–1806]. Though sometimes fee'd as highly in his own lifetime as Reynolds, Stubbs benefited not at all from the eighteenth-century revival of the 1860's and 1870's. If a gentleman's or lady's portrait was of little consequence, when it had left the family, a horse's portrait was of no consequence at all. But towards the accession of Edward VII the Victorian prejudice against sporting pictures vanished mysteriously. The 'nouveau riche' had not only to be a shooting and riding man, but to be surrounded by shooting and riding pictures. Naturally the most sporty and the least artistic works were favoured. But Sir Walter Gilbey, a passionate equestrian, had a true love of Stubbs. His twelve splendid examples were sold in 1915 for about £3,300. *Eclipse and Rider*, which made £735, was actually sold in the U.S.A. in 1929 for £15,500, but to-day this collection of Stubbs pictures might be worth more than £400,000.

In 1951 the horse and jockey picture, *Gimcrack*, which had made £231 at the Gilbey sale, made £12,600 at the dispersal of the 'National' Gallery of British Sports and Pastimes. It was recognised at last that in his uncorrupted integrity Stubbs was one of the very greatest of English masters, if not indeed the greatest of all, who retained all his life the touching almost primitive quality of the young Gainsborough. It would be hard to say what the four pictures illustrating *Shooting* or the painting of the *Wedgwood Family at Etruria* might fetch to-day, but prices for some of Stubbs's least satisfactory subjects have been lively. In 1960 the much too large *Poodle* made £17,000, while *Princess Charlotte's Zebra*, which had made £220 10*s*. in 1923, rose to £20,000 in 1960 after it had been discovered buried in Harrods' depository.

The sale in November 1960 of James Pollard's *North Country Mails at the Peacock, Islington*, for £19,000, demonstrates that the sporting-picture market is still mainly inaesthetic—as it was in the late 1920's, when absurd prices were paid for Sartorius and the elder Herring. But a second exception must be made for Ben Marshall, much less of an artist than Stubbs, but almost as much a poet until, in his old age, he became sentimental and Landseerish (he died in 1835). In 1951 *Sorcery, Winner of The Oaks*, made £4,830, not much more than the £4,200 which was fetched by *Mr. Fermor's Hounds* at the height of the sporting-picture boom in 1926. In 1959, however, *Longwaist, Owner and Rider* made £8,400, a reappraisal which seems overdue.

3. *Taste on the Expense Account, 1952–1960*

We come to the study of a market, which is totally different from anything in this book, a market created by inflated currency, topsy-turvy financial controls and topsy-turvy systems of taxation, the market of the declining Roman Empire of Western man.

In 1952 the English cost of living had already trebled itself since 1939, but of this the salerooms gave remarkably little indication, except in the case of popular ornaments for small homes and standardised paintings that were a little below the attention of millionaires. The change that was to come was fiscal in origin, as indeed had been several of the great market changes of the past. The fortunes of the mid-Victorian subject-painters, for instance, had been made on an expanded market for framed prints, following the repeal of the duty on glass.[1] The English eighteenth-century school boomed in the U.S.A. after 1909, when the 20 percent. tariff on imported art was repealed. And after 1913 there was a boom in modern French painting, following the extension of tariff repeal to living art.

Perhaps the greatest impact of all legislation on the art market had been the Settled Lands Act of 1882.[2] In this case the impact was conventional. It enabled the insecure and, later on in history, the overtaxed, to sell off art treasures. But the legislation of the 1950's encouraged the insecure and the overtaxed to buy them. When it became possible for the Nation to accept works of art in payment of death duties, it was a positive advantage to bequeath works of art rather than money.

Ironically the Act, of which this was a development had deprived the National Gallery of a £47,000 bequest, when it was first passed in 1895. This protest of Mrs. Lyne Stephens was directed against death duties, which amounted to 1 percent. on the first £10,000 and which came to 8 percent. on a million.[3] But the real outcry against the Harcourt death duties was that they were levied for the first time on land and chattels as well as on money. Yet, sixty years later, it required only a slight twist to make this principle an advantage to the owners of art treasures. But this was in fact a step towards the absolute extinction of fine art in private ownership and in public circulation from hand to hand, a process that had already been accelerated in the 1930's with the founding

[1] See pp. 98–9. [2] See p. 176.

[3] Ensor, *op. cit.*, pp. 217–18; Marillier, *op. cit.*, p. 70.

of the National Gallery, Washington. Duveen was the first to see that by persuading his clients to leave their possessions to public galleries, he ensured the safety of his own market against future shocks. When a world slump came, very few of his own prices collapsed in the open light of day.

The logical next step came in the 1950's, when the inferior prizes of the market and the much higher values offered less inducement to endow galleries. To enable the flow into the U.S.A. to continue as it had once done, the Federal revenue authorities decreed that gifts to museums and galleries could be set against the donor's tax liabilities in the year of donation to the extent of 30 percent. But, of course, when matters of aesthetics fall into the hands of lawyers, accountants and politicians, something bizarre can be expected. It seems that the value of the object is assessed by the museum, be it ever so humble, that receives it. The museum may get this free gift if it assesses it high enough for the owner's satisfaction. It seems also that the donor may then keep the object for the rest of his life, notwithstanding the fact that it may by these means have cost him nothing or even have made him a profit. The bill, paid by other taxpayers, is reflected in some of the more abnormal prices that are bid at European auctions. It is the main source of the champagne and television-screen entertainments of the modern saleroom. Moreover, there is little doubt that other governments will follow this example, particularly those which have not yet exhausted every thinkable device for getting rid of taxpayers' money.

It is natural that this type of bidding should be associated largely with modern French painting. An old-master picture of quite obvious importance reaches the world's salerooms nowadays not more than three or four times a year at most. Mushroom museums, on the other hand, need the things that command public attention. It is, of course, a powerful reason for this particular predilection, but not the only one. There is occasionally a genuine belief in the merits of the object itself. In the case of the Impressionists, they were clearly the last school of purely visual painting that was not atrophied by a deadweight of tradition. In the case of the living modern art of to-day, the universal acceptance of Cézanne, who seemed so outrageous barely half a century ago, is an encouragement to speculate in what looks most up-to-date, most daring and most vital.

The new prices began at the Cognacq sale in Paris in 1952 and reached London with the easing of currency-exchange controls in 1956. The nation was prepared for the shock a few years ahead, and it fell lightly. In the winter of 1950 the Royal Academy opened its doors to the exhibition, *l'École de Paris*. The approach was arch and hesitant, the very title suggesting French naughtiness, a vision of old gentlemen in eighteenth-century dress with quizzing glasses, a fallen screen and a nude model. But even the late Granville Fell, editor of the *Connoisseur*, showed himself less outraged than at any time since 1935, even going so far as to illustrate a very small Renoir. By December 1953, the *Connoisseur* had got round to '*Renoir, a world of sensuous beauty*'—a world which it had taken the *Connoisseur* a long time to discover.

At the Gabriel Cognacq sale of 1952 the followers of Cézanne were not represented, but of Cézanne himself there was a still life at £33,700 and a landscape at £20,500. These were the biggest advances; the Degas *Danseuses saluant* was conservatively priced at £11,000 and the Manet portrait at £12,000. Rather higher advances were recorded for Renoir with *Les deux sœurs* at £19,500 and a *Girl's portrait* at £23,000, and for Van Gogh with *Les Chardons* at £16,800. The only advance over pre-war prices which had truly kept pace with the speed of inflation was that of Cézanne, the first of the real moderns, and this was a significant portent.

In 1954 this revaluation began to embrace Cézanne's followers. At the Rees-Jeffreys sale at Sotheby's the Tate Gallery bought Matisse's oil sketch of the *Head of Paul Derain* for £7,035. There was a Soutine at £4,725 and a Picasso water-colour drawing at £4,410. At the Bradley Campbell sale in New York another Soutine made £6,600, Matisse's *Au fauteuil* £4,920 and a Modigliani portrait £5,450. At this stage semi-abstract works advanced less: £2,940 for a Picasso at the Rees-Jeffreys sale, £1,260 each for a Braque and a Juan Gris. Yet within five years, a Braque exercise of his Cubist period was to make over £50,000.

The prices of 1956 included surprising advances by distinctly minor men: £7,350 for a Bonnard and about £5,000 each for a Vuillard and a Utrillo. It was a sign that, as a millionaire's market, the modern French school had now taken the place of the English eighteenth-century portraits in the 1920's. Compared with the large number of modern works at prices over £10,000, the London salerooms in 1952–1956 produced only twelve old masters that made as much. In 1952 there was Constable's *Salisbury Cathedral* at £21,525, a Pieter Breughel at £11,025 and a Frans Hals, bought-in at £11,000. In 1953 there were Gainsborough's *Market Cart* and *Cottage Door*, bought for Paul Getty at £27,000 each, the Ashburnham Claude at £13,000, a quattrocento portrait at £11,000 and a trecento panel from Ashburnham at £10,000. In 1954 the nearest thing to a £10,000 picture was Turner's

Helvoetsluys at £9,240, scarcely dearer than in 1927 and not much dearer than in 1895. In 1955 there was an authenticated small Titian, the truly hideous *Allegory of Prudence*, at £11,550, while Salomon Ruysdael's *Ferry Scene* made £10,800. In 1956 there was the Poussin *Adoration*, now in the National Gallery, at £29,000, an Averkamp *Skating Scene* at the record price of £14,000, and a standard Hobbema at a standard 1920's price of £16,800.

With this list, covering more than three years, may be compared the William Weinberg sale of 10th July 1957, and it was only one of three modern French sales which Sotheby's held that year. In one morning nine pictures changed hands at prices between £11,000 and £31,000, the latter figure being reached by Van Gogh's *Usines à Clichy*, and next to it the same painter's queer pastiche of a Rembrandt *Angel* at £26,000. There followed Monet's *Blue House at Zaandam* and Renoir's *Girl in a Red Blouse* (but with such flabby hands) at £22,000 each, the same price as Seurat's *Le Faucheur*, which was a pretty but ever so slight oil sketch, 16 ins. × 12 ins. A few years before Seurat painted this rare postage stamp, there had been an almighty convulsion over Whistler's dainty 200-guinea *Nocturne*, which looks almost beefy by comparison.

The homage paid to mere autographs at this sale was far more striking than the £17,000 paid for Gauguin's *Bathing Boys* and Manet's *Young Bull in a Field* at £11,000. Three small and bare crayon studies by Seurat made £6,200 between them, while seven early drawings and water-colours by Van Gogh aggregated more than £20,000. Drawn in Holland between 1882 and 1884, they offer not the least hint of Van Gogh's mature style. Provincial, dull, barely works of art at all, they contain about as much promise of genius as the drawings of Adolf Hitler that came under the same hammer three years later. Another of these drawings, the *Paysan bêchant* of 1881, which looks like an unusually stodgy prize-winning drawing from a Public School competition, made £6,500 in 1959, as if it were a Rembrandt or a Dürer. On the other hand, a beautiful and typical Van Gogh landscape drawing, in his developed style, made only £2,200 at Sotheby's in November 1960. There is no accounting for the philatelists of connoisseurship.

In the autumn of 1957 this now extremely popular drama transferred itself to New York. The Georges Lurcy collection was finer than the Weinberg collection, and the £20,000 top prices now became average prices. The sale, moreover, gave some indication of the value of a big Renoir subject picture, since, despite its price, the £71,300 *La Serre* was nowhere near the class of *Les Canotiers* or *Les Enfants de Mme. Charpentier*:

		£
Renoir	*La Serre*	71,300
Gauguin	*Mao Taporo*	64,330
Toulouse-Lautrec	*Aux Ambassadeurs, gens chics*	39,360
	Aristide Bruant aux Ambassadeurs	22,130
Camille Pissarro	*Le Pont Neuf*	20,360
Degas	*Four dancers*	17,900
Alfred Sisley	*Le Loing à Moret*	13,400
	Entrée du village	12,500
Raoul Dufy	*Fantasy view of Paris*	9,300
Matisse	*Dans le boudoir*	9,000
Soutine	*Paysage aux vâches*	6,785

The sale seems (at the end of 1960) to have represented the top of the market for the minor Impressionists. The price of *Mao Taporo* was gigantic, but no surprise, since in June 1957 the shipowner Niarchos had bid £104,630 in Paris for a Gauguin *Still Life with Apples* (but in francs).

During the London season of 1958, the sale of a small Cézanne water-colour, *Le Jardinier Vallier*, for £20,500, was memorable, but every-thing looked small after the Goldschmidt sale of the 15th October. There were only seven pictures in the sale, all first-class of their kind, pictures that made no exacting demands on the eye, and all of them illustrated in colour. No series of works as costly as these had ever been sold at a single auction in all history. But when the prices are reduced to what they would have meant in the days of the gold sovereign, they would not have surprised the late nineteenth century. The £48,000 *La Bergère* of 1890 was a much dearer picture than the £220,000 Cézanne:

		£
Cézanne	*Boy in a red waistcoat*	220,000
Van Gogh	*Public gardens at Arles*	132,000
Manet	*Rue Mosnier aux drapeaux*	113,000
Cézanne	*Les grosses pommes*	90,000
Manet	*Le promenade*	89,000
Renoir	*La Pensée*	72,000
Manet	*Self-portrait*	65,000

It is still too soon to decide whether these values for masters, who seem occasionally to be falling back before their successors, are any longer valid. But, on the strength of the price paid for a lightweight small portrait head, *La Pensée*, the National Gallery raised the insurance valuation on Renoir's *Les Parapluies* to a quarter of a million. As to the successor painters, their rise in value became more apparent five weeks later at the Arnold Kirkeby sale in New York:

		£
Picasso	*Madonna and Child* (early work)	54,285
Cézanne	*Garcon, couché sur l'herbe*	44,500
Renoir	*Jardin à Sorrento*	37,500
Bonnard	*Fenêtre ouverte*	34,140
Renoir	*La couseuse*	31,070
Monet	*Child in a cradle*	30,350
Degas	*Dancers on a landscape stage*	23,680
Matisse	*Fleurs et ceramiques*	23,215
Modigliani	Half-length portrait, male	23,600
	Portrait of Mme. Eynaud-Vaillant	23,250
Pissarro	*Route d'Auvers*	23,425
Van Gogh	*Barge at Arles*	24,150
Signac	*Fishing boats*	12,140
Manet	Half-length portrait of a girl	14,000

An average price of £30,000 for fourteen pictures in a single sale sounds less extravagant when it is realised that the purchasing power was no more than the 5,000 guineas which were normally paid for a well-known Alma-Tadema, Millais or Burne-Jones in the first years of the century—with this difference, that no one bought an Alma-Tadema to reduce his taxes or his death duties.

The following illustrations are from two sales, held at Sotheby's on 6th May 1959 and 1st July 1959. Considering the quality of the works, the values of the Impressionists and Post-Impressionists seem at least to have remained static if not actually to have declined, whereas Picasso and Braque are on the way up:

		£
Picasso	*La belle Hollandaise* (1905)	55,000
Van Gogh	*Bridge at Asnieres* (bought-in)	45,000
Cézanne	*Mme. Cézanne*, portrait	40,000
Braque	*Woman with a mandolin*	36,000
Cézanne	Self-portrait	32,000
Degas	*Three dancers rehearsing*	22,000
Renoir	*Ambroise Vollard as a bull-fighter*	22,000
	Dead pheasant in the snow	19,000
	Portrait, *Misia Sert* (National Gallery)	16,000
Cézanne	*L'assiette bleue*	17,000
Braque	Still-life	15,000
Toulouse-Lautrec	*Return from the shoot*	15,000
	Marcelle Lender	13,000
Monet	*Bassin de Nympheas, Giverny*	13,000
Modigliani	Portrait, *Beatrice Hastings*	12,000

In the following November, however, there were two works sold in London at prices which compared with the unique Goldschmidt sale. Cézanne's *Man in a Blue Blouse* was forced by the competition of the National Gallery to £145,000, while Gauguin's *J'attends ta reponse* made £130,000. But even more impressive was the price of a mere drawing, touched with gouache—Picasso's *Family of Harlequin* at £12,000 was one of the most costly drawings that had ever been sold and far dearer than any of the unique Fra Bartolommeo landscape drawings that reached Sotheby's in November 1957.

The year 1960 saw the same pattern further accentuated, static prices for the last of the 'visual' painters, much higher prices for their followers, such as the £38,000 paid for Modigliani's *Man in a Blue Shirt* and £30,000 for Fernand Léger's semi-abstract *Smoker*. The first price of this kind for a pure abstract painting was paid on 27th April, when Nelson Rockefeller's Braque, the *Violin Composition*, was auctioned for the benefit of the Museum of Modern Art for 145,000 dollars or £51,600. It was the second most costly of fifty lots, the dearest being a straightforward Cézanne *Applescape* at £70,440. Another abstract picture by Braque was sold by Sotheby's in October 1960 for £42,000, but the dearest Picasso at this sale was a realistic work, *Crouching Woman*, at £48,000. The new market evidently finds the abstract works of Braque more attractive, for the dearest, more or less abstract Picasso at this sale, the *Woman in an Armchair*, made £30,000 and not more, while a work of the short-lived but surely very derivative Nicolas de Staël made as much as £13,000.

The same tendency could be seen equally in the market for the native art of this self-deprecating island. At a Sotheby sale in April 1960 the two highest-priced modern English works were both completely geometric abstractions by Ben Nicolson at £1,500 and £1,400 each. No 'visual' work fetched as much. Even Stanley Spencer's *Street in Zermatt* made no more than £1,050, though it must have taken him as long to paint as Holman Hunt's *Scapegoat*, while the best Matthew Smith made £620 and the best Sickert £520. Eccentricity is, however, the only form of intellectual independence the age permits, and in the previous season *Going out at Epsom*, painted by Sir Alfred Munnings in a style that became outmoded soon after 1900, made £3,600.

The disparity in values between old masters and moderns was partly levelled out in 1956–1960 as a result of the dispersal of some famous estates. The Westminster Rubens and the Andrews Gainsborough could be said almost to have restored equilibrium. On the other hand, the Turners and Rembrandts ignored the advent of inflation altogether and, though the following list provides a glimpse of the bottom of the barrel, at least nine items could have fetched as much in the late 1920's:

			£
24.6.59	Rubens	*Adoration of the Magi*	275,000
7.12.60	Frans Hals	*Unknown Cavalier*, bust portrait	182,000
23.3.60	Gainsborough	*Mr. and Mrs. Andrews* (National Gallery)	130,000
24.6.59	El Greco	*St. James*, half-length	72,000
3.4.60	Rubens	*Holy Family*, oil sketch (bt. by Walker Gallery, Liverpool)	50,000
3.4.60	Rembrandt	*Saskia as Juno* (bought-in)	52,500
24.6.59	Frans Hals	*Portrait of Frans Post*	48,000
23.3.60	Rembrandt	*Portrait of young man* (1633)	40,000
18.5.58	El Greco	*Christ healing the blind*	37,800
24.6.59	Claude	*Worship of the Golden Calf*	36,000
		Sermon on the Mount	35,000
18.11.59	Rubens	*Portrait* (bearded man)	35,000
18.11.59	Gainsborough	*Countess of Chesterfield*	34,000
23.3.60	Canaletto	*S. Giorgio Maggiore, Venice*	32,500
24.6.59	Master of the Osservanza, Altarpiece	*Resurrection*	31,000
16.6.57	Lorenzo Costa	*St. Jerome*	28,000
19.1.57	Boucher (N.Y.)	Four small oval panels	25,000
28.11.56	Murillo	*Girl baring her shoulder*	25,000
24.6.59	Van Goyen	*View of Emmerich*	24,000
24.6.59	Titian	*Duke of Urbino and his son*	24,000
27.6.58	Gainsborough	*Duke of Gloucester*	22,050
23.3.60	Rembrandt	*Girl's head*, 1634	22,000
17.10.56	Turner (N.Y.)	*Fort Vimieux*	20,000
23.3.60	Canaletto	*Redentore, Venice*	20,000
30.6.60	Stubbs (Harrods)	*Princess Charlotte's zebra*	20,000
7.12.60	Stubbs	*Baron de Robeck riding*	20,000

Apart from the first three items, this list of pictures which made £20,000 and over in 1956–1960 is exceeded by the principal modern paintings in the Lurcy and Kirkeby sales alone. Higher prices were, of course, paid for old masters outside the saleroom, but the information was not generally published. In 1957 a small head of a girl by Vermeer was said to have been sold by the Duc d'Arenburg to Charles B. Wrightsman for about £400,000. The National Gallery, Stockholm, was said to have given about a quarter of a million for Watteau's *Lute Player*. The price, paid on behalf of the National Gallery for the

Rembrandt *Equestrian Figure* from Panshanger in 1960, may have been nearer £300,000 than £200,000, if remitted death duty is included.

Accepting these figures purely hypothetically, one may ask what to-day would be the cost of the £310,000 *Benois Madonna* of 1914, the £240,000 *Alba Madonna* of 1931, the £225,000 Van Eyck *Three Maries at the Sepulchre*, of 1940? But the question is unanswerable. Firstly, because it is not certain any longer that a Raphael or a Leonardo *Madonna* is worth several times as much as any Vermeer. Proportionate values have changed enormously. In the 1920's it would have been unthinkable that a Rubens altarpiece, if such a thing had come on to the market, should fetch twelve times as much as a Gainsborough whole-length of his most fashionable period. Secondly, because the market has been so starved of first-class old masters since the war that there has been no continuous competition to keep their prices moving. Consequently the more persistent upward movement of some of the modern painters gives a somewhat false impression. If six El Grecos had appeared in one sale, the price of the two El Grecos in this list might have been very much higher.

There is nothing new in this situation. Even now, the London sale-rooms are much less monopolised by the work of the living and the recently dead than they were in the 1870's and 1880's. Some of the prices paid for modern French art in Paris and New York at the end of that period were, as we have seen, higher in real purchasing power than even the Goldschmidt prices in October 1958. But all these valuations of Millet, Meissonier, Breton and Rosa Bonheur have collapsed hopelessly. The modern buyer must therefore be prepared to face that possibility too.

But can such falls repeat themselves? The high-priced pictures of to-day are destined, sooner rather than later, to be frozen off the market. Price must eventually cease to be an indication of a change in taste. When everything of its class is safely tucked away in a museum, the price is forgotten. Whether a picture was bought for the National Gallery in the 1830's for a hundred or two, or whether its companion was bought by Andrew Mellon for the Washington National Gallery in the 1930's for a hundred thousand, is of no consequence to anyone. Few people know the price in any case. The work is there and nothing like it can be found again.

Historians of the changes of taste should not allow a crystal ball to form any part of their library equipment. Forecasts should not be made, but none of the implications of the present should be ignored. Tachist painting and Action painting are a development so seemingly irrational that a large body of critical opinion prefers to keep silent. But look at some of the prices and remember that Braque and Picasso were lucky to get £250 for a picture, even when they were close on the age of fifty and when the critical climate was favourable:

Parke-Bernet Galleries, New York, 27 April, 2960

		£
Georges Mathieu (b. 1921)	*Abstraction* (1951)	1,350
Jean Dubuffet (b. 1901)	*L'ame des sous-sols*	4,820
	Grand jazz-band (1944)	9,650
Hans Hartung (b. 1904)	'*756–12*'	3,915
Pierre Soulages (b. 1919)	*Abstraction*	3,255
Arshile Gorky (1904–1948)	*Abstraction*	2,300

These prices are far from exceptional. Mathieu, who can cover a 15-ft. canvas in a public theatre in twenty minutes, is said to receive up to £5,000 for his larger works. A Hartung abstraction was sold at Sotheby's in November 1960 for £4,200. Gorky was a member of the New York school which produced Jackson Pollock, apparently the most costly of the 'post-abstract' painters. Prices of over £25,000 have certainly been paid privately. It was denied that the Jackson Pollock, acquired by the Tate Gallery through the Heinz Fund in November 1960, cost £20,000. The price, it was retorted, was moderate, in fact a generous gesture at less than £5,000.

It may perhaps be argued that, if painting of this kind becomes universally accepted, then the older sort of abstract picture, which retains the discipline of planned composition and planned colour harmonies, must become old-fogeyish and outdated and that the present very high market for such things must therefore fall. It may also be argued that the present emphasis on the flow of the subconscious is part of the last permitted freedom of expression of the individual. As higher education, regulated from one source, extends its grip over entire populations, art may become purely a vehicle of propaganda and therefore realist as it is in communist countries. This would be a complete reaction from the trend of the past sixty years, and it could happen without any preliminary social revolution. Under those conditions the value of all modern schools of painting would decline indiscriminately.

Another contingency which must be considered is that the acquisition of works of art, as traditionally conceived, may become altogether removed from the reach of the individual buyer. A world without art shops or salerooms is not impossible. But things that are created by the hand of man for no utilitarian purpose will always be acquired as embellishments of life. Something must take the place of the objects that are no longer to be found, even when everything down to the least glass paperweight is in a cultural institution of one kind or another. To collect nothing at all is to descend below the level of magpies and marmots.

PART TWO

SALES ANALYSIS OF THE MOST POPULAR PAINTERS

1760–1960

INTRODUCTION

The lists which follow are not a compendious index of the best-known painters of the world. To make such a list to-day would require perhaps treble the seven large volumes of H. Mireur's *Dictionnaire des ventes*, which do not go beyond 1900. It would also require a small army of research workers. The lists are not an independent work of reference, but a companion to the text. Painters have therefore been included either because they have been fashionable at one time or another or because they have generally been recognised as classical. To have included all the rarities that are seldom found on the market would require more elbow room than this single volume.

Some of the painters whose market these lists illustrate may be thought to have taken up too much space, the English late-eighteenth-century school for instance. But this school did dominate the London salerooms for close on seventy years more than any other school of the past, and the historian is obliged to record the fact. Moreover, if Millais, Landseer and Turner receive rather more attention than such a man of miracles as Vermeer of Delft, it is because they were monarchs of the saleroom in their day and a very curious chapter in the history of taste, which is so often the history of bad taste.

I have endeavoured to prevent the constantly recurring 'saleroom painters' from altogether swamping the rarer items. In Algernon Graves's three precious and very accurate volumes of 1918–1920, William Blake gets three entries and David Cox over 600 entries, which fill sixteen folio pages. It is this sort of thing that I have tried to avoid, but of necessity there will be found a lot of information which is not very topical. Possibly there are only a few people who want to look up Wouverman, Berchem, Teniers, Van Ostade and the Both brothers. But at the beginning of the nineteenth century half the art-loving world thought them the greatest painters that had ever lived. This opinion has changed and the lists show, better than any explanatory text, how this change has made itself felt.

The history of the London art market cannot be studied as a completely separate entity. I have therefore included a fair proportion of foreign sales. I have tried to include, where possible, the actual commission fees which painters earned in the period 1760–1960, and, in the case of old masters, privately negotiated sales and State purchases. The saleroom is never the end of the story. Unfortunately it is seldom possible to discover the end. With early sales the identification of the object is often extremely difficult. With very up-to-date sales there is a strong element of mystery. I will add that any information which can help the work of revision will be most welcome.

Unless otherwise stated, the items refer to London sales. Until 1920 or thereabouts this means with few exceptions sales at Christie's. Such sales are therefore designated simply with the letter C, while Sotheby sales are marked with an S. In the case of other firms, the names are given in brief, but in the case of foreign sales only the name of the city. Normally the first name is the name of the vendor, but where the sale is anonymous the name of the auctioneer is entered. Drawings, when included, appear at the end of the lists, but water-colour paintings are included in the main body under the designation wc. Where the name of the present owner or owners is known to me, this appears at the end of the entry.

I must apologise for a profusion of figures like £2,047 10*s.* and £4,567 10*s.*, but everyone knows that the abolition of the guinea would be a suicidal step towards the decimal system. In the case of foreign sales, the prices have been calculated according to the rates of exchange at the time of sale.

SIR LAWRENCE ALMA-TADEMA. 1836–1913

The great days of this painter began in the 1870's, but he lived a long time and his reputation was singularly unassailable. In spite of a small intellectual movement of disfavour, going back at least to the 1880's, there were writers on art on the eve of the First World War who still found these frigid reconstructions comparable with the greatest masters of the past. The market for Alma-Tadema was fairly strong as late as 1925, but in the winter of 1960 when two of his most famous works reappeared on Christie's walls, they were not even mentioned in the newspapers.

		£
1861	Royal Academy. The childhood of Clothild (see 1872).	420
1870	George Rennie. C. The artist's studio.	472 11s.
1872	Murrieta. C. The childhood of Clothild (see 1861).	1,102 10s.
1874	The Roman picture gallery (see 1903). Commissioned by Ernest Gambart, who was said to have paid £10,000 for the picture and copyright.	
1883	Murrieta (Marquess de Santurce). C. The honeymoon (see 1949).	840
	William Lee. C. The wine (see 1950).	504
	The Exedra.	1,470
	Sandeman. C. Betwixt hope and fear (see 1926).	1,312 10s.
1890	Marquess de Santurce. C. Audience with Agrippa (see 1947).	2,675
1891	Marquess de Santurce. C. 'Amateur Romain'.	2,780
1896	Sir Julian Goldsmid. C. Expiation (see 1940).	2,047
1903	Ernest Gambart. C. The Roman picture gallery (see 1874).	2,625
	Dedication to Bacchus.	5,880
1903	Henry Marquand deceased, New York. A reading of Homer.	6,060
1904	The finding of Moses (see 1935, 1942, 1960). Commissioned by Sir John Aird.	5,250
1909	Holbrooke Gaskell. C. Thou rose of all the roses (see 1930).	1,155
1909	Chantrey Bequest buys 'A Favourite Custom'.	1,750
1913	George MacCulloch. C. The sculpture gallery.	2,730
	Love's jewelled fetter.	1,995
1915	Blakeslee. New York. The sculpture gallery (see 1913).	1,902
1920	C. Aphrodite's cradle.	1,430
1925	Sir W. Denny. C. Love in idleness.	1,050
1926	C. Betwixt hope and fear (see 1883).	398
1929	Hollingsworth. C. A Roman studio.	398
	A Roman scribe (£630 in 1907).	336

		£
1931	S. The Roman picture gallery (see 1874, 1903).	500
1930	C. Thou rose of all the roses (see 1909).	110 5s.
	The Mummy.	89 5s.
1935	Sir John Aird. C. The finding of Moses (see 1904, 1942, 1960).	861
1934	C. The roses of Elagabalus (see 1960).	483
1940	C. Expiation (see 1896).	52 10s.
1941	Sir Max Waechter. C. The frigidarium (£315 in 1946).	210
1942	Sir Jeremiah Colman. The finding of Moses (see 1960).	273 10s.
1945	Edwin A. Fricke, New York. Spring.	900
1947	Mrs. A. J. Mason. C. An audience with Agrippa (see 1890).	94 10s.
1948	S. Strigyls and sponges (£483 in 1904).	32
1950	C. The ring.	194 10s.
	The wine (see 1883).	31 10s.
1958	Lady Lever. S. In the rose garden.	241 10s.
1960	F. W. Reeves. C. Roses of Elagabalus (see 1934) (commissioned in 1888 for £4,000).	105
	The finding of Moses (see 1904, etc.).	252

Fra Giovanni da Fiesole or Il beato Angelico, called FRA ANGELICO. 1387–1455

It will be noticed that in early Victorian times Fra Angelico was several times more expensive than any other quattrocento painter. The Fesch *Last Judgement* was certainly the first primitive picture to make a four-figure price. But as early as the Napoleonic wars Fra Angelico had been the model for the German artistic colony in Rome, the *Nazarener* school. There could be no stronger antithesis to French republican art with its frozen dialectic and its blue-chinned Brutuses than this beatified and dedicated monk, painting all his life on the walls of a monastery. In the late 1840's Johann von Fiesole was not only a long established honorary German, but his works had also begun to appear at Oxford in pale Arundel prints on the walls of Puseyite undergraduates, and in 1850 Dante Gabriel Rossetti painted *Ecce Ancilla Domini.*

		£
1826	Baron Vivant-Denon, deceased. Paris. The Visitation, diptych.	43 9s.
1845	Cardinal Fesch. Rome. The Last Judgement, altarpiece	704
	(see 1885). Resold in 1846 to the Earl of Dudley.	1,500
1854	Marquis Joly de Bammeville. Last Judgement (bought in) (see 1897).	525

		£
1856	Samuel Rogers. C. Holy Family enthroned (probably school of Gozzoli).	325 10s.
1859	Earl of Northwick (Philips). Ss. Cosmas and Damian (see 1886).	77 14s.
1860	National Gallery buys in Rome the San Domenico altarpiece from Fiesole; total cost including export fees.	4,200
	Samuel Woodburn. C. The Virgin at the Last Judgement.	462
1882	Hamilton Palace. C. Two panels, quite small, the Virgin and an angel. National Gallery.	1,312 10s.
1885	Christie's negotiate sale of Earl of Dudley's Last Judgement (see 1845) to the Berlin Museum.	10,000
1886	William Graham. C. Ss. Cosmas and Damian (see 1859). National Gallery, Dublin.	73 10s.
1892	Earl of Dudley. C. Holy Family, two angels.	840
1894	Bourgeois. Paris. National Gallery buys Annunciation.	1,500
1897	Ganet. Paris. Last Judgement (see 1854 and 1923).	1,000
1912	J. E. Taylor. C. Annunciation.	1,785
1923	Sir J. Robinson. C. Day of judgement (bought in) (see 1854, 1897).	3,570
1938	Carl Hamilton. New York. Annunciation (Collection Edsel Ford).	37,400
1957	Rev. A. Hawkes. S. Two small panels of saints.	7,800
1959	S. 8 drawings by disciples of Angelico, formerly William Morris collection.	9,000
1960	S. Small panel, St. Benedict, from San Marco altarpiece, Florence.	9,500

ANTONELLO DA MESSINA. 1430–1478

		£
1807	Celotti. Rome. Man holding a medal.	6 10s.
1849	William Coningham. C. St. Jerome in his study, sold as Van Eyck (see 1894).	162 15s.
1859	Earl of Northwick (Phillips). Alleged self-portrait.	82 19s.
1861	National Gallery buys Salvator Mundi in Genoa.	160
1865	Pourtalès. Paris. Louvre buys the Condottiere portrait, dated 1475.	4,541
1869	Stevens (Philips). Portrait, man in green dress and cap.	157 10s.
1882	Hamilton Palace. C. Man in a black dress.	131 5s.
	Youth in a black cap, dated 1474 (Kaiser Friedrich Museum).	514 10s.
1884	National Gallery buys portrait of a young man, in Genoa.	1,040
1884	National Gallery buys The little Crucifixion from Lady Waterford.	350

		£
1894	Andrew Fountaine. C. Man with clasped hands.	425 5s.
	National Gallery buys St. Jerome (see 1849), from the Earl of Northbrook.	2,500
1934	S. Attributed panel, Abraham with angels.	780

The *Condottiere*, St. Jerome and the small Crucifixion would to-day be worth more than a quarter of a million each.

SIR WILLIAM BEECHEY. 1753–1839

A journeyman painter, who exhibited at the Royal Academy almost continuously between 1776 and 1839 and who owed his knighthood to the poor taste of George III. Beechey could make a 100-guinea fee for a whole-length as easily as Romney, but his works only had a very small share in the huge prices paid for eighteenth-century portraits between the 1860's and 1920's.

		£
1775	C. A small family group.	33 12s.
1798	George III commissions an 18-ft. picture of himself reviewing the Dragoons.	1,260
1860	Wilkie executors. C. Portrait of David Wilkie.	33 12s.
1872	Brodrip. C. Evelina holding a letter.	267 15s.
1886	Addington. C. Same picture.	945
1895	James Pryce. C. Two portraits. Lady Barnard.	1,239
	Frederica, Duchess of York.	1,260
1904	Duke of Cambridge. C. George, Prince of Wales.	1,680
1909	Cuthbert Quilter. C. Mrs. Archer.	934 10s.
1912	C. Princess Mary.	600
1913	C. Mrs. R. Hall.	1,071
	Countess of Breadalbane	3,045
1917	C. Mrs. Hill and her son.	1,837 10s.
	Mrs. Farthing (see 1927).	4,830
1918	Earl of Carnarvon. C. Lady Harriet Stanhope.	5,985*
1919	C. Anne and Augustus Coventry.	1,575
1923	Sir Joseph Robinson. C. Duchess of York (bought in).	1,575
1927	Viscount Curzon. C. Mrs. Farthing (see 1917).	1,995
	Lady Beechey.	1,427 10s.
	Self-portrait.	1,102 10s.
1928	Earl of Abingdon. S. Montague, Lord Norries.	3,400
	The Misses Rush, crowning a bust of Handel.	3,200
	C. Queen Charlotte.	1,992 10s.
1934	C. Master James Hatch, whole-length.	1,449
1939	Randolph Hearst. New York. Mrs. Hill and her son.	724
1950	Campbell Lewis. New York. The Meredith children.	1,072
1961	Mrs. Lilian S. Whitmarsh. New York. The Sterling Family.	2,857

GIOVANNI BELLINI. 1427–1516

A heavily attributed painter. Before the researches of Bernard Berenson, any picture that looked like an early Titian but a bit harder passed as a Giovanni Bellini. Until 1900 such pictures were, with few exceptions, very cheap. But when one considers that, recently, prices of over £15,000 each have been paid for quite rough pen-and-ink sketches, William Beckford's two modest purchases, the *Agony in the Garden* and the *Doge Loredano* should now be worth several hundred thousand pounds each.

		£
1770	Count Bruhl. C. Holy Family and saints.	61 19*s.*
1779	Houghton Hall. Empress Catherine buys Holy Family.	60
1800	Orleans sale (Coxe). Adoration of the Kings (resold 1806, £20 19*s.* 6*d.*).	16 16*s.*
1807	Coxe. Beckford buys Doge Loredano (see 1844).	13 13*s.*
1810	Walsh Porter. C. Narcissus (not identified).	53 11*s.*
1823	Fonthill, ex Beckford (Philips). St. Catherine (see 1848). Bought by Smith.	142 16*s.*
	Agony in the Garden (see 1863), sold as Mantegna.	52 10*s.*
1844	Beckford, Lansdowne Towers, Bath. Doge Loredano. Bought by National Gallery.	630
1848	Duke of Buckingham, Stowe (Philips). St. Catherine (see 1823). Bought by Eastlake.	37 16*s.*
1849	William Coningham. C. Holy Family.	183 15*s.*
1852	W. Jones. C. San Zaccharia altarpiece.	378
	Sir W. W. Murray. St. Francis, view of Assisi (Berlin Museum).	735
1855	National Gallery buys Madonna of the pomegranates.	300
1857	Earl of Shrewsbury. C. The Circumcision (bought-in). (National Gallery, 1879).	170 2*s.*
1859	Earl of Northwick (Philips). Madonna with the parroquet.	315
1863	Rev. Davenport Bromley. C. Agony in the Garden (see 1823). Bought by National Gallery.	630
	Small panel, St. Jerome (see 1948).	19 8*s.*
1865	Pourtalès-Gorgier. Paris. Holy Family and donor.	1,624
1867	Duc de Salamanca. Paris. Holy Family.	2,480
1870	National Gallery buys Peter Martyr, small panel.	280
1872	Le Prince Imperiale. C. Holy Family with green curtain.	630
1874	Alexander Barker. V. The Manfrini Holy Family. (Royal Gallery, Dresden).	756
1876	Wynn Ellis. C. Holy Family and saints, signed (see 1886).	483
1879	Anderdon. C. Miniature Holy Family.	46 14*s.*

		£
1879	Alton Towers. C. (Earl of Shrewsbury). The Circumcision (see 1857). Bought by National Gallery.	79 16*s.*
1882	Hamilton Palace. C. Man in black. Bought by National Gallery. Now called Vincenzo Catena.	525
1886	William Graham. C. Holy Family (see 1876).	745 10*s.*
1887	Roupell. C. The blood of the Redeemer (National Gallery).	472
1892	Earl of Dudley. C. Holy Family, 26 ins. × 19 ins.	1,155
	Lady Eastlake. C. Ludwig Mond buys Holy Family and saints (left to National Gallery, 1924).	535
1904	C. S. Hayne. C. Small Holy Family and donor.	1,176
1915	Duke of Northumberland sells the Feast of the Gods to Carl Hamilton (National Gallery, Washington).	20,000 (?)
1923	Lord Brownlow. C. Adoration of the shepherds.	4,410
1925	Earl of Carnarvon. C. Gentleman in black.	3,570
1927	Holford. C. Portrait of a boy, dated 1490 (Barber Institute, Birmingham).	6,510
1929	Sawbridge Earle Drax. C. Riposo.	7,875
1935	S. Small head, man in black.	2,800
1945	Lord Rothermere. C. Weeping Magdalen.	3,360
1948.	C. St. Jerome, small panel (see 1863). Bought by Barber Institute, Birmingham.	4,830
1957	S. Two wings of a Crucifixion triptych (Collection A. E. N. Clark).	22,000

DRAWINGS

1896	Earl of Warwick. C. Presentation in the Temple.	288 15*s.*
1928	S. Portrait of a young man, black chalk	800
1955	Le Hunte. S. Nativity, pen and wash.	4,000
1958	John Skippe. C. Two pencil studies, Christ at the column, on one sheet.	15,750
1959	C. A sheet of three studies of an apostle.	15,540

BERNARDO BELLOTTO

or the younger Canaletto. 1720–1780

The sale of the Hillingdon Bellottos in 1946 and the exhibition of the views of Warsaw in London in 1954 came as a belated reminder that Bellotto's work could be as good as his uncle's at his best period. In fact, it can even be doubted whether Canaletto Senior painted anything better than those dazzling Warsaw evocations. Bellotto, it will be noticed, is a much cheaper painter, but that does not mean that the commodity is easily available. Works painted throughout by Bellotto's own hand reach the salerooms extremely seldom.

		£
1880	Hampton and Sons. C. View of Dresden.	178 10s.
1883	Prince Narishkin. Paris. Two views of Dresden.	360
1898	Tabourier. Paris. Oratory of the palace, Dresden.	404
1901	C. View of Verona (5 ft.).	199 15s.
1908	Martin Colnaghi. (Robinson, Fisher.) English church at Dresden.	462
1929	Princess Paley. C. Church of San Giovanni e Paolo, Venice.	1,785
1946	Lord Hillingdon. C. Five views of Dresden (each 8 ft. wide). Total £9,817.	
	The dearest (see 1957).	2,362
	The cheapest.	1,365
1947	De Carolis. S. The villa Malcontenta (small).	980
1949	Sir Robert Adeane. C. Courtyard of imaginary palace.	1,155
1950	Mrs. Warwick Bryant. C. Two of the Hillingdon Bellottos resold. The pair	3,990
1953	Alan P. Good. C. Two views of Turin.	3,150
1955	C. Unknown town on a river (18 ins. × 30 ins.).	1,680
1957	S. View of Dresden (see 1946).	2,600

NICOLAS BERCHEM. 1620–1683

One of the first Dutch painters to appeal to eighteenth-century French taste. High prices were paid during the Napoleonic wars both in Paris and in London, and there was a somewhat inexplicable revival between the 1860's and 1880's. The modern demand is almost negligible.

		£
1737	Comtesse de Verrue. Paris. Mountainous landscape.	145
1764	Lalive de Jully. Paris. Travellers on a road.	330
1784	Comte Merle. Paris. Ancien port de Gênes.	480
1785	Resold in London next year. (Auguste Lebrun. C.)	640 10s.
1797	John Trumbull. C. Mountainous landscape, bought by Benjamin West for the King. (Royal Collection.)	945
1806	Wellbore Ellis Agar. C. Château de Bentheim, valued for Lord Grosvenor, who bought the collection.	3,150
1809	Granpré. Paris. Mountainous landscape, bought in.	1,200
1817	Buchanan. C. (ex Talleyrand). Les fagots.	840
1823	Fonthill, ex Beckford (Philips). Embarking provisions.	808 10s.
1831	Reinagle. C. Grand mountainous landscape (see 1912).	420
1840	Sir Simon Clark. C. Landscape with ruins, bought by Sir Robert Peel (National Gallery, 1871).	420
1868	San Donato. Paris. Ancien port de Gênes (see 1784–1785).	1,680

		£
1872	Isaac Péreire. Paris. Animals by a canal.	1,680
1875	Miss Bredel. C. Woman with a distaff.	945
1876	Foster, Clewer Manor. C. Landscape (see 1893).	1,207
1882	Hamilton Palace. C. Landscape, dated 1659.	1,735
1890	W. Wells, Redleaf. C. The ford.	892
1893	Field. C. Landscape (see 1876).	682 10*s.*
1896	Arthur Seymour. C. Muleteers at an inn. (over 6 ft.).	546
1900	C. Grand mountainous landscape (see 1831).	189
1912	Lesser. C. Same picture.	367 10*s.*
1925	Earl of Carnarvon. C. Woody landscape.	252
1928	Holford. C. Le diamant de la curiosité.	420
1937	Victor Rothschild. S. Winter scene in Holland.	200
1950	Col. Clowes. C. Landscape, peasants and cattle.	409 10*s.*
1957	Gunhilda Fisher. S. Extensive wooded landscape (probably record English price for a Berchem since 1882).	900
1961	S. Mountainous Landscape	500

WILLIAM BLAKE. 1757–1828

It was only about 1903 that Blake was regarded as a painter-poet, rather than a poet who amused himself by drawing. By 1929 he was established as a great and rare artist. Though the taste for Blake is American as much as English, it is entirely Anglo-Saxon. Religious mania has never been a very marketable commodity in Paris. My own introduction to Blake, the painter, was at the Linnell sale in 1918, to which my drawing-master sent me on a school half-holiday, an unforgettable experience.

		£
1828	John Flaxman, executor sale. Beckford buys the drawings for Gray's *Elegy*, rediscovered on the demolition of Hamilton Palace, 1919.	
1884	William Russell. C. 18 grisaille heads of poets, painted for Hayley's house at Felpham. 5 to 12 guineas each.	
1882	Samuel Palmer executors. S. National Gallery buys Pitt directing Behemoth.	100
1885	Alfred Aspland. S. Tempera paintings on paper:	
	Christ blessing the children.	16 16*s.*
	Fall of the rebel angels.	6 6*s.*
	Some of the drawings made one shilling each.	
1903	Earl of Crewe. S. 21 tempera paintings for *The Book of Job* with proof plates (see 1949), the series.	5,600
1905	S. 10 drawings for *Paradise Lost*, the series.	2,000
1911	Dilke. C. Queen Catherine's dream (see 1925).	52 10*s.*
	Satan tormenting Job.	157 10*s.*

		£
1914	British Museum buys Bathsheba at the bath.	84
1918	Linnell. C. Melbourne National Gallery buys 102 drawings for the *Divina Commedia*, the series.	7,665
	21 drawings for *The Book of Job*.	3,990
	12 drawings for *Paradise Regained*.	2,100
	Many others.	
1925	S. Philoctetes and Neoptolemus, tempera.	510
1925	S. By the waters of Babylon, tempera.	600
1929	Sydney Morse. C. Queen Catherine's dream, tempera, painted for Lawrence (see 1911).	1,942 10*s.*
	The Devil revealed, wc.	1,890
	The Nativity, tempera on copper.	1,029
1937	C. Christ at the sepulchre, wc.	546
1938	2nd Linnell sale. C. Christ praying with angels, wc.	630
1941	Mrs. Henry Walters. New York. Subject in tempera.	2,520
1946	S. Samson and Delilah, tempera (£23 2*s.* in 1914).	1,100
1949	W. Graham Robertson. C.	
	Job confessing his presumption (£105 in 1903), bought by National Gallery, Edinburgh.	7,770*
	Jacob's ladder, bought by British Museum.	5,460
	The Four and Twenty Elders, bought by Tate Gallery.	6,730
	The Ascension, bought by Fitzwilliam Museum.	7,350
	Many others.	
1957	Col. Gowe-Weston. C. Elijah in a chariot of fire.	4,200
1959	S. The good and evil angels, wc, bought by Cecil Higgins Museum.	2,200
	Mary Magdalene at feet of Christ.	2,050

ROSA BONHEUR. 1822–1899

The lady worked very hard indeed and never has a negligible aesthetic merit been better rewarded. For the English market she manufactured Landseers, even to the point of braving the cooking of the Highlands. For the Franco-American market she made Troyons and super-Troyons. Maybe she is not worth more than an inch, but I cannot resist the spectral posthumous biography which emerges from the rise and fall of Christie's guineas. *Surrealistes* should note that in 1868 she drove Millais in a cab from Fontainebleau Station, dressed up as a priest and wearing the sash of the *Legion d'Honneur*.

			£
1860	I. K. Brunel. C. Breton Oxen.		1,417 10*s.*
1861	Ernest Gambart. C. Spanish Buricaros (see 1940).		1,995
1865	C. Two cattle pictures.	each	2,100
1872	Joseph Gillott. C. Scene in the Pyrenees.		1,890

		£
1886	Dana. New York. The horse fair (16 ft. long),	10,600
	sold to Junius Spencer Morgan for	12,000
	Given to the Metropolitan Museum.	
	C. Smaller replica of same, now in National Gallery.	3,150
1887	John Graham. C. Denizens of the Highlands.	5,827 10*s.*
	A Highland Raid (see 1949).	4,059
	Return from Pasture (see 1935).	2,152
1888	Bolckow. C. Pâturages nivernaises (see 1929).	4,410
	Mr. J. G. Johnson of Philadelphia buys a spotted dog.	3,200
1903	Ernest Gambart, deceased. C. On the alert.	3,255
1906	T. Agnew. C. Sheep in the Pyrenees (£1,260 in 1891).	1,071
1910	Armstrong heirlooms. C. Deer park, Fontainebleau.	241 10*s.*
1929	Sir F. Worsley. C. Pâturages nivernaises (see 1888).	48 3*s.*
1935	Steinkopf. C. Return from pasture (see 1887).	110 5*s.*
1940	Capt. R. A. Brassey. C. Spanish muleteers crossing the Pyrenees (see 1861).	147
1945	Vanderbilt, New York. Flock of sheep, 1878.	675
1946	Mrs. George Martin, New York. Persian leopards, small oils.	276
1949	Baroness Burton. C. A Highland raid (see 1887).	199 10*s.*
1952	Marion Davies, New York. Carting timber in the Pyrenees.	287
1954	Sir Kenneth Clark. C. Highland cattle.	63
	Miss L. Coates. C. Sheep in a pasture.	68 5*s.*

RICHARD PARKES BONINGTON. 1801–1828

In the mid-nineteenth century the market for Bonington's coastal scenes was built up in London, the market for his historical subjects in Paris. *Henri IV and the Spanish Ambassadors* (20 ins. across and hardly more than an oil-sketch) made no less than £3,320 in Paris in 1870. But it was no ordinary oil-sketch. In 1827 it was exhibited in the David-haunted Salon, where it precipitated a revolution —and next year it was bought in by Bonington's father for £84.

Bonington's landscapes and coast scenes have become rare and in the last few years very costly, but they did not escape the decline which overtook the entire early nineteenth-century romantic school in the 1880's.

		£
1829	Bonington executor sale. S. Henri IV and the Spanish Ambassadors (see 1870). Bought in.	84
	Mother and child at prayer.	105
1830	Coutan, Paris. Landscape, bought in but subsequently 'sold to Mr. Reitlinger'.	325
1834	Second Bonington executor sale. C. Grand Canal	409 10*s.*
	Fishmarket	304 10*s.*
	Henri III and the English Ambassadors (see 1860).	105
1835	Duke of Orleans, Paris. Torrent in Dauphine, wc.	328

		£
1849	Moselmann, Paris. Francis I and Duchesse d'Etampes.	268
1853	Demidoff, Paris. The old man, wc.	364
	Anne Page and Slender, wc. (Wallace Collection.)	328
1860	Lord Seymour, Paris. Henri III and the Ambassadors. (Wallace Collection.) (See 1834).	1,960
1869	Delessert, Paris. Francis I and Marguerite of Navarre (Wallace Collection).	1,240
1870	San Donato, Paris. Henri IV and the Spanish Ambassadors (Wallace Collection) (See 1829).	3,320
1872	Joseph Gillott. C. Landscape with timber waggon (see 1935).	540
1875	Sam Mendel. C. Chateau on French coast.	483
1878	Monro of Novar. C. Fishmarket, Boulogne (see 1834).	3,150
	Grand Canal, Venice (see 1834).	3,150
1889	Secrétan, Paris. Low tide (oils).	1,164
1890	Barlow. C. Coast scene, Normandy (see 1917).	1,018 10*s.*
1893	Denain, Paris. Banks of a river.	700
1895	James Price of Paignton. C. Les amoureux.	1,818
1899	Sir John Fowler. C. Coast of Normandy.	1,785
1902	Burton. C. Grand Canal (see 1878) (damaged in fire, see also 1914).	84
	Fisherboys on beach.	1,312 10*s.*
1909	Quilter. C. Grand Canal (wc).	378
1914	Sir Charles Robinson. C. Beach at Dieppe.	504
	Grand Canal (part burnt, see 1878, 1902).	7 7*s.*
1917	Sir David Jardine. C. Coast scene, Normandy (see 1890) (Philadelphia Museum).	441
1922	Holbrooke Gaskell. C. Venice, Dogana and Salute.	1,260
	Fuller-Maitland. C. Chateau de la Duchesse de Berri (see 1960). £462 in 1879.	325 10*s.*
1924	Darrell Brown. C. View near Nantes, 1826 (3-ft. landscape, oils).	2,310
1927	Sir James Ross. C. Fisherfolk, Normandy.	3,150
	Viscount Curzon. C. View in Paris, oils.	1,050
1935	J. G. Coats. C. The timber waggon (see 1872).	1,260
	Fécamps beach.	945
1943	A. T. Reid. C. Beach near Dieppe.	1,470
1946	Pitt-Miller. C. River scene, Picardy.	2,940
1954	Miss L. Coats. View on Seine with barge.	2,520
	River scene.	2,415
1959	H. L. Fison. C. Beach scene.	5,040
	S. Fishing village.	4,200
1960	Charles Russell. S. Château de la Duchesse de Berri, small oils (see 1922).	6,800

PIERRE BONNARD. 1867–1947

Not so much a belated Impressionist as a *Symbolist* who in his earlier work rejected form altogether and was harshly criticised by the original impressionist brotherhood. Not found in the London saleroom before the 1950's, but frequently exhibited in London in the 1920's and 1930's. Before the war £1,000 would have been an exceptionally high price. To-day Bonnard rates higher than Sisley or Pisarro and most of Monet.

		£
1948	Parke-Bernet, New York. Les boutiques, Boulevard de Battignoles.	960
1950	Galerie Charpentier, Paris. Les Mamans.	458
1953	Galerie Charpentier, Paris. Femme nue, 1907.	3,470
1954	Parke Bernet, New York. The yellow screen.	5,000
1954	C. Lady at her toilet.	4,410
1956	S. Vegetable stall.	3,500
1955	Galerie Charpentier, Paris. Femme aux mimeuses.	7,350
1957	S. Nue au tub.	5,500
1957	Sir Walter Fletcher. C. Le petit dejeuner.	5,040
1957	Georges Lurcy, New York. Femme nue.	25,000
	Buste de femme courbée.	17,850
1958	S. Le petit dejeuner.	3,800
1958	Arnold Kirkeby, New York. Vendeuse de fruits.	14,200
	At the stage door.	6,075
	Renée.	6,075
	Same day. Vernon sale. Fenêtre ouverte.	34,140*
1959	Goldschmidt. S. Still life.	13,500
1960	Farmyard, seen over a gate.	14,125
	S. Femme nue.	18,000
	Galerie Charpentier, Paris. Petite route meridionale au Cannet, 1924.	19,270
1961	Galliera, Paris. Poppies in a stone vase.	22,350

ALESSANDRO BOTTICELLI. 1444–1510

Probably the most popular of all quattrocento painters, particularly in England, where he influenced late nineteenth-century art unnecessarily. Quite a number of pictures which were sold as Botticellis were not by his hand, and some can no longer be identified. A group, which hovers in style between Botticelli and Filipino Lippi, was for many years attributed to one Amico di Sandro, an invention of Berenson's, which was later dropped by its author. A painting like *Prima Vera* or *Venus rising from the Sea* would to-day be inestimable, and the £173,600, paid by Mellon in 1931 for the much less exciting Hermitage *Adoration* offers no clue. No Botticelli appears to have made £1,000 before 1867. No five-figure price was paid till the last year of the nineteenth century.

		£
1808	Alexander I of Russia buys the Hermitage Adoration from the Corsini family in Florence (see 1931).	
1811	William Young Ottley. Nativity (see 1837). Bought in.	42
1814	Crown Prince Ludwig of Bavaria buys the Munich piéta from the painter Metzner in Florence.	
1816	Cardinal Fesch sale, Rome. Holy Family.	119 8s.
1824	Ravil, commissaire des armées, Paris.	
	Seven singing angels and Holy Family (from Giustiniani Palace, now Kaiser Friedrich Museum).	100
1825	Vivant-Denon, Paris. Holy Family (roundel).	10 13s.
1837	Young Ottley. Nativity (see 1811). National Gallery, 1878.	25 4s.
1843	Cardinal Fesch, Rome. Holy Family.	66 8s.
1854	Marquis Jolly de Bammeville. C. Holy Family (roundel).	220
	Madonna, Child and St. John. Bought Alexander Barker.	546
1857	National Gallery buys Adoration in a landscape from Baldi collection as Filippino Lippi.	627 8s.
1859	Earl of Northwick (Philips). Portrait of a young man. Bought by National Gallery as a Masaccio.	108 3s.
1867	Count Galli Tassi, Florence. Madonna embracing child. Bought for National Gallery with Pollaiuolo's Tobias (now called a school picture).	1,000
1874	Alexander Barker, executors. C.	
	Madonna embracing Christ.	1,680
	Mars and Venus (National Gallery).	1,050
	Venus with Amorini (National Gallery), now called Jacopo del Sellaio.	1,627
	So-called wife of Botticelli (schoolpiece left to National Gallery in 1906).	262 5s.
	Story of Nastagio, two panels (see 1879). Bought in.	£682 and 997 10s.
1878	Fuller-Maitland. C. Adoration (roundel sold as Filippino Lippi). National Gallery.	800
	Nativity. National Gallery (see 1811).	1,500
1879	Alexander Barker, executors. C. Four cassone panels of story of Nastagio.	1,086
	Including marriage of Paolo's daughter (£294, see 1892).	
	The remainder now in the Prado, Madrid.	
1882	Hamilton Palace. Kaiser Friedrich Museum buys the 88 drawings of the *Divina Commedia* through Henry Bohn, the publisher.	
	Hamilton Palace. C. Adoration, National Gallery (once called Amico di Sandro).	1,627
	Assumption of the Virgin. National Gallery. Now called Francesco Botticini.	4,777 10s.

		£
1885	Beckett Denison. C. Madonna of the pomegranate (National Gallery since 1912).	252
1892	Frank Leyland. C. Marriage of Paolo's daughter (see 1879). Collection Oliver Watney.	1,365
1894	Lady Eastlake. C. Holy Family and St. John (National Gallery. Formerly 'Amico di Sandro').	756
	Earl of Ashburnham. Lucretia (bought privately by Isabella Gardner, Boston).	3,500
1899	Chigi family. Madonna of the Eucharist (Isabella Gardner per Colnaghi).	14,600
1905	Lady Ashburton. C. Holy Family and singing angels (Baltimore Museum).	6,300
1906	Lord Grimthorpe. C. Adoration, roundel (see 1917).	5,250
1911	Sir William Abdy. C. Life of St. Zenobius, one of five panels. Metropolitan Museum per Duveen and Pierpont Morgan.	11,550
1917	Fairfax Murray. Adoration, roundel (see 1906) (school picture).	2,940
1921	Austen. C. Nativity, attributed roundel.	2,152 10*s.*
1927	Holford. C. So-called head of St. Thomas Aquinas (now Abegg Collection, Zürich). Small painting on linen.	10,290
1931	Hermitage Museum. Adoration of the kings (see 1808). Sold through Knoedler to Andrew Mellon (now Washington, National Gallery).	173,600*
1946	Earl Crawford of Balcarres. C. Holy Family with saints, small roundel. Attributed. (Collection Rev. Robert Corbauld).	5,880
1946	Lord Rothermere. C. Lady in profile. Attributed.	5,250
1956	S. Madonna and child with pomegranate (attributed).	3,800
1958	Humphrey Cook (ex Doughty House). S. The Pentecost, attributed.	3,800

FRANÇOIS BOUCHER. 1704–1770

The National Gallery owns only two Bouchers, as if to intimate that this sort of Parisian frivolity belongs to the Wallace Collection. It is difficult to understand M. Blanc's fury against the Marquess of Hertford for buying *dessus de porte* at less than £300 each in 1857; it is still more difficult to understand how, fifty years later, two of these decorative panels could have made nearly £50,000 when a Watteau could scarcely make £7,000. The prices of the 1950's suggest that this market at least has not run riot. Boucher could be a very fine artist at times, most brilliant of all perhaps as a draughtsman, and it is his drawings that appear to be advancing most.

		£
1770	Marquise de Pompadour, Paris. Two panels of nymphs.	392
1844	Baron d'Ivry, Paris. La fête des bergers (see 1884). Bought in (may be an error of Mireur).	3,200
1849	Blessington, Gore House. C. Two portraits of the Princesse de Croy.	£18 18*s.* and £12 12*s.*
1851	Montlouis, Paris. Two pairs of ovals, Diana and Calisto (see 1957)	130
	Angelica and Medora (see 1957).	130
1855	Ralph Bernal. C. Two *dessus de porte.*	64 1*s.*
1857	Patureau, Paris. Two groups of nymphs.	580
	Two panels, Autumn and Spring (Marquess of Hertford, Wallace Collection).	580
1860	Culling Eardley (Paris). Two panels of nymphs.	1,250
1861	King. C. Pan and Syrinx (National Gallery 1880).	94 10*s.*
1874	Alexander Barker. 8 upright panels from Wilton (see 1903).	6,052
1884	Baron d'Ivry, Paris. Fête des Bergers (see 1844).	1,600
	Les Lavandiers.	1,600
1885	Paris. La barraudière.	5,350
1887	Earl of Lonsdale. C. Mme. Pompadour (Louvre per Maurice de Rothschild).	10,395
1889	Secrétan, Paris. Sleep of Venus.	3,400
1903	Reginald Vaile. C. 5 of the Crécy panels from Wilton (see 1874 and 1923).	23,415
	Diana reposing.	3,150
1904	Mrs. Ridgeway, Paris. The Charms of Spring, 4 panels.	14,400
1910	Charles T. Yerkes, New York. Toilet of Venus.	5,100
1918	Vicomte de Curel, Paris. Child eating its supper.	3,500
1923	Sir Anthony de Rothschild. C. Les fêtes Italiennes, 4 cartoons for tapestry.	15,750
	Sir Joseph Robinson. C. The 5 Crécy panels, bought in (Collection Princess Labbia, Cape Town).	18,900
1926	Late Lord Michelham (Hampton's).	
	La pipée aux oiseaux / La fontaine d'amour } The pair, bought by Capt. Jefferson Cohen.	47,250*
1930	C. Jupiter and Calisto (23 ins. × 28 ins.).	4,200
1935	Faucher-Magnan. S. La péche chinoise.	2,400
1937	J. Pierson Gregory. C. 5 *dessus de porte.*	5 for 23,100
1950	Stehli, New York. Pastorale, small oval.	4,640
1954	Galerie Charpentier, Paris. Depart pour la péche.	5,100
1955	Maj.-Gen. F. E. Sotheby. S. The mill and the troutstream, 2 small ovals (see 1960).	2 for 9,800
1957	Mae Rovensky, New York. Diana and Calisto.	2 for 12,500
	Angelica and Medora (see 1851).	2 for 12,500

		£
1958	S. Large landscape with watermill (now, Kansas City Gallery).	15,000
1959	C. The Rhône and the Rhine, 2 *dessus de porte* painted in grisaille. 2 for	4,725
1960	Viscount Ednam. C. The mill and the trout-stream (see 1955). 2 for	10,500

DRAWINGS

1906	Charles Bowyer. C. Venus, large sanguine drawing.	105
1920	Marquess of Lansdowne. S. Nude woman reclining. 8 others exceeded £100 each.	400
1923	S. Reclining nude, heightened chalks.	750
1925	Earl of Carnarvon. C. 2 pastel drawings, ladies in landscape.	1,059
1929	Princesse Paley. C. The young angler, sanguine.	441
1936	Faucher Magnan. S. Design for tapestry.	2,400
1944	Mrs. Joseph Heine, New York. The flute-player. Gouache on vellum.	1,120
1949	Claude Lucas. C. Girl's head and shoulders.	504
1956	Galerie Charpentier, Paris. La rêveuse, pencil and chalk.	960
1959	Mrs. H. Chanter. S. The birth of Venus.	1,100
	Venus and Cupid.	1,400
	Black chalk, heightened white.	
1959	Chrysler-Foy, New York. Baigneuse.	1,250

EUGENE BOUDIN. 1824–1898

A little master who has been inflated into a big master. His light and pretty paintings are often considered to be impressionist, which they are not, although Boudin, then an elderly man, was allowed to exhibit with the Impressionists in 1875. He was a pupil of Isabey, trained in the romantic early 'forties, and even his later work pays homage to the idol of that day, Richard Bonington. The one was a very original person, the other a skilful follower, gifted with a better sense of paint and colour, but with, alas, only one thing to say. There are signs that this market, a creation of the 1950's, is getting under control.

At the end of Boudin's life any of his work could have been had for £50. There was a slow build-up in the early 1900's.

		£
1910	Alexander Young. C. Antwerp, 1871.	136 10*s.*
1912	Harvey. C. Port d'Anvers.	231 10*s.*
1927	W. Thorburn. C. 8 pictures. Port of Rotterdam.	472 10*s.*
1928	C. Beach scene.	546
1929	Vente E.S., Paris. Trouville, beach scene.	1,200
1936	Lawson. S. 23 small beach and harbour scenes.	7,500

		£
1940	S. Au Havre, 1887.	78
	Trouville Plage.	88
1941	Lord Rothermere. C. 2 beach scenes.	872 10*s.*
		431 10*s.*
1942	Andrew T. Reid. S. 18 small pictures.	6,700
1945	M. S. Myers. S. 14 small pictures.	4,735
1951	C. Seascape and paddle steamer.	840
1952	(May) Gabriel Cognacq, Paris. Fête des regattes.	4,800
	(3 others, £1,600–£2,000.)	
	(November) Wildenstein, New York. Plage à Deauville.	2,500
1954	Rees-Jeffreys. C. Port of Antwerp.	3,700
	Les chantiers.	2,100
1955	Sir Edward Cripps. C. Berck Plage.	4,200
	Deauville with figures.	5,040
1956	Sale at Glasgow. Jettées, Trouville.	4,700
	Three others at £3,500–£4,000.	
1957	S. Plage à Trouville, 1867.	7,300
1957	Galerie Charpentier, Paris. Trouville, 1862.	13,800
	Les crinolines.	9,800
1957	Georges Lurcy, New York. À Deauville.	8,214
	À Venise.	8,214
1959	S. Trouville.	1,950
1960	(November) S. Beach scene.	8,000
	(December) C. Trouville.	5,090

GEORGES BRAQUE. *b.* 1881

In the early 1900's painted close to Cézanne and was one of the first to do so. The Cubist works, that are now so costly, were produced between 1908 and 1912. Since the 1920's Braque's style has changed little. Consistence, an attractive colour scheme and no violent demands on the eye are the things that have made Braque the most costly of post-Cézanne painters, but in the 1930's £500 was almost a top price.

		£
1921–3	Sequester sales of Henri Kahnweiler, Paris. According to Maurice Rheims, 118 paintings and drawings by Braque made between them less than £800.	
1937	Hollender and Bernheimer. C.	
	Nue dans un paysage (Maynard Keynes).	220 10*s.*
	Corbeille de fruits (Leicester Galleries).	220 10*s.*
	Nature morte (Zwemmer).	183 15*s.*
1945	Walter Chrysler, New York. Grapes.	672
	Still life with fruit.	672
1946	Parke-Bernet, New York. Vase d'anémones, 1927.	995

		£
1947	S. Etretat, 1930.	280
1950	Parke-Bernet, New York. Apples (small).	428
1954	Rees-Jeffreys. C. Still life.	1,260
1954	Bradley Campbell, New York. Fruit.	4,055
1955	S. Nature morte.	2,310
1957	S. Cubist period composition.	7,800
1957	Georges Lurcy, New York. Sausages on a plate.	4,286
1959	S. Still life	9,100
	Still life.	8,500
	Fruit on a dish	15,000
1959	Walter Chrysler. S. Cubist composition 1910, 'Femme à la mandoline'.	36,000
1960	Benefit sale, Museum of Modern Art, New York. The violin, 1912–13	51,400
	S. Still life, 1946.	42,000

JULES BRETON. 1827–1906

Social realism; pious peasants, funerals, death-beds, frugal meals, heavy labour in the fields. Inspired by Millet's *Angelus* of 1859. Imitated in England by Frank Holl and Luke Fildes among others. Much sustained after 1871 by the French faith in the peasant virtues and by the rich American faith in the French faith etc. Of all the vogues that ever were, now the deadest, but in its day one of the most expensive.

		£
1861	Gambart. C. Reapers (Duke of Westminster).	85 1*s.*
1892	Péreire. Paris. Les glaneuses.	728
1877	C. Going to Mass. Bought in.	430 10*s.*
1885	Senez, New York. Le soir dans un hameau de Finisterre (bought from Durand Ruel for £3,922 plus 20 percent. duty).	3,650
1887	Mary L. Morgan, New York. Les communiantes (bought from Durand Ruel for £9,520 plus 20 percent. duty).	9,520
1888	Spencer. New York. Le soir.	4,100
1889	Secrétan. Paris. Le vanneau.	3,570
1890	Harter. C. Interior of an inn (see 1957).	640 10*s.*
1909	James Garland. C. Le goûter (for U.S.A.).	2,835
1913	Oppenheim. C. The haymaker, 1863.	262 10*s.*
1954	Catherine Butterworth, New York. Peasant love.	236
1956	Metropolitan Museum, New York. Religious procession in Brittany, 1869 ($4\frac{1}{2}$ ft. × 6 ft.).	125
1957	Anderson and Garland, Newcastle. Interior of an inn (see 1890).	150

PIETER BREUGHEL the Elder. 1525–1569

Among all the painters of the Breughel or Brueghel family the only great master, but an exceedingly rare one in the saleroom and almost completely ignored before the present century, except to be confused with Jan Breughel. The price of drawings should be noticed. They are among the great prizes of the old-master market that may be still available.

		£
1882	Hamilton Palace. C. Kermesse.	451
1892	Earl of Dudley. C. Noah and his family.	126
1922	National Gallery buys the Adoration from Guido Arnot.	15,000
1928	S. Village merrymaking.	1,500
1939	Mrs. Frank Holbrook. Flight into Egypt (Collection Count de Seilern).	8,190
1952	Major A. Hope. C. Grisaille panel, woman taken in adultery (£10 in 1834) (Collection Count de Seilern).	11,025
1959	C. Small head of a peasant.	2,730

DRAWINGS

1918	Sir Edward Poynter. S. Watermills.	175
1936	Henry Oppenheimer. C. Kermesse.	630
1949	Claude Lucas. C. Peasant and mule.	1,890
1952	Col. Oliver Probert. C. Rhine scenery (Pierpont Morgan Library, New York).	6,510
1958	Mrs. Huggill. S. Alpine scenery.	7,000

JAN BREUGHEL the Elder or 'Velvet' Breughel. 1568–1625

The little crowded scenes, brightly painted on copper and the somewhat dowdy flowerpieces, the ancestors of all flower paintings, remained extremely cheap until the end of the Second World War. Present-day prices have advanced out of all relation to the plentifulness of the product, but the demand to-day is all for an easily recognised style.

			£
1823	Fonthill (Philips) ex Beckford. Two small paintings of the elements, Air and Water, bought back by Beckford (see 1882).		40 19*s*.
1824	Fyre. C. The Seven Wonders of the world, 7 pictures, attributed to Pieter Breughel, bought by Beckford (see 1848).		157 10*s*.
1848	English and Co. The same.	7 for	137 1*s*.
1857	Mackintosh. C. Flight into Egypt.		401 2*s*.
1865	Oppenheim. C. Two cattle-fairs.		115 10*s*.
			142 12*s*.

		£
1882	Hamilton Palace. C. Apollo, Venus and Cupid (with Rottenhammer).	304 10s.
	Air, and Water (see 1823).	2 for 273
1884	Earl of Dudley. C. The Four Elements.	4 for 194 5s.
1903	C. The Four Seasons, flowerpieces.	4 for 168
	George Field. C. Village fair.	141 15s.
1928	C. Market day, 1612.	315
1933	Z. Walker. C. Flowers in a vase.	131 10s.
1944	S. Flowerpiece.	290
1946	S. Flowerpiece.	1,250
1948	Bernard Eckstein. S. Flowers in coloured glass vase, etc.	1,550
1955	Bernard Falk. C. Holy Family at an inn.	3,150
1956	S. Spring and Summer flowers.	2,800
	Landscape with travellers.	1,800
1957	S. Travellers at an inn.	2,600
	Village scene.	3,200
1959	S. Circular landscape with revellers, 1622.	4,400
	Summer flowers, porcelain bowl.	4,500
	Flowers and stone urn.	5,200
1960	S. Elaborate flowerpiece.	15,000

ANGELO BRONZINO. 1502–1572

A much-attributed painter. Even his genuine works tend to be over-hard and have not been found very sympathetic. There is not likely to be another *Triumph of Love, Time and Folly* in the saleroom. There was no demand for Bronzino's work before the fine portraits of the Hamilton Palace sale of 1882. Bronzino-like portraits should be a good speculation, but they are seldom seen.

		£
1823	Farquhar, Fonthill (Philips). Luiz Gonzaga as a standard-bearer. Bought back by Beckford.	168
1847	Edward Solly. C. Princess Malatesta and her son.	178
1855	Ralph Bernal. C. Duchess Bianca Capella (National Gallery, 1906). 4 others under £10 each.	51
	Lady holding a rosary. V. & A. Museum.	4 10s.
1856	Samuel Rogers. C. Leonora da Toledo.	46 4s.
1860	National Gallery buys *Triumph of Love, Time and Folly*, part of a block purchase, Beaucousin, probably under £200.	
1872	Prince Imperiale. C. Cosimo di Medici (Holloway College).	341 5s.
1882	Hamilton Palace. C. Leonora da Toledo and child (see 1927).	1,837 10s.
	Don Garcia di Medici (see 1885).	1,785
1885	Beckett Denison. C. Don Garcia di Medici (see 1882).	945

		£
1893	Bingham-Mildmay. C. Leonora da Toledo (see 1882).	819
1906	Harry Quilter. C. Leonora da Toledo (see 1893).	551
1912	J. E. Taylor. C. Portrait of a young man (Metropolitan Museum).	11,340
	Second portrait of a young man.	6,090
1927	Holford. C. Leonora da Toledo (see 1882).	1,680
	5 attributed pictures, 150 to 400 guineas.	
1928	Earl of Northesk. C. Lady in black, reading.	892 10*s.*
1948	C. S. Wadsworth, New York. Same picture.	1,286
1957	S. Small head of Cosimo di Medici.	700
1958	John Skippe. C. Drawing, man's head.	577 10*s.*

FORD MADOX BROWN. 1821–1893

Never a very popular Pre-Raphaelite painter, because too Continental in inspiration. Spent much of his life painting murals. His easel pictures are scarce, though not greatly sought after.

		£
1859	B. G. Windus. C. The last of England (see 1862). In Tate Gallery; other versions, Birmingham and Fitzwilliam Museum.	341 5*s.*
1862	T. E. Plint. C. The last of England.	430 10*s.*
	Christ washing Peter's feet (Tate Gallery).	94 10*s.*
	Pretty baa-lambs (see 1956).	26 5*s.*
1865	C. 'Work' (Manchester City Gallery). Bought in.	535 10*s.*
1895	Frederick Craven. C. Elijah and the widow's son.	325 10*s.*
1906	Harry Quilter. C. Watercolour replica 'Work'.	409 10*s.*
1909	Sir Cuthbert Quilter. C. Jacob Foscari in prison, wc (see 1958).	273
1919	C. The Fruits of English Poetry.	315
1923	Anthony Prinzep. C. Jacob Foscari, oils.	564
1924	C. Cordelia's portion.	609
1937	C. Cordelia and Lear, small oil sketch.	120 15*s.*
1938	T. Brocklebank. C. Christ washing Peter's feet (watercolour replica).	210
1956	S. Pretty baa-lambs (see 1862). Bought Ashmolean Museum.	560
1958	Lever Art Gallery. C. Jacob Foscari in prison, wc (see 1909).	89 5*s.*

SIR EDWARD BURNE-JONES. 1833–1898

The pale moonlit maidens, draped round a staircase or shivering in barren landscapes, are no longer the subject of Bloomsbury sniggers. There exists to-day some acknowledgement of the fact that, despite unforceful draughtsmanship and anaemic fuzzy paint, Burne-Jones was a master of rhythmical composition. Burne-Jones has fallen slower and risen quicker than his expensive contemporaries Millais, Leighton and Alma-Tadema, but it would be rash to predict the future of this market.

		£
1862	T. E. Plint. C. Watercolours 20 to 40 guineas.	
1884	C. Offering to Hymen.	94 10s.
1886	Colonel Ellis. C. Fides and Sperantia (see 1934).	577 10s.
1886	William Graham of Stobhall. C.	
	Chant d'amour (see 1898 and 1930).	3,307 10s.
	Laus veneris (see 1957).	2,677 10s.
	The days of creation (6-panel screen) (see 1934).	1,732 10s.
	Mirror of Venus (see 1892).	819
	King Cophetua (Birmingham City Gallery).	766 10s.
1892	Frank Leyland. C. Mirror of Venus (£5,775 in 1898).	3,570
	Cupid and Psyche (see 1934).	945
	The Seasons, 4-leaf screen (see 1956).	1, 205
1895	Craven. C. Hesperides, 4-ft. water-colour.	2,688
1898	Burne-Jones executors (£30,000 sale).	
	Love and the Pilgrim (see 1933 and 1942).	5,775
	Fall of Lucifer.	1,050
1898	Joseph Ruston. V. Chant d'amour (see 1886 and 1930).	3,360
1902	C. The wheel of Fortune (see 1948).	1,207 10s.
1907	Lord Davey. C. Flamma Vestalis.	2,100
	C. S. Goldman. C. The Garden Court.	2,625
1907	William Imrie. C. The tree of forgiveness (see 1918).	1,105
1908	R. E. Tatham. C. Love among the ruins (see 1913 and 1958).	1,653 10s.
1913	McCulloch. C. Love among the ruins (see 1958).	5,040
	Psyche's Wedding (see 1958).	2,730
1918	Duke of Marlborough. C. Beguiling of Merlin (Leverhulme).	2,730
	Garden of Paris	1,150
	Tree of forgiveness (see 1907).	1,575
1922	Rosalind, Countess of Carlisle. S. Annunciation, 1879 (Lever Gallery).	980

Beginning of the decline

1923	Anthony Prinzep. C. Green Summer.	399
1928	Holford. The Syrens (7 ft. × 10 ft.) (Ringling Museum, Sarasota, Florida).	110 5s.

		£
1930	James Ismay. S. Chant d'amour (see 1898).	620
1931	Marchioness Curzon. C. The Hours.	462
1933	Countess Bubna. Love and the Pilgrim (see 1898, 1942).	210
1934	Earl of Faringdon. S. Six angels of Creation (see 1886).	860
	Cupid and Psyche (see 1892).	210
	Fides and Sperantia (see 1885) (Dunedin Gallery).	490
1942	Sir Jeremiah Colman. Love and the Pilgrim (bought in), now in the Tate Gallery (see 1898, 1933).	21
1948	Regendanz. S. The Wheel of Fortune, 4-ft. wc (see 1902).	105
1952	Bulteel. C. The Briar Rose, 3 panels.	609
1956	C. The Seasons. 4-leaf gold screen (see 1892).	65 2*s.*
1957	Mrs. P. L. Agnew. S. Laus veneris (see 1886).	3,400
1958	Mrs. E. M. H. Potten. Love among the ruins (see 1913).	480
	Psyche's wedding (see 1913).	680

ANTONIO CANALETTO. 1697–1768

The movements have been erratic and a little outside the general pattern. Most of his life, Canaletto got only the very meagre remuneration of a topographical painter, but at the time of his death his work commanded relatively high prices, particularly among English collectors. This English taste remained very strong up to the accession of Queen Victoria, when four-figure prices had already been reached. The tremendous popularity of native English painters of the Venetian scene, such as Bonington, Holland, Prout and others, now ruined the Canaletto market. With the exception of Lord Dudley's eccentric purchase of 1873, it was extremely rare for a Canaletto to make more than £300 until 1892. The 90's vogue for Canaletto was inspired by Whistler, but quickly gave way to the superficial pleasures of Francesco Guardi. Interrupted by slump and war, there has been a steady recovery since the Tatton Canalettos of 1928, but the earliest and finest of Canaletto's work is still undervalued to-day.

		£
1724	Duke of Lucca commissions 4 big views of Venice (see 1928).	45
1754	Dr. Richard Meade, London. 2 Venetian views, £33 12*s.* and £34 8*s.* 8*d.*	
1771	Fleming, London. 2 views of Verona, 7 ft. 6 ins. each	260 10*s.*
1795	M. de Calonne. C. Grand Canal.	173 5*s.*
1807	Beckford, sale at old abbey, Fonthill. Venetian view (bought by Sir John Soane).	157 10*s.*
1818	Comte de Claperode, Paris. View from Salute.	720
1838	Hinchcliffe. C. Whitehall (see 1886. Now Duke of Buccleuch).	1,050

		£
1842	Waldegrave. Strawberry Hill (Robins) King's College chapel.	21 10s.
1848	Duke of Buckingham, Stowe (Philips). Venetian view. Bought by Earl of Dudley (see 1892).	105
1856	Earl of Orford. Church of St. Mark.	588 10s.
1860	Rev. F. Leicester. C. Piazza San Marco.	367 10s.
1867	Phipps. C. Procession of barges.	404 5s.
1873	M. Maxwell. C. Grand Canal. Bought Earl of Dudley (see 1892).	3,360
1885	Beckett Denison. C. Walton bridge, 1754.	246 15s.
1886	C. Whitehall (see 1838). Bought in.	588
1892	Earl of Dudley. C. Grand Canal (see 1873).	2,047 10s.
	Venetian scene (see 1848).	2,205
1894	Adrian Hope. C. Venetian scene.	934 10s.
1895	Lord Clifden (Robinson and Fisher). Bridge at Verona.	2,100

Between 1895 and 1927 a period of decline

1898	C. Verona, 5-ft. picture.	840
1901	General Pitt-Rivers. C. 5 Canaletto views of London. The largest, Somerset steps.	215 5s.
	St. James's Palace.	252
1905	Lord Tweedmouth. C. Piazza San Marco.	483
1910	C. Doge's palace.	945
1917	Hope heirlooms. C. Roman forum (early work).	210
1920	Duke of Leeds. C. 6 works of Canaletto's Roman period, average price.	647
1927	Pallavicini (Knight, Frank and Rutley). The Rialto, 31 ins. × 42 ins.	997 10s.
1928	Tatton. C. 4 views of Venice, painted for the Duke of Lucca (see 1725) (Hosman Collection, Montreal). the set	25,750
1930	Major B. Hardy. C. The arsenal at Venice.	3,990
1931	S. View on the Tiber.	2,700
1937	Lovelace. C. Marriage of the Adriatic.	2,100
	Two capriccios, painted at Ockham Park.	3,050
	Eton College Chapel (bought by H.M. the Queen Mother).	1,470
1941	Margam Castle. C. Westminster from the river.	4,620
1947	Proctor Beauchamp. S. A pair of Venetian views. each	3,400
1950	Lord Clinton. S. View towards the Salute, Venice.	2,200
1953	Alan P. Goode. S. San Francesco della Vigna (1744).	7,600
	Mrs. Brackley. S. Architectural capriccio, London.	2,300
	Lady Catherine Ashburnham. S. Doge's palace.	2,800
	Grand Canal.	3,000
	The Baccino.	5,500

		£
1954	S. Late Mrs. V. Carling. Church of the Redentore.	6,800
	San Giorgio Maggiore.	5,500
	S. Lord Trent. The Portello at Padua.	3,600
1955	Falconer Madan. C. Somewhat better version of previous picture.	9,450
1959	S. Piazza San Marco.	5,000
	2 Venetian views. each	7,000
1960	Gibson Fleming. S. View from San Giorgio Maggiore.	32,000
	The Redentore.	20,000

DRAWINGS

1883	Sir Henry Hoare. C. A series of 10 finished drawings of Venice, all of them over 100 guineas. The dearest was Public Festival (see 1936).	267 15*s.*
1925	Mrs. H. Johnstone. C. St. Paul's from Adelphi Terrace.	294
1928	S. Grand Canal, Venice, over 2 ft.	370
1935	Faucher-Magnan. S. Somerset House.	560
	John Heseltine. S. Westminster Bridge under construction.	390
1936	Henry Oppenheimer. C. Ascension festival (see 1883).	840
1957	Blofield. S. View in Padua.	1,550
	Capriccio, coach and monastery.	1,100
	View on the lagoons.	700
1959	Ten Cate. S. Capriccio in the lagoons, pen and wash.	1,300

VITTORE CARPACCIO. 1450–1522

Probably the greatest of the precursors of Titian, next to Giovanni Bellini, but heavily misattributed in Victorian times. The Wentworth Castle *St. Eustace Legend*, the *Meditation on the Passion* and the Oppenheimer drawings are possibly the only certain Carpaccios in this list.

		£
1865	National Gallery buys Holy Family with Saints from Count Mocenigo. Now called 'school of Gentile Bellini'.	3,400
1874	Alexander Barker. C. St. Sebastian.	128 2*s.*
1886	William Graham. C. The garden of souls.	204 15*s.*
1911	Sir William Abdy. C. Meditation on the Passion (with false ascription to Montagna), now Metropolitan Museum.	12,915
1919	Wentworth Castle. C. St. Eustace Legend (bought Duveen), now Thyssen Collection, Lugano.	33,600
1934	A. J. Sulley. C. Endymion.	3,150
1938	T. Brocklebank. C. Salvator Mundi.	1,785

DRAWINGS

		£
1902	Sir J. C. Robinson. A gondolier.	315
1908	S. Sir Edward Poynter. Religious procession.	380
1934	British Museum acquires St. Jerome, study.	630
1936	Henry Oppenheimer. C. Sheet of studies for 10,000 martyrs of Thebaid Legion.	903

ANNIBALE CARRACCI. 1560–1609

At the end of the eighteenth century some of the works of the immortal Annibale were admired as much as any of Raphael's, but his output was profuse and uneven and his prices uncertain. Of his many styles the Titianesque landscapes and the variations on Giovanni Bellini themes seem to-day the most attractive. But at prices that are more often in the 50-guinea region than the 500-guinea region, *les fréres Carrache* no longer receive the 21-gun salute of honorary Frenchmen.

		£
1717	The Regent Duke of Orleans buys the Vision of St. Roche.	840
1754	Dr. Richard Meade. Virgin, child and adoring monk.	63
1770	Ansell. C. Magdalen with angels.	79 16*s.*
1798	*Orleans Exhibition.* St. Roche (see 1717 and 1813).	525
	Toilet of Venus. Earl of Berwick (see 1929).	840
	Repose on the flight to Egypt. Lord Gower (see 1913).	735
	The boatman, landscape (Earl of Carlisle).	630
	Jupiter and Danae (Duke of Bridgewater).	525
	Woman of Samaria (Hibbert) (see 1823).	315
	Vision of St. Francis (see 1953).	525
	Valuations.	
	Descent from the Cross (for Earl of Carlisle).	4,200*
	Bath of Diana (for Duke of Bridgewater).	1,260
1801	Young Ottley. C. Sleeping child Jesus (miniature).	735
	Christ crowned with thorns (Earl Fitzwilliam).	1,155
1801	Alexander Day. St. Gregory at prayer (Lord Radstock).	2,625
	Domine quo vadis (National Gallery, 1826). Sold to Earl of Northwick.	2,100
1810	Walsh Porter. C. Silenus and Pan (National Gallery, 1824).	327 10*s.*
1813	Willett. C. Vision of St. Roche (see 1798). Bought in.	194
1816	Adrian Hope. C. Diana and Actaeon (see 1884).	117 12*s.*
1823	Marquess of Londonderry. C. (Ex Princess Murat). Cupid asleep.	945
1824	National Gallery takes over Angerstein's Apollo and Silenus.	500

		£
1826	National Gallery buys *Domine quo vadis* from Thomas Hamlet as part of block purchase, about £1,500–2,000.	
1833	Nieuwenhuys. C. Coronation of the virgin (see 1856).	367 10*s.*
1846	National Gallery buys St. Anthony from Lord Dartmouth.	787 10*s.*
1856	Samuel Rogers. C. Coronation of the Virgin (see 1937). (Now Denys Mahon collection).	420
1859	Earl of Northwick (Philips). Grand landscape with figures in a boat, sold as Velazquez. (1948, National Gallery, Washington).	60 18*s.*
1884	Philip Miles, Leigh Court. C. Diana and Actaeon (see 1816, 1943, 1952).	462
1886	Nieuwenhuys. C. Vision of St. Roche (see 1813, 1798).	231
1892	Earl of Dudley. C. Man with a skull.	52 10*s.*
1913	Duke of Sutherland. C. Riposo (see 1798).	36 15*s.*
1918	C. The artist as a gardener.	304 10*s.*
1927	Holford. C. Healing the widow's son.	420
	Healing the blind.	110 5*s.*
1929	Earl of Yarborough. C. Toilet of Venus (see 1798).	630
1937	Earl of Lincoln. Coronation of the Virgin (see 1856).	50 8*s.*
1943	G. O. Farrer. C. Diana and Actaeon (see 1884).	420
1945	Earl of Radnor. C. Charity (over 7 ft.).	57 5*s.*
1946	Earl of Ellesmere. C. Infant St. John (£105 in 1798).	47 5*s.*
1946	J. S. Oliver. S. Small portrait, young man in black.	380
1948	Viscount Harcourt. C. Susanna and the Elders.	57 15*s.*
1952	Earl of Lonsdale. C. Whole-length portrait of a gentleman.	126
1952	Marion Davies, New York. Diana and Actaeon (see 1943).	447
1953	Lady Catherine Ashburnham. S. Vision of St. Francis (from Duke of Bridgewater, see 1798).	120
1954	C. Holy Family, St. John and angels.	168
1955	Parke-Bernet, New York. Christ, the Redeemer.	625
1958	John Skippe. C. Drawing in red chalk of a youth.	336

LUDOVICO CARRACCI. 1555–1619

		£
1798	Orleans Exhibition. Vision of St. Catherine, valued for Duke of Bridgewater. (Since 1950, National Gallery, Washington).	630
	Susanna and the elders (National Gallery, 1824).	210
1800	Robert Udney. C. Riposo (from Parma) (see 1953).	1,155
1806	Wellbore Ellis Agar. C. Libyan Sibyl.	267 10*s.*
1817	Beckford, Fonthill (Philips). Same picture, bought in (see 1885).	787
1824	Susanna and the Elders, valued for National Gallery.	600

		£
1832	Lord Mulgrave. C. Lot and his daughters.	105
1885	Beckett Denison. C. Beckford's Libyan Sibyl (see 1817).	105
1913	Duke of Sutherland. C. Christ, crowned with thorns (£63 in 1798).	2 2s.
1923	Lord Brownlow. C. Vision of St. Felix.	157 10s.
1953	Lady Catherine Ashburnham. Riposo, 32 ins. × 22 ins. (see 1800).	1,300

PAUL CÉZANNE. 1839–1906

Unquestionably Cézanne has provided the greatest artistic speculation of the century. At the same time it is an error to suppose that there was a time when the prescient could have got Cézanne's pictures for nothing. Cézanne was not interested in selling his work, which he hoarded up in his remote retreat. Towards the end of his life, when his friends and admirers put some of their acquisitions into the saleroom, they bid each other up sufficiently to create prices which seemed formidable by the standards of the period where 'unfinished' works were concerned. The efforts of Monet secured that *Neige fondante* made £270 in 1899, and that would have seemed quite a lot, to both Whistler and Rossetti. *Garçon au gilet rouge* staggered the world in 1959 at £220,000, but it also staggered the world in 1913 when it made £3,600—as much as an Alma-Tadema.

On the *avant-garde* international market at the end of the First World War a good Cézanne was worth about £5,000. Curiously, there was no advance till the Cognacq sale of 1952, except for two or three pictures sold at rather more than this at the beginning of the Second World War. Cézanne is a painter, of whom there are exceedingly few first-class works which are still not frozen from the market and which can therefore provide further adventures.

		£
1894	Théodore Duret, Paris. 3 from £26 to £35.	
1897	Dr. Chocquet (32 in all), Paris. Mardi gras (Hermitage Museum).	184
	Maison du pendu.	248
	Dessert mort.	146
	Anvers.	105
1899	Count Doria, Paris. Neige fondante.	270
1900	Paris. Nature morte.	280
	Maison à la campagne.	220
1907	Vien, Paris. Nature morte, 1877 (see 1913).	760
1911	Henri Bernstein. Paris. Le paysan (see 1960).	960
	Maison en Provence.	920
1912	Rouart, Paris. Baigneuses (Barnes Foundation).	720
	Nature morte.	280

		£	
1913	Count Mariczell de Nemés, Paris. Nature morte, 1877.	2,180	
	Bathers.	2,025	
	Garçon au gilet rouge (see 1958).	3,600	
	Apples and Buffet at same price each.	1,800	
1919	Octave Mirbeau, Paris. Au fond du ravin.	1,640	
1922	Kelekian, New York. Apples on a plate (Lilian Bliss).	5,000	
1929	First Cézanne in London salerooms. S. Bernard d'Hendecourt. Mont St. Victoire, wc.	400	
1932	Paris. Georges Petit. Apples on a plate.	4,250	
1930	Havemeyer, New York. L'Enlevement, early work.	4,960	
1932	S. Water-colour. Le Dr. Merion.	130	
1934	C. Small water-colour. Apples and biscuits.	78	15*s.*
1939	National Gallery, Melbourne, buys *Route montante.*	9,735	
	Paris, vente HG. Le pilon du roi, landscape.	2,720	
1939	S. Mont St. Victoirc.	4,200	
1940	Parke-Bernet, New York. Mme. Cézanne.	5,700	
1942	Albert Barnes buys The Bathers (in U.S.A.).	14,400	
1945	S. Clearing in Forest, small oil.	1,000	
1946	S. Mountainous landscape, wc.	450	
1946	Van Horne, New York. Mme. Cézanne.	6,200	
1947	C. Water-colour, V-shaped trees.	304	10*s.*
	Pommes et poires.	325	10*s.*
1951	Kemde salerooms, New York. Landscape.	2,054	
1952	(May) Gabriel Cognacq, Paris. Apples and biscuits.	33,700	
	Landscape.	20,400	
1952	(July) C. Two bathers, oil sketch.	2,940	
1954	(October) Parke-Bernet, New York. Mont St. Victoire, wc.	1,167	
	Fontaine à Aix, wc.	1,833	
1956	(June) Galerie Charpentier, Paris. Cinq baigneurs.	16,000	
	Louveciennes, landscape.	10,600	
	Aux Jas de Bouffon.	15,500	
	Water-colour landscape.	5,800	
1957	(June) Ader, Paris. La Clairiere, landscape.	8,600	
1957	(July) Weinberg. S. Mme. Cézanne, small sketch.	14,000	
	L'Entrée du jardin, wc.	7,500	
1958	(March) Koenigs. S. Mont St. Victoire, wc.	7,800	
	O. Edler. Le jardinier Vallier, wc.	20,500	
1958	(October) S. Jacob Goldschmidt. Les grosses pommes.	90,000	
	Garcon au gilet rouge (see 1913).	220,000	
1958	(November) Arnold Kirkeby, New York. Garçon couché sur l'herbe.	44,500	
1959	(May) Baron C. E. Jameson. S. Blue dish and peaches.	17,000	
	Pitt-Millwood. S. Self-portrait.	32,000	

		£
1959	(July) S. Walter Chrysler. Mme. Cézanne, small.	40,000
1959	(November) Mrs. T. Kenefick. S. Le paysan (see 1911).	145,000
	Victor Chocquet.	24,000
1960	(April) A. M. Burden, New York. Les pommes.	72,000
1960	(November) Ralph M. Coe. S. Deserted house at Thelonnet.	38,000

MARC CHAGALL. *b.* 1887

A modernist, but not in the main current of the modern movement, a poet rather than a technically qualified painter, a sort of William Blake of Eastern Europe. The best market is in Germany, which banned Chagall's work between 1933 and 1945.

		£
1939	C. The dream.	10 10*s.*
1943	C. The cloud.	94 10*s.*
1948	Parke-Bernet, New York. Le concert bleu.	925
1949	Von Sternberg, New York. Les amoureux dans les fleurs.	1,178
1955	Stuttgart. The drunkard.	3,000
1957	S. Paysage à Peira Cava.	3,800
1957	Georges Lurcy, New York. Violinist and roses.	4,450
	L'esprit des roses.	4,450
1958	Amsterdam. Violoncellist.	11,500
1959	S. La pendule.	4,500
1959	Charpentier, Paris. The Isba, gouache.	3,400
1960	S. A clown, gouache.	4,200
1960	Ernest Duveen. S. Bouquet of flowers.	12,400
	Galerie Charpentier, Paris. Jeunes filles aux fleurs.	10,718

JEAN BAPTISTE CHARDIN. 1699–1779

A very late starter who did not benefit much from the revival of the eighteenth-century French school in early Victorian times. In fact these most sensitive and poetic paintings did not find their real level until the eve of the First World War. Considering that Millet, who dominated the late nineteenth-century French and American market, owed so much to Chardin, this is not easy to explain. It is certain, however, that this tortured age, which seeks peace in the serenity of Vermeer, would honour a fine Chardin should it ever reach the market. The value of the Metropolitan's *Boulles de savon* would to-day be incalculable.

		£
1786	Desenfans Exhibition. Girl with cherries (now Baron Henri de Rothschild).	5 5*s.*
1789	Farquier. C. Boy drawing (le dessinateur) (see 1876).	6

		£
1859	Comte d'Houdelot, Paris. La serinette.	180
1864	Lord Lyndhurst. C. Mme. Geoffrin seated.	73 10*s.*
1865	Duc de Morny, Paris. La serinette (see 1859).	284
1871	De Boellay. C. Larder and dead game.	79 16*s.*
1873	Paris. La serinette (see 1865).	464
1874	Angerstein. C. Lady with children.	189
1876	Paris. Le dessinateur (see 1789). National Gallery, Stockholm.	928
1888	C. Le chocolat.	110 5*s.*
1903	Reginald Vaile. C. The young princess.	273
	The house of cards (see 1912).	210
1910	C. Interior of a larder.	336
1912	Doucet, Paris. Boulles de savon (Metropolitan Muscum).	13,225
	House of cards (see 1903).	8,360
1919	Vicomte de Curel, Paris. The schoolmistress (1938, National Gallery, Washington).	5,400
1925	George Donaldson (at Hove). Pierrot valeur.	1,995
	House of Cards and *The Lesson*, left to National Gallery, John Webb bequest (1850, £31 10*s.* the pair).	
1931	Andrew Mellon buys a second House of Cards from the Hermitage Museum (now National Gallery, Washington) probably	25,000
1951	Galerie Charpentier, Paris. Les Apprêts du dejeuner.	4,700
1951	Samuel Kress Foundation buys from Prince Lichtenstein *La Gouvernante* and *La Guarde attentive* (Washington National Gallery). about	50,000 each
1959	Hon. E. Iliffe. S. Dead rabbit and game bag. (£35 in 1873) 13 ins. × 33 ins.	2,000

CIMA DI CONEGLIANO. 1460[?]–1517[?]

The early Venetians have always been underpriced. This particularly attractive painter may still be capable of an appearance in the saleroom, probably at less than the cost of a de Stael or a Jackson Pollock. There are several reasons for this, all of them distressing, but none of them new. For instance, in 1882 the most beautiful of the pictures listed below, the *Madonna of the goldfinch*, was obtained for the National Gallery by Sir Frederick Burton with an open bid of £651. Yet only six weeks previously Thomas Holloway had had to go to more than ten times this sum in order to secure that up-to-date and inestimable gem, Edwin Long's *Babylonian marriage market.*

1845	Lord Powerscourt. C. Small Madonna and Child.	54 12*s.*
1858	National Gallery buys Holy Family from M. Rousselle.	339 6*s.*

		£
1859	Earl of Northwick (Philips). St. Catherine (Wallace Collection). (See 1912.)	840
1863	William Russell. C. Holy Family.	69 6*s.*
	Davenport Bromley. C. Holy Family.	52 10*s.*
1870	Boxall buys the *Incredulity of St. Thomas* for the National Gallery in Portogruaro.	1,800
1876	Albert Levy. C. Holy Family in landscape (Wantage Collection).	378
1882	Hamilton Palace. C. Madonna, Child and Goldfinch (sold before 1846 for £64).	651
	St. Jerome.	4,493 10*s.*
	(Both bought for National Gallery, ex William Beckford.)	
1886	William Graham. C. Life of the Virgin, 3 cassone panels.	84
1890	Perkins. C. National Gallery buys Ecce homo (sold as Carlo Dolce).	535 10*s.*
1911	Lady Abdy. C. Holy Family.	1,575
1912	J. E. Taylor. C. Panel from St. Catherine altarpiece. (given to Wallace Collection by Langton Douglas).	2,100
1923	Lord Brownlow. C. Holy Family with saints (since 1943 National Gallery, Washington).	9,660
1927	S. Holy Family.	4,400
1948	C. St. Helena, altar panel. Bought Dr. James Hasson.	2,940

CLAUDE LE LORRAIN or Claude Gellée. 1600–1682

There are five distinct stages in the history of the appreciation of Claude's paintings. First there was the late eighteenth century when Claude became an expensive English taste; then there was the time of the Napoleonic wars when the price of a Claude in London became outrageous; then there was a static period, though at a somewhat lower level, which lasted from 1815 to 1890; then came a period of catastrophic decline between 1890 and 1928, when no Claude could make more than 700 guineas; finally, a recovery, at first slow, but in the 1950's quickening with inflation to the £47,000 *Apollo and the Muses* of 1960.

		£
1737	Mme. de Verrue, Paris. A pair, 'pour l'Angleterre'.	320
1754	Dr. Richard Meade, London. Morning and evening (see 1776 and 1806) (Duke of Westminster Collection).	223 13*s.*
1773	Robert Strange. Departure of Jacob.	420
1776	Blondel de Gagny, Paris. Morning and evening, the pair.	998
1779	Houghton Hall. Empress Catherine buys a Seaport and Apollo and Sibyl (Hermitage Museum). each	600
	George III buys a picture from Desenfans.	1,000

		£
1785	Desenfans. Angerstein buys the National Gallery Embarcation of St. Ursula (see 1824).	2,500
1799	Henry Tresham sells Beckford the Altieri Claudes, the Sacrifice to Apollo and Landing of Aeneas (see 1808, 1884, 1940, 1947). pair	6,825
1803	Erard sells Angerstein the Bouillon Claudes, Embarcation of the Queen of Sheba and Marriage of Rebecca (National Gallery, 1824). the pair	8,400
1806	Wellbore Ellis Agar. Lord Grosvenor buys Morning and Evening (see 1776). Valuation—the pair	6,300
	Also buys Sermon on the mount (see 1959).	525
	Worship of the golden calf (see 1959).	2,100
1808	Harris of Bond Street sells Hart Davis the two Altieri Claudes (see 1884, 1940, 1947).	12,600
1810	Walsh Porter. C. Simon before Priam.	2,887 1*s.*
	The enchanted palace (see 1848).	945
1817	Talleyrand. C. Sunset (looted from Hesse Cassel).	1,260
1824	Angerstein. Government purchases as nucleus of National Gallery (£17,500).	
	St. Ursula (see 1785).	4,500
	Queen of Sheba (see 1803).	5,000
	Marriage of Rebecca (see 1803).	3,500
	Morning.	2,500
	Gates of a seaport (see 1807).	1,995
1829	Lord Gwydyr. C. George IV buys Rape of Europa (Royal collections).	2,100
1832	Erard. C. River scene with cattle (see 1945).	960
1844	Jeremiah Harman. C. Aeneas and his father.	1,837
1846	Higginson of Saltmarshe. C. Landscape (Wallace Collection).	1,470
1848	William Wells of Redleaf. C. The enchanted palace (see 1810, now Wantage Collection).	2,100
1850	Earl of Ashburnham. C. Ponte Molle.	1,890
	Bay of Naples.	1,150
1856	Samuel Rogers. C. The mill (see 1922).	693
1878	Monro of Novar. C. Seaport, man unloading timber.	3,150
1882	Hamilton Palace. C. The Entombment (National Gallery, Dublin).	504
1884	Sir Philip Miles. C. Leigh Court. Landing of Aeneas (see 1808).	3,990
	Sacrifice to Apollo (see 1808).	6,090
	Herdsman and cattle crossing river.	2,047 10*s.*
	For all three pictures see 1940 and 1947.	
1890	Lord Haldon. C. Embarcation of St. Paulina.	913 10*s.*
1908	Knowles. C. Landscape with fishermen.	630

		£	
1914	Coats. C. Juno confiding Io to the care of Argus (Sudeley sale, 1882, £451 10s.).	262	10s.
1919	Earl of Northbrook. C. Ascanius and Silvia's stag.	588	
1922	Burdett-Coutts. C. The mill (see 1856).	220	
1923	C. A grand seaport.	682	10s.
1928	Holford. C. Les bergers musiciens.	1,470	
1929	Lord Yarborough. C. Hagar and Ishmael (see 1935).	735	
	Cattle crossing a river (see 1944).	525	
1930	Lord Carrington. C. Jupiter and Europa.	1,312	10s.
	Viscount Scarsdale. C. Tower on the Tiber.	1,207	10s.
1934	C. Flight into Egypt (National Gallery, Melbourne).	577	10s.
1935	Innes. C. Hagar and the Angel (see 1929).	220	10s.
1937	Leonard Gough. C. Flight into Egypt.	367	10s.
1940	R. B. Brassey. C. Sacrifice to Apollo (see 1884 and 1947).	1,785	
	Landing of Aeneas (see 1884 and 1947).	840	
	Cattle crossing a river (see 1884 and 1947).	1,260	
	All bought by late Duke of Kent.		
1944	C. Cattle crossing a bridge (see 1953).	861	
1945	C. River scene with castle (see 1832).	2,415	
	S. Wooded scene with ruins.	1,150	
1947	Duchess of Kent. C. Sacrifice to Apollo. } Lord Fairhaven.	3,045	
	Landing of Aeneas. } Lord Fairhaven.	2,310	
	Cattle crossing river. } Lord Fairhaven.	1,575	
	Earl of Normanton. C. Woody river landscape.	441	
1953	Lady Catherine Ashburnham. S. Campagna landscape (Birmingham City Gallery).	13,000	
	C. Cattle crossing river (see 1944).	997	10s.
1959	Duke of Westminster. C.		
	Worship of the golden calf. } (see 1806).	36,000	
	Sermon on the mount. } (see 1806).	35,000	
1960	Holker Estates. Apollo and the Muses, $9\frac{1}{2}$ ft. × 6 ft., sold to National Gallery, Scotland.	47,000*	

DRAWINGS

		£
1928	S. Roman Campagna.	340
1932	S. Tiber at Rome.	250
1935	J. P. Heseltine. S. 2 landscapes from *Liber Veritatis*.	210
		240
1936	Henry Oppenheimer. S. Two ships, a small sketch in pen and ink.	735
1948	Alfred Jowitt. S. Landscape.	750
1951	Chatsworth. Album of drawings bought by British Museum.	2,000
1954	Henry Reitlinger. S. Landscape with castle.	440
1957	S. Volume of 64 sketches, animals, figures, etc.	2,500

WILLIAM COLLINS. 1788–1847

Collins had only a modest measure of success in his own lifetime. His extreme ineptitude attracted Farington's notice when he was a student, while its prolongation to adult life can be observed in that curious collection, the Sheepshanks Bequest at the Victoria and Albert Museum. None the less, while romantic landscapes remained in vogue, Collins was among the lords of the mid-Victorian saleroom. For that reason alone he figures in this list.

		£
1813	British Institution. The pet lamb.	147 10*s.*
1826	Morrison buys Fisherman's departure.	367 10*s.*
1827	Lord de Tabley. Sunrise on the seashore.	210
1831	Royal Academy. The morning bath, Cromer (see 1881).	200
1827	Robert Peel buys Frost scene.	525
1846	Gillott buys Early Morning (see 1892).	420
1848	Thomas Baring. C. Boys taking seafowl's eggs (sold after painter's death).	698
1856	G. Yonge. C. The skittle-players (see 1875).	1,218 10*s.*
1863	Bicknell. C. Selling fish.	1,228 10*s.*
1870	Edward Bullock. C. Reluctant departure.	1,470
1872	Gillott. C. Barmouth sands.	1,785
	Cromer sands.	3,780*
1875	Sam Mendel. C. Skittle-players (see 1856 and 1907).	2,415
1879	Maddy. C. Dartmouth, 1821.	1,575
1881	William Sharpe. C. Children in Borrowdale.	2,625
1886	McConnell. C. The morning bath, Cromer (see 1831).	892 10*s.*
1888	Bolckow. C. Skittle-players (see 1875).	1,585 10*s.*
1892	Lord Cheylesmore. C. Early morning (see 1846).	2,205
1894	C. The pet lamb (see 1813 and 1930).	420
	The dead robin (see 1934).	483
1897	Sir John Fowler. C. Sunday morning.	1,449
1900	Peel Heirlooms (Robinson and Fisher). Thames at Richmond (bought Duveen).	2,100
1907	George Hooper. C. The skittle-players (see 1875).	535 10*s.*
1912	C. Mussel-gatherers.	152 10*s.*
1919	Camperdown. C. Red Riding Hood.	430 10*s.*
1924	C. A Cumberland Mill.	115 10*s.*
1930	Samson. C. The pet lamb (see 1894).	162 10*s.*
1934	Beausire. C. The dead robin (see 1894).	78 15*s.*
1944	S. A harvest shower, 1815.	150
	C. Clovelly.	43 6*s.*
1946	Robinson and Fisher. View near Chichester.	252
1949	Baroness Burton. C. Cromer sands (replica).	57 18*s.*
1951	Duke of Bedford. C. View near Hastings, 1825.	116 10*s.*

JOHN CONSTABLE. 1776–1837

An enormous number of sketches and studies have appeared in the salerooms and continue to do so. The entries are therefore mostly restricted to Constable's more important works, which have had a varied history. Absurdly cheap in the painter's lifetime, they rose in the English landscape boom of the 1860's, even though Constable rated lower than Callcott, Stanfield and Collins. There was a much stronger boom in the 1890's, when romantic landscape went out of favour and the realistic Barbizons came in. But the Barbizons stole Constable's thunder, and after them the Impressionists. Between 1918 and 1946 only two Constables made over £2,000 in the saleroom, though £9,000 had been reached in 1895. The post-war boom is impressive. It is doubtful whether there is anything to come comparable with the £44,100 *Young Waltonians*, but the oil sketches, sold in 1960, had advanced as sensationally as any Impressionist work, though Constable is still not an international market.

		£
1810	Lord Dysart buys a 30-guinea landscape.	
1814	Landscape, Lock on the Stour, sold for £20 with some books.	
1819	The white horse and barge on the Stour (see 1855 and 1894).	100
1824	Boat passing through a lock.	150
1825	Haywain, View on the Stour and Yarmouth Sands. (3)	250
1827	The Haywain exhibited at the Salon and sold in Paris.	400
1837	The Cornfield, bought for R.A. by subscribers on Constable's death for £315. (National Gallery.)	
1838	Constable executors sale (Fosters).	
	Old chain pier (see 1949).	44 2*s.*
	Horse and barge on the Stour (see 1855 and 1946).	157 10*s.*
	The lock (1824) (see 1855 and 1946).	131 6*s.*
	Salisbury cathedral from meadows (see 1908).	110 5*s.*
	Vale of Dedham with gipsies (see 1944).	105
	Arundel Castle, 1837 (see 1909.) See 1887.	78 15*s.*
	London from Hampstead.	63
	Weymouth Bay (National Gallery 1910). See 1887.	4 4*s.*
1846	Lord Taunton. C. Salisbury Cathedral (1849 £430 10*s.*)	441
	Vale of Dedham (see 1944) (1849, £157).	357
1855	Charles Burch. C. The Lock (see 1838).	860
	The white horse (see 1819).	630
1860	Miss Morris. C. Stoke by Nayland (Salting Bequest 1910, National Gallery).	105
1861	C. Opening of Waterloo Bridge.	462
1866	George Young. C. The Haywain (see 1824) (National Gallery since 1886).	1,365
1870	Edward Bullock. C. Heath scene (see 1873).	787 10*s.*
	Weymouth Bay.	535 10*s.*

		£	
1872	Gillott. C. Weymouth Bay (Louvre).	735	
1873	Hargreaves. C. Heath scene (see 1870).	1,050	
1881	William Sharp. Hampstead Heath (see 1948).	577	10*s.*
1883	Dunlop. C. Study for the Young Waltonians (see 1944). Bought for Holloway College.	1,249	10*s.*
1886	McConnell. C. Dell in Helmingham Park (see 1954).	1,627	10*s.*
1887	Constable Blundell. C. Weymouth Bay (see 1838). National Gallery 1910.	38	17*s.*
1887	C. Hampstead Heath, 1830.	1,050	
	(May, 1887, *The Times* puts Constable only 8th on the list of high-priced English landscape painters.)		
1893	Lord Revelstoke. C. Hampstead Heath (see 1887).	2,625	
1894	Richard Hemming. C. On the Stour with white horse (see 1855). (National Gallery, Washington, 1941, per Joseph Widener.)	6,510	
1895	Huth. C. Children angling on the Stour (see 1946 and 1951). The Young Waltonians, bought Samuel Montague.	8,925	
1908	Stephen Holland. C. Salisbury Cathedral (Washington National Gallery).	8,190	
1909	Holbrook Gaskell. Arundel Mill and Castle (now at Toledo, Ohio).	8,820	
1910	Mappin. C. Stoke by Nayland (*not* National Gallery).	9,240	
1917	Beecham. C. Salisbury Cathedral, 1823 (see 1927).	6,510	
	(Since 1950 in Metropolitan Museum.)		
	On the Stour (bought in).	6,300	
1918	C. Same picture.	4,200	
1920	Holbrooke Gaskell. C. Same picture.	1,995	
1923	Robinson, Fisher. Embarcation of George IV at Greenwich, nearly 8 ft.	2,520	
1924	S. Landscape near Malvern Hall, (24 ins. × 30 ins.)	980	
1925	Melbourne National Gallery buys Keswick Lake.	735	
1927	Mrs. L. Raphael. C. Salisbury Cathedral (see 1917, etc.).	2,310	
1928	Foster's. Waterloo Bridge.	1,785	
1933	Z. Walker. C. The Dell in Helmingham Park (41 ins. × 50 ins.). (Lowest level since 1886.)	357	10*s.*
1936	National Gallery buys Hadleigh Castle from Percy Moore Turner.	10,000	
	C. Sir Cuthbert Quilter. The edge of the wood.	1,365	
1939	Melbourne National Gallery buys Hampstead Heath quarries.	437	
1941	Mrs. Yates Thompson. S. Willy Lott's house (£346 10*s.* in 1888, now Ipswich Museum).	1,400	
1944	National Gallery, Edinburgh, buys Vale of Dedham with gipsies (see 1838) from Neeld family.	20,000	

		£
1946	Melbourne Gallery buys Dell in Helmingham Park (see 1933).	10,000
1946	Pitt-Miller. C. Constable's father's mill at Dedham.	6,930
	Mrs. Hartee (Philips). Lock on the Stour (see 1855) (Collection Lord Fairhaven).	4,600
	Swaythling Heirlooms. C. The young Waltonians, bought by Walter Hutchinson (see 1893 and 1951).	43,050
1948	Sir Bernard Eckstein. S. Hampstead Heath (see 1881). Bought Fitzwilliam Museum.	13,000
1949	H. A. C. Gregory. S. The old chain pier (see 1838). (Bought in.)	13,500
1951	Hutchinson & Co. The Young Waltonians (1946), bought Sir T. Gilbey.	44,100*
1952	Allen Moorhouse. C. Small view of Salisbury Cathedral. (Huntington library, San Marino, Cal.).	21,525
1954	Catherine Butterworth. New York. Dell in Helmingham Park (see 1886).	9,160
1956	Lenox, New York. Willy Lott's house.	10,500
1958	Miss M. Gore. S. Old Hall, East Bergholt, 1801 (the picture for which Constable told Farington he would charge 3 guineas).	3,800
1959	H. L. Fison. C. Vale of Dedham (23½ ins. × 19 ins.)	9,450
	Smaller version of same scene.	8,925
	Oil sketch of trees (£85 in 1925).	6,825
	There were 15 pictures or sketches, totalling £85,900, having gone up by ten times since the late twenties.	
1959	Westcott. C. Stratford Mill (35 ins. × 51 ins.).	4,620
1960	Lt.-Col. J. F. Constable. S. Small portrait of Constable's sisters, early work.	5,200
	S. 3 small oil sketches. Old barn.	4,000
	Landscape near Dedham.	3,200
	Near Flatford.	2,200

JEAN BAPTISTE COROT. 1796–1875

Corot's work was introduced into the U.S.A. by Knoedler in 1866. In the early 1900's it was widely believed that 5,000 reputed Corots had paid U.S. import duties, whereas not more than 2,000 Corots in the world had been accepted by the experts. In the life by Meiergraefe it was actually stated that Corot signed a number of commercial copies in order to oblige. And yet the market for the 'gout americain' Corots, in which the artist parodied his own style with more and more nymphs and willow groves, remained prodigious. The break in prices did, however, follow very soon after the exhibitions of the impudent Jusseaume forgeries in 1928.

And yet Corot was a very great painter. To-day his more honourable works, the *Venus au bain* and the early Italian landscapes, have at least reached the level of Sisley and Pissarro, but they ought to be much higher, whereas many of the 'nymphs and glades' pictures ought never to have recovered at all.

		£
1873	Durand Ruel. C. A woodscene. Bought in.	131 6s.
1877	Vente Corot, Paris. Highest price £720, important pictures at £400. Early Campagna paintings at £15 or less. The Birdnesters (see 1910).	460
1881	A. B. Stewart. New York. Danse des nymphes.	1,039 10s.
1883	Barlow. C. St. Sebastian. 1867 (see 1903).	1,228 10s.
1886	Defour, Paris. Nymphes et faunes.	2,600
	Mary Morgan, New York. Ramasseuses de bois.	3,000
	Lake Nemi.	2,800
1889	Secrétan, Paris. Biblis (see 1960).	3,360
1890	Dana, New York. Danse des amours.	7,200
1896	Lord Leighton. C. The four times of day, series.	6,300
1903	Milliken. C. St. Sebastian (Louvre) (see 1883).	2,415
1905	Louis Huth. C. Man in a punt.	2,732
1908	Stephen Holland. C. Peasant in a boat.	3,150
1907	Melbourne National Gallery buys 'The bent tree'.	5,750
1910	Andrew Maxwell. The Birdnesters (Havemeyer Collection).	13,650
1910	Charles T. Yerkes. New York. The fisherman (Duveen).	16,100
	Morning (Cyrus McCormack).	10,426
1910	Alexander Young. C. 41 Corots, 14 at over a thousand pounds.	
	L'Abreuvoir	6,510
	Evening glow	5,772 10s.
	Mantes la jolie (see 1924)	4,357 10s.
	Bords de la Cure, Morvan.	3,805
1912	Carcano, Paris. Lake Nemi (bought Senator Clark).	16,800
	Baigneuses des îles Borromées (see 1930 and 1952).	8,400
	Stephens. C. Souvenir d'Italie.	8,820
	Newcombe. New York. Lake Nemi (McCormack).	13,430
1913	Ernest MacMillin. New York. Orpheus and Eurydice.	15,520
1914	Coats. C. Souvenir de Mellifontaine.	6,930
	Ronde des nymphes (bought in) (see 1935).	6,830
1918	Curel, Paris. Lac de Terni.	8,700
1919	Sir George Drummond. C. L'île heureuse.	7,140
	Evening.	5,040
1920	Paris. Venus au bain (see 1956).	6,750
1923	Ernest Ruffer. C. Mantes la jolie (see 1910).	3,465
1924	Duke of Marlborough. C. Ronde des nymphes (see 1914).	2,315

		£
1927	Mrs. B. M. Denison. Lago di Garda.	5,565
	Souvenir de l'ecluze, Artois.	3,570
	Souvenir de Normandie.	2,205
1930	Andersons', New York. Baigneuses des îles Borromées (see 1910 and 1952).	8,440
1935	J. G. Coats. C. Ronde des nymphes (see 1914).	525
	Marais au grand arbre.	992 10*s*.
	Les chênes vertes.	814
1938	Parke-Bernet, New York. Landscape, 'the dearest in five years'.	3,320
1945	Cornelius Vanderbilt, New York. Road by the water.	2,225
	Orpheus.	2,225
1946	Van Horne, New York. Nourrice allaitant (17½ ins. × 13½ ins.). A small picture and not in the popular Corot manner but the first to make £4,000 in 16 years.	4,478
1952	Gabriel Cognacq. Paris. Paysage a Morvans.	4,500
1952	Harrison Williams. New York. Baigneuses des îles Borromées (see 1912 and 1930).	2,500
	Benjamin Levy. New York. Odalisque sicilienne.	6,400
1953	Galerie Charpentier, Paris. View at Volterra.	5,204
1954	Catherine Butterworth. New York. Nymphs and fauns.	6,670
	Parke-Bernet, New York. Orphée.	3,212
1955	Aristide Vagliano. C. Secret de l'amour.	8,400
	La charrette.	8,610
	La cucillette de marguerites.	4,725
	Chemin montant à Gouvieux.	3,475
1956	Goldschmidt. S. Venus au bain. 1876 (Collection Maharanee of Baroda). See 1920.	27,000*
1957	Weinberg. S. Blanchisserie a Chaville, small.	5,720
1958	Ten Cate. S. La ferme au grande chaume, Etretat.	9,000
1958	Parke-Bernet, New York. Girl with pitcher on her head. Very small.	5,720
1959	National Gallery values Hugh Lane's small view of Avignon, bought before 1912 for about £300.	30,000
1960	C. Souvenir d'Italie, small. Campagna landscape.	5,775
	Biblis (see 1889). Bought in.	5,250

Antonio Allegri called CORREGGIO. 1494–1534

In the eighteenth century high prices were paid for copies and schoolpieces under the belief that Correggio had been a prolific worker. In fact he lived only forty years, painted chiefly on walls, and his easel paintings are rarer than those of almost any other painter.

The high eighteenth-century valuation of Correggio was based on the prices paid by Charles I at a time when Correggio was the most powerful influence on living Italian art. In 1834 King Charles's *Education of Cupid* returned to England as the second or third most expensive picture in the world. To-day this picture might be worth several hundreds of thousands, but more on account of the rarity than of the popularity of Correggio.

		£
1746	King of Saxony buys the spurious Magdalen reading (Dresden Gallery).	6,500
1753	Frederick the Great buys the mutilated Leda (Pasquier sale, Paris).	842
1771	Sir William Hamilton asks for Venus, Cupid and Satyr.	3,000
1796	Vandergucht. C. The picture bought by the Earl of Radnor.	630
1798	Orleans Exhibition. Noli me tangere (schoolpiece). Robert Udney (see 1829).	420
	Education of Cupid (copy) (see 1832).	367 10s.
	Jupiter and Danae (schoolpiece) valued for Duke of Bridgewater.	1,050
1800	Orleans sale (Coxe). Copy of the Vièrge au pannier (see 1819).	210
1804	From Novellara Palace, Modena. C. Flight into Egypt. Bought in.	1,575
	Robert Udney. C. The genuine but mutilated Danae (see 1810).	210
1807	Lafontaine. C. Virgin, child and St. John, copy of the picture at Modena, bought by Sir T. Baring and later sold to the Tsar for £4,000.	3,150
1810	Walsh Porter. The mutilated Danae picture (see 1804). Bought in.	2,152
1819	Panne. C. Danae (see 1804, 1810).	324 9s.
	Vièrge au pannier (copy).	262 10s.
	(The original was imported by Wallis from Madrid and refused by the Government at £1,260, see 1824.)	
1824	Angerstein. National Gallery buys Christ on Mount of Olives, copy of Duke of Wellington's picture.	500
	Two fresco fragments of heads (Annibale Carracci?).	500
1825	The real Vièrge au pannier, sold by Nieuwenhuys to the National Gallery (Lapeyrière sale, Paris, £2,500).	3,800
1826	Lord Radstock. C. Madonna and Child, bought Lord Northwick (see 1859). According to Farington, III, page 10, acquired before 1804 for £4,000.	336
1834	Marquess of Londonderry sells the original Education of Cupid and the schoolpiece Ecce homo, both from Princess Murat, ex Duke of Alcudia. 2 for	12,075

		£
1859	Lord Northwick. (Philips.) Madonna (see 1826).	115 10s.
1882	Hamilton Palace. C. Ecce homo, a second replica of the National Gallery picture.	325 10s.
1927	Christ taking leave of His Mother (ex Benson) given by Duveen to National Gallery.	
	Count Pallavicini (Knight, Frank and Rutley). The Madonna of sorrows.	1,995

DRAWINGS

1850	King of Holland. Amsterdam. Head of St. John, red chalk.	91 10s.
1917	Earl of Pembroke, Wilton. S. Infant Saviour in manger.	750
1953	Henry Reitlinger. S. Sheet of studies.	550

FRANCIS COTES. 1725–1770

A neat, attractive portraitist with some of Gainsborough's early manner. Hogarth thought that Cotes painted better than his young contemporary, Reynolds. Others shared this view, and at the end of his short life Cotes rivalled Reynolds's fees. He was rich enough to rent (at 100 guineas a year) the handsome house and garden in newly constructed Cavendish Square which became Romney's. Cotes's portraits, pretty though they are, benefited very little from the Duveen boom of the 1920's. They lacked the necessary combination of frilliness, pomposity and gush. No real recovery since the Second World War.

		£
1870	Colonel Clifford. C. Portrait of Mrs. Marrable.	472 10s.
1883	Society of Sacred Harmony. Portrait of Joshua Bates, the orchestral conductor, and his wife.	73 10s.
1896	C. Portrait, Miss Milles.	682 10s.
1900	Mme. de Falbe. C. Lady St. Aubyn.	546
1904	James Orrock. C. Kitty Fisher.	1,785
1910	C. Mrs. McRae.	1,804 10s.
1912	C. Mr. and Mrs. Benwell, a pair.	1,260
1917	C. Mrs. Colquhoun.	1,995
1919	C. Mrs. Hargreaves.	1,071
1927	Viscount Curzon. C. Countess of Shipbrook.	2,257 10s.
1928	Holford. C. John Simpson of Esslington. Presented by subscribers to National Gallery.	4,200
1928	C. Major-General Philips.	1,575
	Sir J. F. Grey. C. Hon. Booth Grey, 1764.	1,312 10s.
1936	C. Portrait of a lady.	399
1952	Lord Brockett. S. The young cricketers.	2,000

JOHN SELL COTMAN. 1782–1842

The most distinguished painter of the Norwich group, and as a water-colourist to-day at the very top of the market for the early nineteenth-century English school, because his style was honest and independent, and because he seldom indulged in those manifestations of hot air which Turner inflicted on his imitators. This, however, has not always been Cotman's fortune. Because of his intellectual honesty, Cotman lived poor and died mad. The mid-Victorian saleroom honoured with singular perversity his heavy Crome-like oil-paintings and his water-colours not at all. In 1895 the National Gallery paid the staggering price of £2,310 for the brown-looking *Galiot in a gale*. But Cotman's water-colours stayed at dull level prices all through the early twentieth century English water-colour craze, lower than David Cox and Copley Fielding or even Stanfield and Birket Foster. This is gradually being put right.

		£
1843	Cotman executors. C. 4 seascapes in oils, 4 to 8½ guineas.	
1853	Ralph Bernal. S. 3 oil paintings and a water-colour, all under £5.	
1859	Chambers. C. The Hotel de Ville, Basel, wc.	16 16*s.*
1873	John Baker. C. On the Yare, oils. (see 1882).	430 10*s.*
1875	T. Wollner. C. Boscastle Cove, oils.	577 10*s.*
1876	Wynn Ellis. C. Yarmouth Harbour, oil.	420
1882	On the Yare (see 1873). Bought by National Gallery.	315
1885	Mott. S. 40 landscapes, water-colour, in one portfolio.	215 5*s.*
1895	James Pryce of Paignton. C. National Gallery buys Galiot in a gale, oil.	2,310
1901	Sir H. M. Thompson. C. Mouth of a river, oils, over 5 ft.	798
1904	James Orrock. C. Off Portsmouth, oil.	483
1908	C. Homeward Bound, oil.	829 10*s.*
1920	Holbrooke Jackson. C. View on the Burr, oil.	294
1922	T. Brocklebank. C. Caeder Idris, wc. (see 1927).	378
1926	Howarth. C. River scene with castle, wc.	462
1927	C. Caeder Idris, wc (see 1922).	430 10*s.*
1931	C. Norwich market place, 1807, wc.	378
1933	C. Norfolk Coast, oil.	504
1936	C. On the River Greta, wc.	241 10*s.*
1948	S. Heidelberg, wc.	820
1957	Mrs. Agnew. S. Landscape, wc.	1,400
1960	S. Blasting St. Vincent's Rocks, Clifton, 1825, wc.	4,800

GUSTAVE COURBET. 1819–1877

Founder of the French social realist school of painting with a strong accent on toil and misery, forerunner of Millet's later subjects, Bastien Lepage, Breton, l'Hermitte, etc. Also painted numerous nudes, portraits and landscapes in a heavy sombre style, sometimes with a palette knife. Intensely unpopular most of his life, but his big moral pictures captured the age before his death. His market, which was destroyed by the advent of Impressionism, hardly reached England, though he greatly influenced the young Whistler. Courbet's non-didactic pictures are now slowly coming back into favour, but between 1920 and 1950 they were absurdly cheap, probably because of the darkening of his pigments at a time when brilliancy of colour was in demand.

		£
1872	J. de Gilloy. C. The forest.	105
1881	Vente Courbet, Paris. Fighting stags in a forest.	1,950
1883	Sandeman. C. Interior with pot of flowers.	225 15s.
1889	Secretan, Paris. The doe cover, bought by Louvre against competition of Mrs. O. Havemeyer.	3,040
1892	Haro. L'atelier du peintre (gigantic picture), bought in, resold in 1899 for £2,400 (Louvre).	4,000
1913	Mariczell de Nemès, Paris. Venus and Psyche.	3,800
1919	Paris. Mme. des Fosses bids £19,000 for l'Atelier du peintre, acquired for the Louvre later at	21,000
1923	Small painting, The Wave, bought by Melbourne National Gallery.	345
1925	C. Villa of the Duc de Morny at Deauville, 1865.	525
	Tate Gallery buys l'Orage through subscribers.	338
1927	Sir James Ross. C. Seascape, 1872	398
	Mrs. de Beer. C. Deer-hunting.	441
1937	Leonard Gow. C. Les enfants du choeur.	420
1945	Parke-Bernet, New York. Winter landscape.	472
1949	Gallerie Charpentier, Paris. A doe in the snow, 1866.	416
1952	Cognacq, Paris. Femme couchée.	5,820
1957	Weinberg. S. Apples on a plate.	5,500
	S. Hiver au Jura, small.	1,900
1959	Parke-Bernet, New York. Château de Chillon (35 ins. × 45 ins.).	6,785
	S. Le fils du sculpteur Duboeuf.	3,800
	National Gallery, revaluations of Hugh Lane's pictures.	
	Self-portrait.	10,000
	The snowbound coach.	15,000

DAVID COX. 1783–1859

The son of a Birmingham blacksmith, painted water-colours in London most of his life, but after 1840 lived near Birmingham, painting in oils which looked like water-colours. This prompted Birmingham industrialists, like Wadmore and Bullock, to make their first commercial speculation in art, with the result that Cox's work, which had never brought him more than £100 for a picture, soared to fantastic heights, to £3,600 within thirteen years of his death, to close on £5,000 in the early 1890's. Birmingham remained loyal till the middle 1920's, when the entire early nineteenth-century water-colour school folded up. The extent of the decline must be measured by the fact that in 1937 the Tate Gallery was able to get Cox's reputed masterpiece, *The Welsh funeral*, for £257 10*s*.

There are no symptoms of a come-back. Cox specialised in yellow-gold open spaces, windswept and populated with figures gathering unprofitable objects. A Wordsworthian painter with no message for this age.

		£
1842	British Institution. Bettws-y-Coed, Welsh funeral (see 1895).	20
1849	The terrace, Haddon Hall, oil.	36 15*s*.
1860	Briscoe. C. The vale of Clwyd, oil (see 1875, 1892, 1916).	278 5*s*.
1865	Wadmore. C. Cloudy day, wc.	330 15*s*.
1870	Bullock. The hayfield, oil (£52 in 1850) (see 1875).	446
1872	Gillott. C. 6 pictures at over £1,500 each, oils.	
	Bettws-y-Coed (see 1884).	2,207
	Peace and war, harvest field.	3,601
1875	W. Quilter. C. The hayfield (see 1870 and 1882).	2,940
	The vale of Clwyd (see 1860).	1,627 10*s*.
1876	Albert Levy. C. Caer Cennen Castle, oil (1910).	2,625
	Counting the flock (see 1926).	2,415
	Ulverston Sands, wc (see 1924, 1955).	1,732 10*s*.
1882	Edward Hermon. C. The hayfield, down to	1,050
1884	Crompton Potter. C. Bettws-y-Coed (see 1872).	2,677 10*s*.
1889	W. Quilter. C. Vale of Clwyd (see 1860, 1916).	2,415
1892	David Price. C. Vale of Clwyd (see 1860, 1916).	4,725*
1895	Craven. C. Bettws-y-Coed, Welsh funeral (see 1842 and 1937).	2,520
1899	Sir John Fowler. The hayfield, oils (see 1876).	1,310
1900	James Reiess. C. Going to the mill, wc.	2,100
1908	Stephen Holland. C. Lancaster, Peace and war, wc.	945
1909	Holbrook Gaskell. Flying the kite, wc (see 1926).	1,753 10*s*.
1910	Armstrong heirlooms. C. 16 pictures mostly under £500.	
	Caer Cennen Castle (£2,625 in 1876).	441
	Ulverston Sands, wc (see 1924 and 1955).	1,050
1916	Barratt. C. Vale of Clwyd, bought by Fitzwilliam Museum.	4,830

		£
1920	Caer Cennen Castle (£441 in 1910).	2,625
1924	Ernest Ruffer. C. Ulverston Sands, wc (see 1955).	1,596
	Darrell Brown. C. Going to the plough, oil.	997 10s.
1926	Holbrook Gaskell. Flying the kite, oil (see 1933).	4,830
	Counting the flock, wc.	2,625
	Flying the kite, wc.	1,575
1929	Sir P. Waterlow (Knight, Frank and Rutley). View on the Yare, oil.	541 5s.
1933	S. Flying the kite, wc (R. R. Leatham Collection, Belfast) (see 1926).	290
1934	Lord Faringdon. S. Changing pastures, wc.	540
1937	Tate Gallery buys Welsh funeral, wc (see 1895).	257 10s.
1938	C. Going to the hayfield, wc (see 1875, etc.).	309 15s.
1945	Edward Nettlefold. C. 5 from £420 to £630. Going to the hayfield (see 1875, 1938, etc.), wc.	630
1954	G. H. Gaskell. C. Mouth of the Yare.	273
1955	Humphrey Cook. C. Ulverston Sands, wc (see 1876, 1924).	787
1957	C. Going to the hayfield, wc.	65 2s.
1959	C. Wide landscape, wc.	99 15s.

LUCAS CRANACH, the Elder. 1472–1553

Has always been a low-priced painter, chiefly because of the uninteresting nature of most of the works that reach the saleroom. There have been too many square-faced Kurfursts and Electors and not enough of the little Nordic Venuses, as plump as partridges and as God made them except for a necklace or a feather hat.

		£
1854	Marquess Joly de Bammeville. C. Christ blessing the children, apparently the replica of an altarpiece at Naumburg.	158 11s.
1855	Ralph Bernal. C. Prince and Princess of Saxony, others at 20 guineas and under.	57 15s.
1857	Earl of Shrewsbury. National Gallery buys portrait of a lady.	50
1863	C. 2 portraits of a man and wife (see 1938).	57 15s.
1882	Hamilton Palace. C. Portrait of a lady in red (see 1912).	325 10s.
	Judith.	115 10s.
1905	C. 2 small male portraits. each	525
1912	J. E. Taylor. C. Lady in a red dress (see 1882).	504
1914	Lord Ellenborough. C. Melancholia, 1533.	892 10s.

		£
1928	C. Woman taken in adultery.	1,785
	St. Christopher.	1,627 10s.
1930	Ramsden. C. Duke of Saxony.	1,890
1937	Rosenthal. S. Luther and Melancthon, 1556 (by Cranach the Younger, see 1954).	280
1938	Mortimer Schiff. C. Prince and Princess of Cleves (see 1863).	1,050
1954	Sir Felix Cassel. C. Hunt in honour of Charles V, 1545.	2,730
	Gerald Reitlinger. S. Luther and Melancthon (see 1937).	1,600
1959	C. George, Duke of Saxony.	2,100
	Adam and Eve (said to have been sold from Charles I's collection in 1650 for £6).	6,510
1960	S. Portrait of Johann Bugenhagen, bought by Hamburg Kunsthalle.	10,000

CARLO CRIVELLI. 1435–1495

A painter with a very distinct style and perhaps more soundly attributed than most quattrocento masters. No certain Crivelli has been seen in the London saleroom for more than half a century. The value of the Ascoli Annunciation (£325 10s. in 1847) would to-day be unimaginable.

		£
1847	Edward Solly. C. The Ascoli Annunciation (presented to National Gallery in 1864 by Lord Taunton).	325 10s.
1849	William Coningham. C. Holy Family and numerous saints.	945
1852	W. Jones. C. Holy Family, signed inscription.	157 10s.
1859	Pieta, bought in Rome by National Gallery.	303
1861	The blessed Gabriele Ferretti, part of a block purchase from Alexander Barker. National Gallery, about	850
1863	The Madonna della rondine or Matelica altarpiece, bought for National Gallery from Count Luigi de Sanctis.	2,182 11s.
	The Berlin Holy Family (see 1892), bought by Lord Dudley from Alexander Barker.	1,846
1863	Davenport Bromley. C. Small panels.	
	St. George } see 1905.	109 4s.
	St. Dominic } see 1905.	46 4s.
1868	San Donato, Paris. Philips buys the Demidoff altarpiece from Ascoli for National Gallery, 16 ft. × 10 ft.	3,360
1874	Alexander Barker. C. National Gallery buys Immaculate Conception from Rimini.	577 10s.
	Also 2 small panels, St. Catherine and Magdalen.	210
	Three saints in niches.	567

		£
1876	Earl of Dudley. C. Holy Family and saints.	315 5*s.*
1886	William Graham. C. Holy Family.	131 5*s.*
1892	Earl of Dudley. C. (See 1863.) Holy Family, bought by Fairfax Murray for Kaiser Friedrich Museum.	7,350
	Small Pieta (1913, Metropolitan Museum).	346 10*s.*
1905	Lady Ashburnham. C. St. George and St. Dominic (see 1863). (Metropolitan Museum.)	1,575
1923	Sir Joseph Robinson. Holy Family, nearly 5 ft.	1,155
1938	Mortimer Schiff. C. Small triptych (attributed).	398

JOHN CROME (Old Crome). 1769–1821

A housepainter, son of a journeyman-weaver and self-taught except for some advice from Sir William Beechey. Founded the Norwich school and strongly influenced Constable. By sticking fairly close to Wynants, Ruysdael and Hobbema, created the realist as opposed to the romantic (post-Claude, post-Turner) school of English landscape. Until about 1890 Crome's work was valued higher than Constable's. Despite dingy colouring and much repetition, the honesty of his painting saved his work after 1929 from collapsing as badly as most of the early nineteenth-century English landscapes.

'Hobbema was one of the last words he uttered.'

		£
1821	British Institution. Heath scene near Norwich, bought by Sir John Swinburne.	31 10*s.*
1855	John Davies. C. English homestead.	75 12*s.*
1862	National Gallery buys Mousehold Heath from W. Yetts.	420
1864	Bishop of Ely. C. Yarmouth regatta.	294
1867	Wynn Ellis. C. View of Cromer (Collection R. A. Butler).	1,100
1872	Gillott (New York). Wooded landscape.	735
1875	Sam Mendel. C. Road scene (returned as spurious).	1,575
	Watts Russell. C. National Gallery buys Windmill on Mousehold Heath.	157 10*s.*
1879	Anderdon. C. Mill on the Yare (bought Salting, National Gallery since 1910).	120 15*s.*
1885	De Zoete. C. Forest with beaters (see 1946).	609
1894	Captain Selwyn. C. Yarmouth water frolics (Iveagh Trust).	2,730
1904	Louis Huth. C. On the Yare.	1,995
1905	Second Huth sale. C. Road through a wood (see 1917).	3,150
1910	Rev. C. J. Stewart. National Gallery buys The Porringland Oak.	2,700
1913	Billings, New York. The willow tree.	11,700*

		£
1917	Sir Joseph Beecham. C. Road through a wood (see 1905; since 1950, Birmingham City Gallery).	5,565
1923	C. Marlingford Grove.	5,250
1924	Darrell Brown. C. River Wensum at Thorpe.	1,732 10s.
	Moonlight on the Yare.	945
	Yarmouth Harbour.	892 10s.
1927	Mrs. L. Raphael. C. Return of the flock.	2,100
	Sir James Murray. C. Scene on the River Maas.	1,628 10s.
1936	Sir Cuthbert Quilter. C. Storm off Yarmouth.	1,365
1946	Swaythling Heirlooms. C. The beaters (see 1885).	2,100
1954	C. The mill.	6,300
1956	S. Norwich Castle and Cathedral.	260
1961	S. A Norwich backwater, $14\frac{1}{2} \times 19$ in.	8,800

AELBERT CUYP. 1620–1691

At the end of the eighteenth century Cuyp ranked with Berchem as the Englishman's favourite Dutch painter, though the French preferred Paul Potter. Cuyp never fell from favour. Beginning with James Ward and Turner and continuing with Landseer, Troyon, Rosa Bonheur and 'the Dutch Barbizons', he exercised a tremendous influence on nineteenth-century painting, without unfortunately transmitting his light skies and clear colour. When Turner painted Dordrecht he called it 'a challenge to Cuyp'—a challenge which Cuyp has survived. The price of the Duke of Westminster's *Small view of Dort* in 1959 should be noticed. The extremely uneven prices show that Cuyp produced much journeyman work, but three waves of fashion can be detected: during the Regency, during the realist frenzy of the '60's and '70's and during the post-war Dutch prosperity period of the 1920's. As is the case with so many Dutch painters, the high-water mark is still the Holford sale of 1928.

		£
1775	John Bartels. C. The environs of Cleves.	157 10s.
1794	Dundas. C. Banks of a river and figures.	204 15s.
1795	Calonne. C. Cattle watering (see 1958).	147
1801	Lord Bessborough. C. Cattle and trees.	409 10s.

In the 1770's Richard Wilson remarked to the young Beechey that a Cuyp at Christie's might not make 30 guineas, but that he, Beechey, would live to see it fetch ten times as much (Whitley, *Artists and Their Friends*, I, p. 380).

		£
1801	Bryan exhibition (ex Robit). Cattlepiece (Sir Simon Clark).	1,050
1809	Grandpré, Paris. Cattlepiece.	1,300
1817	Talleyrand. C. Romantic landscape (A. Baring).	1,150
1841	Lady Stewart. C. View on the Maas (see 1928).	1,522 10s.
1848	Duke of Buckingham. Stowe (Philips). Philip baptising the eunuch (see 1928, 1947).	1,543 10s.

		£
1857	Patureau, Paris. View of Dordrecht.	1,040
1868	San Donato, Paris. Avenue at Dordrecht.	5,600
1869	Delessert, Paris. Cattlepiece.	3,864
1876	C. Foster of Clewer Manor. Cavalier on a grey horse.	5,040
1886	Blenheim Palace. C. Travellers at an inn.	1,837 10*s.*
1892	Earl of Dudley. C. Big landscape.	1,890
1895	Mrs. Lyne Stephens. C. Landscape with Prince of Orange.	2,100
1907	C. Farm scene.	3,950
1923	Lord Brownlow. C. The Maas at Dordrecht (Duveen) (National Gallery, Washington).	18,735
1925	Earl of Carnarvon. C. View on the Maas.	3,885
1928	Holford. C. Dordrecht from the river (see 1841).	21,000
	Philip Sassoon. S. Philip baptising the eunuch (see 1848 and 1947).	2,600
1937	Leonard Gow. C. Two riders.	3,045
1947	Sir Duncan Watson. Philip baptising the eunuch (see 1948 and 1928, Collection Lord Fairhaven).	5,250
1949	C. E. Towner. C. Landscape.	4,200
1953	Lady Catherine Ashburnham. S. River landscape.	5,500
	Marquess of Zetland. C. Man-of-war loading stores.	6,825
1956	Goldschmidt. S. View on the Maas.	9,000
1959	Duke of Westminster. S. Small view of Dordrecht.	25,500*
1958	Stephen Powys, New York. Cattle watering (the other sort of Cuyp, made £147 in 1795).	625
1960	Van Aalst. C. Average cattlepiece.	3,780

CHARLES FRANCIS DAUBIGNY. 1817–1878

Next to Corot, the most attractive of the Barbizon landscape-painters and the least heavy, but appallingly repetitious. To-day two things seem equally difficult to understand: firstly, that these painstaking and very sincere works should ever have been considered slapdash and unfinished; secondly, that they should ever have become so dear, for the price of *Le retour du troupeau* in 1919 was equivalent to close on £30,000 in to-day's money. Whereas other Barbizon painters, Troyon, Rousseau, Jacques, Diaz, Harpignies, have responded little to inflation, Daubigny is once more in demand at about a tenth of the prices of Sisley and Pissarro.

		£
1860	I. K. Brunel. C. 2 cattle pictures. £16 16*s.* and	11 11*s.*
1874	Forbes. C. Morning.	299 5*s.*
	Evening.	283 10*s.*
1882	Forbes. C. Boats on the Oise.	378
1889	Secrétan, Paris. Retour du troupeau (see 1919).	1,680

		£
1904	C. Women washing clothes.	861
1908	Stephen Holland. C. On the Oise, 2 pictures.	3,675
		3,045
1909	Sir J. C. Day. C. 11 pictures. Banks of the Oise.	1,890
	Banks of a river.	997 10s.
	(Bought George Salting, National Gallery, 1910).	
	E. H. Cuthbertson. C. Paysage dans l'Eure.	2,205
1910	Alexander Young. C. 33 pictures.	
	The ferry (Duke of Marlborough, see 1924).	4,515
	Bords de la Cure.	3,885
	5 others at more than £1,000.	
1914	Coats. C. Le soir (see 1954).	3,870
1919	Sir George Drummond. C. Retour du troupeau (1889).	8,190*
1922	Goldschmidt. C. On the Oise.	1,942 10s.
1924	Duke of Marlborough. C. The ferry (see 1910).	1,995
1926	Holbrooke Gaskell. C. Washing day.	997 10s.
1935	Coats. C. Moonlight on the Oise.	472 10s.
	(6th June) An 8-ft. painting of a flock of sheep at midnight made 3 guineas framed.	
1938	Village near Basnieres, over 5 ft.	175
1939	Randolph Hearst. New York. Les bords de l'Oise.	1,028
1945	Vanderbilt. New York. River landscape.	475
1950	Campbell-Lewis, New York. River landscape.	485
1955	Aristides Vagliano. C. Les pêcheurs au bord de l'Oise.	2,940
1957	C. Landscape with sheep.	1,365
1958	S. Le village de Glouton.	2,000
1959	Duke of Westminster. S. Le point du jour, 1869.	1,850

HONORÉ DAUMIER. 1808–1879

Daumier was a sort of Sunday painter. His life was spent producing cheap lithographs for magazines, and when he painted, his pictures looked like his smoky lithographs translated into oils. There was no fashion for them until at least twenty years after Daumier's death, and he was rarely able to sell them for as much as £50. On the whole they are too numerous and too scrappy to compete with the Impressionist market. Daumier's drawings, which have long been ardently sought after, have become more costly than his paintings. *Le Forgeron* is probably the most costly pure drawing (as opposed to a water-colour) of the nineteenth century that has ever been sold. But Daumier drew like a god.

		£
1877	Vente Corot, Paris. Les curieux devant l'etalage.	60
1890	Heilbuth, Paris. L'avocat et sa cliente.	102

		£
1898	Alexander Reid, Glasgow. Les lutteurs.	156
1899	Count Doria, Paris. Wagon du troisième.	1,860
1910	Alexander Young. C. View over a river.	157 10s.
1912	Rouart. Paris. Les avocats.	1,102
	L'atelier.	888
	Several others.	
1913	Borden, New York. Voiture du troisième (Mrs. Havemeyer).	8,250
1922	Melbourne National Gallery buys Don Quixote reading.	1,450
	Les pieces de conviction.	1,200
1923	National Gallery, Edinburgh, buys self-portrait.	700
1927	Sir James Murray. Voiture du troisième (second version), bought by National Gallery, Canada.	7,350
1929	Bernard d'Hendecourt. S. Actor declaiming (drawing).	940
1946	Van Horne, New York. Le premier bain	3,793
1952	Gabriel Cognacq. Paris. Baigneuses.	5,820
	Deux confrères (drawing).	2,348
1956	Goldschmidt. S. Les baigneurs.	9,000
	Le Forgeron (drawing).	8,500
1959	S. Small male head.	5,500
1960	Louvre buys plaster relief 'Les èmigrés'.	11,200
	National Gallery values Lane's Don Quixote at	50,000

JACQUES LOUIS DAVID. 1748–1825

The very moderate modern prices in this list recall those of Benjamin West, who ranks next to David as the highest fee'd painter in terms of real values, who has ever lived. See page 70.

The enormous commemorative pictures, which won David these fees, are not visitors to the salerooms. David was also one of the greatest of portraitists but, considering how heavily his shadow has hung over official French art, the Paris market has never done him much honour.

		£
1806	Napoleon pays £240 apiece for school replicas of David's portrait to be distributed to the legations abroad.	
1808	Le sacre de l'empereur, painted in 1805–7 (largely by a pupil). Commissioned at £2,600, but £4,000* was actually paid. 20 ft. × 30 ft.	
1814	The Marshals saluting the eagles, completed in 1814. Same size. Total price paid	2,080
1834	Lafitte, Paris. Portraits of Pius VII and Cardinal Caprera. The pair	252

		£
1835	Vente David. The French Government buys the unfinished Serment du jeu de Paume, 24 ft. × 35 ft.	100
1859	Earl of Northwick. Belisarius begging.	110 5s.
1865	Pourtalès, Paris. The same pictures as 1834 (see also 1892).	712
1872	Comte de Rouget, Paris. Death of Socrates (see 1892).	704
1882	Hamilton Palace. C. Napoleon I (formerly Earl of Rosebery, Mentmore, now in U.S.A.).	378
1892	Earl of Dudley. C. Pius VII and Cardinal Caprera.	535 10s.
1899	Vente X, Paris. Small replica of Le sacre de l'empereur.	1,440
1926	Louvre buys complete drawing for 'Le sacre'.	1,200
1930	Havemeyer, New York. Portrait of a girl (Collection Chester Dale).	5,370
1950	Jacques. L. Stein. New York. Telemachus and Eucharis (1818).	1,412
1951	Parke-Bernet, New York. Portrait of Lally Tollendal.	5,160
	Philippe de la Rochefoucauld. New York. Mme. de St. Sernin.	2,860
1959	C. 2 drawings of the Roman Campagna. 2 for	840
1961	Galliera, Paris. Cupid and Psyche, 1817.	20,420

EDGAR DEGAS. 1839–1917

It will be seen in the following list that the incredible prices which were paid for two pictures in 1912 and 1918 were deceptive. The advance in value of Degas's work between 1912 and 1946 was in fact so slow as to be barely perceptible. Even to-day he rates at best far below Renoir and Manet and barely level with Monet and Toulouse-Lautrec. It is fairly easy to see why. In 1900 or thereabouts, Degas was a half-way-house to pure Impressionism and therefore easier to sell than the thorough article. To-day it is the Post-Impressionist pictures that are valued highest; furthermore, much of Degas's work, apart from his light-coloured pastel pictures, begins to wear a sombre mid-nineteenth-century look. It is easy to sell a painter whose works are so much alike that they can be recognised from across the road, but there is always some sort of limit to this market. The pastels seem to sell best.

		£
1872	Society of French artists, Bond Street. Two paintings at 100 guineas each (asking price).	
1874	Vente X, Paris. Tribune des courses, Longchamps.	44
1884	Durand Ruel sells On the stage (Mrs. Potter Palmer).	103 5s.
1889	Henry Hill. C. L'absinthe (now in Louvre).	180
	Maître de ballet.	56 14s.
	(Other dancer pictures at £60 to £70.) Ballet girls.	64
1894	Theodore Duret, Paris. Chevaux au course.	284
	Danseuses à la barre et assises.	300
1895	American Art Society, New York. Les blanchisseuses.	440

		£
1898	Glasgow sale. La toilette, water-colour drawing.	64
1899	C. La Repasseuse.	131 10*s.*
1900	Tavernier, Paris. Le ballet, pastel.	564
1903	Milliken. C. Racehorses awaiting the signal.	682 10*s.*
1905	Charles Galloway. C. The ballet (fan-painting).	273
1912	Rouart, Paris. Danseuses a la barre, sold to Mrs. Montgomery Sears for £19,140, plus commission, presented to the Louvre.	21,000
	On the beach, bought by Hugh Lane (see 1959).	3,310
	Rape of the Sabine women.	2,270
	Repetition de danse.	6,000
	Café concert.	2,068
1913	Second Rouart sale, Paris. Avant le course.	4,186
1914	Roger Marx. C. Atelier de modiste.	525
1918	Sir William Eden. C. La toilette, pastel.	4,650
	Blanchisseuses.	2,415
	Vente Degas, Paris. La famille Bellotti (Louvre).	13,300
	Semiramis (Luxembourg).	2,970
	Malheurs de la ville d'Orleans (Louvre).	2,000
1919	Sir George Drummond. C. Self-portrait.	2,205
1924	Tate Gallery (Courtauld Fund) buys Jeunes Spartiates.	1,200
1925	Tate Gallery (Courtauld Fund). Miss Lola at the Cirque Fernando.	3,350
1926	Tate Gallery (Courtauld Fund). Woman seated, pastel.	3,700
1927	Sir James Murray. C. Deux danseuses.	7,560
1937	Leonard Gow. C. Jockeys sous pluie (Sir Harry Oakes).	3,885
	Melbourne National Gallery buys portrait in oils.	2,275
1938	Tate Gallery buys Woman combing her hair.	4,083 4*s.*
1940	Dancer subject, pastel. Durand-Ruel prices.	6,200
1946	Dancer subject, pastel. Durand-Ruel prices.	7,500
1947	Dancer subject, pastel. Durand-Ruel prices (according to Maurice Rheims).	17,750
1951	Parke-Bernet, New York. Trois jockeys (£900 in 1942).	2,130
1952	Felix Wildenstein, New York. Blanchisseuse, pastel.	3,750
1952	Gabriel Cognacq, Paris. Danseuses saluant, pastel.	11,000
1956	Galerie Charpentier. Ballet scene, oils.	19,000
1957	Galerie Charpentier. Small self-portrait.	7,500
1957	Weinberg. S. Self-portrait, oils on paper.	6,500
	Le jockey blessé, sketch.	5,800
	Georges Lurcy. New York. Four dancers.	17,900
	Russian dancers.	12,500
1958	S. Three dancers, yellow skirts.	11,000
	Arnold Kirkeby. New York. Dancers on landscape stage, oils. 55 ins. × $33\frac{1}{2}$ ins.	23,680

		£
1959	Vahl Rubin. S. Three dancers, pastel.	22,000
	National Gallery values On the beach (see 1912).	50,000
1959	Parke-Bernet, New York. Danseuse sur la scene.	64,288*
1960	Robinson, New York. Trois jockeys (£900 in 1942).	23,230

EUGÈNE DELACROIX. 1798–1863

The greatest of the French romantics has never been an outstandingly high-priced painter. In 1869 *Marino Faliero* and in 1873 *Sardanapalus* made record prices for Delacroix, but they were lower than Landseer's prices and no higher than those of the vacuous Paul Delaroche. And while Delacroix's works never went any higher, historical paintings of the next generation, works by Meissonier and Henri Regnault, have made five times as much in their day.

Apart from Lord Hertford's *Marino Faliero*, only oil sketches and minor works have come the way of English collectors.

		£
1865	Paris. Murder of the Archbishop of Liège (Louvre).	1,400
1868	Khalil Bey, Paris. Les convulsionnaires de Tanger.	1,440
1869	Isaac Péreire, Paris. Marino Faliero (Wallace Collection).	4,000
	Vente X, Paris. Faust and Mephistopheles (Wallace Collection).	304
1870	San Donato, Paris. Christopher Columbus at La Rabida.	1,446
1871	Allon. C. Ophelia (see 1959).	420
1873	Waterloo Wilson, Paris. Sardanapalus (Louvre).	3,840
1877	Oppenheim, Paris. The two Foscari (Louvre).	2,820
1881	Edwards, Paris. Les convulsionnaires (see 1868).	3,800
1883	Salvador, Paris. Burial of Rebecca.	2,040
1889	Secretan. C (not the Paris sale). Columbus at la Rabida (see 1870).	1,152 10*s.*
	The Giaour.	1,312 10*s.*
1890	Crabbe, Paris. Tiger hunt.	3,040
1894	Tavernier, Paris. Entombment of Christ.	3,520
1898	Musée Kums, Paris. La passage du gué.	3,360
1913	Paris. Hercules and Alcestis (£1,470 in 1908).	1,138
	Magdalen in prayer (£700 in 1908).	148
1919	Hamilton Palace. C. Tiger and lion.	483
	Baron d'Erlanger. C. A tiger.	700
	Lion eating a horse (see 1937).	550
1929	Bernard d'Hendecourt. S. Young man in dark blue.	740
1937	Leonard Gow. C. Lion eating a horse (see 1919).	237 12*s.*
1946	Van Horne, New York. Christ on the sea of Galilee.	3,110
	S. The dying Moor, oil sketch.	1,800

		£
1951	Philippe de la Rochefoucauld, New York. Academic nude, 32 ins. × 25 ins.	3,750
1956	Goldschmidt. S. l'Arabe blessé.	9,000
	Portrait of Bernay d'Orville.	8,500
1957	Paris, Charpentier. 2 water-colour studies on one sheet, of an Arab.	2,500
1959	S. Le naufrage, oil sketch.	2,600
	Goodyear. S. Ophelia (see 1871).	6,700
1960	C. Seated Arab, small water-colour.	420
	Galerie Charpentier. Academic nude.	1,896

ARTHUR DEVIS, the Elder. 1708–1787

The two Devises were very different people. The elder Devis painted portraits and conversation-pieces right into the period of Grand Manner portraiture in a simple, honest and very charming Hogarthian manner, though somewhat wooden. The younger Devis executed monumental historical works in the manner of Copley and West and horribly sentimental child-portraits in the manner of Hoppner and Lawrence.

		£
1913	Lady Dorothy Neville. C. Sir Joshua Vanneck and family.	1,942 10*s.*
1921	C. Three gentlemen in a landscape.	73 10*s.*
1932	De Salis. C. The love song, 1759.	2,415
1934	Basil Bourne. S. Conversation piece.	1,500
1936	Earl of Lincoln. C. Children in the park at Tattersall.	672
1940	A. N. Gilbey. C. The Swaine family.	1,207 10*s.*
1946	C. Conversation piece.	3,150
1947	C. Conversation piece at Lord Barrymore's.	1,554 10*s.*
1959	R. W. Lloyd. C. River landscape, two children.	1,890
1959	Fison. S. Three gentlemen in a landscape (see 1921).	4,750

ARTHUR DEVIS, the Younger. 1763–1822

		£
1803	C. The sons of Tippoo Sahib (huge).	420
1809	Greenwich Hospital buys Death of Nelson from Boydell.	1,000
1823	Davidson. (Stanley). Stephen Langton and the barons (according to Graves).	2,100
1824	Oil sketch for Death of Nelson.	105
1936	C. John Arthur Simpson as a small boy.	3,580

PETER DE WINT. 1784–1849

Not the most exciting of the early nineteenth-century water-colour landscape painters, but as a Staffordshire man he commanded a strong Midland market. Conforms to the prevailing pattern, a strong market between the 1870's and early 1920's. Has not stood up to inflation. Between 1849, the year of De Wint's death, and 1862 the bigger water-colours made from £40 to £60.

All the following are water-colours.

			£
1861	C. Windsor Castle, wc.		63
1865	Mozley. C. Cornfield and rainbow, wc.		148 1*s.*
1869	Lord Lonsdale. C. Lancaster.		1,417 10*s.*
1872	Frank Leyland. C. Cornfield.		493
1875	William Quilter. C. Southall.		1,732 10*s.*
1885	Sumner. C. Same picture down to		1,008
1889	Quilter. C. Lincoln (see 1913 and 1941).		1,753 10*s.*
1904	Orrock. C. Epping Forest.		1,071
1911	Sanderson. C. Lowther Castle.		840
1913	Ruxton. C. Lincoln (see 1889).		546
1917	Beecham. C. Cookham.		1,995
1919	C. Bray.		997 10*s.*
1920	Holbrooke Gaskell. C. Bolton Abbey.		1,365
1922	Brocklebank. C. Whitby (nearly 3 ft. long).		840
	Dover from the Deal Road.		892 10*s.*
1926	Holbrooke Gaskell. C. Torksey Castle.		577 5*s.*
	Lynn from Castle Rising.		556 10*s.*
1928	Robinson and Fisher. Bolton Abbey (see 1933).		525
1929	Duckworth. C. Swaledale.		252
1933	S. Bolton Abbey (see 1928).		380
1936	Laird. C. Women cutting corn.		252
1938	C. Going to the cornfield, 1848.		309 15*s.*
1941	C. Lincoln (see 1889). Bought Lincoln Museum.		378
1944	C. Stacking barley, and The Hay Field	each	420
1949	G. W. Lysaght. S. Exeter (over 3 ft.).		750
1956	C. Lock with barge and two peasants.		252
1959	David MacLennan. S. The boulder stone.		320

CARLO DOLCI. 1616–1686

Late eighteenth-century prices are not as high as might be expected. Carlo Dolci's small and pretty Madonnas belonged more to the early Victorian taste. The extraordinary self-portrait within a self-portrait in the Uffizzi suggests some soulful Bavarian *Nazarener* peering benignly through his spectacles. But the *Madonna con stelle* has had its day.

		£
1771	Sir Robert Strange. C. Holy Family.	546
1796	Vandergucht executors. C. Holy Family.	225 15s.
1810	Walsh Porter. C. Madonna with lilies (since 1875 in National Gallery).	315
1840	Sir Simon Clarke. C. St. Matthew writing.	955 10s.
1844	Jeremiah Harman. C. Magdalen.	724 10s.
1850	Earl of Ashburnham. C. Salome (Duke of Westminster).	735
1859	Earl of Northwick. (Philips.) St. John writing the Apocalpyse, bought by Lucien Bonaparte ex Riccardi Palace. Bought in after Agnew had bid £2,100.	2,165
1886	Duke of Marlborough. C. Madonna con stelle. Bought-in (the Earl of Dudley was said to have offered £20,000).	6,930
	Adoration of the Magi. Bought-in.	992 5s.
1892	Earl of Dudley. C. Head of Virgin.	393 15s.
1894	C. Annunciation, drawing.	399 10s.
1912	Driver. C. Madonna offering cherries to the Holy Child.	44 12s.
1945	Neeld. C. Roundel-Madonna.	115 10s.
1947	Major James Hanbury. C. Pair of portraits, two English physicians (Burlington House, 1959).	661 10s.
1951	Lady Melchett. S. Man holding a letter.	240
1954	C. The luteplayer.	315
1957	Cobham Hall. S. Glorification of St. Dominic.	90
1960	Sir John Leslie estates. S. Magdalen washing feet of Christ.	400

Domenico Zampieri, called DOMENICHINO. 1581–1641

Less esteemed in the late eighteenth century than Guido Reni and not highly priced at the Orleans sale, Domenichino's reputation during the collecting mania of the Napoleonic wars rested on two pictures, the *St. Cecilia* and the *St. John*. But his most marvellous works were landscapes in the post-Titian tradition. The landscape from the Orleans Collection in the Burlington House exhibition of 1959 was quite a revelation. But these are very scarce works.

		£
1778	C. Time trampling on youth, 7-ft. picture.	153 6s.
1798	Orleans Exhibition:	
	Valued for the Duke of Bridgewater.	
	Christ bearing the cross (see 1935).	840
	Landscape (see 1935).	525
	River scene (see 1935).	315
	Sold at the Exhibition:	
	Abraham and Isaac (Lord Ward).	157 10s.

		£
	Sibylla Persica (Lord Temple, see 1848).	420
	St. Jerome (Thomas Hope, 1816, £119 14*s*.).	367 10*s*.
1804	C. Robert Udney. Magdalen.	556 10*s*.
	St. Cecilia (see 1882 and 1914).	220 10*s*.
1810	Walsh Porter. C. St. Cecilia (see 1885).	1,837 10*s*.
	Philip Miles said to have paid £12,000 (or guineas) to Hart Davis for the Vision of St. John (see 1884 and 1899).	
1811	Earl of Kinnaird. (Phillips). Bath of Diana.	735
1817	d'Alberg. C. Landscape, bought in.	1,050
1820	Champernowne. C. St. George (National Gallery, 1831).	430 10*s*.
1824	Angerstein. Erminia and the shepherds, valued for the National Gallery.	600
1826	Lord Radstock. C. Tobias and the Angel landscape (National Gallery).	451 10*s*.
1848	William Wells of Redleaf. C. St. Cecilia (see 1810).	609
	Duke of Buckingham, Stowe. Sibylla Persica (see 1798, Hertford, now Wallace Collection).	735
1855	Earl of Suffolk. C. St. Cecilia playing 'cello (bought-in).	525
1882	Hamilton Palace. Another St. Cecilia ex Beckford (see 1804; see also 1914).	189
1884	Miles, Leigh Court. C. Vision of St. John (see 1810). The 12,000 guinea picture was bought in at	735
	and resold 1899 for	105
1912	C. Portrait of Cardinal Barbieri.	147
1914	C. St. Cecilia (see 1882).	36 15*s*.
1927	Holford. C. Magdalen.	168
1935	Earl of Ellesmere. C. The Orleans pictures 1798. Landscape. (Denys Mahon Collection.)	157 10*s*.
	River scene.	63
	Christ bearing the Cross.	42
1952	C. St. Jerome at prayer (1798, 1816) (Denys Mahon Collection).	189
1957	Earl of Darnley, Cobham Hall. S. Entry of Don John of Austria (8 ft.).	90

GERARD DOU or Dow. 1613–1675

This is one of the strong Dutch markets of the early nineteenth century which has not kept abreast of the times. In 1817 Beckford considered Dou 'the greatest Flemish painter in the world' and genuinely expected George III to pay him £3,000 for the *Poulterer's shop* of the National Gallery. The taste for this niggling minuteness was actually French rather than English, yet during the

Dutch revival of the Second Empire, prices hardly went beyond the eighteenth-century level. In 1771 a Gerard Dou was about the most expensive thing you could buy, but prices that were enormous for that age were paid already twenty-five years after Dou's death.

		£
1701	Amsterdam. Interior with woman and child.	320
1719	Amsterdam. Poulterer's shop.	500
1771	Braamkamp. The Hague. The young mother (see 1793).	1,184
1777	Prince de Conti, Paris. The Poulterer's shop.	800
1778	Braamkamp, Amsterdam. Picture in three wings, forming a triptych, lost at sea on way to Empress Catherine.	1,410
1787	Desenfans. London. Woman at a well.	600
1793	Choiseul-Praslin, Paris. The young mother (see 1771).	1,340
1804	Van Leyden. Amsterdam. Hermit in a cave (see 1814).	1,680
1808	Groenwald. Rotterdam. The evening class.	1,750
1810	Coupré, Paris. Beckford's Poulterer's shop.	1,024
1814	Paillet, Paris. Hermit in a cave (see 1804) down to —but Beckford pays £1,500 in Paris for the Poulterer's shop.	600
1818	Buchanan prepared to pay £1,700 for a Dou at The Hague.	
1823	John Smith buys Beckford's Poulterer's shop at the Fonthill sale and resells it to Sir Robert Peel, thence National Gallery, 1871.	1,333 10*s.*
1833	Erard. C. Dou's self-portrait (see 1860).	603 15*s.*
1848	William Wells of Redleaf. C. Lady playing the virginals.	357
1860	Isaac Pereire, Paris. Dou's self-portrait (see 1833).	1,480
1870	Albert Levy. C. The astrologer (fell next year to £714).	798
1883	Narishkin, Paris. The fishmarket.	2,000
1894	Adrian Hope. C. The fluteplayer. (Still the record price after 67 years, 1961).	3,675*
1899	Schubart. Munich. The housewife.	1,800
1914	Grenfell. C. Lady in black.	3,045
1925	George Donaldson. Hove sale. The dentist.	157 10*s.*
1935	Lady Anne Arundel. C. The blind Tobit.	651
1937	Lord Lonsdale. C. Peasant girl, miniature oval.	388 10*s.*
1948	C. An elderly painter, 1649.	1,260
1956	Parke-Bernet, New York. Interior, said to include Rembrandt's mother. (£945, Christie's, 1942.)	1,353 10*s.*
1958	Vienna. Girl at a fountain (Calonne sale, 1795, £96 12*s.*), now	680

RAOUL DUFY. 1880–1953

The grand ancestor of all smart modernist magazine advertisements and the inventor of a successful formula which he must have repeated tens of thousands of times without adding anything to it. Most of Dufy's works are in water-colour gouache and, being recognisable at a range of thirty yards, the demand has become insatiable and a temptation to forgers.

		£
1939	Walter Taylor. C. The boat house. 19 ins. × 15 ins.	35 14*s.*
1940	Eumorphopoulos. S. Falaise.	110
1944	S. Sêchage de Voiles.	200
1949	Michael Astor. S. View of Langres.	350
	Parke-Bernet, New York. Ste. Adresse.	400
1951	Galerie Charpentier, Paris. Orchestre.	612
1954	Galerie Charpentier, Paris. Avenue du Bois de Boulogne.	2,065
1957	Galerie Charpentier, Paris. Deauville races.	8,000
	Antwerp.	6,000
	Moulin de la Galette.	4,500
1957	Georges Lurcy, New York. Imaginary view of Paris, oil.	9,300
1959	S. Landscape.	3,400
	Ascot paddock.	2,400
	Paris, Salle Drouot. Stands at Havre regatta, 24 ins. × 28 ins.	12,500*
1960	S. 13 water-colour panels, intended for the steamer *Normandie*, 1935. The set	19,000
	C. Paddock at Ascot.	1,995
	Riviera scene.	2,310

ALBRECHT DÜRER. 1471–1528

Generally the paintings have been a strong market only when the German galleries have been buying. The drawings, on the contrary, have risen steadily in value and were already remarkably priced for the times in 1881. This was largely due to Dürer's unique position among print-collectors, which goes back to the eighteenth century. Even at that time a Dürer attribution (used very freely) could give a Northern primitive picture a certain status.

		£
1802	Beckford, Fonthill. The presentation of the Virgin and the Circumcision, ex Bracciano Palace (attributions). Bought by Walsh Porter.	147
	(Apparently were in Lord Cawdor's sale, 1800, at	138 12*s.*
1814	Delahante. Adam and Eve, dated 1514, bought by Beckford.	147
1823	Farquhar, Fonthill, ex Beckford. Virgin and the 'running child' from Saragossa.	157 10*s.*

		£
1848	Duke of Buckingham. Stowe. St. Barbara reading.	168
	St. Catherine reading.	157 10*s.*
	Both bought for Earl of Dudley.	
1854	Joly de Bammeville. C. Portrait of a senator, bought by National Gallery. Actually by Baldung Grien.	147
1865	Pourtalès, Paris. Portrait of Emperor Maximilian.	520
1867	Schloss Pommersfeld sale. Head of a man.	3,000
1876	Wynn Ellis. C. Portrait, inscribed *Katerina Furleyer.*	338 2*s.*
1882	Hamilton Palace. Frederick the Wise (Kaiser Friedrich Museum).	388 10*s.*
	Self-portrait, dated 1507 (declared by Waagen to be a copy).	409 10*s.*
1883	Narishkin, Paris. Portrait of Jakob Muffel, bought for Kaiser Friedrich Museum.	3,200
1884	Kaiser Friedrich Museum buys Hieronymus Holzschuher.	10,000
1892	Kaiser Friedrich Museum buys Madonna with the goldfinch from the Earl of Lothian.	10,000
1904	National Gallery buys portrait of Dürer's father, dated 1497, from Marquess of Northampton. Now considered a late copy.	5,000
1944	National Gallery buys Madonna with the Iris from Sir Francis Cook.	12,000
1951	Kress Foundation (Washington National Gallery) buys the Count Czernin portrait from Vienna, reputedly	88,000

DRAWINGS

1881	Charles Sackville Bale. C. The stag-beetle (ex Horace Walpole) (now Tyser Collection).	77
	Head of a young man in chalks.	189
1893	R. S. Holford. S. Two men-at-arms.	635
1896	Earl of Warwick. S. Portrait of Lucas van Leyden.	430
	Young man's head, profile.	410
1902	Sir J. C. Robinson. C. Design for a façade, 1497.	966
	Armorial design.	756
1917	Earl of Pembroke. S. Sheet of animal studies.	1,000
1918	Sir Edward Poynter. S. A young man's head.	2,131 10*s.*
	Figure of Apollo.	1,500
	St. Catherine.	1,100
1922	Max Bonn. S. A dead duck.	2,100
1927	Miss Seymour. S. Portrait, the Slovene girl, Una or Lana Windisch (see 1930).	2,700
1930	Same drawing, bought for British Museum.	5,000
1936	Henry Oppenheimer. C. The three wise virgins.	2,415
1958	Skippe. C. Two horsemen.	4,200

WILLIAM ETTY. 1787–1849

Only during the generation after his death did Etty become a thousand-pound painter. During his lifetime the prejudice against his too solid and realistic nudes was very strong. It must be admitted that the absence of idealisation jarred horribly with the tinsel romantic backgrounds. The value of these works since the 1920's has been almost negligible, but there is a demand for Etty's school studies, painted on millboard. Unfortunately, when this vogue began no one took the trouble to read the statement of the Redgrave brothers that dozens of these unfinished studies were completed by others. Since the Redgraves wrote, the number has increased to hundreds. Hence the failure of this market to advance much.

		£
1828	Scene from *Paradise Lost*. Bought by Marquess of Stafford.	525
1830	Sir Thomas Lawrence. C. Pandora.	110 5*s.*
1834	Venus and her satellites. Sold at Royal Academy (buyer refused £1,600).	315
1845	Thomas Wright. C. To arms, to arms! (in 1849, £472 10*s.*)	409 10*s.*
1852	John Clowe. C. The dance. Large picture.	1,155
1854	C. The destroying angel.	808 10*s.*
1870	Bullock. C. Comus (see 1920).	1,055 10*s.*
1872	Gillott. C. Pluto and Proserpine.	1,050
1877	Baron Grant. C. Pluto and Proserpine (see 1872 and 1934).	745 10*s.*
1880	C. Diana and Endymion (see 1935).	315
1882	Hamilton Palace. C. Prodigal son.	99 15*s.*
1894	Fountaine. C. Judgement of Paris. (Lever Gallery, 1903, £315).	525
1908	C. The world before the flood (see 1932).	241 10*s.*
1919	Sir George Drummond. C. The rescue.	420
1920	C. Scene from Comus (see 1870).	609
1932	C. The world before the Flood (see 1908).	204 15*s.*
	Toilet of Venus. (£430 10*s.* in 1873).	102 18*s.*
1934	Fairfax Rhodes. S. Pluto and Proserpine (1872).	90
1935	C. Diana and Endymion (see 1880).	54 12*s.*
1952	Marion Davies, New York. Venus Anadyomene. Single figure, 15 ins. × 15 ins.	258
1954	Gerald Reitlinger. S. The luteplayer, 1834 (bought 1928, £65).	140
1957	Allen. S. The three Graces. 20 ins. × 30 ins.	220
1958	Baron Llangattock. C. Mrs. Vaughan, fancy portrait.	504

JAN VAN EYCK. 1385–1441

The most miraculous of all the early Flemings. Within the narrow space of less than half a century he has been the cheapest old master in the world and very nearly the dearest. The low esteem of the little Van Eycks, whose brilliance never falters, was all the more remarkable in the middle nineteenth century, since the sale of the panels of the *Adoration of the Lamb* in 1821 was one of the costliest transactions that had ever been recorded. But let the list speak for itself.

		£
1801	Bessborough. C. Alleged self-portrait.	23
1821	Edward Solly sells 6 outer panels from the Ghent Adoration of the Lamb altarpiece to the Prussian Government. (Insured in 1934 for £1,400,000 for the complete altarpiece.)	16,000
1823	Beckford's alleged Van Eyck, the Holy Family with the apple.	75 12*s.*
1828	The Philadelphia St. Francis, bought by Sir William a'Court in Portugal as a Dürer (see 1894) for	8
1842	The National Gallery buys John Arnolfini and his wife from Major-General Hay.	630
1850	King of Holland, Brussels. The Tsar buys the Angel of the Annunciation (Hermitage), see 1931.	448
1851	Lord Middleton. C. National Gallery buys the Man in a red turban through Farrer.	315
1857	National Gallery buys the portrait, 'Timothey, leal souvenir', from Carl Ross, Munich.	189 11*s.*
1872	Frances Cook buys The three Maries at the sepulchre (see 1939).	336
1886	Kaiser Friedrich Museum buys alleged Van Eyck portrait of John Arnolfini from Nieuwenhuys.	399
1894	John G. Johnson buys the Philadelphia St. Francis from Lord Heytesbury (see 1933).	700
1921	Melbourne National Gallery buys the miniature Madonna from Ince Hall.	31,395
1931	Andrew Mellon buys Hermitage Annunciation (National Gallery, Washington). (See 1850.)	103,500
1933	Philadelphia Museum values the St. Francis (1894).	105,000
1940	Sir Francis Cook sells the Three Maries to van Beuningen (Boymans Museum, Rotterdam) (see 1872). £300,000 offered by Hermann Goering.	225,000

KAREL FABRITIUS. 1624–1654

It has been the fate of this very fine but short-lived painter to be mistaken for Rembrandt. When sailing under his own colours, his pictures have therefore been inexpensive. Some rectification seems to be in progress.

		£
1867	National Gallery buys Christ blessing the children, as a Rembrandt from the Suermondt Collection, Aachen.	7,000
1912	C. Meeting of Isaac and Rebecca.	3,255
1920	C. Marriage of Isaac and Rebecca.	1,522 10*s.*
1922	National Gallery buys the View of Delft.	1,800
1924	Brewerton. C. Man in a fur hat, bought for National Gallery by Claude Phillips.	6,615
1925	S. Ruth and Naomi.	830
1937	Mrs. W. Buckley. S. Eli and Samuel (Barent Fabritius).	2,900
1959	Del Mont. S. The de Potter children.	3,400
1960	Van Aalst. C. Small portrait head of Rembrandt.	14,700

HENRI FANTIN-LATOUR. 1836–1904

In the salerooms Fantin-Latour is known almost exclusively as a painter of flowerpieces and still life. In art history he is the author of the once much-esteemed big conversation pieces in the Louvre, *L'Atelier a Battignoles, Homage à Delacroix, Le coin du table*, sedate, lifeless, looking like studio photographs and without much more colour. The flowerpieces on which he depended for a living are at least a little gayer in colour, though obsessed with the pre-Impressionist passion for pearly grey. They are all much alike and all tasteful in an efficient sort of way, and, oddly enough, they are the only pre-Impressionist French paintings of the nineteenth century, apart from Boudin, that are booming. Like Boudin, Fantin-Latour is unmistakable.

In the late '80's and early '90's flowerpieces by Fantin-Latour were sold in London for about 20 guineas each.

		£
1894	C. Roses tremières (see 1948).	52 10*s.*
1902	C. Hyacinths and a plate of fruit.	168
1908	C. Mixed bouquet (see 1946).	420
1912	C. 19 flowerpieces sold, the dearest.	483
1914	Cremetti. C. L'immortalité (conversation piece).	1,680
1920	C. 18 flowerpieces—the dearest.	1,134
1924	Leonard Gow. C. Bourriche des roses.	2,735
	Several others made over £2,000 each.	
1929	C. Mixed flowers.	1,627 10*s.*
	Mixed flowers.	1,522 10*s.*
1931	C. Asters in a green vase. (Lowest level since the late '90's.)	75 12*s.*

		£
1933	A. Cunningham. C. Rose tremières (see 1894 and 1948).	819
1936.	C. 3 pictures, total	2,310
1936–7	50 pictures in one season, none over £800.	
1942	A. T. Reid. 7 pictures make £4,500. Mixed bouquet.	997 10s.
1946	C. A single flowerpiece.	1,995
1948	Sir Bernard Eckstein. C. Roses tremières (see 1933). (Resold Sotheby's, 1950, £2,600.)	4,200
1952	Mrs. Geoffrey Hart. S. 4 small average pieces.	3,700
1954	Sir Henry Veitch Trust. C. Roses.	5,040
	Hollyhocks.	4,620
	Peaches.	3,120
1956	Miss Lucy Norton. S. Roses.	6,500
	Morrison McChlery, Mixed flowers.	4,300
1957	Weinberg. S. Flowerpiece.	6,200
1958	Lady Lever Gallery. C. Flowerpiece.	9,450
	Delphinium imperiale.	6,800
1959	S. Flowers and fruit, large composition.	15,000
	Zinnias.	8,000
1960	Catherine Ionides. C. Small flowerpiece.	5,880

JOHN FERNELEY. 1781–1861

A Regency and early Victorian painter of hunts and equestrian scenes of no particular merit, except an obvious period charm. Yet the great sporting-picture boom of the 1920's treated him as if he were a real painter like Ben Marshall or Stubbs. To-day Stubbs is recognised as one of the very greatest English artists, while Ferneley continues as in the 1920's, to make £2,000 or £3,000, but what pounds! After his death Ferneley sank into such neglect that he was not even listed in Redford's *Art Sales* of 1888.

		£
1892	Richard Watt. C. Rockingham.	220 10s.
	Belshazzar.	210
1894	Richard Hemming. C. The Quorn Hunt meet (nearly 8 ft.).	210
1912	Lowther. C. Boy on a pony with terrier.	420
1925	C. The Quorn Hunt meet (see 1894).	1,575
1928	S. The Belvoir Hunt.	3,100*
	Country race meeting.	2,200
1931	S. The Haworth hounds.	700
1947	Sir James Drummond. C. Hunting scenes. 2 for	2,992 10s.
	Standish-Lucy. C. Frank Hall Standish and hounds.	1,575
1948	Hutchinson and Co. C. The Burton Hunt.	2,400
1951	C. Foxhunting, full cry.	2,100

		£
1953	Matthews-Naper. C. The Quorn Hunt, 1819.	1,890
1955	A. H. Caspari, New York. Ralph Lambton and hounds.	1,430
	Sir Francis Mackenzie and huntsman, etc.	2,325
1957	Wentworth. C. Godfrey Whentworth hunting, 1825.	2,730
1960	Rimington Wilson. C. Charlemagne, dapple grey Arab.	840

A. V. COPLEY FIELDING. 1787–1855

One of the most prolific of English water-colourists and until the collapse of this market in the 1920's almost the highest priced. It must be close on forty years since one of these empty works made over £1,000, and, if to-day they make a hundred or two, it is more from force of habit than inner conviction. Yet the biggest late-Victorian prices were paid for Fielding's oil-paintings which seem even emptier. How could anyone have given 3,000 golden guineas for *Travellers in a Storm*? We are too far from the Romantic Movement to understand either this or the action of the bigoted Salon jury of 1824, who awarded a gold medal to a Copley Fielding oil-painting in the company of Lawrence, Bonington and Constable, no less.

		£
1845	George Knott. C. Byland Abbey, oil.	29 8s.
1852	John Clowe. C. Loch Ettive, wc (£472 10s. in 1901).	50 8s.
1860	William Wells of Redleaf. C. Scene on the Downs (oil).	431
1863	Bicknell. C. 22 watercolours. Marquess of Hertford buys Crowborough Hill (Wallace Collection).	798
1871	E. Radley. C. Landscape in oil, bought in.	834 15s.
1875	W. Quilter. C. Mull of Galloway (oil).	1,732 10s.
	Rievaulx Abbey, wc (see 1912, 1942).	995
1879	Fleming. C. South Downs (oil).	798
1881	William Sharp. C. Travellers in a storm, oil.	3,150*
1892	Murrieta Bros. Scottish landscape, oil.	1,260
1899	Sir John Fowler. C. Sussex Downs, wc.	1,848
1902	Sir Thomas Lucas. C. Bolton Abbey, wc.	1,260
1904	Orrock. C. The Weald of Sussex, wc.	976 10s.
1908	Stephen Holland. Ben More, 1847, wc (see 1959).	619 10s.
1910	Vavasour. C. Bay of Naples, wc.	378 10s.
1912	Ruston. C. Rievaulx Abbey (see 1875, 1942), wc.	504
1913	Woodward. C. Loch Earn, wc.	525
1917	Cooke. C. Arundel, 1838, wc.	1,260
1919	Brassey. C. Sunset at Scarborough, wc.	1,197 10s.
1921	Crawford of Balcarres (Trollope). Brighton Downs, wc.	1,197 10s.
	Tintern Abbey, wc.	1,050
	Lawley. C. Staffa, 1851, wc.	1,365

		£
1922	A. H. Wild. C. Tintern Abbey, 1846, wc.	1,029
1924	C. Highland Loch, wc.	672
1925	C. Staffa, 1843, wc (£588 in 1891).	735
1927	C. Ben Lomond, wc (£357 in 1882).	430 5s.
1928	Glennie. C. Loch Katrine, 1844, wc.	483
1929	C. Scarborough, wc.	441
1932	C. Dunstaffnage Castle, 1851, wc.	367 10s.
1937	Lloyd. C. Dunster Castle, wc.	315
1942	Lord Airedale (Marler and Marler). Rievaulx Abbey (see 1875, 1912), wc.	260
1944	C. Distant view of Lancaster.	399
1946	C. Arundel Castle, 1839, wc.	262 10s.
	Lord Joicey. C. The Vale of Neath, wc, over 3 ft. (£709 10s. in 1879).	336
1948	S. Welsh landscape, wc.	360
1956	Stourton. S. The South Downs, 1855, wc.	150
1957	S. Bridlington Pier, 1842, wc (£455 14s. in 1876).	120
1959	C. Ben More, Isle of Mull, 1847, wc (see 1908).	157 10s.
1960	S. On the Rother, wc.	120

FLEMISH PRIMITIVES
before 1540

Excluding Hans Memling, Jan de Mabuse, Quentin Matsys, Van Eyck, and Van der Weyden, for whom see separate entries.

It is more than thirty-three years since a truly great painting of the Flemish fifteenth century appeared in the London salerooms. But there is still a steady trickle of early sixteenth-century works, good examples of Scorel, Isenbrandt, Van Orley, Joos van Cleve, Patinir and others. Although they cost perhaps twenty times as much as in the early 1900's, they still appear absurdly cheap by the standards of to-day, but that has always been the case with the early Flemish masters. In the days when a Van Eyck could still reach the saleroom, it would make about £300.

		£
1842	Waldegrave, Strawberry Hill (Robins), Horace Walpole's Flemish Primitive, the marriage of Henry VI (so called).	92 8s.
1850	King of Holland. Amsterdam.	
	Dirk Bouts: The Emperor Otho and Empress (?).	750
	Bernard van Orley: 4 panels, life of Job.	534
1855	Ralph Bernal. C.	
	Early Flemish School. Man in black cloak.	20 9s.
	School of Van Eyck. A female saint.	3 3s.
	Magdalene.	11 11s.

		£
1860	National Gallery buys DIRK BOUTS's Entombment from Guicciadini, Milan.	120 14s.
1867	National Gallery buys VAN DER GOES's Holy Family.	228
1876	Dunn-Gardner. C. VAN DER GOES, The Jesse Tree (see 1895).	283 10s.
1882	Hamilton Palace. C. HERRI MET DE BLES: St. Jerome.	178 10s.
1884	William Russell. C.	
	BERNARD VAN ORLEY: Magdalene.	32 11s.
	PATINIR: Madonna in landscape.	31 10s.
	SCHOOL OF VAN EYCK: Entombment (gold ground).	3 13s.
1886	Beresford Hope. C.	
	VAN DER GOES: small Madonna.	94 10s.
	PETRUS CHRISTUS: small Madonna (sold as a Van Eyck). Presented by Marquand to Metropolitan Museum, 1888.	315
	JAN SCOREL: The Three Maries at the Cross.	105
1888	Marquess of Exeter. C.	
	PETRUS CHRISTUS: Holy Family and Carthusian monk, bought as a Van Eyck by Berlin Museum through Fairfax Murray.	2,625
1889	National Gallery buys landscape by JOACHIM PATINIR.	2,000
1892	Earl of Dudley. C.	
	MASTER OF ST. GILES: The Mass of St. Giles (National Gallery, see 1934).	3,570
1894	National Gallery buys the Legend of St. Giles, the companion to Dudley's picture, from the Earl of Northbrook.	2,000
1895	Henry Doetsch. C. BERNARD VAN ORLEY: Triptych (Berlin Museum per Fairfax Murray).	168
	C. VAN DER GOES: The Jesse Tree (see 1876).	640 10s.
1904	Wickham Flower. C. Unattributed portrait of Anne of Brittany. (Bellegambe?)	1,260
1907	Francis Baring. C. JAN SCOREL: Salvator Mundi.	2,730
1910	Stainton. Foster's. HIERONYMUS BOSCH: Christ mocked.	662 10s.
1913	C. VAN DER GOES: 2 wings of a triptych.	1,029
1914	Lord Ellenborough. C. SIMON MARMION: Head of a saint.	2,625
1914	Fairfax Murray. C. HIERONYMUS BOSCH: Adoration of the Magi.	2,205
1917	C. ADRIAEN ISENBRANDT: Triptych.	2,887 10s.
1919	C. MASTER OF THE DEATH OF THE VIRGIN: Triptych.	997 10s.
1922	Ogilby. C. DIRK BOUTS: Crucifixion.	1,732 10s.
1923	C. Attributed to ROBERT CAMPIN: The raising of Lazarus.	1,470
1925	National Gallery buys the Nativity by GEERTGEN TOT SINT JANS from Cassirer, Berlin.	9,000
1927	C. MASTER OF THE FEMALE HALF-FIGURE: Magdalene	1,785
	BERNARD VAN ORLEY: Holy Family.	1,312 10s.

		£
1928	Holford. C. Petrus Christus: The man in a doublet. Bought by Duveen. Left by Andrew Mellon to the National Gallery, Washington.	14,700
	Joos van Cleve: Holy Family.	5,565
	Hieronymus Bosch: Adoration of the Magi.	1,050
1929	Brauer. C. Adriaen Isenbrandt: Nativity.	3,360
1930	Joos van Cleve: Holy Family with saints.	2,415
1934	National Gallery buys Hieronymus Bosch's Christ crowned with thorns.	5,291 7*s.*
	Also the Mass of St. Giles (see 1892).	10,000
1936	C. Dirk Bouts: Ecce homo, panel.	1,627 10*s.*
1938	Mortimer Schiff. C.	
	Isenbrandt: Holy Family.	1,050
	Bernard van Orley: Legend of St. Martin.	1,575
	Jan Mostaert: Lady in brown.	1,837 10*s.*
1940	Countess of Northbrook. C. Gerard David: small Madonna. (£23 2*s.* in 1880).	892 10*s.*
1942	Clarence McKay. C. Adriaen Isenbrandt: small triptych.	5,880
1943	Sir B. Sheffield. C. Jan Scorel: Portrait of Lord Sheffield. 1537.	1,575
1950	Galerie Charpentier, Paris. Master of the Legend of St. Augustine: portrait.	1,760
1952	C. Jan Scorel: Large triptych.	2,400
1953	Lady Catherine Ashburnham. S. Patinir: Landscape with Riposo.	3,600
	Bernard van Orley: David and Bathsheba.	4,200
	Antwerp School, 1518: Adoration of Magi.	4,500
1954	C. Hieronymus Bosch: Procession to Calvary.	3,045
1956	C. Adriaen Isenbrandt: Holy Family.	8,925
	Geoffrey Merton. C. Jan Provost: Triptych, Adoration of the Magi.	4,200
	Andrew Verney. C. Joos van Cleve: Burgomaster and wife.	1,730
	Parke-Bernet, New York. Joos van Cleve: Girl's portrait.	3,928
	S. Patinir: Moses and the burning bush.	1,700
1957	The Metropolitan Museum buys the Merode triptych, probably by The Master of Flemalle. Reputed price	303,500
1957	Earl of Roden. S. Jean Bellegambe: Judith and Holofernes.	2,400
	Paul Baerwald. S. Adriaen Isenbrandt: Holy Family in a landscape.	4,200
	C. Jan Scorel Head of a bishop.	1,995
1958	Duke of Devonshire. C. Colin de Coeter: Departure of St. Romuald.	2,310

		£
	Enthronement of St. Romuald. (National Gallery, Dublin).	4,200
1959	C. GERARD DAVID: The risen Christ.	4,725
	MASTER OF THE EMBROIDERED LEAF: Madonna.	8,400
	Professor Strazza. C. JOOS VAN CLEVE: Weeping Virgin.	5,460
1959	S. JAN SCOREL: Madonna.	2,100
1960	S. MASTER OF THE ST. LUCY LEGEND: Madonna.	2,400

DRAWINGS

1936	Henry Oppenheimer. C. DIRK BOUTS, silverpoint portrait.	4,200
1946	Sterling of Keir. S. BERNARD VAN ORLEY: Hunting party, pen and ink.	460
1948	Alfred Jowitt. S. VAN DER GOES. Hooded Lady.	2,200
	Weyden School, silverpoint head.	4,000

FLEMISH SCHOOL

16th and early 17th Century

Excluding Pieter and Jan Breughel and Antonis Mor

English portraits by visiting Flemings of the late Tudor and early Stuart periods enjoyed a much stronger vogue in the 1920's and even in the 1880's than they do to-day. In fact, this is a much-neglected school, and so are the contemporary Flemish landscapes and subject pictures, the 'Northern Baroque' of which there has been a little selective buying since the war. It has to be added that the mythological subjects are often hideous.

		£
1802	Sir Simon Clark. C. FRANS SNYDERS: Boar Hunt.	100 16*s.*
1824	Angerstein. National Gallery acquires JUSTUS SUSTERMANS, Ferdinand of Tuscany and Duchess (as Velasquez, Philip IV, etc.).	300
1882	Hamilton Palace. C. MARK GEERARTS: The English Peace Commission of 1604 (National Portrait Gallery).	2,520
	ABRAHAM BLOEMART: Christ and woman of Samaria.	105
1882	John Henderson. C. FRANS SNYDERS: The larder invaded.	236 5*s.*
1886	Blenheim Palace. C. DANIEL MYTENS: Earl of Holland.	1,008
	Duke of Buckingham.	735
1898	C. MARK GEERARTS: James I.	262 10*s.*
1902	National Gallery buys JORDAENS's portrait of Waha de Linter.	1,200
1903	C. DANIEL MYTENS: Hermann Boerhave.	840
1906	C. MARK GEERARTS: Arabella Stewart.	262 10*s.*
1907	Hodgson. C. JUSTUS SUSTERMANS: Marchesa Guadagni.	777 10*s.*
1911	C. FRANS SNYDERS: Dead game and lobster.	546
	CORNELIUS DE VOS: Portrait of Spinoza.	165 5*s.*

		£
1919	Hamilton Palace. C. MARK GEERARTS: Lord John Hamilton.	1,785
1921	Lord Willoughby de Broke. C. MARK GEERARTS: Queen Elizabeth.	2,950
1925	Earl of Darnley. C. MARK GEERARTS: Frances Howard, Duchess of Richmond.	1,207 10*s.*
	JACOB JORDAENS: The artist and his wife.	3,980
	FRANS POURBUS: François d'Alencon, 1572.	1,050
1928	Holford. C. JUSTUS SUSTERMANS: Whole-length, Boy in a large hat.	13,125*
	Whole-length of a lady.	7,360
	CORNELIS DE VOS: Lady in black with a fan.	1,785
	ADRIAEN HANNEMAN: Prince Rupert.	3,780
	FRANS POURBUS THE YOUNGER: Infanta Isabel.	1,260
1928	Sir J. C. Grey. C. MARK GEERARTS: Lady in yellow.	1,995
1929	C. MARK GEERARTS: Wife of a yeoman of the jewel house (sold with the dress she is wearing).	4,200
1930	Lord Chesham. C. JACOB JORDAENS: Lady in dark dress with a dog.	2,625
1933	Sir Timothy Eden. C. GERARD SOEST: Portrait, 2nd Lord Baltimore (bought Baltimore Museum).	4,200
1934	A. J. Sulley. C. CORNELIS DE VOS: Lady with children.	1,050
1946	Parke-Bernet, New York. FRANS POURBUS THE YOUNGER: Noblewoman.	1,200
1948	Earl Fitzwilliam. C. JACOB JORDAENS: The artist and his wife.	966
1952	Duke of Northumberland. S. JUDOCUS MOMPER: Mountainous landscape.	1,300
1952	Lord Brockett. S. MARK GEERARTS: Sir Henry Lee, 1600.	1,000
1953	Henry Reitlinger. S. LAMBERT LOMBARD: Miracle of loaves and fishes.	1,520
	BARTOLOMAEUS SPRANGER: Venus and Adonis (£126 in 1923, Robinson and Fisher).	850
1959	Duke of Westminster. S. FRANS SNYDERS: Landscape with fox and herons.	1,600
	James Christie. C. CORNELIS DE VOS: Young woman. 1619.	997 10*s.*
	S. JUDOCUS MOMPER: Landscape with travellers.	1,000
1960	S. FRANS SNYDERS: A larder.	7,600

MYLES BIRKET FOSTER. 1825–1899

'He (Samson) used to say that he had known profiteers during the war, who bought a few Birket Fosters so that after dinner, armed with a big cigar, they could take refuge in contemplating them and having a good cry.'—A. C. R. Carter, *Let me tell you* (1942), p. 69.

The market for pure nostalgia. Lots of children, not armed with space-guns, but apple-cheeked, pinafored and weaving daisy chains in the long grass.

This market seems to flourish towards the end of wars. Practically all are water-colours.

		£
1862	Knowles. C. Gathering primroses.	116 11*s*.
1865	C. Donkey rides.	418 19*s*.
1872	Radley. C. The cross-bow (oil).	420
1877	Knowles. C. Oxford from the Thames.	399
1891	Charles Kurtz. C. The meet (see 1903).	535 10*s*.
1903	C. Same picture.	787 10*s*.
1913	C. Ben Nevis (in 1918 it rose to £1,071).	588
1919	C. Greenwich sunset.	1,680
	(48 pictures sold in 1919.)	
1920	Rouen Cathedral.	1,176
	(46 pictures sold in 1920.)	
1922	C. Rouen Cathedral resold.	1,417 10*s*.
	(76 pictures sold in 1922.)	
1924	Crowther. C. On the Thames at Greenwich (see 1933).	1,942 10*s*.
1930	Barnet Lewis. C. 126 Birket Fosters. 6-ft. landscape.	945
	The Weald of Surrey (see 1945).	567
1933	Machell. C. On the Thames at Greenwich.	630
1936	Only 2 out of 24 exceeded £100.	
1943	Sir W. Thomlinson. C. The sheepfold.	945
	Waterlilies.	861
	Windsor Lock.	819
1945	C. The Weald of Surrey (see 1930). [£577 10*s*. in 1961.]	2,152 10*s*.
1946	Henry Mason. C. View near Dorking.	903
1947	Mrs. Penrose. C. A sure and steady aim.	997 10*s*.
1948	Bernard Eckstein. C. Haymakers.	682 10*s*.
1957	Roxborough. C. The old chair-mender.	609
	On the River Mole.	504
1959	C. Near Dalmally, Argyllshire.	472 10*s*.

JEAN HONORÉ FRAGONARD. 1732–1806

An uneven and temperamental painter and a temperamental market. Since there is nothing more to come like the fabulous panels, *Roman d'amour de la jeunesse*, the tendency is for scrappy works, studies rather than completed pictures. But the wonderful pen-and-wash drawings of Fragonard, the most wildly rococco of all rococco, seem to advance continuously. Between the 1780's and 1850's there was virtually no market at all.

		£
1788	4 of the Pierpont Morgan panels sold to Fragonard's cousin, because Mme. Du Barry had refused them (see 1898, 1915).	142
1841	Perregaux. Paris. The schoolmistress (Hertford).	15 8*s*.

		£
1865	Duc de Morny, Paris. Le souvenir.	1,400
	Plaisirs de l'escarpolette.	1,208
	Both bought by Lord Hertford, now Wallace Collection.	
1870	San Donato, Paris. La fontaine d'amour (Lord Hertford, Wallace Collection).	1,260
1872	Cope. C. Pierrot, bought by Sir Richard Wallace as a Boucher (Wallace Collection).	913 10*s.*
1882	Hamilton Palace. C. Lady in a crimson jacket, oval portrait, once at Fonthill.	472 10*s.*
1898	The 10 panels, Roman d'amour de la jeunesse, bought by Agnew from M. Malvitain and sold to Pierpont Morgan (see 1915). 10 for	64,000
1912	Doucet. Paris. Sacrifice au minotaure.	15,830
	Portrait, Mme. Regieri.	5,500
1915	The 10 panels, Roman d'amour de la jeunesse, sold by Duveen to H. C. Frick. 10 for	205,500
1920	Beurdeley, Paris. Venus et l'amour.	5,000
1937	H. G. Boeche. C. Mlle. Gerard, portrait.	4,095
1952	Count Potocki. S. L'homme à l'epée.	7,500
	Gabriel Cognacq. Paris. Jeune fille aux chiens.	11,000
1955	Major F. E. Sotheby. S. 2 small ovals, La folie.	3,000
	L'amour.	1,500
1959	Mrs. Hubert Chanter. S. Oil sketch for La fontaine d'amour (see 1870).	3,200
	Oval portrait head, Le philosophe.	13,000
1960	George J. Gould. S. Small oil sketch, L'Ecurie de l'ane.	5,500
	Penard y Fernandes, Paris. L'heureux ménage, round panel, only 14 in. diam.	11,663
	Galerie Charpentier, Paris. Hide and seek, oil sketch.	10,970

DRAWINGS

		£
1903	C. A series of 12 charcoal drawings.	1,942 10*s.*
1908	Sir James Knowles. C. Entrance to a park, sepia wash.	693
1935	Faucher-Magnan. S. Le taureau.	1,100
	La Sultane.	780
1937	Comtesse de Greffullhe. S. Tivoli gardens (bistre).	2,900
1938	Mortimer Schiff. C. Tivoli gardens (sanguine).	398
1952	Cognacq, Paris. La Rêveuse (bistre wash).	3,165
1956	S. Le taureau enragé.	1,600
1959	Chanter. S. La resistance inutile (pen and wash).	4,500
	Danae and Jupiter.	4,000
	Les Petards.	2,400
	And others at £1,000 to £2,400.	
	Sketchbook, 141 leaves.	16,500

		£	
1959	Galerie Charpentier, Paris. Le repos dans le Foret (sanguine).	2,152	
1960	S. The kiss in the smoke.	1,700	
	Galerie Charpentier. Le Galant surpris.	1,756	

PIERO DELLA FRANCESCA. 1416–1492

No Piero della Francesca has appeared on the market for 22 years, and the price of the last one would suggest that the National Gallery must own at least two which are worth half a million each. Yet they have been, even by the standards of the time, among the cheapest pictures the gallery ever bought. The most original of all the quattrocento painters was not fully appreciated before the present century.

		£	
1853	Samuel Woodburn. C. A Duke of Urbino receiving the order of the Garter (bought by Earl of Ashburnham).	84	
1861	Uzielli sale, Florence. Eastlake buys the Baptism of Christ for the National Gallery.	241	10*s.*
1866	Eastlake buys the lady with the sharp profile from Egidi in Florence for the National Gallery, now called Alessio Baldovinetti.	160	
1867	National Gallery buys from Lady Eastlake the small St. Michael and the dragon panel, then called Carnavale.	50	
1874	Alexander Barker. C. Disraeli buys the Nativity for the National Gallery.	2,415	
1886	William Graham. C. La bella Simonetta (Alessio Baldovinetti?), bought Donaldson.	525	
1889	Odiot, Paris. Portrait of a lady looking to the left.	540	
1908	Isabella Stewart Gardner buys the fresco fragment, The young Hercules, from Borgo san Sepulchro. about	10,000	
1938	Carl Hamilton sale, New York. Duveen buys the small Doria Crucifixion (sold to Andrew Mellon, probably for about £100,000, now National Gallery, Washington).	77,500	

FRANCESCO FRANCIA. 1450–1517

		£	
1824	Sir Mark Sykes. St. Roche (see 1894).	99	15*s.*
	Bianchetti. Crucifixion from Bologna (see 1847).	94	10*s.*
1841	National Gallery buys the Buonvisi altarpiece and predella, ex Duke of Lucca.	3,500	
1847	Edward Solly. Crucifixion (see 1850).	346	10*s.*

		£
1850	Dernville. C. Solly's Crucifixion (see 1863).	215 5s.
1859	Earl of Northwick (Philips). Portrait of Bartolommeo Bianchini, sold as Raphael (National Gallery, 1910).	99 15s.
1863	C. The Solly Crucifixion (see 1850).	105
1872	Prince Imperiale. C. Young man in black (Fed. Gonzaga) (Metropolitan Museum since 1913).	409 10s.
1874	Alexander Barker. C. Roundel, Holy Family.	682 10s.
1874	Paris sale. Madonna from Guastavillani.	840
1879	Fuller Maitland. C. Holy Family with angels.	278 5s.
1886	William Graham. C. St. Francis (fresco).	136 10s.
1894	Sir Walter Farquhar. C. St. Roche (see 1824).	997 10s.
1902	Carmichael. C. Small Holy Family.	1,050
1912	J. E. Taylor. C. Holy Family.	4,725
1954	Morgan Grenville. C. Small Holy Family.	6,300

FRENCH PRIMITIVES
before 1500

The French have been slow in discovering their own primitive school, partly because of the casual late eighteenth- and early nineteenth-century assumption that all Gothic painting before Dürer was Flemish. But having discovered that they possessed a primitive school, they succeeded in making it very fashionable.

		£
1913	Aynard, Paris. Small head of the Virgin, attributed to JEAN MALOUEL (Carlos de Besteguei, Biarritz).	5,700
1920	Stanley. S. JEAN BOURDICHON: Louis XII, drawing on vellum.	1,000
1922	Paul Cassirer, Berlin. Holy Trinity, *c.* 1410 (National Gallery).	4,750
1925	National Gallery buys the meeting of Joachim and Anne by THE MASTER OF MOULINS.	10,000
1929	National Gallery buys the Wilton diptych with portrait of Richard II, late 14th century.	90,000
1930	J. D. Rockefeller buys two small portrait heads by THE MASTER OF ST. JEAN DE LUZ (per Duveen). According to Behrman, the price was	155,000
1936	Henry Oppenheimer. C. Silverpoint drawing of a papal legate by Jean Fouquet (bought 1920, £2,800), bought Duveen.	10,710
1938	Duke of Norfolk. C. Early 15th-century triptych. Coronation of the Virgin.	4,305
1956	S. Drawing of a portrait head in lead point, by MASTER OF MOULINS.	4,800

WILLIAM FRITH. 1824–1909

In 1896, when Frith was alive and still working a little at the age of seventy-two, the collapse in the value of his pictures was as complete as it has been at any time in the present century. His case was therefore unique among the most highly-priced mid-Victorians, such as Millais, Alma-Tadema, Burne-Jones and Lord Leighton, none of whom lived to see the decline of their market.

Frith's popular style undoubtedly depended more than any other contemporary's on the high value of steel-engraving rights, and these fell with the advent of photographic processes. But a still more potent factor was the growth of the Moral Purpose which would have no truck with Frith's sly anecdotes.

Present-day prices are deceptive owing to the lack of highly finished works of Frith's best period. *Derby Day* and *The Railway Station* might well make more (in devalued pounds) than they brought the painter.

		£
1848	The Gleaner, a small portrait head, sold to Mr. Burt.	157 10s.
1851	Miller of Preston commissions The Old Woman accused of Witchcraft (see 1946).	252
1852	Pope and Lady Montague, sold to John Hargreaves (see 1881, 1906).	367 10s.
1853	Ramsgate sands, sold to the dealer Lloyd (passed on to Queen Victoria, but Lloyd made £3,000 on the engraving and exhibition rights).	735
1854–8	Derby Day. Sold to Jacob Bell, who left it to the National Gallery in 1859. Frith retained the rights, on which he made a further £2,250.	1,500
1860	Tarquand. C. Coming of age in the olden time, originally sold for £400 (see 1924).	1,207 10s.
1862	The Railway Station, commissioned by Flatou. Total paid, including rights.	5,250
1863	The Queen commissions Marriage of the Prince of Wales.	3,150
1864	McArthur. C. Flatou buys back Coming of age, etc., resold 1866 for £1,464 15s. (see 1924).	1,207 10s.
1869	C. Altesidora and Don Quixote (see 1882).	2,100
1870	Charles Dickens's executors. Dolly Varden (see 1956).	1,050
1873	W. Grapel. C. Claude Duval (see 1910).	2,047 10s.
1875	Sam Mendel. C. Supper at Boswell's lodgings. (Fell to £3,150 in 1877.)	4,567 10s.*
1878	Flatou sells The Road to Ruin, 4 pictures (resold Ellis sale, C. 1886, £1,575) (See 1919.) 4 for	6,300
1881	Holdsworth. C. Pope and Lady Montague (see 1906).	1,249 10s.
1890	Cozens. C. Coming of age in the olden time (see 1864).	388
1891	Matthias. C. King Charles II's last Sunday.	1,732 10s.

		£
1896	Simpson. C. The Race for Wealth (5 pictures) (commissioned 1880, made £787 10s. in 1889) (see 1925). 5 for	325 10s.
1906	Sir F. T. Mappin. Pope and Lady Montague (see 1881).	483
1910	C. Claude Duval (see 1875, 1922 and 1946).	651
1913	Lord Holden. C. Merry Wives of Windsor (oil-sketch, £136 in 1872).	15 15s.
1917	Gresham. C. Charles II and Lady Castlemaine.	102 18s.
1919	The Road to Ruin (4, see 1878).	460
1924	Restell. C. Coming of age (see 1860, 1864, 1890, 1949).	1,050
1925	Denning. C. The Race for Wealth, set of 5 (see 1896).	168
1932	C. The salon d'or (commissioned by Flatou in 1872 for £4,000. Rhode Island School of Design).	48 6s.
1946	Pitt-Miller. C. The Old Woman accused of Witchcraft (see 1851).	136
	Ramsgate sands, water-colour version.	336
	Morrison McChlery, Glasgow. Claude Duval (see 1875).	160
1945	S. The Railway Station (5-ft. replica).	250
1949	James Foster. C. Coming of age in the olden time (see 1860, 1924, etc.).	336
1956	C. Dolly Varden (see 1870).	75 12s.
	Angling party, large picture.	84

THOMAS GAINSBOROUGH. 1727–1788

See Chapters 3 and 7. A complete sales analysis of Gainsborough's paintings would require a volume to itself. I have therefore restricted this list chiefly to works whose movement of price can be recorded. I have not been able to trace the final prices in America of some of the most costly Gainsboroughs, but it is probable that something like a dozen Gainsboroughs have changed hands at different times at prices of £50,000 to £150,000.

Gainsborough's fees (according to Professor Waterhouse):

- 1748 portraits 5 to 8 guineas.
- 1755 chimney-piece sized landscapes, 15 and 21 guineas.
- 1758 half-lengths, 15 guineas.
- 1760's Whole-lengths, 80 guineas, half-lengths, 40 guineas, heads, 20 guineas.
- 1770's scale rises to 160, 80 and 40 guineas.
- 1785 Landscape for Prince of Wales, £89 6s.; for Duke of Rutland, 3 for £231.

	£
1788 (or after) Reynolds sells Calonne, The Pig Girl (at Castle Howard).	315
Boydell pays for Cornard Wood (National Gallery).	78 15s.
Macklin pays for Hobinol and Gambaretta.	350

		£
1789	Mrs. Gainsborough, Schomberg House. The Woodman.	525
1796	Buttall. Master Jonathan Buttall, 'The Blue Boy', bought by Nesbitt (resold in 1802 to Lord Grosvenor for £68 5*s.*, see 1921).	36 15*s.*
1797	Gainsborough Executors' sale. Cattle watering at sunset.	101 17*s.*
	The Mall in St. James's Park (see 1829 and 1916).	31 10*s.*
	Haymaker and sleeping girl (Boston Museum, 1893).	29 8*s.*
	Mrs. Graham as a Housemaid, monochrome (National Gallery).	4 14*s.*
1803	Walsh Porter. C. Market cart with figures.	115 10*s.*
1808	Earl of Halifax. C. Gipsies reposing.	163 16*s.*
1814	British Institution exhibition. 4 Sheridan family portraits sold for	525
1823	Davison. C. Figures and cattle in a wood.	142 16*s.*
1803–1827	Best prices are for landscapes. Generally portraits made from 30*s.* to £6.	
1827	Lord de Tabley. C. Fishermen launching boats (Collection of Mrs. Mellon-Bruce).	215 5*s.*
	The Cottage Door (Lord Grosvenor, see 1921).	525
1829	Kinderbee. C. Mall in St. James's Park (see 1797 and 1916).	183 15*s.*
1832	Ewer. C. Crossing the brook.	231
1834	Hallett. C. The Morning walk (see 1859). No opening bid.	
1836	C. Dr. Ralph Schomberg, bought in at £52 10*s.* (see 1862).	
1839	The 'disappearing' Duchess of Devonshire, bought from Mrs. Magennis (see 1876).	50
1841	Colonel Damer. C. The market cart (see 1928).	651
1851	British Gallery of Art. C. Fancy portrait, Repose.	945
1859	Earl of Northwick (Philips). The morning walk (see 1834 and 1954).	756
1862	National Gallery buys Dr. Schomberg and Mrs. Siddons, seated. each	1,000
1867	Wilshire. C. Lord Tweedmouth buys Harvest waggon.	3,147
	Landscape with cattle.	1,890
	(See 1946 for both pictures.)	
	Monro of Novar. C. Lady in a pink dress.	582 15*s.*
1872	Gillott. C. A version of The Cottage Door (now Lord Moyne Collection).	1,081 10*s.*
1873	Colonel Townley. C. The Misses Ramus (see 1887).	6,615
1875	Rev. John Lucy. C. Returning from market (bought by Earl of Dudley, now Cincinatti Art Institute).	5,640
	National Gallery buys Cornard Wood (see 1788).	1,207 10*s.*

		£
1876	Wynn Ellis. C. Agnew buys the problematic Duchess of Devonshire against the Earl of Dudley (stolen, see 1901).	10,605
1882	Lord Normanby. C. Oval portrait, Lady Anne Mulgrave (see 1895).	1,123 10*s.*
1883	Sir Henry Hoare. C. Peasants and colliers. Bought Holloway College.	2,835
1887	James Graham. C. The Misses Ramus (see 1873). (Ferdinand de Rothschild, destroyed by fire.)	9,997
1890	Duke of Somerset. C. Lord Alexander Hamilton in Van Dyck dress, small oval. (now National Trust, Waddesdon Manor).	4,410
1893	Lord Revelstoke. C. Mrs. Drummond of Stanmore (see 1913).	7,035
1894	Gibbons. C. The market cart (see 1841, 1913, 1928).	4,725
1895	James Pryce. C. Lady Mulgrave (see 1882). Collection of Pierre Groult, Paris (see page 189).	10,500
1896	Sir Julian Goldsmid. Dorothea, Lady Eden (A. W. Ericson Collection, New York).	5,250
1901	The stolen Duchess of Devonshire (see 1876), bought by Pierpont Morgan (now Collection of Mrs. Mabel S. Ingalls).	30,000
	or	35,000
1902	The artist's daughters with folios (1917, Art Museum, Worcester, Mass.).	5,880
1903	C. Miss Linley in muslin and yellow (discovered in Worthing, now Philadelphia Museum).	9,450
1904	Duke of Cambridge. C. Maria Walpole, Duchess of Gloucester (Cincinatti Art Institute), cost 50*s.* in 1797.	12,705
1906	Denny. C. Viscountess Tracy (see 1946).	6,300
1907	F. W. Huth. C. Landscape with cattle and figures.	5,985
1910	C. Raphael Franco (a record price for a male portrait).	6,510
1911	Pierpont Morgan buys from Lord Sackville The beggar boy and girl (now in the Clarke Art Institute, Williamstown, Mass.).	37,200
1913	Sir Lionel Philips. C. The market cart (see 1841 and 1928) bought Duveen.	20,160
	H. C. Frick buys the Hon. Frances Duncombe, replica of Longford Castle picture. Reputed price	82,700
1916	Sir Audley Neeld. Duveen buys the Mall in St. James's Park (see 1797, 1829. Frick Library, San Marino, Cal.).	62,000
1921	Henry Huntington buys from Duveen the Duke of Westminster's pictures.	
	The Blue Boy (see 1796, 1802).	148,000*
	The Cottage Door (see 1827).	73,500
1923	Gainsborough's daughters (unfinished), bought by National Gallery.	3,349

		£
1925	The original Duchess of Devonshire, bought from Althorp by Duveen (National Gallery, Washington, Mellon Bequest). Final price exceeded	70,000
1925	Countess of Carnarvon. C. Earl of Chesterfield.	6,825
	Countess of Chesterfield (see 1959).	17,860
1926	Late Lord Michelham (Hampton's). Miss Tatton (National Gallery, Washington, per Mellon).	46,200
	Master Heathcote (Alvan T. Fuller, Boston).	46,100
1928	Elbert Gary, New York. Duveen buys back The market cart (see 1913). Now Toronto Gallery.	74,400
1929	Craggs-Nugent (Puttick's). Lt.-Colonel Craggs-Nugent, bought Baron Thyssen (now Beaverbrook Gallery, Fredericton).	15,250
1935	Joel. C. The Charlton children (see 1948).	3,465
	National Gallery buys Viscount Kilmorey.	5,000
1936	Andrew Mellon buys Mrs. Sheridan from Lord Rothschild via Duveen (National Gallery, Washington).	50,000
1937	David Jardine. C. Crossing the brook.	7,780
	Sir Edmund Davis. C. Lady Louise Clarges, £2,100 in 1895. See also 1942.	1,575
1942	Commander Stopford. C. Coast scene (bought Ipswich Corporation).	798
1942	C. Lady Clarges (see 1937, formerly valued at £25,000).	1,365
1945	C. Fishermen dragging nets (ex Ramsay MacDonald, now Collection of Lord Fairhaven).	5,040
1946	E. J. Wythes. C. Countess Tracy (see 1916).	1,050
	Lord Swaythling. C. Grand landscape (see 1867).	4,830
	The harvest waggon (see 1867). Bought by Barber Institute, Birmingham.	20,475
1946	Humphrey. C. Mr. Humphrey shooting near Sudbury, a very early work (see 1951).	2,520
1947	Proctor-Beauchamp. S. Mouth of the Thames (Melbourne National Gallery).	4,000
1948	Bernard Eckstein. S. The Charlton children (see 1935).	1,600
1951	Hutchinson & Co. C. Mr. Humphrey shooting (see 1946).	4,620
	Baroness Burton. C. Sarah, Countess of Kinnoul.	3,465
	George Drummond (Ashmolean Museum).	3,780
	Mrs. Drummond (Montreal Gallery).	2,730
1953	Tollemache estates. C. The Cottage Door.	27,300
	Crossing the brook. (Collection of Paul Getty).	27,300
1954	National Gallery buys 'The Morning Walk—Mr. and Mrs. Hallett', from Lord Rothschild (see 1834 and 1859).	30,000
1956	Parke-Bernet, New York. Small wooded landscape.	7,300

		£
1958	Earl of Waldegrave. C. Henry, Duke of Gloucester (£6 in 1797).	22,050
1959	Sir John Leigh. S. Earl of Chesterfield.	14,000
	Countess of Chesterfield.	34,000
	(Collection of Paul Getty. See Carnarvon sale, 1925.)	
1960	Andrews. S. Mr. and Mrs. Andrews in a park. Bought by Agnew, later acquired for National Gallery.	130,000*
1960	Sandy Lodge (Knight, Frank and Rutley). The painter's daughter, half-length.	5,500
	S. Landscape. The midday rest.	6,200

PAUL GAUGUIN. 1848–1903

In 1896 Gauguin wrote from Tahiti to his friend, Georges Daniel de Manfreid, proposing to send him 15 completed pictures a year in return for an annual remittance of £96. One of these pictures, offered at £6 10s. each, was sold 63 years later for £130,000. Such a price for a painter who was so tragically and pitifully ignored by his age seems almost an appeasement sacrifice to his shade.

		£
1895	Vente Gauguin, Paris. 49 lots.	
	Manao Tapapau (Conger Goodyear Collection).	36
	Mao Taporo (see 1957).	14 10*s.*
	Waiting for the letter (see 1959).	15
1896	Nevermore. Bought by the composer Delius (Courtauld Gallery).	20
1903	Te Rerioa, sold by Manfreid to Ignace Fayet (Courtauld Gallery).	44
1912	Rouart, Paris. Papeete.	1,302
1924	S. Small self-portrait in spectacles.	95
1926	Duke of Rutland. C. Te fare maorie, 1890.	798
	Manchester Whitworth Gallery buys Brittany scene.	260
1932	C. Small Brittany landscape (resold 1933, £105).	220 10*s.*
1940	Eumorphopoulos. S. Apples in a bowl (Alexander Korda).	170
1943	Leopold Sutro. C. Child portrait 'Jean', pastel.	126
1953	Mrs. M. R. Lousada. C. Apples and flowers on a newspaper.	420
1957	Weinberg. S. Jeunes baigneurs bretons.	17,000
	Mrs. Thompson Biddle. Charpentier, Paris.	
	Apples, 1901 (Collection of Niarchos).	104,630
	Apples and grapes.	36,200
	Pont Aven.	14,300
	Brian Melland. S. Apples ($6\frac{1}{2}$ ins. × 14 ins.).	2,520
	Georges Lurcy, New York. Mao Taporo (see 1895).	64,130

		£
1958	Henry J. Heinz. New York. Small basket of flowers.	19,300
1959	George Goodyear. S. J'attends ta reponse (see 1895).	130,000
1960	Ralph M. Coe. S. Tahiti, landscape with figures.	38,000
	Galerie Charpentier, Paris. La fiancée, 1888, 16 ins. × 13 ins.	9,892

JEAN LOUIS GERICAULT. 1791–1824

The most interesting of all the French romantics who broke away from neo-classicism and the least valued in his own day, in spite of the fact that he was profoundly influenced by English painting. Of all strange things, Gericault was smitten with the contemporary English sporting pictures, transforming the unreal spread-out gallop convention of Wolstenholme, Alken and Ferneley into something truly sinister. Still largely a French market.

		£
1820	Le radeau de la Meduse makes £800 in gate money when exhibited in London.	
1824	Vente Gericault, Paris. Le radeau de la Meduse. (Louvre).	240
1853	Louis Philippe. C. 2 paintings of cuirassiers, the pair	936
1857	Wallace, Paris. Cavalry skirmish (bought Hertford, now in Wallace Collection).	222
1873	Laurent Richard, Paris. Lancier rouge.	470
	L'amazone.	470
1886	Defoer, Paris. Triumph of the Hussars.	800
1889	Secrétan, Paris. Le lancier.	564
	Course libre à Rome.	564
1895	Thomas Woolner. C. Horses racing.	120 15s.
1899	Harris Holbrooke. C. L'attelage.	997 10s.
1935	Coats. C. Prancing grey horse.	283 10s.
1944	S. A dappled horse, small oil.	220
1950	Gallerie Charpentier, Paris. Le berger nu.	644
1951	S. Coronation of Marie de Medici, small oil.	280
1952	Gabriel Cognacq, Paris. Jupiter and Alcmene.	2,962
1960	Galliera, Paris. St. Peter Martyr, after Titian.	1,021

GERMAN PRIMITIVES
before 1530

Until fairly recent times a despised school, it being held that Holbein and Dürer were the only German painters. In modern times a large exodus of dealers' stocks from Germany (after 1933) depressed the market. In the 1950's German primitives tended to return to Germany at prices that were found surprising.

		£
1854	The Krueger Collection. On the Prince Consort's advice, the National Gallery bought 64 pictures for £2,800, but kept only 17 of them. 37 German primitives were sent to Christie's, where they made £230 between them, or less than 6 guineas a picture.	
1885	Rev. Russell Fuller. C. ALTDORFER: Christ visiting His Mother (Lady Ludlow, Luton Hoo).	24 3*s.*
1888	Marquess of Exeter. C. ALTDORFER: Nativity (bought by Charles Butler, now Kaiser Friedrich Museum).	162 15*s.*
1892	Hollingworth-Magniac. C. HANS BURGKMAIR: Portrait of a young man.	99 15*s.*
1895	Henry Doetsch. C. COLOGNE SCHOOL: Adoration.	54 2*s.*
	CHRISTOPHER AMBERGER: Portrait.	113 8*s.*
	CRANACH SCHOOL: Madonna.	42
1896	C. MARTIN SCHONGAUER: Annunciation.	504
1901	C. MICHAEL WOHLGEMUTH: 6 Old Testament panels.	183 15*s.*
1911	Murray-Guthrie. C. MARTIN SCHONGAUER: Three saints in a garden.	1,680
1911	G. E. Dering. C. MASTER OF HOLZHAUSEN: Male portrait.	2,175
1912	J. E. Taylor. C. BARTOLOMAEUS BRUYN: Donors, 2 wings of a triptych.	525
1919	Vernon Wentworth. C. HANS EWARTH: Lady Eleanor Brandon.	1,732 10*s.*
1924	Princess Royal. C. MASTER OF ST. BARTHOLOMEW ALTAR: Small head of a prelate.	1,890
1928	S. MASTER OF THE CARNATION: Adoration.	1,850
	COLOGNE SCHOOL: Passion of Christ, triptych.	3,100
1929	S. ALDEGREVER: Lady in a dark dress.	1,100
1930	Ramsden. C. HANS WARTINGER: Anne of Cleves.	2,205
	S. ANONYMOUS: Portrait of Friedrich Rohrbach, 1532.	1,700
1933	Hirsch. C. AMBERGER: Portrait of Matthaus Schwarz and wife. each	1,575
1937	Rosenthal. S. HANS BURGKMAIR: Young man with long hair.	1,550
1938	Mortimer Schiff. C. JOHANN KOERBECKE: Altarpiece. Said to have been bought for Hitler.	3,570
1945	Lord Bagot. S. GERMAN 15TH-CENTURY SCHOOL: Nativity of Christ.	1,850
1947	Ernest Rosenfeld, New York. HANS BURGKMAIR: Portrait of an architect.	3,250
1953	S. HANS BURGKMAIR: Presentation in the temple.	5,500
	2 panels.	3,600
1956	Metropolitan Museum, New York. SWISS SCHOOL: Conversion of Paul.	2,232

		£
1956	J. Walter. S. HERMAN TOM RING: Double child portrait, dated 1464.	10,000
1957	Mae Rovensky, New York. FABER VON CREUTZNACH: Johann Reys and wife, small pair. 2 for	5,750
1959	S. HANS VON KULMBACH: Half-length male figure.	6,500

DRAWINGS

1922	Max Bonn. S. MASTER OF THE HAUSBUCH: Design for stained glass.	380
	HANS VON KULMBACH: St. Nicholas.	210
1929	C. HANS BURGKMAIR: Aristotle and Thais.	304 10*s.*
1936	Henry Oppenheimer. C. WOLF HUBER: Portrait, Luther.	3,255
	ALTDORFER: Landsknecht.	464
1949	Claud Lucas. C. ANONYMOUS: Crucifixion, 1480.	682 10*s.*
1959	S. MAIR VON LANDSHUT: St. Christopher.	2,500

DOMENICO DEL GHIRLANDAJO. 1449–1494

A much-attributed name in Victorian times. Several of the paintings in this list may be by Bastiano Mainardi.

		£
1857	National Gallery buys Holy Family in Volterra (now called School of Verrocchio).	456 16*s.*
1859	Earl of Northwick (Philips). 5 attributed pictures. Holy Family with goldfinch.	99 15*s.*
1874	Alexander Barker. C. Holy Family and many saints. Bought Marquess of Bath.	367 10*s.*
1876	William Willett buys Giovanna Tornabuoni from Mme. de Sagan (see 1896, 1935).	600
1886	William Graham. C. 4 attributed pictures, small Holy Family.	777
	Count Sassetto and his son.	535 10*s.*
1887	Whatman. C. National Gallery buys portrait of a girl, now called Mainardi.	236 5*s.*
1894	Lady Eastlake. C. Holy Family (National Gallery, Mond Bequest, 1924, now called Mainardi).	1,228 10*s.*
1896	William Willett sells Giovanna Tornabuoni to Sedelmeyer (see 1876, 1907, 1935).	1,600
	Earl of Warwick. S. Drawing, Coronation of the Virgin.	115
1907	Duveen sells Giovanna Tornabuoni (ex Rodolphe Kann) to Pierpont Morgan.	18,000
1923	Sir J. Robinson. 2 panels, life of John the Baptist, bought in.	2,625
1929	Lord d'Abernon. C. Roundel, Nativity.	2,205
	S. Madonna and Child, 31 ins. × 22 ins.	6,000

		£
1935	Pierpont Morgan, Jnr., New York. Giovanna Tornabuoni. Bought by Andrew Mellon, now Thyssen Collection, Lugano.	103,300
1948	Alfred Jowett. S. Drawing of a young man.	3,800

Giorgio Barbarelli or GIORGIONE. 1477–1510

To live for only 33 years is to give a lot of trouble to art experts. At one time anything with a lot of landscape, which was not quite a Titian, was labelled Giorgione. Then there was a time when only three or four pictures were accepted. Since the death of Berenson it has been possible to repeat Giorgione's name in something above a hoarse whisper and American galleries are beginning to be almost daring in their attributions. Some of the paintings in this list are due to be reinstated.

		£
1798	Orleans Exhibition. A replica of the National Gallery Gaston de Foix, valued for Earl of Carlisle (see 1928).	157 10s.
1802	Sir Simon Clarke. C. Cupid stung by a bee (see 1859).	94 10s.
1805	Ex Barberini Palace. C. Lady at her toilet.	586
1820	Benjamin West. C. The Gaston de Foix of the National Gallery (see 1856).	147
1847	Claudius Tarral. C. The Adoration of the Kings (see 1938).	1,543
1855	Samuel Rogers leaves Gaston de Foix to the National Gallery.	
1859	Earl of Northwick (Philips). Hertford buys Cupid stung by a bee (see 1802, Wallace Collection).	1,316 10s.
1870	San Donato, Paris. The supper party, bought by Earl of Dudley.	2,310
1882	Hamilton Palace. C. Venetian general (see 1939).	530 5s.
1885	Henry Bohn. National Gallery buys the Golden Age, now thought to be an early Titian.	1,417 10s.
1892	Earl of Dudley. C. The supper party (see 1870). (It had been knocked by Crowe and Cavalcaselle).	220 10s.
	The Golden Age, school version.	546
1892	Frank Leyland. C. Holy Family.	840
1895	Henry Doetsch. C. Unknown bearded man, sold as Jacopo dei Barbari (Washington, National Gallery).	23 2s.
1897	Unthank. (Robinson and Fisher.) Italian nobleman.	945
1905	Lady Ashburton. C. Young man holding skull.	1,680
1906	C. Nymphs by a river. 39 ins. × 60 ins.	960
1911	Lady Abdy. C. Malatesta da Rimini.	2,572 10s.

		£	
1925	Earl of Darnley. C. Herod receiving head of John the Baptist.	1,785	
1927	Lord Portarlington. C. Spanish nobleman.	861	
1928	Robinson and Fisher. Gaston de Foix (see 1798).	1,575	
1930	Marquess of Lansdowne. C. Alleged portrait of Sansovino, bought in.	966	
1937	The 4 small panels of the Loves of Damon and Thyrsis (said also to be by Previtali), bought for National Gallery.	14,000	
1938	The Adoration of the Kings, bought from Lord Allandale by Duveen (see 1847), sold to Samuel Kress. Since 1941 National Gallery, Washington. Reputed price (Behrman).	103,300	
1939	C. Venetian general (see 1882).	1,207	10*s.*
1944	Neeld. C. St. George and Dragon (attributed).	1,050	
1957	Lord Carew. S. David and head of Goliath, small panel.	2,200	

THOMAS GIRTIN. 1775–1802

An early member of the English water-colour school, this modest young man was a realist rather than a romantic, the inventor of the nineteenth-century technique but not its style, and the man who attracted Turner to water-colours. Naturally he has been underrated. When up to £5,000 was being paid for David Cox and when Copley Fieldings, de Wints and Clarkson Stanfields were fetching several thousands apiece, the best Girtins could be had for a hundred guineas. As in the case of Cotman and Palmer, the balance is at last being redressed.

		£	
1803	Gilpin. C. Ripon Minster.	11	11*s.*
	Girtin's executors sale. Nothing exceeded 25 guineas.		
1864	Allnutt. C. Bridge over the Ouse, York	43	1*s.*
1873	Charles Vine. C. Lichfield.	163	16*s.*
1881	Bale. C. Morpeth Bridge (see 1933).	115	10*s.*
	The River Exe (see 1948).	161	14*s.*
1908	Sir James Knowles. C. Porte St. Denis.	120	15*s.*
1912	C. Ripon Cathedral, 1800.	50	8*s.*
1928	C. Tintern Abbey.	231	
1933	C. Morpeth Bridge (see 1881 and 1948).	325	10*s.*
194[illegible]	S. Eltham Palace (2 guineas in 1828).	250	
1948	Walter Turner. S. Rainbow on the Exe (see 1881).	1,800	
	Morpeth Bridge (see 1933).	1,750	
1955	Miles Thompson. S. York Minster.	980	
1959	H. L. Fison. C. Landscape.	1,470	
1960	S. Fishing village and estuary.	2,100	
	C. Kirkstall Abbey.	472	10*s.*

VINCENT VAN GOGH. 1853–1890

Those who think that they might now be millionaires if only their grandfathers had not bought the Barbizon school should set their minds at rest. In 1900, when a Van Gogh could have been had for under £50, your grandfather would not have known where to look for one. And in 1913 Van Gogh was nearly as dear as Sargent.

		£
1900	Tavernier, Paris. Le dejeuner.	36 8*s.*
	Maison à la campagne.	40
	Blot, Paris. Roses tremières.	44
1913	Nemés, Paris. Still Life.	1,450
1921	Kelekian. New York. Self-portrait (Detroit Art Museum).	1,300
1922	S. Woman spinning, drawing, Dutch period (see 1957).	52
1924	Tate Gallery. Courtauld Fund purchases. Cypress trees.	3,300
	The yellow straw chair.	696
	Sunflowers.	1,304
1926	Tate Gallery. Courtauld Fund purchases View of Arles.	2,100
1927	Sir James Murray. C. Vase of flowers.	1,260
1932	Georges Petit, Paris. Bridge at Arles.	4,620
1935	J. K. Newman, New York. Printemps près d'Arles.	3,100
1939	S. Olive trees at St. Remi.	4,000
1940	Parke-Bernet, New York. Portrait.	3,920
	Melbourne National Gallery buys a male portrait.	2,196
1943	Sutro. S. Park at Arles.	1,550
1948	Regendanz. C. Les fortifs, large water-colour (bought from Cassirer, Berlin, 1926, £300).	1,155
1951	Charpentier, Paris. Pont de Chatou	11,950
1952	Gabriel Cognacq, Paris. Les Chardons.	16,820
1955	Parke-Bernet, New York. Flowers in a glass vase.	12,700
1957	Weinberg. S. Usines à Clichy.	31,000
	Angel's head.	26,000
	Woodcutter (early oil sketch).	6,500
1958	Goldschmidt. S. Public gardens at Arles.	132,000*
	S. Field with yellow flowers.	17,000
1958	Arnold Kirkeby, New York. Barge at anchor.	24,150
1959	Kenefick. S. Barge unloading coal at Arles.	30,000
	Bridge at Asnières. Bought in.	45,000

DRAWINGS

1957	Weinberg. S. 7 early drawings, from £2,200 to £3,300 each.	
1959	S. Man with a hoe, early drawing.	6,500
1960	S. Roofs, 1888.	5,000
	Rewald. S. Old man with an umbrella, early.	3,800
1960	S. Landscape at Arles.	2,200

Francesco Goya y Lucientes
GOYA. 1746–1828

This list can be compared with those of Gainsborough, Reynolds, Romney, Hoppner and Lawrence, which make the portraits of Goya seem remarkably cheap. But then Goya was not pompous or snobbish or sentimental or obsessed with millinery. All this changed in a few minutes in June, 1961, when the Duke of Leeds's portrait of Wellington made £140,000 (since going to press).

It may be added that Goya had some clever imitators, and that these, in the absence of pedigrees for most of his pictures, have been a worse handicap still.

		£
1853	Louis Philippe. C. (ex Hall Standish). Ladies on a balcony.	73 10s.
1873	Lord Dalling. C. 2 paintings, called Youth and Age.	194 5s. 147
1896	National Gallery. Doña Isabel Cobos de Porcel, bought in Madrid.	405
Before 1907	Havemeyer buys the two Sureda portraits. 2 for	1,750
	Portrait of Duke of Wellington.	700
1908	Earl of Clarendon. C. Pepe Ileno, the bullfighter (see 1919).	546
1916	C. A lady in black.	3,465
1919	Sir George Drummond. C. Pepe Ileno (see 1908).	2,628
1925	Henri Bernstein, Paris. Duveen buys Miguel Osorio da Zuniga (the Little Red Boy), see 1928.	10,500
	Melbourne National Gallery. A court lady, very fat.	5,600
1928	Jules Bache pays for the Red Boy (now Washington National Gallery)—after rejecting at £36,000 (Behrman, p. 79).	33,000
1929	Walter Burns. C. The sermon, small oil.	2,940
1930	Mrs. O. Havemeyer, New York. Lady with guitar. (Doubted. Ringling Museum, Sarasota, Fla.)	4,340
1936	Hon. M. Winterfield. S. Gasparini the court tapissier, small portrait.	1,300
1939	Mrs. Evelyn St. George. S. Doña Antonia Zarate (Field Collection, Chicago).	6,800
1941	J. Horace Harding, New York. The child, Victor Guyé.	8,500
1951	Galerie Charpentier, Paris. 2 pendant portraits, the pair	23,650
1952	S. Small oil sketch, Las pobrecitas.	3,800
1953	Galerie Charpentier, Paris. Girl's portrait.	6,650
1957	S. Las pobrecitas (second version).	1,800
	Galerie Charpentier. Portrait of Don Manuel Godoy.	2,860
1958	S. Portrait of lady in mantilla.	2,200

DRAWINGS

		£
1935	Faucher-Magnan. S. The advocate, and Peasant with a musket (see 1950) 2 for	145
1936	Henry Oppenheimer. C. Anglers under a rock.	525
1950	S. The advocate. Peasant with a musket (see 1935). } the pair	680
1957	Koenigs. S. Young girl with two pitchers, signed and inscribed.	3,400
	Galerie Charpentier. 7 drawings.	
	'Watch that step.'	3,675
	Miseries of war.	2,756
	Moving a wounded man.	2,250
	Others, £1,300 to £2,250.	
1960	S. A bearded woman with a child.	1,400
1961	Girl playing with puppies	6,000

JAN JOSEFSZ VAN GOYEN. 1596–1675

Remained one of the cheapest of seventeenth-century Dutch painters until the eve of the First World War, when the subtlety of his transparent, almost monochrome, paint began to be appreciated. At the moment Van Goyen is very much in fashion, but he was a prolific painter who left great numbers of small pretty things. Town-views, like the Duke of Westminster's *Emmerich*, are exceedingly rare. In the late nineteenth century a French, rather than an English, taste.

		£
1771	Sir Robert Strange. C. Landscape with a castle.	47
1837	Duchesse de Berri. C. House by a river.	56 4*s.*
1870	Mecklenburg, Paris. Le rade.	200
1873	Sedelmeyer, Paris. A rough sea.	864
1874	Angerstein. C. Landscape, dated 1630.	294
1881	Waterloo Wilson, Paris. View of Dordrecht.	1,220
1882	Hamilton Palace. C. River with ferry-boat (small).	388 10*s.*
1903	C. River scene (see 1934).	399
1907	Edward Balfour. C. River, church and ferry.	819
1912	C. Castle of Nimuegen, 1647.	1,050
1913	C. River scene.	1,155
1917	Kennedy. C. View of Dordrecht.	1,470
1934	Marquess of Zetland. C. River scene (see 1903).	892 10*s.*
1937	Macdonald. C. Watch-tower by a river, 1644.	2,205
1944	Neeld. C. View of Leyden, 1651.	4,410
1947	Lady Vyvyan. C. View of Gorinchem.	3,255
1953	Alan P. Goode. S. 2 small panels, river scenes.	3,500
		3,600
1959	S. Castle of Montfoort, 1646.	6,000

		£
1959	Duke of Westminster. S. View of Emmerich.	24,000*
1960	Van Aalst. C. View over a town, 1647.	9,425
	2 river scenes.	8,400
		7,350
1960	S. Very small river scene.	3,000

Domenico Theotocopuli, called EL GRECO. 1548–1614

A few El Greco pictures were removed from Spain both by French and English speculators during the Peninsular War. But there was no market for El Greco's most typical works until about 1900, when the false theory was formulated that this true child of the baroque age was a man born out of his time and a sort of forerunner of Cézanne. In the nineteenth century El Greco could sometimes become relatively expensive, but only when his work was confused with Titian or Tintoretto.

		£
1849	William Coningham. C. Portrait, Don Vincenzio Anastagi.	113 10s.
1853	Louis Philippe. C. Don Alvaro de Bassan.	155
	The lady in the fox-fur, or so-called portrait of the artist's daughter (Sterling Maxwell Collection), see 1882.	133
	5 late and developed works (including the 12-ft. Adoration, now National Museum, Bucharest £10) were sold for	64 10s.
1872	Isaac Péreire, Paris. Alonzo de Herrera.	36 12s.
1882	Hamilton Palace. C. Ludovico Cornaro, bought by the National Gallery as Titian—portrait of a Venetian admiral.	619 10s.
1886	William Graham. C. The so-called artist's daughter (see 1853).	304 10s.
1901	Mrs. O. Havemeyer buys in Spain Cardinal Guevara in spectacles.	2,880
	View of Toledo (Metropolitan Museum).	2,880
1906	Durand Ruel buys the Assumption of the Virgin.	3,500
	Resold to Chicago Art Institute.	10,950
1907	Don Abreu. C. Christ at Calvary.	1,995
1912	H. C. Frick buys the Man in Armour from Knoedler.	51,000
1913	Mariczell de Nemés, Paris. Agony in the Garden.	4,950
	Resold to National Gallery, 1919.	5,250
	Holy Family.	7,900
1921	Moneylenders driven from the Temple, bought by J. Quinn.	4,500
1923	Sandeman. C. Christ led to Calvary (Cardiff Museum).	3,360
1926	C. St. Martin dividing his cloak.	1,365

		£
1930	Havemeyer. New York. Small head of St. Peter.	3,200
1939	Mrs. Evelyn St. George. S. St. Catherine.	3,800
1953	Lord Greene. S. Small figure of St. Paul (see 1960).	2,050
1956	Goldschmidt. S. Small figure of Virgin.	14,000
1958	C. Christ healing the blind, replica of early work at Parma, sold as Veronese (see 1960).	37,800
1958	S. Small half-length of St. Philip.	7,000
1959	Del Monte. S. St. James, 27 in. × 21 ins.	72,000
1960	Jacob Polak. S. Half-length St. Paul (see 1953).	5,000
1960	Christ healing the blind (see 1958), lent by Charles Wrightsman to Metropolitan, said to have cost well over	100,000

JEAN BAPTISTE GREUZE. 1725–1805

A very strong early and mid-Victorian fashion. Some of the pictures sold in the 1870's would not fetch a quarter the price to-day. The market was made by the competition of Lord Hertford and Lord Dudley, but it survived both these collectors and did not decline until well into the '90's, when the emphasis was no longer on Greuze's soulful maidens, but on his straightforward portraits, which have now become extremely rare.

By eighteenth-century standards, Greuze was a pretty high priced painter in his own lifetime. Certainly no Reynolds fancy portraits fetched as much at auction, while he lived, as the first five works in this list.

		£
1772	Duc de Choiseul, Paris. Girl carrying a puppy (see 1876).	300
1782	Marigny, Paris. Louis XVI buys L'Accordée.	680
1785	Auguste Lebrun, Paris. Le Père de famille.	367 10*s.*
1785	Marquis de Verri, Paris. Le fils puni.	840
1795	Calonne. C. La prière de l'amour.	840
1815	Prince of Wales buys La trompette.	189
1832	Watson Taylor. C. Girl carrying a puppy (see 1772 and 1876).	703 10*s.*
1845	Cardinal Fesch. Rome. Lord Hertford buys Votive Offering to Cupid (Wallace Collection).	1,540
1846	Hugginson. C. Lord Hertford buys Psyche (Wallace Collection).	1,050
1852	William Wells. C. Girl with basket of eggs.	788
1857	Patureau, Paris. Hertford buys an almost identical Psyche (see 1846).	1,108
1863	San Donato, Paris. La dame de charité.	1,960
1865	Pourtalès, Paris. Innocence.	4,008
	Duc de Morny. La Pelotonneuse (Hertford).	3,660
1870	San Donato, Paris. Hertford buys Les œufs cassées.	5,040
	Fidelity.	3,560
	(Both Wallace Collection.)	

		£
1876	Foster of Clewer Manor. C. Lord Dudley buys Girl carrying a puppy (see 1772, 1832) (since 1892, Lord Bearsted Collection, Upton.)	6,720*
1885	Caraman-Chimay, Paris. La petite dormeuse.	3,600
1893	Field. C. Innocence.	3,045
1894	Adrian Hope. C. Young girl at a window.	3,450
1895	American Art Society, New York. Mlle Olivier.	4,430
1900	Peel Heirlooms. C. Marie Antoinette.	1,417 10s.
1908	Henry Say, Paris. Bacchante.	2,400
1919	Ruxley Lodge. C. Portrait, Barbarie la Courteille.	4,200
1921	C. La belle Blanchisseuse.	1,050
1927	Hon. Mrs. Yorke. C. Les sevreuses.	1,995
1934	Sir E. H. Scott. C. Two little girls.	1,680
1936	Comte de Beaumont. S. Portrait of an actor.	2,000
1939	Randolph Hearst, New York. C. The Dauphin Louis XVII.	2,778
1944	J. P. Morgan, Jnr. Head of a boy.	1,680
1946	Baron d'Erlanger. S. Girl in blue.	1,300
1950	Stehli, New York. La première leçon d'amour.	2,845
	Mlle. Ledoux, half-length.	3,214
1953	Parke-Bernet, New York. Portrait of a boy.	2,232
1957	Ambatiellos. S. Small boy in a white coat.	3,100

FRANCESCO GUARDI. 1712–1793

A Parisian taste of the 1860's which hardly reached London till the 1890's. Spectacular advances took place at the end of both European wars. For the modern market, see page 225.

		£
1857	Richard Wallace, Paris. Grand Canal.	164
	Dogana.	144
1863	Morland. C. Piazza San Marco.	79
1865	Duc de Morny, Paris. Rialto Bridge.	996
	Dogana.	800
1876	Albert Levy. C. Grand Canal.	183 15s.
1880	C. Rialto.	430 10s.
1881	De Beurnonville, Paris. Venice, capriccio.	1,080
1884	Miles of Leigh Court. C. Dogana.	420
1891	Lord Frederick Cavendish-Bentinck. C. 11 pictures, Venice towards the Dogana (see 1948).	756 10s.
1895	S. Lord Clifden. C. Rialto.	745 10s.
1906	Christopher Bushell. C. San Giorgio Maggiore.	1,783 10s.
1907	Hon. Mrs. Ashley. C. St. Mark's Square.	1,575
1915	Lady Charteris. C. Lagoon scene.	2,625

		£
1919	Sir George Drummond. C. Small Venetian fête.	6,510
1935	Faucher-Magnan. S. Island in lagoons.	1,450
1939	Caldwell. S. St. Mark's Square.	2,900
	Three others at over £2,500 each.	
1941	Rothermere. C. 14 in all, The Dogana.	2,520
1943	Sir Berkeley Sheffield. C. Fiesta on the Riva Schiavone.	4,200
1946	Lord Swaythling. C. The Rialto.	3,570
1948	Mrs. MacArthur James. C. Entrance to Grand Canal, very large capriccio (see 1886 and 1891).	10,290
1949	Weston. C. The Salute.	7,560
1955	Major-General Sotheby. S. Lagoon with barge.	7,000
1956	Cuthbert. C. 2 capriccios. 2 for	21,000
1959	S. Lagoon scene.	14,500

DRAWINGS

1891	Cavendish-Bentinck. C. A papal reception (see 1951).	220 10*s*.
1907	C. Piazza San Marco, 14 ins.	199 10*s*.
1920	Fairfax Murray. C. Piazza San Marco.	298
1923	S. Venice, the Salute, pen and bistre, 24 ins.	420
1936	Henry Oppenheimer. C. Landscape capriccio.	567
1937	Comtesse de Greffulhe. S. 2 capriccios.	820
		850
1951	Lady Melchett. S. Papal reception (see 1891).	4,400
1953	Ashburnham. S. Panorama from the Baccino.	4,500
1954	Clive Pascall. S. A puppet show.	3,800
1957	Ryland. S. Festival outside San Marco.	5,000

FRANS HALS. 1584–1666

In his own time and in his own country Frans Hals was a fashionable painter, but between 1760 and 1860 his pictures were all but worthless. It was then discovered that his paintings offered a formula for painting rich city men in black frock-coats. But whereas the modern black-coated portrait fell on evil days soon after 1925, the year of Sargent's death, the momentum of Frans Hals continued. In 1865 the world gasped when Lord Hertford gave more than £2,000 for *The Laughing Cavalier*, which was then about 40 times the value of any Frans Hals. But to judge from the decidedly constipated cavalier of 1960 at £182,000, that picture would to-day be worth more than half a million.

		£
1741	The Earl of Oxford. London. 3 portraits. The dearest at	9 10*s*.
1774	Van Heemskerke, The Hague. The Laughing Cavalier (see 1865).	15

		£
1779	Houghton Hall. The painter's son, bought by Empress Catherine (see 1931).	60
1800	Gildemeester, Amsterdam. The Laughing Cavalier, now at	25
1821	Lady Thomond. C. A lady's portrait.	3 3s.
1833	Nieuwenhuys sells The Laughing Cavalier to Pourtalès.	80
1845	Cardinal Fesch, Rome. Portrait.	27 10s.
1848	Duke of Buckingham. Stowe. 2 portraits (see 1899).	7 7s.
		11 11s.
1855	Bernal. C. Admiral de Reuter.	4
	Lady in a black dress.	2 15s.
1865	Pourtalès, Paris. Hertford buys The Laughing Cavalier (Wallace Collection).	2,040
1870	Blokhuyzen, Amsterdam. Portrait of Dr. Hornbeck.	464
1876	F. A. Keogh. C. National Gallery buys its first portrait.	105
	Albert Levy. C. 4 portraits, the dearest	399
1880	San Donato, Paris. The artist's son.	2,400
1881	Waterloo Wilson, Paris. Pieter Van der Broeke.	3,124
	Scriverius and his wife, a pair (see 1889).	3,200
1885	William Russell. C. A man in black with a still life thrown in (see 1913).	5 5s.
1889	Gwylt. C. George Salting buys Lady with a fan (National Gallery since 1910).	1,680
1889	Secretan, Paris. Pieter van der Broeke (see 1881). (Now Iveagh Trust, Kenwood.)	4,420
	Scriverius and his wife (see 1881).	3,640
1897	Robinson and Fisher's. Gentleman with a ruff.	3,517
1899	C. Reappearance of the Stowe portraits (see 1848). Gentleman.	3,150
	Lady. (Fenway Court Museum, Boston).	2,100
1902	Cholmley. C. The man with gloves (given to National Gallery in 1910).	3,780
1907	Duveen buys The Artist's Family, from Colonel Warde (now Thyssen Collection, Lugano). About	30,000
1908	National Gallery buys the Burgomaster's Family from Lord Talbot de Malahide.	25,000
1910	Charles T. Yerkes, New York. Duveen buys An old woman (sold to H. C. Frick, £31,000. Frick Foundation.)	28,250
1913	Lord Glanusk. S. The man in black (see 1885).	9,000
	Mariczell de Nemés. Paris. Male portrait.	13,135
1919	Drummond. C. Joseph Coymans (Viscount Cowdray Collection).	26,775
	S. Unrecorded portrait.	12,000
1923	Sir J. B. Robinson. Portrait (bought in, now Princess Labbia Collection, Cape Town).	19,950

		£
1931	Andrew Mellon buys the Hermitage portraits. The artist's son (see 1779).	35,000
	The officer at the window.	45,000
1932	S. The smuggler (bought for £3).	3,200
1935	Meinheer and Vrouw Bodolphe, sold to the Metropolitan Museum by J. Pierpont Morgan, Jnr. The two	62,000
1937	Walker estates. (Lofts and Warner.) Seated man with pointed hat.	12,705
1941	Baltazar Coymans, left to National Gallery, Washington, by Andrew Mellon. Valuation at cost price in 1936–7 (Duveen ex Rodolphe Kann).	87,500
1947	R. J. Cooper. C. Hille Bobbe, a Fishwife. First-rate small portrait.	3,360
1952	Walter Burrell. S. So-called portrait of Van Tromp.	11,000
1953	Lionel F. Strauss. New York. Portrait of a gentleman, half-length.	8,750
1959	Oliven. S. Small portrait of Frans Post (Collection of Major Allnatt).	48,000
1960	Warde-Aldam. S. An unknown cavalier, 30 ins. × 24 ins. (bought Koetser, fetched £15 in 1885, now Collection of Major Allnatt).	182,000*

MEINDERT HOBBEMA. 1638–1709

Hobbema has a lot to answer for. His endless, repetitious wooded landscapes, though an important invention, were responsible for imitation not only by the Barbizon school, but by painters who could have done much better, such as Gainsborough, Crome and Constable. In the eighteenth century, when the Dutch Italianisers were in vogue, Hobbema was not appreciated. The boom began in the Regency period and was practically continuous until the record price at the Six sale in 1928. Considering that heavily painted, realistic landscapes in unrelieved green and brown are no longer popular, Hobbema's present-day prices seem unnaturally high. He never painted another *Avenue at Middelharnis*, which soars above the nine other National Gallery Hobbemas.

		£
1776	Lord Montfort. C. Watermill landscape.	59 14*s.*
1800	Gildemeester. Amsterdam. Peasants by a ford.	481 10*s.*
1802	Countess of Holderness. C. The cornfield (a Willem Van der Velde included, see 1880, 1889).	294
1815	The Avenue at Middelharnis, sold in Holland (see 1829).	90
1823	Watson Taylor. C. The Smet van Alpen watermill (see 1854).	997 10*s.*
1824	Sir Robert Peel buys Brederode Castle.	880

		£
1829	Sir Robert Peel buys The Avenue at Middelharnis. And several others, all in the National Gallery since 1871.	840
1829	Zachary. C. The watermill (with Berchem?).	1,207 10s.
1832	Watson Taylor. C. Wooded landscapes, a pair.	1,103 10s.
1844	Jeremiah Harman. Peasants passing a ford (Bearsted Collection).	1,942 10s.
1845	Cardinal Fesch. Rome. Entry to a wood.	1,722
1850	King of Holland, Amsterdam. Hertford buys Watermill (Wallace Collection).	2,250
1854	Mecklenburg, Paris. The watermill (see 1823).	2,900
1857	Patureau, Paris. Windmills (resold in Berlin, 1860, for £4,200, now Kaiser Friedrich Museum).	3,860
1868	San Donato, Paris. Forest.	4,400
1872	Baroness Hodson. Amsterdam. Wooded landscape.	3,740
1875	Bredel. C. Watermill (first £3,000 Hobbema sold in London).	3,225
1876	Schneider of Creuzot, Paris. Watermill.	4,000
1880	San Donato, Paris. The cornfield (see 1802, 1889). Bought by E. Secrétan.	8,400
1882	Hamilton Palace. C. Watermill. Bought Sedelmeyer.	4,252 10s.
1889	Secrétan, Paris. The cornfield (1880) resold.	5,670
	Secrétan, Paris. C. Cattle and figures.	5,460
1890	Perkins. C. The path through the wood (see 1913 and 1915).	3,465
1892	Earl of Dudley. C. Landscape, 1663, painted with A. van der Velde (bought for £3,150).	10,080
1893	George Field. C. A flooded wood (see 1946).	4,725
1899	Sir John Foster. C. Landscape with oaks.	9,555
1901	Blaithwaite. C. Landscape with woods.	9,870
1902	Barchard. C. Landscape with peasants greeting each other. Bought (Salting National Gallery, 1910).	9,660
1913	Oppenheimer. C. The path through the wood (see 1890).	15,750
	Sold next year in Chicago to E. D. Libbey of Toledo. Now Taft Collection.	26,000
1913	Slingelandt, Amsterdam. Landscape with watermills. Given by Queen of Holland to National Gallery, Toronto, in 1950.	14,300
1928	Jan Six. Amsterdam. The house in the wood (Collection of Horace Havemeyer).	33,000*
1930	Earl of Feversham. C. Landscape with sportsmen (since 1950 Metropolitan Museum).	16,800
1933	Mrs. M. Stewart. C. Wooded scene (see 1955).	15,225

		£
1937	Lloyd. C. Anglers.	7,350
	Wooded landscape (£933 10*s.* in 1864).	5,250
1946	Lord Swaythling. C. Flooded wood (see 1893).	11,025
1955	Sir Edward Cripps. C. Wooded scene (see 1933).	6,090
1956	C. Hamlet in the woods (£1,102 10*s.* in 1876).	16,800
	S. Baroness Cassel von Doorn. Flat landscape.	12,500
1960	Van Aalst. C. Wooded river scene.	14,700

WILLIAM HOGARTH. 1697–1764

The factors which have kept Hogarth a cheap market are explained in Chapter Three. The modern prices are deceptive, since none of Hogarth's highly finished subject pictures has appeared in the saleroom since 1922. It would be impossible to estimate the value of *The Marriage à la Mode* series to-day.

		£
1744	Hogarth's sale. Marriage à la Mode, 6 pictures.	126
	Rake's Progress, 8 pictures.	184 16*s.*
	The 4 'Times of day' pictures.	137 1*s.*
1750	March of the Guards to Finchley, raffled for.	967 10*s.*
1796	Cawthorne. C. The 6 Marriage à la Mode pictures (bought Angerstein, see 1824).	1,050
	Hogarth's self-portrait (see 1869).	45 3*s.*
1801	Ireland. C. Polly Peachum in *The Beggar's Opera* (see 1832, 1884).	5 7*s.* 6*d.*
	Bessborough. C. 'Before and after' (see 1959).	35 14*s.*
1802	William Beckford, Fonthill. The 8 Rake's Progress pictures sold to Sir John Soane.	598 10*s.*
1812	Jefferley. C. Beckford buys the 6 Harlot's Progress pictures (4 destroyed in a fire; for remaining 2 see 1876). 6 for	189
1823	Mrs. Garrick. C. Sir John Soane buys the 4 Election pictures.	1,732 10*s.*
	Garrick and his wife (now at Windsor).	74
1824	National Gallery takes over Marriage à la Mode. the six	2,500
1832	Watson Taylor. C. The Shrimp Girl (National Gallery 1884).	42
	Polly Peachum (National Gallery, 1884).	54 12*s.*
	The Beggar's Opera, scene.	73 10*s.*
	Graham children (bought Lord Normanton), see 1934.	94 10*s.*
1838	Lord Northwick. C. The hazard table (bought in).	178 10*s.*
1851	C. The 2 surviving Harlot's Progress pictures, bought by Monro of Novar. The two	66 3*s.*
1867	Monro. C. The same, bought in.	420
		446 10*s.*

Year	Sale	£
1869	H. R. Willett. C. National Portrait Gallery buys Hogarth at his easel (see 1796).	378
1874	James. C. The lady's last stake.	1,585 10*s.*
	Calais Gate (National Gallery, 1891).	945
1878	Monro. C. The Harlot's Progress (2), see 1867, etc.	546
		315
1884	Miles of Leigh Court. C. National Gallery buys:	
	The Shrimp Girl } see 1832.	262 10*s.*
	Polly Peachum } see 1832.	840
1891	Bolckow. C. Duke of Westminster buys Calais Gate and presents it to National Gallery (see 1874).	2,570
1892	Wedderburn. C. Hogarth's servants, oil sketch (£5 15*s.* at Hogarth's widow's sale in 1790), bought National Gallery.	162 15*s.*
1893	Bingham Mildmay. C. The painter's wife.	1,213
1899	Forman. C. Morning in Covent Garden (see 1938).	720
1904	Townshend heirlooms. C. National Gallery buys portrait of Quin, the actor.	794
1905	Louis Huth. C. Taste in high life } see 1921.	1,310
	The Beggar's Opera } see 1921.	1,050
1905	Lord Tweedmouth. C. Assembly at Wanstead House (MacFadden Collection, Philadelphia).	2,833 10*s.*
1909	Tate Gallery buys *The Beggar's Opera.*	1,750
	Dr. Hoadley (£31 10*s.* in 1879).	2,000
1921	C. *The Beggar's Opera* (ex Huth, 1905).	1,050
1930	C. Portrait, Anne Wolstenholme.	2,257 10*s.*
1934	Duveen gives Graham Children to National Gallery (see 1832), price paid said to have been	6,000
1937	Earl of Lincoln. C. Southwark Fair (presented by Sir Harry Oakes to Foundling Hospital).	3,045
1938	Heathcote Heirlooms. C. Morning and Night (see 1899, now at Upton, Viscount Bearsted), the pair	2,522
1942	Sir Edmund Davis. S. The staymaker. Bought by National Gallery.	3,250
1943	Sir B. Sheffield. C. Portrait of Captain Joseph.	1,365
1951	Walter Hutchinson & Co. C. Building a house of cards (bought 1926, £315), oil sketch.	1,785
1958	Sir Francis Cook. S. Portrait of a lady.	1,900
1959	S. Before and after the seduction (see 1801). 2 for	5,500
	A club of gentlemen.	3,000
1961	Duke of Leeds. S. Polly Peachum (replica, see 1884).	30,000*

HANS HOLBEIN the Younger. 1497–1543

While many fairly well-attributed Holbein works have been sold cheaply for the period, there have been few things rarer on the market than an important, absolutely authentic Holbein picture. There were few pictures that had ever fetched £35,000 in 1890 when the National Gallery acquired *The Ambassadors*, and few that had fetched £72,000 in 1910, when they obtained *Christina, Duchess of Milan*. Such works to-day would command several hundreds of thousands of pounds. Even a drawing is likely to make many times as much as the drawings in this short list.

		£
1741	Dr. Meade. Adrian Stokes and Frances Brandon. Bought by Horace Walpole (now Wynn-Finch Collection, called Hans Ewarth), see 1842.	15 14*s*.
1754	Earl of Oxford. Portrait of Erasmus.	110
1785	Desenfans Exhibition. Henry VIII, cartoon for the Barber Surgeons' Company picture.	105
1808	John Lenthall. C. Sir Thomas More's family (copy?), bought in.	1,050
1821	Edward Solly sells Georg Gisze to Prussian Government. About	200
1842	Waldegrave. Strawberry Hill. Adrian Stokes (see 1741).	92 8*s*.
1850	King of Holland, Amsterdam. Portrait of a lady.	416
1855	Ralph Bernal. C. Anne of Cleves (schoolpiece) (see 1930).	183 15*s*.
1881	Waterloo Wilson, Paris. Portrait of Bishop Gardner. Bought by M. Secretan. This was a very bad shot. In 1889 it was resold for £1,200 as a Quentin Matsys.	2,568
1882	Hamilton Palace. C. Small portrait of Edward VI as a boy, bought by Queen Victoria.	798
	Portrait of Edward Seymour, Lord Protector.	514 10*s*.
1885	Duke of Marlborough sells portrait of unknown young man to Prussian Government.	5,250
1890	The Ambassadors. Bought by the National Gallery as part of a block purchase from Longford Castle.	35,000
1897	Millais executors. C. Man's head with black beard, bought by Millais at Dresden Exhibition, 1871, bought for Kaiser Friedrich Museum.	3,150
1905	Hawkins. C. Miniature portrait, so-called Frances Howard (Mrs. Pemberton), see 1935.	2,750
1906	Lord Grimthorpe. C. 2 attributed portraits, Nicolas d'Aubermont and wife.	3,150
1910	National Gallery buys Christina, Duchess of Milan from Agnew (formerly Duke of Norfolk) with aid of anonymous gift of £40,000	72,000

		£
1911	Benjamin Altman buys portrait of Margaret Wyatt, now Metropolitan Museum.	51,650
1929	Lord Yarborough. C. Edward VI as a child (other versions Windsor, Hanover; now National Gallery, Washington, per Andrew Mellon).	9,975
1930	Sir John Ramsden. C. Anne of Cleves (schoolpiece, see 1855).	2,205
	Hurcombs' Rooms. Attributed male portrait.	4,000
1932	Sir W. Blount. C. 2 miniatures of Thomas Cromwell in a locket.	2,047 10*s.*
1934	Boston Fine Arts Museum acquire portrait head of Anthony Butts from Butts family.	12,000
1935	Pierpont Morgan, Jnr. C. Miniature portrait of Mrs. Pemberton, bought in 1905 for £2,750 as portrait of Frances Howard. Given by Duveen to Victoria and Albert Museum.	6,195
1944	Neeld. C. Small alleged portrait of Anne Boleyn.	1,995
1945	Miss Seymour. C. Huge portrait of Henry VIII. Schoolpiece, bought by Walker Gallery, Liverpool.	3,885
1946	Mrs. Berryman. S. Small head of a gentleman in yellow.	3,885
1946	Lord Rothermere. C. Small male half-length.	7,350
1957	Fuller-Maitland. S. 2 medallion portraits.	4,200
1958	C. Miniature portrait, Thomas Cromwell, ex Pierpont Morgan.	1,680

DRAWINGS

1898	C. Lady in a large cap.	294
1902	Sir J. C. Robinson. C. A meeting of delegates.	168
1910	Mrs. W. H. Millais. C. Alleged self-portrait.	204 15*s.*
1917	C. Head of a man. Black and red chalk.	861
1920	Marquess of Lansdowne. S. Bearded man, black and red chalk.	500
1922	Max Bonn. S. A leper and his bell.	600
1926	2 portrait drawings, British Museum per subscribers.	800
1936	Henry Oppenheimer. C. Figure of Tantalus.	1,522 10*s.*
1946	S. Design for a stained-glass window.	1,850
1947	S. Silverpoint, young man wearing chain of beads.	900
1955	Le Hunte. S. Design for stained-glass (Barber Institute).	3,400

PIETER DE HOOCH. 1629–1683

Only a very moderately priced painter during the Dutch boom of the Napoleonic wars. He was virtually a discovery of the 1860's and belongs to the cult of artistic realism then prevalent. In the present century he has been so fantastically outdistanced by the Vermeer cult that one wonders whether this beautiful painter may not be underrated. But the market is not likely to see another picture like the National Gallery's two courtyards.

		£
1777	Paillet, Paris. Interior with figures (see 1958).	27 15s.
1804	Van Leyden, Amsterdam. Woman in courtyard (see 1825).	220
1814	Delahante. C. Music party.	205
1825	Woman in courtyard. Bought by Nieuwenhuys (see 1869).	945
1826	Smith of Marlborough Street sells to George IV:	
	The card party.	600
	Woman in a courtyard.	400
	(Both at Windsor.)	
1848	William Wells. C. Woman in a courtyard with child, bought Lord Overstone.	540 12s.
1861	Scarisbricke. C. The bedchamber (see 1894).	441
1869	Delessert, Paris. National Gallery buys the woman in a courtyard (see 1804, 1825).	1,722
1876	Schneider of Creusot, Paris. Mother with a cradle, bought for Kaiser Friedrich Museum.	5,400
1889	Secretan, Paris. Interior with drinkers.	11,040
1893	Bingham Mildmay. C. Woman cutting bread and butter, (see 1919).	2,940
1894	Adrian Hope. C. The bedchamber (see 1861).	2,257
1900	Mrs. Berger. C. Woman with basket of pears.	1,105
1914	Robinson and Fisher's. Interior with company.	8,610
1917	National Gallery buys The Collation, in Amsterdam.	3,000
1919	Neumann. C. Woman cutting bread and butter (see 1893).	7,980
1928	Six, Amsterdam. Interior with company.	12,500
1937	Lewis Lloyd. C. 2 Interiors with company.	3,045
		2,940
1937	Victor Rothschild. S. Woman in a courtyard with pump. (Baron von Beuningen, now Boymans Museum).	17,500
1941	C. The asparagus-sellers.	2,310
1946	Lord Swaythling. C. Woman nursing a sick child.	7,875
1953	Borthwick Norton. C. Lady with child and maid.	3,360
1954	Catherine Butterworth. New York. Woman nursing a sick child (see 1946).	12,150
1957	C. Soldiers drinking in a barn.	4,095
1958	Louis S. Kaplan, New York. Interior with figures (see 1779).	8,925
1960	Dreesman. Amsterdam. Interior of the town hall.	17,485

JOHN HOPPNER. 1759–1810

Hoppner was regarded as the leading British portrait painter for eighteen years, that is, between Reynolds's death in 1792 and his own. Lawrence, who painted incredibly better, could not charge higher fees until after Hoppner's death. This seems to be the only explanation, apart from the general aesthetic insensibility of this market, for the mirth-provoking prices of the 1913–1930 period. Hoppner's portraits are very shy of the salerooms since the public tumble of *The Tambourine Girl* in 1944.

		£
1806	The sleeping nymph, sold at the R.A. (see 1827).	300
1808	£2,000 made in one year from pupil-copies of his portrait of Pitt.	
1827	De Tabley. C. The sleeping nymph (Lord Egremont, Petworth).	427 10*s.*
1857	Earl of Liverpool. C. Portrait of Pitt (Apsley House).	136 10*s.*
1859	Earl of Northwick. (Philips.) Infancy, girl with dog.	52 10*s.*
1866	Farrer. C. Duchess of Devonshire.	61 19*s.*
1871	C. W. Lewis. Portrait of Pitt.	168
1881	C. Lady Waldegrave. Bought in and purchased by Woods, the auctioneer (see 1906).	24 3*s.*
1888	C. Unknown female portrait.	378
1889	Mrs. Gwyllym. C. Miss Horneck.	2,372 10*s.*
1895	Lord Bridport. C. Huge portrait of Nelson.	2,677 10*s.*
1901	Lady Charles Bruce. C. Louisa, Lady Manners (bought Duveen, see 1926).	14,732 10*s.*
	Mrs. Farthing.	8,400
1902	Robinson and Fisher. Lady Mary Arundell.	8,190
1906	Late T. H. Woods. C. Lady Waldegrave (see 1881).	6,300
	C. Miss Papendieck, a small girl (see 1930).	3,150
1907	Mrs. Manning. C. Mrs. Manning and daughter.	4,200
	C. Susanna Gyll, small head.	4,200
1909	Sir J. D. Millburn. S. Lady Langham (see 1936).	5,250
1910	C. The hurdy-gurdy player (see 1935).	7,927
1913	J. H. B. Christie. C. Phoebe Hoppner (see 1935).	9,765
	Borden, New York. Miss Arbuthnot.	12,500
1914	Duveen sells E. T. Stotesbury The Tambourine Girl (see 1944). Reputed price.	72,300*
1922	Baroness Burdett-Coutts. C. William Pitt.	7,370
1925	Earl of Darnley. C. Child portrait.	10,710
1926	Michelham (Hampdens). Lady Louisa Manners (see 1901).	18,900
1929	Lord Brownlow. C. The Cust brothers (bought in).	10,500
	The Bowden children.	11,550
1930	Breitmeyer. C. Miss Papendieck (see 1906).	14,700

		£
1932	Earl of Durham (at Lambton Castle). Lady Anne Lambton and children (bought in).	23,000
1933	Anderson's, New York. Louisa, Countess of Mansfield.	10,000
1934	Lord Faringdon. S. Master William Russell.	3,400
1935	Solly Joel. C. Duveen buys back Phoebe Hoppner (see 1913).	12,075
	The hurdy-gurdy player (see 1910).	5,040
1936	Spender-Clay. C. Lady Langham (see 1909).	1,732 10*s*.
1938	Lord Stanley. C. Lady Leighton.	2,310
1944	E. T. Stotesbury, New York. The tambourine girl (see 1914).	2,500
1949	Mrs. George Keppel. C. 'Perdita' Robinson.	2,415
1950	Parke-Bernet, New York. Miss Pringle, half-length.	1,250
1951	Gallerie Charpentier, Paris. Girl in white.	1,720
1955	Parke-Bernet, New York. The Macnamara children, small.	1,465
1957	Mae Rovensky, New York. Emilia Lenox.	1,425
1959	R. W. Lloyd. C. Countess of Oxford and daughter, full-sized group, over 7 ft. high.	1,470

WILLIAM HOLMAN HUNT. 1827–1910

The relatively low valuation of the pictures after the sale of the copyright should be noticed. There is a close parallel between the exhibitions of Hunt's religious pictures and those of Benjamin West sixty to seventy years earlier.

		£
1847	Scene from Woodstock. Sold at R.A.	20
1848	Eve of St. Agnes (see 1924).	70
1849	Oath of Rienzi.	100
1850	Bennett gives £168 for Christians escaping from Druids.	
1853	Lord Grosvenor offers £315 for Claudio and Isabella.	
1854	McCracken. C. Two gentlemen of Verona (see 1950).	435
	The Light of the World, bought by Combe.	420
1856	Windus pays £472 10*s*. for The Scapegoat, put-up in 1862 at Christie's and bought in for £498 10*s*.	
1860	Finding of Christ in the Temple (begun in 1854), sold to Gambart with all rights.	5,775
1861	Manchester City Gallery buys The Hireling Shepherd (sold in 1853 for £315, for second version, see 1957).	615
1863	Late Augustus Egg. C. Claudio and Isabella (commissioned in 1850 by Egg for 25 guineas). See 1918.	640 10*s*.
1871	Pocock. C. Dolce fa niente. (Bought in) (see 1938.)	745 10*s*.
1873	C. The strayed sheep (bought in).	1,050

		£
1874	The shadow of death (begun 1869), sold to Agnew with all rights. Manchester City Gallery.	11,000*
1877	Baron Grant. C. The shadow of death (small original version).	1,522 10s.
	Finding of Christ in the temple (small version).	1,417 10s.
1883	Triumph of the Innocents (begun 1874). Picture sold after disposal of copyright (Walker Gallery, Liverpool).	3,675
1886	William Graham. C. The Light of the World, small version.	787 10s.
1887	John Graham. C. The awakening conscience (see 1946).	107
	Finding of Christ in the temple (see 1877).	1,260
1887	Durrant. C. The awakening conscience (see 1946), bought in at	105
1887	Sir Thomas Fairbairn. C. Two gentlemen of Verona (see 1854, 1950), bought in.	1,050
1891	Matthews. C. Finding of Chrsit in the Temple, the finished picture (Birmingham City Gallery). See 1860.	3,570
1909	Quilter. C. The scapegoat (see 1856, 1923).	2,940
1918	Chantrey bequest buys Claudio and Isabella (Tate Gallery, see 1863).	1,000
1919	Holman Hunt executors. C. Mayday on Magdalen Tower (painted 1891, Lever Art Gallery).	1,995
	C. The lady of Shalott.	3,360
1923	Anthony Prinzep. C. The scapegoat (see 1909) (Lever Art Gallery).	4,830
1924	C. Eve of St. Agnes (1848). Bought by Guildhall Gallery.	357
1926	T. Clarke. C. Afterglow in Egypt, small oils (see 1946).	682 10s.
1937	C. Triumph of the Innocents, preliminary picture 4 ft. long (see 1883).	567
1938	T. Brocklebank. C. Dolce fa niente (see 1871).	241 10s.
1946	C. The awakening conscience (see 1887) (Collection Colin Anderson).	210
1946	C. The afterglow in Egypt (see 1926).	52 10s.
1950	Floersheim. C. Two gentlemen of Verona (see 1854).	241 10s.
1953	Wilfred Hall. C. Isabella and the pot of Basil (73 ins. × 45 ins., bought-in, 1871, £549 3s.).	115 10s.
1957	Sir T. Agnew. S. The Hireling Shepherd, 2nd version (see 1861).	2,200

JAN VAN HUYSUM. 1682–1749

Chiefly of interest for the very high prices paid in the late eighteenth century. Huysum's flower-pots seem expensive to-day for what they are, even if the more tasteful but equally mechanical flowerpieces of Fantin-Latour are preferred. The late eighteenth-century prices were indiscriminate. Anything that aped nature closely was as good—Rachel Ruysch, Jan van Os and the young Hewlitt of Bath.

		£
1773	Sale at Amsterdam. Flowerpiece, dated 1740.	320
	Liotard. C. 2 flowerpieces.	1,050
1776	Neumann. Amsterdam. Gouache drawing of flowers.	108
1778	Braamkamp, Amsterdam. A single flowerpiece.	410
1779	Houghton Hall. A pair valued for the Empress Catherine.	1,200
1793	Beckford buys 'a grand assemblage of flowers' (sold 1823 for £362, see 1882 and 1927).	368
1809	Sabatier, Paris. A single flowerpiece.	582
1826	Comte Pourtalès. C. Flowers and sculptured vase.	330 15*s.*
1848	William Wells. C. Flowerpiece (National Gallery, 1875).	420
1867	Lord Derby. C. Flowerpiece (National Gallery since 1869). (The price paid to Nieuwenhuys was £900.)	399
1880	San Donato. Paris. Single flowerpiece.	920
1882	Hamilton Palace. C. Beckford's Assemblage of flowers (see 1793 and 1927).	1,288 10*s.*
1899	Mieville. C. Bouquet.	735
1912	Miss M. Driver. C. Flowers and sculptured vase.	278 5*s.*
1927	S. Beckford's Assemblage of flowers (see 1882).	3,800
1930	Lady Meyer. C. Flowers and terracotta vase.	1,995
1938	Magee. C. Flowerpiece.	2,835
1947	S. Series of 12, painted for Lord Petre in 1730.	13,500
1954	C. A pair of flowerpieces. 2 for	6,090
1960	S. Single flowerpiece (record price).	5,800*

The record price for any seventeenth-century Dutch flowerpiece is probably £6,825, paid in 1958 for a work of Huysum's forerunner Baltasar van der Ast [1590–1666]. But much higher prices are paid for flowerpieces by the Franco-Flemish followers of Velvet Breughel.

JEAN DOMINIQUE INGRES. 1780–1867

Swollen by the fame of his huge public commissions, Ingres's easel pictures fetched high prices in his own lifetime. The quite small picture, *Stratonice*, commissioned by the Duke of Orleans in 1841, made over £2,500 in 1852, at a time when no English painter could command such a price. By the 1890's decline was already visible and, until the sale of *Mme. Moitessier* in 1936, Ingres's paintings were absurdly cheap. Large finished works are now so rare that it is impossible to figure out what would happen to them, except that they would not be likely to rival the Impressionists. Ingres's drawings, on the contrary, have never ceased to advance. They neared the thousand pound mark more than forty years ago. Such a drawing as the *Stamaty Family* in the Louvre should be worth from £10,000 to £15,000.

		£
1841	Perregaux, Paris. Female figure.	63 10s.
1843	Mainmare, Paris. Henri IV and the Spanish Ambassador.	142
1852	Duchesse d'Orleans. Paris. Stratonice.	2,520
1865	Pourtalès. Paris. Raphael painting La Fornarina.	380
1867	Vente Ingres, Paris. Angelica chained to the rock (Luxembourg). Resold 1872 for £2,800.	2,500
	The Odalisque (Louvre).	1,760
	The golden age, oil study.	1,080
1872	Pereire, Paris. Oedipus and the sphinx.	1,025
1889	Secrétan, Paris. Oedipus and the sphinx.	2,800
1918	National Gallery. M. de Norvins, Roger and Angelica, and Oedipus bought at Degas sale. Each about	300
1919	C. Lady in white satin, 1814.	1,427 10s.
1927	Empress Eugenie. C. Louis XV and Moliére, small painting, 1860.	304 10s.
1928	S. Lady in pale blue.	620
1936	National Gallery buys Mme. Moitessier.	14,676*
1950	Charpentier, Paris. Stratonice, small replica.	730
1959	National Gallery values portrait of the Duke of Orleans, Lane Bequest, 1915, at	7,500
1960	C. Female torso, small oil study.	525

DRAWINGS

		£
1867	Vente Ingres, Paris. Study for 'Duke of Alva at St. Gudule'.	92 14s.
1872	Carlin, Paris. Study for Apotheosis of Napoleon.	288
1888	Goupil, Paris. Portrait of Mme. Heudebert-Lescot (see 1919).	252
1894	Paris. Apotheosis of Napoleon (see 1872).	520
1919	Paris. Laboeuf de Montgermont. Mme. Lescot (see 1888).	900
1926	Comtesse de Greffulhe. S. A lady seated.	440
1928	S. Portrait of Mrs. Margaret Badham.	820
1929	Bernard d'Hendecourt. S. Mme. Reiset and daughter.	940
1947	S. Mrs. Woodhead and Rev. Henry Carter (Fitzwilliam Museum).	1,200
1951	Jacques Leon Stern, New York. Portrait of M. Charles Dupaty	732
1959	Gallerie Charpentier, Paris. Mme. Gallois, portrait.	[illegible]
1960	S. Sheet of child studies.	1,000
	Parke-Bernet, New York. Seated nude, pencil.	1,250

JOSEPH ISRAELS. 1824–1911

Very grey and wet and always associated in my mind with memories of mahogany panelling and stale cigar smoke, these dour moralities were bought by a dozen Scottish industrialists. Towards 1909 the industrialists began to die. After a long absence, the big moralities returned to the saleroom. By 1919 they had passed the £5,000 mark, but by 1924 there was no one left to die, and now it was the market that died. It should be realised that, had he been a wise young man, Van Gogh would have spent his life in the firm of Boussod, Valadon selling Joseph Israels.

		£
1865	J. G. Robinson. C. The drowned fisherman (see 1910).	157 10*s*.
1874	J. S. Forbes. 4 at over £750 each. Breakfast time.	861
1876	Albert Levy. 7 pictures. After the storm (see 1903).	1,344 10*s*.
1879	Fenton. C. La fête de Jeanne (see 1908).	1,690 10*s*.
1882	J. S. Forbes. C. Out of darkness into light.	1,102 10*s*.
1895	Keiller. C. Pancake day (see 1910).	945
	Grant-Morris. C. The anxious family.	992 10*s*.
1903	Gurney. C. After the storm.	1,130
1908	Ismay. C. La fête de Jeanne (see 1879).	1,680
1909	Cuthbert Quilter. C. Washing the cradle.	2,362 10*s*.
1910	Andrew Maxwell. C. Pancake day (see 1895, 1923, 1957).	2,835
	Alexander Young. C. 14 pictures by Israels.	
	The drowned fisherman, bought by the Tate Gallery.	4,830
	The fisherman's wife (see 1957).	2,625
1918	Westmacott. C. Grace before meat (see 1951).	3,675
1919	Sir William Drummond. C. Age and infancy.	5,040
1923	Cremetti. Pancake day (see 1910, 1957).	1,942 10*s*.
1924	Ernest Ruffer. C. Grief.	1,102 10*s*.
1951	C. Grace before meat (see 1918).	78 15*s*.
1957	William K. Busch. New York. The fisherman's wife (see 1910).	360
	The three paddlers.	250
1957	A. C. Kenrick. C. Pancake day (see 1910, 1923).	525

ITALIAN SCHOOL

14th century and earlier

The *Trecento*, the gold-background pictures—in the eighteenth century something to amuse eccentrics like Horace Walpole; in the early nineteenth century something to be picked up as a souvenir in Florence or Rome, like a cameo or a box in mosaic-work, and not much dearer, often hung in the servants' bedrooms and forgotten. In the late nineteenth century to be had sometimes for three or four guineas and, if very good, for thirty to fifty. There may be men alive who remember them. To-day almost everything, even if it is only a head 6 ins. square, cut out of an altar tabernacle, gets an attribution to the master of this and that. And there is very little under £2,000.

		£
1804	Colonel Smith. C. Simone Memmi (?): Madonna.	5 6*s.*
1810	Hon. Charles Greville. C. Cimabue: Madonna.	12 12*s.*
	Giotto: Angel-head in fresco.	1 11*s.*
1823	Fonthill, ex Beckford. Orcagna: Crucifixion.	19 9*s.*
1854	Joly de Bammeville. C. Duccio: Crucifixion.	278 5*s.*
1856	Samuel Rogers. C. 2 fresco heads, ex Charles Greville, attributed to Giotto, bought National Gallery.	78 15*s.*
	Holy Family enthroned, Giottesque altarpiece.	325 10*s.*
1859	Earl of Northwick (Philips). 10 pictures attributed to Giotto; the dearest was a choir of angels, now in Musée Condé, Chantilly.	73 10*s.*
1863	Davenport Bromley. C. Attributed to Giotto: Ascension of the Virgin, ex Fesch Collection.	950
	Crucifixion triptych, attributed to Orcagna.	64
	St. George and dragon, attributed to Orcagna.	21
	Duccio: Crucifixion (see 1854).	262 10*s.*
	Simone Memmi: St. Ursula.	118 13*s.*
1879	Alexander Barker. C. Attributed to Orcagna: Octagonal Coronation of the Virgin.	28 7*s.*
1885	W. Fuller Russell. C. Spinello Aretino: Altarpiece of the Crucifixion with side panels, said to have belonged to Beckford.	252
	Many others at £20 to £30.	
	National Gallery buys 2 predella panels by Ugolino da Siena: The Calvary, and Betrayal of Christ. 2 for	26 *s.*
1886	William Graham. C. Cimabue: Resurrection (lunette).	44 21*s.*
	Ascribed Giotto (?): 2 saints in niches.	48 6*s.*
	Taddeo Gaddi: The Descent from the Cross.	21
1892	Earl of Dudley. C. So-called Giotto: Last Supper.	283 50*s.*
1896	C. Taddeo Gaddi: Diptych, saints, 5 ft.	141 15*s.*
1897	Rev. Davenport Bromley. C. Orcagna: Holy Family.	199 10*s.*
1902	National Gallery buys Lorenzo Monaco: Coronation of the Virgin, 7-ft. altarpiece.	2,739
1911	Charles Butler. C. Taddeo Gaddi: Holy Family enthroned.	1,102 10*s.*
1920	Coates Heirlooms. C. Taddeo Gaddi: Holy Family.	5,250
1925	Holden-White. C. Ugolino da Siena: Resurrection.	1,575
1927	Duke of Sutherland. C. Ugolino da Siena: 2 small panels, Resurrection and St. Thomas.	1,522 10*s.*
1929	Bernard d'Hendecourt. S. Master of the St. George Codex: Annunciation, bought by Duveen.	6,500

		£
1929	Brauer. C. PIETRO LORENZETTI: St. Catherine of Alexandria.	1,890
1934	Hon. W. K. Rous. C. ORCAGNA: Coronation of the Virgin.	840
1943	J. Pierpont Morgan, Jnr. C. DUCCIO: Crucifixion, small triptych.	5,670
1946	Earl of Kinnaird. C. MARIANO DI SER AUSTERIO: Resurrection.	2,730
1949	Virgoe-Buckland. S. BERNARDO DADDI: Holy Family with saints.	820
1950	Henry Harris. S. CIMABUE SCHOOL: Tabernacle of 10 panels.	2,400
1953	Lady Catherine Ashburnham. S. RIMINI SCHOOL: Vision of Beata Chiara.	10,000
1957	S. DUCCIO, attributed: Small Madonna.	1,600
1958	Sir Francis Cook. S. GIOVANNI DEL BIONDO: Altarpiece, 1372.	3,200
1959	Prince Lichtenstein. TADDEO GADDI: Annunciation, panel, intended for Toronto, taken over by Agnew.	35,000
1959	Del Monte. S. MASTER OF OSSERVANZA ALTARPIECE: Resurrection, small panel.	31,000
	Marquess of Northampton. C. PARRI SPINELLI: Drawing after Giotto.	6,090
1959	Charles Loeser. S. BERNARDO DADDI: St. Dominic.	2,800
	C. BERNARDO DADDI: Head of Christ (under 10 ins.)	2,940
	BARNA DA SIENA: Small Crucifixion.	2,100

ITALIAN SCHOOL
15th and Early 16th Centuries
Florence and Central Italy

For Fra Angelico, Botticelli, Ghirlandajo, Filippo and Filipino Lippi, Mantegna, Perugino, Piero della Francesca, Pollaiuolo, Signorelli and Verrocchio, see separate entries.

		£
1804	Robert Udney. FRA BARTOLOMMEO: Madonna del Sedia.	66 3*s.*
	Holy Family.	128 2*s.*
1810	Hon. C. F. Greville. C. MASACCIO: Heads of Peter and Paul.	10 10*s.*
	Head of Evangelist.	5 15*s.*
1811	Young Ottley. C. MASACCIO: St. Dominic.	42
	(MASOLINO, see 1950.)	
1820	Champernowne. C. FRA BARTOLOMMEO: Aldobrandini Madonna.	304 10*s.*
	Ascension of Magdalene.	126

		£
1837	Coesvelt. C. FRA BARTOLOMMEO: Holy Family, roundel, bought in.	472
1843	Louis Philippe buys GIOVANNI LO SPAGNA: Nativity (Louvre).	1,000
1846	Higginson. C. BALDESSARO PERUZZI: Adoration, bought in (given to National Gallery, 1849).	525
1849	Coningham. C. MARIOTTO ALBERTINELLI: Creation and Temptation (2).	189
1855	Eastlake buys for National Gallery in Italy:	
	COSIMO ROSSELLI: St. Jerome.	114 17*s.*
	BENOZZO GOZZOLI: Holy Family.	137 16*s.*
1856	Samuel Rogers. C. LORENZO DI CREDI: Coronation of the Virgin (see 1945).	315
1856	Lord Orford. C. National Gallery buys Ascension of the Virgin by GIOVANNI BERTUCCI (called Lo Spagna).	651
1858	National Gallery buys 22 paintings for £7,035 from Lombardi-Baldi family, including UCCELLO's Route of San Romano (probably £300).	
1859	Earl of Northwick. National Gallery buys LORENZO DI CREDI: Virgin adoring child.	315
	Holy Family in landscape.	525
1860	National Gallery buys The lady in profile by ALESSIO BALDOVINETTI.	160
1863	Davenport Bromley. C. National Gallery buys PESELLINO: Trinity.	2,100
1874	Alexander Barker. C. National Gallery buys UMBRIAN SCHOOL: 3 Griselda panels.	624 10*s.*
	BERNARDINO DA SIENA: Madonna enthroned.	525
	PINTURICCHIO: Return of Ulysses (fresco).	2,152 10*s.*
1879	Alexander Barker. C. LORENZO DI CREDI: Holy Family, roundel.	53 10*s.*
	BALDESSARO PERUZZI: Nativity.	47 7*s.*
1881	National Gallery buys FIORENZO DI LORENZO: Triptych (in Perugia).	136 12*s.*
	Mayne. C. PIERO DI COSIMO: Young St. John in profile (Metropolitan Museum, since 1921).	178 10*s.*
1884	William Russell. C. UCCELLO: Tobias and the angel.	69 6*s.*
	National Gallery buys in Siena the Madonna of the Girdle by MATTEO DI GIOVANNI (nearly 11 ft. high, many figures).	2,100
1886	William Graham. C. PIERO DI COSIMO: Triumph of Chastity.	273
	SCHOOL OF GOZZOLI: Adoration, 9 ft.	110 5*s.*
	See Ghirlandajo, Pollaiuolo.	

		£
1887	Lord Methuen. C. National Gallery buys Francesco Bacchiacca: Story of Joseph, 2 panels for	3,150
1889	C. Parri Spinelli: Madonna and Christ.	745 10s.
1892	Earl of Dudley. C. Fra Bartolommeo: Holy Family (see 1837).	535
	Lorenzo di Credi: Holy Family and St. John.	2,520
1895	National Gallery buys Pisanello: Vision of St. Eustace from Earl of Ashburnham.	3,000
1899	Stefano Bardini. C. Pisanello: George and dragon (see 1958).	1,450
	Pesellino: 2 cassone panels (Metropolitan Museum, 1909).	1,200
1902	Sir J. C. Robinson. C. Giovanni di Paolo: Small panel of a Saint.	267 10s.
1905	C. Piero di Cosimo: Young man, small panel.	120 15s.
1910	Octavus Coope. C. Lorenzo di Credi: Round Holy Family.	819
1911	Charles Butler. C. Pinturicchio: Holy Family.	1,102 10s.
	Cosimo Rosselli: St. Nicolas of Bari.	1,155
	St. Catherine.	1,312 10s.
	Paolo Uccello: 2 battle scenes (see 1914).	2,100
1911	Lady Abdy. C. Gentile da Fabriano: Triptych, Adoration of the Magi.	3,832 10s.
1913	Aynard, Paris. Giovanni di Paolo: 6 small panels (see 1943).	7,350
1914	Arthur Grenfell. C. Uccello: The fall of Pisa and the Battle of Anghiari (Ashmolean Museum) (see 1911). 2 for	1,522 10s.
1916	S. Gentile da Fabriano: Triptych.	940
	Canon Sutton. National Gallery buys Masaccio Madonna.	9,000
1922	Maitland. C. Cosimo Rosselli: Holy Family.	1,727 10s.
1923	Sir Joseph Robinson. C. 2 quattrocento panels, Jason and Medea, bought in.	6,510
1927	Holford. C. Pesellino: Madonna with saints (bought Duveen) (Metropolitan Museum, per E. S. Harkness).	16,800
	Alessio Baldovinetti: Portrait of a prelate.	1,732 10s.
	Umbrian School: Girl in profile.	6,825
1929	Lord d'Abernon. C. Bastiano Mainardi: Holy Family (round).	1,995
	Sawbridge-Earle-Drax. C. Filipino Lippi: Holy Family	1,050
	Neri di Bicci: Assumption of the Virgin (over 7 ft. square).	7,350
1934	National Gallery buys 7 panels, Sassetta: Life of John the Baptist (Duveen ex Clarence McKay). 7 for	43,000
1937	Earl of Lincoln. C. Small panel by Piero di Cosimo.	2,625

		£
1942	Wilshere Estates. S. UNKNOWN PAINTER: Portrait of a young man.	3,300
1943	J. Pierpont Morgan, Jnr. MATTEO DA SIENA: Small panel (£65 2s. in 1885, de Zoete sale) (Barber Institute, Birmingham).	5,460
	Before the sale National Gallery buys 4 panels, GIOVANNI DI PAOLO: Legend of John the Baptist.	12,000
1945	National Gallery, BENOZZO GOZZOLI: Holy Family with apples.	6,000
1946	Melbourne, National Gallery buys UCCELLO: Portrait of a lady.	17,000
1950	National Gallery buys 2 panels of saints by MASOLINO (see 1811).	15,750
1951	Christopher Norris. S. PAOLO GIOVANNI FEI: Triptych (see 1956) (£23 2s. in 1906).	2,400
1953	Lady Catherine Ashburnham. S. SANO DI PIETRO: Miracle of San Bernardino.	3,000
	STEFANO SASSETTA: Agony in the garden.	9,000
1955	S. SANO DI PIETRO: Holy Family.	1,800
	MASOLINO: Virgin, triangular gold-ground panel.	3,500
1956	The Louvre buys SASSETTA: Holy Family. Reputed price	50,000
1956	Dr. James Hasson. S. PAOLO GIOVANNI FEI: Triptych (see 1951).	3,570
1958	National Gallery buys UCCELLO: St. George and Dragon, small panel (see 1899).	35,000
	S. NERI DI BICCI: St. Catherine of Alexandria, nearly 6 ft.	2,400
1959	Charles Loeser. S. NERI DI BICCI: Tobias and the Angel.	2,850
1960	Sebastian Powell. S. NERI DI BICCI: 2 small panels.	2,200
	Tibor de Budai. C. BOTTICINI: Holy Family.	3,360
	Myron C. Taylor, New York. UNKNOWN PAINTER: Cassone panel, c. 1450.	3,214
	ANGHIARI MASTER: Cassone panel, Triumph of Aemilius Paulus.	2,500

DRAWINGS

1920	Marquess of Lansdowne. S. PISANELLO: Man hanging from a gallows (see 1936).	410
1921	Earl of Northwick. S. BENOZZO GOZZOLI: Sheet of studies.	395
1929	S. BENOZZO GOZZOLI: Crucifixion, pen and ink.	440
1930	S. BENOZZO GOZZOLI: Draped figure, pen and ink.	390
1936	Henry Oppenheimer. C. PISANELLO: Man hanging from a gallows (see 1920).	1,890
	PISANELLO: Man on a rearing horse.	892 10s.

		£
1949	Claude Lucas. S. PISANELLO: Rider in armour.	2,450
1953	Henry Reitlinger. S. PISANELLO: Statue and rocks (bought 1921 in a mixed lot for £10).	1,600
1955	Le Hunte. S. PISANELLO: Saddled horse.	1,800
	FRANCESCO DI GIORGIO: Donor and two angels, tinted drawing on vellum.	9,500
1957	S. FRA BARTOLOMMEO: Album of landscape drawings. 42 drawings, done before 1517.	100,850
	Sold in separate lots, the cheapest £600, the dearest	8,500
1958	S. SCHOOL OF FRA ANGELICO: 8 drawings.	9,400
1958	Skippe. C. PIERO DI COSIMO: Portrait head.	3,150
1959	Marquess of Northampton. C. FRA BARTOLOMMEO: Adoration of the kings.	6,510

North Italian Primitives

For Crivelli, Francia, school of Leonardo and Venetian school, see separate entries.

		£
1811	Young Ottley. C. MAZZOLINO: Christ disputing with doctors.	189
	MAZZOLINO: Ecce Homo.	450
1823	Fonthill (Philips), ex Beckford. MAZZOLINO: Woman taken in adultery (National Gallery, 1853).	122 17*s.*
1847	Edward Solly. C. MAZZOLINO: Destruction of Pharaoh.	241
	GAUDENZIO FERRARI: Visitation.	399
	GIROLAMO DA TREVISO: Madonna enthroned.	296
1856	Samuel Rogers. C. MAZZOLINO: Christ disputing (see 1811).	525
1857	National Gallery buys BORGOGNONE: Marriage of St. Catherine.	430
1859	National Gallery buys LORENZO COSTA: Holy Family.	880
1863	Davenport Bromley. C. VINCENZO FOPPA: Adoration (National Gallery).	127
1864	National Gallery buys in Verona GIROLAMO DAI LIBRI: Holy Family and St. Anne altarpiece.	1,580
1867	National Gallery buys COSIMO TURA: Madonna enthroned. } from Lady Eastlake.	160
	St. Jerome.	75
1869	National Gallery buys MARCO MARZIALE: Circumcision.	1,005
1874	National Gallery buys COSIMO TURA: Smaller Madonna (Alexander Barker sale).	84
1875	National Gallery buys SOLARIO: Venetian Senator (from Baslini).	1,800

		£
1882	National Gallery buys Ercole Grande: Altarpiece from Ferrara.	2,970
1887	National Gallery buys Ercole di Roberti: Israelites gathering manna (from Ferrara).	650
1891	Cavendish-Bentinck. C. Girolamo dai Libri: Holy Family enthroned (National Gallery, Dublin).	120 15s.
1892	Frank Leyland. C. Francesco Cossa: Adoration with St. Joseph.	987
1894	Lady Eastlake. C. Ercole Grandi: Adoration of the shepherds.	493 10s.
1899	C. Lorenzo Costa: Holy Family enthroned.	210
1901	Arthur Kay. C. Andrea Solario: Annunciation.	2,100
1905	Henry Willett. C. Gaudenzio Ferrari: Holy Family. (see 1955).	194 5s.
1905	Lawrie & Co. C. Francesco da Rimini: Holy Family and Angels (National Gallery, 1907).	504
1911	Sir William Abdy. C. Alvise Vivarini: Adoration.	3,885
	Andrea Solario: Portrait, Giovanni Bentivoglio.	4,200
	Cosimo Tura: Male portrait.	1,890
1919	Hamilton Palace. C. Girolamo dai Libri: Holy Family enthroned (built into the staircase).	2,730
1927	Holford. C. Palmezzano da Forli: Holy Family.	2,100
	Gaudenzio Ferrari: Nativity.	2,520
	Giulio Campi: Isabella d'Este.	1,785
1929	S. Lombard School: Lady in a rich dress.	3,500
	Lorenzo Costa: Young man in black and red.	1,750
1946	Lady Violet Melchett. S. Bartolommeo Montagna: Small head of the Virgin.	8,200
1947	Bromley Davenport. S. Ercole Roberti: St. Jerome.	4,000
1952	Galerie Charpentier, Paris. Domenico Morone: Life of St. Thomas Aquinas.	4,095
1955	S. Gaudenzio Ferrari: Holy Family (see 1905).	1,600
1957	Kincaid Lennox. S. Lorenzo Costa: A cardinal as St. Jerome. Bought in.	28,000
1958	John Skippe. C. Francesco Cossa: Venus embracing Cupid, drawing.	8,400

SIR AUGUSTUS JOHN. 1879–

For the most universally accepted modern and non-academic English painter of the booming 1912–1930 age, it is perturbing to compare these prices with those which were paid for the living favourites of the previous generation. For the lack of support for the British school in the first half of the present century the reader is referred to Chapter Six. But there has always been a healthy interest in John's splendid drawings.

		£
1918	Red Cross sale. C. 'Any portrait' commission (see 1937).	892 10s.
1920	Lord H. Bentinck. Woman with hands clasped. Charcoal drawing.	105
1921	S. 26 drawings fetched £230 (compare 1960).	
1927	Sir James Murray. C. The blue pool, oil. (Aberdeen Art Gallery).	640
1937	C. Portrait (see 1918).	162 15s.
1938	Leopold Albu. C. Portrait, Princess Bibesco (Collection of Paul Getty).	588
1940	Melbourne National Gallery buys portrait, W. Challoner Dowdswell.	2,500
1946	Melbourne National Gallery buys La Belle Jardinére.	1,000
1951	Geoffrey Blackwell. C. Nude model, drawing.	147
1954	Rees-Jeffreys. C. Girl, seated on a wall.	945
1955	Dennis Howarth. C. The woman on the hill.	1,312
1959	Geoffrey Harmsworth. C. Dorelia, drawing.	682 10s.
1960	C. Dorelia, wash drawing.	892 10s.

SIR EDWIN LANDSEER. 1802–1873

Trained in the Regency school of Leslie and Wilkie, Landseer lived into the late-Victorian period, but died rather too soon to share its incredible rewards. It is probable that £10,000 was paid for *The Otter Hunt* in the year of his death, the highest price that was ever given for a modern English picture, apart from its copyright value. Landseer was certainly the king of the English sale-room in the 1870's, 1880's and even early 1890's, though the prices were only a fraction of those that French and American collectors paid for Millet and Meissonier.

There is a mild and very selective revival at the present moment, though in 1960, when the famous *Bolton Abbey* picture received no higher bid than 60 guineas, the catalogue never even gave its history. Landseer's leaden colour persisted all his life, and it seems to express his age, but in fact it was the product of congenital melancholy.

		£
1827	De Tabley. C. Monkey and two dogs.	173 5s.
1834	Lord Charles Cavendish-Bentinck buys Scene of the Old Time at Bolton Abbey (see 1944, 1960).	400
1842	Harvest in the Highlands, sold to Bicknell (see 1863).	420
1843	Sir E. Codrington. C. Dead swan and peacock.	304 10s.
1845	Sheepshanks buys the Highland Drovers.	525

		£	
1851	Lord Londesborough buys The Monarch of the Glen.	362	10s.
1852	William Wells. C. Fallow deer.	635	
	Red deer.	682	10s.
1859	Phipps. C. The Highlander and his daughter (Lord Hertford, now Wallace Collection).	815	
1860	William Wells. C. The stonebreaker's daughter.	1,155	5s.
	I. Kingdom Brunel. Titania and the fairies (see 1883 and 1910).	2,940	
1863	Bicknell. C. Harvest in the Highlands (see 1842).	3,097	10s.
	Crumbs from the rich man's table (Wallace Collection).	2,415	
1868	Edward Betts. C. Braemar, a group of deer (see 1887).	4,200	
1872	Gillott. C. Pointers' to-ho (see 1917).	2,016	
1873	Landseer executors. Lady Godiva's prayer. C. (see 1916).	3,360	
	Baron Grant was said to have paid £10,000 for the Otter Hunt (see 1877).		
1875	Earl of Dudley. C. The deer family.	3,045	
1877	Baron Grant. C. The Otter Hunt (see 1873, 1913) (sold to Lord Holden for £6,215).	5,932	
1880	E. J. Colman. Well-bred sitters.	5,250	
	Man proposes (Holloway College).	6,610	
	The fatal duel, unfinished cartoon, painted in three hours (see 1933, £39 8s.).	5,250	
1883	Lord Brownlow sells Titania to Quilter (see 1910).	7,350	
1884	Lady Otho Fitzgerald. C. The Monarch of the Glen (see 1851, 1892, 1916).	6,510	
1887	Bolckow. C. Braemar (see 1868).	5,197	10s.
1890	William Wells. C. None but the brave (see 1935).	4,620	
	The roebucks (see 1945).	4,042	10s.
1892	Lord Cheylesmore. The Monarch of the Glen.	7,245	
	Resold, Agnew to T. Barratt (see 1916).	8,000	
1894	Richard Hemmings. C. Chevy Chase.	3,937	10s.
	Resold in the following year (see 1923).	5,985	
1896	Hargreaves. C. Pensioners (£1,312 15s. in 1884).	798	
1897	Pender. C. The lost sheep (bought Pierpont Morgan) (see 1943).	3,255	
1907	C. The deer family (see 1875 and 1941).	2,835	
1909	Quilter. Titania and the fairies (see 1883).	2,520	
1910	C. Highland shepherd's home (£1,050 in 1874).	304	10s.
1913	C. The Otter Hunt (see 1873, 1877).	1,260	
1916	Barratt. C. The Monarch of the Glen (now Messrs. Dewar).	5,250	
	Lady Godiva's prayer (see 1873).	943	
1917	Sir Joseph Beecham. C. Pointers' to-ho (see 1872).	136	10s.
1923	Sir J. B. Robinson. Chevy Chase (see 1895 and 1951).	1,050	

		£
1930	C. Taking a buck (£2,047 10*s*. in 1887).	27 6*s*.
1933	Countess Bubna. C. The fatal duel (see 1880).	39 8*s*.
1935	Steinkopf. C. None but the brave (see 1890).	152 10*s*.
1942	Jeremiah Colman. C. The catspaw (£819 in 1912).	136 10*s*.
1943	J. Pierpont Morgan, Jnr. C. The lost sheep (see 1897).	315
1944	C. Scene at Bolton Abbey (see 1834) (see also 1960).	105
1945	C. The deer pass (painted 1852).	546
1945	Lady Wantage. S. The roebucks (see 1890).	440
1951	C. Chevy Chase (1895, 1923).	157 10*s*.
1955	Aristides Vagliano. C. Too hot (small picture, £924 in 1893).	336
1955	Alfred Caspary, New York. Hunters and hounds.	625
1958	Mrs. Barchard. S. Refreshment (donkey eating carrots).	600
1959	C. Old grey mare in a stable (not in the market before).	1,260
1960	C. Scene of the olden time at Bolton Abbey (see 1834 and 1944).	63

NICOLAS LANCRET. 1690–1743

Lancret imitated Watteau, who was only a few years his senior, but Lancret's charm being of a more obvious nature, his pictures fetched more until well into the present century. Lancret's prices followed a pattern common to all the French rococco; a complete eclipse fully a generation before the French revolution, from which there was scarcely a vestige of recovery until the 1840's; a frenzied boom in the 1860's and 1870's through the competition of Dudley, Hertford and the Rothschilds, and a second boom before the First World War, which has been reduced subsequently to life-size.

		£
1770	Paris. 2 pendant panels.	38
1791	Paris. L'Escarpolette, large composition.	4
1845	Marquis de Cypierre, Paris. 2 pendants of a masqued ball at the Trianon.	128 14*s*.
		146
1857	Richard Wallace, Paris. Dog picking up a gold piece.	137
1862	Lord Pembroke, Paris. Dance in a park.	1,040
1869	Fould, Paris. Rendezvous at a fountain.	2,520
1880	George Gipps. C. Fête champêtre.	850 10*s*.
1880	Paris. La ronde champêtre.	2,420
1881	De Beurnonville, Paris. Tire a l'arc.	2,560
1889	Secrétan, Paris. Plaisirs de l'hiver.	1,368
1895	Lyne Stephens. C. Nicaise.	1,365
1899	Broadwood. C. Fête champêtre.	2,572 10*s*.

		£
1903	Reginald Vaile. C. Strolling musicians (see 1946).	2,625
	The swing and the see-saw (see 1946).	1,114 10s.
1908	Henry Say, Paris. Fête champêtre.	11,200
1912	Darnell. C. Mischief.	882
1930	C. Fête champêtre.	3,045
1935	Macdonald of the Isles. S. Les heures du jour, 4 small paintings on copper.	3,885
1945	S. Le tasse de chocolat (bought Dr. James Hasson).	12,500
1946	A. P. Humphrey. C. The swing and the see-saw (see 1903).	1,995
1950	C. Ladies and gentlemen in a garden (24 ins. × 30 ins.).	2,415
1951	Paris. La Marechale de Luxembourg et sa famille.	3,332
1959	Thelma Chrysler, New York. L'Escarpolette (45 ins. × 36 ins.).	10,000

MAURICE QUENTIN DE LATOUR. 1704–1788

The most brilliant of all the pastellists. Observations as for Lancret, but it has been a very long time since a first-rate Latour came on to the market.

		£
1858	Paris. Portrait de Mme. Regnière.	106
1868	Same portrait.	244
1879	Portrait of an engraver.	166
1881	2 pastel portraits, each at	120
1892	Paris. Pastel portrait, Mme. Pompadour.	250
1893	Denain, Paris. Mlle. Salle, danseuse de l'Opéra.	720
1897	Paris. Mme. Rouillé, pastel portrait.	1,262
1912	Doucet, Paris. Pastel portrait, Duval d'Epinoy (bought Henri de Rothschild, now Gulbenkian Foundation)	27,300
1913	Dawkins. C. Pastel portrait, Henry Dawkins.	2,226
1936	Winterfield. S. Pastel portrait. Mme. de la Poplinière.	3,000
1959	S. Mme. Savalette de Lange, pastel.	8,500
1959	Chrysler-Foy, New York. Masque of the artist (12 ins. × 9 ins.).	3,928 10s.
	Head of a girl, smiling.	2,500

Comte Henri de TOULOUSE-LAUTREC. 1864–1901

Before the war Lautrec's prices barely competed with those of the orthodox Impressionists. The stigma of having been an illustrator of magazines and a designer of posters took a long time to overcome. £2,000 was considered a very high price for the finest of Lautrec's gouaches and pastels. To-day Lautrec rates only below Renoir and Manet among the Impressionists. Outside the saleroom, prices as high as £70,000 have been paid, while the *Au salon* of the Musée d'Albi might be worth more than that.

		£
1898	Paris. Deux amies, pastel.	8
1899	Paris. Jeune femme assise.	56
1901	Blot, Paris. 'Melinite', portrait (see 1906). Bought in.	50
	Depeaux, Paris. A sa toilette.	160
	Aux Ambassadeurs, gens chics (see 1957).	78 8*s.*
1905	Paris. Lautrec executors' sale. A Montrouge, oils (bought in).	180
	St. Lazare, gouache (bought in).	156
1906	2nd Blot sale, Paris. Melinite (see 1901).	264
	2nd Depeaux sale. Intérieur de Cabaret.	280
1907	Georges Viau, Paris. La Goulue at the Moulin Rouge.	216
1913	Heim, Paris. 'Ces dames' (oil on millboard).	470
	La Pierreuse.	392
	Au salon (oil and pastel).	312
1914	Roger Marx, Paris. Dans le lit (oil on millboard).	600
	A l'Opéra, drawing, touched in oils.	368
1919	Manzi, Paris. Le leçon de chant.	628
1920	Sevedjan, Paris. Le Moulin Rouge, 4 ft., oils, about	1,100
1922	Kelekian, New York. Portrait of Cipa Godebski, about	820
1925	Tate Gallery, Courtauld Fund. Femme assise.	650
1926	Decourcelle, Paris. Danseuse en scene, long panel, in oils, 80 ins. × 28 ins.	1,850
	Portrait of Alfred la Guigne, small, oils.	780
1946	William van Horne, New York. Gueule de bois, 1889.	7,464
	Femme rousse assise.	6,840
1952	Felix Wildenstein, New York. L'Argent, gouache.	1,950
1957	Charpentier, Paris. Self-portrait.	3,300
	Medallion head for a decoration.	2,300
1957	Georges Lurcy, New York. Aux ambassadeurs, gens chics (see 1900).	39,630
	Aristide Bruant aux Ambassadeurs.	22,130
1958	Galerie Charpentier, Paris. Portrait, M. Manzi, 1899.	10,080
1958	S. Lili Granier, portrait.	15,000
1959	Nygaard. S. Retour de chasse, oil, 1883 (an academic picture).	15,000
	Marcel Lender, rough sketch for a colour lithograph.	13,000
	Medallion head for a decoration.	6,000
1959	Parke-Bernet, New York. Femme rousse dans un jardin.	64,288*
1960	Galerie Charpentier, Paris. Bettine, portrait.	25,450
	Le coucher, 1899.	25,565

SIR THOMAS LAWRENCE. 1769–1830

Before the 1920's there was seldom any question of Lawrence's work competing in the market for Gainsborough and Reynolds. The promotion of Lawrence seems to have been due chiefly to the private taste of Andrew Mellon. The general fall of the English portrait school in the 1930's was therefore followed by some readjustment. To-day the best of Lawrence rates well below Gainsborough, about level with Romney, higher than Reynolds and well above Hoppner, which seems fair enough. Lawrence was an incredibly highly fee'd painter. Some of his 700-guinea commissions of the 1820's may have advanced less than threefold to-day, but for more than forty years after Lawrence's death his portraits could have been bought for 50 guineas or less.

		£
1790	Lawrence, aged 21, gets for Nelly Farren (see 1935),	105
1808	320 guineas for whole-length groups.	
1827	150 guineas for portrait heads, 600–700 guineas for whole-lengths.	
1831	C. Lawrence executors' sale. Self-portrait.	493 10*s.*
	About 150 portraits; mostly unfinished or studies; 2 groups exceeded £200 each, but most were under £30.	
	Woodburn buys Satan summoning his legions (Burlington House).	504
1849	Blessington. C. Half-length of Lady Blessington (see 1899).	336
1859	Earl of Northwick (Philips). William Pitt, whole-length.	147
1863	Bicknell. C. Miss Siddons, small head.	147
1872	Marquis du Blaisel. Mrs. Baring on a sofa.	1,470
1885	V. P. Calmady. C. 'Nature', fancy portrait, bought in.	1,890
1891	C. Miss Murray.	1,270 10*s.*
1896	Angerstein. C. Mrs. Angerstein and child.	2,257
	Mme. Sablukoff and family, large crayon drawing.	1,050
1897	Cholmondely. C. Nelly Farren (Agnew) (bought subsequently by Pierpont Morgan, reputedly for £10,000, see 1935).	2,415
1906	C. Miss West, half-length.	4,200
1907	Peel heirlooms (Robinson and Fisher). Miss Peel or 'Childhood's innocence'.	8,400
1911	Comtesse de Noailles. C. Mrs. Baring and her children (see 1923)	8,400
1912	Doucet, Paris. Portrait of a young girl.	8,800
1913	C. Lady Orde and her child.	6,720
1917	Hope heirlooms. C. Hon. Mrs. Henry Hope.	3,570
	Master Hope, 1826.	4,830

		£
1924	Lady Carnarvon. Mellon buys Lady Templeton and her son through Duveen (National Gallery, Washington). Reputed price 40,000 to	50,000
1926	Late Lord Michelham (Hampton's). 'Pinkie' (Miss Mary Moulton Barrett). Bought Duveen.	77,700
	Subsequently sold to Henry Huntington for about	90,000
1928	Holford. C. Lord Castlereagh (replica, see 1938).	4,410
1930	Barnet Lewis. C. Mrs. R. B. Jones, small oval portrait.	5,460
1932	Earl of Durham (Anderson and Garland). Master Lambton, 'The Red Boy', 1835. Bought in nominally at	95,000
1935	Solly Joel. C. The woodland maid.	9,975
1935	The Metropolitan Museum buys Nelly Farren (see 1897).	41,200
1938	C. Lord Castlereagh (see 1928).	567
1939	Lord Bearsted. C. Red Cross sale. Miss Angerstein.	252
	Earl of Rosebery. C. Duke of Wellington, head.	1,155
1944	E. T. Stotesbury, New York. Lady Singleton.	2,250
	Mrs. Thompson and her son.	1,675
1945	Parke-Bernet, New York. George IV, half-length.	1,507
1946	Cameron of Lochiel. C. Mrs. Murray and child.	1,995
1951	Gallerie Charpentier, Paris. Lady Ellenborough.	1,670
1956	Parke-Bernet, New York. Lady Neeve, half-length.	1,785
1957	Mae Rovensky, New York. Francis Mackenzie, Lord Seaforth.	4,646
1958	Earl of Waldegrave. C. Alleged Miss Siddons, daughter of the actress.	6,300
	Lord Hatherton. C. Mrs. Lyttleton.	4,410

Frederick
LORD LEIGHTON. 1830–1896

Was always considered rather high-class and precious and therefore, in an England which was dominated by the popular print market, nowhere near the highest priced painter. Leighton did indeed live to see his gigantic *Daphnephoria* fetch nearly £4,000, but more than twenty Landseers must have fetched as much, and as many Millais pictures. Those who expect a Leighton revival should have plenty of patience.

		£
1855	Queen Victoria buys Cimabue at the Royal Academy.	630
1863	Mrs. Barwell. The feigned death of Juliet (bought in).	294
1866	Royal Academy. Agnew buys The Sargonsian bride.	1,200
1868	Gambart. C. King David.	420
1874	Frank Leyland. The Sargonsian bride (see 1866 and 1960).	2,677 10*s.*
1875	Sam Mendel. A noble Venetian lady (see 1910).	997 10*s.*

		£
1876	Royal Academy. The Daphnephoria, bought by Lord Revelstoke, see 1893 and 1912 (16 ft. long).	1,500
1880	Mrs. Benzon. C. Cleoboulos instructing his daughter.	1,312 10*s.*
1890	Chantrey Bequest buys Bath of Psyche (Tate Gallery).	1,050
1891	Matthews. C. The music lesson (see 1925).	2,467
1893	Lord Revelstoke. C. The Daphnephoria (see 1913).	3,937 10*s.*
1896	Leighton executors' sale. Perseus and Andromeda.	651
1900	James Reiss. Helen and Rhodos.	2,887 10*s.*
1903	Sir Horatio Davies. C. Moorish garden (see 1930).	199 10*s.*
1906	Lady Ashburton. C. Winding the skein.	1,522 10*s.*
1907	Imrie. Melition (see 1927).	1,260
	Lord Davey. Golden hours (£1,155 in 1888).	262 10*s.*
1909	Cuthbert Quilter. C. Cymon and Iphigenia.	2,310 10*s.*
1910	Armstrong heirlooms. C. Noble Venetian Lady (see 1875).	204 10*s.*
1913	MacCulloch. C. The Daphnephoria (see 1866 and 1893) (Lever Art Gallery).	2,625
	Garden of Hesperides.	2,625
1925	Denny. C. Lord Bearsted buys The Music Lesson (see 1891) (presented to Guildhall Gallery).	3,255*
1926	C. The spirit of the summit ($6\frac{1}{2}$ ft.).	346 10*s.*
1927	C. Melition (see 1907).	262 10*s.*
1930	C. The Moorish garden (see 1903).	199 10*s.*
	The Mother of the Muses (over 4 ft.).	15 15*s.*
1931	C. The Egyptian Slinger (£294 in 1907).	44 2*s.*
1934	Lord Faringdon. S. Venus disrobing.	270
	Daedalus and Icarus.	230
1938	Leopold Albu. C. Cymon and Iphigenia (see 1909). Leeds Art Gallery.	493 10*s.*
1953	C. The light of the harem (4 ft.).	48 6*s.*
1958	Lever Art Gallery. C. Oil sketch for Cimabue (see 1855).	115 10*s.*
1960	Knight, Frank and Rutley. The Sargonsian bride (see 1866 and 1874).	200

LE NAIN

The brothers Antoine 1588–1649, Louis 1593–1648, and Mathieu 1607–1677

The authorships of the three brothers have not been disentangled, nor has the origin of their part-Dutch and part-Italian style of *genre* painting. Considering that in the middle of the eighteenth century the Le Nains were esteemed as highly as any Dutch *genre* painter, their work seems absurdly cheap. But the prices of the very few reliable Le Nain pictures which have reached the open market are no indication of their present value.

		£
1758	Sir Luke Schaub, London. A man piping and his children dancing.	180
1801	Bessborough. C. A group of beggars.	105
1803	Walsh Porter. C. The infant card-players (sold as a Caravaggio).	388 10s.
1840	Sir Simon Clarke. C. The passions.	115 10s.
1875	Miss Bredel. C. Two boys and a girl with music.	493 10s.
1882	Lord Sudeley. C. Peasants and animals, a small pair.	325 10s.
1888	C. Alleged portrait of Tycho Brahe with a book.	210
1894	Sellar. C. The tasting, five children.	110 5s.
1906	C. A company of butchers, large picture.	136 10s.
1908	Sir Robert Loder. C. A children's concert, 1629.	1,333 10s.
1913	A. F. Walter. C. The astronomers.	525
1930	Carrington. C. A group of peasants.	819
1931	Hirsch. C. A merry group, dated 1629.	1,890
1937	Lord Aldenham. S. Les petits chanteurs.	1,100
1944	Neeld. C. Peasants in a landscape.	2,100
1945	Neeld. C. A family group.	2,940
1952	Gabriel Cognacq, Paris. Les petits danseurs.	3,780
1960	Mrs. Dorothy Rhodes. C. Pieta (Mathieu le Nain).	6,090

LEONARDO DA VINCI. 1452–1581

It is possible that the only real Leonardos in this list, apart from the drawings, are the *Virgin of the Rocks* and the *Benois Madonna*. It is nevertheless of some interest to compare what collectors were prepared to pay at different times for works which they believed genuine.

		£
1777	Sir Robert Strange. C. Madonna, Child and St. Joseph.	283
1781	Gavin Hamilton buys The Virgin of the Rocks from the monks of the Conception Brotherhood in Milan for 30 ducats or £15 (sold in 1785 to Lord Lansdowne, who sold it in 1810 to the Earl of Suffolk for 2,000 guineas, see 1879).	
1801	Sir William Hamilton. C. The laughing boy with a puzzle. (Bought by Beckford, see 1823, 1882; now considered a fragment from a larger picture by Bernardo Luini.)	1,365
1801	Alexander Day's exhibition. Christ disputing with the doctors, bought by the Earl of Northwick (National Gallery, Holwell Carr Bequest, 1831). Now considered to be by Luini.	3,150
1803	Walsh Porter. C. Madonna and Child.	840
1811	Duke of San Pietro. C. Portrait of a woman in a green turban or handkerchief. Bought in.	3,150

		£
1813	Buchanan sells Alexander Baring the Virgin, St. John and sleeping child, imported from the Escorial, perhaps	4,000
1825	Christie's offer a copy of the lost Leda and the Swan, imported from Italy (see 1874 and 1879).	7,000
1850	King of Holland, Amsterdam. The Tsar buys the portrait, 'La Columbina' (Hermitage).	3,333
	Holy Family (Hermitage), now called Luini.	1,292
	Duke of Weimar buys the so-called Last Supper studies.	666
	Copy of the lost Leda (Munich Gallery).	2,041
1874	Alexander Barker. Copy of Leda (see 1825) bought in at	178 10*s.*
	Resold in 1879 for	84
1879	National Gallery buys The Virgin of the Rocks (see 1781).	9,000
1888	Lord Monson. C. La Vierge au bas relief (offered to Prussian Government at 12,000 guineas).	2,520
1914	The Tsar buys the Benois Madonna in Paris.	310,400*
1927	Holford. C. Virgin with the carafe. School picture.	2,100
1956	Prince Lichtenstein. An offer of 2 million dollars from the Canadian Government for a Portrait of a Lady was said to have been refused.	714,000

DRAWINGS

1830	Lawrence. C. 8 alleged cartoons for the Last Supper, bought by Woodburn and sold to King of Holland (see 1850). Late copies.	536 14*s.*
1836	Woodburn's Exhibition of the Lawrence Collection. 75 alleged Leonardo drawings offered for	1,500
1850	King of Holland. Amsterdam. 2 sheets of studies.	83 10*s.*
1881	Sackville-Bale. C. Study of a child.	309 15*s.*
1886	Marquess of Breadalbane. C. Girl's head.	204 15*s.*
	Sheet of allegories.	210
	Sheet of figures.	175
1896	Earl of Warwick. S. Silverpoint, girl's head.	480
1912	J. E. Taylor. C. Head of a lady.	105
1917	Earl of Pembroke. S. Man on a rearing horse (see 1936).	735
1926	S. The ermine, emblem of purity, 3½ ins. circle.	800
	Sheet of studies, silverpoint.	760
1927	Holford. S. Horse and rider.	2,500
	Leda, fragment of cartoon on paper.	1,785
1936	Henry Oppenheimer. C. Man on a rearing horse (see 1917).	4,305
1951	Lady Violet Melchett. S. Study for Virgin and St. Anne of the Louvre, black chalk.	8,000
1954	Lady Violet Melchett. S. Head of Leda, grisaille, attributed (see 1927).	3,400

JEAN BASTIEN LEPAGE. 1849–1885

An academic populariser of Millet-like themes, such as the famous *Potato Gatherers* and, despite a life of only thirty-six years, a most powerful influence in England and America. He painted the Prince of Wales, he inspired Marie Baschkirtzev and, somewhat like Cecil Lawson in England, he was regarded as the white hope of realist landscape painting as it foundered before the onslaught of Impressionism. It should be noticed that the soulful Marie Baschkirtzev, going to school in elastic-sided boots, made nearly £3,000 even in 1927.

		£
1882	E. Gray. C. La coquette.	372 12*s.*
1885	C. Pas mêche (see 1913), bought in.	441
1885	Vente Bastien Lepage, Paris. The potato gatherers (see 1913).	1,164
	The beggar.	840
	Annunciation to the shepherds.	952
1889	Dana, New York. Joan of Arc listening to voices.	4,800
1913	MacCulloch. C. Potato gatherers (National Gallery, Melbourne, see 1885).	3,755
	Pas mêche, see 1885.	2,005 10*s.*
	Pauvre fauvette.	1,452 10*s.*
1924	C. Portrait of Mme. Lelegue, 1877.	441
1927	Sir James Murray. C. Going to school.	2,837 10*s.*

CHARLES ROBERT LESLIE. 1794–1859

An American disciple of Benjamin West in his declining years, who introduced into the England of George IV a particularly abominable convention which was to last nearly a century—namely, the pictorial anecdote in historic dress which is really a book-illustration. See Chapter Four. Considering how tremendous was his influence, Leslie's works benefited very little from the inflation of the modern English school in mid-Victorian times.

		£
1821	Mayday in the time of Elizabeth, sold at R.A.	315
1840	Coronation of the Queen, royal commission.	630
1845	G. Knott. C. Scene from *The Vicar of Wakefield* (see 1946).	682 10*s.*
	My Uncle Toby and the widow Wadman (Tate Gallery).	136 10*s.*
1854	Lord Charles Townshend. C. Sterne and the Grisette.	535 10*s.*
1856	Samuel Rogers. C. Sancho and the Duchess (see 1886).	1,176
	The Princes in the Tower (see 1890).	225 15*s.*
1859	Earl of Northwick (Philips). Columbus and the egg.	1,123 10*s.*

		£
1863	Bicknell. C. The Heiress (see 1886).	1,260
1870	Bullock. C. The Rape of the Lock (see 1912).	1,365
1872	Harris. C. Falstaff impersonating the King (see 1877).	1,050
1875	Mendel. C. Scene from Henry VIII.	1,365
1877	Baron Grant. Falstaff impersonating the king.	1,522 10s.
1886	McConnell. C. Sancho Panza and the Duchess (see 1856).	157 10s.
	The Heiress (see 1863).	288 15s.
1890	C. The Princes in the Tower (see 1856).	12 12s.
1910	Octavus Coope. C. Falstaff impersonating the King (see 1872).	126
	Sir F. T. Mappin. Merry wives of Windsor (same price in 1879).	567
1912	John Gibbons. C. The Rape of the Lock (see 1870).	81 18s.
1946	Pitt-Miller. C. Scene from *The Vicar of Wakefield* (see 1845).	241 10s.
	Reading the will.	178 10s.
	Sir Roger de Coverley in church.	115 10s.
1951	Marion Davies, New York. The Minstrel Boy.	258

JOHN FREDERICK LEWIS. 1805–1876

A painter of the post-Bonington romantic school who chose an individual path of his own and who is far from sharing to-day in the neglect of other early Victorian painters of the Oriental scene, such as Muller and Roberts. Lewis was influenced on the one hand by Fromentin and on the other by the Pre-Raphaelites, thereby producing such extremely pleasing works as *Lilium auratum* and *Siesta*. Not many of his oil-paintings, however, are of that brilliant standard and to-day it is Lewis's water-colours that attract most attention. Less than forty years ago the best of them were to be had for a few pounds each.

		£
1855	Ralph Bernal. C. Scene in the highlands, wc.	136 10s.
1860	Burnett. C. The Frank camp, wc. (see 1912 and 1952).	607
1862	Langton. C. The posada } oils.	399
	The bull-fight } oils.	393 10s.
1872	Harris. C. The Arab scribe, wc. (see 1917.	483
1875	William Quilter. C. The school at Cairo), wc.(see 1891).	1,239
	Lilium auratum, oil (see 1892).	1,060 10s.
	The prayer of faith (see 1916 and 1935).	1,176
1875	William Leaf. C. House of the Coptic patriarch (oil). (see 1924).	1,942 10s.
1877	C. The Siesta (oil). See 1923.	1,013 10s.
1891	Matthews. C. The reception, wc. (see 1937 and 1960).	892 10s.
	Intercepted correspondence.	1,764
	The school at Cairo, wc. (see 1875).	1,785

		£
1892	David Pryce. C. Lilium auratum (see 1875), presented, 1911, to Birmingham City Art Gallery.	840
1893	Bowman. C. The Koran commentator, oil (see 1905).	2,677 10*s.**
1895	Thomas Woolner. C. Bezestein bazaar (see 1919).	1,470
1905	Louis Huth. C. The Koran commentator (see 1893).	1,732 10*s.*
1908	Stephen Holland. C. The school at Cairo, wc. (see 1891).	1,312 10*s.*
1912	C. The Frank encampment, wc. (see 1860, 1952).	463
1916	T. Barratt. C. The prayer of faith (see 1875 and 1935).	483
1917	C. The Arab scribe (see 1872).	420
1919	C. Bezestein Bazaar, oil (see 1895).	966
1921	Brassey. C. Siesta, oil (see 1877).	115 10*s.*
	Bought next year for the Tate Gallery.	367 10*s.*
1924	C. The Coptic patriarch's house (see 1875).	651
1935	Steinkopf. C. The prayer of faith, wc (see 1875, 1916).	68 5*s.*
1937	C. The reception, large wc. (see 1891 and 1960).	110 5*s.*
1941	Ethel Barton. S. The Cairo bazaar, 1875, oil, 30 ins. × 20 ins.	10
1946	Pitt-Miller. C. The love missive, 1854.	157 10*s.*
1952	S. The Cairo bazaar, oil, 1876.	75
	The Frank encampment, wc (see 1860).	260
1957	C. Landseer angling, wc.	420
1958	S. The Koran commentator (see 1893, 1905).	900
1959	S. The midday meal, 1875, oil.	900
	Dyson Perrins. S. Cairo, caged doves, wc (£441 in 1885).	300
1960	S. The mendicant, wc (£241 10*s.* in 1894).	150
	C. Indoor gossip (oil).	525
	The Reception, wc (see 1891 and 1937).	840

JOHN LINNELL, SNR. 1792–1882

This dull, kind man lived to the age of ninety, combining in one existence the feats of a boy prodigy who interested the young Turner and Wilkie, of a faithful friend who bought and hoarded Blake's water-colours and of an ancient Druid who reproached Millais for his beastly small girls in pinafores. Having said that, I must add that Linnell's paintings hardly justified the valuation of his contemporaries. They were mostly painted according to a scrappy formula, based on James Ward or Patrick Nasmyth, but more romanticised. Financially, Linnell was incredibly successful, for the great saleroom boom occurred in his own lifetime. Between 1868 and 1879 some thirty-two of his landscapes made four-figure prices in Christie's alone. Even in 1908 *The Timber Waggon* made a successful reappearance at £2,257 10*s.*, but to-day £300 would be a high price for anything by Linnell's hand.

		£
1853	Burch. C. David and the lion.	640 10s.
1864	Threlfall. C. The disobedient prophet.	997 10s.
1868	5 landscapes in the Bigg and Fallows sales made over a thousand guineas each.	
1870	Bullock. C. A storm in harvest. (See 1910.)	1,428
	Woodcutters.	1,365
1872	Gillott. C. Woodcutters.	2,625
	Hampstead Heath (see 1924).	1,748
	Barley harvest.	1,711 10s.
	Eve of the deluge (see 1913).	1,092 10s.
1875	Woolner. C. The last gleam before the storm.	2,625
1879	Fenton. C. A harvest dinner.	1,690 10s.
1883	C. Midday rest.	1,585 10s.
1887	John Graham. C. The sheep drover.	1,972
1890	Hunt. C. Harvest field (see 1914).	1,701
1892	David Price. C. The timber waggon (see 1908).	3,255*
1896	C. The Welsh drovers (see 1910).	1,050
1908	Harry Coghill. C. The timber waggon (see 1892).	2,257
	Stephen Holland. C. Carrying wheat.	1,995
1910	Armstrong heirlooms. C. A storm in harvest (see 1870).	819
	The Welsh drovers (see 1896).	325 10s.
1913	Lord Holden. C. Eve of the deluge (see 1872).	189
	In the following year fell to	28 7s.
1914	Harvest field (see 1890).	525
1924	Darrell Brown. Hampstead Heath (see 1872).	315
1926	R. Clarke. The rainbow, over 6 ft.	189 10s.
1946	Swaythling heirlooms. C. Hillside farm, Isle of Wight.	315
1956	C. Arcadian shepherds (£438 10s. in 1883).	75 12s.

FILIPPO LIPPI. 1406–1469

A much rarer painter than his son, Filippino Lippi. Apart from the two National Gallery pictures, these are probably attributed works.

		£
1849	Coningham. C. Adoration of the Magi.	199 10s.
1854	Joly de Bammeville. C. Vision of St. Bernard, bought by National Gallery as a Masaccio.	400
1857	National Gallery. Holy Family and angel (schoolpiece).	627 8s.
1861	National Gallery buys John the Baptist and saints from Alexander Barker, part of block purchase, about	700
1863	Davenport Bromley. C. A replica version of the above picture.	255 3s.

		£
1879	Brett. C. Adoration of the Magi, round picture.	231
1886	William Graham. C. Holy Family with angels, gold background (bought in Paris, 1885, for £90), sold to Berlin Museum through Fairfax Murray.	661 10s.
1889	Puxley. C. Holy Family.	745 10s.
1892	Frank Leyland. C. Adoration, roundel.	735
1904	S. H. Fraser. C. Small Holy Family.	525
1921	Austen. C. Holy Family and saints.	1,050
1944	Schinasi, New York. Madonna della Stella (from Carmine altarpiece).	7,500
1955	Kay. S. Betrothal portrait (attributed).	2,600

FILIPPINO LIPPI. 1460–1505

Perhaps fewer false attributions than with most quattrocento painters.

		£
1854	National Gallery buys Vision of St. Bernard.	398
1856	Samuel Rogers. C. La bella Simonetta (see 1863, 1892).	194 5s.
1857	National Gallery buys the Rucellai Holy Family.	627 8s.
1858	National Gallery buys small St. Francis panel in Ferrara. about	100
1863	Davenport Bromley. C. Simonetta (see 1856, 1892).	483
1864	Brett. C. Coronation of the Virgin (suspected).	504
1874	Barker. C. Adoration of the Magi (Sir Herbert Cook, Richmond).	735
1892	Earl of Dudley. C. La Simonetta (see 1863).	1,050
	Declanche, Paris. Esther and Ahasueras.	328
1894	Lady Eastlake. St. Catherine.	472 10s.
	Holy Family (see 1938).	525
1911	Charles Butler. C. Cupid and Psyche.	525
	Christ and disciples.	105
1921	Austen. C. Holy Family (called Amico di Sandro).	1,365
1935	Adoration triptych, ex Pierpont Morgan, bought by Metropolitan Museum.	52,000
1938	Carl Hamilton, New York. Holy Family (see 1894), Metropolitan Museum.	25,800
1940	Earl of Balfour. S. Small Madonna.	460
1959	S. Small attributed Holy Family.	1,700

DRAWINGS

1902	Sir J. C. Robinson. Christ and John the Baptist.	157 10s.
1917	Earl of Pembroke. S. Study for a Pieta.	640
1936	Henry Oppenheimer. C. 2 sheets of studies.	1,365
	Figures of saints.	1,890

EDWIN LONG. 1829–1891

Included a *titre de curiosité* to illustrate some of the worst and most expensive pictures of the late Victorian salerooms. Observations will be found on page 160.

		£
1865	Wallis. C. Love has its little cares.	168
1875	Adamson. C. Lazarillo and the blind beggar.	315
1877	Baron Grant. C. Madrid (7 ft.), see 1896.	660 10s.
1882	The Babylonian marriage market (Holloway College) (bought by Edward Hermon in 1878 for £7,350).	6,615
	The Suppliants, 1872.	4,305
1883	Taylor. C. The gods and their makers.	2,625
1891	Before his death, Long refused £5,250 for The Parable of the Sower, 17 ft. × 9 ft. (see 1908).	
1892	James Pryce. C. Diana or Christ, 1881.	2,625
1896	C. Madrid street scene (see 1877).	546
1908	Mrs. Long, deceased. The Parable of the Sower (see 1891).	131 5s.
1911	C. Feast of Anubis.	152 10s.
1915	C. The search for beauty (8 ft. × 6 ft.).	189 10s.
1922	Baroness Burdett-Coutts. 3 portraits of Henry Irvine, commissioned in the 1880's for £2,100.	91 7s.
1961	C. Billetting in Cadiz (£525 in 1882).	52 10s.

LORENZO LOTTO. 1480–1556

Foremost among the underpriced early Venetians, contemporaries of Titian, who became a millionaire's market only after Berenson's studies.

		£
1847	Edward Solly (ex Lucien Bonaparte). C. Venetian family, very Titianesque (left to National Gallery in 1879).	225 15s.
1862	National Gallery buys double portrait, Agostino and Niccolo della Torre.	320
1881	National Gallery buys portrait of the proto-notary Giuliano.	600
1895	Henry Doetsch. C. Altarpiece, Holy Family with saints, recorded by Berenson in 1892.	53 11s.
1902	Stefano Bardini. C. Gentleman holding manuscript and gloves.	420
1927	Holford. C. National Gallery buys Holy Family with St. John (with help of the Benson family).	23,100
1934	S. Allegory, dated 1505.	1,800
1959	Tibor de Budai. C. Half-length male portrait.	3,570

DRAWINGS

		£
1955	A. G. B. Russell. S. Young man, chalk heightened with colours.	8,000
1958	John Skippe. C. Draperies on blue-ground paper.	8,920
	Miracle of St. Lucia, black chalk.	1,575

Jean Gossaert de MABUSE. 1470–1532

Mabuse was one of the few masters of the Northern Renaissance, whom the eighteenth century still remembered. He was therefore as frequently misattributed as Holbein. He is most widely known for a very early and untypical work, *The Adoration of the Kings*, from Castle Howard, a work as crammed with detail as Holman Hunt's *Triumph of the Innocents*. Mabuse should really be judged by his fine Italianising portraits, though these have never been in the highest class of saleroom treasures.

		£
1797	The Adoration of the Kings, sold to Earl of Carlisle by Michael Bryan, having been imported by Van Fulens in 1787 as a Dürer (see 1911).	525
1798	Duke of Argyll. C. Madonna with Child and angel.	4 14*s.*
1802	Countess of Holderness. C. A double portrait.	138 12*s.*
1812	Beckford refuses an Adoration at £68 5*s.*	
1842	Waldegrave, Strawberry Hill. (Robins). Horace Walpole's alleged Marriage of Henry VII.	168
1848	William Wells. C. An old man and his wife (see 1900).	91
1855	Ralph Bernal. C. 7 attributed pictures, between 19 and 65 guineas.	
1859	Earl of Northwick (Philips). Portrait of Jeanne la Folle.	199 10*s.*
	Barrett of Lee Priory. C. Consecration of a priest.	551
1877	Robert Napier. C. Adoration, triptych.	519 15*s.*
1882	Hamilton Palace. C. Same picture.	525
	Labours of Hercules.	525
1899	Methuen. C. So-called children of Henry VII.	556 10*s.*
1900	National Gallery buys double portrait of an old man and his wife (see 1848), now considered a school picture.	4,000
1901	C. Jacqueline de Bourgogne with astrolabe.	2,520
1907	Francis Baring. C. Jean Carondalet (see 1934).	3,850
1908	Same picture, bought by National Gallery.	2,300
1911	National Gallery buys Adoration of the Kings from the Countess of Carlisle (see 1797).	40,000
1912	C. Ss. Catherine and Barbara, 2 wings of a triptych (see 1923).	1,365

		£
1923	C. Same pictures.	1,837 10s.
	Lord Brownlow. C. Mary Tudor, Duchess of Suffolk.	3,990
1925	Earl of Carnarvon. C. Small portrait head.	4,620
1928	Holford. C. Man with a gold chain.	7,140
	Lady Trevelyan. C. 2 small portraits, a donor and his wife.	6,090
1929	C. A king richly attired, 32 ins. × 20 ins.	3,465
1930	George Folliott. S. Dame Elizabeth Bullen (bought as a Holbein. A. L. Nicholson).	15,500
1934	Leopold Hirsch. C. Jean Carondalet (see 1907).	3,150
1946	E. J. Wythes. C. Penance of Count of Toulouse.	1,628 10s.
1950	Allen Fenwick. C. Holy Family at a window, 18 ins. × 14 ins., ex Earl of Northwick, £31 10s. in 1859.	3,570

DANIEL MACLISE. 1811–1870

Began with rather folky Irish peasant scenes in the manner of Mulready and proceeded to vast Shakespearian and mediaevalist compositions, and finally to the big mural paintings of modern history which ruined his health. Pre-eminently Maclise was the painter whose mannerisms provoked the Pre-Raphaelite revolt. The highest paid of all English painters in the 1850's, Maclise lived to see the decline of his works in the saleroom in the next decade. In the present century he became almost worthless, but he has left his mark on children's pantomimes.

		£
1851	Gallery of British Art. The author and the actors.	609
1852	C. Hunt the slipper (see 1946).	695
1854	Royal Academy. Earl of Northwick buys Marriage of Strongbow (see 1859, 1879), 10 ft. × 16 ft.	4,000
1859	Earl of Northwick (Philips). Same picture, bought by Flatou (see 1879).	1,795
	Robin Hood and his men.	1,370 5s.
1858–62	House of Lords murals. Wellington greeting Blucher.	2,500
1860	Henry Wallis. C. Bohemian gypsies, bought in (see 1872).	1,081 10s.
	Holdsworth (Glasgow). The Sleeping Beauty, bought in (see 1865).	1,000
1861	Agnew. C. Ordeal by touch (see 1937).	577 10s.
1865	J. Knowles. The Sleeping Beauty (see 1860).	939 15s.
1872	Gillott. C. The Bohemian gypsies, 7 ft. × 14 ft. (see 1860, 1919).	934 10s.

		£
1879	Roche. C. The marriage of Strongbow (see 1854, 1959). Bought by Richard Wallace and presented to National Gallery, Dublin.	787 10*s.*
1883	Williams. C. Peter the Great in Deptford Dock (Holloway College).	388 10*s.*
1913	Lord Holden. C. The Bohemian gypsies (see 1872).	199 10*s.*
1924	C. A gross of green spectacles, 1854.	157 10*s.*
1937	C. Ordeal by touch (see 1861), 10 ft. × 7 ft., framed.	2 12*s.*
1946	Pitt-Miller. C. Hunt the slipper (see 1852).	210
1954	S. Snap-apple night in Ireland (£304 10*s.* in 1890).	440

NICOLAS MAES. 1632–1698

Observations as for Metsu.

		£
1795	Calonne. S. Woman suckling a child.	74 11*s.*
1811	C. The Eavesdropper, bought by Lord Yarmouth (Wallace Collection).	157 10*s.*
1846	Higginson of Saltmarshe. Woman at a pump (see 1894).	745 10*s.*
1875	Miss Bredel. C. Girl making lace, 1655 (see 1893).	1,785
1888	National Gallery buys The Card Players from Lord Monson.	1,375 10*s.*
1893	Bingham Mildmay. C. The lace-maker (see 1875) (National Gallery, Toronto).	1,730
1894	Adrian Hope. C. Woman at a pump (see 1846).	3,003
1894	Hume Campbell. C. Portrait of Van Levenhoek (National Gallery, Salting Bequest, 1910).	136 10*s.*
1905	Lawrie & Co. C. Portrait of a gentleman.	840
1909	C. A pair of portraits, man and wife.	2,255
1910	Sir George Chetwynd. C. Lady in white by a fountain.	1,152 10*s.*
1917	Marquess of Breadalbane. C. Boy asking for alms.	1,785
1919	C. Old lady, asleep.	2,028 5*s.*
1921	Lord Carbery. C. Family group, 1656.	3,150
1930	Breitmeyer. C. Woman plucking a duck, 1655.	1,890
1937	Lewis Lloyd. C. The workshop.	1,365
1937	Victor Rothschild. S. The maidservant.	1,100
1950	Allen Fenwick. C. Vertumnus and Pomona (16 guineas at Northwick sale, 1859, see 1960).	420
	H. A. Clowes. C. The lace-maker.	2,992 10*s.*
1956	Lady Hillingdon. C. Lady and gentleman, a pair.	1,050
1960	S. A huge family group.	3,200
	Parke-Bernet, New York. Vertumnus and Pomona (see 1950).	425

EDOUARD MANET. 1832–1883

Only Manet's later work was truly Impressionist and, despite the controversy which he created, his most famous works fetched far more in the 1880's than those of the Impressionist brotherhood. Renoir began to rate with Manet only in the present century.

		£	
1872	Two exhibitions held by Durand-Ruel in London. Manet's works, including The Fife-player, were priced at 200 to 400 guineas, but there is no evidence that any were sold.		
1878	Faure. Paris. Polichinelle.	80	
1881	Edwards, Paris. Boy with a sword (see 1894).	364	
1884	Vente Manet, Drouot, Paris. Olympia (see 1890).	400	
	Argenteuil.	500	
	Bar aux Folies Bergères.	234	
	Chez le pere Lathuille (see 1894).	200	
	Serveuse de Bocks.	100	
	Le linge.	320	
	Le balcon.	120	
	Portrait of Emile Faure as Hamlet.	140	
	Le skating.	67	
	Nana (see 1894).	120	
1888	J. G. Johnson buys The Alabama and the Kearsage.	310	
1889	Henri van Cutsem buys Argenteuil (Musée de Tournai).	560	
1890	The Luxembourg Gallery buys Olympia (see 1884).	774	12*s.*
1894	Theodore Duret. Paris. Nana (see 1884).	360	
	Le père Lathuille (see 1884).	320	
	Le repas (G. Vanderbilt).	440	
	Le Torero (Havemeyer).	420	
1894	Durand-Ruel sells Boy with a sword (see 1881, now Metropolitan Museum).	720	
1898	The *Alabama* off Boulogne, bought by O. Havemeyer.	800	
	Le Jardin, bought by O. Havemeyer.	880	
	Durand-Ruel sells Rue Mosnier aux drapeaux (see 1958).	480	
1899	Mme. Chocquet. Paveurs de la Rue de Berne (see 1913).	540	
	Manet dans son atelier.	400	
1902	C. Lady in white.	126	
1903	C. Jettée a Boulogne.	504	
1906	Lord Grimthorpe. C. Jeune fille à la cravate blanche.	257	15*s.*
1912	Rouart, Paris. Buste de femme, bought in.	3,880	
1913	Mariczell de Nemés. Paris. Paveurs de la Rue de Berne.	3,180	
1922	La promenade, sold by Durand-Ruel (see 1957). About	2,000	
1924	Courtauld Fund for Tate Gallery. La serveuse de Bocks.	10,000	
1925	National Gallery, Melbourne. Maison à Reuil.	4,600	
1926	J. J. Cowan. The ship's deck (small oil).	997	10*s.*

		£
1930	Mrs. O. Havemeyer, New York. Marguerite de Conflans.	2,170
1937	Leonard Gow. C. Two roses in a glass.	1,050
1952	Gabriel Cognacq, Paris. Portrait of a young girl.	11,835
	Pelouse a Longchamps.	8,825
1952	Felix Wildenstein. New York. Jeanine Martin (pastel).	10,000
1955	Parke-Bernet, New York. Beach at low tide.	4,820
	Four oranges, $7\frac{1}{2}$ ins. $\times 9\frac{1}{2}$ ins.	5,200
1957	Weinberg. S. Bullock in a meadow.	11,000
1958	Jacob Goldschmidt. S. La promenade (see 1921).	89,000
	Self-portrait with palette.	65,000
	Rue Mosnier aux drapeaux (see 1898).	113,000*
1958	Arnold Kirkeby. New York. Girl in a garden.	14,000
1959	National Gallery values the pictures which Sir Hugh Lane bought for less than a thousand each in 1909–1912.	
	Eva Gonzalez at an easel.	150,000
	Musique aux Tuileries.	200,000

ANDREA MANTEGNA. 1431–1506

Small paintings and therefore, though no one doubted Mantegna's significance, idiotically underpriced. *The Agony in the Garden* reached the National Gallery within the memory of man for £1,500. It could not be worth less than a quarter of a million to-day, probably half a million.

		£
1795	Sir Joshua Reynolds. C. 2 attributed paintings of The Agony in the Garden at £5 each. It is probable that one of them was Beckford's Giovanni Bellini, now in the National Gallery. It is possible that the second was the Mantegna version, also in the National Gallery, which was bought by Coningham at the 1845 Fesch sale.	
1845	Cardinal Fesch. Rome. The Agony in the Garden. About	300
1849	Coningham. C. Same picture, £420, resold in 1851 (see 1894).	252 10*s.*
	The Holy women at the Sepulchre (left to National Gallery in 1892 by Lord Taunton, but now considered a schoolpiece).	134 8*s.*
	The Resurrection (see 1881).	53 10*s.*
1855	National Gallery buys Holy Family enthroned from Roverselli, Florence.	1,125 10*s.*
1859	Earl of Northwick (Philips). 5 attributed pictures at 11 to 52 guineas.	
1860	National Gallery buys a schoolpiece from the Beaucousin Collection, Noli me tangere. About	300

		£
1873	National Gallery buys Triumph of Scipio, a long frieze in tempera on canvas, from Capt. Vyvyan.	1,500
1881	National Gallery buys a schoolpiece from Thibaudeau, Paris, The Resurrection (see 1849).	300
1882	Hamilton Palace. C. Tuccia and Sophonisba, 2 grisaille panels, bought by National Gallery.	1,785
	St. Stephen and St. George, small panels, not recognised as Mantegna, bought by J. E. Taylor, but not in his sale, 1912.	441
1883	National Gallery buys grisaille panel, Samson and Delilah, in a sale of Earl of Sunderland's drawings (for companion piece, see 1917).	2,362 10*s.*
1894	National Gallery buys The Agony in the Garden from the Earl of Northbrook, see 1795, 1845, 1849, 1851).	1,500
1903	The Weber (Berlin) Madonna bought from Dowdswell in London.	4,000
1912	J. E. Taylor. C. 2 small grisaille panels, Judith and Dido (Metropolitan Museum).	16,275
1912	Consul Weber, Berlin. Duveen buys Holy Family enthroned (see 1903). Now Metropolitan Museum.	29,500
1917	Earl of Pembroke, Wilton. 2 grisaille panels, Judith and Holofernes, sold to Joseph Widener, now National Gallery, Washington.	25,000 (?)
1931	Lord Barrymore. C. Small Holy Family.	1,950
1935	C. St. Jerome, small panel.	4,410

DRAWINGS

1893	R. S. Holford. S. Design for a chalice.	185
1896	Earl of Warwick. S. Design for a fountain.	165
1902	Sir T. Carmichael. C. Chalk drawing, man's head.	110 5*s.*
1936	S. Madonna and child, silverpoint.	520

THE MARIS FAMILY

Three Dutch brothers who were the best known of the so-called 'Dutch Barbizon school'. A powerful taste among Scottish industrialists in the 1890's and early 1900's and most formidably priced. The best to-day would seem to be Jacob Maris, who painted a number of straightforward landscapes and townscapes, and the least attractive Mathew Maris, whose family scenes have a banality all their own. Prices were paid equivalent to £20,000 to £42,000 in to-day's money. It is difficult in 1961 to perceive what the owners thought they were getting for all this money. On the other hand, those owners would have something lively to say if they could see the sort of art that fetches from £20,000 to £42,000 now.

JACOB MARIS. 1838–1898

		£
1883	Barlow. C. Canal scene.	367 10*s.*
1897	George James. C. Amsterdam.	1,155
1899	Patterson. C. Seaweed-gatherers.	1,415
1903	Hamilton Bruce. Rotterdam.	2,625
1909	Cuthbertson. C. View over a village.	3,150
1910	Alexander Young. C. Entry to the Zuider Zee (see 1924).	3,150
1913	McCulloch. C. Landscape with windmills (£880 in 1898).	6,930*
1918	Westmacott. C. Amsterdam.	3,780
1920	Glen Coates. C. Hulsdrecht.	1,942 10*s.*
1924	Ernest Ruffer. C. Entry to the Zuider Zee (see 1911 and 1932).	2,887 10*s.*
1927	Sir James Murray. C. The towpath.	1,837 10*s.*
1932	C. Entrance to the Zuider Zee (see 1910, 1924).	75 12*s.*
1935	Coates. C. Dutch town.	840
1944	C. The pet goat.	132 10*s.*
1959	National Gallery values Lane's Girl feeding a bird.	500

MATHEW MARIS. 1835–1917

		£
1903	Hamilton Bruce. C. He is coming.	1,995
1909	Sir J. C. Day. C. The four mills.	3,465
	Feeding chickens.	3,150
1910	Andrew Maxwell. L'Enfant couché.	5,145
	P. M. Inglis. Feeding ducks.	2,835
1918	P. G. B. Westmacott. C. The sisters.	6,510
1920	Glen Coates. C. The young cook.	3,360

WILLIAM MARIS. 1844–1910

		£
1910	Alexander Young. C. Scene near Dordrecht.	2,940
1911	Sir Charles Wakefield. Feeding calves.	3,202 10*s.*
1919	Drummond. C. Girl with a goat and kid.	3,780

BEN MARSHALL. 1766–1835

Completely forgotten between his own time and the late nineteenth century, Ben Marshall's pictures benefited from the indiscriminate boom in English sporting subjects in the 1920's and fell during the 1929–1933 slump, when this market collapsed. Since the end of the war, there has been a disposition to regard Marshall as a genuine painter and not a studio-prop for horsy snobs. This is much overdue.

		£
1812	Marshall charged a standard fee of 50 guineas.	
1891	C. 'The sportsman', portrait of J. C. Shaddick.	210 5*s.*
1907	C. Sportsman and pointer (see 1945).	126
1915	C. Barrington Price. Groom and hunter.	210
1920	C. 5 racing pictures, the dearest	525
1925	Lord Wollavington (sale at Gloucester). The Berkeley Hunt, 1800.	2,205
	Lord Aylwyn. C. Mr. Powlett and his hounds.	1,785
1926	Sale at Banbury. Mr. Fermor's hounds.	4,200
	C. Francis Astley and his harriers.	2,730
	Mares and foals.	3,045
1927	Campbell. S. General Sir H. F. Campbell with gun.	2,400
1929	C. Grimalkin, jockey and trainer.	3,255
1930	C. Priam, jockey and trainer (see 1902).	1,312 10*s.*
1942	Robinson and Fisher's. Gentleman Jackson (see 1951).	609
1943	C. Gentleman on grey hunter.	2,940
1945	C. Sportsman and pointer (see 1907).	2,520
1947	Late Tresham Gilbey. C. Thomas Hilton riding.	3,360
1948	Francis Bowes-Lyon. C. J. V. Grimsted and hounds.	2,310
1951	Hutchinson & Co. Sorcery, winner of the Oaks.	4,830
1955	Alfred Caspary, New York. Lord Jersey's Middleton.	2,232
1959	Mrs. Pritchard. C. Longwaist, owner and rider, 1825.	8,400*
	C. Anti-Gallican and rider.	5,040

JOHN MARTIN. 1789–1854

Martin's huge, gloomy engravings were costly productions which he could not sustain. It is little realised to-day that the paintings from which he made them were among the most fashionable works of the period. In the first quarter of the present century Martin's huge oil paintings and proportionately oversized gouaches were barely worth the price of their frames. To-day there is a small demand.

		£
1813	Royal Academy. Adam's first sight of Eve.	73 10*s.*
1816	British Institution. Joshua commanding the sun (see 1861).	205
1819	Fall of Babylon, bought by Thomas Hope (see 1917).	420
1821	Belshazzar's Feast, bought by British Institution with copyright (see 1857).	1,260
1823	Destruction of Herculaneum, bought by Duke of Buckingham (see 1848).	840

		£
1848	Duke of Buckingham. Stowe. Same picture.	105
1857	Mackintosh. C. Belshazzar's Feast (see 1821).	142 10*s.*
1861	Charles Scarisbrick. C. Joshua commanding the sun.	472 10*s.*
	The Deluge.	157 10*s.*
	The Fall of Nineveh.	215 5*s.*
1869	National Gallery buys Destruction of Pompeii.	200
1913	Thomas Wollner. S. The burning of Troy, 38 ins. × 35 ins.	6
1917	Lord Francis Hope. Fall of Babylon (see 1819).	68 5*s.*
1945	The Great Day of his Wrath, bought by Tate Gallery.	100
1954	Denny. C. The destruction of Pharaoh's host, gouache.	147
1957	C. Valley of Desolation, gouache.	210
1959	C. The return to Paradise, over 6 ft.	199 10*s.*

HENRI MATISSE. 1869–1954

In the late 1950's works by Matisse were among the costlier prizes of the saleroom, yet even in the 1930's it was rare for them to make more than £1,000, while in 1919, when Matisse was fifty years of age, £250 was an exceptionally high fee. On the whole the struggles of the Post-Impressionist generation have been harder than those of the original Impressionists.

		£
1927	L'Atelier rouge, large mural decoration, sold in London.	800
1937	Hollender and Bernheimer. C. Ruisseau au village.	273
	Femme nue devant une fenêtre.	96 12*s.*
1940	Eumorphopoulos. C. Landscape (bought Alexander Korda).	105
1941	Horace Harding, New York. Nature morte.	2,600
1947	Parke-Bernet, New York. Bouquet of anemones.	1,225
1949	Von Sternberg, New York. Cucumbers, 15 ins. × 18 ins.	912
1954	Galerie Charpentier, Paris. La fenêtre ouverte.	4,795
	Bradley Campbell, New York. Au fauteuil	4,920
	Rees-Jeffreys. S. Portrait of Derain (bought by Tate Gallery) (£280 in 1928).	7,035
1955	Parke-Bernet, New York. Gorge du Loup.	3,130
1956	S. Plate of fruit.	4,200
1957	Galerie Charpentier, Paris. Le jabot bleu.	5,200
	Georges Lurcy, New York. Dans le boudoir, 13 ins. × 21 ins.	9,000
1958	Arnold Kirkeby, New York. Fleurs et ceramique.	23,215*
1960	S. Girl seated at window, 1921.	18,750
	C. The drawing lesson.	21,000
	Jacques Sarlie. S. Nude.	8,500
	Tate Gallery buys a huge nude woman. Grant-in-aid.	16,000

QUENTIN MATSYS. 1466–1530

A very freely-used name in the eighteenth and early nineteenth centuries for any late Gothic paintings of the North. Flemish primitives, so attributed, were considerably more expensive than Italian primitives.

		£	
1779	Houghton Hall. Empress Catherine buys The money-lender and his wife (Romerswael?).	200	
1808	Lord Burrell. C. 2 portraits in one frame.	215	
1855	Ralph Bernal. C. Portrait, Don Manuel de Menens.	52	10*s.*
1857	National Gallery buys 2 small panels from King of Holland, Christ and the Virgin.	137	12*s.*
1859	Earl of Northwick. (Philips). Youth reading a letter.	42	
1863	Robert Craig. The artist and his wife, a pair.	90	6*s.*
1880	George Smith. C. Head of the Virgin.	160	13*s.*
	Portrait of an old woman.	162	15*s.*
1886	Ridway. C. Youth reading a letter (see 1859).	115	19*s.*
	William Graham. C. Heads of Jews and soldiers (fragment, sold in 1922 and 1936 as Memling, *q.v.*).	157	10*s.*
1889	Secretan, Paris. Portrait, Bishop Gardner. From Fonthill. Bought as a Holbein.	1,200	
1904	Wickham Flower. C. Holy Family.	1,260	
1907	Massey Mainwaring. C. Alleged portrait, Louis XI.	630	
1918	Linnell. C. Holy Family with saints (National Gallery, 1922).	1,260	
1920	Miss Seymour. C. The Ugly Duchess.	924	
1923	Robinson and Fisher. Small Holy Family.	1,217	10*s.*
1924	Thomas Bodkin. C. Pieta (National Gallery, Toronto).	4,095	
	Sneyd. C. Holy Family enthroned.	4,095	
1927	C. A philosopher, small panel.	735	
1930	Lord Scarsdale. C. Head of the Virgin.	945	

ERNEST MEISSONIER. 1815–1891

In terms of real values, it is certain that no painter has ever seen his work fetch as much in his own lifetime as Meissonier. For, though *Friedland* in its two versions was far surpassed by two of Millet's pictures, Millet himself did not live to see this happen. The version of *Friedland* which was sold in New York in Meissonier's lifetime made the modern equivalent of at least £80,000; the version sold a few months after his death about £125,000.

It was a homage paid to pure dexterity and to the most exact copying of Nature that was conceivable. Just a hundred years previously collectors had succumbed to the same passion by paying the highest prices of the age for the miniature *genre* pictures of Gerard Dou. It appears to be a recurrent symptom, but this is not a tip for the much-discussed year 1984.

		£
1851	Thevenin, Paris. Soldiers throwing dice.	521
1857	Richard Wallace, Paris. Arquebusier (Wallace Collection).	292
1865	Duc de Morny, Paris. Halt before the inn (Wallace Collection).	1,440
	The bravi.	1,148
1869	French Gallery, London. Ruskin buys 'Napoleon in 1814', newly painted, 12 ins. × 9 ins.	1,050
	Delessert, Paris. Les Amateurs.	1,600
1870	Lord Hertford buys Napoleon and his staff (Wallace Collection).	1,302
1876	Taylor, New York. The Maréchale de Saxe and his staff.	2,300
1877	Oppenheim, Paris. The sergeant.	4,000
	Innocence and mischief.	3,520
	George Fox. C. The standard-bearer (see 1900).	777
1880	Kurtz. C. The commercial traveller.	1,312
1881	J. Waterloo Wilson, Paris. Cavalry halting.	5,000
1882	John Ruskin. C. Napoleon in 1814 (see 1869).	6,090
1887	Stewart, New York. Cornelius Vanderbilt buys 'Friedland'.	13,500
1888	Bolckow. C. Refreshment.	2,068 10*s.*
1889	Secrétan, Paris. 17 pictures by Meissonier, Cuirassiers de 1805, bought by Duc d'Aumale.	7,600
1890	Bolckow. C. The Signpainter (paid £8,400).	6,672
	Porto-Riche, Paris. '1814' (see 1927).	5,240
1892	J. Murrieta, London (Marquis de Santurce), sells to Jean Balli a second version of Vanderbilt's huge water-colour, 'Friedland'. It was recalled at the 1913 Balli sale (*q.v.*) that the price had been	20,700*
1892	Crabbe, Paris. Le guide (see 1920).	7,080
	James Pryce. C. L'Atelier de Regnault (see 1914).	1,890
1893	Vente Meissonier, Paris. The etcher.	10,880
1897	'1814', monochrome version. Paris.	3,800
1900	Mrs. Bloomfield Moore. C. The standard-bearer (see 1877).	2,625
1903	Gambart. C. A noble Venetian.	1,453 10*s.*
	Advance guard of an army (see 1930).	535 10*s.*
1913	Jean Balli, Paris. Friedland (see 1892).	6,300
1914	Coates. C. L'Atelier de Regnault (see 1892).	861
1920	C. The guide (see 1892).	5,250
1927	Miss Dennison. C. '1814' (see 1890), bought Lord Camrose.	1,470
	Recit du siège de Bergue op zoom, miniature, 2 ins. across.	315
1930	Samson. C. Advance guard of an army (see 1903).	67 4*s.*
1940	C. Cavalier taking refreshment (6 ins. × 7 ins.).	105

		£
1944	Sir A. Bird (at Solihull). Miniature painting, Gentleman taking snuff.	105
1945	Late Cornelius Vanderbilt, New York. The painter at his easel.	810
1950	Frederick Harris, New York. Arrival at the châteux. (ex Vanderbilt sale).	965
1956	Parke-Bernet, New York. Brigadier de Cuirassiers, oil sketch.	285
1957	Parke-Bernet, New York. En vedette (£545 in 1893).	500

HANS MEMLING. 1430–1494

The name of Hans Memling was used very freely in nineteenth-century attributions. For instance, not one of the eleven Memlings of the King of Holland's sale of 1850 is accepted in the modern canon. A number of moderately priced Flemish primitive pictures have been sold in the present century which are probably no more than schoolpieces, but at least they are in Memling's style.

		£
1823	Fonthill, ex Beckford. Virgin, child and apple, sold as Van Eyck.	74 12*s.*
1830	Sir Thomas Lawrence. C. The death of the Virgin.	74 12*s.*
1838	Zachary. C. Same picture.	84
1850	King of Holland. Amsterdam. 11 pictures (attributed), 2 scenes from the Life of St. Bertin. (Simon Marmion). each	958
	Altar of Charles V.	500
1855	Ralph Bernal. C. Holy Family with missal.	95 11*s.*
1856	Samuel Rogers. C. So called self-portrait (National Gallery, 1876, thought to be by Dirk Bouts).	90 6*s.*
1862	National Gallery buys Holy Family enthroned. Weyer sale, Cologne.	759
1865	National Gallery buys 2 small panels, St. John and St. Lawrence, from Sano, Paris.	480
1872	W. Middleton. C. Triptych with Crucifixion and donors.	910
1874	Alexander Barker. C. Holy Family and saints.	1,365
1892	Frank Leyland. C. Holy Family enthroned.	929
1893	Lord Revelstoke. C. Small Madonna.	1,155
1902	J. L. Propert. C. Very small Madonna and child.	1,134
1912	J. E. Taylor. C. Young man with a letter (see 1945).	3,990
1917	C. Drawing of a youth.	682 10*s.*
1922	Ralph Brocklebank. C. Fragment, Heads of Romans and Jews (sold 1886 as Quentin Matsys, *q.v.*), see 1936.	1,470
1924	Duke of Westminster. C. Holy Family enthroned.	1,837 10*s.*
1924	Melbourne National Gallery buys the Man of Sorrows.	12,500

		£
1925	Earl of Darnley. C. A donor praying, small panel.	1,575
1929	S. Holy Family in church interior, triptych.	1,500
1936	C. Fragment, Romans and Jews (see 1922).	357
1937	Leonard Gow. C. Small Annunciation, triptych.	1,522 10*s.*
1938	Mortimer Schiff. C. Holy Family.	6,510
1939	Anderson's, New York. Descent from the Cross, triptych, formerly R. von Kaufmann, Berlin.	17,130
1945	Parke-Bernet, New York. Young man with a letter (see 1912).	5,403
1955	Leopold Goldschmidt Collection, Paris. Samuel Kress Foundation buys Holy Family and Donors, altarpiece (National Gallery, Washington). about	88,000
1956	S. The two St. Johns, small attributed panel.	1,700

GABRIEL METSU. 1615–1661

That very pretty picture, *The Music Lesson* of the National Gallery, was already a quite expensive work in 1783. But it is astonishing how little Metsu has advanced since the nineteenth century. *La Collation*, for instance, hardly more than doubled its price between 1889 and 1953. The 2 Vermeers, which were cheaper pictures than *La Collation* in the 1889 sale, would to-day be worth two or three hundred thousand pounds each. Metsu was in fact a good painter of the second rank, but how many others have fared much better.

		£
1776	Blondel de Gagny, Paris. Vegetable market, Amsterdam (resold to Louis XVI in 1783 for £722 and now in the Louvre).	1,073
1783	Blondel d'Azincourt, Paris. The Music Lesson (see 1798).	750
1790	C. (One of the first émigré sales.) Traveller at an inn.	210
1798	Bryan. C. The music lesson (see 1783) (1871, National Gallery).	157 10*s.*
1801	Robit, Paris. Lady washing her hands (bought Bryan).	318
	Le corset bleu (bought Hibbert) (see 1829).	340 10*s.*
1817	Talleyrand. C. The duet (see 1840).	525
1829	George Hibbert. C. Le corset bleu.	567
1840	Simon Clarke. C. Le corset rouge.	535 15*s.*
	The duet (bought Robert Peel, now National Gallery).	472 5*s.*
1846	Higginson. C. Woman cleaning fish (see 1937).	504
1861	Scarsbrick. C. Lady with a spaniel.	273
1865	Duc de Morny, Paris. Visite à l'accouchée.	2,000
	Lady with dog.	2,360
1868	San Donato, Paris. La visite.	2,040

		£
1889	Secrétan, Paris. La collation (see 1953).	3,200
	Interior with figures.	2,580
1894	Adrian Hope. C. Lady with a spaniel, small.	1,260
1905	C. Page pouring water at table.	1,942 10*s.*
1913	Steengracht, Paris. The sick child.	14,530*
1925	Earl of Carnarvon. C. Lady drawing a bust.	2,205
1937	Victor Rothschild. S. Woman cleaning fish (see 1846).	2,800
	Lady in white satin with a spaniel (see 1960).	1,350
1950	Col. H. S. Clowes. C. Girl with a mirror.	4,200
1953	Earl of Iveagh. C. The breakfast (see 1889).	7,350
1960	S. Lady with a spaniel (see 1937).	5,000

MICHELANGELO BUONAROTTI. 1475–1564

No certain easel picture has appeared on the market, because it is not certain that Michelangelo painted any. With the drawings it is a different matter. It is interesting to speculate on the price which the British Museum would have to pay to-day for the £600 study for *Adam* of 1926. Should one multiply by 25 or by 50?

		£
1795	Sir Joshua Reynolds. C. Leda and the swan (left to the National Gallery in 1838 and thought to-day to be a copy by Rosso of a lost work). Bought by Lord Berwick.	73 10*s.*
1798	Orleans Exhibition. Holy Family. Bought by Thomas Hope (see 1844).	420
1822	Sir George Beaumont buys in Florence the bas-relief of the Holy Family, presented to the Royal Academy by his heirs in 1830.	1,500
1844	Mrs. Bonar declines £250 from the National Gallery for the Orleans Holy Family, now ascribed to Ghirlandajo (see 1870). Sold to Lord Taunton.	420
1868	National Gallery buys The Entombment, from Macpherson, stolen from the Cardinal Fesch Gallery before 1839 and discovered in a street market in Rome in 1846.	2,000
1870	National Gallery buys the Holy Family (see 1844) from Lord Taunton's executors.	2,000
1960	S. Temptation of St. Anthony, attributed tentatively as a painting made at the age of 13 after an engraving by Martin Schoengauer.	13,000

DRAWINGS

1837 Samuel Woodburn's Exhibition of Lawrence's drawings, 150 alleged Michelangelo drawings dispersed.

		£
1850	King of Holland, Amsterdam. Lawrence's drawings.	
	Death of Phaeton, pen and ink.	75 17*s.*
	Last Judgement, study.	64 2*s.*
	Resurrection, figures.	62 10*s.*
1886	Marquess of Breadalbane. C. David and Goliath, sheet of 4 studies.	205
1896	Earl of Warwick. S. Study in chalk for a Pieta.	1,400
1902	Sir J. C. Robinson. Pieta, pen and ink.	588
1926	British Museum buys a study for The Creation of Adam.	600
1936	Henry Oppenheimer. C. A sheet of studies.	3,570

FRANS VAN MIERIS the elder. 1635–1681

The works of the Mieris family were very much in the finicky French late eighteenth-century taste. They have scarcely fetched more in modern times, unless they have turned out to be unrecognised Vermeers.

		£
1765	London. Man at a window (see 1946).	99 15*s.*
1768	Gaignat, Paris. Le corset rouge (see 1840).	124
1771	Braamkamp. Amsterdam. The Letter.	300
1804	Van Leyden, The Hague. The Pearl Stringer (Windsor).	480
1811	Same picture. Bought by the Prince Regent at Lafontaine's sale, Christie's.	1,050
1817	Talleyrand. C. L'enfileuse de perles.	880
1840	Robert Peel buys Le corset rouge (see 1768), National Gallery since 1871.	320 10*s.*
1841	Perregaux, Paris. The musician.	884
1846	Duval (Philips). The painter and his wife.	945
1857	Patureau, Paris. Interior and figures.	788
1875	Miss Bredel. C. The enamoured cavalier.	4,300*
1892	Earl of Dudley. C. Same picture.	3,570
1937	Lewis Lloyd. C. The violinist.	1,575
	Leonard Gow. C. Man in contemplation.	1,176
1946	Duke of Buccleuch. C. Man at a window (see 1765).	210
1950	Ethel Floersheim. C. A dish of oysters.	441
1957	S. The music lesson.	800
1960	Gallerie Charpentier, Paris. La coquette.	805

WILLEM VAN MIERIS the younger. 1662–1747

		£
1772	Choiseul, Paris. The fisherman.	112
1802	Countess of Holderness. C. The Raree-show.	220 10*s.*
1804	Simon Clarke. C. The cat.	371 14*s.*

		£
1817	Tuffen. C. Interior with figures.	346 10s.
1827	Robert Peel buys the same picture (National Gallery, 1871).	388 10s.
1857	Comte Vidan, Paris. La bonne mère.	492
1868	Rhodes, Paris. Same picture.	816
1875	Rev. John Lucy. C. The grocer's shop.	787 10s.
1892	The Earl of Dudley. C. Same picture.	766 10s.
1895	Henry Doetsch. C. Officer at a window, 1701.	8 19s.
1899	J. Mieville. C. Woman at a spinning wheel.	714
1910	J. E. Fordham. Poulterer's shop.	147
1946	J. Walter. S. Apothecary's shop.	1,080
1955	S. The itinerant showman.	1,200

SIR JOHN MILLAIS. 1827–1896

In spite of his tremendous popularity in the 1880's, Millais was not able to see his pictures rival the posthumous saleroom triumphs of those of Landseer. It is unlikely that he was paid more than 5,000 guineas for even his 'Christmas supplement pictures', but he worked hard and he produced them fast. The modern revaluations are interesting. In 1886, at the extreme height of Millais's popularity, his boyhood work *Christ in the House of His Parents* (the Carpenter's Shop) made only £892 10s. In 1922 it cost the nation £10,500. The determination to like only the Pre-Raphaelite Millais appeared even more strongly in 1946 when the works commissioned by Miller of Preston came under the hammer. *Peace Concluded*, for which Miller had paid £945 in 1856, fell to half that figure, whereas the Pre-Raphaelite *Huguenot*, commissioned in 1852 for £300, rose to £2,100. This seems likely to be the pattern for some time.

		£
1849	Plint buys Christ in the House of His Parents (see 1862, 1878, 1886, 1922 (£10,500).	150
1853	Arden buys The order of release (see 1898).	400
1855	Arden buys The rescue (see 1879).	580
1858	Sir Isumbras at the ford, commissioned by Gambart (see 1912 and 1887).	800
1859	Lord de Grey buys The love of James I of Scotland (see 1917).	1,050
1862	Plint. C. The black Brunswicker (see 1901).	819
	Christ in the House of His Parents (see 1849).	525
	The Royalist (see 1897).	551
1873	John Hargreaves. C. Awake (see 1923).	1,417
1875	Sam Mendel. C. Jephthah's daughter (bought 1867, £4,200, see 1910, 1917).	3,990
	Chill October (bought 1871, £1,000, see 1910).	3,255

		£
1876	Armstrong. C. Hearts are trumps (commissioned 1872, 2,000 guineas, see 1944).	1,365
1877	Baron Grant. C. 4 landscapes at over £1,000 each. Scotch firs.	1,837 10s.
1879	Joseph Arden. C. The rescue (see 1855).	1,312
	The order of release (see 1898).	2,835
1880	E. J. Colman. C. The princes in the tower (Holloway College).	3,990
1883	Dunlop. C. Isabella and Lorenzo (£100 in 1849) (Walker Art Gallery).	1,102 10s.
	Mariana and the moated grange (£150 in 1851).	850 10s.
1886	William Graham. C. The vale of rest (£735 in 1859).	3,465
1887	Kaye Knowles. Over the hills and far away (1876).	5,250
	Sir Isumbras at the ford (see 1858).	1,365
1888	Bolckow. C. The North West Passage (commissioned at £4,930). Now Tate Gallery.	4,200
1892	Coghill. C. Sound of many waters (landscape).	3,045
	Leyland. C. Eve of St. Agnes (see 1942).	2,205
1893	Brocklebank. C. Victory, O Lord.	1,260
1895	Chantrey Bequest buys 'Speak, speak'.	2,000
1897	Plender. C. The proscribed Royalist.	2,100
1898	James Ruston. The order of release (see 1879).	5,250
1900	Reiss. C. The boyhood of Raleigh.	5,250
	Both bought for the Nation by Lady Tate.	
1901	Brassey. C. The black Brunswicker (see 1862) (Lever Art Gallery).	2,782
	'No', 1870 (see 1933).	1,470
1908	Sound of many waters (see 1892).	1,155
	Ismay. C. Murthly Water (£1,572 10s. in 1891).	336
1909	Sir Cuthbert Quilter. C. Murthly Moss (landscape bought from Millais, 1887, £2,000), see 1954.	3,150
1910	Armstrong Heirlooms. C. Chill October (see 1875).	5,040
	Jephthah's daughter (see 1867, 1875).	1,217 10s.
1913	Lord Holden. C. The Bride of Lammermoor (see 1927).	1,597
	George McCulloch. C. Sir Isumbras (see 1858, 1887) (highest price ever bid at auction), bought for Lever Art Gallery, £9,000.	8,190
1915	Wigan. C. An idyll of 1745 (said to have been commissioned at £4,000 in 1885).	1,050
1917	Churchill. C. Love of James I of Scotland (see 1859).	714
	Fairfax Murray. C. Melbourne National Gallery buys The rescue (see 1879).	1,417 10s.
	Jephthah's daughter (National Museum, Wales), see 1910, etc.	1,050

		£
1920	T. Clarke. C. Apple blossoms (£695 in 1922) (Lever Art Gallery).	1,995
1922	Late Mrs. Beer. Tate Gallery buys Christ in the House of His Parents (see 1849, 1883).	10,500*
1923	Cremetti. C. Just awake (see 1873) (see 1929).	451 10s.
	Eve of St. Agnes (see 1892, 1942).	1,575
1926	Shaw. C. Asleep (£1,470 in 1890).	840
1927	C. The Bride of Lammermoor (see 1913 and 1945).	399
1928	S. Murthly Water, landscape (see 1892 and 1930).	250
1929	C. Just awake (see 1923).	525
1930	Barnet Lewis. C. Study for 'The proscribed Royalist' (see 1939).	168
	Samson. C. Murthly Water (see 1892, 1928).	472 10s.
1933	Mitchell. C. 'No' (see 1901).	262 10s.
1935	S. Murthly Water (see 1930, etc.).	685
1939	Sir Edmund Davis. S. Study for The proscribed Royalist (see 1930).	54
1942	Sir Edmund Davis. C. (At Chilham Castle). Eve of St. Agnes (see 1923).	630
1944	Chantrey Bequest buys 'Hearts are trumps' (see 1876).	1,050
	C. 'Yes' (£1,050 in Renton sale. C. 1878).	44
1945	Vanderbilt, New York. The Bride of Lammermoor (see 1913, 1927).	143 10s.
1946	Pitt-Miller. C. The Huguenot (commissioned 1852 at £300).	2,100
	Peace concluded (£945 in 1856).	462
	C. Flowing to the river, landscape (£1,165 10s. in 1880).	14 14s.
1954	Sir Kenneth Clark. C. Murthly Moss (6-ft. landscape) (see 1909, £3,150).	157
1956	Parke-Bernet, New York. Pomona (small girl with apple barrow, 1882, when it cost £2,000).	250
1958	The Lever Art Gallery. C. The violet's message (small picture, £100 in 1852).	840

JEAN FRANÇOIS MILLET. 1814–1875

The king of the great boom in modern painting in the 1880's and the creator of the most costly modern picture ever sold in terms of real money. Yet he died poor and unappreciated within less than a generation of these triumphs. A true painter despite all the hou-ha.

		£
1859	The Angelus (see 1881, 1889), sold for	72
1873	Paris. La femme à la lampe (see 1911).	1,540
1875	A few months before Millet's death, unfulfilled commission for 8 paintings in the Pantheon.	2,000

		£
1876	Vente Millet, Paris. Le tueur de cochons (see 1910).	960
1881	Waterloo Wilson, Paris. L'Angelus (see 1859).	6,400
	Pâturages a Greville.	2,000
1886	Defoer, Paris. The man with a hoe.	2,280
1888	Paris. Les glaneurs (Louvre).	2,080
1889	Secrétan, Paris. L'Angelus (see 1881), bid up by Gauchez for the Louvre against Knoedler.	22,120
	Sale disowned. Subsequently bought by Chauchard and left to the Louvre.	32,000
1890	Chauchard negotiates with Secretan's executors for La Bergère (Louvre). Price according to Maurice Rheims, 1,200,000 francs.	48,000*
1890	Senez. New York. L'Attente.	8,000
1894	Garnier, Paris. La Herse.	3,000
1898	Dana, New York. The turkey keeper.	4,100
1909	Sir J. C. Day. C. The goose maiden, 12 ins. × 9 ins.	5,250
1910	Yerkes, New York. Killing the pig (see 1876).	8,200
1911	La femme à la lampe, reported to have been bought in Holland for H. C. Frick (see 1873).	31,000
1912	Stephens. C. Oedipus taken from the tree, small early work (£441 in 1910), see 1914.	2,450
1914	Coates. C. Guardienne du troupeau (see 1949).	5,880
	Sir James Ross reported to have paid for Oedipus taken from the tree (see 1912).	12,000
1923	Ernest Ruffer. C. Le coup de vent.	1,890
1927	S. N. A. Coates. C. Sleeping nymph and fawn.	651
1929	Hollingsworth. C. L'amour vainqueur (early work).	651
1934	Anderson's, New York. The knitting lesson (see 1945).	3,200
1937	Leonard Gow. C. Le briquet (pastel).	283 10*s*.
1945	Thanhouser, New York. La Fileuse, 15½ ins. × 11½ ins.	1,695
1945	Cornelius Vanderbilt, New York. Return from the well, 1862.	7,500
	The sower, 1850.	6,500
	The knitting lesson (see 1934).	3,125
	La Bergère (see 1956).	2,750
1949	Parke-Bernet, New York. Guardienne du troupeau (see 1914).	965
1956	Parke-Bernet, New York. La Bergère, small pastel version (see 1945).	1,071 10*s*.
1959	Count Zamoyski. S. The woman of Canaan (landscape).	800

AMADEO MODIGLIANI. 1884–1920

I remember M. Zborowski's little room about the year 1922; portrait-heads at £15 to £20, half-length sitters at £50 or £60 and two or three life-sized odalisques, unframed, on the floor at an ambitious £80 each. The stock of the dead painter might have been valued at about £1,000 and to-day it might be worth half a million.

No modern painter's works have advanced as fast, but the reason can be sought in a word, dreaded by modern painters and never mentioned except in contempt by their propagandists: beauty.

At the eve of the Second World War prices as high as £800 had been paid. £500 was more usual for a portrait.

		£
1939	Gallerie Druet, Paris (Salle Drouot). Nu blond.	560
1940	Eumorphopoulos. S. Female portrait.	530
1946	Paris, Salle Drouot. Mme. Zborowski, half-length.	480
1946	Parke-Bernet, New York. Portrait of a woman.	829
1947	At Parke-Bernet, New York. Elena, small head, 1917.	560
1948	At Parke-Bernet, New York. Head of a young girl.	820
1949	At Parke-Bernet, New York. Le grand Nu (nearly 4 ft.).	4,460
1951	Kende Galleries, New York. Same picture.	530
1954	Arthur Campbell, New York. Raimondo, small head.	5,450
1956	At Parke-Bernet, New York. Mme. Hebuterne, small head	3,750
1958	At Parke-Bernet, New York. Another version.	4,100
1958	At Amsterdam. Mme. Czekowska, half-length.	22,000
1958	Parke-Bernet, New York. Half-length male portrait (Collection of Edward B. Robinson).	23,600
	Portrait Mme. Aynaud-Vaillant.	23,250
1959	Portrait of Mme. Hebuterne (small).	11,000
	Portrait of Beatrice Hastings.	12,000
1960	S. Head of Leopold Zborowski.	8,500
	Portrait of a sculptor in a blue shirt.	38,000*
	Girl's head (bought 1926 for under £100).	24,000
	Portrait of a boy.	21,000
1960	C. Girl's head.	10,500
	Small portrait, bought in.	4,400
1960	New York. Gladys Lloyd Robinson. Boy in a green shirt	20,540

DRAWINGS

1954	Gerald Reitlinger. S. Sculptural figure, coloured chalks.	350
1956	Roderick O'Connor, Paris. Caryatide rose, gouache.	2,084
1957	Parke-Bernet, New York. Caryatid, tempera and gouache.	1,486
1960	S. Caryatid figure, green gouache.	2,200
	Rewald. S. Portrait head.	1,000

CLAUDE MONET. 1840–1926

At the end of the nineteenth century, Monet's work rated as high as Manet's and Renoir's and a great deal higher than Degas's. To-day Monet is only a poor fourth on the list. These changes in preference are not easy to account for, except that in a popular market, as opposed to the market of a few rare spirits, Renoir appeals more because his charm is more obvious and Manet because his outlook is more traditional.

		£
1873	Paris. Nature morte.	31 5*s.*
1887	Bonvin. Paris. Le printemps.	72
1890	Paris. Jardin des Tuileries.	84
1892	Michel Levy, Paris. Seine à Rouen.	364
	Arthur Studd (London) buys 'Haystacks'.	200
1894	Mrs. Potter Palmer, Chicago, buys Argenteuil.	310
	Theodore Duret, Paris. Les dindons.	480
1897	Paris. Pont d'Argenteuil.	860
1898	Goupy. Paris. Au jardin.	880
1900	Bonner. New York. 3 views of Rouen Cathedral.	620
		600
		560
1905	Durand-Ruel, London. Hugh Lane buys Vetheuil, effet de neige (National Gallery).	700
1906	Lord Grimthorpe. C. Le phare de l'hospice.	204 15*s.*
1910	Andrew Maxwell. C. Effet de neige.	504
1919	Sir George Drummond. C. Poppy field.	1,312
1920	American Art Association, New York. La Tamise à Londres.	2,900
	Mrs. Charles Hunter. C. Island of San Giorgio, Venice.	630
1924	Courtauld Fund for Tate Gallery. Plage à Trouville.	650
1925	John Singer Sargent. C. Bordighera.	882
1926	Presented to Tate Gallery. Les peupliers.	900
	Dame, assise dans un parc.	525
1927	Sir James Murray. C. Falaises à Fécamp.	1,522 10*s.*
1936	National Gallery, Melbourne, buys Vetheuil, 1878.	1,546
1940	Harcourt Johnstone. S. View in Hyde Park.	640
1944	S. Cliffs at Pourville.	340
1946	Van Horne, New York. The Seine at Bougival.	2,763
1948	Parke-Bernet, New York. Islot à Port Villiers.	2,070
1950	Salle Drouot. Paris. Bridge on the Thames.	684
1957	Galerie Charpentier, Paris. Giverny, 1894.	8,200
	Antibes, 1887.	17,500
	Inondation.	8,300
1957	Weinberg. S. Blue house at Zaandam.	22,000
	Rochers de Belle Isle.	6,000

		£
1958	Parke-Bernet, New York. Monet's child in a cradle.	30,250*
1958	Galerie Charpentier, Paris. Fishing boats, Etretat.	12,120
1959	S. Bassein de Nymphéas à Giverny.	13,000
	Church at Pourville under snow.	14,000
	Venice, 1908.	12,000
1959	National Gallery values Hugh Lane's Snow landscape (£700 in 1905).	15,000
1960	L. N. Villiers. S. Nymphèas à Giverny.	18,000
	Margaret S. Davies. S. Grand Canal, Venice.	19,500
1960	C. Water garden, Giverny.	19,950
1960	Parke-Bernet, New York. Houses of Parliament, 1904.	15,000

ANTONIS MOR
(Sir Anthony More). 1512–1576

A Dutchman, pupil of a Fleming who painted like an Italian, almost like Moroni. His name has been taken much in vain and some of these portraits may not be his own, but in 1926 his *Elizabeth of Valois* made the price of a Holbein, which it was thought to be. Before the 1850's Mor's fine English portraits were almost worthless. They became very costly during the English-portrait boom of the 1920's, but, like Van Dyck, Mor shared the decline of this market.

		£
1810	Campion. Portrait, Sir Thomas Gresham, now National Portrait Gallery (see 1922).	99 15*s.*
1823	Fonthill, ex Beckford. Jeanne d'Archel (see 1858).	17 17*s.*
1842	Waldegrave, Strawberry Hill (Robins). 4 portraits. Thomas Howard, Duke of Norfolk.	42
1855	Ralph Bernal. C. 4 portraits. Elizabeth of Valois (see 1926).	47 5*s.*
1858	National Gallery buys Jeanne d'Archel (see 1823).	200
1859	Earl of Northwick (Philips). 4 pictures. Charles Brandon, Duke of Suffolk.	90 6*s.*
	Resold in 1864. Brett sale. C.	136 10*s.*
1881	De Beurnonville, Paris. Man holding gloves (see 1957).	110
1885	De Zoete. C. Thomas, Lord Seymour.	157 10*s.*
1887	Whatman. C. National Gallery buys head of unknown bearded man.	237 10*s.*
1897	Cholmondeley. C. Elizabeth of Valois (see 1855, 1926).	556 10*s.*
1906	Lord Grimthorpe. C. Lady holding a chain, 1566.	462
1919	C. Edward, Duke of Somerset.	2,940
1922	Baroness Burdett-Coutts. C. Sir Thomas Gresham (see 1810).	630
1925	Earl of Darnley. C. Lady in red, alleged Mary Tudor.	4,410

		£
1926	Bischoffsheim. C. Elizabeth of Valois (see 1856, 1897, Collection of A. F. Philips).	11,025*
	Countess of Carlisle. S. Another Mary Tudor portrait.	5,000
1928	Holford. C. Emanuel Philibert, Duke of Savoy (see 1943).	4,095
1934	Leopold Hirsch. C. Marie de Guise, half-length.	892 10*s.*
1943	C. Duke of Savoy (see 1928).	577 10*s.*
1946	Parke-Bernet, New York. Ottavio Farnese, 1563.	1,231
1957	Scott-Taggart. S. Man holding gloves (see 1881).	1,300
1960	C. Nicolas Granvella.	1,890

GEORGE MORLAND. 1763–1804

This painter follows precisely the pattern of the eighteenth-century revival, though on a much smaller scale than Gainsborough or any of the fashionable portraitists. Morland discovered the Teniers formula, which was later used by Wilkie and his followers, but the artificial sentiment of his works made them unpopular until they were old enough to acquire a period charm. At the present moment Morland's pictures have by no means recovered the position which they held at the time of the sporting-picture boom of the 1920's.

		£
1790	The farmer's stable, commissioned by Macklin.	200
1791	Morland's own sale, numerous works, the dearest—A pig stye.	18 17*s.*
1807	Robert Wedd. C. Horsemen at an inn door.	173 5*s.*
1811	John Whigston. C. Wreck of an Indiaman.	199 10*s.*
1823	General Bloomfield (Philips). A stable.	141 15*s.*
1842	Henry Dobree. C. 9 pictures, 3 of them at over	200
1850	Meigh. C. Pigs in a fodder yard.	90 6*s.*
1863	G. H. Morland. C. Pottery-seller.	288 15*s.*
1871	Brooks. C. Sportsmen halting at an inn (bought in).	393 15*s.*
1873	Pulling. C. Fruits of early industry.	640 10*s.*
1876	Albert Levy. C. Postboys' return (see 1898, 1946).	630
1879	Anderdon. C. Quarry with peasants, bought by National Gallery.	42
1883	Tierney. C. The cottage door, and The press-gang, bought for Holloway College.	399
1886	Addington. C. Trepanning a recruit.	320 5*s.*
1888	H. W. Bolckow. C. Robbing an orchard.	798
1892	C. Cornish wreckers.	840
1895	C. F. Huth. Visit to a child at nurse.	1,102 10*s.*
1898	Robert Rankin. C. The postboys' return (see 1946).	1,312 10*s.*
1905	Louis Huth. C. Higglers preparing for market (see 1930).	2,100
	Lord Tweedmouth. C. Dancing dogs (see 1929).	4,200

		£
1907	Christopher Bushell. C. Happy cottagers.	2,940
1911	C. The public house door (see 1935).	1,785
1917	Beecham. C. Benevolent sportsmen.	5,460
1919	C. The Gypsies' tent.	3,255
1923	W. L. Agnew. C. The farmyard, 1792.	1,785
1928	Fleming. C. The turnpike gate.	3,570
1929	C. Dancing dogs (see 1905).	9,040
1930	Barnet Lewis. C. 29 pictures by Morland. Higglers preparing for market (see 1905). Bought for Tate Gallery.	6,825
	The deserter pardoned.	5,250
1934	Leopold Hirsch. C. Children bird-nesting.	2,940
	Juvenile navigators (see 1948).	2,835
1935	Solly Joel. The public house door (see 1911).	1,890
1946	Swaythling Heirlooms. The postboys' return (see 1876).	4,410
1948	Sir Bernard Eckstein. S. Boys bird-nesting } (see 1934).	5,100
	Juvenile navigators } (see 1934).	5,100
1951	Walter Hutchinson and Co. Same pictures, the pair.	10,920
1956	Parke-Bernet, New York. The Revenue cutter.	1,328
1960	Mrs. Gibson Fleming. S. Coast scene and smugglers.	1,800
	Another coast scene.	1,800
	Farmyard scene.	1,300

GIAMBATTISTA MORONI. 1525–1578

The relatively high prices paid by the National Gallery in the middle nineteenth century are puzzling, since this was the time when many fine Titians were lost to the nation at a few hundreds each. The appeal seems to have been that of a certain slickness and an easily recognisable style. Modern prices are not appreciably higher. The National Gallery owns not less than nine, all of them portraits.

		£
1800	Robert Fagan. Titian's Schoolmaster, bought by Lord Gower as a Titian. Sold by Duke of Sutherland to P. A. B. Widener, now in National Gallery, Washington.	630
1852	William Jones. C. Portrait inscribed Bartolommeo Bongo.	246 15*s.*
1862	National Gallery buys The Tailor in Bergamo.	320
1865	Pourtalés, Paris. National Gallery buys The Lawyer.	528 8*s.*
1876	National Gallery buys 3 large portraits from Baslini, probably members of the Fenaroli family of Brescia. The three	5,000
1882	Hamilton Palace. C. Small portrait head.	178 10*s.*
1890	National Gallery buys whole-length portrait of an Italian nobleman from Longford Castle, part of a block purchase. About	10,000
1905	Laurie & Co. C. Lady at a window.	1,050

		£
1911	Lady Abdy. C. Gentleman holding a book.	1,680
1923	Lord Wimborne. C. Nobleman in blue fur-lined coat.	525
1927	Holford. C. Gentleman in black, half-length.	1,470
1929	Lord Stalbridge. C. Nobleman in armour, 1563.	3,990
	Lord Yarborough. C. Gentleman in black, holding a pen.	1,575
	C. General Mario Benvenuto (Ringling Museum, Sarasota).	2,205

WILLIAM MULLER OF BRISTOL. 1812–1845

By no means the least attractive of the early nineteenth-century landscape painters who followed the Turner-Bonington formula, but to-day of very little value. In the 1930's big, fresh-looking landscapes which had fetched several hundreds each in the late nineteenth century could have been bought for £15–£20. Good examples rarely reach the saleroom nowadays, but they are doubtless in pickle.

		£
1846	Decease sale. Rock tombs of Lycia.	129 3*s.*
1850	Charles Meigh. C. Egyptian temple.	451 10*s.*
1854	C. On the Nile. Tombs of Ben Hassein.	913 10*s.*
1865	Knowles. C. The Slave Market (see 1868).	661 10*s.*
1866	Woodhouse. C. The Acropolis, 1843.	582 15*s.*
1868	Fallows. C. The Slave Market (see 1865).	1,344
1870	Bullock. C. Compton Dando, children sailing boat.	1,312
1872	Gillott. C. The chess-players.	3,202 10*s.*
1874	Heugh. C. Same picture (see 1890, 1931).	4,052*
1876	Albert Levy. The Slave Market (see 1868).	2,898
	Street in Cairo (see 1910).	1,092
1881	William Sharpe. C. Tomb in the water, Telmessus.	2,625
	Arab shepherds.	2,730
1883	Lee. C. Gillingham Church (see 1955).	1,018 10*s.*
1887	Bolckow. C. Tombs of Lycia (see 1846).	3,937 5*s.*
1891	Bolckow. C. The chess-players (see 1872, 1931).	3,202 10*s.*
1895	James Pryce. Carnarvon Castle (Tate Gallery purchase).	2,415
1903	C. Children with a bird trap.	1,680
1910	C. Street in Cairo (see 1876).	168
1913	Mundeford Allen. C. View of Bristol.	84
1927	Knight, Frank & Rutley. Gillingham, boy angling.	441 10*s.*
1931	Bristol City Gallery buys The chess players (£4,052 in 1874).	78 15*s.*
1955	C. Gillingham Church (see 1883).	58 16*s.*
1959	Dyson Perrins. S. Compton Dando, wc.	100
	Pontypool Mill, oil.	130

WILLIAM MULREADY. 1786–1863

It was Mulready, the Irishman, who gave Wilkie's romping peasants the decidedly nostalgic 'childhood memories' twist which dominated early Victorian painting and book illustration. Even kings like a good cry, and George IV bought *The Wolf and the Lamb* (not a bad picture either) when Mulready was thirty-four. He could make 1,000 guineas on a picture, and he lived to see more than that made by some of his pictures under the hammer. But in the 1870's Mulready's market was completely overshadowed by Landseer and the painters of the Turner-Bonington tradition.

		£
1809	According to Farington (*Diaries*, V, 172) the 23-year-old Mulready asked £315 for his Carpenter's shop (see 1954).	
1820	The wolf and the lamb, bought by the King.	525
1827	The cannon, bought by Sir Robert Peel.	500
1838	The convalescent from Waterloo. Bought by the Earl of Northwick (see 1859) (Victoria and Albert Museum).	714
1845	George Knott. C. The widow (see 1881).	420
1850	Charles Meigh. The careless messenger returned (see 1932).	136 10*s.*
1859	Earl of Northwick. (Philips). The convalescent from Waterloo (see 1838).	1,239
1861	Sir John Swinburn. C. Punch.	1,002 10*s.*
1864	Mulready executors. C. The toy-seller (last picture, painted 1862).	1,197
1872	Joseph Gillott. C. Changing horses.	651
1878	Fuller-Maitland. C. National Gallery buys Snow scene.	200
1881	Houldsworth. C. The widow (see 1845).	1,155
1886	MacConnell. C. Idle boys (see 1895).	1,585 10*s.*
1890	William Wells. C. A dog with two minds.	1,218
1893	Ralph Brocklebank. C. Train up a child.	1,386
1895	C. Idle boys (see 1886).	1,050
1900	Peel heirlooms. C. The cannon (see 1827).	1,302
1912	C. The sailing match.	162 15*s.*
1913	Southgate. C. The carpenter's shop (see 1809, 1954).	105
1929	S. A fair (3 ft.).	7
1932	Earl of Durham (at Lambton Castle). The careless messenger returned (see 1850).	10
1954	S. The carpenter's shop (see 1809).	50

ESTEBÁN MURILLO. 1617–1682

The vogue for the most baroque of the Spaniards reached England in the 1750's. There were two great boom periods—in the Napoleonic wars and in the 1830's-60's. To some extent Murillo shared the subsequent decline of his Italian contemporaries, but it must be realised that of the enormous number of Murillo religious subjects only a very few that have reached the salerooms show even traces of his own hand. The rarest things in the salerooms to-day are Murillo's realist paintings of peasant and gypsy life, and for these very high prices may be expected.

		£
1742	Carrignan, Paris. St. John.	115
1768	Gaignat, Paris. Virgin and sleeping child (now in Hermitage Museum, Leningrad).	730
1778	Late Duchess of Bridgewater. C. Good Shepherd (bought in) (see 1801).	619 10*s.*
1779	Houghton Hall. Empress Catherine buys Assumption of the Virgin. } Hermitage Museum	700
	Adoration of the shepherds. } Hermitage Museum	600
1786	Desenfans Exhibition. The flower girl (Dulwich Gallery).	900
1795	Calonne. C. Same picture bought back.	682 10*s.*
	Holy Family (see 1884).	536
1801	Sir Simon Clarke buys from Bryan The Good Shepherd.	2,100
	St. John the Baptist and saints (ex Robit sale, Paris, see 1840).	2,100
	George Hibbert buys Marriage feast of Cana (ex Robit sale, Paris, see 1829).	1,260
1811	Kinnaird buys Wallis's Virgin from Seville (later stolen). In Nemés Collection, 1910.	1,260
1813	Wallis sells the Cadiz Holy Family to Lord Berwick.	2,500
	Wallis sells Jacob and Laban to Lord Grosvenor (see 1859).	3,000
1825	Lord Berwick. C. Cadiz Holy Family (see 1837).	1,890
1829	George Hibbert. C. Marriage feast of Cana (see 1801).	913
1837	National Gallery buys Cadiz Holy Family (see 1813) from Bulkely Owen.	3,675
1840	Sir Simon Clarke. C. The Good Shepherd (see 1801). Bought by James Rothschild.	3,045
	St. John and the lamb (bought by Lord Ashburton and left to National Gallery).	2,100
1846	Higginson. C. Lord Hertford buys Adoration of the shepherds (Wallace Collection).	3,018 15*s.*
1850	King of Holland, Amsterdam. Assumption of the Virgin.	3,000
1852	William Wells. C. Lord Hertford buys Charity of St. Thomas Villanova.	2,992
	Paris. Marshal Soult executors. Immaculate Conception from Seville (bought by Louvre against Tsar of Russia).	24,600*
	St. Peter enchained (Hermitage Museum).	6,020
	Flight into Egypt (see 1845).	2,060
1853	Ex King Louis Philippe. C. 18 pictures. Vièrge à la ceinture.	1,550

		£
1853	Don Andreas da Andrada and his dog (Metropolitan Museum since 1927).	1,020
1857	Patureau, Paris. Louvre buys Virgin and sleeping child.	1,660
1859	Earl of Northwick. Jacob and Laban (see 1813).	1,480 10*s*.
1860	Sir Culling Eardley. C. Immaculate Conception (bought in). This was the highest sum ever bid at an English auction in 1860.	9,450
1865	Pourtalés, Paris. Faith presenting the Eucharist (see 1895).	2,700
1867	Earl of Dudley said to have paid for a peasant scene (see 1892).	3,400
1876	Wynn Ellis. C. Immaculate Conception from Peru, a poor copy said to have cost £4,200 in the 1860's.	430 10*s*.
1878	Monro of Novar. C. St. Anthony and the child Christ.	2,362
1882	Hamilton Palace. C. Infant Christ asleep. Bought for U.S.A.	2,415
1884	Miles of Leigh Court. C. Holy Family (see 1795).	3,150
1892	Earl of Dudley. C. St. Anthony and child Christ (see 1878 and 1957).	1,218
	Peasant figures (see 1867).	1,890
1895	Richard Foster. C. Holy Family (see 1916).	4,200
	Mrs. Lyne Stephens. Faith presenting the Eucharist (see 1865 and 1934).	2,467
1901	Sir H. H. Edwardes. C. Murillo's alleged self-portrait.	2,730
1909	Sir Cuthbert Quilter. C. Immaculate Conception (see 1944).	5,040
1913	Duke of Sutherland. C. St. Justin and St. Rufina, a pair (£241 10*s*. in 1876).	2,310
1914	W. L. Fletcher. C. Holy Family.	2,415
1916	C. Holy Family (see 1895).	6,510
1926	Duke of Portland. C. Holy Family and St. Rosalie.	2,100
1927	Count Pallavicini (Puttick's). Immaculate Conception.	4,000
1928	Holford. C. Gypsy girl baring her shoulder (from Thomas Baring, 1843, see 1956).	5,880
	Portrait of Duke of Medina Celi.	3,360
1933	George Prettyman. C. Christ healing the paralytic (bought ex Soult, 1846, £500, see 1950).	1,522 10*s*.
1934	Lord Faringdon. C. Faith presenting the Eucharist (see 1865, 1895).	840
1935	Earle-Drax. C. St. Francis Xavier (picture rolled up under the seat of Joseph Bonaparte's carriage at the Battle of Vittoria).	399 10*s*.
1937	Kingston House Trust. C. 3 huge canvases made	123 18*s*.
1938	C. 2 huge Immaculate Conception each	1,008
1944	Quilter. C. Immaculate Conception (see 1909).	525
1945	Sir Francis Fremantle. C. Flight into Egypt (see 1852).	3,360

		£
1947	Earl of Dudley, Himmley Hall sale. Virgin adoring child, small.	1,732 10s.
1950	Graham Robertson executors. National Gallery buys Christ healing the paralytic (see 1933).	8,000
1956	Goldschmidt. S. Gypsy girl baring her shoulder (see 1928).	25,000*
1957	Lord Carew. S. St. Peter enchained (replica of Hermitage picture, see 1852).	4,600
	Baerwald. S. St. Anthony adoring infant Christ (see 1892 and 1878).	3,600

PATRICK NASMYTH. 1786–1831

The first wave of English romantic landscape, deriving from Gainsborough and the Dutch school rather than from Claude and Turner. Comparable with James Ward and John Linnell. A short painting life which favoured Surrey and Sussex. Never one of the more costly English landscape painters, Nasmyth has kept his level (but in devalued pounds), probably because of the eighteenth-century flavour which he retained.

		£
1833	Archbutt. C. A view of Harrow.	25 4s.
1848	Sir T. Baring. C. In Hampshire.	210
1859	Earl of Northwick (Philips). Leigh Woods, gypsies (see 1891).	714
1866	Flatou. C. Bristol from Brandon Hill.	761 5s.
1868	James Fallow. C. View at Ringwood.	1,065 15s.
1870	Bullock. C. Boy fishing.	1,218
1872	Gillott. Firth of Forth.	1,123 10s.
1875	Mendel. C. Waterfall at Glen Shirah.	1,470
1887	John Graham. C. Same picture.	1,270 10s.
1891	Matthews. C. Leigh Woods (see 1859).	1,491
1892	David Price. C. View in Surrey, 1829 (see 1910).	2,625
1910	C. Leigh Woods (see 1891).	1,627 10s.
	View in Surrey (see 1892).	2,047 10s.
1913	C. Landscape with windmill.	546
1916	Barratt. C. Woody landscape.	756
1920	Holbrooke Gaskell. C. View near Tunbridge Wells.	1,050
1927	Mrs. L. Raphael. C. View near Haslemere.	2,206
1930	Barnet Lewis. C. Leigh Woods (see 1910).	756
1946	Swaythling heirlooms. C. View near Woburn.	1,207 10s.
1948	Sir Bernard Eckstein. S. Near East Grinstead, 1829.	820
1956	Parke-Bernet, New York. Leigh Woods (see 1910).	535
1960	S. Landscape near Clifton, 1828.	2,100

JEAN MARC NATTIER. 1685–1766

Immensely fashionable in the first quarter of this century. For general observations see entry, Lancret. The first entry is deceptive, since the whole of this school was practically valueless until the 1850's, while Nattier, being a portrait painter and nothing else, recovered even later.

Year	Sale		£
1817	Talleyrand, Paris. Duchesse de Chateauroux.		700
	Marquise de Flaves.		700
	Both bought in (see 1899).		
1855	Bernal. C. Marie Leczynska, 4-ft. portrait.		10 10*s.*
1862	Earl of Pembroke, Paris. Mme. Vallembras.		165 12*s.*
1872	Paris. 4 allegorical heads,	the set	2,082
1887	Lord Lonsdale. C. Mme. Victoire (see 1913).		409 10*s.*
1888	De Beurnonville, Paris. Mme. de Flesselles.		1,800
1890	Crabbe, Paris. Same portrait.		3,000
1892	Earl of Egremont. C. Lady as a water nymph.		1,123 10*s.*
1895	Mrs. Lyne Stephens. C. Lady on clouds with doves.		4,095
1899	Paris. Duchesse de Chateauroux and Mme. de Flaves (see 1817).		1,400
1903	Reginald Vaile. C. Comtesse de Neuburg.		4,725
	Lady with blue scarf.		3,255
1908	C. Marquise de Romilly.		2,940
1913	Lionel Philips. C. Marquise de Tournelle (see 1942).		4,055
	Marquise de Flavacourt.		4,830
	Lord Brooke, 1741 (see 1920).		3,360
	Murray Scott. C. Mme. Victoire (see 1887 and 1920).		2,205
1918	Vicomte de Curel, Paris. Portrait of Courvoisier.		4,400
1920	Asher Wertheimer. C. Lord Brooke (see 1913).		3,675
	Mme. Victoire (see 1913).		995
1926	Bischoffsheim. C. Duc de Ponthievre (bought Duveen).		12,075*
1929	Princess Paley. C. Lady in blue and white.		3,675
1936	Comtesse de Greffulhe. S. Portrait, Comtesse de Ventimille, bought in.		5,200
1942	Lockett. C. Marquise de Tournelle (see 1913).		585
1951	Stehli, New York. Marquise de Ligneris.		3,925
1957	Mae Rovensky, New York. Oval portrait of a lady.		5,350
1959	S. Portrait of Mme. Tocqué, 1741.		6,500
1960	Galliera, Paris. Louis XVI, bust portrait, 25 ins. × 32 ins.		4,223

SIR WILLIAM QUILLER ORCHARDSON. 1835–1910

A man who went through many phases without changing his scrappy, anaemic palette. The inventor of that forgotten monster, the 'problem picture', in modern dress. Once furiously sustained by regional patriotism.

		£
1868	Royal Academy. Shakespearean subject.	400
1877	Royal Academy. The Queen of swords.	1,050
1880	Chantrey Bequest buys Napoleon on the *Bellerophon* (Tate Gallery).	2,000
1895	C. The story of a life.	745 10*s.*
1908	Humphrey Roberts. C. Hard hit, 1879.	3,460
	Holland. C. Replica of Napoleon on *Bellerophon.*	1,680
1910	Octavus Coope. C. The duke's antechamber (see 1942 and 1960).	1,680
	C. The Queen of swords.	1,218
1913	McCulloch. C. Master Baby (National Gallery, Edinburgh.	4,620
	The young duke (see 1915).	4,620
1915	Blaikeslee Galleries, New York. The young duke.	1,900
1917	Churchill. C. The rivals.	1,890
1924	C. The gambler's wife.	315
1926	A. Shuttleworth. C. Glasgow Gallery buys the marriage de convenance.	1,239
1927	Sir James Murray. The Borgia.	924
	The lyric.	840
	Both bought by Dundee Art Gallery.	
1936	W. Quilter. C. The challenge.	178 10*s.*
1939	Sir Edmund Davis. C. Lady Orchardson, half-length.	252
1942	Lord Dovedale. S. The duke's antechamber (see 1910).	330
1954	Baroness Burton. C. Voltaire at the Duc de Sully's supper (National Gallery, Edinburgh).	294
1960	F. W. Reeves. C. The duke's antechamber (see 1910).	50 8*s.*

VAN OSTADE, ADRIAEN. 1610–1685
and
VAN OSTADE, ISAAC. 1621–1649

Two very distinct persons. Adriaen Van Ostade painted the Teniers-like scenes of drunken boors that the eighteenth century found so endearing, but which leave the present age somewhat cold. Isaac Van Ostade, a younger brother, who lived only twenty-eight years, painted rather frilly Italianising landscapes, such as Ibbetson, Wheatley, Morland and others tried to imitate. Most of the pictures which reach the saleroom to-day are by Adriaen Van Ostade and cost no more than they did a hundred years ago.

		£
1777	Randon de Boisset. Paris. Village scene.	600
1798	Bryan-Calonne sale (Philips). A Dutch tavern.	408 10*s.*

		£
1811	Lafontaine. C. A cabaret scene, bought by the Prince Regent, now at Windsor.	1,050
1817	Buchanan buys at Paris Talleyrand sale, Woman and child (see 1926).	525
1823	Erard. Robert Peel buys Village and figures (Isaac Ostade, in National Gallery since 1871).	420
1829	Robert Peel buys the Alchemist, National Gallery.	840
1834	Duchess de Berri, Paris. Tavern.	800
1837	Duchesse de Berri, Paris. Village dance.	880
1844	Harman. C. Robert Holford buys 'After dinner' (see 1928).	1,387
	Penrice. C. Twenty people dancing (see 1928).	1,375
1846	Higginson. C. Cabaret scene.	997 10*s.*
	Village inn (Isaac Ostade).	1,060 10*s.*
1848	William Wells. C. Country inn and horsemen.	1,050
	A country fair (see 1934).	325 10*s.*
1857	Patureau, Paris. Winter scene. (Isaac Ostade).	1,280
1861	Schneider, Paris. Kitchen interior (see 1892). Bought by Earl of Dudley.	4,100
1876	Foster, Clewer Manor. C. Alehouse interior.	3,780
1882	Hamilton Palace. C. Cabaret.	1,837 10*s.*
	(Beckett Denison sale, 1885.	945)
1892	Earl of Dudley. C. Interior of a kitchen (1861).	2,625
1895	Mrs. Lyne Stephens. C. The village inn (Isaac Ostade).	1,743
1907	C. An alchemist.	1,365
1919	Neumann. C. Two figures at a cottage door (Isaac Ostade).	1,102 10*s.*
1923	Wertheimer. C. Farm scene (Isaac Ostade).	1,470
1925	Earl of Carnarvon. C. Woman and child at a door (see 1817 and 1936).	2,100
	Peasants at an inn.	1,470
1928	Holford. C. After dinner (see 1844).	4,200
	Country dance (see 1844 and 1934).	3,675
	2 others over £3,000 each.	
1930	Lord Carrington. C. Skating scene (Isaac Ostade).	2,100
1934	Marquess of Zetland. S. Country dance (see 1928).	1,400
1936	C. Farm scene (Isaac Ostade, see 1923).	1,202 10*s.*
1937	S. Wayfarers at an inn.	1,785
1951	Duke of Bedford. C. Two horsemen before an inn (Isaac Ostade).	2,520
1958	Heywood Lonsdale. C. 'Five boors at a window' (£420 in 1879).	2,520
1958	S. Domestic scene with peasant lovers, small.	3,800

SAMUEL PALMER. 1805–1881

The saleroom pattern of this now very fashionable painter is remarkable indeed. Palmer produced his highly poetic pastoral scenes under the direct inspiration of William Blake, who died when Palmer was twenty-two years old. But in 1837 Palmer married Linnell's daughter and went to Italy, whence he emerged as an ordinary romantic Victorian water-colourist. As such, he commanded moderately good prices towards the end of his own life, whereas his Blake-like works became worthless. In 1925 these early productions were 'put on the map' through the publication of Lawrence Binyon's classical work on Blake's followers. They rose rapidly beyond the £300 mark, only to fall to the low levels of 1940, when good examples were to be had for less than £30. The present recovery began with the sale of the very discriminating Walter Taylor collection in 1948, but the price of *The Weald of Kent* in 1960 was so sensational as to create a completely new level of prices. But it is only the 'Shoreham period' that is wanted, and of this period the monochrome gouache paintings most of all.

			£
1862	Clint. C. Early summer, wc.		47
	Sunset, wc.		26 15*s.*
1875	Mitchell. C. Emily and Valancourt, wc.		105
1881	Giles. C. Twilight (oil).		162 15*s.*
	The gleaning field, wc.		145 15*s.*
1883	Gurney. C. Tityrus, wc.		168
	Glaucus and Lycidas, wc.	each	131 5*s.*
1892	C. Towered cities, wc.		141 15*s.*
1912	Josiah Wilkinson. C. Gleaners, large wc (early).		18 18*s.*
1922	Bainbridge. C. The morning of life, wc.		189
1925	Pawle. C. Sir Guyon at the ford, oil.		141 15*s.*
1926	Melbourne National Gallery buys Carting the Wheat, large wc.		195
1927	Varley. C. Harvest time, wc.		178 10*s.*
	The Golden City, oil (Melbourne National Gallery).		346 10*s.*
1928	W. H. Palmer. C. The cottage window, oil.		283 10*s.*
1929	Morse. S. Bay scene, moonlight, wc.		185
1933	Victor Rienecker. S. Harvesting and milking, wc.	each	50
1934	C. Harvest field, wc (over 3 ft.).		178 10*s.*
1937	C. Same picture.		63
1940	Mrs. Arthur Davey. C. Harvest time, oil.		33 12*s.*
	7 water-colours from 20 to 28 guineas.		
1943	S. The sleeping shepherd, wc.		70
1946	S. Sheep crossing stream, wc.		190
1948	Walter Taylor. S. All water-colours. Taking home grapes.		240
	Harvesting.		230
	Rustic contentment.		220

		£
1954	Henry Reitlinger. S. Sheepshearing (oils).	1,150
	Shepherd resting by his flock (monochrome gouache).	310
1960	Eardley Knollys. S. Weald of Kent (monochrome gouache).	6,000
1961	S. The Evening Star (monochrome gouache).	5,200

Francesco Mazzola
IL PARMEGIANINO. 1504–1540

Expensive in the early nineteenth century; a substitute for the unobtainable Correggio.

		£
1787	Sir John Taylor. C. Holy Family.	425 2*s.*
1780	Jacob More sells Lord Abercorn the Vision of St. Jerome from Citta di Castello.	1,575
1798	Orleans Exhibition. Cupid making his bow (valued for Duke of Bridgewater).	735
1801	Young Ottley. C. Marriage of St. Catherine.	1,627 10*s.*
After 1808	Vision of St. Jerome, sold to Watson Taylor by William Seguier.	7,000 (?)
1823	Watson Taylor. C. St. Jerome, bought by Holwell Carr for the British Institution (transferred to National Gallery, 1838).	3,202
1826	Lord Radstock. C. Alleged self-portrait.	882
1830	Sir Thomas Lawrence. C. Nativity.	112 7*s.*
1838	Earl of Northwick. C. Holy Family with saints.	231
1859	Earl of Northwick (Philips). 6 pictures, Holy Family with Magdalene.	105
1882	Hamilton Palace. C. Miniature Holy Family.	241 10*s.*
1895	Henry Doetsch. C. A Cardinal and his secretary.	21
1913	Duke of Sutherland. C. Young man in crimson doublet.	576
1920	A. Wertheimer. C. Young man in pink.	315
1950	David James. S. A nobleman, half-length.	500
1958	Duke of Devonshire. C. Small Holy Family.	2,205

DRAWINGS

1953	Henry Reitlinger. S. Study of Thaïs.	500
1959	C. Ganymede at an assembly of gods.	2,625

JEAN BAPTISTE PATER. 1696–1736

Watteau school; for general observations, see entries, Lancret and Watteau.

		£
1776	Blondel de Gagny. Paris. Le bal (large).	80
1839	Augustin, Paris. Setting up camp.	260

		£
1857	Patureau, Paris. Concert champêtre.	1,220
1859	Smallbone. C. Garden scene, 13 figures.	71 8*s.*
1862	Earl of Pembroke, Paris. Figures in a park.	1,232
1868	Schaffhause, Paris. A pair of fêtes.	3,500
1874	Alexander Barker. C. Blind man's buff.	535 10*s.*
1881	De Beurnonville, Paris. En campagne.	2,080
1885	Mrs. de Ath. C. Fête champêtre.	2,887
1891	C. Fête champêtre.	1,365
1895	Mrs. Lyne Stephens. C. The swing and the dance, a pair of small ovals (see 1955).	808 10*s.*
1903	Reginald Vaile. C. Pleasures of the country.	2,100
1908	Henri Saye, Paris. Conversation galante.	3,960
1910	C. A pair of fêtes.	2,782 10*s.*
1913	Sir James Murray Scott. C. Fête champêtre.	2,415
1919	C. Fête champêtre.	2,835
1943	Sir Berkeley Sheffield. C. Pair of fêtes.	2,730
1950	Stehli, New York. L'escarpolette.	3,570
1951	Digby. S. A pair of fêtes (see 1943).	4,200
1955	Alcibiades Vagliano. C. The swing and the dance (see 1895).	14,700
1958	Baron Llangattock. C. Bathing nymphs.	5,040

PIETRO PERUGINO. 1446–1524

The prices are highly deceptive. Only one important Perugino in this list has changed hands since 1885. The three panels of the Pavia altarpiece, bought by the National Gallery in 1856 for the then enormous price of £3,571 8*s.*, would be worth over a quarter of a million to-day. On account of his influence on Raphael, Perugino was dearer than other quattrocento painters even in the 1820's.

		£
1795	Sir Joshua Reynolds. C. Marriage of St. Catherine.	6 6*s.*
1800	Orleans sale (Coxe). Predella, sold to Sir Christopher Sykes as a Raphael (see 1931).	63
	Holy Family.	5 5*s.*
1823	Fonthill (Philips), ex Beckford. Holy Family.	33 12*s.*
	(See 1841.) Bought back by Beckford.	294
1825	McGillivray. C. Holy Family and St. John in landscape. Bought by Edward Solly.	71 8*s.*
1841	National Gallery buys Beckford's Holy Family (see 1823), a small panel which was attacked by Ruskin.	800
1847	Edward Solly. C. Christ carrying cross with SS. Thomas and Francis (resold in 1850 for £43 1*s.*).	152 5*s.*

		£
1850	King of Holland, Amsterdam. Holy Family (Louvre).	1,958
1856	Duke of Melzi. National Gallery buys the 3 panels of the Pavia altarpiece.	3,571 8s.
1859	Earl of Northwick (Philips). Holy Family enthroned. Bought from Duke of Lucca, 1844, by the Duc d'Aumale for the Louvre.	367 10s.
1878	Monro of Novar. St. Francis in ecstasy (see 1906).	273
1879	Baron della Penna. National Gallery buys Holy Family with St. Francis and St. Jerome.	3,200
1882	Hamilton Palace. C. Virgin in prayer.	504
	Holy Family (National Gallery, Dublin).	262 10s.
1885	J. Morris Moore sells Apollo and Marsyas to the Louvre as a Raphael.	8,000
1892	Earl of Dudley. C. Christ and woman of Samaria.	1,050
	Baptism of Christ.	545
	Nativity.	736
	Resurrection (predella), since 1911 in Metropolitan Museum.	273
1902	Sir T. G. Carmichael. C. The court of Apollo (see 1934).	735
1906	Cassels. C. St. Francis (see 1878).	346 10s.
1927	Holford. C. Madonna, Child and two cherubs.	4,830
1931	Henry Hirsch. C. Pieta (predella, see 1800), National Gallery, Dublin.	3,990
1931	Andrew Mellon buys the Hermitage Crucifixion triptych, once attributed to Raphael (National Gallery, Washington, 1938).	50,000
1934	F. A. White. C. The Court of Apollo (see 1902), National Gallery, Edinburgh.	2,257
1936	Henry Oppenheimer. C. Apollo (silverpoint drawing).	1,470
1945	John Bass, New York. Small Madonna, 1491.	2,750

SEBASTIANO DEL PIOMBO. 1485–1547

It is hard to believe that this competent imitator of Raphael's developed style should once have been the highest-priced painter in the world. For the full story of *The Raising of Lazarus* see pages 32–3. In modern times a few attributed portraits have appeared on the market, but they have been moderately priced.

		£
1727	The Regent Duke of Orleans buys The Raising of Lazarus from the chapter of Narbonne Cathedral.	960
1798	The same picture, bought by Angerstein at the Orleans Exhibition in London.	3,675
1814	The Louvre offers £10,000.	

		£
1816 (?)	Beckford offers the equivalent of £13,000.	
1824	The British Government pays £8,000. The picture becomes Number One of the National Gallery.	
1847	J. P. Anderdon. The Salutation. Bought in at £913 10*s.* and resold in 1851 (a copy).	420
1849	William Coningham. C. Holy Family, bought by Thomas Baring.	1,890
1850	King of Holland, Amsterdam. Christ at the tomb.	2,466
1852	Marshal Soult, Paris. Christ carrying cross.	1,640
1882	Hamilton Palace. C. Portrait of Clement VII.	236 5*s.*
1885	Duke of Marlborough sells so-called Fornarina portrait to Berlin Museum.	10,000
1894	Earl of Northbrook. National Gallery buys Raphaelesque Holy Family.	2,000
1899	Talleyrand, Paris. Metropolitan Museum buys the portrait of Columbus.	10,000 (?)
1923	Earl of Grafton. C. Cardinal Carondalet. (Thyssen Coll.).	3,255 10*s.*
1946	Earl of Kinnaird. C. Small portrait of Cesare Borgia.	672

PABLO PICASSO. 1881–

The man of many styles and the most popular painter of his age. Until 1960 the high prices were paid only for his more realistic works and the very high prices only for quite early examples. In order to retain some sense of proportion, divide by six and then compare with Millet, Meissonier, Breton and Rosa Bonheur.

		£
1921–3	Paris. Sequester sales of the stock of Henri Kahnweiler. According to Maurice Rheims, 132 paintings and drawings made a total of £1,400.	
1934	Tate Gallery buys a flowerpiece of 1901.	700
1937	Hollander and Bernheimer. C. Portrait of a woman.	157 10*s.*
	Abstract still life (bought in).	105
	Dancers, pen-and-ink drawing.	60 18*s.*
1940	Eumorphopoulos. S. Children, wc.	210
1941	Red Cross sale. C. Three Graces, drawing.	73 10*s.*
1945	J. K. Thanhauser, New York. Les Amants, 1900.	1,060
1946	Parke-Bernet, New York. Un verre d'absinthe, oil, 15 ins. × 12 ins., 1912.	578
1947	Parke-Bernet, New York. Bottles (semi-abstract).	319
	Abstract composition.	400
1948	Parke-Bernet, New York. Les fugitifs.	1,107
1949	Parke-Bernet, New York. La gommeuse (see 1960).	1,250

		£
1952	Percy Moore Turner. S. La Nicoise, portrait of Mme. Helluard.	1,250
1954	Rees-Jeffreys. S. The sibyl, pen-and-wash drawing.	4,410
	Bullfight, small oil.	2,835
1956	Nelson Rockefeller buys Girl with mandolin, semi-abstract.	35,000
1956	Gallerie Charpentier, Paris. The dove, pen drawing.	1,700
1957	Georges Lurcy, New York. Interior, semi-abstract.	3,215
1958	Cronyn, New York. Woman with blue stockings, 1907.	7,500
1958	Josephine Stein. S. Woman in an armchair, 1941.	9,500
1958	Regniault, Amsterdam. Interior, semi-abstract, 1934.	13,000
1958	Arnold Kirkeby, New York. Madonna and child (early realistic work).	54,285
1959	Major Vahl Rubin. S. La belle Hollandaise (1905) (bought since the war for £6,000), Brisbane Gallery.	55,000
1959	S. Bal de mardi gras, 10-ft. stage design.	6,500
	Harlequin of the Cirque Medrano (pen and colour gouache).	12,000
1960	Jacques Sarlie. S. Crouching woman (realist).	48,000
	La gommeuse (see 1949, realist).	30,000
	Woman in armchair.	30,000
	Man with red glove.	26,000
	Still life with candle.	17,000
1960	Gallerie Charpentier, Paris. Charcoal caricature sketch, dated Barcelona, 1899, when Picasso was eighteen years old.	4,607
1961	Barbara Church, New York. Fernande, cubist head, dated 1912.	26,780

CAMILLE PISSARRO. 1831–1903

For the market of the minor Impressionists, see also Sisley. Two or three years ago Pissarro prices seemed disproportionate, but it is too early to say that there has been any readjustment. If these rather dull works are to rate so high, then why not Corot and Daubigny?

		£
1874	Paris. Barrage sur l'Oise.	38
1888	Laroux, Paris. Village under snow.	24
1890	May, Paris. Route à Roquancourt.	50
1894	Nunés, Paris. Winter.	174
1899	Alfred Sisley, Paris. Tuileries in winter.	192
1900	Guasco, Paris. River bank.	328
1912	Rouart, Paris. 5 landscapes, total	944
1924	B. C. Smith. C. Pont Neuf (1901).	141 15s.
1925	Tate Gallery, Courtauld Fund. Boulevard des Italiens.	1,575

1927	Sir James Murray. C. Bords de la Vionne (Melbourne, National Gallery).	£ 1,102 10s.
1933	Tate Gallery, Courtauld Fund. The Louvre under snow.	1,000
1946	Van Horne, New York. Old Chelsea Bridge, 1890.	1,578
1947	Lady Kent. S. Village street.	1,250
1950	Parke-Bernet, New York. Paysan à la Cheyne, La Seine à Paris. each	1,322
1951	C. Winter scene.	567
1952	Parke-Bernet, New York. La Vigne.	2,500
	Poirier en fleurs.	2,657
1953	Parke-Bernet, New York. Jardins du Louvre.	5,000
1954	Rees-Jeffreys. S. Montfaucault.	2,940
1955	Sir Edward Cripps. C. Orchard.	3,990
1957	S. Bassin des Tuileries.	5,500
	Weinberg. S. Bank Holiday at Kew.	9,000
	Jardin à Pontoise.	5,600
1957	Georges Lurcy, New York. Pont Neuf.	20,360
	Country road.	6,430
1958	Parke-Bernet, New York. Route d'Auvers.	23,325*
	Henry Heinz, New York. Aprés-midi, Rouen.	13,650
1959	S. Village à travers les arbres.	12,000
	Soleil couchant à Moret.	10,500
	Quarry à Pontoise.	4,200
1959	National Gallery values Hugh Lane's Marly, 1873 (bought before 1912 for about £300).	14,000
1960	Gladys Robinson, New York. Avant-port de Dieppe.	12,500

ANTONIO POLLAIUOLO. 1432–1498

Not exactly one of the current names of the sale catalogues, but there have been just enough to establish a price pattern. A number of works, which are no longer accepted, have been attributed to this rare master at different times.

1849	William Coningham. C. Apollo and Daphne (National Gallery since 1875).	£ 13 13s.
1856	National Gallery buys Martyrdom of St. Sebastian from Marchese Pucci.	3,155 4s.
1860	Samuel Woodburn. C. Pieta, said to have been signed and dated 1460.	60 18s.
1863	Davenport Bromley. C. A triumph with female captives.	82 19s.
1867	National Gallery buys Tobias and the Angel from Count Tassi, now called Verrocchio. About	500
1874	Alexander Barker. C. Holy Family and goldfinch.	693
1886	William Graham. C. Portrait inscribed Clarice Orsini.	136 10s.

		£
1897	G. P. Boyce. C. Small Holy Family in archway.	446 5s.
1909	Hainauer Collection per Duveen. Girl's profile (Mrs. Gardner. Fenway Court Museum, Boston).	12,000
	A Condottiere (Pierpont Morgan, see 1936).	15,000
1911	Lady Abdy. C. Wanderings of Ulysses, 2 small panels.	1,260
1917	Earl of Pembroke. S. Combat of Hercules, pen drawing.	920
1936	Duveen sells the Condottiere portrait to Andrew Mellon (now National Gallery, Washington), probably	103,300

PAUL POTTER. 1625–1659

The *Market*, which still belongs to the Grosvenor family, cost £1,600 about the year 1807, or nearly as much as Irvine had to pay for Titian's *Bacchus and Ariadne*. Yet during the Second World War Sotheby's sold another of these Potter cow-scapes that had not trebled its price in a hundred and ten years. *Trois belles vaches* was the title of the picture which Louis XVI bought in 1784 for £880. One would have thought he was buying *The Three Graces* at the very least, paying as he did, the value of a couple of hundred quattrocento pictures. One can only conclude that the cow (and Potter's cows had none of the voluptuousness of Cuyp's) was a sacred animal—and in a sense it was.

		£
1772	Duc de Choiseul. Hunt near The Hague.	1,038
1778	Braamkamp. Amsterdam. Cattle picture, lost at sea on the way to the Empress Catherine.	905
1784	Vaudreuil, Paris. Trois belles vaches, bought for the King (Louvre).	880
1798	Bryan, London (Coxe). Cattlepiece, sold to the Duke of Bedford, now Royal Collections.	1,101 10s.
1801	Robit, Paris. Cattlepiece (see 1837).	1,188
1801	Tolozan, Paris. The market (£750 in 1785).	1,080
	Resold in Rotterdam to Lord Crawford for	1,350
1806	C. Same picture (sold to Lord Rendlesham, £1,600, thence to Lord Grosvenor, £1,500. Still in the family).	1,552 10s.
1812	Sir Thomas Baring. The Geldemeester Potter, sold to the Prince Regent (£850 in 1800).	1,600
1823	Watson Taylor. C. Bull and two cows, bought in.	1,270
1829	Lord Gwydyr. C. Cows and a horse.	1,265 5s.
1833	Nieuwenhuys. C. The young bull (see 1942).	1,212 10s.
1837	Duchesse de Berri. Paris. Cattlepiece (see 1801).	1,484
1846	Higginson of Saltmarshe. C. Cattlepiece (Wallace Collection).	976 10s.
1868	San Donato, Paris. Paturage.	4,480
1869	Besborodko. Paris. Bulls fighting.	1,980

		£
1875	Paris. Landscape with animals.	1,800
1884	Miles of Leigh Court. C. Three cows.	451 10s.
1890	Duke of Somerset. C. Dairy farm.	6,090
1903	C. Peasants dancing, 1645 (see 1942).	2,835
1911	Sir William Agnew. C. Three oxen and sheep.	1,550
1913	Steengracht, Paris. Small cattlepiece, bought by Krupp von Bohlen (see 1931).	6,140
1919	L. Neumann. C. Cattlepiece (see 1931).	2,835
1928	Holford. C. The rabbit warren (£409 10s. in 1838).	8,400*
1931	Henry Hirsch. C. Cattlepiece (see 1919).	714
1942	John Walter. S. The young bull (see 1833).	3,500
	Peasants dancing (see 1903).	950
1952	C. Two cows and a goat.	1,050
1958	Parke-Bernet, New York. Head of a bull.	2,321
1959	Duke of Westminster. S. Cavaliers' race.	6,500

NICOLAS POUSSIN. 1594–1665

The French have not always been so anxious to make Poussin a great master as they are to-day. He was an international painter who worked in Rome and who was very highly priced in his own lifetime. There was a revival in the time of the Regent Duke of Orleans in the 1720's and a second, largely English, revival in the Napoleonic period. With few exceptions, the market went very flat between the 1820's and 1920's. But even the record price, paid in 1956, is not high by to-day's standards. There are probably still a few good examples of Poussin's rather large production which may not be frozen from the market.

		£
1715	Duke of Orleans buys The Seven Sacraments. Each picture	685
1742	Carrignan. Paris. Venus and Aeneas.	145
1777	Randon de Boisset, Paris. Bacchanalia (see 1795).	600
1779	Houghton Hall. Empress Catherine buys Moses striking the rock.	900
	Holy Family.	800
	Continence of Scipio.	600
1794	Joshua Reynolds. C. Adoration.	546
1795	Calonne. C. Bacchanalia (see 1807).	913 10s.
	Triumph of David (see 1913).	630
1798	The Duke of Orleans's Seven Sacraments, valued for Duke of Bridgewater. each	700
	Birth of Bacchus (see 1894).	525
	Exposure of Moses (Lord Temple).	840
1801	Young Ottley. C. Sacrifice of Noah.	1,050

		£
1803	Walker. C. Triumph of Bacchus, bought by Angerstein (see 1824).	840
1807	Troward. C. Bacchanalia (see 1795 and 1813).	1,575
1813	Bryan (ex Robit). The Holy Family (Lord Radstock) (see 1826).	1,260
1813	Earl of Kinnaird. C. Bacchanalia, bought in.	1,470
1824	National Gallery purchases from Angerstein Triumph of Bacchus (see 1803).	1,500
1826	Lord Radstock. C. Holy Family (see 1813).	630
1829	National Gallery buys from Thomas Hamlet Bacchanalia (see 1813).	1,500
1842	Waldegrave, Strawberry Hill (Robins). Education of Jupiter.	78 15*s.*
1850	Earl of Ashburnham. C. Triumph of Bacchus.	1,218
	Triumph of Pan (Kansas City Museum).	1,239
	(Last four-figure prices until 1924)	
1881	Waterloo Wilson, Paris. Infancy of Bacchus.	800
1882	Hamilton Palace. C. Entombment (National Gallery, Dublin).	504
1884	Miles of Leigh Court. The plague at Athens.	420
1911	C. Les funerailles de Phocion (Louvre, 1921).	367 10*s.*
1913	Duke of Sutherland. C. Triumph of David (see 1795).	315
	Bacchante and Satyr.	252
1922	Baroness Burdett-Coutts. C. Roman landscape.	630
1924	Duke of Westminster. C. Riposo (now Reinhardt Collection, Winterthur).	6,510
1929	Lord Yarborough. C. Holy Family with St. John.	924
1945	Earl of Radnor. National Gallery buys Worship of the Golden Calf.	12,000
1948	Viscount Harcourt. C. Moses sweetening the waters (Baltimore Museum).	6,930
	Melbourne National Gallery buys from Longford Castle Israelites crossing the Red Sea.	12,000
1951	Samuel Kress Foundation buys Duke of Sutherland's Holy Family (£640 10*s.* in 1810).	25,000(?)
1956	Jocelyn Beauchamp. S. Nativity (Koetser) (subsequently acquired by National Gallery).	29,000
1960	Walter Chrysler, New York. The grateful Father, 21 ins. × 17½ ins. (ex Duke of Westminster Collection).	1,428

SIR HENRY RAEBURN. 1756–1823

A family horde of portraits which appeared at Christie's in 1877 suddenly gave the almost forgotten Scottish painter a market. Rather mysteriously in the early 1900's, the competition of American millionaires made this slick manneriser the rival of Gainsborough for a few years. Raeburn was therefore the worst casualty of the 1929–1933 slump. The revival has been extremely cautious. Since 1934 none of his portraits has passed the £5,000 mark.

		£
1804	Raeburn receiving 100 guineas for whole-length portraits in Edinburgh.	
1810	Caleb Whitefoord. C. His portrait.	2 12*s*.
1863	William Russell. C. Portrait of Walter Scott, bought in (see 1922).	3 5*s*.
1877	Raeburn family sale. C. 28 completed portraits. 49 lots made £6,000. Lady Raeburn.	997 10*s*.
	Second version (see 1905).	640 10*s*.
	Self-portrait (see 1905).	535 10*s*.
	Sir William Scott Elliott (see 1927).	325 10*s*.
1887	Andrews. C. Lady Raeburn.	850 10*s*.
1897	Affleck Frazer. C. Jane Frazer-Tytler.	1,312 10*s*.
1899	C. Innocence.	1,994
	Mrs. Robertson Reid.	1,386
1902	C. A. Barton. C. Two sons of D. M. Binning (National Gallery, Washington).	6,825
	George and Maria Stewart.	3,780
1905	Lord Tweedmouth. Lady Raeburn (see 1877) (Collection of Lady Mountbatten).	9,135
	Self-portrait (see 1877).	4,725
	Mrs. Oswald.	3,780
1907	C. Mrs. Hart, whole-length (see 1913).	6,930
1909	C. Sir John Sinclair (given to National Gallery, Edinburgh).	6,510
1911	C. Lady Janet Trail (Toledo Museum of Art).	14,700
1911	Col. Williamson. C. Mrs. Robertson-Williamson, bought by Duveen (see 1926 and 1954).	23,415
1912	Charles Wertheimer. C. Mrs. Hay (bought Duveen, thence E. T. Stotesbury).	20,260
1913	Blaikeslee Galleries, Chicago. Mrs. Hart (see 1907).	31,000*
1917	Sir Hugh Lane, deceased. C. The McNab in the uniform of the Breadalbane Fencibles (bought by Sir Thomas Dewar, who was reputed to have been offered £50,000 by Duveen in the 1920's).	25,510
1918	Colin Mackenzie. C. Mrs. Mackenzie.	12,600

		£
1919	Second Hamilton Palace sale. C. 11th Duke of Hamilton as a boy.	9,450
1920	Glen-Coates. C. The McDonald children (Lord Bearsted, Upton).	21,000
1922	Baroness Burdett-Coutts. C. Sir Walter Scott (National Gallery, Edinburgh).	9,660
1926	Late Lord Michelham (Hampdens). Mrs. Robertson Williamson (see 1913 and 1954). Bought by Knoedler against Duveen, who tried to buy it back.	24,675
1927	Mrs. Rumbold. S. William Scott Elliott (see 1877) (Jules Bache, New York).	12,600
1929	C. Miss Lilias Campbell.	8,400
1930	C. The Misses Inglis.	7,140
1932	S. Six Mackenzie family portraits made in all One of them fetched £90.	2,290
1933	C. Mrs. Mackenzie (£3,360 in 1918).	882
1934	Leopold Hirsch. C. Lt.-Col. Morrison.	4,620
	The Allen brothers (Sir James Dewar Collection).	11,025
1936	A. J. Sulley. C. Miss Lilias Campbell (see 1929).	945
	Buchanan. C. Andrew Buchanan.	2,730
1938	S. Sir John Fraser.	1,700
1945	Souter-Sanderson. C. William Fullarton.	2,205
1946	C. Lady Harriet Donalson and her son.	2,415
1948	Parke-Bernet, New York. Mrs. Dalrymple.	2,065
1949	Mrs. George Keppel. C. Mrs. Dear.	2,100
1950	Parke-Bernet, New York. Mrs. Mary Russell.	1,500
1951	Mrs. Stocker. C. Alan Maconachie.	1,890
1952	H. W. Sams. C. Alexander Home as a Midshipman.	3,045
	Vernon Prentice. New York. Unknown boy with cherries (£630 in 1908).	4,825
1954	Catherine Butterworth, New York. Mrs. Robertson-Williamson (see 1911, 1926).	5,000
1956	Sterling Stewart. C. Mrs. Andrew Stewart.	3,780
1957	Mae Rovensky, New York. Sir Brooke Boothby.	2,500
	Sir Robert Menzies.	1,600

RAPHAEL. 1483–1520
Raffaello Santi

It might be argued that the continuous high valuation of Raphael was merely a tradition, which began with the King of Saxony's Sistine Madonna, and that people have long ceased to think him the greatest painter in the world. But the fact is that Raphael had everything. He was the tenderest of quattrocento painters and yet he invented the Grand Manner. Till thirty years ago, moreover, there was always a Raphael or two left to keep the market on its toes. And even if you didn't like his paintings, Raphael drew divinely. There are probably no more Raphaels that are not frozen off from the market, though the Earl of Ellesmere's Raphaels at the Edinburgh National Gallery are still in private ownership. The value of a Raphael to-day is therefore a purely abstract problem. But I have no doubt that, little as Raphael may suit the spirit of the age, another Raphael on the market would mean another highest priced picture in the world.

		£
1754	King of Saxony buys the Sistine Madonna (17,000 ducats).	8,500
1795	Reynolds. C. Madonna of Loreto (copy).	99 14s.
1797	John Trumbull. C. Madonna, corset rouge (contemporary replica of Louvre picture), see 1820. Bought by Benjamin West.	890
1798	Orleans Exhibition. Valued for Duke of Bridgewater.	
	La belle vierge. } Earl of Ellesmere, on loan to Edinburgh National Gallery	3,150
	Vierge au pannier. }	1,260
	Madonna del passeggio. }	315
1800	Orleans Exhibition, pictures sold:	
	Virgin lifting the veil (now Duke of Westminster).	735
	Virgin of the House of Orleans (Musée Condé, Chantilly) (see 1869).	525
	Madonna of the tower (National Gallery) (see 1856).	157 10s.
	Road to Calvary, predella panel (National Gallery) (see 1884).	157 10s.
	Agony in the garden, predella panel (Fenway Court, Boston) (see 1856).	44 2s.
	Pieta, predella panel (Fenway Court Museum, Boston) (see 1831).	63
1800	Lucien Bonaparte buys Crucifixion altarpiece from Città Castellana (see 1847, 1892).	800
1801	Alexander Day Exhibition. St. Catherine (see 1839).	2,625
	Garvagh Madonna (see 1865).	1,575
1802–3	Irvine buys 2 early Raphael Madonnas in Florence. Returned to Italy by Buchanan as unsaleable.	830
1806	The Brera Gallery, Milan, buys Betrothal of the Virgin.	2,120
1808	Coesvelt buys the Alba Madonna from de Bourk in Madrid (see 1836).	4,000
	Crown Prince of Bavaria buys the portrait of Bindo Altoviti.	200
1810	Lawrence buys the Aldobrandini Three Graces (see 1885). About	1,000
1811	Lawrence buys Vision of the Christian knight (2nd Young Ottley sale. C. See 1847).	409 10s.

		£	
1818	Sir Thomas Baring sells King of Bavaria Madonna della tenda (Munich Pinakotek).	5,000	
1822	Bonnemaison returns the Spasimo da Palermo of the Escurial to the Spanish Royal family after Buchanan had failed to get £7,350 in London.		
1829	King of Bavaria buys Casa Tempi Madonna in Florence (Munich Pinakotek).	4,000	
1831	Sir Thomas Lawrence. C. The Orleans Pieta (see 1800) (see also 1881, 1896–1900).	131	15*s.*
1836	Coesvelt (London) sells the Alba Madonna to the Tsar (see 1808 and 1931).	14,000*	
1839	National Gallery buys Beckford's St. Catherine (see 1800). About	6,000	
1841	Monro of Novar buys Madonna of the candelabra (1878).	1,500	
1847	Lord Ward buys Cardinal Fesch's Crucifixion altarpiece (see 1800 and 1892), refused by National Gallery at £2,400.	2,240	
1856	Samuel Rogers. C. The Orleans Agony in the garden (see 1922).	472	10*s.*
	The Orleans Madonna of the Tower (bought Mackintosh, left to National Gallery, 1906).	472	10*s.*
1865	National Gallery buys Garvagh Madonna (see 1801).	9,000	
1869	The Tsar buys Costabile Madonna from Perugia (Hermitage Museum).	12,400	
	Delessert sale. Paris. Virgin of the House of Orleans (see 1800, bought Duc d'Aumale, Musée Condé, Chantilly).	6,000	
	Duke of Ripalda offers the Louvre the Colonna altarpiece at £40,000 (see 1901).		
1873	Unnamed sale. Paris. Alleged fresco fragment, God blessing the newly created world.	8,400	
1878	Monro of Novar. C. The Virgin of the candlestick (see 1841), bought in by executors (Baltimore Museum since 1903).	20,475	
1881	Charles Sackville Bale. C. Pieta (see 1831 and 1896–1900).	535	10*s.*
1884	Miles of Leigh Court. C. Lord Windsor buys Road to Calvary (see 1800); sold to National Gallery, 1913.	588	
1885	National Gallery buys Ansidei Madonna from Duke of Marlborough.	70,000*	
	Duc d'Aumale buys late Earl of Dudley's Three Graces (6 ins. × 6 ins.). See 1810, now Musée Condé, Chantilly.	25,000	
1892	Earl of Dudley. C. Emil Mond buys Crucifixion (see 1800, 1847). Left to National Gallery, 1924.	11,130	
1896–1900	Mrs. Whyte of Barron Hill sells the Orleans Pieta (see 1800, 1831) to Mrs. Isabella Gardner (Fenway Court Museum, Boston).	5,000	

Year	Entry	£
1901	J. Pierpont Morgan buys the Colonna altarpiece from Sedelmeyer (see 1869).	100,000
1913	National Gallery buys the Road to Calvary from Lord Plymouth (see 1800, 1884).	4,000
1913	P. A. B. Widener buys the smaller Panshanger Madonna (intended by Duveen for Altman at £155,000).	116,500
1917	Hope Heirlooms. C. The so-called Hope Raphael portrait of Marcantonio Raimondi, bought in 1801 for £99 15*s*. (In 1946 it made £418 19*s*. as a Francobigio.)	4,516
1922	Baroness Burdett-Coutts. C. The Orleans Agony in the garden (see 1800, 1856), bought for Clarence McKay; left to Metropolitan Museum, 1932.	7,350
1927	Pallavicini (Knight, Frank and Rutley). A papal secretary. Small attributed portrait.	3,255
1929	Duveen sells Andrew Mellon the larger Madonna from Panshanger.	172,800
1931	Andrew Mellon buys from the Hermitage Museum through Knoedler the Alba Madonna (see 1808, 1836). National Gallery, Washington.	240,800*
	St. George and the dragon, painted for Henry VII.	152,000
1939	Anderson's, New York. The Madonna of the pinks. Probably a pupil's work, based on the smaller Panshanger Madonna. Left to Art Museum, Worcester, Mass., 1940.	12,400
1950	Frank C. McComber, New York. Attributed Holy Family, 24 ins. × 18 ins.	9,780

DRAWINGS

Year	Entry	£
1837	Samuel Woodburn. 160 drawings (alleged) from the Lawrence Collection, offered at £15,000.	
1850	King of Holland. Amsterdam. One of these same drawings, Christ at the tomb.	575
	Portrait of an old man.	266 10*s*.
1866	Rev. Dr. Wellesley. S. 13 drawings. Holy Family, silverpoint.	600
	British Museum buys Holy Family, pen and ink.	380
1881	Charles Sackville Bale. S. Study for a pieta.	535
1896	Earl of Warwick. S. Man in armour.	355
1907	Lord Davey. C. Mill by a bridge (attributed).	178 10*s*.
1919	C. Alleged self-portrait, leadpoint.	399
1922	Max Bonn. S. Youth. Silverpoint drawing.	250
1951	S. Child, fragment of a cartoon, 15 ins. × 16 ins.	980
1956	Sir John Leslie. S. Two prophets with angels (Lawrence and King of Holland collections), pen and ink.	2,000
1959	John Skippe. C. Head of a child, charcoal (attributed).	420

REMBRANDT VAN RYN. 1606–1669

The most unpredictable of old masters in the saleroom. He has been both overpriced and underpriced according to the standards of different periods. And, until the nation's purchase of the Panshanger horseman in 1960, only one Rembrandt had made £100,000. An enormous output mainly of oil-sketches, a small army of disciples and imitators, a villainous pigment which has reduced most of his works to harmonies in brown and black—there could not be worse obstacles to saleroom success. The wonder is that Rembrandt has been appreciated as much. For seventy years collectors were pretty frightened of him. There have in fact been only three waves of great popularity, and all of them short. In England during the Napoleonic wars; in Germany and America in the 1870's–1880's; universally in the first thirty years of this century, but not maintained since.

		£
1761	Old man in a black hat, bought by Lord Scarsdale (see 1930).	210
1764	Elector of Cologne, Paris. Prodigal son.	240
1772	Duc de Choiseul. Paris. The two philosophers (Louvre). The pair	582
1776	Grot de Grote of Hanover. C. Adoration.	315
1777	Randon de Boisset. Louis XVI buys Supper in house of Emmaus (Louvre).	442
1778	Braamkamp, Amsterdam. Henry Hope buys Miraculous draft of fishes.	436
1779	Houghton Hall. Empress Catherine buys Sacrifice of Isaac by Abraham.	300
	Portrait of Saskia.	300
	(Both Hermitage Museum).	
1792	Moore Slade Exhibition (Orleans Collection). The mill (see 1925).	525
1795	Joshua Reynolds. C. Vision of Daniel.	178 18*s.*
	Susannah and Elders.	163 16*s.*
	(Kaiser Friedrich Museum since 1883.)	
1798	Bryan (ex De Boers) (Coxe). The centurion (Wallace Collection, see 1848).	1,522 10*s.*
	Portrait of a Fleming (see 1946).	210
1800	Orleans sale (Coxe). The cradle, bought Payne Knight.	1,050
	The Burgomaster (see 1848)	315
1801	Bryan Exhibition (ex Robit sale, Paris).	
	The tribute money (see 1840, 1876).	840
	Man in armour.	525
	Woman at a window.	525
1807	Lafontaine. Woman taken in adultery (National Gallery). Price negotiated with Angerstein, £4,000 or £4,200. See 1824.	
1807	Elwyn. C. The Rabbi, bought by Beckford (see 1850).	882

		£
1811	Lafontaine. C. Shipwright and his wife (Royal Collections). Bought for Prince Regent.	5,250
1812	Prince Regent buys Adoration of the Magi (Royal Collections) from Sir T. Baring.	2,800
1816	Ex-Empress Marie Louise, Paris. Noli me tangere.	1,260
1816	Henry Hope. C. Burgomaster Pancras and wife.	290
1824	The Government buys from Angerstein for future National Gallery:	
	Woman taken in adultery (see 1807).	4,000
	Adoration of the shepherds.	1,200
1828	Dutch Government buys The anatomy lesson for The Hague Museum.	3,250
1831	Sir Thomas Lawrence. C. Joseph and Potiphar's wife (Kaiser Friedrich Museum).	498 10s.
	David and Bathsheba (see 1913).	157 10s.
1832	Erard, Paris. So-called 'Van Tromp' portrait (see 1890 and 1927).	684
1840	Simon Clarke. C. Standard-bearer.	840
	Tribute money (see 1801, 1876).	630
1842	Valckenier. Amsterdam. King of Holland buys the two Pelicorne family groups per Nieuwenhuys (see 1850).	3,000
1843	Cardinal Fesch. Rome. Robert Holford buys Lady with a handkerchief (see 1928).	630
	Lord Ward (Dudley) buys St. John preaching (see 1892).	3,080
1844	Harman. C. National Gallery buys the Rabbi (per Farrer).	473 11s.
1848	Duke of Buckingham (Philips at Stowe). The unmerciful servant (The centurion, see 1798), bought by Lord Hertford, Wallace Collection.	2,300
1849	Robert Holford buys Martin Looten (see 1928).	735
1850	Earl of Ashburnham. C. The mathematician, bought in.	1,050
1850	King of Holland, Amsterdam. The two Pelicorne portraits (see 1842; bought by Lord Hertford, Wallace Collection).	1,500
	Beckford's Rabbi (see 1807), Kaiser Friedrich Museum, 1874, see also 1857.	283
	An Oriental (Munich Pinakotek).	375
	Nicolas Ruts (see 1894).	375
1851	Lord Middleton. C. Self-portrait in old age, given by Eastlake to National Gallery.	431
1854	Mecklenburg. Paris. Burgomaster Six.	1,120
1855	Collot, Paris. Nicholas Tulp (bought in).	640
1856	Samuel Rogers. C. Self-portrait.	225 10s.
1857	Patureau, Paris. Beckford's Rabbi (see 1850).	605
1860	Sir Culling Eardley. C. Mr. and Mrs. Elison, a pair (see 1876).	1,840

		£
1861	National Gallery buys self-portrait from Messieurs de Richemont, Paris.	800
1865	Duc de Morny, Paris. Hermann Doomer, the gilder (see 1882).	6,200
	Pourtalés, Paris. A burgomaster.	1,380
1867	National Gallery buys portrait of an old lady from Lady Eastlake.	1,200
1868	San Donato, Paris. An old woman, aged 87.	2,750
1876	Lissingen, Paris. Portrait of an old man.	6,800
	Schneider, Paris. Johannes Elison (see 1860), bought in (see 1956).	2,000
1876	Wynn-Ellis. C. The tribute money (see 1801).	378
1881	San Donato, Paris. Lucretia (see 1913).	5,840
1882	Henry Marquand buys Hermann Doomer (see 1865), plus 20 percent. duty.	12,400
	Hoare of Stourhead. C. Flight into Egypt (National Gallery, Dublin).	514 10s.
1884	Albert Levy. C. (Ex Lord Portarlington.) Man in a black cap. The first four-figure Rembrandt sold in England since 1848.	1,890
1889	Viscount Oxenbridge. C. Death of Lucretia (Institute of Art, Minneapolis).	3,937 10s.
1890	Crabbe, Paris. Portrait of an admiral (£684 in 1832. See 1927).	4,260
1892	Earl of Dudley. C. St. John preaching (see 1843) (Kaiser Friedrich Museum).	2,625
	Samson Wertheimer. C. Henrike Stoffels in bed. (Edinburgh National Gallery.)	5,250
1893	Lord Clifden. C. Burgomaster Six.	5,775
	Vrouw Six.	7,035
1894	Adrian Hope. C. Nicolas Ruts (see 1850 and 1904).	4,935
	Wife of Burgomaster Cardon (see 1914).	1,365
	Earl of Ashburnham sells double portrait, Claes Ansloo and his wife, to the Kaiser Friedrich Museum.	9,000
1899	National Gallery buys Jacob and Margarete Tripp from Lord de Saumarez. The two	15,050
1904	Pierpont Morgan buys Nicolas Ruts (see 1850) from Boni de Castellane (Metropolitan Museum).	30,000
1909	E. W. Parker. C. Descent from the Cross (National Gallery, Washington, 1941, per Widener).	8,190
	Duveen sells Benjamin Altman 3 portraits from the Rodolphe Kann Collection, now in the Metropolitan Museum. First Rembrandts to make £50,000 each. Three for	155,000
1911	Lord Lansdowne sells P. A. B. Widener The Mill (see 1792. Since 1941, Washington National Gallery).	103,300*

		£
1913	Borden sale, New York. Nicolas Ruts (2nd version) (Frick Foundation, New York).	27,000
	Duveen sells to Frick portrait of a merchant.	51,650
1913	Paris, Mariczell de Nemes. Rembrandt's father (Seymour de Ricci Collection).	23,500
1913	Steengracht sale, Paris. Duveen buys David and Bathsheba (see 1831), resold to Benjamin Altman for £50,000, now Metropolitan Museum.	44,000
1917	National Gallery buys The Philosopher from Sir Francis Davies; small picture.	3,784
1920	Ravensworth Castle. C. Baptism of the eunuch.	10,500
1921	Prince Yussoupoff sells Joseph Widener the two portraits in feather hats, National Gallery, Washington, 1941 The pair	103,300
1926	Duveen buys an oval portrait of a young man from Count Wachtmeister, Sweden, dated 1632. According to Behrman, quoting Press reports, Duveen paid 410,000 dollars (National Gallery, Washington, per Widener).	87,406
1927	Sir James Ross. C. Portrait of Van Tromp (see 1832 and 1890. Viscount Cowdray Collection).	33,250
1928	Holford. C. Young man with a cleft chin (Mrs. Charles Payson, New York).	46,200
	Martin Looten, 1632 (see 1849) (Mensing Collection, Amsterdam).	27,300
	Lady with a handkerchief (see 1843). National Gallery, Toronto.	31,500
	Self-portrait with a scabbard (Harry Oakes, Nassau). This still (in 1961) the English auction record for a Rembrandt.	50,400
1929	Comtesse de Behague. C. Descent from the Cross (Ringling Museum, Sarasota).	8,190
	Lord Brownlow. C. Portrait of a warrior.	16,380
1930	Monnell sale, New York. Rabbi in broad hat (Oscar B. Cintas, New York).	15,000
1931	Lord Scarsdale. C. Portrait of an old man (see 1761).	19,950
1931	Andrew Mellon buys The Polish nobleman, and Joseph and Potiphar's wife from the Hermitage, about 50,000 each (National Gallery, Washington).	
1933	National Gallery, Melbourne, buys an oil-sketch for a self-portrait from the Duke of Portland.	21,500
1936	National Gallery, Melbourne, buys The two Philosophers from the same source.	21,250
1937	Mrs. Wilfrid Buckley. S. Self-portrait, bought in.	11,500
1938	Chamberlin. C. Rembrandt's father (bought in, Hove, 1877, for £100. Collection of Sir Edward Mountain).	7,350

		£
1938	National Gallery buys Saskia as Flora from Duke of Buccleuch.	28,000
1940	National Gallery buys Margarete Tripp from Lord Crawford.	20,000
1946	Lord Rothermere. C. Self-portrait (see 1798, portrait of a Fleming). Bought Glasgow Art Gallery.	13,125
1948	Lord Delisle and Dudley. S. Self-portrait as a young man. Bought by Walker Gallery, Liverpool.	13,500
1950	S. Small moonlit landscape.	10,000
	Lord Dovedale. S. Self-portrait. The first since 1928 to exceed £20,000 at auction.	21,000
1951	Nathan Katz, Paris. Self-portrait, aged 56.	12,800
	Edward Hulton. S. Christ at the column.	8,200
1953	Fairbridge Society. C. Self-portrait, bought in.	8,925
	(Sold privately to F. Farkas, New York.)	15,000
1956	Baroness Cassel von Doorn, Paris. Self-portrait.	12,000
	S. The artist's sister, 1634, oval portrait.	16,500
1956	Boston Fine Arts Museum buys Johannes Elison and Maria Bockenole from Eugene Schneider (see 1860 and 1876). The pair	142,000
1956	Parke-Bernet, New York. Rembrandt's father, small head.	4,660
1960	(Formerly Lord Beauchamp.) S. 2 small oval portraits:	
	Young man, 1633.	40,100
	Young woman, 1634.	22,000
1960	Van Aalst. C. Saskia as Juno (discovered in Bonn in 1936, bought in).	52,500
1960	National Gallery buys large equestrian portrait from Panshanger. Treasury contribution.	128,000
	Other contributions, £10,000; full amount not disclosed.	

DRAWINGS

1836	Samuel Woodburn. 200 drawings ex Sir Thomas Lawrence, offered for £1,500 or £7 10*s.* a drawing.	
1881	Sackville Bale. C. Landscape on vellum.	189
	Annunciation.	63
1896	Earl of Warwick. S. Man's head.	150
1902	Sir J. C. Robinson. C. Old man by a roadside.	115 10*s.*
1913	S. Man in a broad hat, pen and wash.	480
1920	Marquess of Lansdowne. S. Another man in a broad hat.	3,300
1922	Max Bonn. S. Woman looking through a window.	1,550
1926	Lord Brownlow. S. Landscape and buildings.	1,550
1928	Holford. C. Maurits Huyghens, finished portrait in heightened chalk.	10,500*
1929	S. A bearded man, red chalk.	1,600
1935	Faucher-Magnan. S. Amsterdam, small sketch.	450

		£
1936	Earl of Warwick. S. Isaac blessing Jacob (see 1951).	450
	Henry Oppenheimer. C. Adoration in a landscape.	735
1948	S. Portrait of Henrike Stoffels.	3,000
1949	Oscar Oppenheimer. S. Sheet of studies (Barber Institute).	4,200
1951	Lady Melchett. S. Isaac blessing Jacob (see 1936).	1,560
1952	Oliver Probert. C. Christ before Caiaphas.	840
1956	Salle Drouot, Paris. Sleeping watchdog.	1,665
1957	Frans Koenigs. S. Old man walking with a stick.	2,300
	Studies of four heads.	3,800
1960	Mensing, Amsterdam. Kostverloren Castle, pen and ink sketch.	7,636
	Koenigs. S. Balaam and the angel.	4,800
1961	S. Shah Jehan and his falconer (after a Mogul miniature).	13,500

GUIDO RENI. 1575–1642

At the end of the eighteenth century the third most expensive picture that had ever been sold since the history of collecting was a Guido Reni, and little more than a schoolpiece at that. While the romantic movement was the enemy of Guido Reni's broad expanses of flat paint, the cult survived Joshua Reynolds by at least two generations, though in the 1840's Reni's name excited actual animosity. By the 1860's the fashion was right out and without the ghost of a revival till a hundred years later. And even now it is not much of a ghost, despite painstaking propaganda—and despite much real merit.

		£
Before 1745	Robert Walpole buys The doctors of the Church.	630
1758	Sir Luke Schaub's sale. Lord Grosvenor buys Virgin and sleeping child.	315
	Henry Furnese sale. S. The 1st Earl Spencer buys a Guido Reni and an Andrea Sacchi. The two	2,200
1773	Bladen. C. Earl of Carlisle buys St. Cristina.	451 10*s.*
1776	Mr. Duncombe of Duncombe Park buys a Guido Reni for	2,000
1779	Houghton Hall. The Empress Catherine buys The Immaculate Conception, ex Marchese Angeli.	3,500*
1798	Orleans Exhibition:	
	Head of Magdalene (Lord Gower, see 1913).	157 10*s.*
	Infant Jesus sleeping on a cross (Duke of Bridgewater).	367 10*s.*
	Magdalene (Henry Hope, see 1957).	420
	St. Apollonia (Troward, see 1832).	367 10*s.*
	Ecce Homo (Hibbert, see 1820, 1866).	157 10*s.*
	Persian Sibyl (Hibbert, see 1848).	315
1800	Prince Justiniani, Rome, asking for St. Anthony, Paul and the Virgin.	3,000

		£
1801	Bryan Exhibition (ex Robit). Magdalene (see 1840).	682 10*s.*
1803	Durazzo family, Genoa, offer family altarpiece.	1,650
1820	Benjamin West. C. Ecce Homo (see 1798), bought in.	735
	Bt. Samuel Rogers for £29 8*s.* (left to National Gallery, 1856).	
1832	Watson Taylor. C. St. Apollonia (see 1798).	420
1840	Sir Simon Clarke. C. National Gallery buys Magdalene.	430 10*s.*
1844	Penrice. C. National Gallery buys Lot and his daughters.	1,680
1845	National Gallery buys Susanna and the elders.	1,260
1848	Montcalm Museum. C. Flora (see 1885).	252 10*s.*
1850	Earl of Ashburnham. C. Bacchus and Ariadne (see 1910).	420
	King of Holland, Amsterdam. St. Joseph.	658
1853	Louis Philippe. C. Vision of St. James.	420
	Resold at Scarisbrick sale, 1861. C.	1,312 10*s.*
1878	Monro of Novar. C. Europa.	220 10*s.*
1882	Hamilton Palace. C. 10 family pictures from 3 guineas to 80 guineas.	
1885	Beckett Denison. C. Flora (see 1848).	48 6*s.*
1894	Andrew Fountaine. C. *Il diamante* or Venus stealing Cupid's bow. Bought in.	1,050
1895	Henry Doetsch. C. Full-length Magdalene.	42
1910	C. Bacchus and Ariadne (see 1850).	9 19*s.* 6*d.*
1913	Duke of Sutherland. C. Head of Magdalene (see 1798, sold with another).	11 11*s.*
	Ecce Homo.	220 10*s.*
1938	C. Half-length portrait, Cardinal di Bonsi.	94 10*s.*
1943	C. Boy in black, oil on paper.	441
1946	Crawford of Balcarres. C. Small head of a sibyl.	252
1954	C. Assumption of the Virgin.	441
1957	Earl of Darnley. S. (At Cobham Hall):	
	St. Theresa.	130
	Magdalene (see 1798).	130
	Liberality and modesty (10 ft.).	65
	Massacre of the innocents.	260
1957	Earl of Yarborough. S. Toilet of Venus, 10 ft.	70
1959	National Gallery buys Prince Lichtenstein's 14-ft. Adoration of the shepherds; said to have cost	10,000

PIERRE AUGUSTE RENOIR. 1841–1919

During the last years of his life Renoir executed a number of fashionable commissions, and at the time of his death his market was already overtaking Sargent's. That alone explains why a Renoir has become the appropriate symbol of great wealth, like the Rubens pictures that were bought by Louis

XVI's *intendants généraux*. It is curious that Renoir's paintings are always described as modern even when they are ninety years old. They are no more modern than Millais's *Mrs. Bischoffsheim*.

		£
1880	Héreau, Paris. Tête de femme.	5 16*s.*
1888	Ledoux, Paris. Fillette au faucon.	58
1894	Théodore Duret. Buste de femme.	196
1895	American Art Society, New York. La lecture.	145
	Paris. Sortie du conservatoire.	62 14*s.*
	Durand-Ruel. Dejeuner des canotiers (see 1923).	300
1897	Vevey. Paris. Femme nue au bord du mer.	240
1899	Comte Doria, Paris. La Pensée (see 1959).	884
	Café concert.	400
	Rentrée au conservatoire.	268
1899	Chocquet, Paris. A la Grenouillère.	800
	Moulin de la Galette.	420
1900	La femme à la chat, said to have been sold for £2,000.	
1907	Metropolitan Museum buys Mme. Charpentier et ses enfants.	3,500
1912	Rouart, Paris. La Parisienne.	2,312
1914	First appearance at Christie's. Femme à la rose.	630
1919	Durand-Ruel sell La loge.	4,000
	(December) 4 pictures auctioned for £7,000 in all.	
1920	American Art Society. New York. Canotiers de Charenton.	5,575
	Dans la prairie.	5,595
	Both bought back by Durand-Ruel.	
1923	Durand-Ruel resell Les Canotiers to Duncan Philips, Washington. According to Maurice Rheims, the price was 200,000 dollars, then worth more than	50,000
1924	Tate Gallery. Courtauld Fund. La première sortie.	7,500
1932	Georges Petit, Paris. Child with a hoop.	4,112
1937	Leonard Gow. C. Pommes rouges, small.	231
1939	Vente H.C., Paris. Les deux soeurs.	1,650
1942	Albert Barnes buys Mussel-fishers of Berneval, in U.S.A.	38,250
1948	S. Gabrielle en rouge (small).	2,200
1948	Parke-Bernet, New York. Baigneuse.	3,750
1951	S. Small half-length of a girl.	2,300
1952	Gabriel Cognacq. Paris. Les deux soeurs (see 1939).	19,400
	Jeune fille.	23,000
1956	Galerie Charpentier, Paris. The rose-trimmed hat.	16,200
	S. La Ferme, small landscape.	6,000
1957	S. Baigneuse (small and slight).	9,500
	Weinberg. S. Girl in red blouse.	22,000
	Galerie Charpentier. Mosquée a Alger.	22,000
	Georges Lurcy, New York. La serre.	71,300

		£
1958	Bérard. S. La fête de Pan.	14,000
	Goldschmidt. S. La pensée (see 1899).	72,000*
1958	Arnold Kirkeby. New York. La couseuse.	31,070
	Jardin a Sorrente.	37,500
1959	Parke-Bernet, New York:	
	Les filles de Durand-Ruel, 32 ins. × 26 ins.	91,075*
	Lady with parasol, 21½ ins. × 25½ ins.	55,000
	Jeune fille au chapeau blanc.	33,070
1959	S. Misia Serte (bought for National Gallery).	12,600
1959	S. Dead pheasant in snow.	19,000
	Ambroise Vollard as Torero.	22,000
	National Gallery values Les Parapluies, bought by Hugh Lane for £1,000 about 1910.	250,000
1960	Schonmann. S. Femme nue dans l'eau.	38,000
	Les deux laveuses.	38,000
	C. Mme. Georges Vailliere (bought in).	12,600
	Galerie Charpentier, Paris. Woman with a muff, drawing in sanguine.	4,750

SIR JOSHUA REYNOLDS. 1723–1792

The strong contemporary preference for Reynolds's subject-pictures rather than for his portraits lasted until the 1850's. But in the revival of interest in eighteenth-century portraits which followed, Reynolds gradually took second place to Gainsborough, a thing which would have been unimaginable in his own day. In the hysterical 1920's Reynolds's portraits competed only very occasionally with the top-ranking Gainsboroughs. To-day Reynolds would appear to be outranked not only by Gainsborough, but also by Romney and Stubbs and perhaps also by Zoffany, and it would have to be a very important sort of Reynolds, if there are any left, which would hold its place against Raeburn or Lawrence.

	Fee for whole-length portraits:	£
1753		63
1769		105
1774		157 10s.
1782		210
	Garrick between Tragedy and Comedy (see 1880).	262 10s.
1779	Holy Family for Earl of Radnor.	1,400
1786	Infant Hercules, struggling with serpents. Commissioned by Empress Catherine (now Hermitage Museum).	1,575
1790	Calonne buys Tragic Muse (see 1823 and 1921).	735
	Macklin commissions Holy Family (see 1829).	525
1795	Calonne. C. The Tragic Muse (see 1823).	336 10s.

		£
1796	Reynolds Executors. Strawberry girl (see 1856).	81 8*s.*
	Perdita (Wallace Collection).	52 10*s.*
	Unclaimed family portraits at 2*s.* 6*d.* per ft.	
1798	Bryan. (Skinner and Dyke). Mrs. Billington as St. Cecilia (see 1956), bought by Henry Hope.	325 10*s.*
1805	Boydell (Tassie). C. Death of Cardinal Beaufort.	527 2*s.*
	Puck (see 1856).	215
	Macbeth and the witches.	378
1809	Lawrence buys Lord Heathfield (National Gallery, 1824).	300
1810	Late Caleb Whitefoord. C. Nelly O'Brien (Wallace Collection).	67 4*s.*
	Charity.	73 16*s.*
1813	John William Willett (Coxe). The strawberry girl (see 1856).	204 15*s.*
1816	Mrs. Piozzi. C. Portrait of Dr. Johnson.	378
1821	Countess of Thomond. C. The Seven Virtues (Lord Normanton, Somerley). 7 for	5,565
	Central panel for The Seven Virtues, The Adoration (Earl Fitzwilliam).	1,575
	Snake in the grass.	535 10*s.*
	Piping shepherd.	430 10*s.*
1823	Watson Taylor. C. Lord Grosvenor buys The Tragic Muse (see 1790, 1795, 1921).	1,837 10*s.*
	Dr. Johnson (see 1816).	483
1828	Carysfort. C. Sir Robert Peel buys Snake in the grass (see 1821).	1,260
1829	Lord Gwdyr. Holy Family (see 1790). National Gallery (now Tate Gallery).	1,995
1834	Sir Robert Peel buys Robinetta (see 1879).	315
1842	Waldegrave, Strawberry Hill (Robins).	
	The lace-makers (the ladies Waldegrave, bought in) (£315 in 1781, see 1952).	577 10*s.*
	Duchess of Gloucester, bought in.	735
1844	National Gallery. The age of innocence, bought at Harman sale, 1844, and presented, 1847.	1,596
1848	Duke of Buckingham, Stowe (Philips).	
	Marquess of Buckingham.	210
	Marquess of Granby.	210
1856	Samuel Rogers. C. Puck (see 1805) (T. W. Fitzwilliam Collection).	1,029
	Cupid and Psyche (see 1922).	756
	Girl sketching (see 1922).	367 10*s.*
	The strawberry girl (Wallace Collection, see 1813).	2,205
	The mob cap (see 1922)	819

		£
1859	Col. E. Paget. C. Mrs. Hoare and child (Wallace Collection).	2,677 10s.
	G. B. Windus. Penelope Boothby (Earl of Dudley).	1,155
1861	C. Miss Carnac (Wallace Collection).	1,795
1863	Bentley. C. Mrs. Hartley and child, bought in (1928, £4,776 10s.).	1,942 10s.
1872	Milligan. C. Metropolitan Museum buys Master Hare.	2,415
1876	Wynn-Ellis. C. Ferdinand Rothschild buys Miss Stanhope (now Waddesdon Manor Trust).	3,150
1879	Lord Lonsdale. C. Robinetta (see 1834).	1,050
1885	Duke of Marlborough sells The Little Fortune Teller (see 1925).	5,250
1886	Lord Rothschild buys Garrick between Tragedy and Comedy. (Rothschild Collection, Rushbrook.) Price reported to exceed	20,000
1888	Bolckow. C. Mrs. Payne Galway carrying a child (bought by Pierpont Morgan).	4,305
1890	Charles Butler. C. Mrs. Butler.	4,725
1894	Seymour Delmé. C. The Delmé family (now National Gallery, Washington, per Pierpont Morgan and Andrew Mellon).	11,550
	Duchess of Montrose. C. Mrs. Matthew (£998 in 1866) (see 1923).	4,410
1896	Goldschmidt. C. Hon. Miss Mary Monckton.	7,875
1905	Lord Tweedmouth. C. Countess of Bellamont.	6,930
1909	Cuthbertson. C. The Snake in the grass (see 1821).	5,145
	Sir Cuthbert Quilter. C. Venus and the piping boy (see 1925 and 1937).	6,730
1912	C. Lady Sarah Bunbury sacrificing to the Graces (Chicago Art Institute).	8,610
	The Misses Paine (Lever Art Gallery).	9,040
1915	Duveen sells Lord Bessborough's Lavinia, Countess Spencer to Henry Huntington, a replica of the Althorp picture. Vindicated in a lawsuit in 1927 (price as given by Behrman, p. 117).	51,600
1919	Camperdown. C. Reynolds in LL.D. robes (see 1942).	5,985
	Duke of Westminster. C. The Tragic Muse (see 1823). Bought in	at 34,600
1919	2nd Hamilton Palace sale. C. 10th Duke of Hamilton.	13,125
	10th Duke of Hamilton as a child.	9,450
	Elizabeth Gunning.	7,350
	Hon. Mrs. Peter Beckford.	7,140
1920	Glen Coates. C. Earl and Countess of Ely (Lord Bearsted, Upton).	11,340

		£
1921	Duveen sells the Duke of Westminster's Tragic Muse to Henry Huntington (now Huntington Library, San Marino, Cal. See 1790, 1795, 1823, 1919).	73,500*
1922	Baroness Burdett-Coutts. C. Cupid and Psyche (see 1856).	2,520
	Girl sketching (see 1856).	5,460
	The mob cap (£819 10*s.* in 1856) (see 1929).	2,100
1925	Countess of Carnarvon. C. Countess of Carnarvon and her son.	9,975
	Earl of Carnarvon.	6,720
	For the two pictures, see 1941.	
1925	The Althorp portraits, sold through Duveen to Henry Huntington:	
	Lady Georgina Spencer.	
	Lady Campden and Lady Lavinia Spencer, twin portrait.	
	The Little Fortune Teller (see 1885).	
	Probably more than £50,000 was paid for each.	
1925	Earl of Darnley. C. Calling of Samuel (Lady Sackville, Knole).	7,036
	Hon. Edward Bligh (see 1951).	3,990
1927	Mrs. Rumbold. S. Mrs. Thomas Rumbold.	13,000
	Sir James Ross. C. Lady Anne Fitzpatrick (Lever Art Gallery. This is still the highest price ever paid for a Reynolds picture in the saleroom).	19,425*
1928	C. Anne, Viscountess Townshend, whole-length.	13,125
	Dame Thompson. C. The Cruttenden children.	7,560
	Leverton Harris. C. Miss Hickey, small head.	7,455
1929	Lord d'Abernon. C. The mob cap (see 1856, 1922) (Collection of Hon. Mrs. Fellows). This is apparently the last Reynolds to have made £5,000 at auction (1961).	6,300
1937	C. Venus and the piping boy (see 1909).	304 10*s.*
1939	C. The Bradyll family, whole-length.	2,100
	Earl of Rosebery. C. Hon. Augustus Keppell.	2,520
	'Offie' Palmer with a muff.	2,520
1941	S. Ino and the infant Bacchus (£276 3*s.* in 1863).	270
	Mrs. Herbert. S. Earl and Countess of Carnarvon (see 1925). The pair, bought in.	400
1942	H. A. Lockett. C. Reynolds in LL.D. robes (see 1919).	2,520
1946	Swaythling heirlooms. C. Captain Winter riding.	1,050
1950	Fitzgerald. C. Miss Charlotte Fish, half-length.	1,522 10*s.*
1951	Edward Hulton. C. Hon. Edward Bligh (see 1925).	2,625
1952	Earl of Halifax. S. Lady Holford, whole length, bought through N.A.C.F. for Temple Newsam Gallery.	2,000
1952	Edinburgh National Gallery buys the Lace-makers (see 1842) from Mrs. Yerborough. Sold to Thwaites the brewer in the early 1900's for £20,000.	

		£
1953	Earl of Iveagh. C. Dr. Johnson reading a book.	3,465
1954	Major Bowes-Daly. C. Hon. J. D. Daly (early work).	1,575
	S. Portrait of Wang-y-Tong.	750
1956	Parke-Bernet, New York. Richard Barwell and his son, whole-length group.	4,270
	Parke-Bernet, New York. Mrs. Billington with a choir of angels (see 1798). Bought by New York Public Library.	2,321 10*s.*
1957	Lord Carew. S. Squire Connolly.	3,050
1960	Walter Chrysler, New York. George Hardinge, M.P., small half-length.	1,074

HUBERT ROBERT. 1733–1808

Not appreciated until late in the nineteenth century and most fashionable in the 1920's and 1930's, when prices were as high as to-day. Considering the sums which are paid for Guardis that appear to have been cut off by the yard, this painter of the later rococo seems underrated.

		£
1870	Paris. The fountain and the cascade, 2 oval panels.	480
1881	De Beurnonville, Paris. Fountain.	221
1882	Moreau-Chanton. Paris. Fountain and monument.	236
1910	C. Building seen through an archway.	220 10*s.*
1921	Earl of Northwick. S. Architectural capriccio, drawing.	160
1926	C. Paysage avec cascade.	1,522 10*s.*
1929	Princess Paley. C. Roman buildings, a pair.	5,880
1935	Faucher-Magnan. S. Les blanchisseuses.	2,500
	Orangerie a Versailles.	1,150
1937	Comtesse de Greffulhe. S. Small pair of landscapes.	2,900
1941	Harcourt-Johnstone. S. Péche à la ligne.	270
1951	Galerie Charpentier, Paris. Terraces, Villa d'Este.	3,940
1956	Parke-Bernet, New York. Les lavandieres. Colonnades antiques. } a pair.	6,785
1957	Ambatielos. S. Ruined temple.	4,500
	Landscape with temple, drawing.	980
	Fountain and aqueduct, drawing.	800
1960	Galliera, Paris. The lawn dressers.	3,620
	Timken, New York. Classical ruins, 29½ ins × 30 ins.	1,963

DAVID ROBERTS. 1796–1864

A most terrible object lesson. In the heyday of mid-Victorian romantic taste, the water-colours of David Roberts, depicting the Near East and Spain, were the delight of kings. His fussy oil paintings of the interiors of churches could make close on £2,000 in the saleroom. But in 1933 one of these interiors, which had been sold in 1891 for £1,470, made 10 guineas, and they have fetched as little as 5 guineas. To-day there is a small revival of interest in Roberts's water-colours, but he was little better than a topographer, and much of his saleroom success was due to the fact that his daughter married the heir of Elhanan Bicknell, the successful speculator.

		£
1838	Earl of Northwick. Sir Robert Peel buys The Israelites leaving Egypt.	225 11*s.*
1853	King Louis Philippe. C. 4 paintings, left by Frank Hall Standish. Church of St. Helena at Bethlehem.	483
1863	Bicknell. C. Interior, Church of St. Gomart, Lierre (Wallace Collection).	1,438 10*s.*
	Square at Tetuan, wc (bought by Bicknell in the 1840's for £21).	430 10*s.*
1865	Davis. C. Interior, St. Stefan's Dom, Vienna.	1,911
1873	Hargreaves. C. Interior, St. Jacques, Antwerp (see 1910).	1,050
1875	Sam Mendel. C. Interior, Seville Cathedral.	1,890
1879	Fenton. C. Interior, Duomo, Milan.	1,470
1881	Houldsworth. C. Piazza San Marco.	1,617
1891	C. Interior, St. Peter's, Rome (see 1942).	1,470
1893	Brocklebank. C. Ruins of Baalbec.	1,627 10*s.*
1897	Sir John Pender. C. Chapel at Dixmude (see 1957).	567
1901	C. Gate at Cordoba, large oil.	152 5*s.*
1903	C. Nile ruins (£346 10*s.* in 1881).	22 10*s.*
1910	C. Interior, St. Jacques, Antwerp (see 1873).	50 8*s.*
1926	Late Lord Michelham (Hampton's). Interior, St. Peter's, Rome (see 1891 and 1942).	630
1933	Countess Bubna. C. Same picture (see also 1942).	10 10*s.*
1940	Countess of Northbrook. C. Interior of St. Gomart at Lierre (2nd version, Bicknell sale, 1863, £577 10*s.*).	5 5*s.*
1942	C. St. Peter's, Rome (see 1891, 1926, 1933).	42
1946	Pitt-Miller. Chancel of St. Jacques, Bruges.	157 10*s.*
1956	Countess of Stafford. C. St. Paul's from the Thames, oil.	240
1957	C. Chapel at Dixmude, wc (see 1897).	105
1959	Lord Brassey. C. The Palace of the Caesars, oil.	231
1960	S. Street of Alcala, Madrid, wc.	180

GEORGE ROMNEY. 1734–1802

Romney was not a very highly esteemed painter in his own day. He was not a Royal Academician, and the most he got, even for his great family groups, was not more than 160 guineas. In Victorian times his reputation almost disappeared.

As late as 1872, Mr. Woods, a partner in Christie's, bought the famous *Stanhope Children* for 28 guineas. To-day Romney by no means shares the limbo of Lawrence, Raeburn, Hoppner and Reynolds. In 1959 *The Bootle Boys* made £8,000. It must be added that in the heyday of the 1920's it might have made over £40,000. Between 1914 and 1926 five Romneys were sold at ultimate prices ranging from £50,000 to £70,000 each.

		£
1787	Anne de la Pole, commissioned for (see 1913).	105
1801	Sir William Hamilton. C. Lady Hamilton as Bacchante (Tate Gallery).	131 5*s.*
1805	Tassie. C. (Boydell Gallery.) The infant Shakespeare.	65 2*s.*
1807	Beckford buys The gypsy.	210
1807	Romney Executors sale. C. Titania (see 1827).	68 5*s.*
	Three half-length Lady Hamiltons. The three	36
	Mrs. Siddons, head.	4 6*s.*
	An unfinished whole-length at 10*s.* 6*d.*	
	Lady Hamilton as Cassandra (see 1929).	38 11*s.*
1810	Hon. C. F. Greville. C. Lady Hamilton as Diana.	136 10*s.*
1827	Lord de Tabley. C. Titania (see 1807).	162 15*s.*
1834	C. Lady Hamilton as Ariadne (see 1944).	57 15*s.*
1854	Lord Charles Townshend. C. Lady Hamilton as Cassandra (see 1807 and 1929).	189
1860	G. Gouldsmith. C. Lady Hamilton as St. Cecilia.	472 10*s.*
1867	Monro of Novar. C. Duchess of Grafton.	236 5*s.*
1872	Alan Swinton. C. Lady Paulett (bought in).	162 15*s.*
	The Stanhope children, bought in and purchased by Woods (see 1906).	29 8*s.*
1873	Butterworth. C. John Wesley.	556 10*s.*
1875	J. Browne. C. Lady Hamilton at a spinning wheel.	808 10*s.*
1879	J. H. Anderdon. C. Mrs. Tickell.	840
	The parson's daughter (bought by National Gallery).	378
1882	Colburn. C. Benedetta Ramus.	1,386
1888	C. Lady Hamilton reading the *Gazette*.	1,310
1889	C. Lady Hamilton in a Welsh hat.	2,850
1890	C. Lady Hamilton as 'Sensibility'.	3,045
	Walter Long. C. Lady Hamilton as Circe.	4,042 10*s.*
1896	Viscount Clifden (Robinson and Fisher). The Spencer sisters, allegory of music and painting.	11,025
1897	John Cooper. C. Two children in a garden.	9,550
1900	Mrs. Berger. C. Charlotte Pearse.	7,350
1902	Eyre. C. Miss Rodbard.	11,025
1903	Beckett. C. Mrs. Blair (National Gallery, Washington).	9,925 10*s.*
1906	T. H. Woods. C. The Stanhope children (see 1872).	4,830
1909	E. H. Cuthbertson. C. Mrs. Blackburne.	5,460
	Sir Cuthbert Quilter. C. Mrs. Jordan (see 1932).	5,040

Year	Sale	£
1913	De la Pole. C. Anne de la Pole (see 1787), bought by Duveen for Lord Michelham (see 1926).	41,370
	Borden, New York. The Willett children.	20,650
1914	Lord de Saumarez. Agnew buys privately for Henry Huntington portrait of Penelope Lee Acton.	45,000
	Henry Huntington pays £20,000 for the Kemble sisters, in reality the Waldegrave sisters, and not by Romney, but by Ozias Humphrey. Having been the subject of a successful lawsuit by Huntington in 1918, it was sold in 1944 for £63.	
1917	C. The Misses Baldwin (see 1920).	3,255
1919	2nd Hamilton Palace sale. C.	
	The Misses Beckford (Huntington library).	54,600
	William Beckford as a boy (Frick Foundation).	16,800
	Alderman Beckford.	13,125
1919	Capt. Henry Beaumont. National Gallery buys the Beaumont family.	13,000
1920	Lord Methuen. C. Sir Christopher and Lady Sykes (double portrait).	28,350
	C. The Misses Baldwin (see 1917).	1,995
1925	Every. C. Sir Edward Every (see 1960).	5,040
1926	Bischoffsheim. C. Lady Lushington.	8,715
1926	Sir W. Bromley Davenport. Mrs. Davenport (now in National Gallery, Washington, bought by Knoedler for Andrew Mellon, who paid about £70,000).	60,900*
1926	Late Lord Michelham (Hamptons). Anne de la Pole (see 1913, bought back by Duveen and sold to Governor Fuller; now Alvin T. Fuller Collection).	46,200
	Lady Hamilton as an ambassadress (bought by Capt. Jefferson Cohen).	42,000
	Lady Elizabeth Forbes.	25,200
	Children of Captain Little.	22,050
1927	Sir James Ross. C. Lady Sullivan (the last of the five-figure Romneys).	17,850
1928	C. Mrs. Anne Warren (see 1934).	6,090
1929	C. Lady Hamilton as Cassandra (see 1807, 1854, 1935).	8,925
1931	C. Richard Mayler.	6,825
1932	Lambton Castle sale. Maj.-Gen. John Lambton.	7,500
	Louisa, Countess of Durham.	8,500
1932	E. Ruffer. Mrs. Jordan (see 1909).	1,680
1934	Leopold Hirsch. C. Mrs. Thomas Raikes.	4,935
	A. J. Sulley. C. Mrs. Anne Warren (see 1928).	819
1935	Solly Joel. C. Lady Hamilton as a Welsh girl (see 1889).	5,460
	Lady Hamilton as Cassandra (see 1929).	1,260
	Mrs. Charteris and her children (Joel was said to have spent £15,000 on this).	588

		£
1939	Bentinck. C. Sir Robert and Lady Milnes (a pair).	7,560
1944	E. T. Stotesbury, New York. The Vernon children.	5,500
	Neeld. C. Lady Hamilton as Ariadne (see 1834).	4,725
1947	Bruce-Williams. S. Sir Thomas Rumbold, half-length.	3,600
1956	Parke-Bernet. Anne, Marchioness Townshend.	4,650
	Parke-Bernet. David Hartley and the American Treaty.	4,270
1957	Mae Rovensky. New York. Playmates, boy and dog (£1,732 10s. in 1899).	2,850
	Mrs. Montague Burgoyne.	3,571 10s.
1959	S. Edward and Randle Bootle.	8,000
	The Leigh family (Melbourne National Gallery).	3,600
	Sir Austen Harris. S. Portrait of George Greaves.	6,000
1960	S. Sir Edward Every, whole-length, 1780 (see 1925).	2,800

SALVATOR ROSA. 1615–1673

A distinctly English cult, based on the craze for Gothic romances. It lasted from the 1790's to early Victorian times, but the neglect of Salvator Rosa until a few years ago is almost unaccountable. In the 1920's his works were sold for a few pounds apiece and are not easy to trace.

		£
1767	Julienne, Paris. Apollo and the Sibyl (see 1850).	485
1779	Houghton Hall. Empress Catherine buys the Prodigal Son (Hermitage Museum).	700
1795	Calonne. C. A seaport (bought by Henry Hope).	536
1798	Bryan, ex Calonne (Coxe). Pythagoras and the fishermen (see 1957).	432 5s.
1801	Young Ottley. C. The finding of Moses (see 1845).	1,575
	Mercury and the woodman (see 1824, 1837).	1,627 10s.
1810	Marquess of Lansdowne. C. Diogenes (bought in) (see 1885).	1,050
	Heracleitus.	997 10s.
1823	Fonthill, ex Beckford (Philips). Job and his companions (see 1912).	441
1824	Mark Sykes. C. Mercury and the woodman (see 1801, 1837).	2,204 10s.
1829	Lord Durham. C. Same picture.	1,680
1837	National Gallery buys Mercury and the woodman from G. Byng.	1,680
1848	Duke of Buckingham. Stowe (Philips). The finding of Moses (see 1801).	1,050

		£
1850	Earl of Ashburnham. Apollo and the sibyl (see 1767). Bought by Marquess of Hertford. (Wallace Collection).	1,785
	St. John preaching and baptism of the eunuch, a pair, bought in (see 1953). 2 for	1,050
1859	Earl of Northwick (Philips). L'Umana Fragilta (see 1958).	346 10s.
1885	Beckett Denison. Diogenes (see 1810).	51 9s.
1892	Earl of Dudley. C. Finding of Moses (see 1848).	472 10s.
1904	Townshend Heirlooms. C. Belisarius (over 9 ft. long), bought in (see 1947).	273
1912	J. E. Taylor. C. Job and his companions (see 1823).	33 12s.
1929	Lord Yarborough. C. Lake scene, nearly 7 ft. (Ringling Museum, Sarasota).	220 10s.
1940	S. The rocky coast of Calabria (£199 10s. in 1849).	99 15s.
1945	Neeld. C. Coast scene with horsemen, small.	157 10s.
1947	Lady Townshend. C. Belisarius (see 1904).	262 10s.
1949	Isabella Weston. C. Coral fishers.	199
1953	Lady Catherine Ashburnham. S. Baptism of the eunuch. (See 1850.) St. John preaching.	6,100
1957	Earl of Darnley, at Cobham Hall. S. Miraculous draft of fishes.	1,700
	Death of Regulus (7 ft. 6 ins.). (According to Farington, bought 1811, £5,250).	4,800
1958	S. Finding of Moses (see 1892).	1,250
1958	Duke of Devonshire. C. Pythagoras and the fishermen (see 1798).	2,940
	Goodheart-Rendel. C. Allegory of justice (10 ft.).	2,100
	Wallace-Cunningham. C. L'Umana Fragilta (see 1859). Now Fitzwilliam Museum.	3,360
	Lord Chesham. C. Small landscape (£7 17s. in 1930).	735
1959	Martin. C. Tobias and the angel, bought later by the National Gallery in Amsterdam.	472 10s.
	Charles Loeser. S. Jason and the dragon (£325 10s. Bessborough sale, 1801).	2,000
1960	Galliera, Paris. The sleeping soldier, 12 ins. × 9 ins.	1,536

DANTE GABRIEL ROSSETTI. 1828–1882

Had only a small and rather precious public in his own lifetime, but a boom began shortly after his death. This already began to collapse before the First World War. There are signs of a slow recovery, but the interest in Burne-Jones seems to be greater than the interest in Rossetti, who is still considered as primarily a poet.

		£
1859	Windus, an early patron, sells a water-colour, 'Lovers', to Gambart for £12.	
1868	Windus. C. Lucrezia Borgia, wc.	73 10s.

		£
1874	Heugh. C. The Annunciation (see 1886).	388 10s.
1877	Heugh. C. Mona Rosa, wc.	105
	Christmas carol, oil.	168
1881	Crompton Potter. C. Lucrezia Borgia, wc (see 1934).	183 15s.
1882	Walker Gallery, Liverpool, buys Dante's Dream at the tomb of Beatrice.	1,575
1883	Rossetti Executor sale. Beata Beatrix, replica (see 1920).	661 10s.
	Giotto painting Dante, wc.	430 10s.
1885	Col. Ellis. C. La bella Mano (see 1909).	855 15s.
	Donna delle finestre (see 1937).	535 10s.
	Venus Verticordia (see 1936).	577 10s.
1886	William Graham. C. Dante at the tomb of Beatrice (see 1898).	1,050
	Ecce ancilla domini (Annunciation) (see 1874). National Gallery.	840
	Beata Beatrix.	1,207 10s.
	La Ghirlandata (see 1898).	1,050
	'Found', 1853.	756
1887	John Graham. C. Pandora, 1871 (see 1956).	577 10s.
1888	W. A. Turner. C. Fiametta, 1878 (see 1956).	1,207 10s.
1892	Frank Leyland. C. Veronica Veronese (see 1903).	1,050
	The Blessed Damosel.	1,029
1898	Joseph Ruston. C. Dante at the bier of Beatrice (see 1886 and 1907).	3,150
	La Ghirlandata (see 1886).	3,150
1903	Reginald Vaile. C. Veronica Veronese (see 1892).	3,954
1907	C. Same picture.	2,883 10s.
	Imrie. C. Dante at the bier of Beatrice (see 1898).	2,520
1909	Sir Cuthbert Quilter. C. La bella Mano (see 1885).	2,100
1916	Tate Gallery buys 10 paintings and water-colours from Rae Collection for £7,910. Average price	790
1920	Fairfax Murray. C. Beata Beatrix replica (see 1883).	293
1925	Mrs. Vipan. C. Beata Beatrix (same picture?).	346 10s.
1926	Holbrooke Gaskell. C. Proserpine.	357
1927	Sir James Murray. C. Bocca Bacciata (see 1935).	168
	Sir James Ross. C. La Ghirlandata (see 1898).	840
1934	Beausire. C. Lucrezia Borgia, 2-ft. water-colour (see 1881).	173 5s.
1935	C. Bocca Bacciata (see 1927).	231
1936	C. Venus Verticordia (see 1885).	105
1937	Lord Aldenham. S. Donna delle finestre (see 1885).	300
1938	C. Dis manibus (£241 10s. in 1874) (see also 1955).	241 10s.
1939	Edmund Davies. C. Paolo and Francesca.	420
1949	S. Rosa triplex, wc.	220
1955	C. Dis manibus (see 1938).	304

		£
1956	Knight, Frank and Rutley. Vision of Fiametta (see 1888).	400
1959	Dyson-Perrins. S. Pandora (see 1887).	221
	The blue bower (1865). First four-figure price since 1909.	1,900

GEORGES ROUAULT. 1871–1958

		£
1935	Roger Fry. S. Head of a clown.	20
1946	S. Head of a judge (Collection of Douglas Cooper).	880
1949	Parke-Bernet, New York. Clown à la rose.	1,070
	Fille de cirque.	824
1950	S. Three clowns.	240
1951	Parke-Bernet, New York. The clown.	930
	Christ before Pilate.	855
1955	Parke-Bernet, New York. Christ et le pauvre.	4,017
1956	S. Head of Christ.	2,400
1958	S. Paysage biblique.	5,000
1958	Parke-Bernet, New York. Crepuscule, Paysage legendaire.	22,215*
1959	S. A clown.	9,500
	A flowerpiece.	4,200
1960	Jacques Sarlie. S. A head.	9,000
1960	Gladys Robinson, New York. Potentate pierrot.	12,500
1960	S. Palace of Ubu Roi.	14,000

THEODORE ROUSSEAU. 1812–1867

Where, said Sir George Beaumont, do you put your *brown tree*? And the art-struck baronet was crushed by Constable with the word *nowhere*. Henceforward and until the Impressionists rediscovered a few home-truths, Nature was painted as green as it looked, unless you went to Italy to avoid it. In France, where Nature had been avoided since Poussin's day, the baleful discovery that a tree was green was made by Theodore Rousseau in a much-abused picture which he sent to the Salon of 1831. For thirty-six years he painted his green, Dutch-looking landscapes, making very little money out of them (much like Constable), but, as the list shows, the posthumous fortunes of this pre-Impressionist were striking enough to deserve recording.

		£
1849	Marquis de Lau, Paris. Paysage au printemps.	604
1858	Louvre buys La clairère.	160
1865	Duke de Morny, Paris. Oaks at Fontainebleau.	336
	Durand-Ruel buys 60 completed pictures and some studies for £5,600.	
1868	San Donato, Paris. Château de Broglie.	388

		£
1868	Executors' sale. Gorges d'Aspremont.	600
1870	Edwards, Paris. Avant la pluie.	1,560
1873	Laurent Richard. Le Givre.	2,404
	8 pictures at £1,000 to £2,000.	
	Nicol. C. Scene near Fontainebleau.	472 10s.
1880	De Beurnonville, Paris. Hauteurs du Valmondois.	2,964
1881	Hartmann, Paris. Marais dans les landes, 1852. Rousseau's reputed masterpiece, bought by the Louvre.	5,160
1889	Secrétan, Paris. The charcoal-burner's hut.	3,050
1898	Fuller-Dana, New York. Same picture.	7,300
1909	Cutherbertson. C. Winding road.	4,830
1910	Charles T. Yerkes. New York. Paysage.	5,220
1913	Senator Clark, reported to have paid for The fisherman	33,000
1945	Cornelius Vanderbilt, New York. River scene.	798
1951	S. Woods at Fontainebleau, 25 ins. × 39 ins.	200
1952	Nuttall, New York. Impending storm.	464
1956	Metropolitan Museum, New York. Evening.	643
1958	Lehman, New York. Small landscape with cows.	1,150
	S. Marais dans les Landes.	2,100
1960	Mrs. Catherine Ionides. C. Landscape.	387 10s.

SIR PETER PAUL RUBENS. 1577–1640

Although Rubens's paintings never have been cheap by the standards of any time, appreciation has varied a great deal. In the second half of the eighteenth century the build-up of the market was purely French. Between the 1790's and 1820's it was English. Between the 1820's and 1860's the market stayed barely level and the pagan subjects declined. There followed a phase of German and Netherlands buying, which culminated in the quite artificial prices paid by the Rothschild family in 1885. Yet the enormous rise in value of all leading painters between the 1880's and 1920's hardly applied to Rubens, because this was not the taste of the Middle West. It was nevertheless extraordinary that the National Gallery was able to get *The Watering Place* in 1926 for no more than £20,000. The £275,000 Westminster *Adoration*, sold in 1959, had been a cheap picture in 1806 when half a dozen real or alleged Rubens pictures had changed hands for five or six times as much. But in 1959 it was realised that this was the last altarpiece, and perhaps the last full-scale completed work of Rubens which could come on the market.

		£
1742	Carrignan, Paris. St. Cecilia.	400
1748	Godefroy, Paris. Adoration.	320
1756	Tallard, Paris. St. Cecilia, sold to Frederick the Great (now Kaiser Friedrich Museum).	802
1768	La Live de Jully, Paris. Helena Fourment and child (Louvre).	832

		£
1768	Randon de Boisset buys The Adoration from Bourg St. Vinox, spending altogether (School picture, see 1853 and 1915).	1,248
1777	Randon de Boisset sells the Louvre Helena Fourment (see 1768), which had cost him £987, for	748
1779	Empress Catherine buys the Houghton Hall Magdalene at the feet of Christ (Hermitage Museum).	1,600
1783	The Westminster Adoration (see 1959), bought in Brussels at the sequester sale of the Soeurs blanches of Louvain.	700
1783–5	Angerstein buys The Rape of the Sabine Women, from Mme. Bosschaert of Antwerp (see 1824). Asking price £3,000, but the price paid was probably	2,500
1795	Joshua Reynolds. C. Self-portrait (ascribed Van Dyck), National Gallery, 1824.	147
	The boar hunt (see 1850, 1894).	174 5s.
1798	Bryan, ex Calonne (Coxe). Diana and nymphs (see 1802).	1,050
	Death of Actaeon.	1,407 10s.
	Sketch for Whitehall ceiling.	231
1792	Orleans Collection. Judgement of Paris, valued for Earl of Kinnaird (see 1815, 1844).	2,100
1800	Orleans sale (Coxe). Landscape with St. George (Morland, later Royal Collections).	1,050
	Thomyris, receiving the head of Cyrus (see 1940).	1,260
	Continence of Scipio (destroyed by fire, 1837).	840
1800–1	James Irvine in Genoa buys The rainbow and Château de Steen landscapes, and The triumph of Caesar, 3 for	1,000
	James Irvine buys The brazen serpent.	1,100
1802	Sir Simon Clarke. C. Diana and nymphs (see 1798).	1,102 10s.
1803	Buchanan. Lady Beaumont buys Château de Steen (left to National Gallery, 1828).	1,500
	Marquess of Stafford buys Allegory of peace and war (presented to National Gallery, 1828).	3,000
1806	Hart Davis buys Conversion of Saul from Hastings Elwyn (resold to Miles of Leigh Court for £5,000, see 1899).	4,300
1806	Lord Grosvenor buys the Louvain Adoration from the Marquess of Lansdowne (see 1783 and 1959).	800
	Lord Grosvenor buys from Wellbore Ellis Agar, Ixion deceived by Juno (see 1910). Valuation	3,200
	Worship of golden calf. Valuation	2,100
1807	Caleb Whitefoord (Coxe). The brazen serpent (see 1800), bought in (see also 1837).	1,260
1810	Walsh Porter. C. St. George landscape, ex Balbi Palace (Royal Collections).	2,152
	Marquess of Lansdowne. C. Venus, Cupid and Vulcan (bought in, see 1834).	1,260

		£	
1815	Henry Tresham. C. The judgement of Paris, ex Orleans Palace (1792, 1844), bought in.	1,575	
1816	Henry Hope. C. Oil sketch, The Assumption (Royal Collections).	262	10s.
	Woman taken in adultery (Duke of Westminster).	2,100	
1818	De Bourk sells Lord Grosvenor the 4 Loeches cartoons (workshop copies, see 1924). The four	10,000	
1820	Champernowne. C. The triumph of Caesar (see 1800 and 1856).	351	15s.
	The horrors of war (oil sketch), see 1856.	162	16s.
1821	George IV buys Château de Laeken from Aynard, Paris.	1,260	
1823	Smith sells Sir Robert Peel Le chapeau de paille (National Gallery, 1871).	3,600	
1823	Watson Taylor. C. The rainbow landscape (see 1800 and 1856, bought by Earl of Orford).	2,730	
1824	Champion. C. Peter receiving the keys, bought for King of Holland (see 1850, Champion paid £5,000).	2,625	
1824	National Gallery buys Angerstein's Rape of the Sabine Women (see 1783–5).	2,500	
1827	Sir Robert Peel buys Triumph of Silenus (National Gallery, 1871).	1,155	
1834	Lansdowne. C. Venus, Cupid and Vulcan (see 1810) (said to have cost £1,575 in the early 1800's).	57	15s.
1837	National Gallery buys The brazen serpent from Bulkely Owen.	3,675	
1840	Sir Simon Clarke. C. Holy Family (bought by Robert Holford).	945	
1844	J. Penrice. C. National Gallery buys Judgement of Paris (see 1792, 1815 ex Lord Kinnaird).	4,200	
1846	Higginson of Saltmarshe. C. Holy Family with Saints Elizabeth and John (Hertford, Wallace Collection).	2,478	
1850	King of Holland, Amsterdam. Lord Hertford buys St. Peter receiving the keys (see 1824), now in Wallace Collection.	1,800	
	The boar hunt (see 1795 and 1894).	1,600	
1853	Lucien Bonaparte. C. The Bourg St. Vinox Adoration (see 1768 and 1915), bought by Bennett.	1,260	
1856	Samuel Rogers. C. The horrors of war (see 1820).	210	
	Triumph of Caesar (see 1820).	1,102	10s.
	Both bought for National Gallery.		
1856	Earl of Orford. C. The rainbow landscape (see 1823), Hertford (Wallace Collection).	4,777	10s.
1860	Sir Culling Eardley. C. Portrait of a lady (bought in).	7,875	
1867	Sale at Schloss Pommersfeld. Charity (bought in) (has remained with Schonborn family).	6,000	

		£
1872	Gillott. C. Family of Rubens.	1,291 10*s.*
1873	Knyff. Antwerp. Antiope (schoolpiece?), bought in.	8,000
1876	Foster of Clewer Manor. C. Holy Family (ex Hart Davis), bought by Ferdinand de Rothschild.	4,200
1880	San Donato, Paris. Portrait of Spinola (replica of Brunswick picture, Chicago Art Institute).	3,240
1882	Hamilton Palace. C. Triumph of Galatea, oval grisaille (bought for National Gallery, 1885, £672).	1,680
	Loves of the centaurs, oval grisaille.	2,100
	Daniel in lions' den, schoolpiece, resold in 1885 for £2,520 and in 1919 for £2,520.	5,145
1884	Miles of Leigh Court. C. Holy Family, bought in (see 1899).	5,250
	Woman taken in adultery (replica).	1,735
	Conversion of Saul (see 1806, 1899), bought in.	3,465
1885	The Duke of Marlborough's private sales:	
	To Alfonse de Rothschild. Helena Fourment (schoolpiece).	22,750
	Rubens and his family (a copyist work).	35,000
	To Ferdinand de Rothschild (now Waddesdon Manor).	
	The garden of Hesperides (regarded by Gluck as a concocted work based on the Prado picture).	26,250
	To the Kaiser Friedrich Museum. Andromeda enchained.	15,000
	The drunkenness of Silenus.	10,000
1886	The Duke of Marlborough. C. Lot and his daughters (see 1911, 1927).	1,942 10*s.*
	Anne of Austria (see 1935).	3,885
	Holy Family (see 1926 and 1946).	1,428
	Return from Egypt, Virgin wearing a hat.	1,575
	Holy Family with cushion.	1,050
	(The last two made £308 10*s.* as a pair in 1934).	
	Venus and Adonis, schoolpiece, offered originally at £15,000. (Bought in, now Metropolitan Museum.)	7,560
1894	Adrian Hope. C. The boar hunt (see 1795 and 1850).	1,743
1899	Sir Cecil Miles. C. Conversion of Saul (see 1884) (Kaiser Friedrich Museum since 1903).	2,625 10*s.*
	Holy Family (see 1884).	3,715
1901	Alfred Buckley. C. Raising from the Cross, oil sketch.	3,360
1911	Charles Butler. C. Lot and his daughters (see 1886 and 1927).	6,825
1910	Charles T. Yerkes. New York. Ixion deceived by Juno (see 1806; now in the Louvre).	6,160

		£
1915	Blakeslee Galleries, New York. The Bourg St. Vinox Adoration (see 1768 and 1853), schoolpiece.	2,689
1919	2nd Hamilton Palace sale. C. Daniel in the lions' den (see 1882).	2,520
1923	Lord Brownlow. C. Flight into Egypt, nocturne, oil sketch.	2,625
1924	Duke of Westminster. C. 3 of the Loeches cartoons (see 1818) (now Ringling Museum, Sarasota), bought in.	2,415
1925	Earl of Darnley. C. Head of an old woman (National Gallery, Toronto).	2,100
1926	C. Holy Family (see 1886 Blenheim sale) (see also 1946).	1,732 10*s*.
1927	Sir James Ross. C. Lot and his daughters (see 1886 and 1911, now regarded as a schoolpiece).	2,205
1928	Holford. C. Erection of the Cross, oil sketch (National Gallery, Toronto).	5,460
1928	Mrs. Leverton Harris. C. Anton Triest, Archbishop of Ghent, small portrait.	9,660
1933	Barrymore. S. 6 oil sketches for a tapestry life of Achilles.	9,200
1935	J. Pierpont Morgan, Jnr. Metropolitan Museum buys Anne of Austria, replica of Prado picture (see 1886).	51,500
1936	National Gallery buys The watering place from the Duke of Buccleuch.	20,000
1936	Currie. C. Portrait, Princess Brigida Spinola Doria.	2,835
1939	Duke of Newcastle. C. Constantine and Maxentius (oil sketch; replica, Orleans and Samuel Rogers sales, £273 in 1856).	1,575
1940	Earl of Harewood. Thomyris and head of Cyrus (see 1800), sold to Boston Fine Arts Museum. Price not disclosed.	
1944	N. W. Neeld. C. Portrait of Pieter Pecquius	16,800
1946	Parke-Bernet, New York. Holy Family (see 1886, £1,428), schoolpiece.	3,769
1946	Earl of Halifax. C. Holy Family and infant St. John, small oil sketch.	6,930
1949	S. Suicide of Dido, oil sketch. Bought at a country auction in 1948, 50*s*.	3,200
1951	Lord Belper. S. Via Crucis (grisaille painting).	5,000
1955	Vanderbilt-Twembly, New York. Philip IV, portrait head.	5,750
1957	Christopher Norris. S. Adoration of the Magi, oil sketch.	14,000
1958	Herbert Guttman. S. Coronation of the Virgin, oil sketch.	7,500
	Mrs. Maud Barchard. S. Oil sketch, Abraham and Melchizedek (Loeches cartoons, see 1818, 1924).	33,000
1959	Duke of Westminster. S. Adoration of the Kings, altarpiece of the White Sisters, Louvain (see 1783, 1806), bought for Major Allnatt at the highest recorded auction price for any picture.	275,000*

		£
1959	Kingston Hall Estates. S. Small head of a bearded man. Oil sketch.	35,000
1960	Duke of Devonshire sells oil sketch, Holy Family, to Walker Gallery, Liverpool.	50,000
1960	Bergander. C. Portrait of Dr. Garnisius, bought in.	11,550

DRAWINGS

1836	Samuel Woodburn's exhibition of Thomas Lawrence's drawings. 150 Rubens studies offered for £3,000.	
1882	Hamilton Palace. C. Portrait of a lady, 1623, red chalk.	111 16*s.*
1902	Sir J. C. Robinson. C. Large study for the Garden of Hesperides.	861
1918	Sir Edward Poynter. S. Double portrait, Rubens and Helena Fourment.	490
1920	Marquess of Lansdowne. C. Girl's head, charcoal.	330
1928	Holford. C. Helena Fourment in crayon and sanguine.	6,825
	Bancroft. S. Susanna Fourment, black and red chalk.	2,650
1936	Henry Oppenheimer. C. 2 studies of a faun.	1,102 10*s.*
	Landscape study.	892 10*s.*
1940	R. Adam Ellis. S. Nymphs bathing.	430
1954	Henry Reitlinger. S. Angel blowing a trumpet.	510
1959	John Skippe. C. Martyrdom of St. Ursula.	787 10*s.*
	Cain cursed by the Lord, red chalk.	777

JACOB VAN RUYSDAEL. 1628–1682

This was the waterfall-and-ruins-Ruysdael who was most popular in the eighteenth century, as opposed to his uncle, Salomon Ruysdael, who painted river scenes and who only really came in with the Van Goyen taste in the 1880's. Of Jacob Van Ruysdael the National Gallery owns at least 20 works, all in their way charming, but these fussy, realistic trees have a lot to answer for.

		£
1798	Bryan, ex Calonne (Coxe). Landscape with bridge (see 1875).	173 15*s.*
1802	Holderness. C. Watermill and church.	682 10*s.*
	Castle of Bentheim (see 1913).	315
1810	Walsh Porter. C. The Mill (Royal Collections) bought for Prince Regent by Lord Yarmouth.	304 10*s.*
1822	The watermill, bought by Robert Peel (National Gallery, 1871).	601
1829	Lord Liverpool. C. View of a breakwater.	530 5*s.*
1843	Tardieu, Paris. Waterfall.	1,000
1850	King of Holland. Amsterdam. Mountainous landscape (Brussels Museum).	1,075

		£
1857	Patureau, Paris. Waterfall (Hertford, Wallace Collection).	1,108
1859	National Gallery buys 2 landscapes from Count Stolberg.	1,187 15s.
		1,069 10s.
1861	Scarisbrick. C. Landscape with ruins (see 1913).	1,312 10s.
1868	San Donato, Paris. Dunes at Scheveningen (see 1893).	2,400
1875	Miss Bredel. C. The ruin, ex Calonne (see 1798) (see also 1892).	2,310
1882	Hamilton Palace. C. Wooded scene.	1,218
1892	Earl of Dudley. C. The ruin (see 1875). (National Gallery, Salting Bequest, 1910).	1,470
1893	Bingham Mildmay. C. Shore at Scheveningen, bought by National Gallery	3,045
1894	Adrian Hope. C. Sheep on a bridge (see 1919).	1,365
1895	Foster of Clewer Manor. C. Coast scene.	4,410
1905	Lawrie & Co. C. A waterfall.	1,316
1910	Earle Drax. C. River scene and cattle.	2,362 10s.
1913	Spencer Hall. C. Castle of Bentheim (see 1948).	4,200
	Landscape with ruins (see 1871).	840
1919	Neumann. C. Ruins.	12,600*
	Sheep on a bridge (see 1894).	9,975
1928	Holford. C. Le coup de soleil (£504 in 1848).	6,300
1937	Lewis Lloyd. C. Woody landscape near Middleburg.	5,460
1948	DeLisle and Dudley. C. Castle of Bentheim (see 1913).	4,200
1950	Col. H. A. Clowes. C. Coast near Scheveningen.	6,195
1953	Tollemache Estates. C. Castle near Amsterdam.	3,045
1960	Charles Russell. S. Wooded landscape and shepherds.	8,500
	Edge of Zuider Zee.	4,500

SALOMON VAN RUYSDAEL. 1600–1670

		£
1771	Sir Robert Strange. C. Ferryboat scene.	34 13s.
1854	Mecklenburg, Paris. Landscape.	320
1872	Luscombe (Forster's). Ferryboat and figures.	170 2s.
1880	San Donato, Paris Banks of the Meuse.	1,004
1881	Waterloo Wilson, Paris. Le bac (Brussels Museum).	1,280
1890	George Perkins. C. Woman with a bundle.	735
1899	Broadwood. C. Scheveningen.	924
1910	C. Frozen river scene, 1653.	1,134
1913	Rev. E. A. Dawkins. Nimeguen.	1,837 10s.
1924	Lord Castletown. C. River scene with boats.	1,732 10s.
1929	C. The ferry.	3,150
1930	Wilbraham. C. Ferryboat, 1649.	1,995
1938	Savile. Rufford Abbey. C. River scene.	4,200

		£
1949	Mrs. Cale. C. River scene.	1,470
1955	S. The ferry, 1650.	10,800
1957	Parke-Bernet, New York. Village and ferryboat, 1650.	6,500
1958	Lord Ardilaun. C. Wooded river scene, 1644.	7,350
1959	Del Monte. S. Halt before an inn, 1644.	8,000
1960	Van Aalst. C. The ferry.	15,750
	Milligan. C. Estuary, 1651.	9,450
1960	Benn. S. River landscape, 1647.	7,000

JOHN SINGER SARGENT. 1856–1925

An American, the last painter practising in England to make money on the heroic scale of the late nineteenth century. Conventional enough in outlook to satisfy the Establishment, Sargent's painting was, at the same time, sufficiently individual to constitute a rarity which he alone could produce. It is hardly more than thirty years since those splashy, almost totally inaesthetic water-colour landscapes were making 3,000 to 4,000 guineas apiece, and an oil sketch 7,000 guineas. And that was real currency. Only very special post-Impressionist works could make the equivalent in the money of to-day.

		£
1887	Chantrey Bequest buys Carnation, Lily, Lily Rose.	700
1905	Sir Henry Irving, deceased. Ellen Terry as Lady Macbeth, 1889, full-length, bought for Tate Gallery.	1,260
1915	President Wilson, portrait commissioned by Hugh Lane for the Red Cross.	10,000
1917	Mrs. Percival Duxbury, portrait commissioned for the Red Cross.	10,000
1920	Mrs. Charles Hunter. C. Venice, Church of the Gesuite, wc. (see 1929).	756
1924	Melbourne National Gallery buys Hospital at Grenada, small oil sketch.	2,205
1925	Sargent executors' sale. C. San Vigilio, oil sketch.	7,350
	Venice, Grand Canal, wc.	4,830
	Don Baltazar Carlos, copy in oil of a Velazquez picture. (£1,995 in 1961.)	6,300
	2 studies, water-colour and pencil, Bedouin chiefs (see	3,570
	1943).	1,102 10*s.*
	74 water-colours, average price. About	2,000
	Unfinished whole-length portrait in oil, Mme. Gautreau, presented by Joseph Duveen to the Tate Gallery, purchase price believed to have been	20,000
1927	Sir James Murray. C. Padre Albera, small oil.	3,780
	Gypsy encampment, small oil.	2,992 10*s.*

		£
1928	Lady Elcho, Mrs. Tempest and Mrs. Adeane, a whole-length group sold in U.S.A. by Capt. R. Wyndham. Metropolitan Museum.	18,000
1929	C. Church of the Gesuite, Venice, wc. (see 1920).	651
1931	C. Majorca, wc., 21 ins.	115 10*s.*
1933	Cora, Countess of Stafford (Curtis and Henson). Full-length portrait of same.	609
1935	J. K. Newman. New York. Portrait, Mme. Errazuriz.	887
1936	Tate Gallery buys The brook, small oil painting.	450
1936	C. Pertud, wc.	504
1936	John M. MacCormack. New York. Mme. Helleu, whole-length.	975
	Atlantic storm, oil.	280
1937	S. Venice, large water-colour.	52
1939	C. Mrs. Charles Hunter, large charcoal portrait.	19 19*s.*
1940	Sir Chartres Biron. S. The Salute, Venice, oil, 18 ins. × 25 ins.	38
1941	Lord Rothermere. C. Garden, Corfu, oil.	168
	Other small oil landscapes, 90 to 100 guineas.	
1942	Late Wilson Steer. C. Venice, inscribed water-colour.	73 10*s.*
1943	Sutro. S. Arab chiefs, 2 studies, wc. (see 1925), originally £4,672 10*s.*	88
1944	S. Large charcoal portrait, Marie Lohr.	5 10*s.*
1946	Parke-Bernet, New York. Beside an Alpine pool, small oil painting.	475
1952	C. San Vigilio, Corfu (see 1925, £7,350).	105
1954	Arthur Campbell, New York. Pertud (see 1936), wc.	339
1956	Parke-Bernet, New York. Mlle. Dehan, small portrait.	1,075
1957	Parke-Bernet, New York. The De Glehns sketching, oil.	1,321
	Parke-Bernet, New York. Pomegranates, Majorca, oil.	984

ANDREA DEL SARTO. 1487–1531

There has been hardly enough of this rare master of the High Renaissance to create a sales pattern. Moreover, few of these paintings now satisfy the experts. It would have been more interesting if something like the National Gallery's *Holy Family* and *Sculptor* portrait had been on the market in modern times

		£
1770	Ansell. C. Holy Family, said to have been copied from Raphael.	372 15*s.*
1802	Desenfans (Skinner and Dyke). Holy Family.	840
1807	Duke of Gloucester. C. Madonna della sacca, bought by Francis Baring.	630

		£
1810	Walsh Porter. C. Virgin, Child and St. John, obtained by Irvine from Aldobrandini Palace. Left to National Gallery, 1831, by Holwell Carr.	1,207 10s.
1811	Young Ottley. C. Charity (see 1847).	504
1820	Champernowne. C. Holy Family with angels.	430 10s.
1823	Princess Murat. C. St. John writing *Revelations*.	472 10s.
1832	Lafitte, Paris. Big altarpiece, Holy Family.	1,120
1847	Anderdon. C. Charity (see 1811).	451 10s.
1850	King of Holland, Amsterdam. Hertford buys Holy Family, St. John and two angels (Wallace Collection).	2,510
1862	National Gallery buys The sculptor portrait in Florence.	270
1878	Monro of Novar. C. Pietà and two angels (see 1898, 1912).	735
1882	Hamilton Palace. C. The Magdalene (see 1911).	357
1898	Ruston. C. Pietà (see 1912 and 1878).	630
1899	Lord Methuen. Self-portrait.	934 10s.
1908	Duke of Sutherland. C. Virgin, Child and St. John (see 1802).	682 10s.
1911	Charles Butler. Magdalene (see 1882).	945
1912	Farrer. C. Pieta (see 1898).	525
1928	C. Portrait of Cardinal Altieri.	1,312 10s.
1936	Oppenheimer. C. Man's head, drawing.	1,785
1957	Mae Rovensky, New York. Small portrait, attributed by Berenson.	2,950
1959	C. Holy Family and St. John, 55 ins. × 48 ins.	2,730

GEORGES PIERRE SEURAT. 1859–1891

Not one of the original Impressionist painters, but a painter who tried to carry their theories a step further under the name of *Pointillisme*. The present-day prices are based on extreme rarity. Seurat lived less than thirty-two years, and painted very few finished pictures. There has been nothing like *Une baignade* on the post-war market, while *La grande jatte* was said to have been insured for a million dollars when it was damaged by fire.

		£
1921	Kelekian. New York. La poudreuse (bought by John Quinn).	1,300
1923	Le cirque, bought by John Quinn (Louvre, 1924).	1,900
1924	Tate Gallery, Courtauld Fund. Une baignade.	3,917
	La grande jatte, bought by F. C. Bartlett, Chicago (destroyed in fire, Museum of Modern Art, 1958).	6,000
1932	S. Small landscape, oil.	160
1947	Parke-Bernet, New York. Marine, small oil.	350
1954	Bradley Campbell, New York. Parade de danseuses (coloured crayons).	2,320

		£
1957	Weinberg. S. Le faucheur, small oil.	22,000
	Study for La grande jatte.	7,000
	Street scene, study.	5,500
	Crepuscule, charcoal drawing.	3,000
1958	S. Study for Une baignade.	12,000
1960	J. Rewald. S. Honfleur, charcoal drawing.	5,000

PAUL SIGNAC. 1863–1935

The other well-known *Pointillist*, but less of a poet and an artist than Seurat.

		£
1952	Parke-Bernet, New York. Quai St. Bernard.	1,606
1957	Georges Lurcy, New York. Beach scene, St. Brieuc.	11,070
	River scene.	6,075
1958	Le Gallais, New York. The mill.	8,930
	Arnold Kirkeby, New York. Bateaux et pecheurs.	12,140
1960	J. Rewald. S. Salle à manger, coloured drawing.	2,200
1960	Galerie Charpentier, Paris. L'Odet a Quimper.	7,165
1961	Galliera, Paris. Port of St. Tropéz.	17,675

LUCA SIGNORELLI. 1441–1523

Plausible small panels are still attributed to this name, but there is no *Return of Ulysses* yet to come. The price of the *Holy Family* of 1901, actually less than *The Circumcision* of 1882, is curious.

		£
1860	Late Samuel Woodburn. C. Riposo.	567
1874	Alexander Barker. C. St. George and Dragon, bought in	252
	Triumph of chastity (National Gallery).	840
	Return of Ulysses (fresco), National Gallery, now called Pinturricchio.	2,152
1879	Alexander Barker. C. St. George and dragon (see 1874 and 1912).	85
1882	Hamilton Palace. C. Circumcision (National Gallery).	3,150
1882	National Gallery buys Nativity from Bardini, Florence.	1,200
1887	Sommervell. C. Feast at Simon's house (National Gallery of Ireland).	178 10*s*.
1892	C. Frank Leyland. Story of Coriolanus (Kaiser Friedrich Museum).	315
1901	National Gallery buys Madonna, Child and saints, nearly 9 ft. high, from E. Volpi, Florence.	2,677 10*s*.
1911	William Abdy. C. Samson slaying Philistines, small panel.	115 10*s*.

		£
1912	Sir William Farrer. C. St. George and dragon (see 1879).	462
1946	Crawford of Balcarres. C. Small Madonna.	1,050
1949	Parke-Bernet, New York. 2 very small panels, Journey to House of Emmaus. 2 for	1,965

ALFRED SISLEY. 1840–1899

Since 1925, when the Tate Gallery acquired *Pont de Moret*, prices have gone up perhaps fifteen times for a painter who was always one of the cheaper Impressionists, being, in spite of his charm, the least original. At the moment the market seems to be very steady, but, as in the case of Pissarro, one may ask why these works should fetch many times as much as the very best of the Barbizon paintings.

		£
1874	Sale in Paris. Bougival.	15 3*s.*
1890	Porto Riche, Paris. Le verger.	46
1893	Coquelin, Paris. Le Loing à St. Mannés.	122
1899	Count Doria, Paris. Early frost.	360
	Dachery, Paris. Noisy le roi.	340
	Marly.	360
	Sisley executors' sale. 25 pictures from £100 to £350.	
1900	Tavernier, Paris. Inondation.	614
1906	Lord Grimthorpe. C. View on the Seine.	168
1925	Tate Gallery, Courtauld Fund. Pont de Moret.	1,200
1927	Sir James Murray. C. Bridge at Sèvres, bought for Tate Gallery.	840
1932	S. Landscape.	110
1941	R. F. Goldschmidt. C. Chantier St. Maury.	315
1942	A. T. Reid. C. Bords de la riviere.	504
1944	S. On the Seine.	370
1945	Thanhauser. New York. Chemin des fontaines.	1,250
1947	Parke-Bernet, New York. La route de St. Germain.	1,125
1952	Felix Wildenstein, New York. La Seine au point du Jour.	3,400
1953	Parke-Bernet, New York. St. Mannés.	4,328
1956	Sir Edward Cripps. S. Country street.	5,460
1957	Weinberg. S. Seine à Paris.	9,000
1957	Georges Lurcy, New York. Entrée du village.	12,500
	Le Loing à Moret.	13,400
	River landscape.	11,070
1960	Cassirer. S. Environs de Marly.	12,500
	S. River landscape.	8,000
1961	Galliera, Paris. Spring near Moret.	19,175*

CHAIM SOUTINE. 1894–1944

A discovery of the 1930's, but appreciation came slowly.

		£
1938	Tate Gallery. Prêtre en soutane	393 15*s.*
1947	Parke-Bernet, New York. Boy in blue, half-length.	500
1948	C. Tulips (see 1952).	210
1949	S. Still life, skinned rabbit.	400
1952	Salle Drouot, Paris. La route rouge.	1,972
	C. Tulips (see 1948).	651
1954	Arthur Campbell, New York. Old mill near Cannes.	6,600
1954	Rees Jeffreys. S. La tricoteuse (see 1957).	4,725
1956	Parke-Bernet, New York. Woman with a dog.	4,400
1956	S. Flowers in a vase.	2,800
1957	S. La tricoteuse (see 1954).	7,500
1957	George Lurcy, New York. Paysage aux vaches.	6,785
1958	Regniault, Amsterdam. Portrait head.	12,000
1960	Galerie Charpentier, Paris. Girl with ducks.	16,000

SPORTING PICTURES

Including Alken, Barraud, John Herring, Senr., Cooper Henderson, James Pollard, Francis and John Sartorius, Deane Wolstenholme, John Wootton, but excluding John Ferneley, Ben Marshall, Stubbs, James Ward, for whom see separate entries.

Although Wootton was at work in the 1730's and Cooper Henderson as late as the 1860's, I have presented these pictures as a group. None of the painters had strong aesthetic merits, but all painted with the same sort of mannerist charm. The vogue for such pictures began in the early 1900's and reached ridiculous proportions in the 1920's, which also saw the zenith of the coloured sporting-print. The present recovery is selective and possibly a little more aesthetic.

		£
1851	C. JOHN BARRAUD: The Badminton hunt.	120 15*s.*
1865	J. F. HERRING, SENR.: C. The Derby; a set of 16. Per picture	172 10*s.*
1872	C. J. F. HERRING: The start of the Derby.	693
1879	Alexander Barker. C.:	
	JOHN SARTORIUS: Set of 6 hunting pictures.	76 13*s.*
	J. F. HERRING: 'Doctor Syntax' and jockey.	68 5*s.*
	'Emilius' and jockey.	70 7*s.*
1884	Lady Otho Fitzgerald. C.:	
	J. F. HERRING: The English homestead.	367 10*s.*
1896	C. J. F. HERRING: Interior of a stable.	819

Year	Sale	£
1910	Sir Walter Gilbey. C. Francis Sartorius, Snr.: Race at Newmarket, 1767 (nearly 7 ft.).	84
	John Sartorius: Death of the fox.	231
1913	C. J. F. Herring: Goodwood, parade and finish. 2 for	866 5*s.*
1920	John Sartorius: Meet of foxhounds.	1,155
1925	Lord Woollavington. C.:	
	J. F. Herring: A pair of racing pictures.	4,200
	A pair of racing pictures.	3,150
1925	C. Wolstenholme: Fox hunting, set of 4.	2,625
1927	Barron. C. Cooper Henderson: Edinburgh-Lancaster mail.	1,202 10*s.*
1927	C. James Pollard: Mail coaches at the Peacock, Islington (see 1960).	168
1928	C. John Wootton: Newmarket, 1736.	2,100
	John Sartorius: The Belvoir Hunt, small pair.	3,255
	'Foxhunter' with rider, 1800.	3,150
	Thomas Oldacre on 'Brush'.	4,935*
	C. W. Barraud: Surrey Staghounds.	1,155
1930	C. James Pollard: Derby and Goodwood Cup, 1833 a pair.	1,680
	Sir O. Wakeman. C. John Sartorius: Hunting subject, 1800.	3,150
1936	C. James Pollard: Outside the Falcon, Waltham Cross.	693
1946	Capt. E. Hale. S. William Barraud: Old Surrey Foxhounds.	2,500
1948	Francis Bowes-Lyon. C. Dean Wolstenholme: Lord Glamis and his staghounds.	2,940
1951	Walter Hutchinson & Co. C. Henry Alken: Grand Leicestershire Steeplechase (8).	1, 050
1955	Alfred Caspary, New York. Cooper Henderson: Leeds-London Royal Mail.	1,336
1956	Parke-Bernet, New York. James Pollard: Hyde Park Corner.	1,033
	Cooper Henderson: All right.	1,158
	Changing hands.	1,158
1959	C. J. F. Herring: Start of the Derby.	3,255
	Start of the Oaks.	3,045
	Charles Theriot. S. John Sartorius: Lord Chesterfield's 'Don Juan'.	2,200
1960	S. Wormold. James Pollard: North Country mails at the Peacock, Islington (see 1927).	19,000*
	Carriage and horses of Smith Barry, Esq.	4,800
1961	Duke of Leeds. S. John Wootton: Newmarket with Royal Family.	5,500
	Others, £1,000 to £4,000.	

CLARKSON STANFIELD. 1793–1867

Of all the followers of Turner and Bonington, purveyors of the Southern romantic landscape, Clarkson Stanfield was the most overrated in mid-Victorian times and the most devalued at the end of the last war. At Christie's alone some 37 of Stanfield's oil-paintings made over a thousand pounds each between 1860 and 1900. The huge contraptions, which could make up to £3,500 seventy years ago, could be had until quite recently for £50 or thereabouts. On the other hand, Stanfield's water-colours, which rarely made more than £400 at the height of his fashion, have fallen much less. Stanfield had been a scene-painter at Drury Lane, and he never forgot it.

		£
1832	Watson Taylor. C. Wreckers off Fort Rouge, Calais.	435 15s.
1838	Bicknell buys the Pic du Midi (see 1872).	735
1845	James Lloyd. C. Castello d'Ischia.	714
	Mazorbo.	425 5s.
1848	Duke of Buckingham, Stowe. Wreckers off Calais (see 1832).	430 10s.
1851	C. Morning after the wreck (see 1872).	924
1860	Houldsworth. C. The Giant's Causeway, bought in.	1,365
1863	Bicknell. C. Pic du Midi (see 1838).	2,677 10s.
	The Beilstein.	1,575
	Shipping near St. Malo.	1,291 10s.
1864–8	9 pictures between 1,200 and 2,100 guineas.	
1868	Stanfield executors. C. 52 water-colours from 50 to 260 guineas.	
1872	Gillott. C. Wooden walls of England (see 1913).	2,835
	Brooks. C. The morning after the wreck (see 1851).	2,940
1877	Baron Grant. C. Battle of Roveredo.	2,520
1881	E. J. Colman. Pic du Midi (see 1863).	2,677 10s.
	Battle of Roveredo (Holloway College).	3,465
1884	Lady Otho Fitzgerald. C. A Guarda Costa (see 1896).	1,995
1892	Lord Cheylesmore. St. Michael's Mount (5 ft. × 8 ft.) (see 1925).	3,150*
1896	Sir Julian Goldsmid. C. A Guarda Costa (see 1884).	2,415
1900	C. A Guarda Costa off Fuentarabia.	1,837 10s.
1903	C. The Stack Rock, Antrim (£661 10s. in 1878).	42
1910	C. The day after the wreck (see 1872).	514 10s.
1913	C. The wooden walls of England (see 1872).	168
1925	S. St. Michael's Mount (see 1892), 8 ft. long.	150
1940	C. Wreckers off Fort Rouge, wc.	7 7s.
1946	C. Rochester Castle, wc.	99 15s.
	Sorrento.	56
1951	S. Isola Bella, oil, 28 ins. × 43 ins. (£661 10s. in 1879).	35

		£
1953	S. The Dogana and Salute, Venice (8 ft. long) (£173 5s. in 1908).	75
1956	S. Salute and Grand Canal, Venice, oil.	110
1958	Lever Art Gallery. C. Coast scene and fishermen, small oil.	504

JAN STEEN. 1626–1679

Since he often painted picturesque low company, Jan Steen was more popular in the late eighteenth century than Peter de Hooch. To-day prices for Jan Steen are very moderate and far below those of the peak period for Dutch pictures, 1913–1919. In 1913 the Rijksmuseum, Amsterdam, bought a picture for the equivalent of £110,000 in modern money.

		£
1774	Greenwood's auction. Tavern and 70 figures.	141 15s.
1800	Alexander Day Exhibition. Girl learning her prayers.	210
1818	Sir Robert Peel buys The music master (National Gallery, 1871).	310
1828	M. N. Zachary. C. Skittle-players (£203 14s. in 1810).	388 10s.
1841	Marquess Campden. C. The school (Marquess of Stafford).	1,092
1844	Jeremiah Harman. C. Dancing to bagpipes.	630
1847	Claudius Tarral. C. Effects of intemperance (see 1878, 1956).	236 5s.
1849	W. W. Hope. C. The poulterer.	525
1864	Oppenheim. C. The card party (£525 in 1870).	294
1872	Cope. C. Courtesan stealing a watch.	1,071
1878	Monro of Novar. C. Effects of intemperance (see 1847 and 1956).	1,312 10s.
1885	Hermann de Zoete. C. Bad company.	1,428
1893	Field. C. The greeting (see 1946).	724 10s.
1900	Peel heirlooms. C. Cabaret with figures.	1,362 10s.
1910	Octavus Coope. The sick lady.	3,412
1912	Norman Forbes Robertson. C. Twelfth Night feast, dated 1662 (see 1934).	2,152 10s.
1913	Steengracht, Paris. Joyous company.	16,700
	Subsequently bought by subscribers for the Rijksmuseum, Amsterdam.	18,370*
1919	L. Neumann. C. The spendthrift.	17,010
1928	Six, Amsterdam. Drinking party.	17,000
1931	Henry Hirsch. C. Twelfth Night feast (see 1912).	1,575
1934	Leopold Hirsch. C. Same picture.	2,625
1935	Macdonald of the Isles. C. Bridal couple's return.	2,520
1946	Lord Swaythling. C. The greeting (see 1893).	7,140

		£
1849	Sir Bernard Eckstein. S. The satyr and the peasant.	3,800
1956	Percy B. Meyer. C. The effects of intemperance (see 1817).	1,890
	Brussels, Palais des Beaux Arts. Joyeuse Compagnie.	4,500
1957	Sir Henry Price. S. Musicians in a tavern.	3,600
1960	Dreesman, Amsterdam. Wedding scene.	9,640

GEORGE STUBBS. 1724–1806

To-day Stubbs ranks among English painters with Gainsborough and Constable. The pictures which fetch £20,000 with some regularity are by no means his masterpieces. For a work like *The Wedgwood Family* it would be impossible to forecast a price, yet as late as the middle 'twenties, no picture by Stubbs could be expected to exceed 700 guineas. Very good ones could be had for 200 guineas, which was less than the painter charged in his own lifetime.

		£
1775	Hon. Charles Dillon. C. Horses fighting.	15 15*s.*
1785	Wildeman. C. Frightened horse, lioness and panther, a pair.	39 18*s.*
1796	Josiah Wedgwood commissions 'The Wedgwood family at Etruria Hall' (Museum, Stoke-on-Trent).	236 17*s.*
1801	Stubbs wins an action against Sir Vane Temple for his fee for a horse-and-rider portrait.	300
1807	Stubbs executors' sale. Thomas Hope fails to win an equestrian picture at	200
1811	General Stewart. C. The Shooting Pieces, small picture in enamel on porcelain.	110
1868	W. K. Gratwicke. C. The Keeper and The Steward, a pair.	388 10*s.*
1876	Horses in a landscape. C.	100 16*s.*
1891	G. A. F. Cavendish-Bentinck. C. 'Gimcrack' (see 1951).	52 10*s.*
1899	C. 4 paintings to illustrate shooting, each 40 ins. × 50 ins. 4 for	945
1902	J. R. F. Burnett. C. 'Eclipse' (see 1915 and 1929).	693
1905	Louis Huth. C. 2 porcelain pictures. Gamekeepers.	756
	Labourers.	546
	Lord Tweedmouth. C. Josiah Wedgwood, riding, 1782.	546
1910	Sir Walter Gilbey. C. Molly Longlegs (see 1947).	25 4*s.*
1915	Sir Walter Gilbey. C. Haymakers.	420
	Reapers (see 1959).	441
	'Eclipse' (see 1901, 1929).	735
	'Gimcrack' (see 1891, 1951).	231
	2nd 'Eclipse' portrait.	430 5*s.*
	7 others at less than £200 each. 12 pictures made about £3,300 between them.	

		£
1923	W. L. Agnew. C. Princess Charlotte's zebra (see 1960).	220 10s.
1927	S. Groom and two hunters.	1,180
	Knight, Frank. 'Shark', rider and trainer.	1,040
1929	Walter Raphael sells 'Eclipse' (see 1915).	7,350
	Said to have been resold in U.S.A. for £15,500.	
	Col. E. F. Hall. C. Huntsmen setting out.	4,410
1932	Ramsden. S. Sir John Ramsden, horse and groom.	750
1937	Comtesse de Greffulhe. S. Hunters in a park.	820
1940	Arthur Lyndley. C. Partridge shooting (on porcelain).	420
1942	C. Harvesters (on porcelain).	577 10s.
1943	Earl of Bolingbroke. C. 'Gimcrack' (see 1915) and 'Turf', a pair of horse portraits with riders.	8,820
1946	Lord Chesham. S. Pair of small horse pictures.	1,850
1947	Tresham Gilbey. C. 'Molly Longlegs' (see 1915).	1,942 10s.
1951	Hutchinson & Co. C. 'Gimcrack' (see 1891, 1915, 1943).	12,600
	'Turf' (see 1943).	5,250
1959	Mrs. Alexander Malcolm. S. Reapers (on porcelain) (see 1915).	13,500
	Stallions, a pair of frieze paintings.	19,000
1960	Earl of Shrewsbury. The poodle.	17,000
	Mrs. Matthew. S. A white spaniel.	2,800
	Harrod's. Princess Charlotte's zebra (see 1923).	20,000
1960	De Robeck. S. Baron de Robeck riding, 1791.	20,000
	M. D. Wyatt. S. Mr. and Mrs. Wilson at a hunt, 1752, a youthful work.	4,000

DAVID TENIERS, the younger. 1610–1674

There are two very striking features concerning the taste for Teniers. The first is that in the late eighteenth century his pictures were among the highest priced in the world, though Teniers himself had once boasted that he had covered three leagues with his brush. The second oddity is that people have been prepared to pay almost precisely the same prices in all ages, and no more, in spite of the devaluation of money. In fact, a Teniers graph is a mildly oscillating horizontal line.

		£
1768	Gaignat, Paris. Cabaret scene.	750
1776	Blondel de Gagny, Paris. The Prodigal Son, bought in.	1,248
1779	Houghton Hall. Empress Catherine buys The Cookshop.	800
1783	Blondel d'Azincourt. The Prodigal Son (see 1776), bought for Louis XVI, now in the Louvre.	1,040

		£
1798	Bryan (ex Calonne). Le Teniers au chaudrons (Duke of Bedford, Woburn).	735
	Le bonnet rouge (see 1928).	367 10s.
1800	Orleans (Coxe). The cabaret and the shepherd (bought by Beckford).	500
1805	Robert Heathcote (Skinner). Kermesse (said to have cost £1,050).	215
1811	Lafontaine. C. Kermesse, bought for the Prince Regent (Royal Collections).	1,732 10s.
1815	Delahante sells the Prince Regent a Village feast (Royal Collections).	1,680
1821	Knight (Philips). Village feast.	420
1829	Lord Gwydyr. C. The Acts of Mercy.	387
1834	Duc de Berri. C. The Fair at Ghent (bought in, see 1837).	1,470
1837	Duchesse de Berri. Paris. Fair at Ghent (see 1834).	645
1840	Simon Clark. C. The Freemasons (see 1872).	661 10s.
1844	Penrice. C. Peasant card-players.	892 10s.
1846	Higginson of Saltmarshe. C. La grande Kermesse.	1,260
1850	Metcalfe. C. Six peasants dancing.	829 10s.
1857	Mackintosh. C. The Prodigal Son (on copper).	850 10s.
1864	Oppenheim. C. Kermesse.	1,522 10s.
1872	Charles Cope. C. The Freemasons (see 1840).	1,575
1882	Hamilton Palace. C. Group in a kitchen.	945
1886	Duke of Marlborough. C. The Teniers Gallery. 117 miniature copies of old masters (see 1959).	2,031 11s.
1892	Samson Wertheimer. C. The guardroom (see 1913).	1,780 10s.
	Village fête.	1,575
1913	Oppenheimer. C. The guardroom (see 1892).	2,100
	The alehouse.	1,260
1919	Neumann. C. Seven Ages of Mercy.	1,575
	Trictrac-players.	1,522 10s.
1925	Earl of Carnarvon. C. The Four Seasons (copper).	630
1927	Hon. Mrs. Yorke. C. The Prodigal Son.	1,785
1928	Holford. C. Le bonnet rouge (see 1798).	3,360*
1937	Lewis Lloyd. C. Cabaret scene.	1,470
1939	C. The Four Seasons (see 1925).	525
1943	Sir Berkeley Sheffield. C. Fortune teller.	1,260
1944	Neeld. C. Temptation of St. Anthony (signed).	1,323
1947	Cooper. C. Skittle-players.	997 10s.
1950	Col. H. S. Clowes. Fête de village.	1,575
1953	Galerie Charpentier, Paris. Temptation of St. Anthony.	3,165
1959	Loeser. S. A single miniature painting from the Blenheim Teniers Gallery (see 1886), reproducing a lost Giogione.	2,600

		£
1960	S. Village scene and figures.	750
	Mountains and hermit's cave.	750
	Galerie Charpentier, Paris. The alchemyst.	2,686

GERARD TERBORCH. 1617–1681

Tightly painted and rather wooden, Terborch's pictures were the quintessence of French taste at the end of the eighteenth century, but much less appreciated in England. The record prices in the present century—and they are staggering—have been paid in Paris and Amsterdam. Nor must one forget *The Peace of Munster*, that singularly stodgy work which in 1868 became one of the ten most expensive pictures in the world.

		£
1790	C. Lady in satin, drinking.	225 15*s.*
1800	The love-letter (Windsor). Bought by Francis Baring.	450
1802	Holderness. C. Family group.	325 10*s.*
1804	Van Leyden, Amsterdam. Talleyrand buys The Peace of Munster.	640
1807	Talleyrand, Paris. Lady with a lute and companions.	787 10*s.*
1826	C. Same picture bought by Robert Peel (National Gallery, 1871).	966
1837	Duchesse de Berri. Paris. The Peace of Munster (see 1804).	1,820
1848	Casimir Perrier. C. Old woman reading (Hertford, Wallace Collection).	640 10*s.*
1868	San Donato, Paris. The Peace of Munster (see 1837), bought by Richard Wallace; given to National Gallery, 1872.	7,200
1878	Monro of Novar. C. The glass of lemonade.	1,942 10*s.*
1895	Lyne-Stephens. C. Officer courting.	2,047 10*s.*
1904	C. Lady with a letter.	1,680
1913	Six, Paris. Mother combing her child's hair.	13,850
1923	Sir J. B. Robinson. C. Interior and figures.	3,150
1928	Six, Amsterdam. Lady with gallants.	25,000*
1928	C. Lady at her toilet.	1,522 10*s.*
1937	Comtesse de Greffulhe. S. The message.	1,900
1946	Melbourne National Gallery buys portrait of a lady.	5,000
1955	Viscountess d'Abernon. C. Hermanna van der Cruysse.	1,260

GIAMBATTISTA TIEPOLO. 1693–1770

Perhaps the most truly splendid figure of the Venetian revival, but the Victorian prejudice against Tiepolo's unabashed paganism died hard. At the Beckett Denison sale in 1885, when the National Gallery acquired its first two Tiepolos for £162 16*s.*, Redford, in *The Times*, dismissed Tiepolo as 'that facile decorator of the later Venetian school'. Until very recently, Tiepolo's paintings, despite their habitual fine condition, have been absurdly cheap in comparison with his pen-and-ink drawings; and the latter, it is shameful to have to add, are cheap compared with the journalese productions of the younger Tiepolo, Giandomenicho.

		£
1859	Earl of Northwick (Philips). Coriolanus and the Roman matrons.	13 13s.
	St. Vincent de Paul.	59 17s.
1878	Monro of Novar. C. Holy Family, 8 ft.	99 15s.
	Martyrdom of St. Agnes.	105
1885	Beckett Denison. C. National Gallery buys 2 pendant pictures of Henry IV at Canossa (formerly Earl of Dudley, £152 10s.).	162 15s.
1891	Cavendish-Bentinck. C. National Gallery buys Deposition from the Cross.	157 10s.
1893	C. Immaculate Conception (see 1908).	540 15s.
1905	Capel Cure. C. The finding of Moses (small).	262 10s.
1908	A. Hitchens. C. The Immaculate Conception (see 1893).	430 10s.
1910	Earle Drax. C. Adoration of the Magi.	735
1911	Consul Weber, Barlin. 2 panels from a Crucifixion.	13,000
1918	T. F. White. C. The Trojan horse (National Gallery).	2,250
1927	Pallavicini (Knight, Frank & Rutley). An Oriental with fair beard.	1,212 10s.
1928	Chrisovelonni. C. Rebecca at the well.	2,625
	The woman taken in adultery.	2,415
1933	Melbourne National Gallery buys Banquet of Cleopatra.	25,000
1935	Faucher-Magnan. S. Apotheosis of the poet Soderini, oil sketch.	920
1936	S. A halberdier (nearly 7 ft.).	1,400
1938	G. L. Durlacher. C. Girl with a parrot.	1,365
1941	Robinson and Fisher. Virgin's head, small.	294
1948	Sir Bernard Eckstein. S. Bacchus and Ariadne, small oil sketch (see 1955).	1,400
1952	Galerie Charpentier, Paris. Sacrifice of Iphigenia.	5,308
1955	S. Bacchus and Ariadne (see 1948).	2,600
1960	S. Baron von Pollnitz, Christ and woman of Samaria.	7,500
	Edward Washer. Diogenes (small head) (San Francisco, Cal., 1939, £50).	2,800
1960	Gladys Robinson, New York. Triumph of the Church (oil monochrome sketch, 2½ ft. × 3½ ft.).	3,210
1960	Galerie Charpentier. Beauty abducted by Time (over 7 ft.).	25,360

DRAWINGS

1885	S. 350 drawings, bought by the Victoria and Albert Museum.	12

		£
1929	Bernard d'Hendecourt. S. Flight into Egypt.	400
1935	Faucher-Magnan. S. 2 studies, Apollo protecting the arts.	340
		420
1949	S. Holy Family with St. Joseph.	340
1953	Lord Greene. S. Head of a young man, red chalk.	580
1956	Salle Drouet, Paris. Head of a young man, pen and wash.	2,250
	Death of Seneca, pen and wash.	1,000

GIANDOMENICHO TIEPOLO. 1727–1804

From *The Childhood of Pulcinello*, an album of 150 pen-and-wash drawings which was offered in the early 1920's for £500.

		£
1953	Henry Reitlinger. S. Drawing from this series.	640
	Another from the same series.	620
1956	Hanning Philips. C. Home life of Pulcinello.	920
1959	S. Pulcinello at school.	1,700

Jacopo Robusti
IL TINTORETTO. 1518–1599

Tintoretto never recovered from the pasting he received in Reynolds's discourses, and in the 1850's even the intensive propaganda of *The Stones of Venice* could not create a market for him. Or perhaps it would be more truthful to say that Tintoretto's easel works had never been popular at any time. The distortions (half way to El Greco), the impure pigments, the oil-sketch character of most of the works, the difficulty of determining schoolpieces—all have contributed. The post-war pictures in this list are of the attributed kind.

		£
1795	Joshua Reynolds. C. Christ washing feet of disciples (see 1882).	52 10*s.*
1795	C. The raising of Lazarus (see 1927, 1947).	168
1800	Orleans (Coxe). Bryan buys in The origin of the Milky Way (Childhood of Hercules) (see 1892).	52 10*s.*
1814	Delahante. C. Jupiter and Leda.	220 10*s.*
1856	Samuel Rogers. C. The miracle of the slave, oil sketch (see 1922).	430 10*s.*
1859	Earl of Northwick (Philips). 5 attributed pictures, 12 to 38 guineas.	
1882	Hamilton Palace. C. Venetian admiral (Vincenzo Morosini) (see 1924).	1,155

		£
1882	Christ washing feet of disciples (see 1795) (in two pieces and in very bad condition), bought by Burton for the National Gallery (80 ins. × 160 ins.).	157 10*s.*
1886	William Graham. C. Jupiter, nursed by nymphs.	420
1890	Earl of Darnley. National Gallery buys Origin of the Milky Way (see 1800).	1,312 10*s.*
1893	Bingham-Mildmay. C. A Venetian admiral.	903
1895	Henry Doetsch. C. Agostino Barbarigo, half-length.	99 15*s.*
1905	Capel Cure. C. Bartolommeo Capello (see 1929).	120 15*s.*
1910	Mrs. Arthur Severn. Metropolitan Museum buys The Doge Mocenigo presented to the Saviour, ex Ruskin Collection.	10,000
1911	Charles Butler. C. Moses striking the rock.	787 10*s.*
1913	Mariczell de Nemes, Paris. The woman taken in adultery.	10,850
1922	Baroness Burdett-Coutts. C. The miracle of the slave, oil sketch (see 1856).	840
1924	National Gallery buys Vincenzo Morosini (through National Art Collections Fund) (see 1882).	14,000
1926	Sir W. Bromley Davenport. C. Apollo and Marsyas.	2,205
1927	Holford. C. Raising of Lazarus (see 1795).	3,360
	Man in black at a table.	3,045
	Gentleman at a window.	2,100
	David and Goliath.	2,625
1927	Melbourne National Gallery buys Pietro Loredano.	14,000
1928	At Robinson and Fisher's. Diana and Endymion.	4,310
1929	Lord Yarborough. C. Pieta, small oil-sketch.	3,675
	S. A member of the Capello family, portrait (see 1905).	8,000
1932	Glogowski. S. Unknown portrait.	1,600
1944	National Gallery buys Departure of John the Baptist for the desert.	12,000
1946	Earl of Kinnaird. C. Conversion of Paul.	1,050
1947	Lord Rothermere. C. Raising of Lazarus (see 1927).	4,830
1956	S. Miracle of loaves and fishes.	1,600
1959	C. Senator in red robes.	2,520
	Mrs. Walter Burns. S. Family group, over 8 ft.	2,520
1960	Gladys Robinson, New York. Small head of a prelate.	5,000

JAMES TISSOT. 1836–1902

A Frenchman who came to England in 1871 and who painted anecdotal pictures, but charmingly in a manner deriving from Whistler and Manet. He had a modest vogue in his lifetime and was even reputed to have made a £1,000 fee on occasions. But it was decided at his death that he had not created High Art. Furthermore, his own admirers were antagonised by the religious paintings of his last years. By the 1920's Tissot's poetic and evocative paintings were hardly worth the price of their frames. A revival began in the 'thirties and to-day the better sort of Tissot should make over a thousand pounds.

		£
1873	Murrieta. C. On the Thames, bought in (see 1883).	598 10s.
1874	Lord Powerscourt. C. Avant le depart.	945
1875	Barlow. C. The world and the cloister.	367 10s.
1876	The railway station.	388 10s.
1881	Houldsworth. C. The reply, bought in.	787 10s.
1883	Murrieta. C. On the Thames (see 1873).	273
1888	Charles Waring. C. Les adieux.	231 10s.
	William Lee. C. Visitors to the National Gallery (see 1929).	157 10s.
1903	Branch and Lees. The captain's daughter.	183 15s.
1913	Lord Holden. C. Waiting for the Fourth.	44 2s.
1928	Tate Gallery buys The visit.	40
1929	C. Visitors to the National Gallery (see 1888).	21
	Tate Gallery buys The picnic.	200
1937	Chantrey Bequest buys The ball on shipboard.	600
1940	C. In Kew Gardens.	73 10s.
1945	Chantrey Bequest buys The party on board a man-of-war.	2,500
1947	C. Reading the news.	304 10s.
1951	C. Henley Regatta.	945
1954	C. Waiting for the ferry.	1,627 10s.
1957	C. Amateur circus.	1,207
	Hide and seek.	892 10s.

Tiziano Vecellio
TITIAN. 1480?–1576

There have really been only three periods when Titian has been estimated at his true worth in England: in the reign of Charles I, under the Regency of George IV and since 1929. The fantastic neglect of the Victorian age was due to a failure to appreciate a painter who never in his life descended to cheap emotionalism. Unlike Rubens, Titian has never appealed to the common man. One of the most singular features of the great Orleans picture speculation of 1798–1800 was the failure of these new buyers to take up the several fine and cheap Titians. But for the intensive efforts of Duveen, the same phenomenon might have repeated itself in the present century.

		£
1785	Earl of Dover offers for Benjamin West's spurious Titian, The death of Actaeon (see 1820)	1,300
1787	Sir John Taylor. C. Holy Family and saints, said to have belonged to Charles I.	493 10s.

		£
1795	Sir Joshua Reynolds. C. The Entombment.	168
1798	Orleans Collection. Valuations for the Duke of Bridgewater (now collection of Earl of Ellesmere):	
	Diana and Actaeon (at National Gallery, Edinburgh).	2,625
	Diana and Calisto (at National Gallery, Edinburgh).	2,625
	Allegory of human life (at National Gallery, Edinburgh).	630
	Venus à la coquille (at National Gallery, Edinburgh).	840
	Portrait, Clement VII (see 1946).	420
	Orleans Collection sales:	
	Philip II and his mistress. Earl Fitzwilliam.	1,050
	Rape of Europa. Lord Berwick (see 1896), Fenway Court, Boston.	735
	Smaller Diana and Actaeon (now Harewood Collection).	210
	Perseus and Andromeda. Bryan (now Wallace Collection).	326 10s.
	Noli me tangere. Thomas Hope (see 1820, National Gallery).	330
	Venus and Adonis. Fitzhugh (see 1884, 1899).	420
	Riposo. Henry Walton (see 1842 and 1927).	262 10s.
	Penitent Magdalene. Thomas Maitland (see 1929).	367 10s.
1801	Alexander Day Exhibition, ex Colonna Palace. Angerstein buys Ganymede (schoolpiece).	1,500
	Venus and Adonis.	2,750
	(See 1824).	
1807	Earl of Kinnaird buys Bacchus and Ariadne from Buchanan, bought from Aldobrandini Palace, possibly for £1,900 by James Irvine). Price according to Farington,	3,150
1810	Campion. C. Rape of Europa (see 1798, 1896).	309 15s.
1810	Walsh Porter. C. Ariadne in Naxos (copy of Prado picture?).	1,575
1813	Earl of Kinnaird (Philips). Bacchus and Ariadne, bought in. Sold subsequently to Thomas Bazely (see 1824).	2,625
1815	Page Turner. C. Perseus and Andromeda (see 1798), bought by Lord Yarmouth. Wallace Collection.	362
1817	Edward Solly buys Titian self-portrait in Venice (Berlin Museum since 1821).	300
1820	Benjamin West. C. Death of Actaeon, bought in. (Acquired 1783. In 1899 it made £210).	1,785
	Champernowne. C. Noli me tangere (see 1798). Left by Samuel Rogers to National Gallery, 1856.	330 15s.
1824	National Gallery buys from Angerstein, Jnr., The Ganymede (schoolpiece).	2,000
	Venus and Adonis.	3,500

		£
1826	National Gallery buys Bacchus and Ariadne from Thomas Hamlet as part of block purchase, probably	5,325*
1826	Lord Radstock. C. Salome and head of St. John.	1,890
1842	C. Riposo in landscape (see 1798).	430 10*s.*
1849	Coningham. C. Tarquin and Lucretia (Fitzwilliam Museum).	525
1847	Claudius Tarral. C. Daniello Barbaro (see 1928).	39 18*s.*
1850	King of Holland, Amsterdam. Philip II and his mistress (see 1798).	833
1852	Soult, Paris. The tribute money, bought by National Gallery (now called Paris Bordone).	2,604
1852	Dawson Taylor. C. The Rape of Europa (see 1798, 1896). National Gallery attacked by Morris Moore for not bidding.	288 10*s.*
1856	Samuel Rogers. C. Apotheosis of Charles V (see 1927).	283 10*s.*
1869	C. So-called Titian's daughter, whole-length.	845 5*s.*
1870	San Donato, Paris. Duke of Urbino and his son (see 1959).	700
1876	C. Man in a red cap (see 1914).	94 10*s.*
1882	Hamilton Palace. C. Holy Family with St. John (resold Beckett Denison sale. C. 1885, for £325 10*s.*).	1,207 10*s.*
1884	Miles, Leigh Court. C. Venus and Adonis (see 1798 and 1899).	1,764
1892	Earl of Dudley. C. Holy Family, bought by Ludwig Mond and left to National Gallery, 1924.	2,520
1896	Earl of Darnley. Isabella Stewart Gardner buys The Rape of Europa (see 1798, 1810, 1852) (now Fenway Court Museum, Boston).	20,500
1899	Sir Cecil Miles. Venus and Adonis (see 1798, 1884).	420
1903	E. F. Milliken. C. Giorgio Cornaro, portrait.	4,725
1904	Sir George Donaldson sells the so-called portrait of Ariosto to the National Gallery, bought by the Earl of Darnley in the early nineteenth century.	30,000
1906	Man with a red cap (see 1876), bought by Hugh Lane.	2,170
1911	Charles Butler. Tarquin and Lucretia (schoolpiece, bought in, 1879, £273).	2,730
1912	J. E. Taylor. C. The lace-maker (£136 10*s.* in 1881).	3,750
1913	Portrait of Philip II, dated 1554, sold by Hugh Lane to Mrs. J. Thomas Emery (Cincinnatti Art Institute).	60,000
1914	Arthur M. Grenfell. C. Man with red cap (see 1906).	13,650
	Bought back by Hugh Lane and sold to H. C. Frick in 1915 (Frick Foundation).	50,000
1914	Caterina Cornaro, bought by Herbert Cook from Crespi Collection as a Giorgione.	36,000
1924	Portrait of a friar, bought by National Gallery, Melbourne.	7,950
1925	Earl of Darnley. C. Venus and Adonis (see 1798, 1884, 1899), now Metropolitan Museum.	2,415

		£
1925	Joseph Widener buys the Althorp version of this picture, now National Gallery, Washington.	50,000 (?)
1926	Corry sale, Esher. The apotheosis of Charles V (see 1856), bought by National Gallery.	11,000
1927	Holford. C. A second Caterina Cornaro (Böhler Collection, Lucerne).	4,200
	The Orleans Riposo (see 1798, 1842).	3,570
1928	Tatton. C. Daniello Barbaro (see 1847).	7,560
1929	Duke of Northumberland sells the Cornaro family to the National Gallery.	122,000
1929	Lord Brownlow. C. The Magdalene (see 1798).	4,620
	Navagero family portrait (male head).	3,255
1930	Marquess of Lansdowne. Man with a short beard.	8,505
1931	Andrew Mellon buys the Hermitage Museum's Venus with a mirror.	112,250
1932	Duveen buys Venus and the lute-player from Earl of Leicester, Holkham, bought by the Metropolitan Museum, New York, in 1936.	About 100,000
1936	Knight, Frank and Rutley. Lady in brown dress.	3,990
1948	Knight, Frank and Rutley. Bianca Capella, attributed portrait.	3,760
	C. Small attributed Holy Family.	3,990
1953	Tollemache Estates. Man with a letter.	6,510
1955	Francis Howard. C. Small allegory of prudence.	11,550
1959	Duke of Westminster. S. Duke of Urbino and his son (see 1870).	24,000

CONSTANTIN TROYON. 1810–1865

'The French Cuyp' was a highly prized painter in the London of the 1880's and 1890's. His cattle scenes rated with Landseer's Highland pictures and higher than Millais's landscapes, and his market lasted until the First World War. Yet, long before their recognition of their Impressionists, the better French critics had preferred the lighter touch of Corot and Daubigny. It is difficult to understand today the hold which Troyon had over the tycoons' market in England and America. He handled rich, heavy paint with ability, yet he seems incapable of advancing far from the Cuyp formula. He had a certain pioneering value, but this became overrated, as so often is the case. *Les hauteurs de Suresnes*, which had once been considered Troyon's masterpiece, was sold in 1944 for the price of two cases of black market whisky. But there has been a moderate recovery.

		£
1860	Gambart. C. Cattle on the seashore.	136 10*s.*
1870	Creswick. C. Coast scene with boats.	609
1873	Sir J. Pender. C. Landscape with cattle.	1,417

		£
1883	William Lee. C. Cattle, evening.	1,995
1887	Charles Waring. C. The ferry.	3,675
	Bolckow. C. The watercart (bought for £40).	2,100
1889	Secrétan, Paris. La descente des vaches (see 1927).	2,200
	Le passage du Gué (see 1927).	4,800
	Secrétan, London. C. Les hauteurs de Suresnes (see 1944).	3,045
	La guarde-chasse.	2,940
1890	Bolckow. C. Going to market.	4,930
1895	Mrs. Lyne Stephens. C. Dogs and gamekeepers.	2,992 10s.
1899	Mieville. C. Dairy farm.	6,720
1902	William Waring. C. Cattle and sheep.	7,350
1910	Alexander Young. C. Vaches aux pâturages (see 1927).	6,090
	Charles T. Yerkes, New York. Coming from market.	8,275*
1914	Coates. C. 2 cattle landscapes.	6,090
		5,775
1918	C. The plough.	1,155
1919	Sir J. Drummond. C. Summer storm.	1,575
1922	C. Glade in a forest (7 ft. 6 ins. × 5 ft.).	105
	C. Going to market (small version).	252
1927	Hon. Mrs. Dennison. C. Le passage du gué (see 1889).	472 10s.
	Sir James Ross. La descente des vaches (see 1889).	567
	Sir James Murray. C. Vaches aux pâturages (see 1910).	577 10s.
1933	C. Woods and meadows.	120 15s.
1944	J. Pierpont Morgan, Jnr. C. Les hauteurs de Suresnes (see 1889).	126
1952	Parke-Bernet, New York. Going home, evening.	71 10s.
1955	Vagliano. C. The farm pond (12 ins. × 15½ ins.).	630

JOSEPH MALLORD WILLIAM TURNER. 1775–1851

Unlike Constable, Turner has not kept pace in general with the inflation of the times. Later Impressionist Turners on the grand scale seem unlikely to appear in the saleroom, but the early and now very brown seascapes and Claude pastiches fetch less than at the turn of the present century. The big Swiss and Rhineland water-colours are dearer than in 1912, but at best they have barely doubled in value. On the other hand, small water-colours and oil-sketches make prices which would have been impossible during the boom years 1863–1913 when size was the yardstick of value.

		£
1799	Angerstein buys watercolour, Carnarvon Castle.	42
1800	William Beckford buys The fifth plague in Egypt.	157 10s.
1801	Duke of Bridgewater buys Dutch boats in a gale.	262 10s.

		£
1806	Falls of the Rhine (now Boston Fine Arts Museum).	367 10s.
	Lord de Tabley buys Walton Bridges (see 1845).	210
1813	Sir John Swinburn buys Mercury and Herse (see 1897).	577 10s.
	Walter Fawkes buys a view of Dort, challenge to Cuyp (see 1937).	525
1824	George IV buys Battle of Trafalgar (Royal Collections).	630
1827	De Tabley. C. Turner buys back Sun rising through mist (National Gallery, 1856).	513
1835	John Nash. C. Cowes harbour.	283 10s.
1844	Elhanan Bicknell buys Palestrina (see 1863).	1,050
	Offers £1,600 for Sun rising through mist.	
1845	Thomas Wright. C. Walton bridges (see 1890, 1904, 1917).	703 10s.
1848	Newington Hughes. C. Sheerness (see 1890).	593
1850	Charles Meigh. French coast (Fort Vimieux), bought by Lenox of New York (see 1956).	693
1853	Broderip. C. The Dogana, Church of San Giorgio, commissioned for Chantrey, 1841.	1,155
1854	James Wadmore. C. Cologne.	2,100
	Harbour at Dieppe.	1,942 10s.
	Guardship at Nore (see 1893, 1945).	1,606 10s.
1860	H. A. J. Monro (Novar). C. The Grand Canal (see 1875).	2,626
1863	Bicknell. C. Palestrina (see 1844), bought in (see 1881).	1,995
	Re-sold by Bicknell's executors in 1865.	2,205
	Helvoetsluys (see 1954).	1,680
	Antwerp, van Goyen in search of a subject (see 1887, 1912).	2,635 10s.
	Port Ruysdael (see 1919 and 1960).	1,995
	Lucerne (see 1869), wc, commissioned 1842, £84.	735
1867	Monro of Novar. C. Modern Italy, bought in (see 1878).	3,466
1869	Smith. C. Lord Dudley buys Lucerne, wc (see 1863).	1,029
1870	Bullock. C. Dudley buys Venice, Dogana and Salute (see 1899).	2,688
1872	Joseph Gillott. C. Walton bridges (see 1845 and 1890).	5,250
	Thames and Medway (now Washington National Gallery, per Widener).	4,567
	Kilgarran Castle, bought by Metropolitan Museum, N.Y.	2,835
	John Ruskin. C. Grand Canal and Rialto (see 1875).	4,000 10s.
	Water-colours, Gillott Sale	
	Bamborough Castle, bought by Earl of Dudley.	3,307 10s.
	Heidelberg and Ehrenbretstein (Heidelberg, see 1908). each	2,782 10s.
1875	Mendel. C. Grand Canal and Rialto (see 1860), Agnew.	7,350
	Sold to Earl of Dudley, £8,055 (see 1885).	

		£
1878	Monro of Novar. C. Ancient Italy.	5,450
	Modern Italy (see 1867).	5,260
	Rome from the Aventine.	6,142 10*s*.
	Piazza San Marco.	5,460
	Van Tromp's Shallop (see 1946).	5,460
1884	Cosmo Orme. C. 4 early water-colours make £3,297. Considered a slump price, since £4,200 had been offered in 1872.	
1885	On the death of Earl of Dudley, Cornelius Vanderbilt was said to have paid for the Grand Canal (see 1875)	20,000
1887	John Graham. C. Antwerp (see 1863) (Frick Foundation, bought 1912).	6,300
1890	William Wells of Redleaf. C. Sheerness (see 1848) (Lady Wantage Collection).	7,450
	Ayscough Fawkes. Lucerne from Fluellen (see 1959), wc.	2,310
	Bolckow. C. Walton bridges (see 1845, 1872, 1904, 1918).	7,450
1893	Earl of Essex. C. The Nore (see 1854, 1945).	4,305
1895	James Pryce of Paignton. Helvoetsluys (see 1863, 1927, 1954).	6,720
	Lake Zug, wc (see 1959).	1,156
1896	Julian Goldsmid. C. Rockets and blue lights (see 1910).	3,885
1897	Sir John Pender. C. 4 Turners for £30,000.	
	Mercury and Herse (see 1813, 1946).	7,875
	Wreckers off Cumberland coast.	7,980
	State procession at Venice.	7,350
	Venice, the Giudecca (£2,100 in 1863). (See 1930).	7,140
1899	Fowler. C. Venice, the Dogana and Salute (see 1870, 1927).	8,610
1904	James Orrock. C. Walton bridges (see 1890, 1917).	7,350
1906	W. R. Cassels. C. Rape of Europa (£309 15*s*. in 1872).	6,720
1908	Stephen Holland. C. Mortlake Terrace (see 1913).	13,250
	Mrs. Pound. C. The storm.	5,775
	The morning after.	8,085
1908	C. Heidelberg, wc (see 1872).	4,410
	Constance, wc (see 1917).	2,310
1909	Holbrooke Jackson. C. Burning of Houses of Parliament (McFadden Collection, Philadelphia).	13,125
	Parkes. C. East Cowes Castle (see 1913).	6,825
1910	Charles T. Yerkes. New York. Rockets and blue lights, bought by Duveen for U.S.A.	26,500
	Dream of Venice.	12,000
1912	J. E. Taylor. C. Red Rigi, wc (£8,295 in 1928).	2,100
	Blue Rigi (see 1942), wc.	2,835
	Carisbrook Castle (see 1930), wc.	1,995

		£
1913	Borden, New York. Duveen buys East Cowes Castle (now Frick Foundation) (see 1909).	21,700
	Mortlake Terrace (see 1908), sold to Frick, about	30,800*
1917	National Gallery, Melbourne, buys Walton bridges (see 1806, 1890, 1904).	3,675
1917	Sir Joseph Beecham. Constance, wc (see 1908).	4,252
	Mouth of Grand Canal, wc (see 1942).	2,572
	Windsor Castle, wc (£1,785 in 1908).	3,360
1919	Sir George Drummond. C. Zürich, wc (£1,260 in 1877).	6,510
	Port Ruysdael (see 1863 and 1960).	6,720
1919	Camperdown. C. Bonneville, wc (see 1930).	3,780
1926	Lord Burgh. C. View near North Court, Isle of Wight.	6,247 10*s.*
1927	Sir James Ross. C. Venice, the Dogana and Salute (see 1870, 1899).	30,450*
	(Still the auction record for any Turner picture.)	
	Helvoetsluys (see 1895, 1954).	8,925
1929	Lord Yarborough. C. Vintage festival at Macon.	9,030
1930	Barnet Lewis. C. Bonneville, wc (see 1919).	1,517
	C. P. Allen. C. Lausanne from Le Signale, wc (£1,732 in 1912).	577 10*s.*
	Carisbrook Castle, wc (see 1912).	892 10*s.*
1930	Monell, New York. Venice, the Guidecca (see 1897).	17,000
1935	A. A. Allen. S. Lake Thun, wc (£1,417 10*s.* in 1912).	294
1936	Cuthbert Quilter. C. Adonis parting for the chase (£4,200 in 1909).	3,360
1937	W. R. Fawkes. C. Dortdrecht, challenge to Cuyp (see 1813), bought in.	6,510
	C. Lausanne from Le Signale, wc (see 1930 and 1942).	546
1942	Walter Jones. C. Red Rigi (see 1912, 1929).	1,155
	Blue Rigi (see 1912).	1,575
	Mouth of the Grand Canal, wc (see 1917).	357
	Mainz, wc (£1,207 10*s.* in 1912), Barber Institute.	577 10*s.*
	Lausanne from Le Signale, wc (see 1930, 1937).	483
1945	S. The Nore (see 1893).	1,785
1946	Lord Swaythling. C. Mercury and Herse (see 1897).	2,625
	Thomas Pitt-Miller. C. Van Tromp's shallop (see 1878).	2,730
	Quillebœuf, wc.	3,465
1954	Miss L. Coates. C. Helvoetsluys (see 1863, 1927).	9,240
1956	Lenox, New York. Fort Vimieux (see 1850).	20,000
	Staffa, Fingal's Cave, bought 1845.	17,200
1958	S. Spiez, small water-colour.	3,400
	Tell's chapel at Fluellen, wc.	2,100
1959	Mirrielees. C. Lake Zug, wc (see 1895).	11,028*
	Lake Lucerne wc, (see 1869, 1890).	11,550*
	Record prices for Turner's water-colours.	

		£
1959	H. L. Fison. C. Mountains with cattle, small oil.	8,925
1960	Parke-Bernet, New York. Port Ruysdael (see 1863 and 1919).	11,072
1960	S. Bedford, wc (£504 in 1878), small.	5,500
	Llanthony Abbey, wc.	5,000
	Bellinzona, wc.	3,500

MAURICE UTRILLO. 1883–1955

Began as a fairly straightforward Impressionist painter, but developed a sort of shorthand style of his own. Works of obvious, though not very profound, charm, tailing off very badly indeed after the First World War; so much so that forgeries are not easy to detect. Before 1950 it was unusual for these works to fetch more than £500.

		£
1928	C. La rue Boyer, 1913.	525
1939	C. Tour St. Jacques.	54 12*s.*
1940	Sir Chartres Biron. S. Village church.	72
1942	Charles T. Reid. C. Village church, 1914.	504
1944	Pincus Brennen, New York. Paysage de Banlieu.	1,040
1946	Parke-Bernet, New York. A presbytery, Corsica.	678
1947	Parke-Bernet, New York. Rue Mont Cenis.	525
1949	H. A. C. Gregory. S. The barracks.	950
1950	Galerie Charpentier, Paris. Derriere la maison.	1,130
1951	Parke-Bernet, New York. Suburban street.	768
1952	Parke-Bernet, New York. Moulin à Montmagny.	1,175
1953	Salle Droot, Paris. Le Lapin Agile, Montmartre (see 1958).	2,050
1954	Galerie Charpentier, Paris. Rue St. Vincent.	2,860
1956	Parke-Bernet, New York. Small town in the Paris Banlieu.	5,175
1957	Galerie Charpentier, Paris. Rue Sancelles.	9,350
1957	Weinberg. S. Street in Montmartre (see 1960).	9,200
1958	Parke-Bernet, New York. Le Lapin Agile, Montmartre (see 1953).	10,000
1959	S. A château.	6,000
	Church under snow.	4,500
	Street scene.	6,800
1959	Salle Drouot, Paris. Montmartre, snow scene.	12,500
1960	C. Eglise Sacre Cœur, Montmartre.	7,350
	Street in Montmartre (see 1957).	6,300
	S. Escalier de la Reine Berthe, Chartres.	7,800
1961	Barbara Church, New York. Rue de Crimée, 1910, 40 ins.	18,507

ADRIAEN VAN DE VELDE. 1635–1672

An able, derivative painter, much influenced by his masters, Wouvermans and Paul Potter, and therefore very much in the eighteenth-century taste. The National Gallery owns eight, but the once brisk market is practically extinct.

		£
1776	Blondel de Gagny, Paris. Landscape with figures.	624
1777	Randon de Boisset, Paris. Cattlepiece.	832
1811	Lafontaine. C. Lord Yarmouth buys Peasants and Cattle reposing, for the Prince Regent (bought from Smet van Alpen for £688).	1,890
1833	Nieuwenhuys. C. Large landscape.	1,375 10*s.*
1840	Sir Simon Clark. C. Peasant at a ford, bought by Robert Peel (National Gallery, 1871).	798
1846	Higginson of Saltmarshe. C. Mercury and Argus.	493 10*s.*
1864	Oppenheim. C. Woman and cattle at a ford.	451 10*s.*
1875	Miss Bredel. C. A miniature cattlepiece.	4,515*
1876	Foster, Clewer Manor. C. A view on the Rhine.	3,150
1890	William Wells. C. Three cows, two goats.	987
1896	Sir E. Dean Paul. C. Maternal occupation.	798 10*s.*
1903	Sir E. Page Turner. C. Woman washing her feet.	367 10*s.*
1928	Holford. C. Pastoral scene, 1663.	651
1953	Borthwick Norton. C. Woody park.	787 10*s.*

WILLEM VAN DE VELDE. 1633–1707

An English taste which dates from the days when Van de Velde held appointments from Charles II and James II. Rather more saleable in modern times than Adriaen van de Velde, but none the less deadly monotonous. The National Gallery owns 16, among which the ships at anchor appear much more satisfactory than the ships in storms.

		£
1772	R. Ansell. Seapiece from the Braamcamp Collection.	315
1785	Desenfans. A calm.	294
1803	Walsh Porter. C. Seafight.	430 10*s.*
1811	Lafontaine. Lord Yarmouth buys Fleet at anchor for Prince Regent (Royal Collections).	997 10*s.*
1823	Watson Taylor. C. A calm (National Gallery, 1871).	409 10*s.*
1833	Nieuwenhuys. C. On the Zuider Zee.	531 15*s.*
1840	Sir Simon Clark. C. Becalmed fleet.	976 10*s.*
1843	Sir B. Codrington. C. Fishing boats and jetty.	1,548 15*s.*
1844	Jeremiah Harman. C. Le coup de canon.	1,449

		£
1846	Higginson of Saltmarshe. C. Men-of-war in a calm, bought by Hertford, Wallace Collection.	1,764
1859	Earl of Northwick (Philips). Fleet becalmed (see 1896).	651
1864	Anderson. C. Dutch fleet off the Texel.	682 10s.
1873	Herbert. Dutch yacht and men-of-war.	766 10s.
1876	Foster, Clewer Manor. C. A calm.	2,367 10s.
1882	Hamilton Palace. C. A calm, ship saluting (resold, 1885, £829 10s.).	1,365
1891	Lord Haldon. C. Departure of Charles II.	1,963 10s.
1896	C. Fleet becalmed (see 1859).	525
1908	Henry Say, Paris. Dutch fleet.	1,020
1914	Gomme. C. Fleet at anchor.	2,625
1927	Hon. Mrs. Yorke. S. Dutch fleet at anchor.	1,825
1928	Holford. C. Small fleet at anchor.	4,410
1937	Victor Rothschild. S. Ships in a calm.	2,100
1954	Sir Felix Cassel. C. Dutch fleet near Brielle.	3,990
1958	Baroness Cassel von Doorn. New York. Fleet at anchor.	15,000*
1958	S. Fishing boats, very small.	5,500
1960	S. Fleet at anchor.	13,000

SIR ANTHONY VAN DYCK. 1599–1641

It is impossible to assess the present position of Van Dyck, since nothing of the first quality has changed hands in the past thirty years. Van Dyck has generally been a dull market, the exceptions being the late eighteenth and early nineteenth centuries and the first quarter of the present century, when there was even an occasion on which a Van Dyck became the costliest picture in the world, a thing which it would be hard to imagine to-day. Van Dyck lived only forty-two years, and all but a very few of the many hundreds of surviving Van Dyck portraits must have been painted merely under his direction or by his apprentices.

		£
1736	Robert Walpole buys Holy Family from Princess of Friesland.	1,400
1741	Earl of Oxford. Sir Kenelm Digby, portrait.	63 5s.
1756	Tallard, Paris. Rinaldo and Armida (£80 in 1652).	280
1768	Gaignat, Paris. Portrait of Bouchardot.	368
1771	Comte de la Güiche. Equestrian Charles I, hunting.	708
	Commissioned in 1635 for £200. Bought by Mme. Du Barry and sold to Louis XV in 1775 (now Louvre).	960
1775	Robert Strange. C. Christ, Virgin and saints.	304 10s.
1779	Houghton Hall. Robert Walpole's Holy Family (see 1736) sold to the Empress Catherine.	1,600
	12 portraits, mostly at £200, including Philip, Lord Wharton, with a spear (Hermitage Museum, see 1931).	

		£
1787	Sir John Taylor. C. Samson and Delilah (Dulwich Gallery).	735
1790	Gaston, Duke of Orleans, bought by Lord Radnor (Longford Castle, replica of Chantilly picture).	630
1798	Bryan (ex Calonne at Coxe's). Portrait of Van der Geest, bought by Angerstein through Farington, see 1824.	357
1800	Orleans sale (Coxe). Family of King Charles, schoolpiece, bought by Duke of Richmond and still at Goodwood.	1,050
1801	Robit, Paris. The Earl of Arundel.	150
	This was a missing Orleans picture, re-sold to Duke of Bridgewater (now in U.S.A.).	525
1804	Buchanan. C. Treble portrait of Charles I from Genoa, bought in (now Royal Collections, per William Wells, 1814).	514
1810	Walsh Porter. C. St. Sebastian (National Gallery, Toronto).	852 10*s.*
	Holy Family.	787 10*s.*
1811	Lafontaine. C. Healing the lame (Royal Collections), negotiated price, either £3,000 or	3,990
1814	Delahante. C. Stoning of Stephen, bought Lord Egerton, still at Tatton.	735
1816	Henry Hope. C. Self-portrait as Paris (Wallace Collection).	378
	Gaston, Duke of Orleans (Royal Collections).	409 10*s.*
1820	George IV buys Marriage of St. Catherine (schoolpiece) from M. de Burtin, Brussels (Royal Collections).	2,625
1824	Angerstein. National Gallery buys Expulsion of Theodosius (after Rubens).	2,500
	Portrait of Van der Geest (see 1798).	700
1826	Lord Radstock. C. Portrait of Spinola (Pierpont Morgan, Jnr., 1931).	357
1833	Nieuwenhuys. C. Frans Duquesnoy (Fiammingo), probably schoolpiece, now in U.S.A.	362 5*s.*
1844	Jeremiah Harman. C. Self-portrait.	430 10*s.*
1848	William Wells. C. Wife of Simon de Vos (Wallace Collection).	787 10*s.*
1850	King of Holland, Amsterdam. The 2 Leroy portraits, bought by Lord Hertford (Wallace Collection).	5,300
1850	Earl of Ashburnham. C. Don Livio Odescalchi.	525
1860	Sir Culling Eardley. C. The Snyders family, bought in. Possibly a replica of picture at Cassel.	1,050
1861	Lord Morley. C. The Bolingbroke family, bought in. May be replica of Rothschild picture.	1,742 10*s.*
1882	Hamilton Palace. C. Prince of Phalsburg (Lord Rosebery, Mentmore).	2,100

		£
1882	Duchess of Richmond and her son (resold, Beckett Dennison sale, 1885, for £892 10*s*.).	2,047 10*s*.
	10 attributed pictures in all.	
1885	Private sales, Duke of Marlborough:	
	To National Gallery: Equestrian Charles I.	17,500
	To Earl of Pembroke: Lady Morton and Mrs. Killigrew.	5,250
	To Sedelmeyer: Family of Duke of Buckingham.	10,500
1886	Duke of Marlborough. C. 11 attributed pictures:	
	Time clipping Cupid's wings (see 1887).	241 10*s*.
	Suffer little children (National Gallery, Toronto).	840
	Maria, Duchess of Richmond (Earl of Pembroke).	1,207 10*s*.
1890	Duke of Somerset. C. Henrietta Maria (schoolpiece).	1,050
1897	Baron de Hirsch. C. Boy in purple and green.	1,680
	Late Sir John Millais. C. Time clipping the wings of love (see 1886), now Musée Jacquemart-André.	1,105
1900	Peel Heirlooms. C. The Genoese senator and his wife (ex Balbi Palace, 1802), bought by Robert Peel in the 1830's for £800 (Kaiser Friedrich Museum). The pair	24,250
1905	Lady Ashburton. C. Charles I and Henrietta Maria, a pair, apparently replicas, bought Duveen. 2 for	17,850
1906	The Cattaneo family portraits, sold by Cesare Imperiale and sold by Knoedler to P. A. B. Widener, now National Gallery, Washington. 5 pictures, including portrait of Elena Grimaldi-Cattaneo, which alone fetched	103,300*
1907	Giovanni Cattaneo and Marchese Carnevari, sold to H. C. Frick.	Price unknown
1907	National Gallery buys the smaller portraits, Giovanni and Elena Cattaneo. The pair	27,000
1909	Widener buys the alleged Lady Brook and her son from the Earl of Warwick, actually Paolina Adorno (Washington, National Gallery).	Price unknown
1914	H. C. Frick buys the Duke of Abercorn's Paolina Adorno from Duveen (Frick Foundation).	82,400
1919	2nd Hamilton Palace sale. C. Portrait, 1st Earl of Denbigh (see 1938).	6,615
1921	Stowe (local sale). Baron de Vieuville, bought in.	8,075
1922	From Lucas family, Panshanger, National Gallery buys the Villiers brothers (bought in 1862 for £30).	15,000
	National Gallery, Melbourne, buys Countess of Southampton.	17,800
1923	Lord Brownlow. C. Anton Triest, Bishop of Ghent, sold by Duveen to Henry Huntington.	29,400
1927	Duveen buys Henrietta Maria and Geoffrey Hudson, the dwarf. Sold to Randolph Hearst, now at Los Angeles (from Earl of Northbrook).	77,500

		£
1927	C. A Genoese officer, half-length.	13,125
1928	Holford. C. The Abbé Scaglia (Collection of Lord Camrose), bought by Robert Holford from Francis Baring in 1843 for under £500. English auction record for a Van Dyck.	31,500
1928	Marchesa Balbi, sold to Andrew Mellon, now National Gallery, Washington. over	50,000
1928	Mrs. Bissett. C. 1st Earl of Peterborough.	9,975
	Countess of Peterborough.	4,725
1929	Lord Brownlow. C. Jacques Leroy (Collection of Mrs. Benjamin F. Jones, Pittsburg).	17,850
1931	Stroganov sale, Berlin (Soviet Government). 2 half-length portraits.	33,000
1931	Hermitage Museum. Andrew Mellon buys Philip, Lord Wharton, with a spear (see 1779), now in National Gallery, Washington.	45,000
1938	Melbourne National Gallery buys portrait of 4th Earl of Pembroke from Wilton.	12,500
	Viscount Fielding. C. 6 portraits for £8,552, Lord Denbigh (see 1919).	1,995
1945	Proctor-Beauchamp. C. Bacchanalia (after Poussin).	2,415
1948	Earl Fitzwilliam. C. Rinaldo and Armida, bought by Los Angeles County Museum.	4,830
1952	Borthwick-Norton. C. Female half-length.	2,940
1954	Marquess of Linlithgow. C. Ecce Homo, bought for Barber Institute, Birmingham.	8,400
1955	Ruth Vanderbilt-Twembly, New York. Duchess of Arensburg and child.	6,725
	Francis Howard. C. Genoese nobleman, 29 ins. × 24 ins.	6,090
1956	Goldschmidt. S. Two heads of a Negro, oil sketch.	7,800
1958	Duke of Devonshire. C. St. Judas Thaddeus, small panel.	5,775
	Earl of Ancaster. S. Small portrait of a man in sculptural oval.	7,000
1960	Heywood-Lonsdale. C. Portrait of unknown lady with a chain girdle.	6,300

DIEGO VELAZQUEZ. 1599–1660

Although *Admiral Pulido Pareja* was sold as early as 1790 for the respectable sum of £600, the Englishman had little idea what a Velazquez ought to look like until the end of the Peninsular War. In the 1840's Velazquez began to be expensive when many painters, Wilkie among others, admired the rich impasto of his paint. The slow recognition of Manet and Whistler helped the Velazquez market and made him the ideal painter of the *fin du siècle*. Since the legendary sale of *The Rokeby Venus* in 1906, even higher prices have been paid, but expertise, particularly that of the exacting Beruete y Moret, played havoc with some of the older attributions.

		£
1779	Houghton Hall. The Empress Catherine buys portrait of Innocent X (see 1931).	60
1790	Vandergucht sells the Earl of Radnor Admiral Pulido Pareja (see 1890).	600
1813	J. B. S. Morritt of Rokeby buys the Escurial Venus from Buchanan, imported by Wallis. Price probably about	1,000
	Marquess of Lansdowne buys Duke of Olivarez and self-portrait from Buchanan (see 1888) The pair	630
1846	National Gallery buys The Boar Hunt from Lord Cowley.	2,200
1850	King of Holland. Philip IV and Duke of Olivarez, bought by the Tsar, now Hermitage Museum. 2 for	3,240
1853	Louis Philippe. C. London, National Gallery buys Adoration of the Shepherds, now considered a schoolpiece.	2,060
	Marquess of Hertford buys Baltazar Carlos at the riding school (Wallace Collection).	1,680
1856	Samuel Rogers. C. Baltazar Carlos riding (replica of Duke of Westminster's picture, Wallace Collection).	1,270 10*s*.
	Philip IV as a young man, schoolpiece (see 1942).	215 5*s*.
1856	Earl of Shrewsbury, Alton Towers. Philip IV (Holford Collection until 1928, now Ringling Museum, Sarasota), disputed picture.	129 3*s*.
1859	Earl of Northwick (Philips). 9 attributed pictures. Equestrian portrait, Don Luiz de Haro (James de Rothschild).	966
1865	Pourtalés, Paris. National Gallery buys Orlando Muerto, disputed picture.	1,549 4*s*.
	San Donato, Paris. Head of Philip IV in old age, National Gallery.	1,200
1867	Duc de Morny, Paris. Infanta Isabel (see 1895).	2,040
1877	Duc de Salamanca, Paris. Philip IV (see 1895).	2,840
1881	Henry Sackville Bale. C. Don Baltazar Carlos (schoolpiece, Metropolitan Museum, 1889, per Henry G. Marquand).	871 10*s*.
1882	Hamilton Palace. C. Beckford's whole-length Philip IV brought back from Spain by General Dessoles (National Gallery).	6,300
1890	Earl of Radnor. Longford Castle. National Gallery buys Admiral Pulido Pareja (see 1790). Part of block purchase.	10,000
1893	Lord Clifden. C. Mariana of Austria (see 1909, 1936).	4,305
	Infanta Maria Teresa.	1,260
	Isabel de Bourbon (see 1895).	2,625

		£
1895	Mrs. Lyne Stephens. C. Infanta Isabel (see 1867).	4,510
	Philip IV (see 1877).	409 10s.
1902	Arthur Kaye. C. The grape-seller.	2,625
1904	S. E. Frazer. C. Don Baltazar Carlos (sold same year to Boston Fine Arts Museum).	1,575
1906	The Escurial Venus or Rokeby Venus, bought from the Morritt family by Agnew and bought by subscribers for the National Gallery (see 1813).	45,000
1909	Sir Cuthbert Quilter. C. Mariana of Austria (see 1893, 1936), bought in at	2,415
1911	The Schloss Lichtenegg version of the Dulwich Gallery Philip IV, bought by H. C. Frick through Agnew.	82,000
1913	Mrs. Collis Huntington buys Duke of Olivarez through Duveen (Huntington Library, San Marino, Cal.).	82,700
1923	Sir Joseph Robinson. C. Two princesses.	2,205
1927	Pallavicini (Knight, Frank and Rutley). The nutcracker, small attributed early work.	1,985
1928	Holford. C. Philip IV (see 1856), schoolpiece (Ringling Museum, Sarasota).	3,465
1936	Sir Cuthbert Quilter. C. Mariana of Austria (see 1909) (Rockhill Nelson Gallery, Kansas City).	5,880
1942	S. Small head of Philip IV (see 1856).	450
1945	Neeld. C. Portrait of a man (attributed).	2,940
	Parke-Bernet, New York. Small head of a girl.	7,537
1949	Viscount Cowdray. S. Count Olivarez, 1624.	11,000
1959	C. The dwarf Pertusato (attributed).	2,205

VENETIAN SCHOOL

Late 15th and 16th centuries

Excluding Giovanni Bellini, Carpaccio, Cima da Conegeliano, Giorgione, Lorenzo Lotto, Moroni, Tintoretto, Titian, Veronese, for which see separate entries.

Perhaps the most remarkable feature of this list is the prices, ranging between £400 and £800, which were paid in the early and mid-nineteenth century for minor early sixteenth-century Venetian painters when many works of Titian and Tintoretto were going for less. Obvious charm has always been expensive. But to-day the early Venetians seem to be the cheapest pictures on the market.

		£
1769	Sir G. Colebrooke. JACOPO BASSANO: The vintage.	173 5s.
1776	Biondi. C. GIOVANNI DA PORDENONE: Holy Family.	139 10s.

		£
1779	Houghton Hall. Empress Catherine buys:	
	PARIS BORDONE: Two women.	200
	PALMA VECCHIO: Adoration of the shepherds.	250
	JACOPO BASSANO: A winter piece.	100
1795	Calonne (Skinner). BARTOLOMMEO SCHIDONE: Holy Family.	210
1798	Orleans Collection, valuations:	
	PALMA VECCHIO: Doge of Venice, for Duke of Bridgewater.	420
	SCHIAVONE: Christ before Pilate, for Duke of Bridgewater.	262 10*s.*
	JACOPO BASSANO: Circumcision (Lord Gower).	105
1800	Orleans sale (Coxe). PALMA VECCHIO: Venus and Cupid.	54 12*s.*
1803	Graves. C. SCHIAVONE: Holy Family.	262 10*s.*
1804	C. PALMA GIOVANE (Borghese Palace): Assumption of the Virgin.	828 10*s.*
	SCHIAVONE: St. John and St. Joseph, bought in.	714
1806	Duke of Novellara. C. BATTISTA DA PORDENONE: Woman accused of adultery, bought by Marquess of Stafford.	546
1810	Walsh Porter. C. JACOPO BASSANO: Conversion of a princess.	325 10*s.*
1823	Fonthill, ex Beckford (Philips). PALMA VECCHIO: Martyrdom of a saint, large picture.	36 15*s.*
1833	Erard. C. PALMA VECCHIO: Holy Family.	77 14*s.*
1845	Andrew Geddes. C. ANDREA SCHIAVONE: Holy Family with saints.	441
1853	Samuel Woodburn. C. National Gallery buys PALMA VECCHIO: Warrior adoring the Virgin, sold as Giorgione.	525
1855	National Gallery buys:	
	PORDONENE: Portrait of Pelegrino Morosini.	60 9*s.*
	MARCO BASAITI: St. Jerome.	43 14*s.*
1856	National Gallery buys:	
	BARTOLOMMEO VIVARINI: Holy Family.	97
	JACOPO BASSANO: The Good Samaritan (Samuel Rogers. C.).	241 10*s.*
1858	National Gallery buys:	
	BONVICINO MORETTO: A nobleman.	360
	BASAITI: Madonna of the meadow.	651
1859	Earl of Northwick (Philips):	
	PALMA GIOVANE: Holy Family.	168
	BONVICINO MORETTO: St. Bernard and other saints (National Gallery).	517 10*s.*
1861	National Gallery buys PARIS BORDONE: Portrait of a lady.	257 13*s.*
1863	Rev. Davenport Bromley. C.:	
	PALMA VECCHIO: Sacred and profane love.	441 10*s.*
	VINCENZO FOPPA: Adoration (National Gallery).	127 1*s.*

		£
1864	National Gallery buys:	
	PAOLO MORANDO: St. Roche and angel. FRANCESCO BONSIGNORI: Venetian senator. } the two for	880
1867	National Gallery buys:	
	PAOLO MORANDO: Holy Family.	900
	FRANCESCO BONSIGNORI: 2 portraits.	160
1872	Prince Imperiale. C. PARIS BORDONE: Girl at dressing-table (Earl of Dudley).	735
1874	Alexander Barker. C.:	
	ANDREA PREVITALI: Holy Family, bought for Dresden Gallery.	693
	ANDREA SCHIAVONE: Holy Family (National Gallery).	189
1878	National Gallery buys GIOVANNI SAVOLDO: Magdalen at the Tomb.	350
1879	National Gallery buys AMBROGIO BORGOGNONE: 3 panels dated 1501. 3 for	1,200
1882	Hamilton Palace. C. BERNARDO LICINIO: Holy Family.	451 10s.
1884	Sir P. Miles, Leigh Court. C. BONIFAZIO DI PITATI: Adoration of the Magi (National Gallery).	383 5s.
1885	Harkness. C. BARTOLOMMEO VIVARINI: Holy Family.	115 10s.
1886	National Gallery buys BONIFAZIO DI PITATI: Holy Family, altarpiece.	750
1886	William Graham. C. PALMA GIOVANE: Adoration of the shepherds.	278 5s.
	DOSSO DOSSI: Orlando Furioso.	262 10s.
1891	Cavendish-Bentinck. C. VINCENZO CATENA: Holy Family and St. Catherine.	141 15s.
1892	Earl of Dudley. C. PALMA GIOVANE: Holy Family.	682 10s.
	MARCO BASAITI: Holy Family with St. Catherine.	871 10s.
	BONIFAZIO DI PITATI: Holy Family and saints.	1,018 10s.
1894	Lady Eastlake. C. GENTILE BELLINI: Madonna enthroned (National Gallery).	692 10s.
1895	Henry Doetsch. C. CARIANI: Adoration.	105
	SAVOLDO: Portrait of a nobleman.	126
1896	Lord Leighton. C. National Gallery buys SCHIAVONE: Jupiter and Semele.	168
1899	Mrs. Higgins. C. PARIS BORDONE: Baptism of Christ.	1,123 10s.
1905	Capel Cure. C. BASAITI: Portrait of a young man.	882
1911	Sir William Abdy. C. BARTOLOMMEO VIVARINI: Small Adoration of the Magi.	3,920
1911	Charles Butler. C. BARTOLOMMEO VENEZIANO: Holy Family with St. Elizabeth.	1,205
	Holy Family and saints.	892 10s.
	ANDREA PREVITALI: Holy Family and donor.	787 10s.

		£
1912	J. E. Taylor. C. FRANCESCO SALVIATI: Portrait of a nobleman.	3,750
	JACOPO BELLINI: St. Dominic and donor.	1,365
1917	S. DOSSO DOSSI: Portrait of Duchess of Ferrara (see 1927).	1,850
1920	Miss Seymour. C. AMBROGIO DI BORGOGNONE: Holy Family, triptych.	1,680
1923	Lord Brownlow. C. GENTILE BELLINI: Portrait of Bartolommeo Colleoni.	3,675
1927	Holford. C. BARTOLOMMEO VENEZIANO: Portrait.	11,025
	BONIFAZIO DI PITATI: Santa Conversazione.	1,575
	GIOVANNI DI CALCAR: Gentleman in black.	2,415
	GIROLAMO ROMANINO: Portrait, Francesco Franceschini.	2,205
1927	S. DOSSO DOSSI: Duchess of Ferrara (see 1917).	1,850
1929	Lord Brownlow. C. BATTISTA DOSSI: Orlando Furioso.	3,150
	S. PARIS BORDONE: Lady in fur-lined cloak.	1,550
1944	Schinasi, New York. VINCENZO CATENA: Nobleman.	742
1945	Earl of Radnor. C. PARIS BORDONE: The painter's daughter.	651
1946	Crawford and Balcarres. C. SAVOLDO: Portrait of a gentleman.	420
1948	A nobleman. S. JACOMETTO VENEZIANO: A Benedictine nun.	1,450
1951	Lady Violet Melchett. S. VINCENZO CATENA: Holy Family and saints.	1,106
1953	Lady Catherine Ashburnham. S. BARTOLOMMEO SCHIDONE: Young girl with hornbook.	1,200
1955	S. AMBROGIO BORGOGNONE: Nativity.	2,400
1956	Michael Tennant. C. ANDREA DI PREVITALI: Holy Family and saints.	1,890
	Parke-Bernet, New York. PALMA VECCHIO: Venetian nobleman, small head.	1,607
1957	Francis Coughlan. S. ANTONIO VIVARINI: Polyptich.	2,200
1958	Duke of Devonshire. C. ANDREA SCHIAVONE: Marriage of Cupid and Psyche.	4,725
	Gunhild A. Fisher. S. MARCO BASAITI: Benediction of Jesus.	11,500
	C. PALMA GIOVANE: Venetian senator and his son.	1,680
1959	Charles Loeser. S. BARTOLOMMEO VENEZIANO: Holy Family, dated 1502.	4,600
	S. Attributed JACOPO BELLINI: Small Nativity, bought in.	15,500
	Duke of Westminster. S. JACOPO BASSANO: Holy Family.	1,800
	John Skippe. C. GIOVANNI DA PORDENONE: St. Christopher, pen-and-wash drawing.	2,205

		£
1960	S. FRANCESCO SAVOLDO: Temptation of St. Anthony.	12,000
	Gladys Robinson, New York. DOSSO DOSSI: Allegory of love, 62 ins. × 50 ins.	6,070
	Galliera, Paris. ANDREA SCHIAVONE: Annunciation.	3,437

JAN VERMEER
of Delft. 1632–1675

The extraordinary fortunes of these tremendous works are described in Chapters Five and Seven and require no further comment.

		£
1696	Anonymous sale, The Hague. 21 pictures, mostly identified, were sold at prices from £2 10*s*. to £15.	
1719	Amsterdam. The woman with the pitcher (see 1907).	10 10*s*.
1797	Nyman, Amsterdam. The geographer (1885, Staedel Institut).	11
1800	Geldemeester, Amsterdam. The astronomer (now Collection of A. de Rothschild).	28 10*s*.
1810	Smet van Alpen, Amsterdam. The singing lesson (now Frick Foundation).	51
1813	Muelman, Amsterdam. Woman with the pitcher (see 1907).	175
	The lace-maker (Louvre) (see 1870).	7
1822	Lapeyriere, Paris. La liseuse (Rijksmuseum) (see 1839, 1902).	42 10*s*.
	Stinstra, Amsterdam. Rijksmuseum buys The great view of Delft.	242
1837	Duchesse de Berri, Paris. Lady and servant (Frick Foundation).	16
1839	Sommariva, Amsterdam. La liseuse (see 1822 and 1902).	73 10*s*.
1848	Casimir Perrier. C. Girl weighing gold (see 1910), bought in (National Gallery, Washington, per Joseph Widener).	68 5*s*.
1870	Blockhuyzen, Rotterdam. Louvre buys The lace-maker (see 1813).	51
1872	Robiano, Brussels. The letter-writer (Metropolitan Museum, per Pierpont Morgan).	16
1872	Isaac Pereire, Paris. The geographer (see 1797).	652
1874	Kaiser Friedrich Museum buys Girl with the pearl necklace (sold by Thoré-Buerger to Suermondt).	800
1876	Goldschmidt, Paris. Toilet of Diana (The Hague Gallery), sold as a Nicolas Maes).	193
1877	Vernon. C. Woman with a pewter ewer, sold as a Metsu (see 1888).	404 5*s*.

		£
1888	Lord Powerscourt sells The woman with a pewter ewer to Henry Marquand, reputedly for £2,000, now in the Metropolitan Museum.	
1889	Secrétan, Paris. Le billet doux (Otto Beit Collection).	2,580
	Lady and servant (Frick Foundation).	2,480
1892	National Gallery buys Lady standing at the virginals from Messrs. Lawrie.	2,400
1900	Brussels Museum buys Man in black (doubtful).	780
1902	Amsterdam Rijksmuseum buys La liseuse through subscribers (see 1822, 1839).	3,750
1906	De Gez, Brussels. P. A. B. Widener buys The girl with a flute and a Chinese hat (National Gallery, Washington), part of block purchase.	30,000
1907	Six, Amsterdam. The woman with a pitcher (La Laitiere), bought for the Rijksmuseum at a price reputed to be close on £50,000.	
1910	Segur-Perrier, Paris. P. A. B. Widener buys The Girl weighing gold (see 1848). Price probably in region of £30,000.	
1922	Joseph (Robinson and Fisher). Officer and laughing girl (1925, Frick Foundation).	4,200
1930	Six, Amsterdam. The street in Delft, bought by Sir Henri Deterding and presented to the Rijksmuseum.	75,000
1931	Andrew Mellon buys The girl with the red hat (National Gallery, Washington).	Over 100,000
1937	Boymans Museum, Rotterdam, buys Christ in the house of Emmaus (with the aid of Baron Beuningen), *forgery by Van Meegeren.*	55,000
1959	Prince d'Arenburg, Meppen, private sale to Charles Wrightsman, New York, per Rosenberg and Stiebel. Girl's head, 18 ins. × 16 ins., sold in Rotterdam in 1816 for 3 florins.	About 400,000

Paolo Caliari called IL VERONESE. 1528–1588

It is difficult to determine how far the hostile propaganda of Sir Joshua Reynolds was responsible for the low valuation of Veronese in England at the end of the eighteenth century. Pictures that had made £600 and more in Paris reached 150 guineas in London with difficulty. In the 1850's there were some high prices, but they were paid for works on the monumental scale. Works of moderate size, being in the nature of oil-sketches for Veronese's great decorative compositions, have stayed cheap to this day.

		£
1747	Pontchartrain, Paris. Presentation in the Temple.	345
1751	Same picture.	605
1788	Antrobus. C. Woman taken in adultery.	191
1798	Orleans Exhibition. 17 attributed works, valued for Duke of Bridgewater:	
	Venus and Adonis (see 1946).	157 10*s.*
	But it had been valued for Duke of Orleans at	657
	Venus and Mars united (see 1903), bought by Hastings Elwyn.	315
	Veronese between virtue and vice, bought by T. Hope.	367 5*s.*
	Wisdom accompanying Hercules, bought by T. Hope.	525
	Christ and disciples (see 1913). Valued for Lord Gower:	210
1800	Orleans Collection sale (Coxe):	
	The four allegories (see 1890), bought by Lord Darnley.	135 10*s.*
	Venus and Mars, bought by William Willett (see 1813).	262 10*s.*
	Rape of Europa (National Gallery, 1831), schoolpiece.	210
1801	Young Ottley. Marriage of the Virgin.	588
1810	Walsh Porter. C. Venus and Cupid (see 1840).	808 10*s.*
1813	William Willett. C. Venus and Mars (see 1800).	52 10*s.*
1815	Comyn. C. Vision of St. Helena (see 1878) (in 1816 £106, in 1860 £283 10*s.*).	162 15*s.*
1823	Fonthill, ex Beckford (Philips). St. Jerome at prayer.	315
1840	Sir H. Clarke. C. Venus and Cupid (see 1810).	325
1845	Joshua Bates. C. Cephalus and Procris (see 1927).	745 10*s.*
1855	National Gallery buys The adoration of the Magi, nearly 12 ft. high, from A. Toffoli, Venice.	1,977
1856	Samuel Rogers. C. Magdalene at the feet of Christ (see 1922).	399
1857	National Gallery buys The family of Darius from Count Vittore Pisani, Venice (15½ ft. long).	13,650
1870	San Donato, Paris. A Venetian lady.	1,208
1878	Monro of Novar. C. National Gallery buys Vision of St. Helena (see 1815, 1816, 1860).	3,465
1891	National Gallery buys The four allegories from the Earl of Darnley (see 1800). 4 for	5,000
1903	Lord Wimborne. C. Venus and Mars united (see 1798), Metropolitan Museum (£8,000 in 1910).	6,300
1913	Duke of Sutherland. C. Christ and disciples (see 1798).	1,427 10*s.*
	Venetian nobleman and bishop.	1,050
1922	Albert Fletcher. C. Magdalene at the feet of Christ (see 1856), now National Gallery, Toronto.	1,785
1927	Holford. C. Cephalus and Procris (see 1845), also known as Celedonian boar hunt.	1,680
	Diana and Actaeon.	1,470

		£
1946	Earl of Ellesmere. C. Venus lamenting death of Adonis (see 1798).	1,995
1947	Sir Herbert Cook. Melbourne National Gallery buys The rewards of philosophy.	30,000
1951	Mrs. H. F. Buxton. Holy Family with saints.	8,000
1957	Mrs. Parkinson. S. The woman taken in adultery.	9,800

DRAWINGS

1902	Sir J. C. Robinson. Marriage of St. Catherine.	120 15*s.*
1917	Earl of Pembroke. S. Venus crowned with fame.	1,650
1929	Bernard d'Hendecourt. S. Man seated, black chalk.	330
1955	A. G. B. Russell. S. Gondolier (chalk).	1,600
	Head of a Negro (chalk).	2,100
1958	John Skippe. C. Seated lady, chalk on blue paper.	1,155

ANDREA DEL VERROCCHIO. 1435–1488

A rare and much attributed master, still capable of making an appearance in the saleroom in the present century. Best known as a sculptor and the teacher of Leonardo da Vinci.

		£
1844	Jeremiah Harman. C. Holy Family (attributed).	105
1856	Samuel Rogers. C. A lady of the Soderini family, sometimes called La Simonetta (see 1892).	194 5*s.*
1857	National Gallery buys schoolpiece, Virgin adoring child Christ (sold in Florence as Ghirlandajo).	455 16*s.*
1867	National Gallery buys Tobias and the angel, schoolpiece (sold by Baslini in Florence as Pollaiuolo).	500
1892	Earl of Dudley. C. La Simonetta (see 1856).	1,050
1894	Farquhar. C. Holy Family (sold as Pesellino).	451 10*s.*
1911	Charles Butler. C. Same picture. (Metropolitan Museum, 1913, via Benjamin Altman.)	6,300
1926	S. Sheet of studies, head and two hands, leadpoint.	330
1953	Mrs. E. L. Scott. S. Small head of the Virgin.	11,000

Marie Louise
VIGÉE-LEBRUN. 1755–1842

The painter who most completely expresses the smallness and the tidiness of French painting under the full impact of neo-classicism. Even with a *Princess Talleyrand* at £17,600 in roaring 1912, the lady appears cheap alongside her English contemporaries. The fact is that the French themselves preferred the freedom and the swagger of the English school of portraiture. In this very sale there was an expensive Lawrence. In Mme. Vigée-Lebrun's own day, it was the other way round. After the Peace of Amiens, when she came to England, the social world was captivated with her enamel-like finish. No question here of leaving the draperies to the apprentice. And she charged two or three times as much as Hoppner or Lawrence.

		£
1789	Laborde, Paris. Mme. Lebrun and her daughter (Louvre).	360
	Portrait of Hubert Robert.	360
1804	Duchess of Dorset, whole-length, painted in London.	525
1845	Cypierre, Paris. Girl at a piano.	16
1868	D'Espagnac, Paris. Portrait of a young man.	204
1870	Reiset, Paris. Family group, 1776.	1,140
1874	C. A lady singing with a harp.	50 8*s.*
1878	Duclos, Paris. Mme. Royale as a milkmaid.	960
1887	Earl of Lonsdale. C. Lady with a dog.	168
	De Salnote, Paris. A young girl.	960
1895	Mrs. Lyne Stephens. C. A lady on a green divan.	2,362 10*s.*
1907	Mrs. Finch. C. Duchesse de Piennes, small head, 1789.	2,520
1912	Doucet, Paris. Princesse de Talleyrand (Collection of Henri de Rothschild).	17,600
1915	Knight, Frank and Rutley. Self-portrait.	6,960
1926	Bischoffsheim. C. Mme. du Barry.	1,365
1934	A. J. Sulley. C. Alexandrine Brogniart.	2,730
1938	Bourbon-Massimo. S. Marie Antoinette, small head.	600
1944	Mrs. Joseph Heine, New York. La fillette aux cerises.	3,100
1946	Baron d'Erlanger. S. Duchesse de Grammont.	1,150
1947	Mary Thompson, New York. Mme. Lebrun and her daughter, 1789.	6,250
1949	Parke-Bernet, New York. Mme. Elizabeth of France.	4,735
1956	Stehli, New York. Portrait of Gabriel de St. Aubin.	3,215
1959	Parke-Bernet, New York. Princess Poniatowska.	2,321

EDOUARD VUILLIARD. 1868–1940

The second generation of Impressionists, painting originally like Bonnard in a 'symboliste' style which almost ignored form. His later works (less in demand) came to terms with patrons who wanted their families and interiors depicted with rather more realism. The larger works used to fetch from £500 to £1,000 in the 1930's, but, though they have advanced remarkably, they have not kept pace with the post-Cézanne painters.

		£
1933	Tate Gallery, Courtauld Fund, buys Le toit rouge.	236 15*s.*
1935	C. Une femme lisant (gouache).	107 2*s.*
1939	Henri Canonne, Paris. La conversation.	195

		£
1940	C. Same picture.	189
1947	C. La fenêtre ouverte.	924
1950	S. Beach scene.	300
1954	Galerie Charpentier, Paris. Femme au chien.	2,940
1956	S. Small interior.	1,200
	Chez les Hessels.	2,200
1957	Parke-Bernet, New York. Chez les Hessels.	4,800
1957	Georges Lurcy, New York. Les Tuileries.	25,000*
1958	Arnold Kirkeby, New York. Au bord de la Seine.	8,000
1959	National Gallery values Lane Bequest picture, The Mantelpiece, bought before 1912 for about £300.	8,000
1959	Parke-Bernet, New York. Le salon.	9,855
1960	C. Portrait of René Blum, 1912.	4,410
	Gladys Robinson, New York. La loge (pastel).	11,120
	John Rewald. S. Jeune fille assise, brush drawing.	4,400

FRED WALKER. 1840–1875

The vogue for the laboured landscapes with figures of this now somewhat forgotten painter is linked with the Millais-landscape cult. The fact that the high prices held until the 1920's may have derived from identification with the Barbizon School and its Dutch imitators. He was a sort of English pre-Impressionist painter, but suffered badly from the mid-nineteenth-century habit of painting water-colours to look like oils and *vice versa*. The cult also had a great deal to do with the fact that he died young.

		£
1874	Benson. C. The old gate (see 1908).	1,050
1886	William Graham. C. The bathers (see 1909).	2,625
	The vagrants (Tate Gallery).	1,858 10*s.*
1887	William Leech. C. Water-colours, Spring.	2,100
	Autumn.	1,050
1892	Lehmann. C. Marlow ferry, wc (see 1908, 1945).	1,175
1908	Tatham. C. The harbour of refuge, wc (see 1912).	2,709
	The violet field, wc (see 1920, 1937).	1,680
	The old gate (see 1874), bought by Tate Gallery.	1,575
1908	Stephen Holland. C. Marlow ferry (see 1892, 1917).	2,835
	Cookham (£472 10*s.* in 1885), wc.	1,680
1909	Sir Cuthbert Quilter. The bathers (see 1918).	3,045
1912	Sir William Agnew gives The harbour of refuge (see 1908) to the Tate Gallery, having refused £10,000 from the Duke of Westminster.	
1917	Miss Misa. C. (Red Cross sale.) The plough, bought by Lady Wernher. Luton Hoo.	5,670*

		£
1917	Sir Joseph Beecham. C. Marlow ferry (see 1908, 1945).	2,625
	Fishmonger's shop, wc.	1,260
1918	Mrs. Kenneth Clark. C. The bathers (see 1909).	2,205
1920	Glen Coates. C. The violet field, wc (see 1908, 1937).	1,995
	Small replica of The plough.	1,995
1923	Sir Cuthbert Quilter. C. The seafarers.	672
1937	C. The violet field (1908, 1920).	210
1945	C. Marlow ferry (see 1908).	798
1957	C. The plough, wc version (2 ft. long).	147

JAMES WARD. 1769–1859

He was born within five years of the death of Hogarth, and his granddaughter, the last of a dynasty of painting Wards, died in 1925. A man who bridges three distinct epochs must have many styles. He painted rather stodgy Hoppner-like family groups, Dutch cattle pictures, early-nineteenth-century hunting pictures and wildly romantic mountain scenery, but Ward's most individual style, as shown in the famous *Fighting Bulls*, derived from Rubens's landscape, *The Château de Steen*, which Ward was able to study in 1803.

		£
1811	Fitzherbert. C. Sheep washing.	120 15*s.*
1821	British Institution. Allegory of Waterloo. Presented to Greenwich Hospital.	1,050
1827	Lord de Tabley. Lake and tower at Tabley Park.	199 10*s.*
1829	Ward executors. C. Cattlepiece, 'Emulation of Paul Potter', bought in.	220 10*s.*
1862	G. R. Woods. National Gallery buys Bull, cow and calf.	1,500
1878	Lord Ribblesdale. National Gallery buys Gordale Scar.	1,500
1884	National Gallery buys Harlech Castle.	350
1905	C. Portrait, Miss Georgina Musgrave.	1,680
1919	C. Same picture.	7,140*
1920	Harland Park. C. The Red Lion, Paddington, with coaches, 1790.	567
1926	At Robinson, Fisher's. Combat between 'Shannon' and 'Chesapeake.'	157 10*s.*
1929	C. A livery stable.	1,222 10*s.*
1935	S. Michael Bryan and his family (Henry Reitlinger Foundation, Maidenhead).	150
1936	C. Huntsmen setting out.	298
1938	Berkeley-Levett. C. John Levett, shooting, 1812.	1,470
1951	Outside the Bunch of Grapes tavern, coaches.	651
1959	C. Lioness and heron, mountainous landscape.	630
1960	S. Snow scene with shooting party.	5,800

ANTOINE WATTEAU. 1684–1721

Even in his own lifetime Watteau was appreciated in England. Although he invented the style of painting associated in France with the rococo, his successors were financially much more successful and when neo-classicism arrived Watteau was either forgotten or detested. By all the rules, Watteau should have been restored to popularity after the restoration of the monarchy, but, in fact, the taste of the Restoration was for the High Renaissance in furniture and for a vague imitation of the great Venetians in painting. It was the bourgeois monarchy of 1830–1848 that brought back Watteau, but the poor condition of his pictures has always told against him in the salerooms, whose triumphs have been reserved for Fragonard and Boucher.

			£	
1754	Richard Meade, London. 2 fêtes.	The pair	94	10*s.*
1776	Blondel de Gagny. Les Champs Elysées.		270	
		In 1783	332	
1791	Auguste Lebrun, Paris. 2 fêtes champêtres (bought for £416 in 1780).		100	
1802	Desenfans (Skinner). The Dulwich Gallery fête champêtre, sold for less than £100.			
1812	Claude Joseph Clos, Paris. Fête champêtre.		16	
1823	Fonthill, ex Beckford (Philips). The four ages	4 for	56	14*s.*
1826	Vivant-Denon, Paris. Carnival.		26	
1828	Lord Carysfort. C. 2 miniature masquerades (see 1875 and 1924).		63	
1833	La Neuville. C. Italian fair and mountebank, bought in.		309	10*s.*
1845	Cardinal Fesch, Rome. Fête in a park. Le repos de chasse. Sold as a pair (see 1852, 1865).		1,175	
1848	Comte de Morny (Philips). Les Champs Elysées (see 1776), bought by Lord Hertford (Wallace Collection).		945	
1852	Duc de Morny, Paris. Fête in a park (see 1845) (Wallace Collection).		1,000	
1853	Louis Philippe. C. Landscape with actors (Hertford).		735	
1856	Samuel Rogers. C. The music lesson (Wallace Collection).		173	15*s.*
1857	Patureau, Paris. Les deux Cousines.		2,200	
1865	Duc de Morny, Paris. Plaisirs du bal.		1,480	
	Repos de chasse (see 1845).		1,240	
	Both bought for Lord Hertford (Wallace Collection).			
1873	Thomas Norris. C. Les delices de la campagne.		1,239	
1875	Lucy. C. 2 miniature masquerades (see 1828, 1924).		535	10*s.*
1878	Monro of Novar. C. Les deux marquises.		2,625	
1886	Paris. L'Enseigne de Gersaint (Schloss Charlottenburg).		350	
1891	Mrs. James. C. L'occupation selon l'age (Lord Seymour).		5,460	

		£	
	L'accord parfait (National Gallery, Murray-Scott Bequest).	3,675	
1893	Bingham-Mildmay. C. Bal champêtre.	3,517	10*s.*
1895	Mrs. Lyne Stephens. C. La gamme d'amour (National Gallery, Wernher Bequest, 1914).	3,517	10*s.*
1897	De Goncourt, Paris. 3 small pieces, all under	1,000	
1899	C. La Musette.	1,434	
	Broadwood. C. L'accordée du village.	1,365	
1904	C. H. T. Hawkins. C. Guitar-player surprised.	2,520	
1907	Gabbitas. C. La contredanse.	2,625	
1910	Melbourne National Gallery buys Les jaloux.	3,000	
1913	Murray Scott. C. Fête champêtre (now in U.S.A.).	6,510	
1918	C. La marriée du village.	2,940	
1924	Sir Edward Scott. C. 2 miniature masquerades (see 1828, 1875).	3,265	
1945	Neeld. C. L'ile de Cythere, small schoolpiece (see 1957).	2,625	
1951	Henry E. Stehli. New York. Fête du Dieu Pan, 26 ins. × 32 ins.	4,465	
1957	Mae Rovensky, New York. L'ile de Cythere (see 1945).	6,250	
1959	S. Ex Duke of Cambridge. La rêve de l'artiste, said to have been completed by Schall.	2,800	

DRAWINGS

		£	
1891	Mrs. James. C. 12 lots. Sheet of 5 women's heads.	682	10*s.*
	Sheet of 3 studies of Mme. Duclos.	367	10*s.*
	Sheet of 3 studies, Girl dressing.	283	10*s.*
	Others at 120 to 230 guineas each.		
1908	Sir James Knowles. S. Lady with fan.	350	
1911	C. Two ladies, sanguine and white.	1,648	10*s.*
	3 Negro heads, one sheet (see 1922).	1,213	10*s.*
1922	Max Bonn. S. 3 Negro heads (see 1911).	3,200	
1926	Comtesse de Behague. Study of head and two hands.	760	
1931	Miss Ferrers. S. 3 large sanguine figure studies, one sheet.	1,550	
1935	Faucher-Magnan. S. 3 sheets of sanguine figure studies. Each	1,300	
	Study of hands.	620	
1937	Comtesse de Greffulhe. S. Sheet of studies.	5,800*	
1938	Mortimer Schiff. C. A Moor's head, sanguine.	945	
	Three ladies.	756	
1948	S. Sanguine drawing. Savoyard peep-show man.	1,300	
1954	Andrew d'Antal. S. Sheet of studies, 3 children, chalk.	2,700	
1956	Salle Drouot, Paris. Study of two girls, sanguine.	2,000	
1959	S. Study of two reclining figures, chalk.	900	

GEORGE FREDERICK WATTS. 1817–1904

An eminent Victorian who was far from achieving eminent Victorian prices. Watts, however, did not take much trouble to sell his pictures. He led a sheltered life, and it was his intention that the nation should enjoy the vast Scythian mass-burial of his works which the curious may find at Compton, near Guildford. There are, I believe, the beginnings of a Watts revival favouring his early portraits more than the vast allegories that resemble a Veronese, boiled in fog.

		£
1873	Rutley. C. Portrait of a lady with a fan.	126
1883	Tom Taylor. C. Blanche with a violin.	267 10*s.*
1886	William Graham. C. Diana and Endymion.	913 10*s.*
1887	Hilditch Richards. C. Eve of peace (see 1898, 1934).	947 10*s.*
	Love and life (see 1913).	1,155
	Love and death (see 1890, 1913).	1,155
1890	William Carver. C. Una and the Red Cross knight (see 1958).	1,732
	Love and death (see 1913).	1,381 10*s.*
	Rider on the white horse.	1,522 10*s.*
	Replica of 'Hope' (see 1913, 1942).	483
1898	Ruston. C. The eve of peace (see 1887, 1934).	1,417
1905	Louis Huth. C. Daphne.	1,742 10*s.*
1907	Lord Davey. C. Little Red Riding Hood.	1,310
	'For he had great possessions' (see 1924).	1,050
1913	George MacCulloch. C. Fata Morgana (see 1934).	1,783 10*s.*
	J. Ruston. C. Hope, replica (see 1890, 1942).	1,575
	Love and life (see 1890).	860
	Love and death (see 1887).	1,050
1917	Lord Ranksborough. C. Neptune's horses.	867 10*s.*
	Dawn (see 1934).	608 10*s.*
1919	Sir James Drummond. C. Eve.	630
1924	Sir T. Devitt. C. 'For he had great possessions' (see 1907).	173 5*s.*
1927	Mrs. Beer. C. Orpheus and Eurydice (6 ft.) (same price in 1908).	336
1934	Lord Faringdon. S. The eve of peace (see 1898).	210
	Ellen Terry, portrait.	320
	Sir Galahad, 1862.	820
	Dawn (see 1917).	240
1934	Col. Fairfax Rhodes. S. Fata Morgana (see 1913).	240
	The rain cloud (£420 in 1906).	10
1939	Edmund Davis. C. Creation and denunciation of Adam and Eve.	75 12*s.* 35 4*s.*
1942	Jeremiah Colman. C. Ariadne.	160
	Hope (replica, see 1913).	94 10*s.*

		£
1946	S. Olympus on Ida (nearly 5 ft.).	160
1956	C. Tennyson, portrait.	210
1958	Lady Lever. C. Una and the Red Cross knight (see 1890).	157 10*s.*

ROGIER VAN DER WEYDEN. 1400–1464

		£
1801	Bessborough. C. Beckford buys Exhumation of St. Hubert (bought back at Fonthill sale, 1823, for £81 5*s.*, see 1868).	96 12*s.*
1850	Charles Meigh. C. Dream of Pope Sergius (see 1938).	112 7*s.*
1868	National Gallery buys Exhumation of St. Hubert from Lady Eastlake (see 1801 and 1823).	1,500
1872	W. Middleton . C. Holy Family and saints.	113 8*s.*
1911	Lady Abdy. C. Small triptych.	945
1918	Linnell. C. Small head of a monk (9 ins. × 7 ins.).	1,995
1919	Palmer. C. Holy Family, altarpiece.	4,200
1922	Louis Fry. C. Adoration of the Magi.	2,415
1927	(or earlier) Holford. Lady in a coif, sold to Andrew Mellon, now National Gallery, Washington.	20,000 (?)
1938	Mortimer Schiff. C. Dream of Pope Sergius (see 1850), Baron von Beuningen, Boymans Museum, Rotterdam.	14,700
1942	S. Small Nativity (schoolpiece).	960
1948	Alfred Jowitt. S. Drawing in metal point of unknown man.	4,000
	Earl of Southesk. C. Altarpiece, Nativity, over 6 ft.	3,150
1959	C. Mass of St. Gregory, small panel.	12,600

BENJAMIN WEST. 1738–1820

In the second half of the eighteenth century Benjamin West made more money than any painter in the world—and on works which to-day would have difficulty in making ten shillings a foot. He was nevertheless an extremely inventive painter whose influence was felt for more than a century. American patriotism has created a market for West's portraits and some of his historical paintings in the present century, but the market has not responded to inflation.

		£
1768	George III buys The departure of Regulus.	420
1771	Lord Grosvenor buys a version of The death of Wolfe (now Ottawa Gallery).	400
1779–83	8 paintings for Windsor: The triumphs of Edward III.	
	3 paintings cost each	1,365
	5 cost each	525 to 630

1783–1801	9 pictures for the Chapel Royal, Windsor.	£
	8 pictures cost each	1,050
	1 picture cost	1,265
1794	Altarpiece for Royal Naval College, Greenwich. Total fee, including preliminary study.	1,431 5s.
1803	Designs for Windsor stained-glass window.	2,100
1805	Tassie. C. (Boydell Shakespeare Gallery.) King Lear.	215 5s.
	Ophelia.	131 5s.
1811	British Institution buys Christ healing the sick (National Gallery, 1826).	3,150
1814	West believed to have refused £10,000 for Christ rejected by Caiaphas (30 ft. × 16 ft.).	
1829	West Gallery (Robins). Christ before Caiaphas.	3,150
	Death on the pale horse.	2,100
	Both bought in. Pennsylvania Academy, Philadelphia, since 1839.	
	14 huge paintings from the Chapel Royal, Windsor, which had been returned by George IV to West's family.	
	Moses receiving the laws.	546
	The cheapest, Noah sacrificing, made	26 5s.
1851	Sir R. Harvey (at Stoke Court):	
	Penn's treaty with the Indians (see 1929).	441
	The death of Nelson.	892 10s.
1893	Thomas Price. C. Hon. Mrs. Shute-Barrington, portrait.	341 5s.
1900	At Emery's Rooms. Capture by bandits.	1,785
1901	Balnain Trust. C. The death of General Frazer. Pair of large pictures.	283 10s.
1917	Peel heirlooms. C. Self-portrait.	346 10s.
1921	Monckton. S. Death of Wolfe, 1776 (8 ft.).	250
1926	Lord Worsley. S. Portrait of Benjamin Franklin (Metropolitan Museum).	3,300
1927	S. Portrait of Sir Joseph Banks.	330
1929	Craggs-Nugent (Puttick's). Penn's treaty with the Indians (see 1851).	378
	Death of Wolfe, another version.	378
1945	Neeld. C. General Kosciusko in London, 12 ins. × 16 ins. (£42 in 1829.)	210
1959	Duke of Westminster. S. Battle of La Hogue.	2,000
	General Monk receiving Charles II.	1,500
	Elijah raising Shunamite's son.	800
	Jacob blessing Ephraim and Manasseh.	1,000

JAMES ABBOTT McNEILL WHISTLER. 1834–1903

A market that has been well sustained by American patriotic buying, but there have been too many small, scrappy works in the saleroom to maintain a continuous interest. There have been really no works with any feeling of completeness about them since the Edmund Davis sale of 1939. It may be doubted whether certain of the prices, created by the Whistler *furore* which preceded the First World War would hold up to-day, when the famous Nocturnes appear, not individual and rebellious, but painfully ladylike.

		£
1873	Mrs. Louis Huth, whole-length portrait commission.	630
1876	C. Valparaiso (see 1890).	215 5*s.*
1878	Grosvenor Gallery. Old Battersea Bridge (see 1886).	157 10*s.*
1886	William Graham. C. Old Battersea Bridge (see 1905).	63
1890	William Howell. C. Rose Corder, whole-length.	241 10*s.*
	Valparaiso (see 1876).	126
1891	Glasgow Corporation buys portrait of Thomas Carlyle.	1,050
1892	The Luxembourg buys 'Whistler's mother'.	200
1892	Frank Leyland. C. Princesse du pays de Porcelaine (see 1905).	441
1894	George Street. C. The music room.	199 10*s.*
1903	Paris. Nocturne à Venise.	735
1904	Charles Freer buys from Obach 'La princesse du pays de Porcelaine' (see 1892).	5,250
	Also the contents of Leyland's peacock room, an 'art nouveau' decoration on leather, etc.	13,000
1905	Irving. C. Charles Freer buys portrait of Henry Irving as Hamlet.	5,040
	Tate Gallery buys Old Battersea Bridge (see 1878, 1887).	2,000
1916	Thomas Way. S. The little white girl, bought for Tate Gallery through the Studd Bequest.	2,000
1919	Sir George Drummond. C. La note rouge (oil).	945
	Duveen was reported to have paid for 'Lady Meux, harmony in pink and grey' (Frick Foundation).	41,300*
1934	Lord Aberconway (Robinson, Fisher). Almond blossoms.	483
1936	O'Malley. C. Battersea, nocturne in blue and gold (see 1939).	945
1937	Leonard Gow. C. Tillie, wc.	173 5*s.*
	Dancing girl, wc.	183 15*s.*
	Brady, New York. Mrs. Archibald Campbell, oil sketch.	372
1939	Sir Edmund Davies. C. At the piano, 1860.	6,405
	Symphony in white, No. III (Barber Institute).	3,465
	Battersea, nocturne (see 1936).	682 10*s.*
1944	S. Millman's Row, small oil (see 1957).	630

		£
1946	S. Symphony in red.	390
	Beach scene.	220
1950	C. 'Three figures, pink and grey.'	735
1957	S. Millman's Row (see 1944).	1,000
1958	Frances Welch, New York. The Thames from Battersea Bridge, small oil.	1,607

SIR DAVID WILKIE. 1785–1841

An immensely formative artist but, since his death, never a very popular one. Those who had been in a state of uncontrolled ecstasy over Wilkie's dingy, crowded pastiches of Morland and Teniers were inclined to view Wilkie's streaky, almost Impressionist later style unfavourably, yet it is just these works, *The First Earring* among them, which excite a little interest to-day.

		£
1806	Sir George Beaumont buys The blind fiddler.	50
1813	The Prince Regent buys Blind man's buff.	525
	Angerstein buys The village festival (see 1824).	840
1816	The Duke of Wellington commissions The Chelsea Pensioners (completed 1824).	1,260
1824	The village festival, bought by National Gallery.	800
1830	George IV buys picture of his reception of the Scottish nobility at Holyrood.	1,680
1832	Sir Robert Peel buys John Knox preaching.	1,260
	Earl of Mulgrave. C. Rent day.	787 10*s.*
1839	Lady Baird Preston commissions The finding of Tippoo Sultan's body ($11\frac{1}{2}$ ft. × 9 ft.).	1,575
1842	Wilkie executors. C. The school (see 1887).	756
	The rabbit on the wall (see 1876).	735
1848	William Wells. C. Distraining for rent, bought in (see 1890) (bought for £420 in 1813).	1,102 10*s.*
1850	King of Holland, Amsterdam. The Irish whiskey still (see 1950).	841
1853	C. Benvenuto Cellini and the Pope.	997 10*s.*
1855	Foster. The first ear-ring (now Tate Gallery).	295
1860	C. The cotter's Saturday night (see 1897, 1908).	257 10*s.*
1865	J. Knowles. C. The errand boy.	1,102 10*s.*
1872	J. Gillott. C. The penny wedding (see 1877).	735
1876	Wynn Ellis. C. The rabbit on the wall (see 1842).	1,050
1877	Baron Grant. C. The penny wedding (see 1872).	359 2*s.*
	Napoleon and the Pope.	1,890
1887	John Graham. C. The school (see 1842).	1,732 10*s.*

		£
1890	W. Wells (Redleaf). C. The village festival, replica.	1,890
	Distraining for rent (see 1848).	2,310*
1893	Ralph Brocklebank. The letter of introduction, 1814.	2,152 10s.
1897	Sir John Pender. C. The cotter's Saturday night (see 1860, 1920).	1,362 10s.
1908	Sir John Ismay. C. Same picture (see 1920).	1,188
1912	C. The Spanish mother.	588
1913	Lord Joycey. C. The pedlar (see 1959).	420
	Card-players.	504
1920	Glen Coates. C. The cotter's Saturday night (see 1897).	945
	The bride at her toilet.	924
1921	C. The china-mender, small painting.	115 10s.
1926	Lord Burgh. C. Small oil study for The Chelsea Pensioners.	215 5s.
1937	Victor de Rothschild. S. Guess who it is (1824).	160
	Portraits, Colonel and Mrs. Deare. 2 for	315
1950	Lord Crichton. C. The Irish whiskey still (see 1850).	483
1958	S. Oil sketch for The letter of introduction, 1814.	160
1959	C. The pedlar (see 1913).	1,732 10s.
	Smith-Cunningham. C. The Turkish letter-writer (£446 5s. in 1842, £420 in 1895).	525

RICHARD WILSON. 1714–1782

Considering that Wilson had been obliged to sell many of his best landscapes for forty guineas, the prices which were paid a generation after his death were impressive. Wilson's works came in and went out with the Claude fashion, but in the 1870's they benefited in a modest way from the eighteenth-century cult and they benefited again in the 1920's. To-day his work seems underpriced, but it is many years since anything of the importance of *The Thames at Twickenham* has appeared in the salerooms.

		£
1755	Duke of Gloucester commissions The children of Niobe (see 1806, 1876, 1961)	157 10s.
1765	2 large landscapes sold to Sir Robert Blake (see 1807). 2 for	168
1801	Purling. C. Villa of Maecenas.	262 10s.
1806	Duke of Gloucester. C. The children of Niobe (see 1755).	840
1807	2 landscapes, bought by Mr. Brockwood (see 1765).	400
1816	Roberts. C. Solitude, bought in.	250 4s.
1827	Lord de Tabley. C. View over the Arno (see 1875).	493 10s.
	Tabley Hall and Park.	204 15s.
1841	Marquess Camden. C. Italian landscape.	246 15s.
1844	Jeremiah Harman. C. Rome from the Ponte Molle.	325 10s.

		£
1856	Samuel Rogers. C. Hadrian's villa, 1765.	141 15*s.*
1865	Cooper Smith. C. Lake Albano, bought in.	420
1875	Watts Russell. C. View over the Arno (see 1827 and 1895).	1,890
1876	Wynn Ellis. C. Children of Niobe (see 1806).	451 10*s.*
1879	National Gallery buys oil sketch, 'On the Wye'.	26 5*s.*
1882	Hamilton Palace. C. View of Rome.	1,050
1886	J. Bentley. C. Apollo and the seasons.	425 5*s.*
1888	Andrews. C. According to A. C. R. Carter, the slump in Wilson's work had become so severe that 12 oil paintings were sold for £525.	
1895	James Pryce. C. View on the Arno (see 1827, 1875).	651
1899	J. Mieville. C. Sion House.	556 10*s.*
1909	E. W. Parker. C. Solitude.	367 10*s.*
1916	Robinson, Fisher. Gallery landscape.	252
1920	Harland-Peck. C. View of Tivoli, 4 ft.	441
1927	C. Lake scene with figures.	703 10*s.*
1928	Holford. C. The River Dee.	4,305
1929	Captain Ford. C. 17 pictures made over £20,000.	
	Lake Nemi.	3,255
	Near Dolgelly.	1,785
	The Thames at Twickenham.	6,720
1930	S. Pembroke town and Castle, bought for National Museum of Wales, Cardiff.	1,900
1937	Earl of Lincoln. C. National Gallery buys a pendant to the same picture.	1,029
1946	Parke-Bernet, New York. River scene with ruins.	900
1948	Earl Fitzwilliam. C. Near Gravesend, artist sketching.	1,312 10*s.*
1953	Tollemache Estates. C. Holt Bridge on the Dee.	3,465
	Extensive landscape.	3,250
1954	Earl of Dartmouth. C. Finished drawing of the Tiber, Rome, commissioned 1754.	504
1957	C. Doldabarn Castle.	3,150
1961	Bonham's rooms. Children of Niobe (see 1806, 1876).	2,100

PHILIPS WOUVERMAN. 1614–1688

Wouverman was not quite the most expensive Dutch painter in the late eighteenth century, but in England he was the most generally accepted favourite and the most frequently imitated. He never went out of fashion in the nineteenth century, but prices rose only very moderately above those of the Regency period, while to-day these works, even at their best, fetch no more than they did in a very different currency some hundred and thirty years ago. Yet fine examples are certainly becoming very rare.

		£
1767	Julienne, Paris. The stag hunt (see 1772).	695
1768	Gaignat, Paris. Marche aux chevaux (see 1834, 1837).	605
1777	Duc de Choiseul. The stag hunt (see 1767).	860
	Randon de Boisset, Paris. Chasse au hareng (see 1928).	500
1790	A French nobleman. C. Landscape with figures.	556 10*s.*
1801	Robit, Paris. The horse fair (see 1768, 1834).	646
1805	Robert Heathcote. C. A pair of riding scenes (had cost £1,155).	604 5*s.*
1808	Choiseul Praslin. Paris. La ferme aux colombiers.	837
1811	Lafontaine. C. The Prince Regent buys The hay harvest.	1,785
1817	Talleyrand. C. La ferme aux colombiers (see 1808).	1,260
1823	Watson Taylor. C. Banks of a river.	1,195
1834	Duc de Berry, Paris. The horse fair (see 1801), bought in (bought in again 1837, £1,484).	2,100
1854	Mecklenburg, Paris. The horse fair finally comes to rest with the Marquess of Hertford (Wallace Collection).	3,200
1859	Earl of Northwick (Philips). Miseries of war.	1,086 15*s.*
1864	Oppenheim. C. Departure for the chase.	903
1875	Miss Bredel. C. Canal scene.	1,281
1876	Foster, Clewer Manor. C. La port-drapeau.	1,312 10*s.*
1892	Earl of Dudley. C. Sportsmen halting at an inn.	3,675
1910	Octavus Coope. C. La charette embourbée.	945
1914	Grenfell. C. Door of a cabaret.	861
1919	Neumann. C. Halt of sportsmen.	1,102 10*s.*
1925	Earl of Carnarvon. C. Soldiers on the march.	1,102 10*s.*
1928	Holford. C. La chasse au hareng (see 1777) (bought in, 1841, by Robert Holford for £409 10*s.*).	4,200*
1937	Victor de Rothschild. S. Outside a lonely inn.	850
1940	Robert Brassey. C. The fortune-teller (£630 in 1872).	315
1944	Neeld. C. Outside a blacksmith's.	1,627 10*s.*
	2 other riding scenes at (each)	1,155
1946	E. J. Wythes. The stag-hunt, over 6 ft.	840
1956	C. Sportsmen buying fish.	630
1958	Miss Barchard. S. Haymakers.	2,100
1959	A. Rolfe. S. Hawking party taking leave of hostess.	4,200
1960	Galliera, Paris. Landscape.	2,600

JOHANN ZOFFANY. 1733–1810

Possibly no eighteenth-century English painter, not even Benjamin West, could make as much money as Zoffany in his prime. In 1772–1774 he received from the King £1,500 for his travelling expenses and £800 for the picture, when he made his fussy, overcrowded work, *The Tribuna in the Florence Gallery.*

Zoffany's journey to India was said to have made him £36,000 in the year 1785 alone. Yet for seventy-three years after his death, not one of his pictures made £100. Even in the 1920's Zoffany had only a modest share in the huge prices for eighteenth-century pictures. The ability to use the 'tight brush' of the Dutchmen, which had brought him such high esteem, was little admired when the free and flowing brush was so much in demand. But it may be noticed that in 1960 one of his family groups made £7,000. No Reynolds whole-length or group had made as much in thirty-three years.

		£
1811	Zoffany executors. C. (Robins.) Garrick in *The Provoked Wife*.	98 18*s*.
	Scene from *Speculation*.	32 11*s*.
	Doratt. C. Dr. William Hunter lecturing, bought in at	210
1823	Fonthill, ex Beckford (Philips). Garrick in *The Farmer's Return* (see 1932).	33 12*s*.
	3 more in Watson Taylor and 6 in Mrs. Garrick sales. Only one exceeded £50.	
1856	C. Scene from *Merchant of Venice*, bought in.	147
1875	C. Portrait of David Garrick.	34 13*s*.
1883	Sacred Harmonic Society. C. Portrait of Dr. Arne.	115 10*s*.
1898	C. Colonel Mordaunt's cockfight at Lucknow (see 1926).	220 10*s*.
1905	Henry Irving. C. Portrait of Garrick.	441
1912	C. Portrait of Gainsborough.	294
1922	Countess of Carlisle. C. Garrick in *The Alchemyst*.	5 4*s*.
1926	Lord Burgh. C. R. H. Bennett, Esq., at a window.	1,850
	Colonel Mordaunt's cockfight (see 1898).	760
1928	C. The Young family.	7,350
	S. The Colmore family.	5,000
	Portrait group.	2,450
1929	S. The Duke of Northumberland with Mr. Selby.	1,500
	Lord Yarborough. C. Garrick in *The Farmer's Return* (see 1823).	3,570
1929	Lord Sherburn. C. The Dutton family.	7,350
1930	C. The Bradshaw family (National Gallery, Toronto).	5,880
1932	Lambton Castle (Anderson and Garland). *The Farmer's Return* (smaller version).	900
1936	Sir Philip Sassoon. S. Family of Sir William Younge.	3,150
1938	Viscount Lee of Fareham. National Gallery buys Mrs. Oswald of Auchincruive.	5,000
1939	Lord O'Hagan. C. The Townely Gallery (Burnley Museum, Staffs).	1,312 10*s*.
	Townely and his friends.	168
1945	C. Family of Rev. Christopher Fawcett.	2,100
1948	S. Garrick, Aiken and Bramsby in *Lethe* (Birmingham City Gallery).	1,850

		£
1956	Parke-Bernet, New York. Blowing bubbles.	1,964
	Two children in Oriental costume.	1,518
	William Hodgson and family.	1,250
1960	Lady Lister. S. Unknown family group, small.	5,000
	P. A. Lewis. S. The Laurie family, 1771.	7,000

BIBLIOGRAPHY

At different times attempts have been made to tabulate the prices of pictures. In 1824 William Buchanan printed a number of sale-lists which he had himself recorded. A good many prices were printed in John Smith's *Catalogue raisonné* of Flemish and Dutch pictures between 1829 and 1842. Charles Blanc in his *Trésor de la curiosité* of 1858 published a series of Paris sale-lists which went back more than a hundred years. The first attempt at a systematic sales-analysis of *all* painters was made by George Redford in the second volume of his *Art Sales* of 1888. Unfortunately, it was so carelessly compiled as to be largely useless—in marked contrast to that absolute goldmine of information, the huge first volume of this work. In 1896 W. L. Roberts made a painstaking analysis of all Christie sales up to that year, but only sale-by-sale, without any indexing.

Only one work of this kind has set out to be really comprehensive. The seven folio volumes of Dr. H. Mireur were completed in 1911, but only traced the history of pictures (he included drawings and engravings) to the year 1900. Here again the standard of accuracy was very uneven and, since Mireur included English and American sales, the rate of exchange was sometimes at fault. The last attempt was made in 1918–1921 by Algernon Graves. This rare three-volume work is both accurate and clearly presented, but, alas, painfully parochial. It was restricted to English sales, but an inordinate amount of space—in fact, the greater part—was monopolised by the English nineteenth-century school.

Graves terminated his researches with the year 1910. The last fifty years can only be followed by direct access to the sale-catalogues or by the use of the annual volumes of *Art Prices Current*, *The Year's Art* and the *Connoisseur*. But of course a great deal has happened outside the saleroom, and for this information the works listed below have all been of value:

ALEXANDER, BOYD *Life at Fonthill from the correspondence of William Beckford.* Translated and annotated. London, 1957.

ALLEN, FREDERICK LEWIS *The Great Pierpont Morgan.* New York, 1949.

AMERICAN ART NEWS Monthly magazine, consulted here for years 1910–1920.

ART JOURNAL, London, 1849–1911 Consulted mainly for second half of nineteenth century.

BELL, C. F. *A list of works contributed to public exhibitions by J. M. W. Turner, R.A.* London, 1901.

BEHRMAN, S. N. *Duveen.* London, 1952.

BLANC, CHARLES *Le trésor de la curiosité, tiré des catalogues de ventes,* 2 vols. Paris, 1858.

BREDIUS, A. *Rembrandt, Gemaelde.* Phaidon Verlag, Vienna, 1935.

BUCHANAN, WILLIAM *Memoirs of painting, with a chronological history of the importation of pictures by the Great Masters into England since the French Revolution*, 2 vols. London, 1824.

CARTER, A. C. R. *The Year's Art*, 1882–1947 (edited by Carter since 1886). *Let me tell you*, 1942.

CAVALLI, GIAN CARLO *Guido Reni, Cronologia, catalogo, etc.* Rome, 1955.

COLLINS, WILKIE *Memoirs of the life of William Collins*, 2 vols. 1858.

CONNOISSEUR, THE Monthly magazine of art. Consulted here for years 1930–1954.

COOPER, DOUGLAS, AND BLUNT, ANTHONY *The Courtauld Collection, a catalogue and introduction.* 1954.

CUNNINGHAM, ALAN *The life of Sir David Wilkie*, 3 vols. 1843.

DICTIONARY OF NATIONAL BIOGRAPHY.

DUBUISSON, A., AND HUGHES, C. E. *Richard Parkes Bonington.* 1924.

DUNN, H. TREFFY *Recollections of Rossetti and his circle.* 1904.

EBERLEIN, KURT CARL *Die Malerei der Deutscher Romantiker.* Munich, 1928.

ENSOR, R. C. K. *England, 1870–1914.* Oxford, 1936.

FARINGTON, JOSEPH *The Farington Diary, 1793–1817*, edited by James Greig, 8 vols. London, 1922–1928.

FINBERG, A. J. *The life of J. M. W. Turner.* Oxford, 1939.

FORSTER, HENRY ROMSEY *The Stowe catalogue, priced and annotated.* London, 1848.

FRITH, WILLIAM POWELL *My autobiography and reminiscences*, 3 vols. 1888.

GALT, JOHN *The life and works of Benjamin West*, 2 vols. 1820.

GARLICK, KENNETH *Sir Thomas Lawrence*, English Master series. 1954.

GAUNT, WILLIAM *The Pre-Raphaelite tragedy.* London, 1942.
Victorian Olympus. London, 1955.

GISSING, A. G. *Holman Hunt, 1827–1910, a biography.* London, 1936.

GLUCK, GUSTAV *Van Dyck. Des Meisters Gemaelde. Klassiker der Kunst*, 2nd edition. 1931.

GRANT, COLONEL M. H. *A chronological history of the old English landscape painters in oil*, 2 vols. 1926, supplementary volume, 1947.

GRAVES, ALGERNON *Art Sales.* 3 vols. 1918–1921.
(with W. V. Cronin) *A history of the works of Sir Joshua Reynolds*, 4 vols. 1909.

GRONAU, GEORG *Correggio. Des Meisters Gemaelde. Klassiker der Kunst.* Leipzig, 1907.

HAMILTON PALACE COLLECTION *Illustrated priced catalogue*, public edition. London, 1882.

HAYDON, BENJAMIN ROBERT *Autobiography and memoirs.* Introduction by Aldous Huxley. London, 1927.

HERMITAGE MUSEUM, LENINGRAD *Catalogue of paintings (Russian text).* Latest edition, 1958.

HOLMES, SIR CHARLES, AND BAKER, C. H. COLLINS *The making of the National Gallery, 1824–1924.* London, 1924.

JAMESON, MRS. *Companion to the most celebrated private galleries of art in London*, 2 vols. 1844.

KAY, SYDNEY J. *John Constable, his life and work*. London, 1948.

LESLIE, C. R. *Memoirs of the life of John Constable Esq., R.A.*, 1843. Edited by the Hon. Andrew Shirley. 1937.

MANSON, J. B. *Sir Edward Landseer*. 1922.

MARILLIER, H. C. *Christie's, 1766 to 1925*. London, 1926.

MAYER, AUGUST L. *Murillo, Des Meisters Gemaelde. Klassiker der Kunst*. Leipzig, 1913.

MEIER-GRAEFE, JULIUS *Corot*. Berlin, 1930.

MILLAIS, JOHN GUILLE *The life and letters of Sir John Everett Millais*, 2 vols. 1899.

MIREUR, DR. H. *Dictionnaire des ventes des tableaux, dessins, gravures*, 7 vols. 1901–1911.

NATIONAL GALLERY *Catalogue of pictures*, 86th edition. 1946.

NATIONAL GALLERY, MILLBANK *Illustrated Guide*, British School. 1925.

OLDENBOURG, RUDOLF *P. P. Rubens. Des Meisters Gemaelde. Klassiker der Kunst*. Berlin, 1931.

OPPÉ, PAUL A. *Early Victorian England, Oxford, 1934*. Section, Art, Vol. II, pp. 102–176.

PENDERED, MARY L. *John Martin, painter*. London, 1923.

REDFORD, GEORGE *Art sales. A history of sales of pictures and other works of art, etc.*, 2 vols, folio. London, 1889.

REDGRAVE, RICHARD AND SAMUEL *A century of British painters*. Phaidon edition, 1947, based on 2nd, 1890, edition.

REYNOLDS, SIR JOSHUA *Fifteen Discourses delivered to the Royal Academy*, 1769–1791.

RHEIMS, MAURICE *La vie étrange des objets*. 1959.

ROBERTS, W. L. *Memorials of Christie's, a record of art sales from 1766 to 1896*, 2 vols. London, 1896.

ROSENBERG, ADOLF *Raffael. Des Meisters Gemaelde. Klassiker der Kunst*. Leipzig, 1906.

ROYAL ACADEMY OF ARTS *Italian art and Britain*. Catalogue, Winter Exhibition, 1959–1960.

RUSKIN, JOHN *Modern painters*, 1843–1861, 5 vols.

SAARINEN, ALINE B. *The Proud Possessors*. New York, 1858.

SMITH, JOHN *Catalogue raisonné of the works of the most eminent Dutch, Flemish and French painters*, 9 vols. 1829–1842.

SMITH, JOHN THOMAS *Nollekens and his times*. 1828. Republished, 1920, 2 vols., with copious notes by Wilfred Whitten.

SPARROW, W. SHAW *George Stubbs and Ben Marshall*. 1929.

SUTTON, DENYS *Christie's since the war, 1945–1958*. London, 1959.

TAYLOR, FRANCIS HENRY *The Taste of Angels*. New York, 1948.
Pierpont Morgan as collector and patron, 1837–1913. New York, 1957.

TORRINGTON, JOHN BYNG, VISCOUNT. *The Torrington Diaries, 1781–1794*, ed. C. Bruyn Andrews, 4 vols. 1934–7.

VALENTINER, WILLIAM R. *Unknown masterpieces in public and private collections.* 2 vols, folio. London, 1930.

WAAGEN, GUSTAV FRIEDRICH *Treasures of art in Great Britain.* London, 1854.

WALLACE COLLECTION. *Catalogue of pictures and drawings,* 15th edition. 1928.

WALPOLE, HORACE, 4TH EARL OF ORFORD *Letters, ed.* Peter Cunningham, 9 vols. Edinburgh, 1906.

WATERHOUSE, PROFESSOR ELLIS K. *Reynolds,* 1941. *Gainsborough,* 1958. } English Master painters.

WHITLEY, WILLIAM T. *Artists and their friends in England, 1700–1799,* 2 vols. London, 1928.
Art in England, Vol. I, *1800–1820.* Cambridge, 1928.
Art in England, Vol. II, *1821–1837.* Cambridge, 1930.

INDEX—I

ARTISTS

INDEX—II

COLLECTORS, DEALERS AND OTHERS

The dates are those of the chief auction sales